A MODERN HISTORY

OF

NEW LONDON COUNTY

CONNECTICUT

EDITOR-IN-CHIEF

BENJAMIN TINKHAM MARSHALL, A.M., D.D.

PRESIDENT OF CONNECTICUT COLLEGE, NEW LONDON

VOLUME I

1922

LEWIS HISTORICAL PUBLISHING COMPANY,
NEW YORK CITY

FOREWORD

The early history of New London County has been well covered by Miss Caulkins' histories of Norwich, and of New London, in various local addresses on special occasions, and in more formal articles prepared for the 200th anniversary of the founding of Norwich Notable amongst these was the historical address of Daniel Coit Gilman, delivered at Norwich on September 7, 1859 To enumerate the special papers delivered at the meetings of the New London County Historical Society, at the dedication of monuments and public buildings of the county, on patriotic occasions, on the 250th anniversary of the town of Norwich (1909), and in almost countless addresses on special topics given before interested audiences in churches and halls, not to mention the many excellent contributions of the press, would in itself be an arduous task, interesting though it might be

Very few parts of our country are more filled with historical associations. Indian legends, mingled with a vast amount of verifiable Indian history; Revolutionary stories, with a record of honorable action surpassed nowhere; loyal patriotism in the days of the Civil War, under the leadership of Governor Buckingham, himself a resident of Norwich, all these offer a wealth of material to the investigator. Out of the great mass of historical writings inspired by such a splendid past there looms up a background, a heritage of memories, that should urge on every citizen of New London County today to better citizenship, to more devoted public service.

From some of these records and addresses we have quoted—they were written by men and women who were near the events described—for we believe that true patriotism is a deep sentiment toward one's native land, not simply a series of outward acts This abiding sentiment of affection and unselfishness in a people, as in an individual, is rooted in memory. By the memory of earlier days, by knowledge of the sacrifices of earlier patriots who made liberty possible for us, will the true spirit of Americanism be best nourished. Nor is the Indian history without value. Even if, in the light of history, "the noble red man" of Cooper's novels seems a somewhat idealized figure, surely nowhere else in America may be found a better typical picture of the early relations of the white settler and the aborigine. We see them both at their best and at their worst. We have the grim picture of John Mason as he leads his resolute forces on to the utter destruction of the Pequots, and we have the picture of Uncas in all things, "Wauregan," living in unbroken amity with the Norwich colonists; we learn of Samson Occum, the Mohican who visited England and brought back ten thousand pounds to Dartmouth College. The present work, then, aims to emphasize only such features of the early history of our country as are helpful to the modern reader in visualizing the days of occupation, of settlement, and colonial development, the essential background by which to emphasize modern conditions.

Our history for the last fifty years, inasmuch as this has not been printed in any one volume, will be described with greater minuteness. It is hoped that this portion of the work may be helpful for some years to come as a storehouse of information.

Among the well informed persons who have labored in this undertaking, the principal place is to be given to Professor Henry A. Tirrell, Principal of the Norwich Free Academy, as the author of the exhaustive chapter on Education, and writer on other topics. Other more important papers and of enduring value are those on "Church History," by Rev. Henry W. Hulbert, D.D., Pastor of the First Church of Christ, Groton; on "Medicine, Physicians and Surgeons," by Charles B. Graves, M.D., former President Connecticut State Medical Society; on "Insurance," by Walter F. Lester, President New London County Mutual Fire Insurance Company; on "Volunteer and Paid Fire Departments," by Howard L. Stanton, Chief Norwich Fire Department, and on "Old Families and Old Homes of Norwich" and kindred topics," by Mrs. Edna Miner Rogers, Regent of Faith Trumbull Chapter, D. A. R.

The publishers of the History, The Lewis Historical Publishing Company, through its agents, editors and official staff, has secured and arranged all the genealogical and biographical matter proper, which appears in the work, and for this material the Editor-in-Chief bears no responsibility.

CONTENTS

CHAPTER I

GENERAL FACTS ABOUT NEW LONDON COUNTY

The Early Towns—Natural Features of the Region—The Indian Occupants—First White Settlers—Illuminating Documents from the Past.

New London County, occupying the southeastern part of Connecticut, is bounded on the east by the State of Rhode Island, on the south by Long Island Sound, on the west by Middlesex and Tolland counties, and on the north by Hartford, Tolland and Windham counties.

The county, with an area of approximately seven hundred square miles, is composed of twenty-one towns, Bozrah, Colchester, East Lyme, Franklin, Griswold, Groton, Lebanon, Ledyard, Lisbon, Lyme, Montville, New London, North Stonington, Norwich, Old Lyme, Preston, Salem, Sprague, Stonington, Voluntown, Waterford; and has a population (census of 1920) of 155,311.

This county was one of the first four counties of the State, organized in 1666, and originally included a considerable part of the present Middlesex county, extending as far west as Clinton. Of the five first cities of Connecticut chartered in 1784, New London county had two, New London and Norwich. Of the twenty-one towns of the county:

New London was settled as "Pequot" in 1646; named from London, England, and authorized as a town in 1658.

Stonington was settled in 1649 and named Stonington in 1666.

Norwich, named from Norwich, England, in 1659, was settled by a Saybrook colony in 1660.

Lyme, named from Lyme Regis, England, in 1667, was set off from Saybrook in 1665

Colchester was settled and named from Colchester, England, in 1699.

Preston was named in 1687 from Preston, England.

Lebanon, named from Lebanon in Syria, was incorporated in 1700.

Groton, set off from New London in 1704, was named from the English home of Governor John Winthrop in 1705.

Voluntown, "Volunteers Town," named in 1708, was settled in 1719.

Bozrah, with Biblical name, was set off from Norwich in 1786.

Franklin, set off from Norwich, in 1786, was named for Benjamin Franklin.

Lisbon, set off from Norwich in 1786, was named from Lisbon, Portugal.

Montville, set off from New London in 1786, took the French name of "Mount Ville."

Waterford, set off from New London in 1801, took a name descriptive of its nature.

North Stonington was set off from Stonington in 1807.

Griswold, named from Governor Roger Griswold, was set off from Preston in 1815.

N.L.—1-1

Salem, named from Salem, Massachusetts, was set off from Colchester, Lyme, and Montville in 1879.

Ledyard, named from Colonel William Ledyard of Fort Griswold fame, was set off from Groton in 1836.

East Lyme was set off from Lyme and Waterford in 1839.

Old Lyme was set off from Lyme in 1855, and named Old Lyme in 1857.

Sprague, named from its founder, William Sprague, was set off from Lisbon and Franklin in 1861.

The following note is prefixed to the list of Connecticut towns printed in the Connecticut Register and Manual (1920).

Until 1700, almost the only official action of the colonial government (General Court) in regard to town organization, was to authorize the town name, usually chosen by its leading man, from his home in England. In October, 1700, we find implied or quasi incorporation, such as exists to this day, in the records: "This assembly doth grant to the inhabitants of the town of Lebanon all such immunities, privileges and powers, as generally other townes within this Colonie have and doe enjoy" The authoritative legal definition of a town in England, contemporary with the earliest Connecticut settlements, is given in the first edition of "Coke's Commentaries upon Littleton," published 1628; "It can not be a town in law, unless it hath, or in past time hath had, a church, and celebration of Divine services, sacraments and burials." The church bodies which moved bodily with their pastors from Massachusetts to Connecticut, proceeded to exercise the secular powers which we regard as those of the town, but the English township is known by its ecclesiastical name of parish. Several of our towns were first set off as parishes, from great town tracts; yet the town in Connecticut colony essentially separated church and state in government, in that it never restricted political suffrage to church-members. As to dates, the official colonial records are followed, as soon as they begin, 1636.

For the beauty and variety of its natural scenery, New London county is excelled by very few regions of equal area. Its southern shore, from the broad sweep of the Connecticut river eastward along a coast of singular charm, with its jutting points and its alluring inlets; by Niantic bay, which Governor Winthrop, as he looked off from the heights above, called one of the most beautiful spots he had ever seen, outward to the majestic estuary of the Thames with its noble harbor; still eastward by the beautiful islets of Noank and Mystic till that point is reached where the States of Rhode Island, New York and Connecticut meet near the harbor of Stonington, is as wonderful today as when the Indians gazed upon its beauties.

And the scenery of the coast is matched by the wooded hills, the rushing streams, the placid lakes, the rich valleys, farther inland. The summer visitor today is found in all parts of the county, not only in the summer colonies built up near the coast, but in many a broad estate whose owner is content to preserve the forest, the rockbound glens, the rich verdure that Nature has so generously supplied.

The chief waters of the county besides its large ponds and lakes are the Connecticut, Thames, Shetucket, Quinnebaug, Yantic, Pawcatuck, Mystic, Poquonock, and Niantic rivers, all flowing in a general southerly course to the Sound. Its navigable waters and its abounding water power have contributed largely to its economic development, from the early days when extensive commerce sprang up with all quarters of the globe, to the later times when manufacturing founded the fortunes of many of its citizens. With such natural advantages Connecticut enterprise and ingenuity have made possible a growth far beyond the expectations of the men of even fifty years ago. One part of this history will be devoted to this remarkable expansion of recent years.

No true conception of the growth of the county is possible without an understanding of the character and customs of the early settlers, the difficulties they had to overcome, their relations with the Indians, their participation in the broader colonial interests, in the Revolutionary War, in the affairs of the State and Nation.

The first settlers, many of them of Pilgrim stock and practically all of them of Puritan origin, had the same deep religious convictions and the same stamina that other New England colonists had. They had inherited from their Anglo-Saxon ancestors a genius for self-government, which, checked by the Stuart despotism in England, burst into bloom in the new life of a New World Hardships were endured and overcome Yet in the midst of a severe struggle for existence, they never lost sight of the great things of life. Religion, education, and morality were the strong supports of local governments founded on law and order. Difficulties strengthened their characters both individually and collectively. It may well be said that the menace of hostile Indians was one of the main incentives to cooperation amongst the early settlers of New England.

The Pequot War was undoubtedly the first step toward the settlement of New London county, for it was not until that tribe had been virtually annihilated that it was safe for colonists to settle in this region. Of the many anecdotes connected with the war, some will be given in the histories of separate towns. We print a general survey from Hurd's "History of New London County":

The territory was preoccupied by the Pequots a powerful tribe of Indians belonging to the widespread Algonquin or Delaware race. This powerful tribe had by their cruelty become the dread of the whites far and near. Rendered bold by numbers, and jealous of every encroachment, they had resolved upon nothing less than the utter extermination of the whites, and shrank from no means, however appalling, which might conduce to the accomplishment of their bloody purpose. Massachusetts had in 1634, with much effort, induced them to allow the peaceable settlement of certain portions of their domain, and to offer satisfaction for former outrages. But the natives were slow to fulfill the conditions of this treaty, and Captain Endicott was sent out by the Massachusetts colony, at the head of ninety men, to enforce the treaty and to chastise them for their past offenses.

This ill-advised expedition failed utterly of its objects, and only tended to exasperate the Pequots, who during the succeeding fall and winter were untiring in their attempts to league the other Indians with them in a war of extermination against the whites, and redoubled their own efforts to rid

themselves of the noxious strangers Savages lurked in every covert, and
there was no safety for life or property. The colonists could not travel
abroad, or even cultivate their fields, but at the peril of their lives. Their
cattle were driven off, their houses burned, the navigation of the river was
seriously impeded, and even the fort at Saybrook was in a state of constant
siege By spring the situation had become critical in the extreme. Nearly
thirty murders had been committed, and utter ruin threatened the colony
unless decisive measures should at once be taken. In this emergency a
General Court was convened at Hartford on the 11th of May, 1637, at which
it was decided to proceed at once to an offensive war against the Pequots,
and for the first campaign to send out a force of ninety men under Capt. John
Mason, then in command of the fort at Saybrook.

About this time, Mason and the warrior Uncas met and formed a
temporary alliance, which was, however, destined to continue without serious
interruption for a long series of years, and prove of great and lasting benefit
to the settlements. Uncas was related both by birth and marriage to the
Pequot royal family, but soon after his marriage he became involved in difficulties, the nature of which is not exactly known, which resulted in his
banishment to the Narragansett country. He was afterwards permitted to
return, but a recurrence of the same troubles led to his banishment for a
second and even a third time. He thus at length became permanently exiled
from his own people, and we find him upon the Connecticut river, near the
infant settlements of Hartford and Windsor, in the spring of 1637, at the head
of about seventy warriors. Both Mason and Uncas were eminently fitted to
be military leaders, each of his own race. Mason possessed marked military
tastes which had been developed and trained in the wars of the Netherland
under Lord Fairfax, while Uncas, by nature brave and shrewd, had, as a
member of the royal family of a strong and warlike nation, abundant opportunity to acquire a thorough knowledge of the methods of Indian warfare
An alliance of two such representative men of the two races then competing
upon American soil could not fail to make an impress upon their peculiar
surroundings Uncas agreed to join the expedition with his warriors, and
the united forces embarked at Hartford on the 20th of May of the same year
and proceeded to drop down the river. In the course of the voyage the
Indians had opportunity to demonstrate their fidelity, which had been unjustly
suspected by some As the water in the river was low and the passage tedious,
the Indians were at their own request allowed to disembark and proceed
along the bank. When near Saybrook, they met and defeated a party of
Pequots, killing seven and taking one prisoner. After their arrival at Saybrook, the commandant of the fort, still distrustful of Uncas, addressed the
sachem as follows "You say you will help Captain Mason, but I will first
see it; therefore send twenty men to Bass river, for there went last night
six Indians there in a canoe; fetch them, dead or alive, and you shall go with
Mason, or you shall not." Uncas did as he was required His warriors
found the enemy, killed four of them, and took another prisoner. This exploit
of the sachem was regarded by Lieutenant Gardiner as a sure pledge of his
fidelity.

Captain Mason had received instructions to land at Pequot Harbor, but
his military judgment led him to sail direct to the Narragansett country and
make his attack upon the enemy from a point whence they would least expect
it. He accordingly proceeded thither, and·on Saturday, May 30th, towards
evening, dropped anchor off the shores of the Narragansett As there was a
strong northwest wind, they remained on shipboard until Tuesday, when
Mason landed and marched directly to the residence of Canonicus, the Nar-

ragansett chief, and informed him of his design of attacking the Pequots in their strongholds, and demanded a free passage through the Narragansett country. The request was readily granted, and Miantonomoh, nephew of Canonicus, suggested that the numbers of the English and Mohegans were too small for an invasion of the Pequot country, and volunteered to send two hundred of his braves with the expedition, though he did not himself offer to accompany them

On the following morning the vessels were manned with a small force, as a larger could not be spared, and were ordered to sail for the mouth of Pequot river. The land force, consisting of seventy Englishmen, and sixty Mohegan warriors under Uncas, with the addition of two hundred Narragansett volunteers, commenced its march westward. After proceeding about twenty miles through a rough country, with only a narrow Indian foot-path for their passageway, they arrived at a place called Nehantic, where they remained overnight. When the English resumed their march on the following morning they were overtaken by others of the Narragansett people, so that they were followed, as they supposed, by near five hundred warriors. As the day was warm and the way rough, several of the men fainted from exposure and want of food. After a march of about twelve miles they reached a ford in the Pawcatuck river, where a halt was made for rest and refreshment. It had been ascertained that the majority of the Pequot warriors were in two forts or inclosures of palisades, one of which was commanded by Sassacus in person, and both regarded by the Indians as within and without impregnable. Mason had originally designed to divide his forces and attack both places simultaneously, but from information received during the halt upon the Pawcatuck he learned that the forts were situated at too great a distance apart to allow of a division of his force, and he decided to advance at once upon the fort on Pequot Hill. The Narragansetts, on learning of his design to attack Sassacus in his stronghold, were smitten with deadly fear. "Sassacus," they said, "was all one god, and could not be killed." So great was their trepidation that a hundred of their number beat a precipitate retreat, and reported in the Providence plantation that the English had all fallen.

At this time Mason called Uncas to him, and asked him what he thought the Indians would do. "The Narragansetts," replied this brave sachem, "will all leave us," "but as for himself 'he would never leave us'; and so it proved, for which expression I shall never forget him. Indeed, he was a great friend, and did great service." The Pawcatuck was the last boundary before the country of the Pequots, and as the Narragansetts found themselves nearing the strongholds of their dreaded rivals, their timidity increased and all but a handful turned back. The Mohegans, however, encouraged by their chief, mustered the courage to proceed. The small army advanced cautiously till towards evening, when they came to a little swamp between two hills, near what are now called Porter's Rocks, where they halted for the night. Rising at an early hour on the following morning, they reached the fortress a little before daybreak. The plan of attack had been so arranged that Mason was to approach the enemy through the main entrance on the northeast side with one division, while Underhill was to make an attack on the southwestern entrance with his division. Uncas with his force was to form an outer line to act as circumstances might indicate. When within a rod or two of the fort a dog barked, and the alarm was given. The troops rushed on, discharging their muskets through the palisades, and then forced an entrance. Mason, with his party, drove the Indians along the main avenue of their fortress towards the west till they were met by Underhill and his division, who had effected an entrance upon that side, when, finding themselves between two fires, they were forced to retreat to their wigwams, where a desperate resistance was made. For a few moments the conflict seemed doubtful, when Mason, realizing the gravity of the situation, hit upon the expedient of burning out the foe, and snatching a brand from the fire applied it to the dry matting of a wigwam. The fire spread with great rapidity, and the whole seventy wigwams were soon in flames. The English retired without the wigwams, and Uncas and his followers formed a circular line close in the rear of the English. The consternation of the Pequots was so great that but few attempted to escape. About six or seven were made prisoners by the English, eighteen were captured by the Mohegans, and seven only made their escape. It so happened that one hundred and fifty warriors from the other fortress were this night in the fort upon Pequot Hill, which made the victory still more complete.

This famous encounter occurred on Friday, June 5th. The same day, at an early hour, the small fleet entered Pequot Harbor. As Mason's force was about to move in the direction of the vessels, a party of Indian warriors approached them from the other fort, but one or two volleys from their trusty weapons served to keep them at a safe distance. The few Narragansetts that hung upon the rear of the little column as it moved steadily up the hill were not slow in making their appearance when the contest was decided, evincing all the courage of tried veterans. They finally accompanied Captain Mason to the harbor, and afforded some assistance to those who conveyed the wounded. The total loss on the part of the English was two killed and twenty wounded.

Sassacus at this critical period was in the fortress on Fort Hill, where he was loudly denounced by his warriors as the procuring cause of their late disaster at the other fort. The Pequots at this fort were also greatly exasperated at the course of Uncas and his followers, and caused all of their near relatives to be slain, except seven who made their escape.

On the day after the battle, a council of the Pequot nation was held to decide upon their future course of action, and after a hasty deliberation they resolved to leave their country, but not till they had destroyed their fortress and wigwams and such remaining property as could not be carried away. The principal band, headed by Sassacus in person, fled westward and did not make any considerable halt till they had reached a large swamp in Saco, the present township of Fairfield. Thither they were pursued by Captain Mason and his faithful ally Uncas. Captain Stoughton also accompanied the expedition in command of a company from Massachusetts. The fugitives were discovered in their new quarters, and were without difficulty routed and utterly dispersed. Sassacus did not risk a halt at the swamp, but with a few of his followers fled directly to the Mohawk country for a safe retreat, but was there slain by the nation, and his scalp was sent to Connecticut as a trophy. As a result of the swamp fight and the death of their late chieftain, the Pequot nation became nearly extinct. Although powerless for harm, the few remaining fugitives were pursued with unrelenting malignity by the English. Even the surrounding tribes were not permitted to harbor them with impunity, but were required by treaty and otherwise to effect, if possible, their utter annihilation. The Pequots were not allowed to dwell in their old homes, to visit the graves of their fathers, or to be called Pequots any more. Lastly, the conquered territory was not to be claimed by the sachems, but to be considered as the property of the English of Connecticut, as their own by right of conquest.

The expedition against the Pequots is the most remarkable recorded in

Knows All men that Onkos Onanece Attawan
sachems ... mohuyen have bargained sold
... over and doe by these presents sell and passed
over unto the Towne and Inhabitants of norwich
nine miles square of land being & being at mohayen
and the parts thereunto adjoyneing with all ponds [brooks]
woods quaries mines with all royalties priviledges and
appurtenances thereunto belonging to them the sd Inha
=bitants of norwich theire heires & successors forever
the sd land are to be bounded as followeth (viz) to
the southward on the first side of the great River
yt line is to be gin at the Brooke falling into the
head of Trading Cove, and soe to run nest north [east]
seven miles from thence the line to run nest north
nine miles and on the east side the aforesd
for the southward the line is to joyne with
River bounds as it is now laid out and soe to run
New London bounds from the foxe River, and soe from
east two miles from thence to Run nor noreast nine miles
thence the line is to Run nor north nine
and from thence the western lines ... Considera
miles to mut with the sd Onkos Onanece and Attawan
=on ... acknowledge to have received of the parties
... doe acknowledge the full & just sume of seventy
pounds and doe promise and engage our selves heires
=ties aforesd ... Bargin and sale
and successors to warant the sd parties theire heires and successors
to the aforesd ... from all claimes and molesta
and them to defend
=ation from any whatsoever in witness whereof wee
have heereunto set to our hands this
sixth of June Anno 1659   Onkos [mark]

Wittnes heerunto
John Mason   Onaneco [mark]
Thomas Tracy   Attawanboot [mark]

This deed ... is Recorded
in the Countrey Record August
20th 1683 as attest
John Allyn secy

DEED FROM MOHEGAN INDIANS, TRANSFERRING NINE MILES SQUARE OF LAND
(TOWN OF NORWICH), RECORDED IN COUNTY RECORD BOOK, AUGUST 20, 1663

American history and one which for boldness of plan and brilliancy of execution may well claim a place among the most daring exploits of universal history. The Pequots outnumbered Mason's forces ten to one, and the day might have been lost had it not been for the faithful service of Uncas and his followers.

Uncas, as lineal descendant of the royal family, laid claim to the sovereignty of the conquered territory, and while by the terms of the treaty the portion upon the Sound was given up, his claim to the remainder of the Pequot country was admitted by the English, and he was acknowledged as the lawful sachem of a territory embracing the northern half of New London and the southern half of Windham and Tolland counties. Some of the surviving Pequots had been assigned him by the terms of the treaty, and many former tributaries of the vanquished tribe yielded their allegiance to him, and added to his power, but his greatest source of strength lay in the favor of the English, which he had fairly won

His rapid rise and growing favor greatly excited the envy of surrounding chieftains, especially of those of the Narragansetts and their allies, the Connecticut River Indians, and they were untiring in their efforts to effect his overthrow. At first they endeavored to cause a rupture between Uncas and the English, but failing in this scheme they next attempted to take his life by assassination. Several fruitless endeavors of this kind were made, but in these diabolic attempts upon his life he was more than a match for them; their calumnies and their murderous designs were made to recoil upon their own heads. Failing in their secret plotting, their enmity ripened into open warfare. In the summer of 1643, only six years after the rout at Mystic Fort, Miantonomoh, at the head of six or seven hundred warriors, suddenly appeared in the very heart of the Mohegan country by a succession of rapid marches. He moved proudly to the contest, doubtless with the assurance that his numerical superiority and the suddenness of his irruption would secure for him an easy victory over his foe and rival. But Uncas was not to be overcome by a surprise. He hastily collected a band of about three hundred warriors and met the invaders upon his own territory. on the Great Plain, probably in the vicinity of the present Fair Grounds in Norwich. He felt the necessity, however, of resorting to strategy in his present emergency, and hence proposed a parley, which was accepted, and the two chieftains met on the plain between their respective armies. Uncas then proposed that the fortunes of the day should be decided by themselves in a single combat, and the lives of their warriors spared, saying, "If you kill me, my men shall be yours, but if I kill you, your men shall be mine."

Miantonomoh disdainfully replied, "My men came to fight, and they shall fight." Uncas on this immediately gave a preconcerted signal to his followers by falling flat upon the ground. At that instant a shower of arrows were discharged upon the enemy, and, raising the war-cry, the Mohegans rushed forward with Uncas at their head, dashing so unexpectedly upon the invading column of warriors that a widespread panic ensued, resulting in their precipitous and headlong flight without even a show of resistance The retreating force was pursued in its flight to Sachem's Plain, in the direction of the fords of the Shetucket, at which place Miantonomoh became the prisoner of Uncas. About thirty of the Narragansetts were slain, and among the prisoners were a brother of Miantonomoh and two sons of Canonicus. Uncas kindly treated his royal prisoner, and without any unnecessary delay took him to Hartford and surrendered him into the hands of the English. His case was laid before commissioners of the United Colonies at their meeting in Boston in September, and the question was there debated whether it was right and proper to put the prisoner to death As the commissioners were unable to agree, the question was by them referred to an ecclesiastical council, which gave its verdict in favor of his execution. It was further decided that the sentence should be carried into effect by Uncas, but without torture. After furnishing a sufficient force to prevent the recapture of the prisoner, Miantonomoh was surrendered into the hands of Uncas, who took him to the place of capture, where he was stricken down by Waweequa, a brother of Uncas. A monument now marks the site of this tragical event. The Narragansetts at several different times invaded the Mohegan country, impatient to avenge the death of their late chief, but Uncas and his followers were uninjured on account of the aid of the English, which was always extended.

It is noteworthy that the first settlements in the county, at New London and Norwich, were made under the leadership of some of the most influential men of New England. John Winthrop, the younger, who received a grant at Fisher's Island, given first by Massachusetts in 1640, confirmed by Connecticut in 1641, and by New York in 1668, received from Massachusetts in 1644 a grant of a "plantation at or near Pequot." Here he lived from 1646 till he was chosen governor of the Colony of Connecticut in 1657. He it was who secured in 1662 that famous charter from Charles II which was saved from Sir Edmond Andros by hiding it in "The Charter Oak." John Mason, of whom we shall have more to say, was one of the early leaders of the Norwich settlement.

Under such stalwart leaders as these, the young communities grew and flourished, till by the end of the seventeenth century towns were found at New London, Stonington, Norwich, Lyme, Preston, Colchester, and Lebanon. From these towns were set off the other fourteen towns as stated above.

The story of the Charter has been told by Mr. Daniel Howard in a document on Connecticut history issued by the State Board of Education:

At the time when Connecticut was settled and when her infant settlements formed their first written constitution, the king of England paid very little attention to what was being done in this new State On the other hand, the people of Connecticut paid very little attention to their connection with England. They did not even mention England or the king in the constitution that they drew up in 1639.

England at that time was very poorly governed. Her king was a tyrant who tried to rule by illegal methods. The people would not submit to such a rule, and in 1639 they put their king to death. No one wonders under such conditions why Connecticut made no mention of the fact that she belonged to England No wonder also that the king paid little attention to Connecticut, for he had troubles enough at home. From 1649 to 1660 England had no king. The people who were at the head of the English government had so many troubles on their side of the ocean, however, that they, too, paid little attention to Connecticut.

In 1660 a great change in affairs took place. In that year a new king, Charles II, came to the English throne. With him came peace and order in England. The new government had time to look abroad and it was sure to give its attention to what was going on in America. Connecticut thought it was wise for her to maintain friendly relations with the new king. She must have his permission to carry on her government, and she might need his protection to shield her from the Indians, the Dutch, and other enemies. Accordingly, in 1661 the Connecticut people took the necessary steps to win the king's favor They declared that their settlements were English, and that they themselves being the king's faithful subjects owed allegiance to the English crown.

The next step was to send Governor Winthrop to England with a petition for a charter. The king was a good-natured man, fond of honors and attentions, and at the same time desirous of adding to his wealth and revenue. So when Governor Winthrop presented him with the ring that the king's father had given to the governor's grandfather, his heart was touched with gratitude and affection. When the governor told him that the land which the settlers had bought of the Indians and fought for at the peril of their lives was now a fertile and populous territory capable of adding much to the wealth and income of his kingdom, he was favorably impressed. Lord Say, Lord Seal, and other friends, aided Governor Winthrop in persuading the king to grant the charter and in 1662 it received the royal signature. Governor Winthrop received two copies of the charter. One of these he sent to America immediately. The other copy he kept in his possession and brought it to Hartford himself. How the people at Hartford, Windsor and Wethersfield rejoiced! New Haven at first objected to being united to the three river towns, for she had hoped to remain a separate colony. Soon, however, she accepted the situation, and all the Connecticut towns were happily united under one government.

Under this liberal charter the colony grew and prospered for the next twenty-five years. The form of government was popular, for the people were required simply to make no laws contrary to those of England. The charter guaranteed to the colony substantially the same rights and privileges that the people had claimed for themselves when they made the constitution of 1639. It was the people's ideal of what a charter ought to be, for it granted all they had asked and even wished for. No wonder they regarded it as a priceless blessing.

Neither is it any wonder that the people were filled with anxiety and distress when a new king, James II, came to the throne of England and tried to take from them this precious charter. The new king believed that it would be a good thing to unite all the New England settlements into one strong colony under an able English governor. In this way they would be better prepared to defend themselves against their Dutch, French, and Indian neighbors.

The king did not stop to inquire whether this change in government would please the people of New England or not. In 1686 he sent Sir Edmund Andros to Boston as governor, with instructions to seize the charters of Rhode Island and Connecticut and annex those colonies to Massachusetts and the rest of New England. From Boston the new governor sent to Governor Treat at Hartford asking that the charter of Connecticut should be sent to him.

Failing to obtain the charter in this way, Governor Andros determined to go to Hartford himself and demand it. Attended by several members of his council, two trumpeters, and a body-guard of red-coated soldiers, he left Boston. Traveling on horseback, they reached the Connecticut river at a point opposite Wethersfield in the afternoon of October 31, 1687. The ferry boat took them to the other side of the river, where a troop of Hartford soldiers met them and escorted them to Hartford with all the pomp and dignity befitting the reception of a royal governor. At Hartford, Governor

Treat, his assistants, and the members of the General Assembly, received them with courtesy and respect. In the evening the General Assembly was in session to hear what Governor Andros had to say. He was escorted to the governor's seat and the Assembly listened to his message. He demanded that the Charter of Connecticut should be given to him and that it should no longer be a separate colony.

Governor Treat made an eloquent and touching plea in reply. He pictured the toil, the hardship, and the sufferings of the early settlers. He told how they had fought with tribes of murderous savages, how they had turned the wilderness into a land of happy homes, how they had obtained their cherished charter, growing and prospering under its protection until relinquishing it would be like giving up life itself.

Still Governor Andros insisted that the charter must be surrendered. There it lay upon the table around which they were sitting. How could the charter be saved? Suddenly the candles were extinguished. There were no matches in those days, and it took some time to relight the candles. When this was done the charter was missing.

What had become of it? Governor Andros never knew, but we know that good friends of Connecticut carried it away and hid it. Andros had no right to demand it, and the Connecticut Assembly were determined that he should not obtain it.

Captain Joseph Wadsworth was the man who carried it away. Believing that the English governor would try to find it, he tried to think of a safe place in which to hide it. He hid it finally in the hollow trunk of a large oak tree standing near the home of Samuel Wyllys.

Equally interesting is Mr Howard's account of Colonial life at that time:

For us to go back to the old colonial days and visit the people who then lived in Connecticut is, of course, impossible, yet we must go back at least in imagination if we are to understand the kind of life they lived.

Let us suppose that we are on a journey through Connecticut a few years before the time when Governor Andros tried to deprive the people of their charter. How strange it seems that everybody travels either on horseback or afoot. We see neither steam nor electric cars nor automobiles, and the people do not even own carriages or wagons. How poor the roads are! They are little better than beaten paths through the woods and fields. Men are at work on their farms, harvesting their crops, and cutting down trees in order to clear new land to plant next year. The homes are mostly grouped in villages and look very much alike.

In the center of almost every house is a great stone chimney ten or twelve feet square from the floor of the cellar up to the floor of the second story, above which it decreases in size as it approaches the roof. In the center of the front of the house is a door opening into a hall from which a stairway leads to the second story. On the right and left are doors opening from the hall into large rooms on each side of the chimney. In the rear of the chimney is another large room. One of these rooms is the kitchen, which in most cases is also the living room of the family. The other large rooms are used for parlors or guest rooms, and the smaller sleeping rooms are up stairs.

We see no stoves, but on three sides of the chimney are huge fireplaces. In the kitchen fireplace is an iron crane on which hang two great kettles. The oven is built into one side of the fireplace. The sides of the rooms are plastered, but the joists and floor overhead are not covered, and nails are driven into the joists to serve as hooks on which to hang small articles. The windows have small diamond-shaped panes of glass set in frames of lead. The floors have no carpets. The furniture is plain and useful rather than ornamental. In one room is a spinning wheel and a hand loom on which the farmer's wife and daughters spin the wool that has been cut from the backs of the sheep, and weave it into cloth from which to make garments for the family.

After the evening meal, eaten from pewter and wooden dishes by the light of tallow candles in the great kitchen, we enjoy listening to the stories told by farmers and their neighbors as they sit about the great fireplace, some of them cracking nuts and others making brooms and various useful articles. We hear strange news of what has happened during the day. A man has been arrested for swearing and has had to stand in the pillory one hour and then receive a whipping. Another man has had to sit for hours in the stocks to punish him for drunkenness.

Last night farmer Jones had five sheep killed by a wolf, and today he and his sons have been hunting for the beast that did the damage. Tomorrow farmer Smith is to begin building a barn and his neighbors are going to the "raising" to help erect the framework, for it is their custom to be friendly and give their services to a neighbor on such occasions. On the morrow we go to the "raising," and late in the afternoon, when the framework of the barn has all been put in place and securely pinned together, we sit down at the great tables and enjoy the feast prepared by Mrs. Smith and her daughters. All go home early, for tomorrow is Sunday, and in Connecticut the observance of the Sabbath begins on Saturday at sunset. Family worship is followed by religious instruction given to the children and to the servants.

On Sunday morning a drum beats and everyone goes to church. The minister and the congregation all carry their muskets. Why? Because hostile Indians are liable to attack them at any minute. Sentinels and guards watch outside the door during the sermon, which lasts two hours. After luncheon, the congregation returns for another long sermon. The tithingman with his long rod tipped at one end with brass and at the other with a rabbit's foot, prevents anyone who is weary from going to sleep. An old man becomes drowsy. He is gently touched upon the head with the brass end of the rod and awakes with a start. In another pew a lady is awakened by having her face brushed by the rabbit's foot. Though these good people could not help becoming tired and sleepy, they had a high regard for their pastor's teaching, for it was to him that they went for advice and counsel not only for their religious life but for almost every question that arose regarding what was right and proper in their social life and customs.

The life of these early settlers was quiet, healthful, and happy. They labored industriously and contentedly on their farms and in the forests. All that they earned was their own to use and enjoy. They made their own system of government and laws, and enjoyed the justice and liberty that these gave them. They believed in education for themselves and for their children. Their moral and religious character made them trust and respect one another and earned them the respect and esteem of people in other colonies.

What sort of people these early settlers were may be judged by a love letter sent in 1674 by Rev. Edward Taylor, of Massachusetts, to Miss Elizabeth Fitch, daughter of Rev. James Fitch, the first clergyman settled in Norwich:

Wethersfield, Mass., 8th day of the 7th month, 1674.

My Dove:—I send you not my heart, for that I hope is sent to Heaven long since, and unless it has awfully deceived me it hath not taken up its lodgings in any one's bosom on this side the royal city of the Great King; but yet the most of it that is allowed to be layed out upon any creature doth safely and singly fall to your share. So much my post pigeon presents you with here in these lines. Look not (I entreat you) on it as one of love's hyperboles If I borrow the beams of some sparkling metaphor to illustrate my respects unto thyself by, for you having made my breast the cabinet of your, affections as I yours mine, I know not how to offer a fitter comparison to set out my love by, than to compare it unto a golden ball of pure fire rolling up and down my breast, from which there flies now and then a spark like a glorious beam from the body of the flaming sun. But alas! striving to catch these sparks into a love letter unto yourself, and to gild it with them as with a sun beam, and, that by what time they have fallen through my pen upon paper, they have lost their shine and fall only like a little smoke thereon instead of gilding them. Wherefore, finding myself so much deceived, I am ready to begrudge my instruments, for though my love within my breast is so large that my heart is not sufficient to contain it, yet they can make it no more room to ride into, than to squeeze it up betwixt my black ink and white paper. But know that it is the coarsest part that is couchant there, for the finest is too fine to clothe in any linguist and huswifry, or to be expressed in words, and though this letter bears but the coarsest part to you, yet the purest is improved for you. But now, my dear love, lest my letter should be judged the lavish language of a lover's pen, I shall endeavor to show that conjugal love ought to exceed all other love. 1st, appears from that which it represents, viz: The respect there is betwixt Christ and his church, Eph 5th, 25th, although it differs from that in kind; for that is spiritual and this human, and in degree, that is boundless and transcendent, this limited and subordinate; yet it holds out that this should be cordial and with respect to all other transcendent. 2d, Because conjugal love is the ground of conjugal union, or conjugal sharing the effects of this love, is also a ground of this union 3d, From those Christian duties which are incumbent on persons in this state as not only a serving God together, a praying together, a joining in the ruling and instructing their family together, which could not be carried on as it should be without a great degree of true love, and also a mutual giving each other to each other, a mutual succoring each other in all states, ails, grievances; and how can this be when there is not a love exceeding all other love to any creature? And hereby if persons in this state have not love exceeding all love, it's with them for the most part as with the strings of an instrument not tuned up, when struck upon makes but a jarring, harsh sound. But when we get the wires of an instrument equally drawn up, and rightly struck upon, sound together, make sweet music whose harmony doth enravish the ear: so when the golden strings of true affection are struck up into a right conjugal love, thus sweetly doth this state then harmonize to the comfort of each other and to the glory of God when sanctified. But yet, the conjugal love most exceed all other, yet it must be kept within bounds, for it must be subordinate to God's glory; the which that mine may be so, it having got you in its heart, doth offer my heart with you in it as a more rich sacrifice into God through Christ, and so it subscribeth me,

Your true love till death,

EDWARD TAYLOR.

This for my friend and only beloved, Miss Elizabeth Fitch, at her father's house in Norwich.

No more interesting description of Colonial life at this time can be found than "The Journal of Madame Sarah Knight," the record of a journey from Boston to New York in 1704. Inasmuch as Madame Knight was a resident of Norwich and New London for many years, we print the journal entire:

Monday, Octb'r. ye second, 1704. About three o'clock afternoon, I begun my Journey from Boston to New Haven; being about two Hundred Mile. My Kinsman, Capt. Robert Luist, waited on me as farr as Dedham, where I was to meet ye Western post.

I visitted the Reverd. Mr. Belcher, ye Minister of ye town, and tarried there till evening, in hopes ye post would come along. But he not coming, I resolved to go to Billingses where he used to lodg, being 12 miles further. But being ignorant of the way, Madm Billings, seeing no persuasions of her good spouses or hers could prevail with me to Lodg there that night, Very kindly went wyth me to ye Tavern, where I hoped to get my guide, And desired the Hostess to inquire of her guests whether any of them would go with mee. But they being tyed by the Lipps to a pewter engine, scarcely allowed themselves time to say what clownish—(Here half a page of the MS. is gone.)—Pieces of eight, I told her no, I would not be accessary to such extortion.

Then John shan't go, sais shee. No, indeed, shan't hee; And held forth at that rate a long time, that I began to fear I was got among the Quaking tribe, beleeving not a Limbertong'd sister among them could out do Madm. Hostes. Upon this, to my no small surprise, son John arrose, and gravely demanded what I would give him to go with me? Give you, sais I, are you John? Yes, says he, for want of a Better; And behold! this John look't as old as my Host, and perhaps had bin a man in the last Century. Well, Mr. John, sais I, make your demands.

Why, half a pss. of eight and a dram, sais John. I agreed, and gave him a Dram (now) in hand to bind the bargain. My hostess catechis'd John for going so cheap, saying his poor wife would break her heart—(Here another half page of the MS. is gone.)—His shade on his Hors resembled a Globe on a Gate post. His habit, Hors and furniture, its looks and goings Incomparably answered the rest.

Thus Jogging on with an easy pace, my Guide telling mee it was dangero's to Ride hard in the Night. (which his horse had the sence to avoid) Hee entertained me with the Adventurs he had passed by late Rideing, and eminent Dangers he had escaped, so that, Rembring the Hero's in Parismus and the Knight of the Oracle, I did'nt know but I had mett wth a Prince disguis'd. When we had Ridd about an how'r, wee come into a thick swamp, wch. by Reason of a great fogg, very much startled mee, it being now very Dark. But nothing dismay'd John: Hee had encountered a thousand and a thousand such Swamps, having a Universal Knowledge in the woods; and readily Answered all my inquiries wch were not a few.

In about an how'r, or something more, after we left the Swamp, we come to Billinges, where I was to Lodg. My Guide dismounted and very Complasantly help't me down and shewd the door, signing to me wth his hand to Go in; wch I Gladly did—But had not gone many steps into the Room, ere I was Interogated by a young Lady I understood afterwards was the Eldest daughter of the family, with these, or words to this purpose, (viz.) Law for mee—what in the world brings You here at this time a night?—I never see a woman on the Rode so Dreadfull late, in all the days of my versall life. Who are You? Where are You going? I'm scar'd out of my witts—with much now of the same Kind. I stood aghast, Prepareing to reply, when in comes my Guide—to him Madam turn'd, Roreing out. Lawfull heart, John, is it You?—how do do¹ Where in the world are you going with this woman? Who is she? John made no Ansr. but sat down in the corner, fumbled out his black Junk, and saluted that instead of Debb; she then turned agen to mee and fell anew into her silly questions, without asking me to sitt down.

I told her she treated me very Rudely, and I did not think it my duty to answer her unmannerly Questions But to get ridd of them, I told her I come there to have the post's company with me to-morrow on my Journey, &c. Miss star'd awhile, drew a chair, bid me sitt, And then run up stairs and putts on two or three Rings, (or else I had not seen them before,) and returning, sett herself just before me, showing the way to Reding, that I might see her Ornaments, perhaps to gain the more respect. But her Granam's new Rung sow, had it appeared, would affected me as much. I paid honest John wᵗʰ money and dram according to contract, and Dismist him, and pray'd Miss to shew me where I must Lodg. Shee conducted me to a parlour in a little back Lento, ᵂᶜʰ was almost fill'd wᵗʰ the bedstead, ᵂᶜʰ was so high that I was forced to climb on a chair to gitt up to yᵉ wretched bed that lay on it, on ᵂᶜʰ having Strecht my tired Limbs, and lay'd my head on a Sad-colourd pillow, I began to think on the transactions of yᵉ past day

Tuesday, October yᵉ third, about 8 in the morning, I with the Post proceeded forward without observing any thing remarkable, And about two, afternoon, Arrived at the Post's second stage, where the western Post mett him and exchanged Letters. Here, having called for something to eat, yᵉ woman bro't in a Twisted thing like a cable, but something whiter; and laying it on the bord, tugg'd for life to bring it into a capacity to spread; wᶜʰ having wᵗʰ great pains accomplished, shee serv'd in a dish of Pork and Cabbage, I suppose the remains of Dinner. The sause was of a deep Purple, wᶜʰ I tho't was boil'd in her dye Kettle; the bread was Indian, and every thing on the Table service Agreeable to these. I, being hungry, gott a little down, but my stomach was soon cloy'd and what cabbage I swallowed serv'd me for a Cudd the whole day after

Having here discharged the Ordnary for self and Guide, (as I understood was the custom.) About Three afternoon went on with my Third Guide, who Rode very hard; and having crossed Providence Ferry, we come to a River wᶜʰ they Generally Ride thro'. But I dare not venture; so the Post got a Ladd and Cannoo to carry me to tother side, and hee rode thro' and Led my hors The Cannoo was very small and shallow, so that when we were in she seem'd redy to take in water, which greatly terrified mee, and caused me to be very circumspect, sitting with my hands fast on each side, my eyes stedy, not daring so much as to lodg my tongue a hair's breadth more on one side of my mouth then tother, nor so much as think on Lott''s wife, for a wry thought would have overestt our wherev: But was soon put out of this pain, by feeling the Cannoo on shore, wᶜʰ I as soon almost saluted with my feet: and Rewarding my sculler, again mounted and made the best of our way forwards The Rode here was very even and yᵉ day pleasant, it being now near Sunsett. But the Post told mee we had neer 14 miles to Ride to the next Stage, (where we were to Lodg.) I askt him of the rest of the Rode, forseeing wee must travail in the night. Hee told mee there was a bad River we were to Ride thro', wᶜʰ was so very firce a hors could sometimes hardly stem it: But it was but narrow, and wee should soon be over. I cannot express The concern of mind this relation sett me in: no thought but those of the dang'ros River could entertain my Imagination, and they were as formidable as varios, still Tormenting me with blackest Ideas of my Approaching fate—Sometimes seing my self drowning, otherwhiles drowned, and at the best like a holy Sister Just come out of a Spiritual Bath in dripping Garments.

Now was the Glorious Luminary, with his swift Coursers arrived at his Stage, leaving poor me with the rest of this part of the lower world in darkness, with which wee were soon Surrounded. The only Glimmering we now had was from the spangled Skies, Whose Imperfect Reflections rendered every Object formidable. Each lifeless Trunk, with its shatter'd Limbs, appear'd an Armed Enymie; and every little stump like a Ravenous devourer. Nor could I so much as discern my Guide, when at any distance, which added to the terror.

Thus, absolutely lost in Thought, and dying with the very thoughts of drowning, I come up with the post, who I did not see till even with his Hors: he told mee he stopt for mee; and wee Rode on Very deliberately a few paces, when we entered a Thickett of Trees and Shrubbs, and I perceived by the Hors's going, we were on the descent of a Hill, wch, as wee come neerer the bottom, 'twas totaly dark wth the Trees that surrounded it. But I knew by the Going of the Hors wee had entred the water, wch my Guide told mee was the hazardos River he had told me off, and hee, Riding up close to my Side, Bid me not fear—we should be over Imediatly. I now ralyed all the Courage I was mistriss of, Knowing that I must either Venture my fate of drowning, or be left like ye Children in the wood. So, as the Post bid me, I gave Reins to my Nagg; and sitting as Stedy as Just before in the Cannoo, in a few minutes got safe to the other side, which hee told mee was the Narragansett country.

Here We found great difficulty in Travailing, the way being very narrow, and on each side the Trees and bushes gave us very unpleasant welcomes with their Branches and bow's, wch wee could not avoid, it being so exceeding dark. My Guide, as before so now, putt on harder than I, wth my weary bones, could follow, so left mee and the way behind him. Now Returned my distressed apprehensions of the place where I was: the dolesome woods, my Company next to none, Going I knew not whither, and encompassed wth Terrifying darkness; The least of which was enough to startle a more Masculine courage. Added to which the Reflections, as in the afternoon of ye day that my Call was very Questionable, wch till then I had not so Prudently as I ought considered. Now, coming to ye foot of a hill, I found great difficulty in ascending; But being got to the Top, was there amply recompenced with the friendly Appearance of the Kind Conductress of the night, Just then Advancing above the Horisontall Line. The Raptures wch the Sight of that fair Planett produced in mee, caus'd mee, for the Moment to forgett my present wearyness and past toils, and Inspir'd me for most of the remaining way with very diverting tho'ts, some of which, with the other Occurances of the day, I reserved to note down when I should come to my Stage. My tho'ts on the sight of the moon were to this purpose:

Fair Cynthia, all the Homage that I may
Unto a Creature, unto thee I pay;
In Lonesome woods to meet so kind a guide,
To Mee's more worth than all the world beside.
Some Joy I felt just now, when safe got o're
Yon Surly River to this Rugged shore.
Deeming Rough welcomes from these clownish Trees,
Better than Lodgings wth Nereidees
Yet swelling fears surprise; all dark appears—

Nothing but Light can disipate those fears.
My fainting vitals can't lend strength to say,
But softly whisper, O I wish 'twere day.
The murmur hardly warm'd the Ambient air,
E're thy Bright Aspect rescues from dispair:
Makes the old Hagg her sable mantle loose,
And a Bright Joy do's through my Soul diffuse.
The Boistero's Trees now Lend a Passage Free,
And pleasant prospects thou giv'st light to see.

From hence wee kept on, with more ease yn before; the way being smooth and even, the night warm and serene, and the Tall and thick Trees at a distance, especially wn the moon glar'd light through the branches, fill'd my Imagination wth the pleasant delusion of a Sumteous citty, fill'd wth famous Buildings and churches, wth their spiring steeples, Balconies, Galleries, and I know not what: Grandeurs wch I had heard of, and wch the stories of foreign countries had given me the Idea of.

Here stood a Lofty church—there is a steeple,
And there the Grand Parade—O see the people!
That Famouse Castle there, were I but nigh,
To see the mote and Bridg and walls so high—
They'r very fine! sais my deluded eye.

Being thus agreeably entertain'd without a thou't of any thing but thoughts themselves, I on a suden was Rous'd from these pleasing Imaginations, by the Post's sounding his horn, which assured mee he was arrived at the Stage, where we were to Lodg: and that musick was then most musickall and agreeable to mee.

Being come to mr. Havens', I was very civilly Received, and courteously entertained, in a clean comfortable House; and the Good woman was very active in helping off my Riding clothes, and then ask't what I would eat. I told her I had some Chocolett, if shee would prepare it; which with the help of some Milk, and a little clean brass Kettle, she soon effected to my satisfaction. I then betook me to my Apartment, wch was a little Room parted from the Kitchen by a single bord partition; where, after I had noted the Occurances of the past day, I went to bed, which, tho' pretty hard, Yet neet and handsome. But I could get no sleep, because of the Clamor of some of the Town tope-ers in next Room, Who were entred into a strong debate concernign ye Signifycation of the name of their Country, (viz.) Narraganset. One said it was named so by ye Indians, because there grew a Brier there, of a prodigious Highth and bigness, the like hardly ever known, called by the Indians Narragansett: And quotes an Indian of so Barberous a name for his Author, that I could not write it. His Antagonist Replyed no—It was from a Spring it had its name, wch hee well knew where it was, which was extreem cold in summer, and as Hott as could be imagined in the winter, which was much resorted too by the natives, and by them called Narragansett, (Hot and Cold,) and that was the originall of their places name —with a thousand Impertinances not worth notice, wch He utter'd with such a Roreing voice and Thundering blows with the fist of wickedness on the Table, that it pierced my very head. I fretted, and wish't 'um tongue tyed; but wth as little succes as a friend of mine once, who was (as she said) kept a whole night awake, on a Jorny, by a country Left. and a Sergent, Insigne and a Deacon, contriving how to bring a triangle into a Square. They kept calling for tother Gill, wch while they were swallowing, was some Intermission; But presently, like Oyle to fire, encreased the flame. It set my Candle on a Chest by the bed side, and setting up, fell to my old way of composing my Resentments, in the following manner:

> I ask thy Aid, O Potent Rum!
> To Charm these wrangling Topers Dum.
> Thou hast their Giddy Brains possest—
> The man confounded wth the Beast—
> And I, poor I, can get no rest.
> Intoxicate them with thy fumes:
> O still their Tongues till morning comes!

And I know not but my wishes took effect; for the dispute soon ended wth 'tother Dram; and so Good night!

Wednesday, Octob'r 4th. About four in the morning, we set out for Kingston (for so was the Town called) with a french Docter in our company. Hee and ye Post put on very furiously, so that I could not keep up with them, only as now and then they'd stop till they see me. This Rode was poorly furnished wth accommodations for Travellers, so that we were forced to ride 22 miles by the post's account, but neerer thirty by mine, before wee could bait so much as our Horses, wch I exceedingly complained of. But the post encourag'd mee, by saying wee should be well accommodated anon at mr. Devills, a few miles further. But I questioned whether we ought to go to the Devil to be helpt out of affliction. However, like the rest of Deluded souls that post to ye Infernal denn, Wee made all posible speed to this Devil's Habitation; where alliting, in full assurance of good accommodation, wee were going in. But meeting his two daughters, as I suposed twins, they so neerly resembled each other, both in features and habit, and look't as old as the Divel himselfe, and quite as Uglv, We desired entertainm't, but could hardly get a word out of 'um, till with our Importunity, telling them our necesity, &c they call'd the old Sophister, who was as sparing of his words as his daughters had bin, and no, or none, was the reply's hee made us to our demands. Hee differed only in this from the old fellow in to'ther Country: hee let us depart. However, I thought it proper to warn poor Travailers to endeavour to Avoid falling into circumstances like ours, wch at our next Stage I sat down and did as followeth:

> May all that dread the cruel feind of night
> Keep on, and not at this curs't Mansion light
> 'Tiss Hell: 'tis Hell! and Devills here do dwell:
> Here dwells the Devill—surely this's Hell
> Nothing but Wants· a drop to cool yo'r Tongue
> Cant be procur'd these cruel Feinds among.
> Plenty of horrid Grins and looks sevear,
> Hunger and thirst, But pitty's banish'd here—
> The Right hand keep, if Hell on Earth you fear!

Thus leaving this habitation of cruelty, we went forward; and arriving at an Ordinary about two mile further, found tollerable accommodation. But our Hostes, being a pretty full mouth'd old creature, entertain'd our fellow travailer, ye french Docter, wth Inumirable complaints of her bodily infirmities; and whisperd to him so lou'd, that all ye House had as full a hearing as hee; which was very divirting to he company, (of which there was a great many,) as one might see by their sneering. But poor weary I slipt out to enter my mind in my Jornal, and left my Great Landly with her Talkative Guests to themselves.

From hence we proceeded (about ten forenoon) through the Narragansett country, pretty Leisurely; and about one afternoon come to Paukataug River, wch was about two hundred paces over, and now very high, and no

N.T.—1-2

way over to to'ther side but this I darid not venture to Ride thro, my courage
at best in such cases but small, And now at the Lowest Ebb, by reason of
my weary, very weary, hungry, and uneasy Circumstances. So takeing leave
of my company, tho' wth no little Reluctance, that I could not proceed wth
them on my Jorny, Stop at a little cottage Just by the River, to wait the
Waters falling, wch the old man that lived there said would be in a little
time, and he would conduct me safe over. This little Hutt was one of the
wretchedest I ever saw a habitation for human creatures. It was supported
with shores enclosed with Clapbords, laid on Lengthways, and so much
asunded, that the Light come throu' every where; the doore tyed on wth a
cord in ye place of hinges: The floor the bear earth, no windows but such
as the thin covering afforded, nor any furniture but a Bedd wth a glass Bottle
hanging at ye head on't; an earthan cupp, a small pewter Bason, A Bord wth
sticks to stand on, instead of a table, and a block or two in ye corner instead
of chairs. The family were the old man, his wife and two Children; all and
every part being the picture of poverty. Notwithstanding both the Hutt and
its Inhabance were very clean and tydee: to the crossing the Old Proverb,
that bare walls make giddy hows-wifes I Blest myselfe that I was not one
of this misserable crew, and the Impressions their wretchedness formed in
me cauesd mee on ye very Spott to say:

> Tho' Ill at ease, A stranger and alone,
> All my fatigu's shall not extort a grone.
> These Indigents have hunger wth their ease;
> Their best is wors behalfe then my disease
> Their Misirable hutt wch Heat and Cold
> Alternately without Repulse do hold,
> Their Lodgings thyn and hard, their Indian fare,
> The mean Apparel which the wretches wear,
> And their ten thousand ills wch can't be told,
> Makes nature er'e 'tis midle age look old.
> When I reflect, my late fatigues do seem
> Only a notion or forgotten Dreem

I had scarce done thinking, when an Indian-like Animal come to the door,
on a creature very much like himselfe, in mien and features, as well as Ragged
cloathing; and having 'litt, makes an Awkerd Scratch wth his Indian shoo,
and a Nodd, sitts on ye block, fumbles out his black Junk, dipps it in ye
Ashes, and presents it piping hott to his muschecto's, and fell to sucking
like a calf, without speaking, for near a quarter of an hower. At length the
old man said how do's Sarah do? who I understood was the wretches wife,
and Daughter to ye old man: he Replyed,—as well as can be expected, &c.
So I remembred the old say, and suposed I knew Sarah's case. Butt hee
being, as I understood, going over the River, as ugly as hee was, I was glad
to ask him to show me ye way to Saxtons, at Stoningtown; wch he promising,
I ventur'd over wth the old mans assistance; who having rewarded to content,
with my Tattertailed guide, I Ridd on very slowly thro' Stoningtown, where
the Rode was very stony and uneven. I asked the fellow, as we went, divers
questions of the place and way, &c. I being arrived at my country Saxtons,
at Stonington, was very well accommodated both as to victuals and Lodging,
the only Good of both I had found since my setting out. Here I heard there
was an old man and his Daughter to come that way, bound to N. London;
and being now destitute of a Guide, gladly waited for them, being in so good
a harbour, and accordingly, Thirsday, Octobr ye 5th, about 3 in the afternoon, I sat forward with neighbor Polly and Jemima, a Girl about 18 Years
old, who hee said he had been to fetch out of the Narragansetts, and said
they had Rode thirty miles that day, on a sory lean jade, wth only a Bagg

under her for a pillion, which the poor Girl often complain'd was very uneasy.

Wee made Good speed along, wch made poor Jemima make many a sow'r face, the mare being a very hard trotter; and after many a hearty and bitter Oh, she at length Low'd out: Lawful Heart father! this bare mare hurts mee Dingeely, I'me direfull sore I vow; with many words to that purpose: poor Child sais Gaffer—she us't to serve your mother so. I don't care how mother us't to do, quoth Jemima, in a pasionate tone. At which the old man Laught, and kik't his Jade o' the side, which made her Jolt ten times harder.

About seven that Evening, we come to New London Ferry: here, by reason of a very high wind, we mett with great difficulty in getting over—the Boat tos't exceedingly, and our Horses capper'd at a very surprizing Rate, and set us all in a fright; especially poor Jemima, who desired her father to say 'so jack' to the Jade, to make her stand. But the careless parent, taking no notice of her repeated desires, She Rored out in a Passionate manner· Pray suth father, Are you deaf? Say 'so Jack' to the Jade, I tell you. The Dutiful Parent obey's; saying 'so Jack,' 'so Jack,' as gravely as if hee'd bin to saying Catechise after Young Miss, who with her fright look't of all coulers in ye Rain Bow.

Being safely arrived at the house of Mrs. Prentices in N. London, I treated neighbour Polly and daughter for their divirting company, and bid them farewell; and between nine and ten at night waited on the Revd Mr. Gurdon Saltonstall, minister of the town, who kindly Invited me to Stay that night at his house, where I was very handsomely and plentifully treated and Lodg'd; and made good the Great Character I had before heard concerning him; viz. that hee was the most affable, courteous, Genero's and best of men

Friday, October 6th. I got up very early, in Order to hire somebody to go with mee to New Haven, being in Great perplexity at the thoughts of proceeding alone; which my most hospitable entertainer observing, himself went, and soon return'd wth a young Gentleman of the town, who he could confide in to Go with mee; and about eight this morning, wth Mr Joshua Wheeler my new Guide, takeing leave of this worthy Gentleman, Wee advanced on towards Seabrook. The Rodes all along this way are very bad, Incumbered wth Rocks and mountainous passages, wch were very disagreeable to my tired carcass, but we went on with a moderate pace wch made ve Journy more pleasent But after about eight miles Rideing, in going over a Bridge under wch the River Run very swift, my hors stumbled, and very narrowly 'scaped falling over into the water; wch extreemly frightened mee But through God's Goodness I met with no harm, and mounting agen, in about half a miles Rideing, come to an ordinary, were well entertained by a woman of about seventy and vantage, but of as Sound Intellectuals as one of seventeen. Shee entertain'd Mr. Wheeler wth some passages of a Wedding awhile ago at a place hard by, the Brides-Groom being about her Age or something above, Saying his Children was dreadfully against their fathers marrying, wch shee condemned them extreemly for.

From hence wee went pretty briskly forward, and arriv'd at Saybrook ferry about two of the Clock afternoon; and crossing it, wee call'd at an Inn to Bait, (foreseeing we should not have such another Opportunity till we come to Killingsworth.) Landlady comes in, with her hair about her ears, and hands at full pay scratching Shee told us shee had some mutton wch shee would broil, wch I was glad to hear; But I supose forgot to wash her scratchers; in a little time shee brot it in: but it being pickeld, and my Guide said it smelt strong of head sause, we left it, and pd sixpence a piece for our

Dinners, wch was only smell. So wee putt forward with al speed, and about seven at night come to Killingsworth, and were tollerably well with Travillers fare, and Lodgd there that night.

Saturday, Oct. 7th, we sett out early in the Morning, and being something unaquainted wth the way, having ask't it of some wee mett, they told us wee must Ride a mile or two and turne down a Lane on the Right hand; and by their Direction wee Rode on but not Yet comeing to ye turning, we mett a Young fellow and ask't him how farr it was to the Lane which turn'd down towards Guilford. Hee said wee must Ride a little further, and turn down by the Corner of uncle Sams Lott. My Guide vented his Spleen at the Lubber; and we soon after came into the Rhode, and keeping still on, without any thing further Remarkabell, about two a clock afternoon we arrived at New Haven, where I was reccived with all Possible Respects and civility. Here I discharged Mr. Wheeler with a reward to his satisfaction, and took some time to rest after so long and toilsome a Journey; And Inform'd myselfe of the manners and customs of the place, and at the same time employed myselfe in the affair I went there upon.

They are Govern'd by the same Laws as wee in Boston, (or little differ-ing,) thr'out this whole Colony of Connecticot, And much the same way of Church Government, and many of them good, Sociable people, and I hope Religious too: but a little too much Independant in their principalls, and, as I have been told, were formerly in their Zeal very Riggid in their Admin-istrations towards such as their Lawes made Offenders, even to a harmless Kiss or Innocent merriment among Young people. Whipping being frequent and counted an easy Punishment, about wch as other Crimes, the Judges were absolute in their Sentances. They told mee a pleasant story about a pair of Justices in thoes parts, wch I may not omit the relation of.

A negro Slave belonging to a man in ye Town, stole a hogs head from his master, and gave or sold it to an Indian, native of the place. The Indian sold it in the neighbourhood, and so the theft was found out. Thereupon the Heathen was Seized, and carried to the Justices House to be Eramined. But his worship (it seems) was gone into the field, with a Brother in office, to gather in his Pompions. Whither the malefactor is hurried, And Complaint made, and satisfaction in the name of Justice demanded. Their Worships can't proceed in form without a Bench: whereupon they Order one to be Imediately erected, which, for want of fitter materials, they made with pompions—which being finished, down setts their Worships, and the Male-factor call'd, and by the Senior Justice Interrogated after the following man-ner. You Indian why did You steal from this man? You sho'dn't do so—it's a Grandy wicked thing to steal. Hol't Hol't, cryes Justice Junr, Brother, You speak negro to him. I'le ask him. You sirrah, why did You steal this man's Hoggshead? Hoggshead? (replys the Indian,) me no stomany. No? says his Worship; and pulling off his hatt, Patted his own head with his hand, sais, Tatapa—You, Tatapa—you; all one this. Hoggshead all one this. Hah! says Netop, now me stomany that. Whereupon the Company fell into a great fitt of Laughter, even to Roreing. Silence is co-manded, but to no effect: for they continued perfectly Shouting. Nay, sais his worship, in an angry tone, if it be so, take mee off the Bench.

Their Diversions in this part of the Country are on Lecture days and Training days mostly; on the former there is Riding from town to town. And on training dayes The Youth divert themselves by Shooting at the Target. as they call it, (but it very much resembles a pillory,) where hee that hitts neerest the white has some yards of Red Ribbin presented him, wch being tied to his hattband, the two ends streeming down his back, he is Led away in Triumph, wth great applause, as the winners of the Olympiack Games. They generally marry very young: the males oftener as I am told under twentie than above; they generally make public wedings, and have a way something singular (as they say) in some of them, viz. Just before Joyning hands the Bridegroom quitts the place, who is soon followed by the Bridesmen, and as it were, dragg'd back to duty—being the reverse to ye former practice among us, to steal ms Pride.

There are great plenty of Oysters all along by the sea side, as farr as I Rode in the Collony, and those very good. And they Generally lived very well and comfortably in their famelies. But too Indulgent (especially ye farmers) to their slaves· sufering too great familiarity from them, permitting ym to sit at Table and eat with them, (as they say to save time,) and into the dish goes the black hoof as freely as the white hand. They told me that there was a farmer lived nere the Town where I lodgd who had some difference wth his slave, concerning something the master had promised him and did not punctualy perform; wch caused some hard words between them; But at length they put the matter to Arbitration and Bound themselves to stand to the award of such as they named—wch done, the Arbitrators Having heard the Allegations of both parties, Order the master to pay 40s to black face, and acknowledge his fault. And so the matter ended: the poor master very honestly standing to the award.

There are every where in the Towns as I passed, a Number of Indians the Natives of the Country, and are the most salvage of all the salvages of that kind that I had ever Seen: little or no care taken (as I heard upon enquiry) to make them otherwise. They have in some places Landes of their owne, and Govern'd by Law's of their own making;—they marry many wives and at pleasure put them away, and on the ye least dislike or fickle humour, on either side, saying "stand away" to one another is a sufficient Divorce. And indeed those uncomely Stand aways are too much in Vougue among the English in this (Indulgent Colony) as their Records plentifully prove, and that on very trivial matters, of which some have been told me, but are not proper to be Related by a Female pen, tho some of that foolish sex have had too large a share in the story.

If the natives committ any crime on their own precincts among themselves, ye English takes no Cognezens of. But if on the English ground, they are punishable by our Laws. They mourn for their Dead by blacking their faces, and cutting their hair, after an Awkerd and frightfull manner; But can't bear You should mention the names of their dead Relations to them: they trade most for Rum, for wch theyd hazzard their very lives; and the English fit them Generally as well, by seasoning it plentifully with water.

They give the title of merchant to every trader; who Rate their Goods according to the time and spetia they pay in: viz. Pay, mony, Pay as mony, and trusting. Pay is Grain, Pork, Beef, &c. at the prices sett by the General Gourt that Year; mony is pieces of Eight, Ryalls, or Boston or Bay shillings (as they call them,) or Good hard money, as sometimes silver coin is termed by them; also Wampom, vizt. Indian beads wch serves for change. Pay as mony is provisions, as aforesd one Third cheaper then as the Assembly or Genel Court sets it; and Trust as they and the mercht agree for time.

Now, when the buyer comes to ask for a comodity, sometimes before the merchant answers that he has it, he sais, is Your pay redy? Perhaps the Chap Reply's Yes: what do You pay in? says the merchant The buyer having answered, then the price is set; as suppose he wants a sixpenny knife, in pay it is 12d—in pay as money eight pence, and hard money its own price,

viz. 6d   It seems a very Intricate way of trade and what Lex Mercatoria
had not thought of

Being at a merchants house, in comes a tall country fellow with his
alfogeos full of Tobacco; for they seldom Loose their Cudd, but keep Chewing
and Spitting as long as they'r eyes are open,—he advanc't to the midle of the
Room, makes an Awkward Nodd, and spitting a Large deal of Aromatick
Tincture, he gave a scrape with his shovel like shoo, leaving a small shovel
full of dirt on the floor, made a full stop, Hugging his own pretty Body with
his hands under his arms, Stood staring rown'd him, like a Catt let out of a
Baskett   At last, like the creature Balaam Rode on, he opened his mouth
and said: have You any Ribinen for Hatbands to sell I pray?   The Questions
and Answers about the pay being past, the Ribin is bro't and opened   Bump-
kin Simpers, cryes "its confounded Gay I vow"; and beckning to the door,
in comes Jone Tawdry dropping about 50 curtsees, and stands by him: hee
shows her the Ribin.   "Law, You," sais shee, "its right Gent, do You, take
it, tis dreadfull pretty"   Then she enquires, "have You any hood silk I pray?"
wch being brought and bought, "Have You any thred silk to sew it wth"
says shee, wch being accomodated wth they Departed   They Generaly stand
after they come in a great while speachless, and sometimes dont say a word
till they are askt what they want, which I impute to the Awe they stand
in of the merchants, who they are constantly almost Indebted too; and must
take what they bring without Liberty to choose for themselves; but they
serve them as well, making the merchants stay long enough for their pay.

We may Observe here the great necessity and bennifit both of Education
and Conversation; for these people have as Large a portion of mother witt,
and sometimes a Larger, than those who have bin brought up in Cities; But
for want of emprovements, Render themselves almost Ridiculos, as above.
I should be glad if they would leave such follies, and am sure all that Love
Clean Houses (at least) would be glad on't too   They are generaly very
plain in their dress, throuout all ye Colony, as I saw, and follow one another
in their modes; that You may know where they belong, especially the women,
meet them where you will.

Their Cheif Red Letter day is St Election, wch is annually Observed
according to Charter, to choose their Govenr: a blessing they can never be
thankfull enough for, as they will find, if ever it be their hard fortune to
loose it.   The present Governor in Connecticott is the Honble John Winthrop Esq. A Gentleman of an Ancient and Honourable Family, whose Father
was Govenor here sometime before, and his Grand father had bin Govr of
the Massachusetts.   This gentleman is a very curteous and afable person,
much Given to Hospitality, and has by his Good services Gain'd the affections
of the people as much as any who had bin before him in that post.

Decr. 6th   Being by this time well Recruited and rested after my Journy,
my business lying unfinished by some concerns at New York depending
thereupon, my Kinsman, Mr. Thomas Trowbridge of New Haven, must needs
take a Journy there before it could be accomplished, I resolved to go there
in company wth him, and a man of the town wch I engaged to wait on me
there.   Accordingly, Dec. 6th we set out from New Haven, and about 11
same morning came to Stratford ferry; wch crossing, about two miles on
the other side Baited our horses and would have eat a morsell ourselves, But
the Pumpkin and Indian mixt Bred had such an Aspect, and the Bare-legg'd
Punch so awkerd or rather Awfull a sound, that we left both, and proceeded
forward, and about seven at night come to Fairfield, where we met with good
entertainment and Lodg'd; and early next morning set forward to Norowalk,
from its halfe Indian name North-walk, when about 12 at noon we arrived,

and Had a Dinner of Fryed Venison, very savoury Landlady wanting some pepper in the seasoning, bid the Girl hand her the spice in the little Gay cupp on ye shelfe. From hence we Hasted towards Rye, walking and Leading our Horses neer a mile together, up a prodigios high Hill; and so Riding till about nine at night, and there arived and took up our Lodgings at an ordinary, wch a French family kept. Here being very hungry, I desired a fricasee, wch the Frenchman undertakeing, managed so contrary to my notion of Cookery, that I hastened to Bed superless, And being shewd the way up a pair of stairs wch had such a narrow passage that I had almost stopt by the Bulk of my Body; But arriving at my apartment found it to be a little Lento Chamber furnisht amongst other Rubbish with a High Bedd and a Low one, a Long Table, a Bench and a Bottomless chair,—Little Miss went to scratch up my Kennell wch Russelled as if shee'd bin in the Barn amongst the Husks, and supose such was the contents of the tickin—nevertheless being exceeding weary, down I laid my poor Carkes (never more tired) and found my Covering as scanty as my Bed was hard. Anon I heard another Russelling noise in Ye Room—called to know the matter—Little miss said shee was making a bed for the men, who, when they were in Bed, complained their leggs lay out of it by reason of its shortness—my poor bones complained bitterly not oeing used to such Lodgings, and so did the man who was with us; and poor I made but one Grone, which was from the time I went to bed to the time I Riss, which was about three in the morning, Setting up by the Fire till Light, and having discharged our ordinary wch was as dear as if we had had far Better fare—wee took our leave of Monsier and about seven in the morn come to New Rochell a french town, where we had a good Breakfast. And in the strength of that about and how'r before sunsett got to York. Here I applyd myeslf to Mr. Burroughs, a merchant to whom I was recommended by my Kinsman Capt. Prout, and received great Civilities from him and his spouse, who were now 'both Deaf but very agreeable in their Conversation, Diverting me with pleasant stories of their knowledge in Brittan from whence they both come, one of which was above the rest very pleasant to me viz. my Lord Darcy had a very extravagant Brother who had mortgaged what Estate hee could not sell, and in good time dyed leaving only one son. Him his Lordship (having none of his own) took and made him Heir of his whole Estate, which he was to receive at the death of his Aunt. He and his Aunt in her widowhood held a right understanding and lived as become such Relations, shee being a discreet Gentlewoman and he an Ingenios Young man. One day Hee fell into some Company though far his inferiors, very freely told him of the Ill circumstances his fathers Estate lay under, and the many Debts he left unpaid to the wrong of poor people with whom he had dealt. The Young gentleman was put out of countenance—no way hee could think of to Redress himeslf—his whole dependance being on the Lady his Aunt, and how to speak to her he knew not—Hee went home, sat down to dinner and as usual sometimes with her when the Chaplain was absent, she desired him to say Grace, wch he did after this manner:

> Pray God in Mercy take my Lady Darcy
> Unto his Heavenly Throne,
> That Little John may live like a man,
> And pay every man his own.

The prudent Lady took no present notice, But finishd dinner, after wch having sat and talk't awhile (as Customary) He Riss, took his Hatt and Going out she desired him to give her leave to speak to him in her Clossett, Where being come she desired to know why hee prayed for her Death in the manner aforesaid, and what part of her deportment towards him merritted such desires. Hee Reply'd, none at all, But he was under such disadvantages that nothing but that could do him service, and told her how he had been affronted as above, and what Impressions it had made upon him. The Lady made him a gentle reprimand that he had not informed her after another manner, Bid him see what his father owed and he should have money to pay it to a penny, And always to lett her know his wants and he should have a redy supply. The Young Gentleman charm'd with his Aunts Discrete management, Beggd her pardon and accepted her kind offer and retrieved his fathers Estate, &c. and said Hee hoped his Aunt would never dye, for shee had done better by him than hee could have done for himself.—Mr. Burroughs went with me to Vendue where I bought about 100 Rheem of paper wch was retaken in a fly-boat from Holland and sold very Reasonably here—some ten, some Eight shillings per Rheem by the Lott wch was ten Rheem in a Lott. And at the Vendue I made a great many acquaintances amongst the good women of the town, who curteosly invited me to their houses and generously entertained me.

The Cittie of New York is a pleasant, well compacted place, situated on a Commodius River wch is a fine harbour for shipping. The Buildings Brick Generaly, very stately and high, though not altogether like ours in Boston. The Bricks in some of the Houess are of divers Coullers and laid in Checkers, being glazed look very agreeable The inside of them are neat to admiration, the wooden work, for only the walls are plasterd, and the Sumers and Gist are plained and kept very white scowr'd as so is all the partitions if made of Bords. The fire places have no Jambs (as ours have) But the Backs run flush with the walls, and the Hearth is of Tyles and is as farr out into the Room at the Ends as before the fire, wch is Generally Five foot in the Low'r rooms, and the peice over where the mantle tree should be is made as ours with Joyners work, and as I supose is fasten'd to Iron rodds inside. The House where the Vendue was, had Chimney Corners like ours, and they and the hearths were laid wth the finest tile that I ever see, and the stair cases laid all with white tile which is ever clean, and so are the walls of the Kitchen wch had a Brick floor. They were making Great preparations to Receive their Govenor, Lord Cornbury from the Jerseys, and for that End raised the militia to Gard him on shore to the fort.

They are Generaly of the Church of England and have a New England Gentleman for their minister, and a very fine church set out with all Customary requsites There are also a Dutch and Divers Conventicles as they call them, viz. Baptist, Quakers, &c They are not strict in keeping the Sabbath as in Boston and other places where I had bin, But seem to deal with great exactness as farr as I see or Deall with. They are sociable to one another and Curteos and Civill to strangers and fare well in their houses. The English go very fasheonable in their dress. But the Dutch, especially the middling sort, differ from our women, in their habitt go loose, were French muches wch are like a Capp and a head band in one, leaving their ears bare, which are sett out with Jewells of a large size and many in number. And their fingers hoop't with Rings, some with large stones in them of many Coullers as were their pendants in their ears, which You should see very old women wear as well as Young.

They have Vendues very frequently and make their Earnings very well by them for they treat with good Liquor Liberally, and the Customers Drink as Liberally and Generally pay for't as well, by paying for that which they Bid up Briskly for, after the sack has gone plentifull about, tho' sometimes good penny worths are got there. Their Diversions in the Winter is

Riding Sleys about three or four Miles out of town, where they have Houses of entertainment at a place called the Bowery, and some go to friends Houses who handsomely treat them. Mr. Burroughs cary'd his spouse and Daughter and myeslf out to one Madame Dowes, a Gentlewoman that lived at a farm House, who gave us a handsome Entertainment of five or six Dishes and choice Beer and metheglin, Cyder, &c. all which she said was the produce of her farm. I believe we mett 50 or 60 slays that day—they fly with great swiftness and some are so furious that they'le turn out of the path for none except a Loaden Cart. Nor do they spare for any diversion the place affords, and sociable to a degree, they'r Tables being as free to their Naybours as to themselves.

Having here transacted the affair I went upon and some other that fell in the way, after about a fortnight's stay there I left New-York with no Little regrett, and Thursday, Dec. 21, set out for New Haven with my Kinsman, Trowbridge, and the man that waited on me about one afternoon, and about three come to half-way house about ten miles out of town, where we Baited and went forward, and about 5 come to Spiting Devil, Else Kings bridge, where they pay three pence for passing over with a horse, which the man that keeps the Gate set up at the end of the Bridge receives.

We hoped to reach the french town and Lodg there that night, but unhapily lost our way about four miles short, and being overtaken by a great storm of wind and snow which set full in our faces about dark, we were very uneasy. But meeting one Gardner who lived in a Cottage thereabout, offered us his fire to set by, having but one poor Bedd, and his wife not well, &c. or he would go to a House with us, where he thought we might be better accommodated—thither we went. But a surly old shee Creature, not worthy the name of woman, who would hardly let us go into her Door, though the weather was so stormy none but shee would have turnd out a Dogg. But her son whose name was Gallop, who lived Just by Invited us to his house and shewed me two pair of stairs, viz. one up the loft and tother up the Bedd. wch was as hard as it was high, and warmed it with a hott stone at the feet I lay very uncomfortably, insomuch that I was so very cold and sick I was forced to call them up to give me something to warm me. They had nothing but milk in the house, wch they Boild, and to make it better sweetened wth molasses. which I not knowing or thinking oft till it was down and coming up agen wch it did in so plentifull a manner that my host was soon paid double for his portion, and that in specia. But I believe it did me service in Cleering my stomach. So after this sick and weary night at East Chester, (a very miserable poor place,) the weather being now fair, Friday the 22d Dec. we set out for New Rochell, where being come we had good Entertainment and Recruited ourselves very well. This is a very pretty place well compact, and good handsome houses, Clean, good and passable Rodes, and situated on a Navigable River, abundance of land well fined and Cleerd all along as wee passed. which caused in me a Love to the place, wch I could have been content to live in it. Here wee Ridd over a Bridge made of one entire stone of such a Breadth that a cart might pass with safety, and to spare—it lay over a passage cutt through a Rock to convey water to a mill not farr off. Here are three fine Taverns within call of each other, very good provision for Travailers.

Thence we travailed through Merrinak, a neet, though little place, wth a navigable River before it. one of the pleasantest I ever see—Here were good Buildings, Especialy one, a very fine seat, wch they told me was Col Hethcoats, who I had heard was a very fine Gentleman. From hence we come to Hors Neck, where wee Baited, and they told me that one Church of England parson officiated in all these three towns once every Sunday in turns throughout the Year, and that they all could but poorly maintaine him, which they grudg'd to do, being a poor and quarelsome crew as I understand by our Host; their Quarelling about their choice of Minister, they chose to have none—But caused the Government to send this Gentleman to them. Here wee took leave of York Government, and Descending the Mountainos passage that almost broke my heart in ascending before, we come to Stamford, a well compact Town, but miserable meeting house, wch we passed, and thro' many and great difficulties, as Bridges which were exceeding high and very tottering and of vast Length, steep and Rocky Hills and precipices, (Buggbears to a fearful female travailer.) About nine at night we come to Norrwalk, having crept over a timber of a Broken Bridge about thirty foot long, and perhaps fifty to ye water. I was exceeding tired and cold when we come to our Inn, and could get nothing there but poor entertainment, and the Impertinant Bable of one of the worst of men, among many others of which our Host made one, who, had he bin one degree Impudenter, would have outdone his Grandfather. And this I think is the most perplexed night I have yet had. From hence, Saturday, Dec. 23, a very cold and windy day, after an Intolerable night's Lodging, wee hastened forward only observing in our way the Town to be situated on a Navigable river wth indifferent Buildings and people more refind than in some of the Country towns wee had passed, tho' vicious enough, the Church and Tavern being next neighbours. Having Ridd thro a difficult River wee come to Fairfield where wee Baited and were much refreshed as well with the Good things wch gratified our appetites as the time took to rest our wearied Limbs, wch Latter I employed in enquiring concerning the Town and manners of the people, &c. This is a considerable town, and filld as they say with wealthy people—have a spacious meeting house and good Buildings But the Inhabitants are Litigious, nor do they well agree with their minister, who (they say) is a very worthy Gentleman.

They have aboundance of sheep, whose very Dung brings them great gain, with part of which they pay their Parsons sallery. And they Grudg that, preferring their Dung before their minister. They Lett out their sheep at so much as they agree upon for a night, the highest Bidder always caries them, And they will sufficiently Dung a Large quantity of Land before morning. But were once Bitt by a sharper who had them a night and sheared them all before morning—from hence we went to Stratford, the next Town, in which I observed but few houses, and those not very good ones. But the people that I conversed with were civill and good natured. Here we staid till late at night, being to cross a Dangerous River ferry, the River at that time full of Ice, but after about four hours waiting with great difficulty wee got over. My fears and fatigues prevented my here taking any particular observation. Being got to Milford, it being late in the night, I could go no further; my fellow travailer going forward, I was invited to Lodg at Mrs. ————, a very kind and civill Gentlewoman, by whom I was handsomely and kindly entertained till the next night The people here go very plain in their apparel (more plain than I had observed in the towns I had passed) and seem to be very grave and serious. They told me there was a singing Quaker lived there, or at least had a strong inclination to be so, His Spouse not at all affected that way Some of the singing Crew come there one day to visit him, who being then abroad, they sat down (to the woman's no small vexation) Humming and singing and groneing after their conjuring way— Says the woman are you singing quakers? Yea says They—Then take my squalling Brat of a child here and sing to it says she for I have almost split my throat wth singing to him and cant get the Rogue to sleep They took this as a great Indignity, and mediately departed. Shaking the dust from their Heels left the good woman and her child among the number of the wicked. This is a Seaport place and accommodated with a Good Harbour, But I had not opportunity to make particular obesrvations because it was Sabbath day—This Evening.

December 24. I set out with the Gentlewomans son who she very civilly offered to go with me when she see no parswasions would cause me to stay while she pressingly desired, and crossing a ferry having but nine miles to New Haven, in a short time arrived there and was Kindly received and well accommodated amongst my Friends and Relations

The Government of Connecticut Collony begins westward towards York at Stamford (as I am Told) and so runs Eastward towards Boston (I mean in my range. because I dont intend to extend my description beyond my own travails) and ends that way at Stonington—And has a great many Large towns lying more northerly. It is a plentiful Country for provisions of all sorts and its Generally Healthy . No one that can and will be dilligent in this place need fear poverty nor the want of food and Rayment.

January 6th Being now well Recruited and fitt for business I discoursed the persons I was concerned with. that we might finish in order to my return to Boston. They delayd as they had hitherto done hoping to tire my Patience But I was resolute to stay and see an End of the matter let it be never so much to my disadvantage—So January 9th they come again and promise the Wednesday following to go through with the distribution of the Estate which they delayed till Thursday and then come with new amusements. But at length by the mediation of that holy good Gentleman, the Rev. Mr. James Pierpont, the minister of New Haven, and with the advice and assistance of other our Good friends we come to an accommodation and distribution, which having finished though not till February, the man that waited on me to York taking the charge of me I sit out for Boston. We went from New Haven upon the ice (the ferry being not passable thereby) and the Rev Mr. Pierpont wth Madam Prout Cuzin Trowbridge and divers others were taking leave wee went onward without any thing Remarkabl till wee come to New London and Lodged again at Mr Saltonstalls—and here I dismist my Guide. and my Generos entertainer provided me Mr. Samuel Rogers of that place to go home with me—I stayed a day here Longer than I intended by the Commands of the Honble Govenor Winthrop to stay and take a supper with him whose wonderful civility I may not omitt. The next morning I Crossed ye Ferry to Groton, having had the Honor of the Company. of Madam Livingston (who is the Govenors Daughter) and Mary Christophers and divers others to the boat—And that night Lodgd at Stonington and had Rost Beef and pumpkin sause for supper The next night at Haven's and had Rost fowle. an the next day wee come to a river which by Reason of Ye Freshetts coming down was swell'd so high wee feard it impassable and the rapid stream was very terryfying—However we must over and that in a small Cannoo. Mr. Rogers assuring me of his good Conduct. I after a stay of near an how'r on the shore for consultation went into the Cannoo. and Mr. Rogers paddled about 100 yards up the Creek by the shore side. turned into the swift stream and dexterously steering her in a moment wee come to the other side as swiftly passing as an arrow shott out of the Bow by a strong arm . I staid on ye shore till Hee returned to fetch our horses, which he caused to swim over himself bringing the furniture in the Cannoo. But it is past my skill to express the Exceeding fright all their transactions formed in me. Wee were now in the colony of the Massachusetts and taking Lodgings at the first Inn we come to had a pretty difficult passage the next day which was the second of March by reason of the sloughy ways then thawed by the Sunn Here I mett Capt John Richards of Boston who was going home, So being very glad of his Company we Rode something harder than hitherto, and missing my way in going up a very steep Hill, my hors dropt down under me as Dead; this new surprize no little hurt me meeting it Just at the Entrance into Dedham from whence we intended to reach home that night. But was now obliged to gett another Hors there and leave my own, resolving for Boston that night if possible. But in going over the Causeway at Dedham the Bridge being overflowed by the high waters comming down I very narrowly escaped falling over into the river Hors and all wch twas almost a miracle I did not—now it grew late in the after-noon and the people having very much discouraged us about the sloughy way wch they said wee should find very difficult and hazardous it so wrought on mee being tired and dispirited and disapointed of my desires of going home that I agreed to Lodg there that night wch wee did at the house of one Draper, and the next day being March 3d wee got safe home to Boston, where I found my aged and tender mother and my Dear and only Child in good health with open arms redy to receive me, and my Kind relations and friends flocking in to welcome mee and hear the story of my transactions and travails I having this day bin five months from home and now I cannot fully express my Joy and Satisfaction. But desire sincearly to adore my Great Benefactor for thus graciously carying forth and returning in safety his un-worthy handmaid.

The country suffered little from the ravages of King Philip's War, new settlers continued to arrive, the population grew, the new generation took up the tasks of clearing the land, tilling the soil, and carrying on the various crafts needed in a small community.

A list of the names of the original families of these towns will include many names familiar to students of American History—names prominent in the Colonial period, in the Revolutionary War, and in the development of our whole country as the pioneers spread westward to Pennsylvania, Ohio, and ultimately on to the Pacific Under the history of each town will be found the names of early settlers.

Before 1710 New London county had furnished for Connecticut three Governors, and two Chief Justices of the Supreme Court.

Though the founders were closely allied, there seems to have been much rivalry between New London and Norwich in early days. The first and only magistrate of the county during his lifetime was John Mason, of Norwich, and he usually held his court at home. After his death, a New London man was appointed. There was for many years an effort on the part of Norwich to have sessions of the Superior Court held in Norwich half the time The first county court house was located in New London in 1724 After the burning of New London in 1781, a new one was erected at the head of State street. Norwich became a "half-shire" town in 1734, and soon erected a jail with whipping post and pillory near by. Its court house of 1829 was burned in 1865, and replaced soon after by the present court house at the "Landing."

It is hard for the present generation to realize how closely knit were Church and State in these colonial days. Dr Daniel Coit Gilman, later president of Johns Hopkins, at that time librarian of Yale College, delivered at Norwich in September, 1859, at the celebration of the 200th anniversary of Norwich, an address which is a mine of information on matters pertaining to the early history of New London county. We quote his words regarding religious conditions at the close of the seventeenth century:

I have already said that the first manuscript records of the church have perished. One curious printed document has lately been discovered, bearing date 1675, which is interesting in its bearing on the history of these times. The only complete copy with which I am acquainted belongs to Mr. George Brinley, of Hartford, who has kindly permitted me to bring it before you It is an old fashioned duodecimo of 133 pages, printed in 1683, bearing on its title page the autographs of Increase Mather and of Mather Byles. It contains three distinct treatises; the first, "An explanation of the solemn advice, recommended by the council in Connecticut colony to the inhabitants in that jurisdiction"; and the third, "A brief discourse proving that the first day of the week is the Christian Sabbath." Both of these are attributed to Mr. Fitch. Appended to the former is "The Covenant, which was solemnly renewed by the church in Norwich, in Connecticut colony, in New England, March 22, 1675." The volume is introduced by a letter from Increase Mather, "to the reader," in which he says that "the reverend and worthy author had no thought of publishing these brief and nervous discourses until such time as others did importune him thereunto," and proceeds to comment on their scope and character.

The circumstances which attended this "renewal" are worthy of mention. The war with King Philip was then raging. Norwich, though much exposed by its situation on the frontier, had freely contributed more than its quota to the active army; so freely, indeed, that the General Court sent on from Hartford ten men, from New Haven eight, and from Fairfield eight, "to lye in garrison at Norwich," as a guard to the inhabitants. So great was the danger in those days that the watch in each plantation was ordered "at least an hour before day, to call up the inhabitants, who should forthwith rise and arm themselves, march to the fort, and stand guard against any assault of the enemy until the sun be half an hour high in the morning." Under these circumstances, on the 13th of March, Mr. Fitch writes to the council in Hartford. After acknowledging the receipt of a letter from the council, with their orders for a fast day, he continues:

"Blessed be the Lord who hath moved your hearts in so necessarie and seasonable worke. We intend, God willing, to take that very daye, solemnly to renew our covenant in our church state, according to the example in Ezra's time, and as was sometimes practised in Hartford congregation by Mr. Stone, not long after Mr. Hooker's death. If other churches doe not see cause to doe the same, yet wee hope it will not bee offensive; but doe verily conclude if y be rule for y practise, this is a time wherein the Providence of God does in a knocking and terrible manner call for it."

The covenant evinces the same spirit, and to some extent it employs the same phrases as this letter. After a general recognition of the displeasure of God, as displayed "by blasting the fruits of the earth and cutting off the lives of many by the sword, laying waste some plantations and threatening ruin to the whole," the covenant is renewed in seven particulars, which may be condensed as follows:

1. All the males who are eight or nine years of age shall be presented before the Lord in his congregation every Lord's day to be catechised, until they be about thirteen in age.

2. Those who are about thirteen years of age, both male and female, shall frequent the meetings appointed in private for their instruction, while they continue under family government or until they are received to full communion in the church.

3. Adults who do not endeavor to take hold of the covenant shall be excommunicated.

4. Brethren shall be appointed to admonish those parents who are negligent of their children.

5. The Lord's supper shall be celebrated once in every six weeks.

6. Erring brethren are to be rebuked.

7. Finally, "seeing we feel by woful experience how prone we are soon to forget the works of the Lord, and our own vows; we do agree and determine, that this writing or contents of it, shall be once in every year read in a day of fasting and prayer before the Lord, and his congregation; and shall leave it with our children, that they do the same in their solemn days of mourning before the Lord, that they may never forget how their fathers, ready to perish in a strange land, and with sore grief and trembling of heart, and yet hope in the tender mercy, and good will of him, who dwelt in the burning bush, did thus solemnly renew their covenant with God: and that our children after us, may not provoke the Lord and be cast off as a degenerate off-spring, but may tremble at the commandment of God, and learn to place their hope in him, who although he hath given us a cup of astonishment to drink, yet will display his banner over them, who fear him.

Speaking of the religious awakening that took place in New London county in the earlier part of the eighteenth century, Rev. Mr. Northrop says:

The awakening took deep root in New London county, where the Separatist movement was pronounced, and the knell of dis-establishment began to be sounded. . . . New religious ideas come in, and the established Congregational Church of Connecticut undergoes dissolution and gives place to the rights of free worship. And with the freer and wider thinking begins a better thought of the outside world. Some of the most fruitful beginnings of the great modern missionary movement had their origin right here on this soil, and so it has come to pass that New London county has the distinction of having given more for the evangelization of the world than any other county in the United States.

CHAPTER II

THE BEGINNINGS OF EDUCATION

Education Recognized as a First Necessity—First Free School—Other Schools and Early Teachers—Contrasts Between the Old and New Systems of Education—The Norwich Tests—School Legislation—Provision for the Indians.

In view of the great importance of education in the development of New England as a whole, no less in our county than elsewhere, we interrupt our narrative history to insert a review of educational progress in New London county. In order that we may discuss this subject in a broad sense, we prefix a brief definition of education from the standpoint of history.

Education is the process by which an individual comes into possession of some part of human progress and thus fits himself to take part in the life of his own generation. This process, in a normal person, is taking place most of the time from birth to death.

We are all creatures of the past; in physical appearance, in traits of body and mind, in desires, and in powers, we are the "heirs of all the ages" of human evolution. As there is abundant evidence that man has improved from his original condition, we may fairly say that the inheritance of each generation from the preceding one has steadily increased in value as human experience has covered new fields of action. Each generation progresses, first by acquiring the gains of former generations, then by new experiences of its own.

Somewhat after the beginning of written language the accumulation of records of the past became so great that specially trained men were needed to preserve and interpret these records. And so great has been the increase in the amount and complexity of human progress, that great institutions have arisen to secure for humanity the perpetual possession of its most valuable gains.

These gains may be grouped under two heads: first, gains in aims; secondly, gains in powers. Under these two topics may be grouped, I believe, all the progress of every epoch of history as well as that of every individual in any epoch. Let us then briefly subdivide human aims and human powers.

In so far as man's aims are affected by a belief in the supernatural, we group them under the name of Religion. In so far as his aims affect his dealings with his fellow men we may group them under the head of Morality. The moral code has on the one side the sanction of the institution of Religion, and on the other side the support of the institution of Government.

Human powers may be subdivided into knowledge, or power in understanding; efficiency, or power in action; emotion, or power to feel and appreciate. It is evident then that the great institutions of mankind exist for the purpose of educating man in these aims and powers. The progress of humanity is the aggregate gain of individuals in spiritual inspiration, in moral desires, in respect for law, in power to enjoy what is best, in sympathy for others, in the virtues and habits that promote efficiency, in the understanding necessary to direct one's efforts intelligently.

The School is that institution which exists primarily for the distribution of knowledge. Now the mass of human knowledge has become so great that no one can hope to put into practice more than a very small part of it. It is necessary therefore that the individual choose a time when he will begin to put his attention on the details of his life work rather than on the broader understanding of human progress. This point of time marks the division between his liberal culture and his technical training.

When shall technical training begin? No one knows. The answer will vary with the individual's powers and opportunities. It is fair to say that liberal culture should be prolonged until its further continuance would interfere with the technical efficiency of the individual.

But even technical information will be of little use to an individual unless he has the personal virtues that make him efficient. Strength of will, tact, good habits, and many other qualities, are to be ranked even higher than understanding. In modern times, therefore, the school has become in miniature a world of itself, in which the right minded pupil may learn lessons of morality, lessons of personal power, as well as lessons in understanding and appreciation.

Besides the four great institutions there are other tremendous forces at work moulding the lives of individuals and communities; Literature, Painting, Music, the Press, and too many other forces to mention have today a greater influence than ever before in the history of the world.

A full definition of education, then, in its broadest sense, would be something like this:—Education is the process whereby the individual, through the Home, the Church, the State, the School, and through all the remainder of his environment, learns his own noblest capabilities, learns to obey moral law, gains power to do, and understanding to direct that power.

In treating those facts which it is most advisable that a man entering into life should accurately know, Ruskin says:

I believe that he ought to know three things: First, Where he is; secondly, Where he is going; thirdly, What he had best do, under those circumstances.

First: Where he is.—That is to say, what sort of a world he has got into; how large it is; what kind of creatures live in it, and how; what it is made of, and what may be made of it.

Secondly: Where he is going—That is to say, what chances or reports there are of any other world besides this; what seems to be the nature of that other world. . . .

Thirdly: What he had best do under the circumstances.—That is to say, what kind of faculties he possesses; what are the present state and wants of mankind; what is his place in society; and what are the readiest means in his power of attaining happiness and diffusing it. The man who knows these things, and who has had his will so subdued in the learning them, that he is ready to do what he knows he ought, I should call educated; and the man who knows them not, uneducated—though he could talk all the tongues of Babel.

The men who settled Connecticut believed that every one should be able to read the word of God. Every church therefore had its teacher as well as its preacher. In advance of any Colonial legislation relating to common schools, almost every settlement had its teacher for part of the year at the most. The first laws did little more than guarantee the practice common in most towns. The settlers realized that the system of government dimly outlined in the "Mayflower Compact" of 1619, expanded in the Fundamental Orders of 1639, which to us of today stands forth as the "first written constitution known to history" and the foundation for republican form of government, made universal education essential to self-preservation.

Connecticut was the first State in the Union to set apart and establish a fund for the support of common schools. This was done after the sale of the "Western Reserve" lands in 1795 for $1,200,000. By the Constitution of 1818, Article 8, Par. 2, this fund is forever set apart for public schools:

§ 2 The fund, called the "School Fund," shall remain a perpetual fund, the interest of which shall be inviolably appropriated to the support and encouragement of the public or common schools throughout the state, and for the equal benefit of all the people thereof. The value and amount of said fund shall, as soon as practicable, be ascertained in such manner as the General Assembly may prescribe, published and recorded in the Comptroller's office; and no law shall ever be made authorizing said fund to be diverted to any other use than the encouragement and support of public or common schools, among the several school societies, as justice and equity shall require.

The first law relating to common schools in Connecticut was enacted by the town of New Haven in 1641, and provided for a free school to be supported out of "the Common Stock." The next law was passed in Hartford in 1643, providing a free school for the poor children, with tuition charge for those able to pay. In 1646 a compilation of laws of the colony shows that every township of fifty families should maintain a school, and any town of one hundred families a grammar school. After the union of New Haven and Connecticut under the charter of 1662, many acts were passed relating to common schools. In 1700, every town of seventy families was required to maintain constantly a schoolmaster able to teach reading and writing. Towns of smaller size had to keep a school half the year. A grammar school was required in every shire town. The rate for school expenses was fixed at a minimum of forty shillings for every 1,000 in the county lists, and, if insufficient, was to be further secured by joint levy on inhabitants and parents of children. School committees, as distinct from other town officers, are first mentioned in 1708.

Parishes were recognized as school districts, though under general control of the towns. The close connection between churches and schools was possible because the population was homogeneous. But gradually came about a system of the separation of the church and school. By 1798, schools were managed by themselves as school societies or districts. The gradual return to town management by the consolidation of school districts followed the change of school laws in 1856. The types of schools of course changed as school laws became better adjusted to the needs of growing communities. In the various communities grew up private schools alongside the common elementary school. As types of such schools may be mentioned those described by Miss Caulkins in her "History of Norwich":

The schools in Norwich were neither intermitted or neglected during the Revolutionary War. An institution of higher grade than elementary was sustained in the town-plot through all the distractions of the country. It called in many boarders from abroad, and at one period, with Mr. Goodrich for its principal, acquired considerable popularity. This school is endorsed by its committee, Andrew Huntington and Dudley Woodbridge, in 1783, as furnishing instruction to "young gentlemen and ladies, lads and misses, in every branch of literature, viz., reading, writing, arithmetic, the learned languages, logic, geography, mathematics," &c. Charles White, teacher

The exhibitions of the school were commonly enlivened with scenic representations and interludes of music. A taste for such entertainments was prevalent. The young people, even after their emancipation from schools, would sometimes take part in theatrical representations. We learn from the town newspaper that in February, 1792, a select company of young ladies and gentlemen performed the tragedy of "Gustavus" and "The Mistakes of a Night" at the court-house.

The school-ma'am of former times, with her swarming hive of pupils, was an institution of which no sample remains at the present day. She was a life-long incumbent, never going out of one round of performance: always teaching little girls and boys to sit up straight and treat their elders with respect; to conquer the spelling-book, repeat the catechism, never throw stones, never tell a lie; the boys to write copies, and the girls to work samplers. If they sought higher education than this, they passed out of her domain into finishing schools. Almost every neighborhood had its school-ma'am, and the memory is still fresh of Miss Sally Smith at the Landing, and Miss Molly Grover of the Town-plot.

Dancing-schools were peculiarly nomadic in their character; the instructor (generally a Frenchman) circulating through a wide district and giving lessons for a few weeks at particular points. Reels, jigs and contra-dances were most in vogue; the hornpipe and rigadoon were attempted by only a select few; cotillions were growing in favor; the minuet much admired. In October, 1787, Griffith's dancing-school was opened at the house of Mrs. Billings in the town-plot. He taught five different minuets, one of them a duo, and another a cotillion-minuet. His lessons were given in the morning, with a scholars' ball once a fortnight. Ten years later, J. C. Devereux was a popular teacher of the dance. He had large classes for several seasons at the court-house, and at Kinney's hotel in Chelsea.

In 1799, a school for young ladies was opened in the house of Major Whiting upon the Little Plain, by Mrs. Brooks, who devoted herself especially to feminine accomplishments, such as tambour, embroidery, painting in water-colors, instrumental music, and the French language. She had at first a large number of pupils from this and the neighboring towns, but the attendance soon declined, and the school was relinquished. In general the young ladies at such schools only remained long enough to practice a few tunes on the guitar, to tambour a muslin shawl and apron, or embroider a scripture scene, and this gave the finishing stroke to their education

It was common then, as it is now, for parents with liberal means to send both their sons and daughters from home to obtain greater educational advantages. Young ladies from Norwich often went to Boston to finish their education, and now and then one was placed under the guardian care and instruction of the Moravian sisterhood in their seminary at Bethlehem, Pennsylvania.

In 1782 an academical association was formed in the western part of the town-plot, consisting of forty-one subscribers and one hundred shares of rights. The old meeting-house of the Separatists was purchased and repaired for the use of this institution. The first principal was Samuel Austin, and the range of studies included Latin and Greek, navigation and the mathematics. Two popular school-books then just issued were introduced by Mr. Austin into this school—Webster's "Grammatical Institutes," and "Geography Made Easy," by Jedidiah Morse. Mr. Morse was himself subsequently a teacher in this institution, which was continued with varying degrees of prosperity for thirty years or more. Alexander Macdonald, author of a school-book called "The Youth's Assistant," was one of its teachers. He died May 4, 1792, aged forty. Newcomb Kinney was at one time the principal, and had for his usher John Russ of Hartford, afterward member of Congress from 1819 to 1823 In 1800, Sebastian C. Cabot was the chief instructor. This school was kept in operation about thirty years. After it ceased, the lower part of the building was occupied by the public school, and the upper part, being suitably prepared, was in use for nearly twenty years as a Methodist chapel.

Dr. Daniel Lathrop, who died in 1782, left a legacy of £500 to the town for the support of a free grammar school, upon certain conditions, one of which was that the school should be kept during eleven months of each year. A school upon this foundation was opened in 1787, and continued for about fifty years. The brick school-house upon the green was built for its accommodation. Its first teacher was Ebenezer Punderson But the most noted of its preceptors and the one who longest held his place was Mr. William Baldwin, an excellent instructor, faithful and apt to teach, but a rigid disciplinarian, and consequently more respected than beloved by his pupils, until after-life led them to reverse the decisions of earlier days. The young have seldom judgment and generosity sufficient to make them love those who control them for their good.

In 1843 the Lathrop donation was relinquished, with the consent of the legislature, to the heirs-at-law of Thomas Coit, a nephew of Dr. Lathrop, to whom by the provision of the testator's will it was in such case to revert. The investment had depreciated in value, and the restrictions with which the legacy was incumbered made it, in the advanced state of educational institutions, more of a hindrance than a help. The school had been for many years a great advantage to the town, but having accomplished its mission, it quietly ceased to be.

Evening schools of short duration, devoted to some special study, were not uncommon The object was usually of a practical nature, and the students above childhood. The evening school of Consider Sterry, in 1798, covered, according to his program, the following range of instruction: "Book-keeping in the Italian, American and English methods, mathematics, surveying and plotting of lands; price is. 6d per week Navigation and the method of finding longitude by lunar observations and latitude by the sun's altitude, one dollar for the complete knowledge."

Few men are gifted by nature with such an aptitude for scientific research as Consider Sterry. His attainments were all self-acquired under great disadvantages. Besides a work on lunar observations, he and his brother prepared an arithmetic for schools, and in company with Nathan Daboll, another self-taught scientific genius, he arranged and edited a system of practical navigation, entitled "The Seaman's Universal Daily Assistant," a work of nearly three hundred pages. He also published several small treatises, wrote political articles for the papers, and took a profound interest in freemasonry.

In June, 1800, a school was inaugurated at the brick house on the Little Plain, with Mr. William Woodbridge for the principal. The assembly room was fitted up with desks and benches for an academical hall; both sexes were admitted, and the whole was under the supervision of a board of four citizens—Joseph Howland, Samuel Woodbridge, Thomas Fanning, Thomas Lathrop. But the situation was too remote from the centers of population, and after a trial of two or three years this school was relinquished for want of patronage.

A select school for young persons of both sexes was long sustained in the town-plot, but with varying tides of prosperity and decline. After a void of two or three years, it was revived in 1803 by Pelatiah Perit, who had just then graduated from Yale College, and was only eighteen years of age. Lydia Huntley, afterwards Mrs. Sigourney, was one of his pupils.

Among other teachers of the town-plot, who were subsequently honorable and noted in their several callings, the following are well remembered: Daniel Haskell, president of the Vermont University; Henry Strong, LL.D., eminent in the law; John Hyde, judge of county court, judge of probate, etc.; Dr. Peter Allen, a physician in Ohio; Rev. Joshua L. Williams, of Middletown; J. Bates Murdock, afterwards an officer of the Second War with Great Britain; Phineas L. Tracy, who from 1827 to 1833 was Member of Congress from Genesee county, New York.

A proprietary school was established at the Landing in 1797, by twenty-seven heads of families. The school-house was built on the slope of the hill above Church street, and the school was assembled and organized by the Rev. Walter King. David L. Dodge was the first regular teacher. In 1802, the Rev. Thomas Williams was the preceptor. He was noted for his assiduous attention to the health and morals as well as the studies of his pupils. He drilled them thoroughly in the "Assembly's Catechism," anl used with his younger classes a favorite manual called "The Catechism of Nature." Other teachers of this school were Mr. Scarborough, Ebenezer Witter, John Lord (president of Dartmouth College), George Hill, and others. But no one retained the office for so long a term as Dyar T. Hinckley, of Windham, a man of earnest zeal in his profession, who was master of desk and bench in Norwich for twenty years or more, yet never removed his family or obtained a regular home in the place. He was a schoolmaster of the old New England type, devoted to his profession as an ulterior pursuit, and expending his best energies in the performance of its duties.

Schools at that period consisted uniformly of two sessions a day, of three hours each, with a half-holiday on Saturday. Mr. Hinckley, in addition to this, had sometimes an evening or morning school, or both, of two hours each, for pupils not belonging to the day-school. The morning hours were devoted to young ladies, and from an advertisement of May, 1816, giving notice of a new term, we ascertain the precise time when the class assembled: "Hours from 5 o'clock to 7 A. M." Let no one hastily assume that this early summons would be neglected. Living witnesses remain to testify that it drew a goodly number of young aspirants who came out, fresh and vigorous, at sunrise or a little later, to pursue their studies.

Another institution that made its mark upon society was the Chelsea Grammar School, organized in 1806, but not incorporated till 1821, when it was impowered to hold real estate to the value of $20,000. The school-house was on the side-hill opposite the Little Park, in Union street. This institution continued in operation, with some vacant intervals, about forty years, securing for its patrons the benefits of an academical education for their children without sending them home. Many prominent citizens of Norwich here received their first introduction to the classics, the sons in numerous instances taking possession of seats once occupied by their fathers.

No complete list of the preceptors has been obtained; but among the remembered names are several that have since been distinguished in literary and professional pursuits—Dr. Jonathan Knight, of New Haven; Charles Griswold, of Lyme; Jonathan Barnes, Wyllis Warner, Roswell C. Smith, Rev. Horace Bushnell, D D., and Rev. William Adams, D.D. These men were all young at the time. The preceptors of most schools, here and elsewhere, at that period, were college graduates, accepting the office for a year, or at most for two or three years, between taking their degree and entering upon some other profession. But teachers to whom the vocation is but a stepping-stone to something beyond on which the mind is fixed, however faithful and earnest in their present duties, can never raise an institution to any permanent standard of excellence. It is well therefore that these temporary undertakings should give way to public schools more thoroughly systematized and conducted by persons who make teaching a profession.

In Chelsea, beginning about 1825, a series of expedients for enlarging the bounds of knowledge afford pleasing evidence of the gradual expansion of intellect and enterprise. A lyceum, a circulating library, a reading club, a society for mutual improvement, and a mechanics' association, were successively started, and though most of them were of brief duration, they were cheering tokens of an advance in the right path.

The Norwich Female Academy was incorporated in 1828. This institution was greatly indebted for its origin to the persevering exertion of Mr. Thomas Robinson, who was the principal agent of the corporation. The brick hall erected for its accommodation stood on the hill facing the river, higher than any other building then on the declivity. Neither court-house nor jail had gained a foothold on the height, which was well forested, and toward the north surmounted by a fine prospect station, overtopping the woods, and known as Rockwell's Tower. The academy had the rugged hill for its background, but on other sides the view was varied and extensive; and when at recess the fair young pupils spread in joyous freedom over the height, often returning with wild flowers and oak-leaf garlands from the neighboring groves, neither poetry nor romance could exaggerate the interest of the scene.

The most prosperous year of this academy was 1833, when the number of pupils amounted to nearly ninety, many of them boarders from other places. But the exposed situation of the building, and the rough, steep ascent by which only it could be reached, were adverse to the prosperity of a female academy, and it soon became extinct—disbanded by wintry blasts and icy foot-paths.

In her "History of New London," Miss Caulkins thus covers the early history of public education in New London:

The town school located on this spot was the free grammar-school, which had for its main support the Bartlet and other public revenues, and had been originally established further up the hill, on Hempstead street, but had descended from thence about 1750. It was now removed a few rods to the north, and placed in the highway fronting the Erving lot (Church street in that part not having been opened), with no wall or inclosure around it, these not being deemed at that time necessary. The dwelling houses in this part of the town were few, and the neighboring hills and fields were the playground of the boys In the rear was the Hallam lot, extending from Broad street to the old meeting-house square, with but one building upon it, and that in its north-east corner. A little more distant, in the rear of the court-house, was the Coit "hollow-lot," shaded by large trees, and enriched with a rivulet of pure water (where Cottage street now runs). Still further back was a vacant upland lot (known as Fosdick's or Melally's lot), containing here and there a choice apple-tree, well known to schoolboys; this is now the second burial ground.

We have heard aged people revert to these scenes, the days when they were pupils of the free grammar-school, under the sway of "Master Owen"; when a house of worship had not given name and beauty to Zion's Hill, and only a cellar and a garden, tokens of former residence of one of the early settlers of the town, were to be seen on the spot where the Trott man-sion now stands. (This is supposed to have been the place where stood the house on Charles Hill, fortified in the time of the Indian war. The present house was built by Samuel Fosdick, at the head of Niantic river, but taken apart, brought into town, and erected in 1786. It has been occupied by J. P. Trott, its present owner, more than half a century.) Later than this (about 1796) General Huntington broke ground upon the hillside and erected his house (now Hurlbutt's), in the style called cottage ornée. Beyond this, on the present Coit property, was a gushing spring, where the eager schoolboy slaked his thirst and cooled his heated brow; and not a quarter of a century has elapsed since the space now occupied by the Williams mansion and grounds was an open, irregular hillside over whose rugged surface troops of children, as they issued from the school-room, were seen to scatter in their various sports, like flocks of sheep spreading over the hills.

In the year 1795, the old school-house, a low, red building of one room, with a garret above, entered by a flight of stairs and a trap door, where refractory pupils were committed for punishment; and with desks and benches, which, though made of solid oak, were desperately marred by ink and knife, was abandoned, and the school removed to a larger building of brick, erected for its accommodation in the highway, south of the court house, where it fulfilled another period of its history, of nearly forty years. Here the chair of instruction, or more properly the throne (for the government was despotic), was occupied after 1800 by Dr. Dow, the number of whose subjects usually amounted to about 150, though sometimes rising to 200.

In 1833, a new and much superior edifice was erected for the grammar school on a lot south of the Second Congregational Church, chiefly through the exertion and liberality of Joseph Hurlbut, to whom a vote of thanks was rendered by the town, October 9th, 1833 In this building the Bartlet or grammar school is still continued under the care of the town, but the fund is inadequate to its support and the pupils are taxed to supply the deficiency.

The most noted teachers of this school since 1750, those whose office covered the longest term of years, were John Owen (the remains of "Master Owen," were laid in the second burial ground, but no memorial stone marks the spot If a sufficient number of his old pupils are yet upon the stage of life to undertake the charge, it would be a creditable enterprise for them to unite and raise some simple but fitting monument to his memory. He was for many years both town and city clerk)—and Ulysses Dow; both were peculiar characters, and each remained in office nearly forty years. The former died in 1801, aged sixty-five; the latter in 1844, aged seventy-eight.

The Union School was an establishment incorporated by the General Assembly in October, 1774. The petition for the act was signed by twelve proprietors, who state that they had "built a commodious school house, and for several years past hired and supported a school-master." The original proprietors were Richard Law, Jeremiah Miller, Duncan Stewart, Silas Church, Thomas Allen, John Richards, Robinson Mumford, Joseph Cristophers, Marvin Wait, Nathaniel Shaw, Jr., Roger Gibson, Thomas Mumford.

This school was intended to furnish facilities for a thorough English education and the classical preparation necessary for entering college. The school-house stood on State street, and by the subsequent opening of Union street was made a corner lot. This was a noted school in its early days, yielding a larger income than ordinary schools, and the station of preceptor was regarded as a post of honor. It has been heretofore stated that Nathan Hale held that office in 1775, and that he left the school to enter the army. He was the first preceptor after the act of incorporation. A few only of his successors can be named. Seth Williston, a graduate of Dartmouth College and since known as a divine of considerable eminence, was in charge for two years. Jacob B. Gurley, from the same seminary, succeeded Williston in May, 1794, and was the principal for three years. (Mr. Gurley is a native of Mansfield, Connecticut, but since 1794 a resident of New London, where he began to practice as an attorney in 1797.) Ebenezer Learned, a native of the town, and a graduate of Yale College, filled the chair of instruction in 1799. Knight, of the Medical College of New Haven, Olmstead of Yale, Mitchell of the University of North Carolina, and many other names of note, are among the teachers after 1800.

The school house was taken down and the land sold after 1830, and in 1833 a reorganization took place, a new charter was obtained, and a brick school house flourished for a few years, but could not be long sustained. The Bartlet and common schools gathered in the great mass of pupils; the number wishing to pursue a more extensive system of education was small, and the Union School, an old and venerated establishment, was discontinued. In 1851 the building was sold to the Bethel Society, by whom it has been converted into a commodious house of worship.

No provision seems to have been made for the education of females in anything but needle-work, reading, writing, and the first principles of arithmetic, until the year 1799. A female academy was then built by a company of proprietors, in Green street, and incorporated by the legislature. It continued in operation, with some intervals of recess, about thirty years. The property was then sold and the company dissolved in 1834. A new female academy was built the same year on Broad street, and the system of instruction commenced by Rev. Daniel Huntington. This institution has hitherto met with fair encouragement. Since 1841 it has been in charge of H. P. Farnsworth, principal. The pupils are arranged in two departments, and for a few years past the average number has been about eighty.

Private schools of similar nature were found in other towns of the county, and will be mentioned in the town histories. Higher education was sought by many leading men. Miss Caulkins gives a list of eighty-six names of men native to New London who had received a college education up to the year 1850. A similar list for Norwich may be found in the "Norwich Jubilee

Volume," and includes over 130 names. Beginning with the middle of the nineteenth century have come steady advances in educational methods and equipment The legislation of the State has promoted this by State aid and by compulsory school laws. To describe adequately the progress made in education in New London county for the past fifty years would involve a discussion of educational progress in all civilized lands, and especially in the United States The laws relating to the schools in Connecticut fill over 200 pages of printed matter. New statutes are enacted with each new legislature. In general, it must suffice to say that Connecticut aims to keep pace with country-wide educational progress, but is far less centralized in policy than many States. Consequently there have survived in our county an unusual number of schools that are the products of local initiative rather than of State patronage or State control. The word "Progress" covers the history of education in New London county for the past seventy-five years.

In answer to some people who feel that the new "frills" have been brought into our grammar schools at the expense of the "Three R's," the following paper was prepared and printed in the "School Review":

THE NORWICH TESTS, 1862-1909

In spite of the conclusive evidence of the well-known "Springfield tests"* of four years ago, one still hears not infrequently a lament that "the good old days" are gone It may not be amiss, therefore, for me to submit to the readers of the "School Review" a brief account of another series of tests recently given in a Connecticut community, covering a period of about fifteen years later than that covered by the Massachusetts inquiry.

In 1906, shortly after the preliminary report of the Springfield tests, we decided to try some of our old examination papers on present-day pupils of Norwich, Connnecticut. An arithmetic paper of 1856 was set before an eighth-grade division of the Broadway Grammar School of this city. Since we had the original papers of fifty years ago, we were able to make an exact comparison of results The eighth-grade pupils of 1906 had still more than a year's work in grammar school before taking our regular entrance examinations. The results were as follows:

	1856	1906
Pupils examined	73	27
Members attaining 100 per cent	3	4
Lowest mark	40 per cent	10 per cent
Average mark	75 per cent	88 per cent
Average age	15¼	13½

In other words, the pupils of 1906 though two years younger than the pupils of 1856 did much better work on the very examination for which the pupils of 1856 had been prepared. A result so surprising led us to doubt our own tests. It was thought that possibly the division of pupils of 1906 was a picked division, or that possibly the school did not represent the average of our grammar schools; for, still retaining the antiquated system of district management, we have no such uniformity of grammar school work as is found in many communities. We resolved accordingly to make another test that should better represent our whole community and our average pupils. We sent out to three of our largest districts papers in arithmetic, geography, history, and grammar, given as entrance examinations in 1862 and 1863.

These examinations were given in February. 1909, without previous warning or preparation, and under supervision of school principals, who, in making their returns, were ignorant of the results of 1862-63, and likewise of each others results It was declared by each principal independently that his own pupils would have done much better if the tests had been taken later in the year, after reviews had been completed. The papers given were as follows:

---

* See *The Springfield Tests*, issued by the Holden Book Cover Co , Springfield, Mass.

ARITHMETIC

1. A man bought a house for $4,000, and paid $250 for repairs, and sold it so as to gain 10½ per cent on his investment For how much did he sell it?
2. How much is 3/4x2/3x7/9 divided by 2/5x8/11x5/8.
3. Required, the simple interest on $90 36 for 3 years 6 months 12 days, at 6 per cent.
4. If six yards of cloth cost £4 13s what will 11 yards cost?
5. Find the amount of $304 56 for four years, at 7 per cent, simple interest
6. Subtract 3x4 7/8 from 9x5 2/3.
7. What is the sum of 5 1/2, 6 2/3 and 7 1/4 in decimal numbers?
8. Reduce 0.425 to a vulgar fraction in lowest terms.
9. How many yards of carpeting ¾ yard wide will cover a floor 27 feet long and 16 feet wide?
10. A load of hay weighs 2,625 lbs. What is it worth at $15 per ton?

GEOGRAPHY

1. Where is Chicago situated? Cairo? Memphis? Pensacola? Richmond?
2. Where is Pike's Peak.
3. On what waters would you sail from Norwich to Baltimore?
4. What separates the Red Sea from the Mediterranean?
5. What is the length of a degree of longitude?
6. What are the principal ports of the United States, south of Norfolk, Virginia?
7. Name the principal mountain ranges of Europe.
8. Draw a map of Virginia.
9. Through what State does the Connecticut River flow?
10. When it is noon at Norwich, what time is it 15° east of this place?

HISTORY

1. What were the motives which induced the colonists of Virginia and of New England to form settlements in America?
2. What did Penn make the basis of his institutions?
3. What was the cause of the Revolutionary War?
4. What foreign assistance had the Americans during the Revolution?
5. When was the battle of Bunker Hill fought?
6. When was the Constitution adopted?
7. For what reasons was war declared by the United States against Great Britain in 1812?
8. In whose administration was Louisiana annexed to the United States, and from whom purchased?
9. What was the Missouri Compromise?
10. Which of the States is called the Old Dominion?

GRAMMAR

1. Give the principal parts of the verb *to love*, and write out the inflection of the tenses of the indicative mode
2. Decline *John, James,* and *men.*
3. Write a sentence concerning General Lyon, which shall contain a relative clause.
4. Is the following sentence correct? If not, make it so "I done the best I could"
5. "I intended to have been there." Is this sentence correct? If not, make it so.
6. In the following stanza parse the words in italics :

> The *muse,* disgusted at an age, *and* clime
> *Barren* of every glorious theme,
> In distant lands now waits a better time,
> *Producing* subjects worthy fame

7. Analyze the stanza
8. Compare *Good, bad, little,* and *strong.*
9. Give the principal parts of *go, strike, run, rise,* and *sit*
10. Name and define tenses.

It will be noted that in the fourth question of the arithmetic paper the table of English money is involved. Since we no longer require this in our entrance tests it is not usually taught in our grammar schools. Again in the eighth question the term "vulgar" fraction is used, a term superseded by "common" fraction in most of our textbooks. In history likewise the tenth question involves a term no longer taught in our schools. In one of the schools a substitute question was given instead of the fourth, and the word "common" instead of "vulgar." No suggestion was made, however, as to the tenth question in history. In the other two schools no comment whatever was made on any of the questions, and many pupils registered a flat failure on questions that they would have answered if worded in today's terms. The results of the tests may be tabulated as follows:

School	I	II	III	Total 1909	Total 1862-63
Number	31	25	35	91	88
Age	14	14	14	14	15
Arithmetic	95%	90%	85%	90%	54%
Geography	85%	80%	70%	78%	66%
History	77%	82%	71%	76%	57%
Grammar	85%	74%	75%	78%	63%
Combined Average...........				80%	60%

I cannot say that the results were at all surprising in view of the previous tests of 1906. But that the average pupil of Norwich grammar schools today, at the age of fourteen, is better fitted in all subjects than was the average pupil of fifteen forty odd years ago, shows most clearly that modern fads have not brought with them a loss of the much-praised disciplinary studies of former times

Even without the formal tests, a comparison of the old examinations with those set today for entrance to our school is sufficient to show the greater advancement of modern pupils. I do not submit for this brief sketch any samples of our present papers, but have taken pains to collect such samples from a number of the best high schools of New England. In every case the examinations of today are more difficult than those of forty or fifty years ago.

But someone may ask—as Cicero has it—"Did not the teachers of an earlier day, even if they were not so well trained or so skillful as those of today, did they not, after all, succeed in giving the pupil a stimulus to effort, a spirit of ambition, that modern teachers fail to give? See the great men that have come from those schools."

The reply must be that only time can tell what sort of men will come from the schools of today. Doubtless it has always been true, and always will be true, that men of great natural ability and energy will rise to prominence, whether schools be good or bad. The only pertinent question is whether the greatness of our leaders of today can be traced to the excellence of their grammar school training. Have we any evidence that their teachers roused them to power of thought?

A survey of the entrance records of those alumni of this school who have shown great intellectual power fails to suggest any such power at the end of their grammar school training. A few, out of many, examples must suffice for illustration. One of the greatest oriental scholars of this country was able to secure only 65 in geography and 62 in grammar on such examinations as are printed above. Another alumnus, who stood among the very leaders of his college class and has risen to a position of prominence in many public affairs, secured marks of 55 in grammar, 60 in arithmetic, and 65 in geography. A professor of history in one of our greatest universities was marked 39 in grammar, and 60 in arithmetic, though he showed even then his natural bent for history by getting a mark of 90. A well-known editor received 62 in grammar. A prominent judge secured 60 in history. But further examples are needless to show that the grammar schools of their day did not rouse such men to intellectual achievements

Another lesson is easily learned from the perusal of old records—it is unsafe to estimate a child's mental capacity by the casual blunders he may make, even if they seem to us colossal. To conclude that because a boy cannot locate the Nile River he is therefore entirely ignorant of geography is as unsafe as it is common today in the writings of critics of our schools. To infer that because a boy makes some stupid blunders in judgment in his examinations he is therefore unable to reason at all, is equally unwise. What can be said of the intelligence of a boy who could make the following answers in history?

    1 When was the battle of Bunker Hill fought? *Ans.* 1492
    2. When was the Constitution adopted? *Ans.*: The same year
    3. For what reasons was war declared by the United States against Great Britain in 1812? *Ans.*: Admission of Texas into the United States.

Yet in other studies, and in general intelligence, this boy seemed to be above the average of his class

One suspects that much so-called disciplinary study was of a wooden and mechanical sort. Those were the days when pupils memorized geometry propositions by number, recited history verbatim, and memorized in Latin grammar exceptions that they would never meet in their reading of Latin. The only argument in defense of the older grammar school training that seems sound may be stated somewhat as follows: All effort that ends in success has a strengthening effect on character. The grammar schools of bygone days made learning difficult. Therefore they built up character.

For the few boys or girls who won the fight, surmounted the difficulties of poor instruction. and worked out their own salvation, undoubtedly the process was a strengthening one but for the mass of the pupils the process was not worthy of comparison with that of our modern schools

On the whole the tests show us, not that we are perfect, for our imperfections are glaring and discouraging, but that we must look for aid to the best educational thought of the present and future in our own land and abroad, rather than to a past system on which we have made many improvements

Speaking in broad terms, the progress since 1856 might be grouped under the following heads: Better trained teachers, better text books, better school buildings and equipment, better supervision, better teaching methods, compulsory attendance laws, graded schools, evening schools, continuation schools, trade schools, high schools, medical inspection, better financial support of schools, education of the deaf, care of the defective and the orphaned and destitute, restriction of child labor, and many forms of welfare work closely connected with education. These improvements are of course not peculiar to our county, but have been worked out in many cases with a view to the special needs of a given community.

New London county, too, has a history rich in private generosity. An unusual number of institutions have been started by private bequests. As a part of our outline of education we take pleasure in tracing the history of some of these foundations. It is well for us to remember, however, that, with all the modern devices for making education and life itself an easy process, there is grave danger that in many cases the young people of today fail to attain the strength of character and mind that comes through over-coming difficulties and hardships.

The summary given below, based on a report of the State Board of Education, shows the course of legislation since 1700, a period of 215 years. Most of this legislation deals with support and maintenance.

Support of Public Schools.—The system of public instruction in Connecticut in 1700 embraced the following:

1. A tax of "forty shillings on every thousand pounds of the lists of estates," was collected in every town with the annual tax of the Colony, and payable proportionately to those towns only which should keep their schools according to law;
2. A school in every town having over seventy families, kept eleven months in the year, and in every town with less than seventy families, kept for at least six months in the year;
3. A grammar school in each of the four "head county towns" to fit youth for college, two of which grammar schools must be free;
4. A collegiate school, toward which the general court made an annual appropriation of £120.

In 1773 an act was passed granting all the moneys that should arise from the sale of seven townships, in what is now Litchfield county (viz.: Norfolk, Goshen, Canaan, Cornwall, Kent, Salisbury and Sharon), to the towns of the colony then settled for the support of schools, "to be divided in proportion to the number of their polls and ratable estate." The amount realized from the sale of all these townships cannot now be determined. Norfolk was sold for £6,824 10s.; Kent for £1,225 19s. In the revised statutes published in 1750, the "Act for educating and governing children" remains nearly the same as it was in 1650 with the addition made in 1670. The "Act for appointing, encouraging, and supporting Schools" was the same as in 1700, with the additions mentioned above. In 1754 the amount to be paid from the treasury was reduced to 10s. on each £1,000; in 1766 it was raised to 20s.; and in 1767 it was restored to 40s., where it remained till 1820.

In May, 1766, the selectmen in each town were authorized to collect any sums which remained unpaid at that date for excise on liquors, tea, etc., and pay the same to the school committee in the several towns and societies, to be set apart as a fund to be improved for the encouragement of schools. And at the October session, 1774, the treasurer of the colony is directed to pay out to the several towns the principal sums paid in by them as excise money, together with the interest due at the time of payment, "which moneys shall be appropriated to the use of schools " The money received from this source, with that received from the sale of the townships in Litchfield county, constituted the principal part of the so-called School Society funds.

By the Charter of 1662, given by Charles II., Connecticut was bounded on the north by the Massachusetts line, and on the south by the "sea" (Long Island sound), and extended from Narragansett bay to the "South sea" (Pacific ocean). The parts of this territory covered by the grants already made to New York and New Jersey were never claimed by Connecticut; and the part covered by Pennsylvania was given up to the claims of that State; the remaining portion was held by Connecticut till after the Revolutionary War, when it was all ceded to the United States, except about 3,300,-000 acres in what is now the northwestern part of Ohio. The territory was known as the "Western Reserve," or the "Lands west of Pennsylvania." In May, 1795, an act was passed appropriating the interest on the moneys which should be received on the sale of these lands to the support of schools, "to be paid over to the said societies in their capacity of school societies according to the lists of polls and ratable estate of such societies respectively." The societies here referred to were formerly known only as parishes or societies, and later as ecclesiastical societies. This act recognizes them in a distinct capacity and denominates them school societies.

The "lands west of Pennsylvania" were sold August, 1795, for $1,200,000, by a committee appointed for that purpose, and their report was accepted by the legislature in October of the same year.

The first apportionment of the income of the school fund was made in 1779. In March, 1800, the dividends were $23,651. Up to this time the fund was managed by the committee that negotiated the sale. In 1800, three persons, with the treasurer, were appointed "managers" of this fund In 1810 Hon. James Hilhouse was appointed commissioner of the school fund. During the fifteen years of his administration the annual dividend averaged $52,061.35, and the capital was increased to $1,719,434.24.

In 1810 the expense of keeping a district school above the amount of public money, was apportioned according to the number of days of attendance of each person at school; in 1811 this was so altered as to authorize the apportionment according to the number of persons attending.

In 1820 an act was passed providing that the appropriation of $2 upon every $1,000 (40s. on every £1,000) in the list of each school society should not be paid whenever the income of the school fund equalled or exceeded $62,000, which it did the next year From this date the income of the fund was apportioned to the several school societies and districts according to the number of persons over four and under sixteen in each, on the first Monday of August in each year.

In 1836 the United States revenue was in excess of the expenditures, and Congress directed all the surplus except $5,000,000, to be divided and deposited with the several States, according to their representation in Congress.

The amount thus appropriated was $37.468,859.97, but owing to the financial revulsions only three-fourths of this amount was paid to the States. This State received as its share $764,670.60. At the session of the legislature the same year an act was passed requiring this money to be distributed among the several towns in the State in proportion to their population, and that one-half at least of the entire income received from such funds should be annually appropriated for the promotion of education in the common schools. This is denominated the "Town deposit fund." The amount actually distributed to the several towns was $763,661.83.

In 1841 an act authorized the school societies to divide the public money either according to the number of persons in the districts between four and sixteen, or according to the number who had attended the school; but no district was to receive less than $50; and dividends from the school fund were not to be paid to any district unless its school had been kept at least four months of the year. It was also provided that "two or more adjoining school districts might associate together and form a union district with power to maintain a union school, to be kept for the benefit of the older and more advanced children of such united district." In 1842 the act constituting a board of commissioners was repealed.

In 1846, the act passed in 1841 requiring the school societies to appropriate to each district at least $50 was amended, making the amount $35, provided there were not less than twelve children in the district

In 1854, each town was required "annually to raise by taxation a sum equal to one cent on the dollar on their grand list (as made up at that time) for the support of schools," and the whole amount to be annually distributed to the several school societies within each town, under the direction of the selectmen and town treasurer When the amount of public money received by any district was less than thirty-five dollars, it was to be increased to that amount from the money raised by the town for the purposes of education, and the year for school purposes was to end on the 28th of February.

In 1858, school districts were authorized to fix a "rate of tuition" not exceeding two dollars for any term; but they might exempt therefrom all persons whom they considered unable to pay the same, and the town was to pay the amount abated. In 1862 this was raised to six dollars a year, and to twelve dollars for high schools.

In 1860 the amount to be raised by the town for schools was fixed at not less than three-tenths of a mill on the dollar, which is about the same as the amount fixed in 1854. In 1866 this was raised to four-tenths. In 1861 an act provided that the amount raised by towns for school and the income of the town deposit fund should be distributed under the direction of the selectmen and school visitors; but that no district should receive less than thirty-five dollars of the public moneys.

In 1868 the amount to be raised by the town was "such sums as each town may find necessary to make the schools free, not less than six-tenths of a mill on the dollar," and in addition to four-tenths of a mill before required; and the public money, with the exception of so much as was necessary to make the amount to each district fifty dollars, was to be divided "according to average daily attendance."

In 1869 the amount to be raised by the towns was fixed at not less than one mill on the dollar; sixty dollars to be apportioned to each district, and the balance of the public money to be "divided according to aggregate attendance."

In 1871 an annual appropriation was made from the State treasury of a sum equal to fifty cents for each person between four and sixteen years of age, to be paid to the several towns with the dividends of the school fund.

In 1872 the legislature voted an appropriation to schools from the State treasury "equal in dollars to one-half the number of persons between four and sixteen years of age." In 1872 the sum of $1.50 for every person between the age of four and sixteen was voted.

In 1893 an act was passed providing that when the income of the school fund did not warrant the payment of seventy-five cents per enumerated scholar, making with $1.50 a grant of $2.25 to the towns for each enumerated child, the deficiency should be paid from the State treasury. In 1897 it was directed that the income of the school fund be covered into the treasury, and that $2.25 be paid to the towns for each enumerated child.

In 1903, an act was passed giving towns having grand lists of less than $500,000, a grant from the State treasury upon the basis of average attendance in addition to the grant of $2.25 per child enumerated to enable them to make an expenditure of $25.00 per child in average attendance for support of schools. Each of these towns was required to expend the proceeds of a four-mill tax for the support of the schools. This act was amended in 1907 so that all towns having grand lists of less than $1,000,000 could obtain the grant. In 1909 this law was further amended so that all towns having grand lists of less than $1,750,000 could obtain the grant. The tax rate for towns having lists under $500,000 was reduced to three mills; those having lists over $500,000 and less than $1,000,000, three and one-half mills; those having lists over $1,000,000 and less than $1,250,000, four mills; and those having lists over $1,250,000 and under $1,750,000, six mills. In 1911 this law was again amended so that all towns having grand lists under $2,500,000 could obtain the grant. Those having lists under $500,000 were required to expend two and one-half mills; those having lists over $500,000 and less than $1,000,000, three mills; those having lists over $1,000,000 and less than $1,500,000, three and one-half mills; those having lists over $1,500,000 and less than $2,000,000, four and one-half mills; and those having lists over $2,000,000 and under $2,500,000, six mills.

District System. In May, 1717, the obligation heretofore imposed on towns of seventy families to maintain a school for eleven months, was extended to parishes or ecclesiastical societies having that number of families; and parishes having less than seventy families were to maintain a school

for half the year; and the majority of householders in any parish were authorized to lay taxes for the support of the school.

In October, 1766, a law was passed authorizing each town and society
to "divide themselves into proper and necessary districts for keeping their
schools, and to alter and regulate the same from time to time, as they shall
have occasion, which districts shall draw their equal proportion of all public
moneys belonging to such towns or societies, according to the list of each
respective district therein." In his report of 1853, Dr. Henry Barnard says
that "this act, with the operation of other acts transferring to school societies
the direction and control of schools, which should have been confined to towns,
has resulted in distributing the means of education most unequally over the
state, and lowering the standard of education."

In 1794 school districts were authorized "by vote of two-thirds of all the
qualified voters, passed at a meeting called for that purpose, to lay a tax to
build a schoolhouse, and to locate the same, and to choose a collector."

In May, 1798, the school societies were invested with the powers, and
subjected to the duties, which the former laws had given to and required of
towns and ecclesiastical societies relative to the same objects, and from this
date they are known in law as school societies—with territorial limits sometimes co-extensive with a town, or in some cases a part of a town, and in
other cases parts of two or more towns. These school societies not only had
the control of schools, but generally of the burying grounds within their
limits. In the revision of the laws respecting schools made in 1799, these
societies are required to appoint "overseers or visitors," whose duties were
nearly the same as those now required of school visitors. School societies
were authorized to form school districts, and these districts to tax themselves
for the purpose of building and repairing school houses, to appoint a clerk,
a treasurer, and a collector; but the "committee to employ teachers and
manage the prudentials" was appointed by the school societies. School societies were authorized to institute and support schools of higher order. The
law did not specify how long a time in each year the schools should be kept
open.

In 1886, towns were authorized to direct their school visitors to purchase
at the expense of the town the text books and other school supplies used in
the public schools. This act provided that the books and supplies should
be loaned to the pupils of the public schools free of charge.

In 1886 the employment of children under thirteen in mechanical, mercantile, and manufacturing establishments was forbidden, and the State Board
of Education was authorized to enforce the law. In 1895 the age was changed
to fourteen. Under this law children under fourteen and unemployed children
between fourteen and sixteen are sent to school by the agents of the State
Board of Education.

In 1889, towns were authorized to discontinue small schools, and in 1893,
school visitors were authorized to provide transportation for children wherever any school was discontinued.

In 1893, women were given the right to vote for school officers, and also to vote upon any matter relating to education or to schools In the same year women were made eligible to serve on the board of directors of any public library or on the Connecticut Public Library Committee.

In 1893, the State Board of Education was directed to appoint a committee to be known as the "Connecticut Public Library Committee," and in 1895 acts were passed providing for the expenses of said committee and for annual appropriations for public libraries.

In 1897 it was enacted that children residing in towns whose grand list was less than $900,000 might, with the consent of the school visitors, attend a non-local high school, and that a tuition fee not exceeding two-thirds of $30 should be paid from the State treasury. In 1899 the $900,000 limit was removed so that all towns might receive the State grant for scholars attending non-local high schools

In 1903, the State was authorized to pay one-half the expense of conveying children to and from non-local high schools, provided that not more than twenty dollars be paid by the State for each scholar conveyed.

In 1921 the sum to be refunded towns for high school tuition was increased to $50.

In 1899 it was provided that the eyesight of the pupils in the public schools should be tested annually, and in 1901 this law was modified so that after 1904 the test should be made triennially.

Supervision.—In 1903, the supervision of schools was authorized   Two or more towns together employing not less than twenty-five nor more than fifty teachers were authorized to form a supervision district which should continue for three years at least, and employ a superintendent of schools. The State was required to pay one-half of the annual salary of the superintendent provided that one-half did not exceed $800. This act also provided that upon the petition of the school board of any town employing not more than ten teachers, the State Board of Education should appoint an agent who should discharge the duties of superintendent of schools in said town   Any town for which a superintendent was appointed under this act was required to pay one-quarter of the salary of the superintendent, and the State was required to pay three-quarters   In 1907. this act was so amended that any town having not more than twenty teachers could petition the State Board of Education to appoint an agent to discharge the duties of superintendent, the town to pay one-quarter of the salary and the State three-quarters   A further amendment to this act was made in 1909 so that towns having over twenty and not more than thirty teachers could appoint a superintendent of schools and obtain one-half of the salary of said superintendent from the State, provided the half should not exceed $800 per year   Another amendment provided that the State should pay the entire salary of superintendents appointed for towns having not more than twenty teachers.

Trade Schools.—In 1907, the establishment of free public schools for
N L—1-4

instruction in the principles and practice of trades was authorized. The State Board of Education was authorized to expend a sum not to exceed $50,000 for the support and maintenance of not more than two schools. No action was taken under the provisions of this law, and it was repealed in 1909, when an act authorized the State Board of Education to establish two schools, and providing an annual appropriation of $50,000 for their support.

In 1913, the act of 1909 was amended so that town school committees and district boards of education could establish and maintain schools or courses of instruction in distinct trades, useful occupations and avocations, and obtain from the State annually a grant not to exceed fifty dollars per pupil in average attendance. This amendment also provided that the sum of $125,000 should be appropriated for the maintenance of such schools.

Model Schools.—In 1913, the State Board of Education was authorized to organize one school in each town having twenty teachers or less as a model school for observation and instruction of training classes conducted by the supervisor, and it was provided that the board might pay the teacher not to exceed three dollars per week, provided that the town in which the model school is located should pay not less than ten dollars a week or not less than the wage which was paid for teaching in said school during the previous year.

In "An Act concerning schools," passed in 1839, a school district is for the first time declared to be a "body corporate, so far as to be able to purchase, receive, hold, and convey any estate, real or personal, for the support of schooling in the same, and to prosecute and defend in all actions relating to the property and affairs of the district." This act also empowered school districts to appoint their committees. It named the branches (the same as those now required) which a person must be found qualified to teach before he could receive a certificate from the school visitors. This act also provided that any school society might "apportion the public money among the districts, either according to the number of persons between four and sixteen, or according to the amount of attendance for a period of six months in each year." It was also provided that school districts might tax themselves to the amount of $30 the first year and $10 each year afterwards for school libraries; and that two or more districts might associate for supporting a high school. In 1856, school societies were abolished, and their property and their obligations transferred to towns.

In 1865 towns were authorized to consolidate their school districts; and the act constituting the State Board of Education was enacted. The act making the principal of the normal school ex-officio superintendent of common schools was repealed.

In 1870 the time schools must be kept in each year was made at least thirty weeks in districts in which there were twenty-four or more persons between four and sixteen years of age; and twenty-four weeks, at least, in other districts; and the appropriation of funds was to be made under the direction of the school visitors and selectmen.

In 1888 the towns were required to maintain schools thirty-six weeks in each year in districts numbering one hundred or more children, and twenty-four weeks in other districts. In 1889 this was changed to thirty-six weeks for districts enumerating fifty or more, and thirty weeks for other districts. In 1895 thirty-six weeks was prescribed for all schools.

In 1909, the district system was abolished in fifty-seven towns. Ninety-one towns had voluntarily consolidated their districts previous to the passage of this act and several had obtained special legislation under which consolidation in part had been established

Normal Schools.—In 1849, the State Normal School was established at New Britain. In 1889, a second normal school was established at Willimantic. In 1893, normal schools were authorized at New Haven and Bridgeport. In 1895 so much of this act as provided for a normal school at Bridgeport was repealed. In 1903, a normal school at Danbury was established.

In 1909, an act was passed providing that the State Board of Education may at all times maintain, in any of the normal schools, one student, selected on the basis of scholarship and general fitness, from each town in the State having a valuation of less than one and one-half million dollars. The board was authorized to pay the living expenses of each student, not to exceed $150 in any one year. Each student was required to enter into an agreement with the State Board of Education to teach in one of the towns from which such students are nominated or appointed for a period of three years after graduation unless excused by the State Board of Education.

In 1882 was enacted a law requiring "instruction concerning the effect of intoxicating beverages" if "twelve persons of adult years" petitioned the school visitors therefor. If the visitors did not grant the petition, an appeal to town meeting was provided In 1886 physiology and hygiene relating especially to the effect of alcohol on the human system were made obligatory subjects and put on the same plane as reading and writing; school officers were required to examine teachers in these subjects. In the same year the State Board of Education was authorized to prescribe the books and to prepare a text-book and charts to be distributed to schools without charge. Under the law about forty thousand copies of a text-book were distributed. In 1893 the "nature of alcoholic drinks and narcotics" became an obligatory study. Graded text-books must be used in every school and studied by all pupils. In the lower grades one-fifth of each book must be devoted to "the nature and effects" of alcohol and narcotics; in higher grades the books must contain at least twenty pages relating to the subject. Massing these pages at the end of a book is not compliance with the law Teachers must have an examination as to the "effects and nature of alcoholic drinks upon the human system." Failure to comply with the provisions of the law is "sufficient cause" for forfeiture of public money

In 1884, the State Board of Education was authorized to grant certificates of qualification to teach in any public school in the State and to revoke the same. In 1895, an act provided that certificates granted by the State Board of Education should be accepted by local boards in lieu of any other examination.

In 1885, the establishment of evening schools was provided for by law. Provision was made thereby for the instruction of persons over fourteen years of age in spelling, reading, writing, geography, arithmetic, and such other studies as might be prescribed by the board of school visitors. A grant of $1.50 per child in average attendance was fixed by this act to be paid from the treasury of the State. In 1893, this law was amended so that it was compulsory on every town and school district having ten thousand or more inhabitants to establish and maintain evening schools. It was provided that no person over fourteen and under sixteen years of age should be employed in any manufacturing, mercantile, or mechanical occupation in any town where evening schools were established, unless he had attended an evening school twenty consecutive evenings in the current school year and was a regular attendant. The State grant was increased to $3 per pupil in average attendance. One hundred sessions of a school was required as a condition of obtaining the State grant.

In 1895, the law was amended so that only seventy-five sessions were required to obtain the grant, and the grant was reduced from $3 per child in average attendance to $2.25. A further amendment of the law was made in 1909 so that on petition of at least twenty persons over fourteen years of age, instruction in any study usually taught in a high school might be introduced. The last legislation in Connecticut (1921) has been compiled by the State Board of Education and the report may be secured by application to the Commissioner of Education. It is too voluminous for us to print in this chapter.

We have spoken of the importance placed on education by the early settlers, and have enumerated many such schools in New London and Norwhich. The settlers also felt a responsibility for the welfare of the Indians. Many of these aborigines were suffering from drunkenness and ignorance, and it was not easy to get them to take an interest in a higher life. The pastors in New London and Norwich did their best. We submit a curious document, signed by the Mohegan Chief, Uncas.

When King Charles the First sent his red-faced well-beloved cousin "a Bible to show him the way to heaven, and a sword to defend him from his enemies," Uncas valued the latter gift much more than he did the former. But I am happy to bring forward one new fact to show that he was not at all times indifferent to the other present. It has often been stated that Uncas uniformly opposed the introduction of Christianity among the people of his tribe. Within a few days past an original document has come to light which bears important testimony on this interesting question. It is nothing less than a bond in which, under his own signature, the sachem promises to attend the ministrations of the Rev. Mr. Fitch, whensoever and wheresoever he may choose to appoint. This paper is so remarkable that I shall take the liberty of reading it in full. If we cannot call it the sachem's creed or confession of faith, it is at least his covenant·

Be it known to all men and in special to the Authority of The Colony of Conecticott That I Uncas sachim of the Munheags, now resident in Pamechaug doe by these presents firmly engage and binde my selfe, that I will from time to time and at all times hereafter, in a constant way and manner attend up Mr. James Fitch Minister of Norwich, at all such seasons as he shall appoint for preaching and to praying with the Indians either at my now residence, or wheresoever els he shall appoint for that holy service, and further I doe faithfully promis to Command all my people to attend the same, in a constant way and solemn manner at all such times as shall be sett by the sayd Mr. James Fitch minister, alsoe I promis that I will not by any wayes or meanes what soe ever, either privatly or openly use any plots or contriveances by words or actions to affright or discourage any of my people or others, from attending the Good work aforesayd, upon penalty of suffering the most grevious punishment that can be inflicted upon me, and Lastly I promis to encourage all my people by all Good wayes and meanes I can, in the due observance of such directions and instructions, as shall be presented to them by the sayd Mr James Fitch aforesayd, and to the truth hereof this seaventh day of June in the year one thousand six hundred seventy and three I have hereunto set my hand or mark.

Wittnesed by us   mark
    John Talcott   The   *   of Uncass
    Tho· Stanton. Ser.
    Samuell Mason

Let us look with charity, my friends, upon this promise, remembering that every man, red face and pale face alike, is accepted "according to that which he hath, and not according to that which he hath not."

Of interest in education on the part of New London county citizens, the following is a proof, quoted from Dr Gilman's address

Yale College is even more indebted to Norwich Before it was chartered by the State, Major James Fitch (another son of Reverend James) gave to the new collegiate school a farm of 637 acres of land, and offered the glass and nails for a house. The following is his proposal.

Majr Fitch's Generosity Proposed 1701.—In that it hath pleased y Lord our God as a token for Good To us and children after us to put it into the hearts of his faithfull ministers: to take soe great paines, and be at soe consideiable charge for setting up a coledgeat schoole amongst us and now for farther promoating, of this God pleasing worke I humbly, freely and heartily offer, on demand to provid glass for a house and if people doe not come up to offer what is reasonable and needfull that I will than provid nails of all sorts: to be used in building a houes and hall: 21y I give a farme, 637 Acrs of land and when I come home I will send ye draft and laying out to Mr. Danl. Taylor that he may make such a Deed proper in such a case the farme of value at 150 £ l will alsoe take some pains to put it in a way of yearely profitt 30 £ charge I hope will bring 20 £ p yeare in a little time.

Newhaven October 16 1701   JAMES FITCH.

It was this noble gift which insured at that time the establishment of the now venerable institution. Not many years after, Dr. Daniel Lathrop, beside a large donation to the public school of his native place, gave £500 to the college without limitations; and within the memory of most of those now present, Dr. Alfred E. Perkins, impressed with the thought that "a true university in these days is a collection of books," gave a fund of $10,000 to the college library in New Haven, thus perpetuating his name in grateful remembrance, and exerting an influence which will increase till the college and the country are no more. Three citizens of Norwich, "to the manner born," have thus given to Yale College the largest donations which, at each successive time, its treasury had received from any individual, and their example has been followed by many others, giving in proportion to their means.

The most remarkable of the attempts to civilize the Indians is doubtless that of Rev. Eleazer Wheelock of Lebanon. The remarkable results of his effort with Samson Occum is shown in the following account of the origin of Dartmouth College, taken from Hurd's "History of New London County, Connecticut":

In 1735, Eleazer Wheelock, a clergyman of fine talents, of earnest character, and of devoted piety, was settled over the Second Congregational Church, in the north part of the town of Lebanon. Like many other ministers of the day and afterwards, he had several young men in his family, whom he taught the higher branches of English and in the classics.

In December, 1743, a young Mohegan Indian, about twenty years of age, Samson Occom, whose name has since become more famous than that of any other of the tribe, unless perhaps the first Uncas, applied to Mr. Wheelock for admission among his scholars. Occom was born in 1723, at Mohegan, and grew up in the pagan faith and the rude and savage customs of his tribe. During the great religious awakening of 1739-40 he had become convinced of the truth of Christianity, and deeply alarmed for his own lost condition. For six months he groaned in the gloom of his darkness, but then light broke into his soul, and he was seized with an irresistible impulse to carry this great light to his benighted race, and to become a teacher to his lost brethren, and with his heart swelling with this impulse he now stood before Wheelock, asking to be instructed for this great work.

It was not in the heart of Wheelock to resist this appeal, and he at once admitted him to his school and family with open arms, and in the spirit of his mission. Occom had already learned the letters of the alphabet, and could spell out a few words, and such was his zeal and devotion to study that in four years he was fitted to enter college; but his health had been so impaired by intense application, and lacking also the means, he never entered. Leaving school, he returned to his tribe, preaching and teaching salvation through Christ alone, with power and effect, supporting himself meantime, like the rest of his tribe, by hunting and fishing, and the rude Indian arts of making baskets and other Indian utensils, and occasionally teaching small Indian schools, but during all this time still pursuing his own studies in theology and Bible literature.

In this mission he visited other tribes. In 1748 he went over to Long Island and spent several years there among the Montauk, the Shenecock, and other tribes, preaching and teaching with great success. At one time a great revival occurred under his labors there, during which many Indians were converted. August 29, 1759, he was ordained by the Suffolk Presbytery of Long Island, and was ever after regarded as a regular member of that ecclesiastical body.

The case of Occom and its instructive results attracted wide attention from the first start, and Mr. Wheelock determined to open his school to other Indian youths who desired to engage in and be fitted for the same work, and in a short time it became exclusively an "Indian School" for missionary purposes, so that by 1762 he had more than twenty Indian students preparing for the conversion of their countrymen.

This new movement attracted the earnest attention of the leading clergymen and Christian philanthropists throughout all New England and the Northern colonies. To all who looked with anxiety for the conversion and civilization of the aborigines of this part of North America, this school was long considered the brightest and most promising ground of hope. Notes of encouragement came pouring in from various sources throughout all the New England colonies, from ministers' councils, from churches, and from eminent leaders and philanthropists, with money contributions, cheering on the movement, and all aiming to increase the numbers in training, and to give to the school a wider sweep in its influence. Probably no school in this or any other land or age ever awakened so widespread and intense an interest or seemed freighted with such a precious and hopeful mission as did then this little parochial school, kept in the obscure parsonage of a country minister.

In 1765 a general conference of the friends of the school was held, at which it was determined to send Samson Occom to England to show to our English brethren there what Christianity had done for him, and what it could do for the natives of North America, and that Rev. Nathaniel Whitaker, of Norwich, should go with him, to enlist co-operation in the cause and to solicit contributions in its aid. Occom was then forty-three years old, well educated, and spoke English clearly and fluently. His features and complexion bore every mark of his race, but he was easy and natural in social manners, frank and cordial, but modest in conversation, and his deportment in the pulpit was such as to command deep attention and respect. He could preach extemporaneously and well, but usually wrote his sermons. Such, then, was this son of the forest, and such his sublime mission to the English mother-land—to convert the natives of a pagan continent to Christianity and civilization through the ministry of pagan converts of their own race.

His appearance in England produced an extraordinary sensation, and he preached with great applause in London and other principal cities of Great Britain and Scotland to crowded audiences. From the 16th of February, 1766, to the 22d of July, 1767, he delivered between three and four hundred sermons, many of them in the presence of the king and the royal family and the great nobles of the land. Large contributions were taken up after each of these discourses: the king himself gave £200, and in the whole enterprise £700 sterling were collected in England and about £300 in Scotland.

This success resulted in transferring Wheelock's Indian School to New Hampshire, which it was thought would be a better place for an Indian seminary, as being more retired and less exposed to disturbing influences than the more thickly settled colony of Connecticut. It was then incorporated as Dartmouth College (taking its name from the pious and noble Earl of Dartmouth, whom Occom's mission in England had warmly enlisted in the cause), for the special object and purpose of educating and training Indian youths for the ministry and missionary work of their race, but after the death of Eleazer Wheelock, its founder and president, and especially after the death of his son, John Wheelock, who succeeded him as president, its original and distinctive character as an Indian seminary gradually changed until it became, as it still remains, assimilated in character and purpose with the other colleges of the country; and so the glowing dream, the fervid zeal, and the sanguine hopes and expectations of its great-souled founders faded away

In 1771, a Mohegan Indian, named Moses Paul, was tried at New London and condemned to death for the murder, in a drunken brawl, of Moses Clark. A large assembly of English and Indians collected to witness the execution. At the request of the prisoner, Samson Occom was appointed by the authorities to preach a funeral sermon in the presence of the poor wretch, as was the custom of the time, just before he was launched into eternity. Upon his own coffin, in front of the pulpit, sat the doomed man Next around him were seated his brethren of the Mohegan tribe, the audience filling the rest of the church, a great crowd surrounding it, and a military company acting as guard.

The sermon is still preserved in the library of the Connecticut Historical Society at Hartford (Pamphlet No. 225), the text from Romans vi. 23: "For the wages of sin is death; but the gift of God is eternal life through Jesus Christ our Lord." It is not eloquent, it is not grand oratory, but it is something higher than eloquence, and in its sad and solemn moaning over the degraded and lost condition of his race, in their pagan darkness, their wickedness, the awful consequences of drunkenness, their besetting sin, it has all the moving power and pathos of a Hebrew wail

The first part of the discourse dwells at length upon the peculiar meaning and significance of the term "death," as used in the text, its endless character, and was addressed to the audience at large, and rising with the vastness of the idea, he exclaimed, "Eternity! O Eternity! Who can measure it? Who can count the years thereof? Arithmetic fails, the thoughts of men and angels are drowned in it. How shall we describe eternity? To what shall we compare it? Were a fly to carry off one particle of this globe to such a distance that it would take ten thousand years to go and return for another, and so continue till he had carried off, particle by particle, once in ten thousand years, the whole of this globe and placed it in that distant space, just as it is now here, after all this, eternity would remain the same unexhausted duration! And this eternal death must be the certain portion of all impenitent sinners, be they who they may, Negroes, Indians, English, or what nation soever, honorable or ignoble, great or small, rich or poor, bond or free, all who die in their sins must go to hell together, 'for the wages of sin is death.'"

He next addressed the doomed prisoner upon his coffin, pointed out to him the enormity of his crime, and how by drunkenness, and by despising the warnings and counsels of Christian teachers, he had been led to it; explained to him the way of salvation, urging him with pathos and earnest energy at once to accept it, and like the dying thief upon the cross beside the crucified Saviour, to throw himself upon the mercy of that same Saviour, and so, even at the eleventh hour, escape eternal death.

He then turned to the Mohegans present "My poor kindred!" he exclaimed, "you see the woful consequences of sin by seeing this, our poor, miserable countryman, now before us, who is to die for his sins and his great crime, and it was especially the sin of drunkenness that brought this destruction and untimely death upon him There is a dreadful woe denounced from the Almighty against drunkards; and it is this sin, this abominable, this beastly sin of drunkenness that has stript us of every desirable comfort in this life. By this sin we have no name or credit in the world; for this sin we are despised, and it is right and just, for we despise ourselves. By this sin we have no comfortable houses, nor anything comfortable in our houses, neither food, nor raiment, nor decent utensils; we go about with ragged and dirty clothing and almost naked, most of the time half starved, and obliged to pick up and eat such food as we can find; and our poor children suffering every day, often crying for food, and we have nothing for them, and in the cold winter shivering and crying, pinched with cold. All this comes from the love of strong drink. And this is not all the misery and evil we bring upon ourselves by this sin, for when we are intoxicated with strong drink we drown our rational powers, by which we are distinguished from the brute creation; we unman ourselves, and sink not only to a level with the beasts of the field, but seven degrees beneath them, yea, we bring ourselves to a level with the devils; and I don't know but we make ourselves worse than the devils, for I never heard of a drunken devil."

He closed his discourse with a fervid exhortation to his Mohegan brethren to break off from their sins, and especially from their besetting sin of drunkenness, by a gospel repentance: to "take warning by the doleful sight now before us," and from the dreadful judgments that have befallen poor drunkards. "You that have been careless all your day now awake to righteousness and be concerned for your never-dying souls." Fight against all sin, and especially against your besetting sin, "and above all things believe in the Lord Jesus Christ, and you shall have eternal life, and when you come to die your souls will be received into heaven, there to be with the Lord Jesus and all the saints in glory, which God in His infinite mercy grant, through Jesus Christ, our Lord Amen"

In 1786 he gathered a few Mohegans and several other Indians from other tribes in Connecticut, Rhode Island, and Long Island, and went with them to Oneida county, New York, and there formed the nucleus of the clan afterwards known as the Brothertown tribe among the Six Nations. He continued as their minister, acting also as a missionary among the Six Nations, until his death, which occurred in July, 1792 more than three hundred Indians following him mournfully and tearfully to the grave.

Another young Mohegan, Joseph Johnson. educated in Wheelock's school, became also a preacher of great power and influence. He was sent early as a missionary to the Six Nations of New York, and afterwards co-operated with Occom in the establishment there of the Brothertown clan. At the breaking out of the war of the Revolution the Six Nations, a powerful and warlike Indian confederacy, were at first much inclined to favor the English side and to become the allies of the British forces of Canada, and to this end were strongly tempted by the insidious wiles of British emissaries, backed by the glittering display and lavish use of British gold.

Against this danger both Johnson and Occom exerted the whole weight of their great moral powers and their wide influence, the former especially appealing for help, in averting this impending danger, to Governor Trumbull and other friends here, and to the Assembly His zeal and patriotic efforts attracted the attention of Gen Washington, and while at Cambridge, directing the siege of Boston, he wrote him a letter with his own hand, dated Feb. 20, 1776, thanking him for his patriotic and important services, and in closing he says, "Tell the Indians that we do not ask them to take up the hatchet for us unless they choose it, we only desire that they will not fight against us. We want that the chain of friendship should always remain bright between our friends, the Six Nations, and us We recommend you to them, and hope by spreading the truths of the gospel among them it will always keep the chain bright."

Another remarkable illustration of the importance of education to our forefathers is found in a sermon of Rev. Dr. Nott, pastor of the Franklin church from 1782 till 1852. This pastorate of seventy years, linked with those of Rev. Benjamin Lord and Rev. Dr. Strong of Norwich, forms a note-worthy chain of human lives. Together they served their parishes 187 years! One succeeded another in turn in such a manner that these three men, each well acquainted with the successor in the ministry though not in the same parish, covered, and might well have conveyed by word of mouth, the history of New London county from 1717 to 1852! The sermon referred to was delivered on the fiftieth anniversary of Dr. Nott's settlement at Franklin. He says:

That I have contributed to the general improvement of my people in knowledge, par-ticularly the children and youth—as I have statedly visited the schools twice, usually three times a year, and likewise taught many of the young men Arithmetic, English Grammar, and Geography—I presume none will question. In the mean time, I trust I have con-tributed, in a degree, to the improvement of many others More than forty young men, in whole or in part, have fitted for college under my direction; twenty belonged to this town. A considerable number of the whole entered quite advanced in standing. About half a dozen of the scholars, who belonged to different colleges, have likewise spent con-siderable time with me; some of them a term or two. About the same number of young gentlemen have studied theology with me. A large number of school-masters, and some persons who have studied physic, made merchants, mechanics, and farmers, I have aided, more or less, in their education. I would be far from saying: "By the strength of my hand I have done it, and by my wisdom" I would, with the most lively gratitude, say, I have done it by the strength of that Almighty Being' "Who raiseth up the poor out of the dust, and lifteth the beggar out of the dunghill, and I mention it in this public manner that he may have the glory. (Since I began to fit for college, April, 1774, I have contributed something towards the education, as nearly as I can recollect, of between two and three hundred gentlemen, ladies, or children) As a little wheel in mechanism sometimes puts in motion one much larger, I have been instrumental, in the hand of Divine Providence, of bringing forward into public life some persons who have given a far wider spread to knowledge than I was ever able to do; and some, who now hold in society, and in the Church of Christ, a respectable standing. A wheel in the middle of a wheel O, the depths of the riches both of the wisdom and knowledge of God! How unsearchable are his judgments, and his ways past finding out.

The first music school in this country was founded by Mr. Oramel Whit-tlesey at Salem, in 1835, under the name of Music Vale Seminary, and was maintained with great success for over forty years. Here were educated in music many hundred young women from different parts of the country.

At the time when public high schools were starting in Massachusetts under the leadership of Horace Mann and others, public-spirited citizens in New London county had founded or soon afterwards founded private insti-tutions of high school grade. As time has passed, these institutions have survived, doing their work under private management, partly by means of their original funds and partly by funds given by the public for the secondary education of boys and girls. It is a curious fact that of the seven private schools recognized by the State of Connecticut as doing satisfactorily the work of a public high school, five are found in New London county. A brief statement about each school has been prepared by the principal or by a trustee of each and will be found elsewhere in this work.

CHAPTER III

AN ERA OF UNREST

The War for Independence—The Battle of Groton Heights—Narratives of Jonathan Rathbun, Rufus Avery and Stephen Hempstead—The British Fleet off New London —The War Marks the Beginning of Manufacture and Whaling.

Much of the detail of local history will be found under the separate histories of various towns. New London county sent its full quota and more for every colonial enterprise. It was a large partaker in all the efforts that make Connecticut history glorious. We quote from Mr. Daniel Howard:

In the days of the Revolution, "Brother Jonathan" of Lebanon was Washington's right hand man. It used to be the custom to call the United States "Brother Jonathan," just as we now call the country by the nickname of "Uncle Sam." We do not know who was the first man to apply the name to our country, but it was George Washington who caused the name to be adopted.

When the Revolutionary War broke out in the thirteen colonies there was one governor and only one who joined the patriots in their struggle against the British king and his tyranny. That Governor was Jonathan Trumbull of Connecticut. When we read of what he did to help Washington and his army, we can realize why Washington loved him, trusted him, and looked to him for help and advice whenever he was in trouble.

The War for Independence began in 1775, and Governor Trumbull was among the first men to encourage volunteers to go to Boston and Cambridge in order to help form the American army. The next year, when Washington's army went to New York, more than half of his 17,000 men were from Connecticut. Throughout the six years of the war, Washington depended upon Jonathan Trumbull more than he did upon any other man to help him collect troops, provide food, clothing, and ammunition, write letters to committees of safety for their advice and assistance in carying on the war, and to do everything that was necessary to keep the soldiers and the patriots united and loyal to the army and its commander-in-chief. Washington soon formed the habit of saying whenever he needed advice or assistance, "Let us consult Brother Jonathan." "Brother Jonathan" seemed to represent the whole country, and in time public speakers, poets, authors, newspaper men, in fact everybody, came to use "Brother Jonathan" as a nickname for the United States.

Nathan Hale's name will be honored as long as America endures. It was April 20, 1775, in the Union Grammar School at New London, about thirty boys were busy with their lessons. We can imagine how diligently they were working, for many of them were anxious to enter college, win honors, and eventually become as popular and highly esteemed as was their young teacher, whom they idolized. This teacher was Nathan Hale.

Young Hale, although not quite twenty years of age, had already won high reputation as a scholar, a teacher, a thinker, and a leader among the people. He was born in the town of Coventry, June 6, 1775. He grew up in a typical Connecticut home. Having been prepared for college by his good pastor, he was graduated from Yale University in 1773 with the highest honors. The first year after his graduation he taught in the little red school house at East Haddam. His success there led to his engagement the next

year as teacher of the fine new grammar school at New London. He was
tall, broad-shouldered, graceful. Intelligence beamed from his large blue
eyes, and noble, good-natured face. A leader in athletics among the boys, a
leader in the discussion of public questions among the men, it was no wonder
that everybody loved him.

The political troubles between the American Colonies and England had
made him a bold and outspoken patriot, and often since the day he entered
college his eloquent words had roused his hearers to the highest enthusiasm
in defense of their rights and liberties. On this particular morning his
thoughts were with his pupils and their schoolroom discussions. Suddenly
there was heard the sound of excited voices in the street One window was
open, and the boys caught some words that filled them with excitement
The teacher counseled them not to let their thoughts wander from their
lessons.

The noise and excitement outside the building continued. The boys were
too much disturbed to work, and the teacher himself found that he was
as anxious as the boys to know what was happening He closed his school,
and with his boys rushed toward the crowd that had surrounded the statue
of King George A man on horseback was speaking, but Hale was too far
away to hear what he was saying. When the speech was finished, the crowd
sent up a great shout. "What is it all about " asked Hale. "Haven't you
heard? It is a message from Lexington, where the British have fallen on our
brothers and sought to cut them to pieces. Yesterday there was a battle."
"Has it come to that?" asked Hale in astonishment. "Hush! Hark! he is
going to speak again. No, he is falling from his horse. This way!! Bring
him into the tavern. Give him something to revive him. No wonder after
such a ride!" Another man addressed the crowd: "Let all who wish to form
some plan to help Massachusetts, meet me tonight at Miner's Tavern "

Hale went to his lodgings. He was so absorbed with the terrible news
that had come from Lexington that he thought no more of school. In the
evening he joined the throng of serious, thoughtful men, assembled at Miner's
Tavern. After listening to an earnest speech by the Hon. Richard Law, Hale
asked permission to speak. He ascended the platform and began to talk. As
they listened to his eloquence and observed his manly bearing, his hearers
forgot all else in their desire to seize their muskets and swords and march to
the aid of their countrymen in Massachusetts. Hale closed with these words.
"Let us not lay down our arms until we have gained our Independence!"
Independence! That was a new thought. But it was a thought that would
soon be in thousands of minds.

That night Hale made arrangements to go with the two companies of
soldiers who were to be sent to Cambridge. The following morning they
left New London at sunrise. At Cambridge, Hale became a favorite with the
officers and men For months he worked hard to train and exercise his company of soldiers, and his bravery, daring and resourcefulness won compliments from his commander-in-chief, Washington.

The next year, 1776, Washington's army moved from Boston to New
York and fought the British at Long Island. The British won the battle,
and the Americans were forced to retreat to Harlem Heights, leaving New
York City in the hands of the enemy. Washington was in great distress.
If he only knew the plans of the British, he might prepare his army to meet
them. If he could learn just how the city was fortified and guarded, he
might then capture it There was only one way to get the needed information.
He must send a spy into the British camp. That spy must be no ordinary
soldier. He must be skilled in military affairs, able to make drawings and

descriptions of the fortifications, capable of understanding and reporting everything he saw, and above all else fearless and willing to risk his life.

Washington asked Colonel Knowlton to endeavor to find such a man among the officers. Colonel Knowlton called the officers together and asked for a volunteer to undertake the dangerous task. No one responded. It was the disgrace of being a spy that held them back. The Colonel pleaded eloquently for someone to undertake the work on which the fate of the whole army might depend. Still, no answer. Nathan Hale, who had just risen from a sick bed, was seen approaching. He asked, "What is going on?" They told him. Without a moment's hesitation, he exclaimed: "I will undertake it."

Captain Hull, his friend and former classmate in college, exclaimed, "You do not know what you say. You a spy!" Another of the officers cried out, "There is someone other than you for such service." "Who?" asked Hale. There was no answer.

Hale repeated his offer, saying, "I wish to be useful, and every kind of service for the public becomes honorable by being necessary." His brother officers said no more. That afternoon Hale reported to Washington and received his instructions. With a friend he left the room and walked from Harlem Heights to Norwalk, fifty miles up the Sound on the Connecticut shore. There he disguised himself as a Tory schoolmaster, and alone boarded a sloop that took him to Huntington, Long Island. Having landed near the Widow Chichester's tavern, and knowing this to be a resort for Tories and friends of the British, he passed by and made his first stop at the home of William Johnson, about a mile from his landing place. After resting a few hours and obtaining such information as he could about the journey he wished to make, he set out for the British camp, claiming to be looking for a position to teach. He visited the British camp on Long Island, and crossed over to New York City, where the British had taken full possession since he left Washington's headquarters. Here he spent some days visiting with the soldiers. All this time he was studying the plans of the fortifications, and whenever he had an opportunity to be alone he drew sketches and wrote out in Latin descriptions of what he had seen.

When he could learn no more, with these maps and sketches concealed in his shoes, he started on his homeward journey. In safety he found his way back to Huntington, where he arrived in the morning, and expecting a boat to meet him. It was very early when he arrived, and seeing no boat he decided to go to the Tory tavern for breakfast. At the tavern he talked with the Tories, but he did not notice that one of them left the room after he entered. Several hours later a boat was seen approaching. The Tories at once scattered, fearing the boat might contain Connecticut Yankees, whom they did not wish to meet. Hale assured them that the Yankees would not hurt a poor schoolmaster, and offered to go and see what they wanted.

We can imagine how eagerly he hastened to the edge of the water, expecting to meet his friends, but alas! what a disappointment! When he was within range of the boat's crew a dozen men leveled their guns at him and cried, "Surrender or die!" He was trapped.

The man who had left the tavern was a Tory relative who had recognized him and sent word to a British ship. The commander of this ship had sent the boat to capture Hale. He was at once rowed to the guardship, "Halifax." "Are you a captain in the Continental army?" asked the commander. "I am," replied Hale. "Why are you disguised?" was the next question. There was no answer. "Search him," ordered the commander. The papers and drawings were found in his shoes. That settled it. He was a spy.

Hale was sent at once to the headquarters of General Howe in New York City. Howe was dumbfounded "Why did you, a man of learning and fine appearance, attempt this sort of work?" Hale answered, "I am serving my country, and for that reason I will do any service that my country demands." Howe admired his spirit, and this thought came into his head. "What a gain if this man would serve us Surely ambition and place can tempt him." "I will grant you full pardon, if you will join the British army, and you shall be speedily promoted to a high position." Hale answered, "Nothing so increases my loyalty to my country as this temptation to forsake her." "Then you must die for her," was the grim response of General Howe

Turning to his desk, he wrote out the commitment, which directed William Cunningham to receive Nathan Hale, keep him in custody until morning, and then see that he was hanged by the neck until dead A British officer then conducted Hale to the quarters of Cunningham, the provost marshal. This cruel and brutal man was in the habit of treating his prisoners most shamefully. He would insult them, kick them, and parade them up and down the corridors, with Richmond, his negro hangman, carrying a coil of rope behind them Many were hanged in the yard back of the jail and their bodies left to dangle for hours where other prisoners would see them and shudder at the sight.

This man questioned Hale as to his age and history, and read the death warrant telling him that he was to die at daybreak. Every minute of that time would be needed to say good-bye to his father, brothers, and sisters, and to write a last loving letter to Alice Adams Ripley, the young lady who waited in her Connecticut home, longing and hoping for the time when he would return from the war and make her his wife. He asked that his hands might be untied and that he might have a light and some writing materials. The heartless Cunningham refused his request. Hale asked for a Bible. Again he was refused with jeers and insults. He was placed in his cell, and after Cunningham had fallen into a drunken stupor, a kind-hearted British officer who was his guard furnished him materials and a light. The hours of that sad night were passed in writing his last letters to the dear ones at home.

At daybreak the provost came. The prisoner had not slept, but was ready. He handed his letters to Cunningham, who opened them, read them, tore them into fragments, and stamped upon them, saying the rebels should never see such letters No one should ever know that a man died with such courage. Oh, the anguish that pierced the soul of Nathan Hale! Yet he gave no sign of his feelings.

He was ordered to prepare for the death march. He asked for a clergyman, but his request was refused The line of march took him through a vast crowd of men and women to the place of execution in Colonel Rutger's apple orchard Hale, clothed in white, with his arms bound behind him, was preceded by a file of soldiers The soldiers formed a hollow square, with an apple tree in the center. Underneath the tree the grave had been dug. The hangman placed his ladder against a limb of the tree and adjusted the rope. Four negroes placed the coffin beneath the hanging noose. Hale was ordered to stand upon the coffin. While the final preparations were being made, he stood with his manly form erect and his beautiful face illuminated with the glow of courage and heroism Even the hardest of the soldiers were awed by the sight Cunningham hoped to destroy the impression produced by the sublime spectacle and called to Hale to make his last confession

The martyr, whose face had been turned upward in prayer, after casting upon Cunningham a look of unutterable contempt, turned his eyes to the spectators The women were sobbing and the men had turned away their faces. All became silent and his voice, strong, full, and ringing with the energy of courage and patriotism, uttered these immortal words: "I only regret that I have but one life to lose for my Country!" The provost was stunned His rage almost choked him. As soon as he could collect himself he roared, "Swing the rebel off!"

Noble, heroic death! Thus passed away the martyred patriot spy, but his name will live forever and furnish us with an inspiration for great and noble deeds.

The battle of Groton Heights has often been described. But the account found below, by Jonathan Rathbun, has been out of print for fifty years:

I was born in Colchester, Connecticut, in 1765. When 16 years of age, I joined as a volunteer a company of militia, belonging to my native town, and marched to the relief of New London, intelligence having just reached us of an attack on that place by the British under the conduct of the traitor Benedict Arnold We left home to the number of about one hundred men early in the morning of the 7th of September, 1781, the day after the battle. On our arrival in New London we witnessed a scene of suffering and horror which surpasses description. The enemy were not to be found, but they had left behind them the marks of their barbarism and cruelty. The city was in ashes More than one hundred and thirty naked chimneys were standing in the midst of the smoking ruins of stores and dwelling houses. Very little property had escaped the conflagration except a part of the shipping which, on the first alarm, was sent up the river. But though the city was destroyed, it was far from being deserted. Numerous companies of militia from the neighborhood were pouring into the town; and the inhabitants, who had fled from their burning dwellings, were returning to gaze with anguish on the worthless remains of their property. Women were seen walking with consternation and despair depicted in their countenances, leading or carrying in their arms their fatherless and houseless babes, who in a few short hours had been bereaved of all that was dear on earth Their homes, their provisions and even their apparel, were the spoils of the enemy or lay in ashes at their feet. Some were inquiring with the deepest distress for the mangled bodies of their friends, while others were seen following the carts which bore their murdered fathers, husbands or brothers to the grave. More than forty widows were made on that fatal day. Never can I forget the tears, the sobs, the shrieks of woe which fell from the kindred of our brave countrymen who then gave their lives to achieve our national independence. It was my melancholy duty to assist in the burial of the dead, which brought me directly into the midst of these heart-rending scenes where the wife first recognized her husband, the mother her son, the sister her brother, in the body of a mangled soldier, so disfigured with wounds and clotted with blood and dust as to be scarcely known! Often on my visits to New London have I walked near the spot where I helped to inter my slaughtered countrymen; and, though many years have since rolled away, the recollection is still fresh in my mind, awakening anew the strong feelings of sympathy I then felt, and rousing into activity the love of my country.

I recollect several interesting facts connected with the capture of Fort Griswold and the burning of New London, which I believe are not mentioned in the narratives of Messrs Avery and Hempstead.

After the capture of the fort and the massacre which followed, the enemy laid a line of powder from the magazine of the fort to the sea, intending to blow up the fort, and complete the destruction of the wounded within and around it. Stillman Hotman, who lay not far distant, wounded by three strokes of the bayonet in his body, proposed to a wounded man near him to crawl to this line and saturate the powder with their blood, and thus save the magazine and fort, and perhaps the lives of some of their comrades not mortally wounded. He alone succeeded in reaching the line, where he was found dead lying on the powder, which was completely wet with his blood. I do not find his name among the killed in the list of Mr. Avery.

Another fact of a different character was currently reported at the time and deserves to be recorded to the deeper disgrace of the infamous Arnold. He had a sister living in New London, with whom he dined on the day of the battle, and whose house was set fire to, as is supposed, by his orders, immediately afterwards. Perhaps he found her too much of a patriot for his taste. and took this step in revenge.

The next year, 1782, I was led by the spirit which the scenes I had witnessed in New London had fanned into a flame, to leave my father's house and the peaceful pursuits of agriculture, and to enlist as a private in the Connecticut State troops. Never shall I forget the impressive circumstances under which I took the soldier's oath. With five others of my townsmen who enlisted with me, I was marched into the meeting house on the first Monday in April, it being Freeman's Day, and there in the presence of a large concourse of people we swore to discharge our duty faithfully. We were ordered to Fort Stanwich, in Stamford, Connecticut, where I remained during all but the last month of my term of service. Here I was subjected to the usual hardships of military life. Many a time have I been out for several days on scouting parties, sometimes to the distance of twenty-five miles. These were not only attended with fatigue, cold and hunger, but with no little peril of life. On one occasion a rifle ball passed through my hat and cut away the hair of my head, but a kind Providence protected me.

A party of fourteen men under Lewis Smith were surprised by a body of mounted troops to the number of sixty, by whom they were ordered to surrender. Lewis Smith, perceiving the hopelessness of resistance against such an overwhelming force, inquired of the British officer in command whether if they should surrender they would be treated as prisoners of war. The answer was, "Yes," but no sooner had they lowered their muskets than the enemy shot them down.

As a specimen of the hardships to which the private soldier in time of war is constantly liable, I may mention the following: One evening the orderly sergeants passed around among the men and with a whisper commanded us to equip ourselves without noise, and then we were marched out of the fort to a woods two miles distant and ordered to lie down on the frozen ground, where we passed a bitter cold night with only a single blanket and our overcoats to protect us. We afterwards learned that this step was taken to avoid the enemy, who it was reported were that night to attack the fort with an overwhelming force. From such exposures and hardships as these my constitution received a shock from which I have never recovered. The sickness of my father was considered a sufficient reason for giving me a discharge; and after eleven months' service I left Stamford for Colchester. On reaching home I was immediately taken sick, and for six months was unable to do any business. From that time mingled mercies and misfortunes have attended me. The infirmities thus contracted in the service of my country disabled me from arduous manual labor, and much of my life has therefore been spent in trade and other light employments. My heaviest misfortune, however, has been the sickness of my excellent wife, who for forty years has been confined to her bed, and for whose medication and comfort, with the other expenses of my family, the earnings of my industry have proved insufficient, especially since the infirmities of old age have come upon me. But of none of these things do I complain. They are wisely appointed, and have been greatly alleviated by the kindness of a generous community. I mention them for the sole object of interesting my countrymen in my present effort to supply my wants through this little book.

The following narrative by Rufus Avery, orderly sergeant under Captain William Latham, containing an account of the transactions at New London and Groton on the 6th of September, 1781, is in his own words:

I had charge of the garrison the night previous to the attack. The enemy had not yet appeared near us, nor did we expect them at this time more than ever; but it is true "we know not what shall be on the morrow." About 3 o'clock in the morning, as soon as daylight appeared, so as I could look off, I saw the fleet in the harbor, a little distance below the light house; it consisted of thirty-two in number—ships, brigs, schooners and sloops. It may well be imagined that a shock of consternation and a thrill of dread apprehension flashed over me. I immediately sent for Capt. William Latham, who was captain of said fort, and who was near by. He came and saw the fleet, and sent notice to Colonel Ledyard, who was commander of the harbor, and also of Forts Griswold and Trumbull. He ordered two large guns to be loaded with heavy charges of good powder, &c. Captain William Latham took charge of the one which was to be discharged from the northeast part of the fort, and I had to attend the other on the west side, and thus we as speedily as possible prepared to give alarm to the vicinity, as was to be expected in case of danger, two guns being the specified signal for alarm in distress. But a difficulty now arose from having all our plans communicated by a traitor! The enemy understood our signal was two regular guns, and they fired a third, which broke our alarm, and caused it to signify good news or a prize, and thus it was understood by our troops, and several companies which were lying back ready to come to our assistance in case of necessity were by this measure deterred from coming. The reader may well suppose, though time would not permit us to consider or anticipate long, that the sense of our helplessness without additional strength and arms was dreadful; but the trying events of the few coming hours we had not known! Colonel Ledyard now sent expresses from both forts, to call on every militia captain to hurry with their companies to the forts. But few came; their excuse was that it was but a false alarm, or for some trifling alarm. The enemy's boats now approached and landed eight hundred officers and men, some horses, some carriages and cannon, on the Groton side of the river, about 8 o'clock in the morning; and another division on the New London side, below the light house, consisting of about seven hundred officers and men. The army on Groton banks was divided into two divisions. Colonel Ayres took command of the division southeast of the forts, consisting of about half, sheltering them behind a ledge of rocks about one hundred and thirty rods back; Major Montgomery, with his division about one hundred and fifty rods from the fort, behind a high hill. The army on New London side of the river had better and more accommodating land to march on than that on Groton side. As soon as their army had got opposite Fort Trumbull, they divided, and one part proceeded to the city of New London, plundered and set fire to the shipping and buildings, the rest marched down to Fort Trumbull. Captain

N L.—1-5

Adam Shapley, who commanded, seeing that he was likely to be overpowered by the enemy, spiked his cannon and embarked on board the boats which had been prepared for him in case of necessity; but the enemy were so quick upon him that before he and his little handful of men could get out of the reach of their guns, seven men were badly wounded in the boats. The remaining ones reached Fort Griswold, where, poor fellows, they met a mortal blow

Ayres and Montgomery got their army stationed about 9 o'clock in the morning. When they appeared in sight, we threw a number of shots among them, but they would immediately contrive to disappear behind their hills. About 10 o'clock they sent a flag of truce to demand the surrender of the fort. When the flag was within about forty rods from the fort, we sent a musket ball in front of them, and brought them to a stand. Col. Ledyard called a council of war to ascertain the minds of his officers and friends about what was best to be done in this momentous hour, when every moment indicated a bloody and decisive battle. They all agreed in council to send a flag to them. They did so, choosing Capt. Elijah Avery, Capt. Amos Staunton, and Capt. John Williams, who went immediately to meet the British flag and receive their demand, which was to give up the Fort to them. The council was then inquired of what was to be done, and the answer returned to the British flag was that "the Fort would not be given up to the British." The flag then returned to their division commanded by Ayres, but soon returned to us again; when about a proper distance our flag met them and attended to their summons, and came back to inform Col. Ledyard that the enemy declared that "if they were obliged to take it by storm, they should put the Martial Law in full force," that is, "what they did not kill by ball, they should put to death by sword and bayonet!" Col. Ledyard sent back the decisive answer that "we should not give up the Fort to them, let the consequences be what they would."

While these flags were passing and repassing, we were exchanging shots with the British at Fort Trumbull, as they had got possession of it before the battle commenced in action at Fort Griswold. We could throw our shot into Fort Trumbull without any difficulty, but the British could not cause theirs to enter Fort Griswold, because they could not aim high enough. They had got possession and in use some of our best pieces and ammunition, which were left in Fort Trumbull, when Captain Shapley left it and retreated. About 11 o'clock in the morning, when they perceived what we were about to do, they started with both their divisions, Colonel Ayres advancing with his in solid columns. As soon as they reached the level ground and in a proper range, we saluted them with an eighteen-pounder, then loaded with two bags of grape shot Capt. Elias H. Halsey was the one who directed the guns, and took aim at the enemy. He had long practiced on board a privateer, and manifested his skill at this time. I was at the gun with others when it was discharged into the British ranks, and it cleared a very wide space in their solid columns It has been reported by good authority that about twenty were killed and wounded by that one discharge of grape shot. As soon as the column was broken by loss of men and officers, they were seen to scatter and trail arms coming on with a quick step towards the fort, inclining to the west We continued firing, but they advanced upon the south and west sides of the fort Colonel Ayres was mortally wounded. Major Montgomery now advanced with his division, coming on in solid columns, bearing around to the north, until they got east of the redoubt or battery, which was east of the fort, then marching with a quick step into the battery. Here we sent among them large and repeated charges of grape shot which destroyed a number, as we could perceive them thinned and broken. Then they started for the fort, a part of them in platoons, discharging their guns; and some of the officers and men scattering, they came around on the east and north side of the fort. Here Major Montgomery fell, near the northeast part of the fort. We might suppose the loss of their commanders might have dismayed them, but they had proceeded so far, and the excitement and determination on slaughter was so great, they could not be prevented. As soon as their army had entirely surrounded the garrison, a man attempted to open the gates; but he lost his life in a moment, before he could succeed. There was hard fighting and shocking slaughter, and much blood spilt before another attempt was made to open the gates, which was at this time successful; for our little number, which was only one hundred and fifty-five, officers and privates (the most of them volunteers), were by this time overpowered. There was then no block house on the parade as there is now, so that the enemy had every chance to wound and kill every man. When they had overpowered us and driven us from our station at the breastwork into the fort, and Colonel Ledyard saw how few men he had remaining to fight with, he ceased resistance. They all left their posts and went on to the open parade in the fort, where the enemy had a fair opportunity to massacre us, as there were only six of us to an hundred of them! This, this was a moment of indescribable misery! We can fight with good hearts while hope and prospects of victory aid us, but, after we have fought and bled, and availed nothing, to yield to be massacred by the boasting enemy "tries men's hearts!" Our ground was drenched with human gore, our wounded and dying could not have any attendance, while each man was almost hopeless of his own preservation; but our country's danger caused the most acute anxiety. Now I saw the enemy mount the parapets like so many madmen, all at once, seemingly. They swung their hats around, and then discharged their guns into the fort, and those who had not fallen by ball they began to massacre with sword and bayonet. I was on the west side of the fort, with Capt. Edward Latham and Mr C Latham, standing on the platform, and had a full view of the enemy's conduct. I had then a hole through my clothes by a ball, and a bayonet rent through my coat to the flesh. The enemy approached us, knocked down the two men I mentioned, with the britch (breech) of their guns, and I expected had ended their lives, but they did not. By this time that division which had been commanded by Montgomery, now under charge of Bloomfield, unbolted the other gates, marched into the Fort, and formed into a solid column. I at this moment left my station and went across the parade towards the south end of the barracks. I noticed Col. William Ledyard on the parade stepping towards the enemy and Bloomfield, gently raising and lowering his sword as a token of bowing and submission; he was about six feet from them when I turned my eyes off from him, and went up to the door of the barracks and looked at the enemy, who were discharging their guns through the windows. It was but a moment that I had turned my eyes from Col. L. and saw him alive, and now I saw him weltering in his gore! Oh, the hellish spite and madness of a man that will murder a reasonable and noble-hearted officer, in the act of submitting and surrendering! I can assure my countrymen that I felt the thrill of such a horrid deed more than the honorable and martial-like war of months! We are informed that the wretch who murdered him exclaimed as he came near, "Who commands this fort?" Ledyard handsomely replied, "I did, but you do now," at the same moment handing him his sword, which the unfeeling villain buried in his breast! The column continued marching towards the south end of the parade, and I could do no better than to go across the parade before them, amid their fire They discharged three platoons, as I crossed before them at this time. I believe there were not less than five or six hundred of the British on the parade, and in the Fort They killed and wounded every man they possibly could, and it was all done in less than two minutes! I had nothing to expect but to drop with the rest, one mad looking fellow put his bayonet to my side, swearing, "by Jesus he would skipper me!" I looked him earnestly in the face and eyes, and begged him to have mercy and spare my life! I must say, I believe God prevented him from killing me, for he put his bayonet three times into me, and I seemed to be in his power, as well as Lieut Enoch Staunton, who was stabbed to the heart and fell at my feet at this time. I think no scene ever exceeded this for continued and barbarous massacre after surrender. There were two large doors to the Magazine, which made a space wide enough to admit ten men to stand in one rank. There marched up a platoon of ten men just by where I stood, and at once discharged their guns into the Magazine among our killed and wounded, and also among those who had escaped uninjured, and as soon as these had fired, another platoon was ready, and immediately took their place when they fell back. At this moment Bloomfield came swiftly around the corner of the building, and raising his sword with exceeding quickness, exclaimed, "stop firing! or you will send us all to Hell together!" I was very near him when he spoke. He knew there must be much powder deposited and scattered about the Magazine, and if they continued throwing in fire we should all be blown up. I think it must, before this, have been the case, had not the ground and everything been wet with human blood. We trod in blood! We trampled under feet the limbs of our Countrymen, our neighbors and dear kindred. Our ears were filled with the groans of the dying, when the more stunning sound of the artillery would give place to the death shrieks. After this they ceased killing and went to stripping, not only the dead, but the wounded and those who were not wounded They then ordered us all who were able to march, to the N. E. part of the parade, and those who could walk to help those who were wounded so bad as not to go of themselves Mr Samuel Edgcomb Jr. and myself were ordered to carry out Ensign Charles Eldridge, who was shot through the knee joints; he was a very large, heavy man, and with our fasting and violent exercises of the day, we were but ill able to do it, or more than to sustain our own weight; but we had to submit We with all the prisoners were taken out upon the parade, about two rods from the Fort, and ordered to sit down immediately, or they would put their bayonets into us The battle was now ended. It was about 1 o'clock in the afternoon, and since the hour of eight in the morning, what a scene of carnage, of anxiety, and of loss had we experienced!

The enemy now began to take care of their dead and wounded. They took off six of the outer doors of the barracks, and with four men at each door, they brought in one man at a time. There were twenty-four men thus employed for two hours, as fast as they could walk. They deposited them on the west side of the parade, in the Fort, where it was the most comfortable place, and screened from the hot sun which was pouring down upon us, aggravating our wounds, and causing many to faint and die who might have lived with good care. By my side lay two most worthy and excellent officers, Capt. Youngs Ledyard, and Capt. N. Moore, in the agonies of death. Their heads rested on my thighs, as I sat or lay there. They had their reason well and spoke. They asked for water. I could give them none, as I was to be thrust through if I got up. I asked the enemy, who were passing by us, to give us some water for my dying friends and for myself As the well was near they granted this request; but even then I feared they would put something poison into it, that they might get us out of the way the sooner; and they had said, repeatedly, that the last of us should die before the sun set! Oh what revenge and inhumanity pervaded their steeled hearts! They effected what was threatened in the summons, sent by the flag in the morning, to Colonel Ledyard, "That those who were not killed by the musket, should be by the sword," &c. But I must think they became tired of human butchery, and so let us live They kept us on the ground, the garrison charged, till about two hours had been spent in taking care of their men; and then came and ordered every man of us that could walk, to "rise up." Sentries were placed around with guns loaded, and bayonets fixed, and orders given that every one who would not, in a moment, obey commands, should be shot dead or run through! I had to leave the two dying men who were resting on me, dropping their heads on the cold and hard ground, giving them one last and pitying look Oh God, this was hard work They both died that night. We marched down to the bank of the river so as to be ready to embark on board the British vessels There were about thirty of us surrounded by sentries. Captain Bloomfield then came and took down the names of the prisoners who were able to march down with us. Where I sat, I had a fair view of their movements. They were setting fire to the buildings and bringing the plunder and laying it down near us. The sun was about half an hour high. I can never forget the whole appearance of all about me. New London was in flames! The inhabitants deserted their habitations to save life, which was more highly prized. Above and around us were our unburied dead, and our dying friends. None to appeal to for sustenance in our exhausted state but a maddened enemy—not allowed to move a step or make any resistance, but with loss of life—and sitting to see the property of our neighbors consumed by fire, or the spoils of a triumphing enemy!

Reader, but little can be described, while much is felt There were still remaining, near the fort, a great number of the British who were getting ready to leave. They loaded up our large ammunition wagon that belonged to the fort with the wounded men that could not walk, and about twenty of the enemy drew it from the fort to the brow of the hill which leads down to the river The declivity is very steep for the distance of thirty rods to the river As soon as the wagon began to move down the hill, it pressed so hard against them that they found they were unable to hold it back, and jumped away from it as quickly as possible, leaving it to thrash along down the hill with great speed, till the shafts struck a large apple tree stump, with a most violent crash, hurting the poor dying, and wounded men in it, in a most inhuman manner. Some of the wounded fell out and fainted away; then a part of the company where I sat, ran and brought the men and the wagon along. They by some means got the prisoners who were wounded badly into a house nearby belonging to Ensign Ebenezer Avery, who was one of the wounded in the wagon. Before the prisoners were brought to the house the soldiers had set fire to it, but others put it out, and made use of it for this purpose. Captain Bloomfield paroled, to be left at home here, these wounded prisoners, and took Ebenezer Ledyard, Esq., as hostage for them, to see them forthcoming when called for.

Now the boats had come for us who could go on board the fleet. The officer spoke with a doleful and menacing tone, "Come, you rebels, go on board." This was a consummation of all I had seen or endured through the day This wounded my feelings in a thrilling manner. After all my sufferings and toil, to add the pang of leaving my native land, my wife, my good neighbors, and probably to suffer still more with cold and hunger, for already I had learned that I was with a cruel enemy. But I was in the hands of a

higher power—over which no human being could hold superior control—
and by God's preservation I am still alive, through all the hardships and
dangers of the war, while almost every one about me, who shared the same,
has met either a natural or an unnatural death. When we, the prisoners, went
down to the shore to the boats, they would not bring them near, but kept
them off where the water was knee deep to us, obliging us, weak and worn
as we were, to wade to them. We were marched down in two ranks, one
on each side of the boat. The officer spoke very harshly to us, to "get aboard
immediately." They rowed us down to an armed sloop, commanded by one
Captain Thomas, as they called him, a refugee tory, and he lay with his
vessel within the fleet. As soon as we were on board, they hurried us down
into the hold of the sloop, where were their fires for cooking, and besides
being very hot, it was filled with smoke. The hatch-way was closed tight,
so that we were near suffocating for want of air to breathe. We begged them
to spare our lives, so they gave us some relief, by opening the hatch-way and
permitting us to come up on deck, by two or three at a time, but not without
sentries watching us with gun and bayonet. We were now extremely
exhausted and faint for want of food; when after being on board twenty-four
hours, they gave us a mess of hogs brains; the hogs which they took on
Groton banks when they plundered there.

After being on board Thomas's sloop nearly three days, with nothing
to eat or drink that we could swallow, we began to feel as if a struggle must
be made, in some way, to prolong our existence, which, after all our escapes
seemed still to be depending. In such a time, we can know, for a reality, how
strong is the love of life. In the room where we were confined were a great
many weapons of war, and some of the prisoners whispered that we might
make a prize of the sloop. This in some way was overheard, and got to the
officer's ears, and now we were immediately put in a stronger place in the
hold of the vessel; and they appeared so enraged that I was almost sure we
should share a decisive fate, or suffer severely. Soon they commenced calling
us, one by one, on deck. As I went up they seized me, tied my hands behind
me with a strong rope-yarn, and drew it so tight that my shoulder-bones
cracked and almost touched each other. Then a boat came from a fourteen-
gun brig, commanded by one Steele. Into this boat I was ordered to get,
without the use of my hands, over the sloop's bulwarks, which were all of
three feet high, and then from these I had to fall, or throw myself into the
boat. My distress of body and agitated feelings I cannot describe; and no
relief could be anticipated, but only forebodings of a more severe fate. A
prisoner with an enemy, an enraged and revengeful enemy, is a place where
I pray my reader may never come They made us all lie down under the
seats on which the man sat to row, and so we were conveyed to the brig;
going on board, we were ordered to stand in one rank by the gunwale, and
in front of us was placed a spar, within about a foot of each man. Here we
stood, with a sentry to each of us, having orders to shoot or bayonet us if
we attempted to stir out of our place. All this time we had nothing to eat
or drink, and it rained and was very cold. We were detained in this position
about two hours, when we had liberty to go about the main deck Night
approached, and we had no supper, nor anything to lie upon but the wet deck.
We were on board this brig about four days, and then were removed on board
a ship commanded by Capt. Scott, who was very kind to the prisoners. He
took me on to the quarter deck with him, and appeared to have the heart of
a man. I should think he was about sixty years of age. I remained with
him until I was exchanged. Capt. Nathaniel Shaw came down to N. York
with the American flag, after me and four others, who were prisoners with

me, and belonged to Fort Griswold, and who were brave, and fine young men. Gen. Mifflin went with the British flag to meet this American flag. I sailed with him about twenty miles   He asked me many questions, all of which I took caution how I answered, and gave him no information. I told him I was very sorry that he should come to destroy so many, many brave men, burn their property, distress so many families, and make such desolation. I did not think they could be said to be honorable in so doing. He said "we might thank our own countrymen for it." I told him I had no thanks for him. I then asked the Gen. if I might ask him a few questions. "As many as you please." I asked him how many of the army who made the attack upon New London and Groton were missing? As you, sir, are the commissary of the British army, I suppose you can tell. He replied "that by the returns, there were two hundred and twenty odd missing, but what had become of them he knew not." We advanced, and the flags met and I was exchanged and permitted to return home. Here I close my narrative; for, as I was requested I have given a particular and unexaggerated account of that which I saw with mine own eyes.

The author of the following narrative of events, Stephen Hempstead, entered the service of his country in 1775, and arrived in Boston on the day of the battle of Bunker Hill. He was at Dorchester Point; was on Long Island at the time of the retreat of the American army; and was also a volunteer in the first ships that were to destroy the "Asia," 84-gun ship, and a frigate lying above Fort Washington   In this attempt they were unsuccessful, although grappled to the enemy's vessel twenty minutes   For the bravery displayed by them they received the particular thanks of the commanding officer in person and in general orders, and forty dollars were ordered to be paid to each person engaged. He was afterwards wounded by a grapeshot while defending the lines at Harlem Heights, which broke two of his ribs. He continued in the service, and was again wounded on the 6th of September, 1781   He formerly resided in New London. He enjoyed the reception of General LaFayette in that place during his last visit to this country, and within a few years wrote this account in full, for publication:

On the morning of the 6th of September, 1781, twenty-four sail of the enemy's shipping appeared to the westward of New London harbor. The enemy landed in two divisions, of about 800 men each, commanded by that infamous traitor to his country, Benedict Arnold, who headed the division that landed on the New London side, near Brown's farms; the other division, commanded by Col. Ayres, landed on Groton Point, nearly opposite   I was first sergeant of Capt. Adam Shapley's company of State troops, and was stationed with him at the time, with about 23 men, at Fort Trumbull, on the New London side. This was a mere breastwork or water battery, open from behind, and the enemy coming on us from that quarter, we spiked our cannon, and commenced a retreat across the river to Fort Griswold in three boats. The enemy was so near that they overshot us with their muskets, and succeeded in capturing one boat with six men commanded by Josiah Smith, a private. They afterwards proceeded to New London and burnt the town. We were received by the garrison with enthusiasm, being considered experienced artillerists, whom they much needed; and we were immediately assigned to our stations. The Fort was an oblong square, with bastions at opposite angles, its longest side fronting the river in a N. W. and S. E. direction. Its

walls were of stone, and were 10 or 12 feet high on the lower side and surrounded by a ditch. On the wall were pickets, projecting over 12 feet; above
this was a parapet with embrasures, and within a platform for the cannon,
and a step to mount upon, to shoot over the parapet with small arms. In the
S. W. bastion was a flag-staff, and in the side near the opposite angle was
the gate, in front of which was a triangular breastwork to protect the gate;
and to the right of this was a redoubt with a three-pounder in it, which was
about 120 yards from the gate. Between the Fort and the river was another
battery, with a covered way, but which could not be used in this attack, as
the enemy appeared in a different quarter. The garrison with the volunteers
consisted of about 160 men. Soon after our arrival, the enemy appeared in
force in some woods about half a mile S. E. of the Fort, from whence they
sent a flag of truce, which was met by Capt Shapley, demanding an uncon-
ditional surrender, threatening at the same time to storm the Fort instantly
if the terms were not accepted. A council of war was held, and it was the
unanimous voice that the garrison were unable to defend themselves against
so superior a force. But a militia Colonel who was then in the Fort and
had a body of men in the immediate vicinity said he would reinforce them
with 2 or 300 men in fifteen minutes, if they would hold out; Col. Ledyard
agreed to send back a defiance, upon the most solemn assurance of immediate
succor. For this purpose, Col. —— started, his men being then in sight;
but he was no more seen, nor did he even attempt a diversion in our favor.
When the answer to their demand had been returned by Capt. Shapley, the
enemy were soon in motion, and marched with great rapidity, in a solid
column, to within a short distance of the Fort, where, dividing the column,
they rushed furiously and simultaneously to the assault of the S. W bastion
and the opposite sides. They were, however, repulsed with great slaughter,
their commander mortally wounded, and Major Montgomery, next in rank,
killed, having been thrust through the body whilst in the act of scaling the
walls at the S. W. bastion, by Capt. Shapley. The command then devolved
on Col. Beckwith, a refugee from New Jersey, who commanded a corps of
that description. The enemy rallied and returned the attack with great vigor,
but were received and repulsed with equal firmness. During the attack a
shot cut the halyards of the flag, and it fell to the ground, but was instantly
remounted on a pike pole. This accident proved fatal to us, as the enemy
supposed it had been struck by its defenders, rallied again, and rushing with
redoubled impetuosity, carried the S. W. bastion by storm. Until this moment, our loss was trifling in number, being 6 or 7 killed, and 18 or 20
wounded. Never was a post more bravely defended, nor a garrison more
barbarously butchered. We fought with all kinds of weapons, and at all
places with a courage that deserved a better fate. Many of the enemy were
killed under the walls by throwing simple shot over them, and never would
we have relinquished our arms, had we had the least idea that such a catastrophe would have followed. To describe this scene I must be permitted to
go back a little in my narrative. I commanded an 18-pounder on the south
side of the gate, and while in the act of sighting my gun, a ball passed through
the embrasure, struck me a little above the right ear, grazing the skull, and
cutting off the veins, which bled profusely. A handkerchief was tied around
it and I continued at my duty. Discovering some little time after that a
British soldier had broken a picket at the bastion on my left, and was forcing
himself through the hole, whilst the men stationed there were gazing at the
battle which raged opposite to them, cried, "my brave fellows," the enemy
are breaking in behind you," and raised my pike to despatch the intruder,
when a ball struck my left arm at the elbow, and my pike fell to the ground.

Nevertheless I grasped it with my right hand, and with the men, who turned and fought manfully, cleared the breach. The enemy, however, soon after forced the S. W. bastion, where Capt. Shapely, Capt. Peter Richards, Lieut Richard Chapman and several other men of distinction, and volunteers, had fought with unconquerable courage, and were all either killed or mortally wounded, and which had sustained the brunt of every attack. Capt. P. Richards, Lieut. Chapman and several others were killed in the bastion, Capt. Shapely and others wounded. He died of his wounds in January following.

Col. Ledyard, seeing the enemy within the fort, gave orders to cease firing, and to throw down our arms as the Fort had surrendered. We did so, but they continued firing upon us, crossed the fort and opened the gate, when they marched in, firing in platoons upon those who were retreating to the magazine and barrack rooms for safety. At this moment the renegade Colonel B. commanding, cried out, who commands this garrison? Col Ledyard, who was standing near me, answered, "I did sir, but you do now," at the same time stepping forward, handed him his sword with the point towards himself. At this instant I perceived a soldier in the act of bayoneting me from behind. I turned suddenly round and grasped his bayonet, endeavoring to unship it, and knock off the thrust—but in vain. Having but one hand, he succeeded in forcing it into my right hip, above the joint, and just below the abdomen, and crushed me to the ground. The first person I saw afterwards was my brave commander, a corpse by my side, having been run through the body with his own sword by the savage renegade. Never was a scene of more brutal wanton carnage witnessed than now took place. The enemy were still firing upon us in platoons, and in the barrack rooms, which were continued for some minutes, when they discovered they were in danger of being blown up, by communicating fire to the powder scattered at the mouth of the magazine, while delivering our cartridges; nor did it then cease in the rooms for some minutes longer. All this time the bayonet was "freely used," even on those who were helplessly wounded and in the agonies of death I recollect Capt. Wm Seymour, a volunteer from Hartford, had 13 bayonet wounds, although his knee had previously been shattered by a ball, so much so that it was obliged to be amputated the next day. But I need not mention particular cases. I have already said that we had 6 killed and 18 wounded previous to their storming our lines; 85 were killed in all, 35 mortally and dangerously wounded, and 40 taken prisoners to New York, most of them slightly hurt.

After the massacre, they plundered us of everything we had, and left us literally naked When they commenced gathering us up together with their own wounded, they put theirs under the shade of the platform, and exposed us to the sun, in front of the barracks, where we remained over an hour. Those that could stand were then paraded, and ordered to the landing, while those that could not (of which number I was one) were put in one of our ammunition wagons, and taken to the brow of the hill (which was very steep, and at least 100 rods in descent), from whence it was permitted to run down by itself, but was arrested in its course, near the river, by an apple tree. The pain and anguish we all endured in this rapid descent, as the wagon jumped and jostled over rocks and holes is inconceivable; and the jar in its arrest was like bursting the cords of life asunder, and caused us to shriek with almost supernatural force. Our cries were distinctly heard and noticed on the opposite side of the river (which is a mile wide), amidst all the confusion which raged in burning and sacking the town. We remained in the wagon more than an hour, before our humane conquerers hunted us up, when we were again paraded and laid on the beach, preparatory to embarkation.

But by the interposition of Ebenezer Ledyard (brother to Col. L.), who humanely represent our deplorable situation, and the impossibility of our being able to reach New York, 35 of us were paroled in the usual form, being near the house of Ebenezer Avery, who was also one of our number, we were taken into it. Here we had not long remained before a marauding party set fire to every room, evidently intending to burn us up with the house. The party soon left it, when it was with difficulty extinguished and we were thus saved from the flames. Ebenezer Ledyard again interfered and obtained a sentinel to remain and guard us until the last of the enemy embarked, about 11 o'clock at night. None of our own people came to us till near daylight the next morning, not knowing previous to that time that the enemy had departed.

Such a night of distress and anguish was scarcely ever passed by mortal. Thirty-five of us were lying on the bare floor—stiff, mangled, and wounded in every manner, exhausted with pain, fatigue and loss of blood, without clothes or anything to cover us, trembling with cold and spasms of extreme anguish, without fire or light, parched with excruciating thirst, not a wound dressed nor a soul to administer to one of our wants, nor an assisting hand to turn us during these long tedious hours of the night; nothing but groans and unavailing sighs were heard, and two of our number did not live to see the light of the morning, which brought with it some ministering angels to our relief. The first was in the person of Miss Fanny Ledyard, of Southold, L. I., then on a visit to her uncle, our murdered commander, who held to my lips a cup of warm chocolate, and soon after returned with wine and other refreshments, which revived us a little. For these kindnesses she has never ceased to receive my most grateful thanks and fervent prayers for her felicity.

The cruelty of our enemy cannot be conceived, and our renegade country-men surpassed in this respect, if possible, our British foes We were at least an hour after the battle, within a few steps of a pump in the garrison, well supplied with water, and, although we were suffering with thirst, they would not permit us to take one drop of it, nor give us any themselves Some of our number, who were not disabled from going to the pump, were repulsed with the bayonet, and not one drop did I taste after the action commenced, although begging for it after I was wounded, of all who came near me, until relieved by Miss Ledyard. We were a horrible sight at this time. Our own friends did not know us—even my own wife came in the room in search of me, and did not recognize me, and as I did not see her, she left the room to seek for me among the slain, who had been collected under a large elm tree near the house. It was with the utmost difficulty that many of them could be identified, and we were frequently called upon to assist their friends in distinguishing them, by remembering particular wounds, &c. Being myself taken out by two men for this purpose, I met my wife and brother, who, after my wounds were dressed by Dr Downer, from Preston, took me—not to my own home, for that was in ashes, as also every article of my property, fur-niture and clothing—but to my brother's where I lay eleven months as help-less as a child, and to this day I feel the effects of it severely.

Such was the battle of Groton Heights; and such, as far as my imperfect manner and language can describe, a part of the sufferings which we endured. Never, for a moment, have I regretted the share I had in it; I would for an equal degree of honor, and the prosperity which has resulted to my country from the Revolution, be willing, if possible, to suffer it again.

Stephen Hempstead.

The following note in Allen's history of the "Battle of Groton Heights"

shows that even today there is considerable doubt as to just how Colonel
Ledyard was killed. Mr. Allyn's subscript to the note of Harris indicates
again the lack of conclusive evidence on this point:

Since this transaction there has ever existed in the public mind great
uncertainty as to who was the murderer of Colonel Ledyard, the odium being
divided between Major Bromfield, who succeeded Major Montgomery in
command of the British troops on that occasion, and Captain Beckwith, of
the 54th regiment. No person who actually witnessed the deed survived the
battle,* or if any did they left no account of it behind them; and therefore
the version of the manner of Ledyard's death commonly received as the correct one is but merely a conjecture, at the most. By this, the deed is ascribed
to the officer who received Ledyard's surrender of the fort, supposed by the
greater number to have been Major Bromfield; others at the time, and for
a long time subsequent, laid the infamous transaction to the charge of Captain
Beckwith, supposing him to have been the officer who met Ledyard and
demanded the surrender.

Let us consider the matter a little, and see if we be able to reconcile the
known facts and strong probabilities in the case, with this generally received
opinion. Upon the entry of the British officer to the fort, and at his demand
of who commanded it, Colonel Ledyard advanced to answer, "I did," etc., at
the same time tendering him the hilt of his sword in token of submission.
It is obvious that in this action Colonel Ledyard must have presented the
front of his person to that officer. Now, had the latter, in taking the surrendered sword, instantly (as all accounts charge him with having done)
plunged it into him, is it not also evident that it must have entered in front
and passed out of the back of his person? The vest and shirt worn that day
by Colonel Ledyard, preserved in the Wadsworth Athenaeum at Hartford,
upon examination reveal two rough, jagged openings, one on either side, a
little before and in a line with the lower edge of the arm-holes of the vest.
The larger of these apertures is upon the left side; the difference in size
between it and that on the right corresponds with the taper of a sabre blade
from hilt to point, showing conclusively that the weapon entered from the
left and passed out at the right, and that the person by whom the wound was
inflicted must have stood upon the left side of the wearer when the plunge
was made. These holes are marked: that on the left as "where the sword
entered," and that on the right as "where the sword came out"—so marked,
doubtless, by the person who presented these memorials to the society, a near
relative of Colonel Ledyard, and who considered them as the marks of the
fatal wound. These are the only marks visible upon the garment. It is a
reasonable supposition that when the British officer entered and thundered
his demand he carried his drawn sword in his right hand; for we can scarcely
imagine an officer rushing unarmed into a place of such danger and demanding a surrender. Now, in case he did so carry his sword, he must necessarily

---

* Mr. Harris is in error here, I believe, as I myself have heard this action described
by three people whose fathers saw the murder, and often told of it to their children
(see notes on Andrew Gallup and Caleb Avery). This being the case, most of the
ground for Mr. Harris's argument is taken away. The argument, though ingenious, is
not conclusive, since no one can by reasoning be certain what positions would be
taken in moments of such excitement. The most natural positions are those which
agree with the popularly received account, as men of military experience and education I think, will agree.—A

either have sheathed, dropped, or changed it to his left hand, in order to receive Ledyard's with the right; and this hardly seems possible. We must therefore suppose that he received it in his left hand; and if so, does it not appear as most unreasonable that, having a sword in either hand, he would have used that in his left with which to make the thrust? Yet he must have done so if it was by his own sword that Ledyard met his death. Neither does it appear possible that in the heat and excitement of the engagement, coolly calculating the chances, he would have passed around to the left of his victim for the purpose of making the wound more surely fatal—the only reason for which we can suppose it to have been done.

We have seen from the position occupied by the parties that the wound, if inflicted instantly on the surrender of the sword, must have been given in front; the marks in the vest conclusively prove it to have been given in the left side. We have seen the awkward position of the officer with his own sword in his right and Ledyard's in his left hand—a situation almost precluding the idea of his making the stab with the latter. We have also seen that no person who witnessed it left any testimony regarding the affair, and that all the commonly received version of it is based upon is really but the surmises of a people wrought almost to desperation by their losses and wrongs, who in the first moments of exasperation would naturally attribute an act of such enormity to the commander as the representative of the enemy. Now, after considering all these facts and probabilities, is it not a more rational conclusion that the wound was given by a by-standing officer—a subaltern or aid, perhaps—than that it was inflicted by the officer to whom Ledyard offered his sword? It certainly so appears to us. But in case that, despite all these reasons for believing that officer innocent of the crime, he was really guilty of the two to whom it has been charged, against but one is there any evidence to sustain the charge, and this is purely circumstantial. Captain Beckwith acted as aid to Lieutenant-Colonel Ayres on the day of the battle, and was the officer sent to demand the surrender of the fort. He, with Lord Dalrymple, was sent by Arnold as bearer of despatches to Sir Henry Clinton, and in all probability furnished the account of the battle for Rivington's Gazette, which appeared in that paper before the remainder of the expedition had reached New York. In this account, in which the details of the conference regarding the surrender are given with a minuteness with which only an eye-witness could give them, personal malice toward Colonel Ledyard is a salient feature, which the most unobservant reader cannot fail to notice. The writer appears to have considered the flag and the officers bearing it insulted in the conference; and in his reference to the garrison, and to Colonel Ledyard in particular, he expresses himself in the most contemptuous and bitter terms.

If he was the officer to whom the surrender was made, it is possible that on beholding the man who he fancied had insulted him he allowed his rage to supplant his manhood, and, forgetting his military honor, plunged his sword into his vanquished enemy. From Miss Caulkins' "History of New London" we learn that he afterward passed through New York on his way to Barbadoes. While there he was charged by the newspapers of that city with the murder, which he indignantly denied. A correspondence was opened between him and a relative of Colonel Ledyard in reference to the question, when he produced documents which exculpated him. In view of this, however, as between him and Major Bromfield, circumstantial evidence is strongly in favor of the latter, who doubtless could have furnished as full documentary proof of his innocence, had he been called upon for it.—H.

AN ERA OF UNREST

The population of New London county had grown by 1800 to about 40,000, Stonington at that time being its largest town. Commerce was carried on extensively with the West Indies and with South America and Europe. The war between England and France was at that time a source of much profit to New England, but with the Embargo Act of 1807 the shipping interests of the county were hard hit. It is small wonder that the Federalists opposed Jefferson's policy.

One wonders, of course, why New England, in spite of impressment of our seamen by the Mother Country and her renunciation of a well settled shipping rule, was so luke-warm in its animosity against her and so hostile to France. The reasons are three: In the first place, the French privateers of the West Indies and their depredations on New England commerce; secondly, Jefferson was at the same time a French adherent, and author of a commercial policy the stupidest conceivable from our standpoint. He had called a halt in navy making and had forced on the country the embargo and non-intercourse acts. But the third reason was by far the most important, viz.: The feeling in every real New England man that Great Britain was fighting the battle of Christendom against Bonaparte. "Suppose England has changed her maritime rules," our fathers said, "let us in at the game, no matter what rule she makes. Give us seaway, and give us a port ahead—we will find our way in. Never mind the cruising frigates or the blockade, actual or on paper. If we are caught, ours the loss."

The thought that, after all, Old England might not win hung like a cloud over every New England hamlet. Open the limp sheets of those old Connecticut journals. Even in our actual fighting days from 1812 to 1815, clippings from the English papers that slipped in via Halifax were what people wanted most to read—not news of Chippewa and Lundy's Lane. Wellington and Napoleon were the real figures on the world's stage. And our grandfathers judged rightly.

Such were the feelings that gave birth to the Hartford Convention. Have we in Connecticut anything to apologize for in that gathering? If so, it doesn't appear in its journal—and Theodore Dwight was an honest man. Do we wish it had never met? If that page were taken from New England history, we should always miss something—a rare sample of her sober courage, her four-square view of things as they are. If other events—the treaty, and Jackson at New Orleans—had not come near at the time of its adjournment, its name would never have been spoken with a sneer or written with nullification in the context.

But with the end of the war of 1812 came the dying out of the Federalist party and a new era for industrial New England. The New England of commercial prosperity soon took up manufacturing on a large scale. New London and Stonington still had their thriving fleets of merchantmen and whalers, concerning which we quote from an article by Miss Charlotte M. Holloway, in the "Connecticut Quarterly":

The first ship fitted out from New London was the "Rising Sun," Squire, captain, 1784; but the voyage was not a long nor eventful one, and to the ship "Commerce," rather, which cleared from New London February 6, 1794, is due the honor of having been the pioneer of the New London whaling fishery, and the first to make for southern latitudes, and after a cruise of fifteen months it returned July 6, 1798, with a full cargo of oil. It would have been interesting to know more than the meagre record of the name of the captain, Ransom, but the "Commerce" after another voyage was put into the West Indian trade, and was lost off Cape Henry, December 25, 1799. Gen. William Williams, of the Williams family noted for benefactions to the city, had also sent out the "Criterion," which was successful, but for some reason, though endeavor was made to form a company in New London to prosecute whaling, the published call in "Green's Gazette" met with insufficient response, and the project languished till 1805, when Dr. Samuel H. P. Lee purchased the "Dauphin," built by Joseph Barber, at Pawkatuck Bridge, especially for whaling. Dr. Lee organized a whaling company, but it is not alone through service to her commerce that New London is debtor to this noble man, for in the terrible yellow fever epidemic of 1798 which decimated the population, he remained at his post working day and night to save life and stimulating others to heroism and endurance. Soon three ships were in commission—the "Daphne," "Leonidas" and "Lydia"—and their catches were sufficient to warrant the company in continuing; but there came the deterrents of the Embargo and the War of 1812. So that the real birth of the whale fishing in New London can be dated from 1819, when Thomas W. Williams fitted out the "Mary" (Captain Davis), Daniel Deshon and others the "Carrier," Douglas, and the "Mary Ann," Inglis; in 1820, the "Pizarro," Elias Coit; 1821, the brig "Thames" and the ships "Commodore Perry" and "Stonington," the latter so large that it was made a stock enterprise, divided into shares of one thirty-second each. Both ships sailed the same year around the Horn, and after an absence of twenty-eight months brought back, the "Carrier" 2,100 and the "Stonington" 1,550 barrels. By 1827 there were six ships fitted out by T. W Williams, and N. and W. W. Billings had three—the "Commodore Perry," which was the first copper-bottomed whaler sent from this port, and the "Superior" and the "Phoenix." The "Commodore Perry" made seventeen voyages and the "Stonington" thirteen before they were broken up in 1848. The "Neptune," which T. W. Williams bought in 1824, was built in 1808, and had returned from an unsuccessful voyage when it was purchased from its New Bedford owner for $1,650. After its addition to the New London fleet it made more than twenty voyages. It was in the "Neptune," 1829, that Capt. Samuel Green, the oldest living whaling captain in New London, made his first voyage. His last was in the "Trident," in 1871, and so frightful was his experience that he determined, should he escape, never again to risk his life in the fatal trap which had caught so many good men and ships. In September the fleet of 34 vessels was gathered in a narrow strip from two hundred yards to half a mile in width, from Point Belcher to two or three miles south of Wainright Inlet. The whaling had been fairly good, and despite the warnings of the Esquimaux, who told them the ice was closing in, they remained until the wind changed and the ice floes were driven upon them; the vessels were crushed, the crews abandoned them, glad to save their lives, and after untold hardships, from the 29th of August to the 14th of September, when they abandoned the vessels, the devoted masters and crews started to reach the "Arctic" and another vessel which was free of the ice.

From this firm and New London the first steam whaler was sent to the whaling grounds, and the first steam sealer. In the whaler "Pioneer," Capt.

Ebenezer Morgan, better known as "Rattler" Morgan, was made the best whaling voyage on record; sailing June 4, 1864, for Hudson's Bay, she returned September 18, 1865, with 1,391 barrels of whale oil, and 22,650 pounds of whalebone, a cargo worth $150,000, while the outlay for vessel and fitting was but $35,800 This was the best whaling voyage ever made. The principle on which whaling was conducted was co-operative, the owners furnishing ship, outfit, and providing for the honoring of the captain's drafts; the captain was quite often a part or whole owner. Capital had two-thirds of the gain and the other third was divided proportionately among the officers and men. There being no wages settled, every incentive was furnished for diligence, and somtimes a bonus was offered to the first man who sighted a whale. There were very many daring and successful whalers from New London; indeed, the solid comfort and foundation of many of her homes came from the splendid fortitude and perseverance of these heroes of the sea. There were no more brave and successful captains than the three brothers Smith— Capt. Robert Smith, who was killed on his sixth voyage, in 1828, while capturing a whale; Capt. Frank Smith, in seven successive voyages, in 1831-37, brought home 17,301 barrels of oil; and Capt. James Smith, the third brother, made fame and fortune, but left whaling for commander of a packet between Honolulu and San Francisco. Capt. "Jim" Smith, of the "Manhansett," who is really known wherever a college boy goes for his skill and urbanity, is the youngest ex-whaler in New London. The names of Morgan, Smith, Blydenburgh, Davis, Chapell, Green, Ward, Tinker, Buddington, Hempstead, Baker, Brown, Allyn, Spicer, Fuller, Rice, Benjamin, Tyson, Pendleton, Fish, and others are sure to be thought of when whaling is mentioned. Today there is very little done, save for the obtaining of whalebone, and whaling is practically a past industry as far as New London is concerned.

The water power of the county soon began to turn the wheels of cotton mills. The race of merchants still continued to thrive, but the cotton industry added to population more rapidly. In 1840 Norwich was the largest town of the county. During the early part of the nineteenth century many a man left the county to engage in foreign trade and return with his "pile"

In the interesting life of Daniel Wadsworth Coit, edited by his nephew, Mr. William C. Gilman, may be found a very interesting proof that the Pilgrim blood still ran in the veins of their descendants. The indenture, signed and sealed by all the parties to it, bound his employers to teach him "the trade, art, and mystery of a merchant"; he on his part, and his father for him, agreeing that "he shall of his own free will and accord his master faithfully serve, his secrets keep, and his lawful commands everywhere readily obey; shall not contract matrimony; shall refrain from vice, and from business on his own account; and in all things shall behave himself as a faithful apprentice ought to do during his term of service." His only compensation was to be his board and washing The theory was that the employer stood in the place of a parent to the apprentice, was interested in his welfare, gave him special opportunities for advancement and improvement, with a commercial education that was a full equivalent for his services. By this system, now almost obsolete, except as it may be suggested by the youthful experience of Admiral Sir Joseph Porter in "Pinafore," he received a training that was invaluable in the important and complicated transactions in which he was concerned in later years. The art of writing a faultless business letter, acquired early in life, was an accomplishment not to be despised, in which he excelled.

The particular duties of the youngest clerk, as he describes them, were "to open the store at an early hour, to sweep and dust the floors, to make fires throughout the winter, and not infrequently to roll empty hogsheads and barrels through the streets for packing, and to shoulder and carry goods from one part of the city to another." If the hours were no more than sixty minutes long there were more working hours in twenty-four than there are now, and that work was often carried well into the night, appears by letters to his parents, written when he was "so sleepy he could hardly keep his eyes open." His career is embodied to some degree in the "Notes of Daniel Wadsworth Coit," as follows:

> 1787—November 29. Born, Norwich, Conn.
> 1803—Apprenticed to merchants in New York.
> 1808—Began business on his own account.
> 1818—September 27. Sailed from New York for Peru.
> 1819—January 14. Arrived at Lima.
> 1820—April Sailed from Guayaquil for Gibraltar.
> 1820—September 27. Arrived at Gibraltar.
> 1820-22—Traveled in Spain, France, and England.
> 1822—June. Sailed from London for South America.
> 1822—October. Arrived at Buenos Ayres.
> 1822—December. Crossed the Andes to Valparaiso.
> 1823—December. Arrived at Lima.
> 1828—June. Sailed from Lima for New York.
> 1829—May. Sailed from New York for England.
> 1829-32—Traveled in Europe.
> 1832—June. Returned to Norwich.
> 1833—October. Visited Grand Rapids.
> 1834—September 1. Married Harriet Frances Coit.
> 1834-41—Lived in New York and New Rochelle.
> 1841-47—Lived in Norwich
> 1848—January. To Mexico for Howland and Aspinwall.
> 1849—March. From Mexico to San Francisco.
> 1849-52—In business in San Francisco.
> 1852—June. Returned to his home in Norwich.
> 1876—July 18. Died, Norwich.

From the above it can be seen that he left home in 1818 to be gone ten years! That he left again in 1829 to be gone three years; traveled; lived in Norwich, 1841-1847; left home for four years, and returned to remain twenty-four years, dying at the age of eighty-nine!

CHAPTER IV

LITTLE KNOWN FACTS ABOUT NEW LONDON COUNTY

The Beginnings of Railroads and Telegraphs—Old-Time School Reminiscences—Celebrities in All Walks of Life.

The history of New London County in education has been touched upon. Its history in banking, in the professions, in public improvements, in religious affairs, in industrial development, and in various other aspects of community life, will be discussed in special articles. It is fair to say that the county has been progressive in its activities.

As early as 1800 was built the turnpike between Norwich and New London, "the first turnpike built in the United States," states Dr. Dwight in his "Travels." Adams Express Company was started as an enterprise in Norwich and New London. Regular steamship connection with New York started as early as 1816. The tunnel on the Norwich & Worcester railroad, just outside of Norwich, is the first railroad tunnel constructed in the United States. The Norwich & Worcester railroad was one of the earliest in the country. As early as 1847 a telegraph company was started by citizens of New London and Norwch. The railroad from New London to New Haven (1849-52) completed the first railroad connection between Boston and New York. The New London, Willimantic & Springfield railroad was built by 1850. In whaling and seal fisheries the hardy navigators of New London and Stonington were pioneers in southern waters. The Rogers Brothers were captain and sailing master of the "Savannah," the first steamship to cross the ocean. The abundant water power of the county gave it an early start in manufacturing, especially in the paper and cotton industries. The two largest steamships ever built in America, "The Minnesota" and "The Dakota," each of 3,300 tons, were built in Groton.

In the Civil War the county was the home of the Connecticut War Governor, and sent far more men than its quota. In the period of reconstruction after the war, New London county throve in wealth and population. To recount the new enterprises started, the patents granted to men of the county, the public improvements made, would be beyond the scope of this outline history of the county. Suffice it to say that by 1910 the population had increased to 91,253.

The effects of steam transportation by land and sea were soon felt in the prosperity of the county. Before 1850, the Norwich & Worcester, the New London Northern, the New York, Providence & Boston railroad, the Shore Line, had been chartered, and regular steamboat service established with New York. The age of steam brought prosperity and increasing population. The census of 1860 shows a population of over 60,000 in the county. Schools had been built generally, college training had become not unusual, the press had developed, New London county still continued to furnish men of influence in the nation. Before 1850 the county had sent eight men to be governors of Connecticut, five men to be chief justices of the Supreme Court of the State, and three United States Senators, and twelve members of Congress. From the old home had gone forth men who made their mark in other parts of the Union.

What life was at that time may be seen by a letter sent to Norwich by Donald G. Mitchell, "Ik Marvel," called "Looking Back at Boyhood":

I pity those young folks who pass their early years without having any home knowledge of gardens or orchards City schools and city pavements are all very well; but I think if my childish feet had not known of every-day trampings through garden alleys or on wood walks, and of climbings in hay-lofts or among apple boughs when fruit began to turn, half of the joys of boyhood, as I look back at them, would be plucked away.

So it happens, that when I am asked for some reminiscences of those early days, gone for sixty years or more, the great trees that sheltered my first home stir their branches again. Again I see the showers of dancing petals from the May bloom of apple or peach trees strewing the grass, or the brown garden mold, with a little of that old exultation of feeling which is almost as good as a prayer—in way of thanksgiving

I think I could find my way now through all the involvements of new buildings and new plantings on ground that I have not visited for fifty years, to the spot where the blood peach grew, and where the mulberry stood and the greengage loaded with fruit in its harvest time, and the delightful white-blooming crab, lifting its odors into the near window of the "boys' room."

Then there was a curiously misshapen apple tree in the far orchard, with trunk almost prone upon the ground, as if Providence had designed it for children to clamber upon What a tree it was to climb! There many a time we toddlers used to sit, pondering on our future, when the young robins in the nest overhead would be fully fledged, catching glimpses, too, before yet leaves were fully out, of the brown hermitage or study upon the near wooded hillside, where my father, who was a clergyman, wrought at his sermons.

It is only a dim image of him that I can conjure up as he strode at noontime down the hill. Catching up the youngest of us with a joyous, proud laugh, he led the toddling party—the nurse bringing up the rear—in a rollicking procession homeward

A more distinct yet less home-like image of this clergyman I have in mind as he leaned over the pulpit of a Sunday, with a solemnity of manner that put one in awe, and with an earnestness of speech that made the Bible stories he expounded seem very real.

But the sermons of those days were very long for children. It must have been, usually, before the middle of the discourse that I went foraging about the square pew, visiting an aunt who almost always had peppermints in her bag, or in lack of this diversion I could toy with the foot-stove under my mother's gown, or build fortifications with the hymn-books.

The "lesser" Westminster Catechism also, with which we had wrestlings, was somewhat heavy and intellectually remote. But it was pleasantly tempered by the play of the parlor fire, or the benignly approving smiles when answerings were prompt. In summer weather the song of a cat-bird or brown-thrasher in the near tulip-tree chased away all the tedium of the Westminster divines, or perhaps lifted it into a celestial atmosphere.

The Bible stories, though, as they tripped from my mother's tongue, were always delightful. I thought then, and still think—at sixty-nine!—that her ways of religious teaching were by many odds better than that of the Westminster divines. And there were some of her readings from the hymn-book that tingle in my ears today.

That compulsory Bible-reading, chapter after chapter, and day by day, so common in well-regulated families of those times, has for me a good many ungrateful memories. Wrathful, unwholesome burnings were kindled by this enforced rote reading of a book wherefrom gladsome and hopeful splendors ought to shine.

Of other earliest reading I remember with distinctness that great budget of travel and adventure, good for week-days or Sunday, called "The Pilgrim's Progress." Mercy, and Great-heart, and Christian, and Giant Despair, too, were of our family. Nor can I cease to call to mind gratefully the good woman (Maria Edgeworth) who in the earliest days of our listening to stories made us acquainted with the "Basket-maker's" children who scotched the carriage wheels, and with "Lazy Lawrence" and "Eton Montem."

At what precise age I went to my first school I cannot say. It may have been five or six. A roundabout blue jacket with bell buttons I know I had, and a proud tramp past the neighbors' houses.

The mistress was an excellent woman, everybody said, with a red ruler and discipline, and spectacles A tap from her spectacle-case was a summons every morning to listen to her reading, in quiet monotone, of a chapter in the Bible; after which, in the same murmurous way, she said a prayer.

She taught arithmetic out of Colburn, I think, and Woodbridge's Geography to the older ones, but her prime force was lavished upon spelling We had field-days in that, for which we were marshalled by companies, toeing a crack in the oaken floor. What an admiring gaze I lifted up upon the tall fellows who went with a wondrous glibness through the intricacies of such words as "im-prac-ti-ca-bil-i-ty"!

The mistress had her own curious methods of punishment; and I dimly remember how an obstreperous boy was once shut under the lid of the big writing-desk—not for very long, I suspect. But the recollection of it, and of his sharp wail of protest, gave a very lively emphasis to my reading, years after, of Roger's story of the Italian bride Ginevra who closed the lid of a Venetian chest upon herself in some remote loft where her skeleton, and her yellowed laces, were found years afterwards by accident.

Another of the mistress's methods of subduing masculine revolt was in tying a girl's bonnet upon a boy's head I have a lingering sense now of some such early chastisement, and of the wearisome pasteboard stiffness, and odors of the bonnet!

Of associates on those school benches, I remember with most distinctness a tallish boy, my senior by two years or so, who befriended me in many skirmishes, decoyed me often into his leafy dooryard, half-way to my home, where luscious cherries grew, and by a hundred kindly offices during many succeeding years cemented a friendship of which I have been always proud. A photograph of his emaciated, but noble face, as he lay upon his death-bed in Paris, is before me as I write

Another first school which I knew as privileged pupil—not esteeming the privilege largely—was in the old town of Wethersfield, where I went on visits to my grandfather. I remember his great shock of snowy white hair, and how he was bowed with age. He wore most times long gray hose, with knee buckles, and a huge coat like those in Franklin pictures, whose pockets were often bulged out with a biscuit or an ear of corn. With these he loved to pamper his white pony, or other favorite beast

The school to which the old gentleman introduced me solemnly was near by, and of the Lancastrian order. Mr. Joseph Lancaster had come over from England not many years before to indoctrinate America.

There was great drill of limbs and voices; but what specially impressed me was a long tray or trough of moistened sand, where we were taught to print letters. I think I came there to a trick of making printed letters which was never lost.

There was a quiet dignity about Wethersfield streets in that day. There were great quiet houses before which mighty trees grew—houses of the Welles, of the Chesters, of the Webbs—in some of which Washington had lodged in his comings or goings.

It was through that quiet Wethersfield street, and by way of the "Stage" office at Slocomb's Hotel in Hartford, that I must have traveled first to Judge Hall's Ellington school. There for six ensuing years, off and on, I wrestled with arithmetic and declamation, and Latin and Greek. It was a huge building—every vestige gone now—upon a gentle eminence overlooking a peaceful valley town. I am sure some glimpses of the life there must have found their way into some little books which I have had the temerity to publish.

The principal, a kindly, dignified old gentleman, lived apart, in a house amongst gardens and orchards; but the superintendent, the English master, the matron and the monitors, were all housed with us, and looked sharply after discipline

When I hear boys of near kith complaining of the hardships they endure, I love to set before them a picture of the cold chambers opening upon the corridors in that huge building.

We dressed there by the dim light coming through ventilators over the doors, from lamps swinging in the hall. After this it was needful to take a swift rush out of doors, in all weathers, for a plunge into the washroom door, where we made our ablutions Another outside rush followed for the doors opening upon the dining-hall, where morning prayers were said. Then an hour of study in a room reeking with the fumes of whale-oil lamps went before the summons to breakfast.

There were two schoolrooms The larger was always presided over by a teacher who was nothing if not watchful. The smaller was allotted to a higher range of boys, and here the superintendent appeared at intervals to hear recititations.

I shall never forget the pride and joy with which I heard the superintendent—I think it was Judge Taft, thereafter Attorney General, and Minister to Russia—announce, once upon a time, my promotion to the south school-room. Frank Blair, the general of Chickamauga, was a bench-mate with me there. Once upon a "composition" day we were pitted against each other; but who won the better marks I really cannot say.

Teacher Taft was an athlete. He could whip with enormous vigor (some boys said). but I have only the kindest recollections of him. I used to look on with amazed gratification as he lifted six "fifty-sixes," strung upon a pole, in the little grocery shop past which we walked on our way to swim in Snipsic Lake.

What a beautiful sheet of water it was in those days! Its old shores are now all submerged and blotted out by manufacturers' dams. What a joyous, rollicking progress we made homeward, of a Saturday afternoon, with the cupola and the great bulk of building lifting in our front against the western sky!

The strong point of the teaching at Ellington was, I think, Latin I am certain that before half my time there was up, I could repeat all the rules in Adams' Latin Grammar *verbatim*, backward or forward.

As for longs and shorts and results and quantities and the makeup of a proper hexameter, these were driven into my brain and riveted. Even now I am dimly conscious on uneasy nights, of the *Quadrupedante putrem sonitu* making its way through my dreams with the old schoolboy gallop.

I could stretch this screed farther, but the types forbid. The home, with a glimpse of which I began the paper, had been broken up a long time before the high school experience came to an end. Later, in the spring of 1837, the shattered, invalid remnant of its flock was sailing homeward from a winter in Santa Cruz. In July of the same year I set off from Ellington, by the "Hartford, Ware and Keene Dispatch Line" of stages, seated beside the driver, with twenty dollars in my pocket and my trunk on the roof of the coach, to enter Yale College.

The military history of the county will be given elsewhere. The great "war governor," William A. Buckingham, was a resident of Norwich, born at Lebanon.

Since Civil War days, the county has grown in population to over 155,000 in 1920. The remarkable feature in the growth of population of the country for the past fifty years has been the influx of foreign born. This county, like the rest of New England, has been engaged in absorbing a mixed foreign population into the institutions with which they are unfamiliar. The great instrument for doing this has been the public school system, which will be treated of in a special chapter on education.

The county history is very rich in biography. Sketches of the lives of many famous individuals are inserted hereinafter. The list is by no means exhaustive, for it is safe to say that no equal area and population in our country is richer in ties of relationship with the makers of American history.

Alexander Von Humboldt once wrote that, "judged by the number of centenarians," a semicircular region with New London as its center and a radius of fifteen miles was "the most healthful spot on the globe."

The first railroad tunnel in America was made in this county.

From New London county have come ancestors of at least six Presidents: Fillmore, Grant, Garfield, Hayes, Cleveland, and Harding.

The father of Oliver Perry, of Lake Erie fame, and of Matthew Perry, who made the historic voyage opening up Japan to western civilization, kept a store in Norwich.

The two largest vessels ever built in America, the "Minnesota" and "Dakota," said to be each of 3,300 tons burden, were built at Groton.

Dartmouth College was founded in what was then Lebanon, now the town of Columbia, in Windham county.

The oldest burial ground in the county is in New London, dating from 1653.

Wolves were once so abundant in the county that the early settlers paid a bounty of twenty shillings for each one killed.

The commerce of New London was at one time excelled by only two ports in the country—Boston and New York.

The Shaw mansion in New London was constructed by Acadians driven from home at the time described by Longfellow in "Evangeline."

The first Naval Expedition sent out by the Continental Congress left New London in January, 1776.

The "Savannah," officered by the Rogers Brothers of New London, was the first vessel to "steam" across the Atlantic.

Silas Deane, who was appointed one of the Peace Commission at the end of the Revolutionary War, came from Preston.

In early days in this county, as elsewhere, churches were often founded by lotteries, and the expenses of installing clergymen frequently included a considerable item for "liquor."

Stephen Whitney, one of the promoters of the Great Pacific railway, came from this county, as did President Tuttle, of the Boston & Maine railroad.

Andrew Jackson visited Norwich at the dedication of the Uncas Monument. He pronounced the parade one of the longest he had seen in a place of the size (the boys circled around behind him and rejoined the procession in a well nigh endless chain).

The two leading men of the colony of Connecticut, John Winthrop, the younger, and John Mason, were long residents of this county

This county contains two of the five oldest cities in the State, and is one of the four original counties in Connecticut.

In 1799 New London was almost depopulated by yellow fever.

Three citizens of Norwich have given to Yale College the largest donations which, at each successive time, its treasury had received from any individual These men were Major James Fitch, Dr. Daniel Lathrop, and Dr. Alfred E. Perkins.

Norwich has an unpleasant distinction in one instance in being the birthplace of Benedict Arnold There is nothing to be added.

Avery Waitstill, a native of Groton, removed to North Carolina, where in 1775 he became a member of the Mecklenburg Convention, and as such was one of the signers of the famous Mecklenburg Declaration of Independence

James Cook Ayer, the father of the "patent medicine" business, was born in Groton. He established a medicine factory in Lowell, and accumulated a fortune estimated at $20,000,000 For years he published and distributed free five million copies of "Ayer's Almanac," largely devoted to advertising his goods. For some years before his death, he was confined in an asylum, his brain having become affected.

Isaac Backus, a Baptist minister, was born in Norwich, 1724 He led in the "Separatist" movement, for years held to open communion, but at length abandoned it He was a voluminous writer on historical as well as religious subjects. For thirty-four years he was a trustee of Rhode Island College, now Brown University.

Anna Warner Bailey, born in Groton, 1758, and died there in 1850, wife of Captain Elijah Bailey, of that place, witnessed the massacre by the British at Fort Griswold, September 6, 1781 The next day she visited the spot, searching for an uncle, whom she found fatally wounded, and to whom she brought his wife and child. When the British were threatening New London in July, 1813, "Mother Bailey," as she was known, aided the patriots by tearing up garments for cartridge making

Edward Sheffield Bartholomew, born in Colchester, 1822, died in Italy, 1858, a sculptor of great ability, performed his work in Rome during his later years. Many of his productions are in the Wadsworth Gallery, Hartford.

Dr. Timothy Dwight, twelfth president of Yale College, was a native of Norwich, son of James Dwight, and grandson of Timothy Dwight, the third president of the institution. It was under the presidency of him whose name heads this paragraph, that the college received the legal title of University. President Dwight was highly successful in extending the curriculum of the institution, and in advancing its material interests. He was a member of the American committee for the revision of the English version of the Bible from 1872 to its completion in 1885. He was the author of several volumes, notably one on "The True Ideal of an American University," which appeared serially in 1871-72 in "The New Englander," of which he was then editor, and which had much to do in effecting the transition of Yale from a collegiate to a university status.

Daniel Coit Gilman, first president of Johns Hopkins University, was born in Norwich, July 6, 1831.

Frederick Stuart Church, famous as a painter and etcher, was a resident here

Jedidiah Huntington, soldier of the Revolution and one of the signers of the Declaration of Independence, was born in Norwich, August 4, 1743, and died in New London, September 25, 1818 Jabez Huntington, his father, was a wealthy merchant and a patriot leader; he served three years in the Revolutionary army, and only leaving it on account of failing health The son, a Harvard graduate, entered the army as a captain in April, 1775, two years later was made a brigadier-general, and served in New York and Pennsylvania until the close of the war, and was breveted major-general. He was a member of two courts-martial—that which tried General Charles Lee, and that which convicted Major André He was sheriff of New London county, State treasurer of Connecticut, and collector of customs at New London He was one of the founders of the Society of the Cincinnati, and a man of deep piety and charitable disposition

The famous explorer, John Ledyard, was a native of Groton, born in 1751, son of John and Mary (Hempstead) Ledyard, his father a ship captain. Young Ledyard was a mere child when his father died, and he was brought up in the home of his grandfather. At the age of eighteen, his benefactor having died, Ledyard entered Dartmouth College as a divinity student, with a desire to fit himself for missionary work among the Indians, to whom he was so drawn that he soon abandoned his studies and made his abode among them. This was the beginning of his venturesome career. Making a canoe voyage down the Connecticut river to Hartford, he went on to New London, where he shipped as a common sailor in a vessel bound for Gibraltar. There he enlisted in the British army, and after his discharge therefrom voyaged to the West Indies and thence to New York and London. In the latter place he fell in company with Captain Cook, who was preparing for his third and what was destined to be his last great voyage. The two were mutually pleased with each other, and the younger man became the commander's most trusted lieutenant, and was by his side when Captain Cook was killed on one of the Hawaiian Islands, February 14, 1779. Returning with the expedition to England by way of Kamtchatka, the British authorities in accordance with its naval rules took from Ledyard his notes of the expedition. For two years Ledyard remained in the British navy, leaving it at the outbreak of the Revolution rather than do battle against his countrymen. In 1784 he conceived an idea of fitting out an expedition to explore the northwestern American coast, and visited Spain and France in hopes of securing necessary means, but without success. Finally, at London, he found friendly scientists who furthered his purpose, and he voyaged to Finland and thence to St. Petersburg, where he started for Siberia, but under suspicion of being a spy was harried out of Russia into Poland. Returning to London, an expedition was outfitted for him to explore the interior of Africa, and he sailed in June, 1788, but at Cairo sickened and died, January 17, 1789. His notes of travel were of value, and to this day his narrative of Captain Cook's voyage is famed for its vividness and brilliance. He was a nephew of William Ledyard, who was brutally murdered by the Tory Major Bromfield, at Fort Griswold, Groton Heights, Connecticut, after its surrender, in 1781.

Isaac H. Bromley, whom Chauncey M. Depew spoke of as "a most conscientious journalist, and with whom no personal relations interfered with what he felt was a public duty," was born at Norwich, March 6, 1833, and died there, August 11, 1898; his parents were Isaac and Mary (Hill) Bromley. He was also married in Norwich, to Adelaide, daughter of Jabez and Clarissa T. Roath. He was admitted to the bar, but journalism claimed the greater part of his life work. During the Civil War he was a captain in the 18th Connecticut Regiment. In 1858 he established the Norwich "Morning Bulletin," and conducted it until 1868, when he left it to become editor and part owner of the Hartford "Evening Post." After leaving the paper last named he served in turn on the editorial staff of the New York "Sun" and "Tribune," and after ten years on the latter paper became editor of the "Commercial Advertiser," a position which he relinquished to accept appointment as a government director of the Union Pacific railroad, serving as such until 1884, when he took the editorial management of the Rochester "Post-Express." In October, 1891, he returned to the New York "Tribune," with which he was associated until a few months before his death. He was one of the organizing members of Sedgwick Post, G. A. R., of Norwich.

Charles Harold Davis, one of America's foremost landscape painters, a native of Massachusetts, following ten years' professional studies in France and other art centers, for five years resided continually at Mystic, winter as well as summer, painting directly from nature. His fame is world-wide.

Samson Occum is a name famous in association with what became Dartmouth College. He was a Mohegan Indian living in New London county, who was converted and educated by Eleazer Wheelock, the founder of the above named institution. Occum came to fame as a preacher, and was a valuable aid to his instructor in his educational work and in laying the foundations of schools and academies In 1766 Occum and Rev. Nathaniel Whitaker, of Norwich, visited Great Britain and raised nearly £12,000 (a large sum in those days) for these purposes.

Rev. Lyman Abbott, famous as divine and author, and especially as an exponent of the so-called liberal theology, born in Roxbury, Massachusetts, was fitted for college in Norwich.

Bela Lyon Pratt, the well-known sculptor, was a native of Norwich, a son of George and Sarah Victoria (Whittlesey) Pratt, his father one of the most accomplished lawyers in Connecticut. Young Pratt began drawing and modeling at home while but a child, and received his technical training in the School of Fine Arts of Yale University, in the Art Students' League of New York City under St. Gaudens, and in Paris under Chapin and Falguiere, finally entering the Ecole des Beaux Arts at the head of his class and winning three medals and two prizes. He was soon afterward made instructor in modeling in the Muesum of Fine Arts, Boston. Among his many fine works are some of great local interest—the Avery bust, "the Puritan," at Groton, and the bronze statue of John Winthrop at New London.

Christopher R. Perry, who served with credit in both the American army and navy during the Revolution, was for a time a resident of Norwich, where he conducted a store. Two of his sons are among the most conspicuous figures of their day—Oliver Hazard Perry, the "Don't give up the ship" hero of Lake Erie during the war with Great Britain in 1812-14; and Matthew Galbraith Perry, who crowned a notable naval career with the opening up of Japan to the commerce of the world.

The brilliant Commodore Stephen Decatur, of Tripoli fame, and captor of the British frigate "Macedonian," was for a long period during the war of 1812-14 an enforced sojourner in the Thames river, the mouth of which was blockaded by a squadron of the enemy. His fall in the duel with Commodore Barron is one of the pitiful tragedies of our naval history.

Henry Ward Beecher was a frequent visitor to our county, and scenes and reminiscences of Norwich figure throughout his famous "Star Papers."

Lebanon was the home of the famous Trumbull family, which had as one of its most distinguished representatives Colonel John Trumbull, of Revolutionary fame, but more famous as the historical painter of that stupendous period, most of which are in the Art Gallery at Yale University.

Dr. William Thompson Lusk, one of the world's greatest physicians, and a distinguished professional instructor and author, was born in Norwich, May 23, 1838, and died June 12, 1897, son of Sylvester Graham and Elizabeth

Freeman (Adams) Lusk. His father was a well-known merchant, senior member of the Norwich firm of Lusk, Lathrop & Co. The son received his elementary education in the city of his birth, but on account of an eye affection was obliged to leave college in his freshman year. Going to Switzerland for treatment, and experiencing benefit, he studied medicine in Heidelberg and Berlin. Returning home he entered the army shortly after the outbreak of the Civil War, and served about two years, rising to a captaincy. At Bull Run, under fire, he carried his wounded captain from the field. He completed his professional studies at Bellevue Medical College, New York City, and graduated valedictorian of his class. He then pursued post-graduate studies in Edinburgh, Paris, Vienna and Prague. On his return home he engaged in practice in Bridgeport, Connecticut, later locating in New York City, where he held first rank as an operator and instructor. He was the first in America to successfully perform the Caesarian section, which he repeated on several occasions with a very small percentage of mortality. He was a prolific professional writer, and one of his principal works, "Science and Art of Midwifery," was translated into French, Italian, Spanish, Arabic and other languages.

The village of Lyme was the birthplace of the distinguished lawyer and jurist, Morrison R. Waite, who succeeded Salmon P. Chase as Chief Justice of the United States Supreme Court, appointed by President Grant.

Governor William Alfred Buckingham, famous as one of the "War Governors" of the Civil War period, and one of the most trusted of President Lincoln's supporters, was born May 28, 1804, in Lebanon, New London county. He was educated in the local schools and at Bacon Academy, Colchester. He taught school for a time, afterward serving as clerk in a store in Norwich. After similar service for a short time in New York City, he returned to Norwich, and established a drygoods business, afterward becoming a large and successful manufacturer of ingrain carpets, and then of rubber shoes. He was mayor of the city for four terms; and in 1858 was elected governor, to which office he was returned for eight consecutive terms. At the opening of the Civil War, he was the first governor to send to the front a completely equipped regiment, pledging his personal credit to cover the expense until the legislature could be assembled. The successive quotas of troops were always more than filled, and under his leadership the State contributed to the army and navy almost one-half of her able-bodied population. President Lincoln and Secretary of War Stanton held him in the highest esteem. The war having ended, Governor Buckingham declined further service as such, and was elected to the United States Senate, in which he served with conspicuous ability until his death, February 5, 1875, a short time before the end of his senatorial term. He was one of the founders of the Broadway Congregational Church of Norwich and of the Norwich Free Academy, and was devoted to religious and charitable work. His home in Norwich was purchased by Sedgwick Post of the Grand Army of the Republic, and is known as the Buckingham Memorial.

Donald Grant Mitchell, who as "Ik Marvel" gave untold delight to readers of a generation now well nigh passed away, with his "Dream Life" and "Reveries of a Bachelor," was a native of Norwich, born April 12, 1822, son of Pastor Mitchell, of the Second Congregational Church in Norwich, and grandson of the distinguished Judge Stephen M. Mitchell, of Western Reserve fame. After graduating from Yale, finding his health somewhat impaired, he passed three years on the farm of his grandfather, in Salem, where he undoubtedly received impressions of rural beauties and pleasures which he later pictured so beautifully in his writings. He traveled on foot in England for more than a year, and out of his observations wrote his "Fresh Gleanings; a New Sheaf from Old Fields." Meantime he had taken up law studies, but unable to bear office confinement, made another voyage to Europe, and was in Paris during the revolution of 1848. Returning home, he engaged in literary work, as founder and editor of "The Lorgnette," a weekly; and then producing in turn the two volumes entitled above, and for which he is most famous. In 1854 President Pierce appointed him Consul to Venice, and where he collected material of which he made good use in volumes and magazine contributions written later. His earlier works were published under his nom de plume of "Ik Marvel," but when he came to "My Farm of Edgewood" and "Rural Studies," and others, he assumed his proper name. All his writings were characterized by tender yet manly sentiment, and his descriptions of rural life were enlightening and inspiring.

The name of Oliver Wendell Holmes awakens a pathetic interest in connection with that of Abraham Lincoln. About the time that gem of American literature, Dr. Holmes' "Autocrat of the Breakfast Table," was appearing serially in "The Atlantic Monthly," then in its second year, the delightful essayist and poet wrote "The Last Leaf," one stanza of which appealed so deeply to the martyred President that he frequently repeated it:

"The mossy marbles rest
On the lips that he has pressed
    In their bloom;
And the names he loved to hear
Have been carved for many a year
    On their tomb."

Dr. Holmes was born in Cambridge, Massachusetts, and finished his literary education at Harvard. His grandfather, a resident of Woodstock, wrote as follows in his diary under date of August 4, 1803, as quoted in the "Life of Oliver Wendell Holmes," by John More, Jr.: "Mrs. Temperance Holmes, my much honored and beloved mother (she was therefore Oliver Wendell Holmes' grandmother), was born at Norwich in Connecticut, A. D. 1733. . . . My mother was an admirer of learning, though she received her education in a part of the town of Norwich (Newent parish) which did not probably furnish her any signal advantages at school, yet she had a mother who was at once a school and library to her." It is worthy of note that Holmes, in his "Autocrat of the Breakfast Table," speaks of the "Coit Elms" of Norwich.

Edmund Clarence Stedman, who ranked very high as a poet and essayist, lived in Norwich during all his boyhood. He was born in Hartford, son of Edmund Stedman, a merchant of that city; his mother was Elizabeth C. Dodge, the poetess. His father died when he was but two years old, and he was sent to his great-uncle, James Stedman, at Norwich, and where he began and continued his education until his sixteenth year, when he entered Yale College. An incident of his literary career was his service as a correspondent of the "New York World," from the Army of the Potomac, during the Civil War. He became a member of the New York Stock Exchange, and much of his most excellent literary work was accomplished during the hours that most busy men give to recreation. During his later years he gave himself entirely to literary work.

Lydia Sigourney, an author and poet who has been called "the American Hemans," was a native of Norwich, born September 1, 1791, only daughter of Ezekiel and Sophia (Wentworth) Huntley. She was an ardent student from her very youth, and became proficient in Latin and Greek. In association with Miss Ann M. Hyde, she opened a select school for young ladies, and made it so much of a success that after four years, at the earnest solicitation of leading families in Hartford, she removed her school to that city. When about twenty-four, on the suggestion of a friend, she published "Moral Pieces in Prose and Verse," a collection of her occasional writings. The volume was well received, and paved the way for her life occupation. In 1819 she gave up her school, and became the wife of Charles Sigourney, a merchant of Hartford. Her husband, a most congenial mate, failed in both health and business, and out of necessity she gave herself unreservedly to pen work, becoming one of the most voluminous writers of her day, her published volumes numbering nearly sixty, and her contributions to magazines and periodicals some two thousand. Much of her verse work was on the solicitation of friends, on special occasions, and generally unrecompensed. She was a graceful writer, and all that she produced was marked with lofty sentiment. She was a devoted friend of the sorrowing and afflicted, and in Hartford her memory is held as highly in honor for her charitable work as for her literary talent. She lived many years in widowhood, and died at Hartford, June 10, 1865, in her seventy-fifth year.

Captain Samuel Chester Reid, one of the most brilliant officers of the old American Navy, was born in Norwich, August 25, 1783. His father, Lieut. John Reid, of the British Navy, was taken prisoner at New London on a night in October, 1778, while in command of a night boat expedition sent out from the British squadron. While in custody, he resigned his commission, and on being exchanged took sides with the Americans. In 1781 he married Rebecca Chester, a descendant in the fourth generation of Captain Samuel Chester, of the British Navy, who settled in New London. Her father, John Chester, was among the American soldiers at Bunker Hill, and afterward a member of the Connecticut convention which ratified the Constitution of the United States. Such was the parentage of Samuel Chester

BRICK TAVERN, NORWICH WHERE WASHINGTON RESTED THE NIGHT OF JUNE
30, 1775. SITE NOW OCCUPIED BY NORWICH SAVINGS SOCIETY.

BIRTHPLACE OF MRS. LYDIA HUNTLEY SIGOURNEY, ONE OF THE MOST GIFTED
OF THE EARLIER AMERICAN WRITERS, NOW THE RESIDENCE OF WILLIAM

Reid. Following in the footsteps of the father, he took to the sea at the age of eleven, but was soon among the prisoners taken during the difficulties between France and the United States. Later he served under Commodore Truxton. In the war of 1812 he held the rank of captain, and as commander of the brig "General Armstrong" performed one of the most notable feats in naval annals, off Fayal, fighting with his nine guns and ninety men a British squadron of three vessels with 130 guns and 200 men, finally scuttling his ship rather than surrender. Swimming ashore, he was taken into custody by the Portuguese authorities, who refused to surrender him to the British, and out of which refusal grew an extended diplomatic discussion which was finally settled by Louis Napoleon as arbitrator, who decided against the American claim as to neutral rights. The gun with which Reid sank his vessel was presented to the United States by the King of Portugal. In peace times Captain Reid performed services of the highest usefulness—the invention and construction of the signal telegraph at the Battery in New York and the Narrows between the upper and lower bays; and the perfecting of the pilot boat system at Sandy Hook. He designed the American flag as it is today—the thirteen stripes representing the original States, and a star for each of all The flag of his designing was first raised over the National Hall of Representatives in Washington City on April 13, 1818. Captain Reid married Mary, daughter of Captain Nathan Jennings, of Willington, Connecticut, who fought at Lexington, crossed the Delaware with Washington, and was commended for gallantry at Trenton.

Mrs. Leland Stanford, wife of the late Senator Stanford of California, was a member of the Lathrop family of Norwich In memory of a son who died at the age of sixteen, named for the father, Senator and Mrs. Stanford founded the Leland Stanford University, contributing for the purpose an eighty-three thousand acre tract of land, valued at eight millions of dollars.

Francis Hopkinson Smith, a most talented artist, excelling in water color landscapes, also successful as an author and platform lecturer, added to his varied accomplishments surpassing skill as a mechanical engineer, his most famous piece of work in that line being the foundation and pedestal of the Statue of Liberty in New York harbor. He was the designer and builder of the Race lighthouse off New London, a task which occupied him for six years. He was a native of Maryland.

Richard Mansfield lived in New London some years before his death. His widow, whose stage name was Beatrice Cameron, continues to make it her legal residence.

David Ames Wells, an economist of the highest rank, a native of Massachusetts, was for many years identified with Norwich, which was his place of residence for over twenty years, and where he died, November 5, 1898. He was known as a high-class mechanician and inventor before coming into the field in which he attained international repute; one of his inventions was the machine for folding book and newspaper sheets, and which is practically the same as used at the present time. Giving his attention to taxation problems, he produced his economic work, "Our Burden and Our Strength" (1864), which was an important factor in the restoration of the government credit, which had been seriously inspired during the Civil War. This led to his being appointed chairman of a congressional commission to devise a revenue taxation system, and which eventuated in the creation of a special Commissioner of the Revenue, and his appointment as such official. Among his important public services were the redrafting and perfecting of the internal revenue laws, the introduction of the stamp system for taxes on tobacco, liquors, etc.; and the organization of the Bureau of Statistics of the United States Treasury Department. From a Protectionist, he became a Free Trader, and to this was due his failure of reappointment to his revenue commissionership, in 1870. However, that year he was called to the chairmanship of a commission on the New York State tax laws, for which he prepared two elaborate reports and a revised code. In 1872 he became a lecturer on economics in Yale University. The remainder of his life was passed in railroad arbitrations and railroad and canal taxation questions, and in writing various volumes on these and similar topics.

The Rev. Horace Bushnell, a divine of the loftiest spirituality and a graceful author, in young manhood was a school teacher in Norwich. His "Nature and the Supernatural," published in 1858, daring in its time, became profoundly suggestive in the vast field now illumined by the revelations of evolution. This was but one of several fine volumes from his pen. His clerical life was passed with the North Congregational Church in Hartford, but he was frequently heard in public addresses in principal eastern cities. In 1855, his health being seriously impaired, he visited California, and was there tendered the presidency of the State University, which he declined. In 1859 he resigned his pastorate in Hartford, and devoted himself to literary labors. He died in Hartford, February 17, 1876.

John Fox Slater, a liberal contributor to educational and other philanthropic objects, was a native of Rhode Island, but his life was principally passed in Norwich. He was a principal figure in manufacturing enterprises, displaying therein a capacity similar to that of his distinguished uncle, Samuel Slater, "the father of American manufactures." He was chiefly instrumental in the establishment of the Free Academy in Norwich, for which as a tribute to his memory, two years after his death in Norwich, May 7, 1884, his son, William Albert Slater, erected a memorial building. Mr. Slater's greatest benefaction was his gift of a million dollars in 1882 as a fund for industrial education of the freedmen—the blacks emancipated during the Civil War by President Lincoln.

Joseph Lemuel Chester, antiquarian, born in Norwich, 1821, after some years devoted to journalism in Philadelphia, went to England and died in London, May 28, 1882. He took up his residence there in order to search out the genealogical history of early New Englanders, and among his works was "Marriage, Baptismal and Burial Registers of the Collegiate Church or

Abbey of St. Peter, Westminster," in which edifice a tablet to his memory was placed after his death.

Thomas Winthrop Coit, Episcopal clergyman, was born in New London, June 28, 1803, and died in Middletown in 1885 After occupying several important rectorates and college lectureships, he became a professor in the Divinity School at Middletown. He made many contributions to church literature, and was regarded as one of the best scholars and ablest writers of his denomination.

John Lee Comstock (1789-1858), born in Lyme, was an industrious writer of text-books on the natural sciences, and a skilled draughtsman, making most of the illustrations for his books. His "Mineralogy" was used at the West Point Military Academy, and his "Natural Philosophy," which was republished in London and Edinburgh, had a sale of nearly nine thousand copies

Erastus Corning (1794-1872), born in Norwich, became one of the leading ironmasters and bankers of his day. His master work was in the development of the railroad system of the State of New York and of Hudson river transportation. He held various public offices, including several terms in Congress.

John Gardiner Calkins Brainard, of New London (1796-1828), studied for the bar, but forsook it for journalism. He wrote much verse which brought him a certain celebrity. His brother, Dr. Dyar Throop Brainard, a physician (1810-1863), was a chemist, and an eminent botanist.

Mary Lydia (Bolles) Branch, her husband a lawyer in New York, beginning in 1865 wrote much for periodicals, principally stories and verse for young people.

John Newton Brown (1803-1868), born in New London, Baptist clergyman, held pastorates in Providence, in Massachusetts, New Hampshire and Virginia. In Boston he edited the "Encyclopedia of Religious Knowledge," which was republished in England. He was afterward editor of the "Christian Chronicle" and the "National Baptist," and was editorial secretary of the Baptist Publication Society.

Asa Burton (1752-1836), was born in Stonington and passed his childhood there and in Preston. He became a Congregational minister, was noted as a theological teacher, and prepared some sixty young men for the ministry. He published a volume on "First Principles of Metaphysics, Ethics, and Theology."

George Deshon, born in New London (1823), was a West Point graduate, a room-mate of Gen. U. S. Grant. He was converted to Catholicism, and resigned from the army to enter the Order of Redemptorists, and was one of its most efficient missioners.

The Daboll family of Groton was remarkable for three generations of most useful men. Nathan Daboll (1750-1818), was a famous teacher, and instructed as many as fifteen hundred persons in navigation. His treatise on arithmetic, published at New London in 1799, was long a standard text-book, as was also his "Practical Navigator." In 1773 he began the publication of the "Connecticut Almanac." His son Nathan (1782-1863) was a State legislator; he aided his father compiling his "Arithmetic," and published the "Almanac" from the death of the father and until his own. His son, of the same name, was also a State legislator, aided his father in both of the works before named, and also continued the "Almanac." Celadon Leeds Daboll, another son of the second Nathan, was an inventor and was father of the application of the principle of the clarionet to the construction of the fog-horn as a coast signal. This device was perfected by his brother, Charles Miner Daboll, in the steam fog-horn.

James Deane, Indian missionary (1748-1823), born in Groton, during the Revolutionary War was an Indian interpreter at Fort Stanwix, and later was employed by Congress to pacify the northern Indians. He wrote an essay on Indian mythology, which has been lost.

Charles Wheeler Denison (1809-1881), born in New London, edited a newspaper there before he was of age. He became a minister, and edited "The Emancipator," the first anti-slavery paper published in New York City. He was a potent advocate of the Union during the Civil War, before the cotton operatives in England.

CHAPTER V

THE CITY OF NEW LONDON

Its Founding—First House Lot Owners—The Winthrops—Dealings with the Indians—
During the Revolutionary War—Development of Whaling—Some Remarkable Voyages—The War of 1812—Steam Navigation—Early Newspapers—Manwaring Hill.

From "The Edelwiss," a poem by John G Bolles, the following extract
is taken, illustrative of the river Thames, and of incidents in the history of
New London and vicinity:

> But I do love my own fair Thames,
>   E'er fed by living fountains
> And noble streams of Indian name
>   Upspringing in the mountains.
>
> All gliding through the valleys sweet
>   To that delightful river,
> By airy wing of zephyr touched,
>   I've seen its waters quiver,
> While jauntily upon its breast
> My little skiff would rock and rest;
> And I have seen its quiet depths
>   Reflecting cloud and sky,
> And gazed along its winding course
>   Far as could reach the eye,
> Where, nestled 'mid the distant hills,
>   Its cradled waters lie.
> I ne'er beheld a lovelier scene,
> Or skies more bright, or hills more green,
> Or blissful morning more serene,
> While islands in the distance rest
> As emeralds on the water's breast.
> The traveler, with admiring eyes,
> Exclaims, "Can this be Paradise?"
>
> There towers that lofty monument
>   On Groton's tragic height,
> To mark the spot where martyrs fell
>   Undaunted in the fight.
>
> There Ledyard sleeps, and many a score
>   Of heroes each renowned,
> Who midst the battle's wildest roar
>   Were firm and foremost found.
>
> Amid the storm of fire they sang
>   "Columbia shall be free,"
> And every whizzing bullet rang
>   For honor, liberty.

Allyns and Edgecombs left their plow
    To win immortal fame,
And glory sets on many a brow
    I need not call by name.

Let Hempstead's memory be bright
    Who wrote the battle's story,
Wounded and bruised and down the steep
    Hurled in that wagon gory;

And left for dead among the dead
    Till, touched by gentle hands,
He saw his wife and rose again
    To live long in the land.

'Twas there Decatur with his fleet
    Held hostile ships at bay,
And guarded well the sacred place
    Where patriot ashes lay.

The town of New London is at once the oldest and the smallest in area of New London county. Its boundaries are the same as those of the city of New London, namely: On the north, the town of Waterford; on the east, the town of Groton, from which it is separated by the estuary of the Thames river, forming beautiful New London harbor; on the south by Long Island Sound; on the west by Waterford

Its founder, John Winthrop the younger, was the son of the John Winthrop who, leading the second Puritan emigration from England, became governor of the Massachusetts Bay Colony. The son John, born in 1606, spent the years 1622 to 1625 at the University of Dublin. At the age of twenty-one (1627) he served under the Duke of Buckingham in France, was married in 1631, and the same year arrived in Massachusetts. After the death of his first wife in 1634, he returned to England, married again in 1635, and returned to take charge of the settlement at Saybrook in 1636; from Massachusetts he obtained a grant of Fisher's Island in 1640, confirmed by Connecticut in 1641, and later by New York in 1668. In 1644, shortly after his first settlement on Fisher's Island, he obtained from Connecticut a grant of a plantation "at or near Pequod." This grant he began to occupy in 1645.

The Natal Day of New London is thus described by Miss Caulkins:

At a General Court held at Boston, 6th of May, 1646 Whereas Mr. John Winthrop, Jun., and some others, have by allowance of this Court begun a plantation in the Pequot country, which appertains to this jurisdiction, as part of our proportion of the conquered country, and whereas this Court is informed that some Indians who are now planted upon the place, where the said plantation is begun, are willing to remove from their planting ground for the more quiet and convenient place appointed—it is therefore ordered that Mr. John Winthrop may appoint unto such Indians as are willing to remove, their lands on the other side, that is, on the east side of the Great River of the Pequot country, or some other place for their convenient planting and subsistence. which may be to the good liking and satisfaction of the said Indians, and likewise to such of the Pequot Indians as shall desire to live there, submitting themselves to the English government, &c.

And whereas Mr. Thomas Peters is intended to inhabit in the said plantation,—this Court doth think fit to join him to assist the said Mr. Winthrop, for the better carrying on the work of said plantation. A true copy. &c.—(New London Records. Book VI.)

The elder Winthrop records the commencement of the plantation under date of June, 1646:

A plantation was this year begun at Pequod river by Mr. Winthrop, Jun , (and) Mr. Thomas Peter, a minister, (brother to Mr. Peter, of Salem,) and (at) this Court, power was given to them two for ordering and governing the plantation, till further order, although it was uncertain whether it would fall within our jurisdiction or not. because they of Connecticut challenged it by virtue of a patent from the king, which was never showed us. It mattered not much to which jurisdiction it did belong, seeing the confederation made all as one, but it was of great concernment to have it planted, to be a curb to the Indians.

The uncertainty with respect to jurisdiction hung at first like a cloud over the plantation. The subject was discussed at the meeting of the commissioners at New Haven in September, 1646. Massachusetts claimed by conquest, Connecticut by patent, purchase and conquest. The record says:

It was remembered that in a treaty betwixt them at Cambridge, in 1638, not perfected, a proposition was made that Pequot river, in reference to the conquest, should be the bounds betwixt them, but Mr Fenwick was not then there to plead the patent, neither had Connecticut then any title to those lands by purchase or deed of gift from Uncas.

The decision at this time was, that unless hereafter. Massachusetts should show better title, the jurisdiction should belong to Connecticut. This issue did not settle the controversy. It was again agitated at the Commissioners' Court, held at Boston, in July, 1647. at which time Mr Winthrop, who had been supposed to favor the claims of Massachusetts, expressed himself as "more indifferent," but affirmed that some members of the plantation, who had settled there in reference to the government of Massachustts and in expectation of large privileges from that colony, would be much disappointed if it should be assigned to any other jurisdiction.

The majority again gave their voice in favor of Connecticut, assigning this reason—"Jurisdiction goeth constantly with the Patent."

Massachusetts made repeated exceptions to this decision. The argument was in truth weak, inasmuch as the Warwick Patent seems never to have been transferred to Connecticut, the colony being for many years without even a copy of that instrument The right from conquest was the only valid foundation on which she could rest her claim, and here her position was impregnable.

Mr. Peters appears to have been from the first associated with Winthrop in the projected settlement, having a co-ordinate authority and manifesting an equal degree of zeal and energy in the undertaking. But his continuance in the country, and all his plans in regard to the new town, were cut short by a summons from home inviting him to return to the guidance of his ancient flock in Cornwall. He left Pequot, never to see it again, in the autumn of 1646. In November he was in Boston preparing to embark.

Mr. Winthrop removed his family from Boston in October, 1646; his brother, Deane Winthrop, accompanied him. They came by sea, encountering a violent tempest on the passage, and dwelt during the first winter on Fisher's Island. Some of the children were left behind in Boston, but joined their parents the next summer, at which time Mr. Winthrop, having built a house, removed his family to the town plot. Mrs. Lake returned to the plantation in 1647, and was regarded as an inhabitant, having a home lot assigned to her and sharing in grants and divisions of land as other settlers, though she was not a householder. She resided in the family of Winthrop until after he was chosen governor of the colony, and removed to Hartford. The latter part of her life was spent at Ipswich.

Governor Winthrop, of Massachusetts, regarded the new plantation with great interest. As a patriot, a statesman and a father, his mind expatiated upon it with hope and solicitude. A few days after the departure from Boston of his son, with his family, he wrote to him. "The blessing of the Lord be upon you, and He protect and guide you in this great undertaking. . . . I commend you and my good daughter, and your children, and Deane, and all your company in your plantation (whom I desire to salute,) to the gracious protection and blessing of the Lord."

To this chapter may properly be added the relation of a romantic incident that occurred at an early period of the settlement, and which had an important bearing on the western boundary question that subsequently threw the town into a belligerent attitude toward Lyme.

In March, 1672, when the controversy in respect to bounds between New London and Lyme was carried before the legislature, Mr. Winthrop, then governor of the colony, being called on for his testimony, gave it in a narrative form, his object being to show explicitly that the little stream known as Bride Brook was originally regarded as the boundary between the two plantations. The preamble of his deposition is in substance as follows:

When we began the plantation in the Pequot country, now called New London, I had a commission from the Massachusetts government, and the ordering of matters was left to myself. Not finding meadow sufficient for even a small plantation, unless the meadows and marshes west of Nahantic river were adjoined, I determined that the bounds of the plantation should be to the brook, now called Bride Brook, which was looked upon as certainly without Saybrook bounds. This was an encouragement to proceed with the plantation, which otherwise could not have gone on, there being no suitable accommodation near the place.

In corroboration of this fact, and to show that the people of Saybrook at first acquiesced in this boundary line, the governor related an incident which he says "fell out the first winter of our settling there." This must have been the winter of 1646-47, which was the first spent by him in the plantation. The main points of the story were these:

A young couple in Saybrook were to be married; the groom was Jonathan Rudd The governor does not give the name of the bride, and unfortunately the omission is not supplied by either record or tradition. The wedding day was fixed, and a magistrate from one of the upper towns on the river was engaged to perform the rite; for there was not, it seems, any person in Saybrook duly qualified to officiate on such an occasion. But, "there falling out at that time a great snow," the paths were obliterated, traveling obstructed, and intercourse with the interior interrupted; so that "the magistrate intended to go down thither was hindered by the depth of the snow." On the seaboard there is usually a less weight of snow, and the courses can be more readily ascertained. The nuptials must not be delayed without inevitable necessity. Application was therefore made to Mr. Winthrop to come to Saybrook and unite the parties. But he, deriving his authority from Massachusetts, could not legally officiate in Connecticut. "I saw it necessary (he observes) to deny them in that way, but told them for an expedient for their accommodation, if they come to the plantation it might be done. But that being too difficult for them, it was agreed that they should come to that place, which is now called Bride Brook, as being a place within the bounds of that authority whereby I then acted; otherwise I had exceeded the limits of my commission."

This proposition was accepted. On the brink of this little stream, the boundary between the two colonies, the parties met Winthrop and his friends from Pequot, and the bridal train from Saybrook. Here the ceremony was performed, under the shelter of no roof, by no hospitable fireside; without any accommodations but those furnished by the snow-covered earth, the overarching heaven, and perchance the sheltering side of a forest of pines or cedars. Romantic lovers have sometimes pledged their faith by joining hands over a narrow streamlet; but never, perhaps, before or since, was the legal rite performed in a situation so wild and solitary and under circumstances so interesting and peculiar.

We are not told how the parties traveled, whether on horseback, or on sleds or snow-shoes; nor what cheer they brought with them, whether cakes or fruit, the juice of the orchard or vineyard, or the fiery extract of the cane. We only know that at that time conveniences and comforts were few, and luxuries unknown. Yet simple and homely as the accompaniments must have been, a glow of hallowed beauty will ever rest upon the scene. We fancy that we hear the foot tramp upon the crisp snow; the ice crack as they cross the frozen stream; the wind sighs through the leafless forest; and the clear voice of Winthrop swells upon the ear like a devout strain of music, now low, and then rising high to heaven, as it passes through the varied accents of tender admonition, legal decision and solemn prayer. The impressive group stand around, wrapped in their frosty mantles, with heads reverently bowed down, and at the given sign the two plighted hands come forth from among the furs and are clasped together in token of a lifelong, affectionate trust. The scene ends in a general burst of hearty hilarity.

Bride Brook issues from a beautiful sheet of water known as Bride Lake or Pond, and runs into the Sound about a mile west of Giant's Cove. In a straight line it is not more than two miles west of Niantic Bay. The Indian name of the pond, or brook, or of both, was Sunk-i-paug, or Sunkipaug-suck.

The names of those who first received house lots in the new settlement numbered thirty-six: John Gager, Cary Latham, Samuel Lathrop, John Stebbins, Isaac Willey, Thomas Miner, William Bordman, William Morton, William Nicholls, Robert Hemstead, Thomas Skidmore, John Lewis, Richard Post, Robert Bedeel, John Robinson, Deane Winthrop, William Bartlett, Nathaniel Watson, John Austin, William Forbes, Edward Higbie, Jarvis Mudge, Andrew Longdon, William Hallett, Giles Smith, Peter Beesbran, James Bemis, John Fossecar, Consider Wood, George Chappell. Of these grants not all were taken up; apparently Watson, Austin, Higbie, Hallett, Smith, Busbraw, Fossecar, and Wood did not settle in the town. Mudge and Chappell came a little late, as did Jonathan Brewster, Thomas Wells, Peter Blatchford, Nathaniel Masters, all by 1650. The location of the lots may be found in Miss Caulkins' "History of New London." A considerable colony of people came with Rev Mr Blinman from Gloucester. Other settlers came in from time to time, and by the end of 1651 the settlers from Cape Ann had received house lots. The original town plot is thus described by Miss Caulkins.

The first home lots were laid out chiefly at the two extremities of the semicircular projection which formed the site of the town. Between these were thick swamps, waving woods, ledges of rock, and ponds of water. The oldest communication from one to the other was from Mill Brook over Post Hill, so called from Richard Post, whose house lot was on this hill, through what is now William street to Manwaring's Hill, and down Blackhall street to Truman street was the harbor's north road. Main street was opened, and from thence a cut over the hill westward was made (now Richards and Granite streets). Bank street was laid out on the very brink of the upland, above the sandy shore, and a space (now Coit street) was carried around the head of Beacon Cove to Truman street, completing the circuit of the town plot. No names were given to any of the streets for at least a century after the settlement, save that Main street was uniformly called the Town street, and Bank street the Bank. Hempstead street was one of the first laid out, and a pathway coincident with the present State street led from the end of the Town street west and northwest to meet it. Such appears to have been the original plan of the town. The cove at the north was Mill Cove; the two coves at the south, Bream and Close. Water street was the beach, and the head of it at the entrance of Mill Cove, now Sandy Point

In 1657 Mr Winthrop removed to Hartford, as governor of the Colony. The patent of New London issued by Deputy Governor Robert Treat gives the names of seventy-seven men, but Miss Caulkins is of the opinion that at that time (1704) there must have been approximately one hundred and sixty full-grown men in the town.

It is not the purpose of this volume to enter into the full details of early history, which have been so admirably compiled for New London and Norwich by Miss Caulkins. We print such selections rather to give a general picture of this period of county history. The names found on the rate lists, in the town records, and in various public places, are names famous in the history of New England, and indeed of the United States as a whole. The descendants of these settlers have been the builders of America. From Hurd's "History of New London County" we print the will of Mary Harris, "one of the oldest wills extant in the county":

The last Will and Testament of Mary Harries, taken from her owne mouth this 19th of Jan , 1655.

I give to my eldest daughter, Sarah Lane, the bigest brass pan, and to her daughter Mary, a silver spoone. And to her daughter Sarah, the bigest pewter dish and one silken riben. Likewise I give to her daughter Mary, a pewter candlesticke.

I give to my daughter, Mary Lawrence, my blew mohere peticote and my straw hatt and a fether boulster. And to her eldest sonne I give a silver spoone To her second sonne a silver whissle. I give more to my daughter Mary, my next brasst pann and a thrum cushion. And to her youngest sonne I give a pewter bassen.

I give to my youngest daughter, Elizabeth Weekes, a peece of red broad cloth, being about two yards, alsoe a damask livery cloth, a gold ring, a silver spoone, a fether bed and a boulster. Alsoe, I give to my daughter, Elizabeth, my best hatt, my gowne, a brass kettle, and a woolen jacket for her husband. Alsoe, I give to my daughter Elizabeth, thirty shillings, alsoe a red whittle, a white apron, and a new white neck-cloth. Alsoe, I give to my three daughters aforesaid, a quarter part to each of them, of the dyaper table-cloth and tenn shillings apeece.

I give to my sister Migges, a red peticoat, a cloth jacket, a silke hud, a quoife, a cross-cloth, and a neck-cloth.

I give to my cosen Calib Rawlyns ten shillinges

I give to my two cosens, Mary and Elizabeth ffry, each of them five shillings.

I give to Mary Barnet a red stuff wascote.

I give to my daughter, Elizabeth, my great chest. To my daughter, Mary, a ciffer and a white neck-cloth. To my sister, Hannah Rawlin, my best cross-cloth. To my brother, Rawlin, a lased band. To my two kinswomen, Elizabeth Hubbard and Mary Steevens, five shillinges apeece.

I give to my brother, Migges, his three youngest children, two shillinges sixe pence apeece.

I give to my sonne Thomas, ten shillinges, if he doe come home or be alive.

I give to Rebekah Bruen, a pynt pott of pewter, a new petticoate, and wascote wch she is to spin herselfe; alsoe an old byble, and a hatt wch was my sonn Thomas his hatt.

I give to my sonne Gabriell, my house, land, cattle, and swine, with all other goodes reall and psonall in Pequet or any other place, and doe make him my sole executor to this my will. Witness my hand,

The mark X of MARY HARRIES.

Witness hearunto· John Winthrop, Obadiah Bruen, Willm Nyccolls.

An account of the estate left by John Winthrop, Jr., will show how wide were the interests of these early settlers:

John Winthrop, Esq., the patron and founder of New London, and governor of Connecticut for nearly eighteen years, died in Boston, April 5th, 1676. He had been called to Boston to attend the meeting of the commissioners, to which he was the delegate from Connecticut. His remains were deposited in the tomb of his father, in the cemetery of King's Chapel, where afterward his two sons were gathered to his side. His wife, who deceased not long before him, is supposed to have been buried in Hartford.

Governor Winthrop's family consisted of the two sons so often mentioned, Fitz-John and Wait-Still, and five daughters. The sons were residents in New London at the time of their father's decease. Wait-Still succeeded his brother as major of the county regiment, but at a period ten or twelve years later, removed to Boston. Lucy, the second daughter, the wife of Edward Palmes, belongs to New London; but her death is not on record, neither is there any stone to her memory in the old burial-ground, by the side of her husband. It is therefore probable that she died abroad, and from other circumstances it is inferred that this event took place in Boston, after the death of her father, in 1676. She left a daughter Lucy, who was her only child, and this daughter, though twice married, left no issue. Her line is therefore extinct.

The very extensive landed estate of Governor Winthrop, which fell to his two sons, was possessed by them conjointly, and undivided during their lives. Fitz-John, having no sons, it was understood between the brothers that the principal part of the land grants should be kept in the name, and to this end be reserved for John, the only son of Wait Winthrop. These possessions, briefly enumerated, were Winthrop's Neck, 200 acres; Mill-pond farm, 300; land north of the town of Alewife Brook and in its vicinity, 1,500; land at Pequonuck (Groton), 6,000; Little-cove farm, half a mile square, on the east side of the river—these were within the bounds of New London. On Mystic river, five or six hundred acres; at Lanthorn Hill and its vicinity, 3,000; and on the coast, Fisher's Island and its Hommocks, and Goat Island. Governor Winthrop had also an undisputed title from court grants to large tracts in Voluntown, Plainfield, Canterbury, Woodstock and Saybrook, amounting to ten or twelve thousand acres. He also claimed the whole of what was called Black-lead-mine Hill in the province of Massachusetts Bay, computed to be ten miles in circumference. Magnificent as was this estate in point of extent, the value, in regard to present income, was moderate. By the provision of his will, his daughters were to have half as much estate as his sons, and he mentions that Lucy and Elizabeth had already been portioned with farms. The above sketch of his landed property comprises only that which remained inviolate as it passed through the hands of his sons, and his grandson John, the son of Wait, and was bequeathed by the latter to his son, John, John Still Winthrop, in 1747.

Reference has already been made to the relations of Uncas and the early settlers of the county. After the destruction of the Pequot power, the few survivors of the tribe, having been distributed amongst the Narragansetts and the Mohegans, were settled, some in what is now Westerly, some in what is now Waterford and New London, under the name "Nameaugs." These remnants of a once powerful tribe suffered under the severe treatment meted out to them by Uncas, who disliked Governor Winthrop for his protection of the "Nameaugs."

The jealousy of Uncas precipitated several conflicts with the settlers at New London. When the commissioners of the United Colonies (noteworthy as a step toward the Albany Congress and toward later confederation) were asked by Governor Winthrop to free the Pequots from the control of Uncas, they refused to do so, but reprimanded and fined Uncas for misdeeds.

Until the settlement of Norwich, Uncas led an unsettled life, evading the attacks of his Indian foes and disputing with his white neighbors regarding his rights. The commissioners, after many attempts at settling Indian affairs, made certain awards of lands to the surviving Pequots, which awards were never carried out by the towns concerned. After the charter of 1662, whereby Stonington became a part of Connecticut, the settlement of Indian affairs became subject to the General Court of Connecticut. The records of the General Court show a long list of petitions and awards pertaining to the Indian affairs of New London county, extending over a period from 1662 to Revolutionary times. The early history of Groton and Stonington shows that the Pequots were provided with reservations and treated as wards of the State.

The Mohegans, for their fidelity at all times, were more generously treated by the State, admitted to full citizenship finally (1873), and granted absolute ownership of certain lands, much of the rest of the tribal domain being sold from time to time to settlers of New London, Norwich, and adjoining towns.

Of the primitive life of the settlers we get many glimpses, by the votes of town meetings, wills, and diaries. We find in the town records the following entry:

Memorandum: that upon the 16th day of January, 1709-10, being a very cold day, upon the report of a kennel of wolves, mortal enemies to our sheep and all our other creatures, was lodged and lay in ambuscade in the Cedar Swamp, waiting there for an opportunity to devour the harmless sheep; upon information whereof, about thirty of our valiant men, well disciplined in arms and special conduct, assembled themselves and with great courage beset and surrounded the enemies in the said swamp, and shot down three of the brutish enemies, and brought their heads through the town in great triumph.

The same day a wolfe in sheepe's cloathing designed to throw an innocent man into the frozen water, where he might have perished, but was timely prevented, and the person at that time delivered frome that danger.

As the subject of wolves is thus again introduced, we may observe that at this period and for thirty years afterward a wolf-hunt was a customary autumnal sport. From ten to forty persons usually engaged in it, who surrounded and beat up some swamp in the neighborhood. Mill-pond Swamp and Cedar Swamp were frequently scoured for wolves in November or the latter part of October. George, son of John Richards, had a bounty of £11 for wolves killed during the year 1717; these were probably insnared. The bounty had been raised to twenty shillings per head. The bounty for killing a wildcat was three shillings.

The settlement at New London prospered, till at the outbreak of the Revolutionary War it numbered approximately 6,000 New London's part in that struggle has been fully set forth elsewhere. The Shaw Mansion, the Nathan Hale School, Fort Trumbull, the many anecdotes of local happenings, are rich in historic interest. Miss Caulkins remarks:

So many of the inhabitants of New London had been trained as fishermen, coasters, and mariners, that no one is surprised to find them, when the trying time came, bold, hardy, and daring in the cause of freedom. In all the southern towns of the county—Stonington, Groton, New London, Lyme—the common mass of the people were an adventurous class, and exploits of stratagem, strength, and valor, by land and sea, performed during the war of independence by persons nurtured on this coast, might still be recovered sufficient to form a volume of picturesque adventure and exciting interest. At the same time many individuals in this part of the country, and some, too, of high respectability, took a different view of the great political question and sided with the Parliament and the king. In various instances families were divided; members of the same fireside adopted opposite opinions and became as strangers to each other; nor was it an unknown misery for parents to have children ranged on different sides of the battle-field. At one time a gallant young officer of the army, on his return from the camp, where he had signalized himself by his bravery, was escorted to his home by a grateful populace that surrounded the house and filled the air with their applausive huzzas, while at the same time his half-brother, the son of the mother who clasped him to her bosom, stigmatized as a Tory, convicted of trade with the enemy, and threatened with the wooden horse, lay concealed amid the hay of the barn, where he was fed by stealth for many days.

This anecdote is but an example of many that might be told of a similar character.

The position of New London was such that it was easily blockaded, and constantly threatened with destruction. Many fleets of hostile ships sailed by. Many a privateer slipped out of the harbor in spite of the blockade. "So great, however, was the vigilance of the British squadron on the coast that not a single prize was brought into the harbor of New London from 1776 to 1778." Of the famous attack of Arnold on the town, Miss Caulkins says:

Although New London had been repeatedly threatened, no direct attack was made upon the town till near the close of the war in 1781. General Arnold, on his return from a predatory descent upon the coasts of Virginia, was ordered to conduct a similar expedition against his native State. A large quantity of West India goods and European merchandise brought in by various privateers was at this time collected in New London, the quantity of shipping in port was also very considerable, and among the prizes recently taken was the "Hannah" (Captain Watson), a rich merchant ship from London bound to New York, which had been captured a little south of Long

Island by Capt. Dudley Saltonstall, of the "Minerva," privateer. The loss of this ship, whose cargo was said to be the most valuable brought into America during the war, had exasperated the British, and more than any other single circumstance is thought to have led to the expedition At no other period of the war could they have done so much mischief, at no other had the inhabitants so much to lose.

The expedition was fitted out from New York, the headquarters of Sir Henry Clinton and the British army The plan was well conceived. Arnold designed to enter the harbor secretly in the night, and to destroy the shipping, public offices, stores, merchandise, and the fortifications on both sides of the river, with such expedition as to be able to depart before any considerable force could be collected against him Candor in judging forbids the supposition that the burning of the town and the massacre at Groton fort entered into his original design, though at the time such cruelty of purpose was charged upon him and currently believed. As flowing from his measures and taking place under his command, they stand to his account, and this responsibility is heavy enough without adding to it the criminal forethought.

The official report by Arnold reads as follows:

Sound, off Plumb Island, 8th Sept., 1781.

Sir,—I have the honor to inform your Excellency that the transports with the detachment of troops under my orders anchored on the Long Island shore on the 5th instant, at two o'clock P. M., about ten leagues from New London, and having made some necessary arrangements, weighed anchor at seven o'clock P. M. and stood for New London with a fair wind At one o'clock the next morning we arrived off the harbor, when the wind suddenly shifted to the northward, and it was nine o'clock before the transports could beat in At ten o'clock the troops in two divisions, and in four debarkations, were landed, one on each side of the harbor, about three miles from New London, that on the Groton side. consisting of the Fortieth and Fifty-fourth Regiments and the Third Battery of New Jersey volunteers, with a detachment of yagers and artillery, were under the command of Lieut.-Col Eyre. The division on the New London side consisted of the Thirty-eighth Regiment, the Loyal Americans, the American Legion, refugees, and a detachment of sixty yagers, who were immediately on their landing put in motion, and at eleven o'clock, being within half a mile of Fort Trumbull, which commands New London Harbor, I detached Capt. Millett, with four companies of the Thirty-eighth Regiment, to attack the fort, who was joined on his march by Capt Frink with one company of the American Legion At the same time I advanced with the remainder of the division west of Fort Trumbull, on the road to the town, to attack a redoubt which had kept up a brisk fire upon us for some time, but which the enemy evacuated on our approach. In this work we found six pieces of cannon mounted and two dismounted. Soon after I had the pleasure to see Capt. Millett march into Fort Trumbull, under a shower of grape-shot from a number of cannon which the enemy had turned upon him; and I have the pleasure to inform your Excellency that by the sudden attack and determined bravery of the troops the fort was carried with the loss of only four or five men killed and wounded Capt. Millett had orders to leave one company in Fort Trumbull, to detach one to the redoubt we had taken, and join me with the other companies. No time was lost on my part in gaining the town of New London. We were opposed by a small body of the enemy, with one field-piece, who were so hard pressed that they were obliged to leave the piece, which, being iron, was spiked and left.

As soon as the enemy were alarmed in the morning we could perceive they were busily engaged in bending sails and endeavoring to get their privateers and other ships up Norwich River out of our reach, but the wind being small and the tide against them they were obliged to anchor again. From information I received before and after my landing, I had reason to believe that Fort Griswold, on Groton side, was very incomplete, and I was assured by friends to government, after my landing, that there were only twenty or thirty men in the fort, the inhabitants in general being on board their ships and busy in saving their property.

On taking possession of Fort Trumbull, I found the enemy's ships would escape unless we could possess ourselves of Fort Griswold. I therefore dispatched an officer to Lieut.-Col. Eyre with the intelligence I had received, and requested him to make an attack upon the fort as soon as possible, at which time I expected the howitzer was up and would have been made use of. On my gaining a height of ground in the rear of New London, from which I had a good prospect of Fort Griswold, I found it much more formidable than I expected, or than I had formed an idea of, from the information I had before received. I observed at the same time that the men who had escaped from Fort Trumbull had crossed in boats and thrown themselves into Fort Griswold, and a favorable wind springing up about this time, the enemy's ships were escaping up the river, notwithstanding the fire from Fort Trumbull and a six-pounder which I had with me. I immediately dispatched a boat with an officer to Lieut.-Col. Eyre to countermand my first order to attack the fort, but the officer arrived a few minutes too late. Lieut.-Col. Eyre had sent Capt. Beckwith with a flag to demand a surrender of the fort, which was peremptorily refused, and the attack had commenced. After a most obstinate defense of near forty minutes, the fort was carried by the superior bravery and perseverance of the assailants. On this occasion I have to regret the loss of Maj. Montgomery, who was killed by a spear in entering the enemy's works; also of Ensign Whitlock, of the Fortieth Regiment, who was killed in the attack. Three other officers of the same regiment were wounded. Lieut.-Col. Eyre, and three other officers of the Fifty-fourth Regiment, were also wounded, but I have the satisfaction to inform your Excellency that they are all in a fair way to recover.

Lieut.-Col. Eyre, who behaved with great gallantry, having received his wound near the works, and Maj. Montgomery being killed immediately after, the command devolved on Maj. Bromfield, whose behavior on this occasion does him great honor. Lieut.-Col Buskirk, with the New Jersey volunteers and artillery, being the second debarkation, came up soon after the work was carried, having been retarded by the roughness of the country. I am much obliged to this gentleman for his exertions, although the artillery did not arrive in time.

I have enclosed a return of the killed and wounded, by which your Excellency will observe that our loss, though very considerable, is short of the enemy's, who lost most of their officers, among whom was their commander, Col. Ledyard. Eighty-five men were found dead in Fort Griswold and sixty wounded, most of them mortally; their loss on the opposite side must have been considerable, but cannot be ascertained. I believe we have about seventy prisoners, besides the wounded who were left paroled.

Ten or twelve ships were burned, among them three or four armed vessels, and one loaded with naval stores; an immense quantity of European and West India goods were found in the stores, among the former cargo of the "Hannah," Capt. Watson, from London, lately captured by the enemy, the

whole of which was burnt with the stores, which proved to contain a large quantity of powder unknown to us. The explosion of the powder and change of wind, soon after the stores were fired, communicated the flames to part of the town, which was, notwithstanding every effort to prevent it, unfortunately destroyed.

After the Revolution, New London developed its fisheries and commerce and became a famous whaling center. With its shipbuilding and coasting trade, New London became a center of trade for merchants further inland. Trade with the West Indies sprang up and flourished One hundred and fifty sail of merchant vessels entered and cleared at the port of New London. The first collector of the port was Gen. Jedediah Huntington, of Revolutionary fame The war of 1812 greatly interfered with this commerce, but at the close of the war commerce again revived. In 1816 was made the first trip from New York to New London by steam. The time, twenty-one hours, was considered remarkable. Two natives of New London, Capt. Moses Rogers and Capt Stevens Rogers, were the first to navigate a steam vessel across the Atlantic. The "Savannah" made the trip to Liverpool in twenty-one days, starting May 26, 1819.

To Miss Caulkins' History we are indebted for an outline of the whaling industry:

In tracing the whale fishery, so far as it has been prosecuted by the people of Connecticut, back to its rise, we come to the following resolve of the General Court at Hartford, May 25th, 1647: "If Mr Whiting with others shall make trial and prosecute a design for the taking of whale, within these liberties, and if upon trial within the term of two years, they shall like to go on, no others shall be suffered to interrupt them for the term of seven years."

The granting of monopolies and exclusive privileges was the customary mode of encouraging trade and manufactures in that day. Of Mr Whiting's project nothing further is known. Whales in the early years of the colony were often seen in the Sound; and if one chanced to be stranded on the shore, or to get embayed in a creek, the news was soon spread, and the fishermen and farmers from the nearest settlements would turn out, armed with such implements as they possessd, guns, pikes, pitchforks, or spears, and rush to the encounter. Such adventures, however, belong more particularly to the south side of Long Island than to the Connecticut shore

A whale boat is mentioned in an enumeration of goods before the end of the seventeenth century, and this implies that excursions were sometimes made in pursuit of whales, but probably they were not extended much beyond Montauk. Even at the present day a whale sometimes makes its appearance in the eastern part of the Sound.

We have no statistics to show that the whale fishery was on except in this small way, from any part of the Connecticut coast, before the Revolutionary War At Sag Harbor, on the opposite coast of the Sound, something more had been done. It is said that as far back as 1760, sloops from that place went to Disco Island in pursuit of whales; but of these voyages no record has been preserved. The progress of whaling from the American coast appears to have been pursued in the following order:

1st Whales were killed on or near the coast, and in all instances cut up and dried upon land Boats only used.

2nd. Small sloops were fitted out for a cruise of five or six weeks, and went as far as the Great Banks of Newfoundland.

3rd. Longer voyages of a few months were made to the Western Islands, Cape Verde, West Indies and Gulf of Mexico.

4th. After 1745, voyages were made to Davis' Straits, Baffin's Bay, and as far south as the coast of Guinea.

5th. After 1770, voyages were made to the Brazil Banks, and before 1775 vessels both from Nantucket and Newport had been to the Falkland Islands. Nantucket alone had at that time 150 vessels and 2,000 men employed in the whaling business. Some of the vessels were brigs of considerable burden.

The war totally destroyed the whale fishery, and the depression of business after the war prevented it from being immediately resumed. In Nantucket it revived in 1785, under legislative encouragement. This brings us to the period when the first whaling expedition into south latitude was fitted out from Long Island Sound.

In the year 1784 we find the following notice in the "New London Gazette": "May 20. Sailed from this port, sloop 'Rising Sun,' Squire, on a whaling voyage." Of this voyage there is no further record; it was probably of the short description At Sag Harbor a more extended expedition was undertaken the same year. Nathaniel Gardiner and brother fitted out both a ship and a brig on a whaling adventure They were both unsuccessful, but this is supposed to have been the first expedition after whales from Long Island Sound into south latitudes. In 1785, Messrs. Stephen Howell and Benjamin Hunting, of Sag Harbor, purchased the brig "Lucy," of Elijah Hubbard, of Middletown, Connecticut, and sent her out on a whaling voyage, George McKay, master. The same season the brig "America," Daniel Havens, master, was fitted out from the same place. Both went to the Brazil Banks.

1785.—The "Lucy" returned May 15th, with 360 barrels. The "America" returned June 4th, with 300 barrels These arrivals were announced in the "New London Gazette," in the marine list kept by Thomas Allen, who thereupon breaks forth: "Now, my horse jockeys, beat your horses and cattle into spears, lances, harpoons and whaling gear, and let us all strike out; many spouts ahead! Whales plenty, you have them for the catching."

The first vessel sailing from New London on a whaling voyage to a southern latitude was the ship "Commerce," which was owned and fitted out at East Haddam, on Connecticut river, but cleared from New London February 6th, 1794. An attempt was made to form a whaling company in New London in 1795, and a meeting called at Miner's tavern for that purpose, but it led to no result. Norwich next came forward, and sent out on a whaling voyage a small new ship built in the Thames river, below Norwich, and called the "Miantinomoh." She sailed from New London September 5th, 1800 (Captain Swain), and passing round Cape Horn, was reported at Massafuero August 9th, 1801. She spent another year on the South American coast, but in April, 1802, was seized at Valparaiso by the Spanish authorities and condemned, the ship "Tryal," Coffin, of Nantucket, sharing the same fate.

In 1802, the ship "Despatch," Howard, was fitted out at New London, to cruise in the south seas after whales; but the voyage was not repeated. The year 1805 may therefore be considered as the period when the whaling business actually commenced in the place, and the ship "Dauphin" the pioneer in the trade. This vessel was built by Capt. John Barber, at Pawkatuck Bridge, with express reference to the whale fishery. Her burden was two hundred and forty tons, and when completed she was filled with wood and sent to New York for sale. Not meeting with a purchaser, she returned and came into New London Harbor in the autumn of 1804. Here a company was formed, chiefly through the exertions of Dr. S. H. P. Lee, the first mover in the enterprise, who bought the ship and fitted her for whaling.

The "Dauphin," Capt. Laban Williams, sailed for the Brazil Banks September 6th, 1805, and arrived with her cargo June 14th, 1806. Dr. Lee then bought the ship "Leonidas," in New York, and fitted her also for whaling. Both ships sailed in August; Williams in the "Leonidas," and Alexander Douglas in the "Dauphin" The "Dauphin" arrived in April, 1807, full The "Leonidas" arrived in June, 1807, 1,050 barrels.

In 1807 the ship "Lydia" was bought in New York, and put into the business. The three ships went to the coast of Patagonia. The "Lydia" (Douglas) arrived June 9th, 1808, 1,000 barrels. The "Dauphin" (Sayre) arrived June 13th, 1808, 900 barrels. The "Leonidas" (Wm. Barnes) arrived June 23d, 1808, 1,200 barrels. The "Leonidas" left six of her crew on the uninhabited island of Trinidad; they had landed for refreshment, and the weather becoming very boisterous, the wind blowing off from the island and so continuing for many days, the vessel sailed without them. In July, the schooner "Experiment" (S. P. Fitch) was sent to bring them away. The "Leonidas" (Douglas) sailed again August 31st, 1808.

The embargo, non-intercourse and war, following close upon each other from this period, entirely broke up this, as well as every other species of commerce. The West India trade, which in former times had been the source of so much wealth and prosperity to the town, was never again extensively revived. After the conclusion of peace, only a few vessels were engaged in that traffic, and every year diminished the number. The whale fishery seemed to offer itself to fill the void of this declining trade.

In 1819 the whaling business was commenced anew by T. W. Williams and Daniel Deshon; the first officers employed consisted principally of persons who had gained some experience in the former short period of the business between 1805 and 1808 The brig "Mary" (James Davis) was sent out by Williams; the brig "Mary Ann" (Inglis) and the ship "Carrier" (Alexander Douglas) by Deshon. The "Mary" came in the next season, June 7th, and brought the first results of the new enterprise. She was out ten months and twenty days, and brought in 744 barrels of whale-oil and 78 of sperm. The "Carrier" brought 928 barrels of whale; the "Mary Ann" only 59

In 1820, the brig "Pizarro" (Elias L. Coit) was added to the fleet, and in 1821 the brig "Thames" (Bernard) and the ship "Commodore Perry" (Davis) The last-named vessel was built in 1815, at East Greenwich, Rhode Island, but coppered in New London, after she was engaged in the whaling business. It was the first time that this operation was performed in the place, and the "Commodore Perry" was the first copper-bottomed whaling vessel sent from the port. On her first voyage she was out eight months and four days, and brought in 1,544 barrels of whale oil and 81 of sperm

The "Carrier" (O. Swain), 340 tons burden, was the first vessel from the port that went out on the long voyage for sperm whale. She sailed for the Pacific Ocean February 20th, 1821, and arrived July 12th, 1823, with 2,074 barrels. In November, 1821, sailed also for the Pacific the new ship "Stonington" (Ray), built at Stonington, but sent from New London. In 1822 the ships "Connecticut," "Ann Maria" and "Jones" were added to the fleet, and in 1824 the "Neptune." The four brigs and the ship "Carrier," after making three and four voyages each, were withdrawn from the business; and as no other vessels were added till 1827, at the commencement of that year the whaling list of the port consisted of six ships only—three of them right whale and three sperm cruisers. Of these, five were fitted out by T. W. Williams, and the "Commodore Perry" by N. and W. W. Billings, who were then just launching into the business, and who purchased the same year the "Superior" and the "Phenix."

A fine ship that has for many years braved the storms of ocean cannot be regarded with indifference. She has a history which, if it could be written, would be full of interest. A few brief notes respecting the older ships belonging to the port may therefore be acceptable.

The "Commodore Perry" made seventeen voyages, and the "Stonington" thirteen. They both gave out, and were broken up in 1848. The "Connecticut" was condemned in a foreign port in 1848, was sold, and is still afloat in the Pacific Ocean. The "Ann Maria" was run down by a French whaler in the Indian Ocean in 1842. The "Jones" made sixteen voyages, and was condemned in 1842. The "Neptune" and "Superior," two ships that belonged to the whaling fleet of New London in 1852, were both built in 1808. The "Superior" was built in Philadelphia, and purchased by N. and W. W. Billings in 1827; the "Neptune" in New Bedford, and purchased by T. W. Williams in 1824, for $1650. She had just returned from an unsuccessful whaling voyage, fitted out from New York, and, being sixteen years old, the sum paid for her was considered fully equal to her value. She sailed on her first voyage from New London, June 7th, 1824, has made eighteen voyages, and is now absent (1852) on her nineteenth, having been forty-four years afloat. She has been more than once during that period rebuilt, but has not lost her identity; her keel, stern-post and some of her floor-timbers belong to the original frame.

No other service admits of such rapid promotion as whaling. In 1821, Robert B. Smith went captain of the "Mary." His experience in the business had been gained in two voyages only, but he proved to be one of the most successful and enterprising masters in the trade. He was the first to reach the amount of 2,000 barrels in one voyage, which he did in the "Ann Maria" in 1823, the second time that he went out commander. He was absent eight months and twenty-two days, and brought in 1,919 barrels of whale and 145 of sperm. In his sixth voyage he was unfortunately drowned in the Pacific Ocean, being drawn overboard by a whale, to which he had just made fast with his harpoon and line, December 28th, 1828. Captain Smith's four brothers pursued the same line of enterprise.

Capt. James Smith made ten voyages as captain, and several of them were eminently successful. In three successive voyages in the "Columbia," made to the island of Desolation, from which he returned in 1840, 1842, and 1844, he brought in each time more than 4,000 barrels of oil.

Capt. Franklin Smith, another of the brothers, made the most successful series of voyages to be found in the whaling annals of the port and probably of the world! In seven voyages to the South Atlantic, in the employ of N. and W. W. Billings, and accomplished in seven successive years, from 1831 to 1837, inclusive—one in the "Flora," one in the "Julius Cesar," and five in the "Tuscarora"—he brought home 16,154 barrels of whale, 1,147 of sperm. This may be regarded as a brilliant exhibiton of combined good fortune and skill. Two subsequent voyages made by him in the "Chelsea" were also crowned with signal success. These nine voyages were accomplished between June, 1830, and August, 1841.

Capt. John Rice was one of the crew of the brig "Mary" in 1819, and sailed commander of the "Pizarro," June 9th, 1822. He is still in the service (1852), in date of commission the oldest whaling captain of the port.

The single voyage that perhaps before any other merits special notice is that of the "Clematis" (Capt. Benjamin), fitted out by Williams and Barnes, and arriving July 4th, 1841. She was out ten months and twenty-nine days; went round the world, and brought home 2,548 barrels of oil. This voyage, when the time, the distance sailed, and the quantity of oil brought home are considered in connection, merits to be ranked among remarkable achievements

There is no associated line of business in which the profits are more equitably divided among those engaged in it than in the whale fishery. The owners, agents, officers and crew are all partners in the voyage, and each has his proportionate share of the results. Its operation, therefore, is to enlarge the means and multiply the comforts of the many, as well as to add to the wealth of the wealthy. The old West India trade, which preceded it, was destructive in a remarkable degree to human life and health, and engendered habits of dissipation, turbulence, and reckless extravagance. The whaling business is a great advance upon this, not only as it regards life, but also in its relation to order, happiness and morality. The mass of the people, the public, gained by the exchange.

In 1845, the whaling business reached its maximum; seven vessels were added that year to the fleet, which then consisted of seventy-one ships and barks, one brig, and five schooners. In January, 1846, the "McLellan," of 336 tons, was purchased by Perkins and Smith, with the design of making an experiment in the Greenland fishery. This made the seventy-eighth vessel sailing from New London in pursuit of whales, and ranked the place more than 1,000 tons before Nantucket in the trade. New Bedford was still far ahead, but no other port in the world stood between.

The "McLellan" has made six voyages to Davis' Straits; but the seasons have been peculiarly unfavorable, and she has met with little success. She is now absent (1852) on her seventh voyage.

Employed in the whale fishery from New London: 1820, one ship, three brigs, 950 tons. 1846, seventy-one ships and barks, one brig, six schooners, 26,200 tons; capital embarked, nearly $2,000,000. In 1847, the tide began to ebb; the trade had been extended beyond what it would bear, and was followed by a depression of the market and a scarcity of whale. The fleet was that year reduced to fifty-nine ships and barks, one brig and six schooners: total, sixty-six; tonnage, 22,625. In 1850, about fifty vessels were employed, or 17,000 tons, and the capital about $1,200,000 In 1849 and 1850, twenty-five whaling captains abandoned the business and went to California. Value of imports from the whale fishery, as exhibited by the custom-house returns: 1850, $618,055; 1851, $1,109,410

The following table of imports of whale and sperm oil into the port of New London, from 1820 to 1851, inclusive, and most of the statistics of the whale fishery since 1820, are taken from the Whaling Record of Henry P. Haven, which exhibits the date, length, and results of every whaling voyage made from New London since that period:

Year	Ships and Barks	Brigs	Schooners and Sloops	Barrels of Whale Oil	Barrels of Sperm Oil
1820	1	2	0	1,731	78
1821	0	3	0	2,323	105
1822	1	4	0	4,528	194
1823	4	2	0	6,712	2,318
1824	3	2	0	4,996	1,924
1825	4	0	0	5,483	2,276
1826	2	0	0	2,804	88
1827	5	0	0	3,375	6,166
1828	3	0	0	5,435	168
1829	9	0	0	11,325	2,205

1830	14	0	0	15,248	9,792
1831	14	0	0	19,402	5,487
1832	12	0	0	21,375	703
1833	17	0	0	22,395	8,503
1834	9	1	2	12,930	4,565
1835	13	1	0	14,041	11,868
1836	12	1	0	18,663	3,198
1837	17	0	1	26,774	8,469
1838	15	0	3	25,523	3,426
1839	15	1	2	26,278	4,094
1840	17	2	1	32,038	4,110
1841	15	1	2	26,893	3,920
1842	16	1	3	28,165	4,055
1843	20	0	0	34,677	3,598
1844	18	1	3	39,816	2,296
1845	21	0	0	52,576	1,411
1846	13	1	2	27,441	1,306
1847	35	0	2	76,287	4,765
1848	20	1	1	54,115	3,606
1849	17	0	3	38,030	1,949
1850	17	0	0	36,545	1,603
1851	26	0	2	67,508	2,914

Shortest voyage, ship "Manchester Packet," 1832; seven months and nineteen days (not including voyages of the "McLellan" to Davis' Straits). Longest voyage, ship "William C. Nye," arrived February 10th, 1851; out fifty-seven months and eleven days. Largest quantity of oil in one voyage, ship "Robert Bowne," 1848, 4,850 barrels. Largest quantity of whale-oil in one voyage, ship "Atlantic," 1848, 4,720 barrels. Largest quantity of sperm-oil in one voyage, ship "Phoenix," 1833, 2,971 barrels. Largest quantity of oil imported in any one ship, ship "Neptune," 27,845 whale, 2,710 sperm.

In 1847, the number of vessels employed from New London in freighting, coasting and home fisheries was 171, viz, nine ships and barks, three brigs, fifty-six schooners, 103 sloops and smacks, whole burden, 12,300 tons.[*] The number of seamen employed in the whale fishery and domestic trade was about 3,000.

The year 1849 was distinguished by the general rush for California; nineteen vessels sailed for that coast from New London, but of these one schooner was fitted in Norwich, and two or three others were in part made up from adjoining towns. The statistics of the business with California for two years have been estimated as follows ("New London Democrat"): Sent in 1849, four ships, three barks, twelve schooners; 3,745 tons. Passengers, 152; seamen, 186. Value of goods: merchandise, $3,228; domestic products, $70,418; domestic manufactures, $45,520.

Sent in 1850, one ship, one brig, three schooners; 803 tons. Passengers, 15, seamen, 53. Value of merchandise, $1,905; domestic products, $19,598; domestic manufactures, $10,524.

About fifty persons from New London went in steamers or vessels from other ports. (Nine or ten vessels sailed for California from Mystic.) The whole number that went from the place to California in those two years, as

* From statistics furnished the Harbor and River Convention, at Chicago, in December, 1847, by T. W. Williams.

seamen and passengers, could not have been less than 450.

Of the effect of the war of 1812 on New London, Miss Caulkins tells many interesting anecdotes. One instance must serve:

Varied and numerous were the events of the town and neighborhood during these three successive years of constant rigorous blockade. The sloop "Juno," Captain John Howard, continued to ply back and forth between New London and New York during the whole war with but a single serious accident; that was the loss of her mast by a shot of the enemy after being driven into Saybrook Harbor. Her enterprising commander was well acquainted with the Sound, made his trips during the darkest nights and in severest storms, guided often by the lantern lights of the enemy's ships as he repeatedly ran through their blockading squadron. He was narrowly watched and several times pursued by their boats and barges, but always eluded capture. Sometimes when too closely pursued, a spirited fire from his cannon, four pieces of which he always carried on deck, only to be used in defense, would drive away his pursuers and secure his little craft from further molestation. The fact that the enemy were fully apprised of his times of departure and expected arrival, and in fact all his movements, through the newspapers, which they could easily obtain, renders it the more remarkable that she escaped their vigilance

It is remarkable that during the whole war not a man in Connecticut was killed, notwithstanding the long and vigorous blockade and the many encounters between detachments of the enemy and the inhabitants   One person only, a Mr. Dolph, lost his life on the waters of the coast, off Saybrook, while engaged with others in recovering two prizes taken by the enemy.   Such a fact appears almost miraculous

Commodore Decatur entertained the hope that some opportunity would offer for his escape with his vessels during the winter, and watched for an opportunity favorable to his design   His vessel dropped down and remained at anchor opposite the town, and quietly remained waiting for some remissness of vigilance on the part of the enemy   At length the favorable time seemed to have arrived. A dark night, a favorable wind, and fair tide, all gave every expectation of success   But just as the little fleet were about to start, "blue-lights" appeared on both sides of the river. Such an unusual occurrence gave strong suspicions that these were concerted signals to the enemy, and notwithstanding every preparation had been made with the most profound secrecy, the commodore considered himself betrayed, and relinquished his intentions, making no further effort to run the blockade. Although he was firm in his belief that his intentions were thus signaled to the enemy, it was indignantly denied by the citizens that any traitorous designs existed, and that the lights were accidental, or that those who reported them to the commodore were mistaken   He, however, removed his two large vessels up the river, where they were dismantled and only a guard left on board The "Hornet" remained at New London, and subsequently slipped out of the harbor, and, eluding capture, reached New York in safety.

The restoration of peace in 1815 was an occasion of general rejoicing. Our enemies became friends, and receptions, balls, and public rejoicings signalized the event, in which the officers of the British squadron cordially participated, and who were as cordially received by the citizens of the town. Such was the close of the war of 1812.

We extract from Miss Caulkins' history the following accounts of early enterprise:

The first regular line of steamboats from New York to New London was established in 1816. On the 28th of September in that year, the "Connecticut" (Bunker) arrived from New York in twenty-one hours, which was regarded as a signal triumph of steam, the wind and a swell of the tide being against her. In October the regular line commenced, making two trips per week to New Haven   The "Fulton" (Captain Law) was running at the same time between New York and New Haven. The price of passage was five dollars to New Haven, and from thence to New York, four dollars. Steam propellers, carrying principally freight, but some passengers, commenced navigating the Sound in 1844. The first was the "Quinebaug."

In one respect New London stands in honorable connection with the history of steam navigation. Capt. Moses Rogers, the commander of the steamship "Savannah," the first steam vessel that ever crossed the Atlantic, and Capt. Stevens Rogers, sailing-master of the same and brother-in-law of the captain, were both natives of New London. The "Savannah" was built in New York, under the direction of Captain Rogers, for a company in Savannah, and was a full-rigged ship of about 350 tons burden, and furnished with an engine of eighty or ninety horse-power, by which she made about eight knots to the hour. She sailed for Savannah, May 26th, 1819, for the sole purpose of making the grand experiment of ocean steam navigation. Mr. Scarborough, of Savannah one of the company that owned the steamer, asserted that they had no other object in view; that anticipating the use of steam-enginery in that line, and having a surplusage of profit on hand from some successful operations of the company, instead of dividing it, they built and fitted out the "Savannah," in order to give to America the honor of making the first attempt to navigate the Atlantic by steam.

The passage to Liverpool was made in twenty-two days, fourteen by steam and eight by sails, the latter being used solely through the prudence of the captain to save the consumption of fuel, lest some emergency might occur and the supply be exhausted. From Liverpool the steamer proceeded to Copenhagen, and from thence to Stockholm and to St Petersburg. At these ports she excited universal admiration and interest. Lying at anchor like a public vessel, with no business to accomplish, no port charges to defray, no cargo to take on board, her stay was a continued reception of visitors, and her whole passage through the Baltic might be likened to a triumphant procession. Bernadotte, King of Sweden, and the Emperor of Russia, with their nobles and public officers, not only came on board to examine the wonderful American steamer, but tested her performance by short excursions in the neighboring waters. On the return home, the last place left in Europe was Arendel, in Norway, from whence the passage to Savannah was made in twenty-five days, nineteen by steam and six by sails.

Capt. Moses Rogers gained his experience as a steam engineer on the Hudson river, where he had been engaged in some of the earliest experiments in propelling vessels by steam. After his return from the voyage in the "Savannah," he took command of a steamboat running on the Great Pedee river, and died suddenly at Cheraw, South Carolina, September 15th, 1822, at the age of forty-two years.

Capt. Stevens Rogers is now an officer of the customs in New London, and from him the foregoing account of the first voyage by steam across the Atlantic is derived He has in his possession a massive gold snuff-box presented to him by Lord Lyndock, an English nobleman who took passage in the steamer from Stockholm to St. Petersburg, through an arrangement made for him by Mr. Hughes, the American Minister at the Swedish court. On the inside of the lid is the following inscription: "Presented by Sir Thomas Graham, Lord Lyndock, to Stevens Rogers, sailing-master of the steam-ship 'Savannah,' at St. Petersburg, October 10th, 1819."

Capt. Moses Rogers, among other costly presents, received from the Emperor of Russia an elegant silver tea-urn. The log-book kept during this voyage is deposited in the National Institute at Washington.

The development of New London county since the Civil War days has been mostly along the lines of manufacturing, though many of our smaller towns are still chiefly agricultural in their interests. Special articles have been prepared on many topics, but in general it may be said that our enterprises are characterized by their variety. The main industries are cotton and woolen manufactures, with many others of great importance, among them the making of quilts, of leather goods, of paper, of bleaching and printing, of shipbuilding, the making of engines, of velvet, of machinery of many sorts, of cutlery, of guns, of hardware, of birch and witch hazel oils, of menhaden oil, of silk, of soap, of lace, and many other articles too numerous to mention The inventive genius of the Connecticut Yankee has been revealed in our county as clearly as in the rest of the State.

The account of early newspapers is likewise of interest. The first newspaper of the town bore the following title: "The New London Summary, or The Weekly Advertiser, With the Freshest Advices, Foreign and Domestic."

At the close of the paper was the notification, "Printed by Timothy Green" It was a folio sheet; the size of the page about twelve inches by eight, with two columns of print. The heading was adorned with an ornamented cut of the colony seal, with the escutcheon of the town added by way of crest, viz., a ship in full sail. The first number was issued August 8th, 1758. The editor died August 3d, 1763, and the paper was discontinued.

2. "The New London Gazette," with a stamp of the king's arms, appeared in November, 1763. The size was considerably increased, the print arranged in three columns, and the price 6s. per annum, one-half to be paid on the delivery of the first number. This was in fact the same paper under another name, being a continuation by Timothy Green, nephew and assistant of the former publisher; but as the numerical series of the summary was not continued, the numbers being commenced anew, it may be classed as another paper. It was soon enlarged in size, and the name changed in the course of a few years to "The Connecticut Gazette." This had been the title of the first newspaper in the colony, established in New Haven, 1755, by James Parker and Co, John Holt, editor, but discontinued in 1767, and there being then no paper in the colony bearing that title, it was adopted by the pro-

prietor of the New London paper. In 1789 Mr Green took his son Samuel into partnership with him, and the "Gazette" was issued by Timothy Green and Son to 1794, when Samuel Green assumed the whole business. In 1805 he retired a while from the paper, and it was issued by Cady and Eells (Ebenezer P. Cady and Nathaniel Eells). In May, 1808, it was resumed by Green, and continued to January, 1838, when it passed for two years into the hands of John J. Hyde, who was both editor and publisher. In 1840 it reverted to the former proprietor, or to his son, S. H. Green, and was conducted by the latter to July, 1841. The next editor was A. G. Seaman, by whom it was continued about three years, after which the existence of the "Gazette" entirely ceased. It had been issued regularly under the name of the "Gazette" for more than eighty years.

We would here notice that the Spooner family, which is connected with the history of newspapers in this country, was linked both by marriage and occupation with the Greens. Judah P. Spooner and Alden Spooner, early printers in Vermont, were sons of Thomas Spooner (who came to New London from Newport in 1753), and brothers-in-law of Timothy Green. Alden Spooner (2d), son of the first-named of the brothers, was a native of New London. He is known as the editor of the "Suffolk Gazette," published at Sag Harbor from 1804 to 1811, and of the "Long Island Star," which he conducted from 1811 to his death, a period of about thirty-five years.

Charles Miner, long a noted printer in Wilkes-Barre, Pennsylvania, obtained his knowledge of the business in the "Gazette" office at New London. He was for a number of years a member of Congress, and has left an enduring memorial of his talents and research in the "History of Wyoming," of which he is the author.

Green's "Connecticut Register" was first published in 1785, and again in 1786; it was then intermitted for one year, but has regularly appeared every year since, making, inclusive of 1852, seventy-six volumes.*

After the year 1750, the Greens annually printed an "Almanac or Astronomical Diary." The first numbers were prepared by James Davis, and calculated for the meridian of New London. Next to the series of Davis, they reprinted the "Boston Almanac" of Nathaniel Ames, until 1766, when Clark Elliott, a mathematician and instrument maker who had settled in New London, commenced an independent series of almanacs which were at first published with his own name but afterward with the assumed one of Edmund Freebetter. This change is said to have been caused by a mistake which Elliott made in one of his astronomical calculations, which so much disconcerted him that he refused ever after to affix his name to the almanac. He died in 1793, and Nathan Daboll, of Groton, began his series of almanacs with that year, which were continued by him during his life, and have been

---

* Col. Samuel Green, for so many years editor and proprietor of the "Gazette," though no longer a resident in New London, is still living (1852), eighty-four, realizing that happy enjoyment of health, cheerfulness and prosperity which is designated as a green old age.

prepared by successors of the same name and family to the present year, 1852.

Nathan Daboll was a self-taught mathematician. He compiled an arithmetic which was extensively used in the schools of New England, and a system of practical navigation that was also highly esteemed He opened a school in New London for the common and higher branches of mathematics, and the principles of navigation. He died in Groton, March 9th, 1918, aged sixty-eight

3. "The Weekly Oracle, printed and published by James Springer, opposite the Market," was the title of a newspaper commenced at New London in October, 1796, and continued four years.

4. "The Bee, printed and published by Charles Holt " This paper was commenced June 14th, 1797, and discontinued June 30th, 1802. The editor immediately issued proposals for publishing a paper with the same title at Hudson, New York. "The Bee" may therefore be considered as transferred to that place. This paper was a prominent organ of the Democratic party, and under the administration of the elder Adams the editor was arrested for a libel, tried by the United States Court then sitting at New Haven, and under the provisions of the sedition law condemned to six months' imprisonment and to pay a fine of $200. Charles Holt was a native of New London; he died in Jersey City, opposite New York, in August, 1852, aged seventy-eight.

5. "The Republican Advocate," established in February, 1818, continued about ten years. It was first issued by Clapp and Francis (Joshua B. Clapp and Simeon Francis), but after four or five years the partnership dissolved. Francis removed to the west, and for a number of years published a newspaper in Springfield, Illinois Clapp continued the "Advocate" alone until about the close of the year 1828, when he sold the establishment to John Eldridge. The latter changed the name to "The Connecticut Sentinel," but the publication was not long continued.

6. "The People's Advocate, and New London County Republican." This paper was commenced August 26, 1840, with the immediate object in view of promoting the election of William Henry Harrison to the presidency. The proprietor was Benjamin P. Bissell. The editor for 1840, John Jay Hyde; for 1841, Thomas P. Trott. Bissell then took the whole charge of the paper till his death, September 3d, 1842. In 1843, J. G. Dolbeare and W. D. Manning appeared as associate editors and proprietors, but the next year Dolbeare assumed the sole editorship In November, 1844, he commenced the first daily paper published in New London; it was a folio sheet, the page twelve inches by nine, and called "The Morning News." In April, 1848, the "Advocate" and the "News" were merged in the "Weekly and Daily Chronicle," which, commencing a new series of numbers and bearing a different name, must be considered as altogether a new undertaking.

7 "The New London Democrat" was commenced March 22d, 1845, by J. M. Scofield and S D Macdonald; but the second editor retired with the publication of the forty-fourth number. January 1st, 1848, Scofield, in con-

nection with the "Democrat," commenced a daily paper entitled "The Morning Star." He has since emigrated to California, having assigned his whole
printing establishment, January 1st, 1849, to D. S. Ruddock, the present editor
and proprietor of the "Star and Democrat."

8. "The New London Weekly and Daily Chronicle" were first issued in
May, 1848, by C. F. Daniels and F. H. Bacon, an association which continued
for three years. Since August, 1851, C. F. Daniels has been sole editor and
proprietor.

The above are all the serial publications of the town that have been
continued long enough to count their existence by years. Transient undertakings for a special purpose, and some occasional papers not issued at regular
intervals have been omitted.

The following passage is selected from an article by Miss Charlotte M.
Holloway, written in 1897:

New London fairly teems with well authenticated anecdotes of the Revolution. and it is hard to pass through the older part of the town without finding objects of interest; but the Revolutionary part of local history has been
so thoroughly covered that but passing mention can be made of the houses
which stood in that period.

On Main street are the Guy Richards, corner Main and Richards streets;
the Red Fox Tavern, where Washington stopped in 1756; the Episcopal parsonage. the home of Mather Byles; and the Burbeck house, all between Federal and Masonic streets   The latter was the home of Maj.-Gen. Henry
Burbeck, brevet brigadier-general of the United States army, the founder of
the United States Military Academy, and second chief of artillery, and the
man who did so much to bring that branch of service to its splendid rank.
He served with distinction in the Revolution, was a personal friend of Washington. served with great distinction as chief of artillery to General Wayne
in the war with the Miamis, was thanked in general orders, and in 1800 was
in military command of all the Atlantic seaboard and Eastern and Middle
States, with his headquarters at Washington, and in 1801 began the Academy
at West Point   After a faithful, continuous service in the most useful and
arduous labor for the advancement of the army, he was retired, and devoted
himself to his home in New London.   On July 4, 1846, he was made president
of the Massachusetts Society of the Cincinnati.   He died in October, 1848,
and the Cincinnati erected the fine shaft to his memory in Cedar Grove.   The
town had a taste of his quality.   It had decreed that the three elms which
stand before the house should fall.   The General determined they should not,
and when he placed himself before them, gun in hand, and swore to shoot
the first who touched them, he persuaded the selectmen that he was right.
Within the old house now dwell his sons. William Henry, a member of the
Cincinnati and the Sons of the American Revolution; John; and Charlotte,
who is nearing one hundred years, an honorary member of the Lucretia Shaw
Chapter, D. A. R., which has three daughters of Revolutionary soldiers on
its list.

The Hempstead house, built and fortified in 1678, is the third oldest in
the State.   It was the home of Sheriff Hempstead, famous for his skill and
courage, and of the Joshua whose diary is such a mine of gossip and information.   It is preserved faithfully. as it was known to generations of Hempstead, its quaint interior unmarred by modern touch by its owner, the well-

known author, Mary Bolles Branch, a descendant of Hempsteads. The old stone house wreathed with ivy, its neighbor, was built by Huguenots, in 1697.

On the plateau of Manwaring Hill, commanding a magnificent view of the Sound, a site of surpassing beauty, stands the old Manwaring manor. Since 1660 the land has been in possession of the family. No one has read Miss Caulkins' "History of New London" without being impressed with the limpid clearness of her style and the pleasant humor which made her digress occasionally from the dry-as-dust pathway of fact to pluck some of the fragrant flowers of tradition. Frances Manwaring Caulkins was born in New London, April 26, 1795, and died here, February 3, 1869 Through her father she was a descendant of Hugh Caulkins, who came with Richard Blinman, the first minister of the colony. On her mother's side her ancestry was noted in early English history, Sir Ranulphus de Manwaring being justice of Chester in 1189-99; another, Sir William, was killed in the streets of Chester, defending Charles I, October 9, 1644 For thirty generations the Manwarings held Over Peover, the family seat. Her father died before she was born, and her uncle, Christopher Manwaring, a gentleman noted for generosity, culture and literary tastes, was exceedingly fond of his talented niece, aiding her with his library, and for seven years she dwelt with him. When she desired to teach, he set apart a room, still called her schoolroom. He married for his second wife Mary Wolcott, a noted beauty, and daughter of the famous Wolcott family. The widow of his son, Dr. Robert Alexander Manwaring, Ellen Barber Manwaring (daughter of Noyes Barber, for eighteen years Congressman from this district, the friend of Henry Clay, Daniel Webster and William Henry Harrison, who was to have had him in his cabinet), occupies the mansion with her only son, Wolcott B Manwaring.

No landmark in New London is more interesting than its old mill The following poem by M. G. Brainard, in the "New London Day," is rich in suggestion:

THE OLD MILL AT NEW LONDON

The same old mill that Winthrop built;
　Few were the men that saw it rise;
Today it passes on their life,
　Transmitted through the centuries.

In quietude this lowly house
　Has stood beside the peaceful glen,
And seen the busy years go by,
　Full of the toils of busy men.

Has stood through revolution's blood
　Recorded Arnold's guilty raid,
And looked on England's ships of war,
　From out its oft secluded shade,

Has seen our churches and our schools
　With tower and spire rise one by one;
Has heard the chimes of Sabbath bells
　Ring out their call from sire to son.

Has heard the rising city's din,
　The railroad's shriek, the steamboat's call.
Yet never through the tumult lost
　The dash of its own waterfall.

And men have come and men have gone,
  Houses been built and homes laid low;
And now, the same old mill-stone turns
  E'en as two centuries ago.

How many through this wild ravine
  Have wandered in their youthful day,
And where the water rushed between,
  Have skipped from rock to rock their way.

Then, from the miller's humbler door,
  With borrowed cup, have rushed in haste
To where the ever-flowing trough
  Poured for each thirsty lip a taste.

How many by the placid pond,
  The little wharf, the dainty bridge,
Have watched the willows as they dipped
  Their fringes in the water's edge.

Or, lingering near this quiet spot
  In the soft moonlight pale and still,
Have listened to the water's gush
  And drank the peace of the old mill

Some changes—'tis not all the same;
  The years could never leave us all;
Time's footsteps make their impress felt,
  However silent be their fall

Some little, low, deserted room,
  With lacy cobwebs hanging o'er
Some widening rifts among the laths
  Show what was once that is no more.

And still the water wends its way
  With rush and gush of happy sound,
And throws its arch of sparkling spray,
  And pushes the big wheel around.

Long may the ancient mill-stone grind!
  Long may the ancient mill be seen!
Long wave the trees, long flow the pond!
  Long rest the rocks in their ravine!

Long, through the narrow, open door
  And little window o'er the wheel,
May sunshine gleam upon the floor
  O'er golden heaps and bags of meal.

Soft be the touch of rushing time,
  Swift as they need the prompt repairs;
Reverent the care shall pass thee on
  As thou hast been, to waiting years

CHAPTER VI

THE CITY OF NORWICH

Its Founding—First Settlers—Development of the Town—During the Revolution—
Reminiscent Letters from Former Residents—Beginnings of Manufacturing—Early
Newspapers—The Jubilee of 1859—Abraham Lincoln Visits the City—Roll of Noted
People—Description of the Town by Henry Ward Beecher.

The following is from the pen of Edmund Clarence Stedman:

THE INLAND CITY (1851)

Guarded by circling streams and wooded mountains
  Like sentinels round a queen,
Dotted with groves and musical with fountains,
  The city lies serene.

Not far away the Atlantic tide diverges,
  And, up the southern shore
Of gray New England, rolls in shortened surges,
  That murmur evermore.

The fairy city! not for frowning castle
  Do I extol her name;
Not for the gardens and the domes palatial
  Of Oriental fame;

Yet if there be one man who will not rally,
  One man, who sayeth not
That of all cities in the Eastern valley
  Ours is the fairest spot;

Then let him roam beneath those elms gigantic,
  Or idly wander where
Shetucket flows meandering, where Yantic
  Leaps through the cloven air,

Gleaming from rock to rock with sunlit motion,
  Then slumbering in the cove;
So sinks the soul from Passion's wild devotion,
  To the deep calm of love

And journey with me to the village olden,
  Among whose devious ways
Are mossy mansions, rich with legends golden
  Of early forest days;

Elysian time! when by the rippling water,
  Or in the woodland groves,
The Indian warrior and the Sachem's daughter
  Whispered their artless loves;

Legends of fords, where Uncas made his transit,
    Fierce for the border war,
And drove all day the alien Narragansett
    Back to his haunts afar;

Tales of the after time, when scant and humble
    Grew the Mohegan band,
And Tracy, Griswold, Huntington and Trumbull,
    Were judges in the land.

So let the caviler feast on old tradition,
    And then at sunset climb
Up yon green hill, where, on his broadened vision
    May burst the view sublime!

The city spires, with stately power impelling
    The soul to look above,
And peaceful homes, in many a rural dwelling,
    Lit up with flames of love;—

And then confess, nor longer idly dally,
    While sinks the lingering sun,
That of all cities in the Eastern valley
    Ours is the fairest one.

The town of Norwich is bounded on the north by Sprague and Franklin, on the east by Lisbon and Preston, on the south by Preston and Montville, and on the west by Bozrah and Franklin The original town of nine miles square has lost its area by the setting off of Bozrah, Franklin and Lisbon in 1786, and by the loss of a portion of the present Preston in 1687. The deed of the town land was executed by Uncas, Owaneco, and Attawanhood June 6, 1659, and reads as follows:

Deed of Norwich.

Know all men that Onkos, Owaneco, Attawanhood, Sachems of Mohegan have Bargined, sold, and passed over, and doe by these presents sell and pass over unto the Towne and Inhabitants of Norwich nine miles square of land lying and being at Moheagan and the parts thereunto adjoyneing, with all ponds. rivers, woods, quarries, mines, with all royalties, privileges, and appurtenances thereunto belonging, to them the said inhabitants of Norwich, theire heirs and successors forever—the said lands are to be bounded as followeth. (viz.) to the southward on the west side of the Great River, ye line is to begin at the brooke falling into the head of Trading Cove, and soe to run west norwest seven miles—from thence the line to run nor north east nine miles, and on the East side the afores'd river to the southward the line is to joyne with New London bounds as it is now laid out and soe to run east two miles from the foresd river, nor norwest nine miles to meet with the western line.
——In consideration whereof the sd Onkos, Owaneco and Attawanhood doe acknowledge to have received of the parties aforesd the full and juste sum of seventy pounds and doe promise and engage· ourselves, heirs and successors, to warrant the sd bargain and sale to the aforesd parties, their heirs and successors, and them to defend from all claimes and molestations from any

whatsoever.—In witness whereof we have hereunto set to our hands this 6th of June, Anno 1659.

UNKOS
OWANECO
ATTAWANHOOD

Witness hereunto, John Mason, Thomas Tracy.

This deed is recorded in the Country Booke, August 20th, 1663: as attests John Allyn, secretary. The bounds of this tract, as more particularly described in the first volume of the Proprietors' Records, were as follows:

The line commenced at the mouth of Trading Cove, where the brook falls into the cove; thence W. N. W. seven miles to a Great Pond (now in the corner of Bozrah and Colchester), the limit in this direction being denoted by a black oak marked N that stood near the outlet of "Great Brook that runs out of the pond to Norwich river," thence N N. E. nine miles to a black oak standing on the south side of the river (Shetucket), "a little above Maw-mi-ag-waug"; thence S. S. E. nine miles, crossing the Shetucket and the Quine-baug, and passing through "a Seader Swamp called Catantaquck," to a white oak tree, marked N. thirteen rods beyond a brook called Quo-qui-qua-soug, the space from the Quinebaug to this tree being just one mile and fifty-eight rods; thence S. S. W. nine miles to a white oak marked N, near the dwelling-houses of Robert Allyn and Thomas Rose, where Norwich and New London bounds join; thence west on the New London bounds, crossing the southern part of Mr. Brewster's land, two miles to Mohegan river, opposite the mouth of Trading Cove brook where the first bounds began.

Such were the bounds, as reviewed and renewed in October, 1685, by an authorized committee, accompanied by the two sachems and some of the chief men of Mohegan. The former deed of 1659, with the boundaries thus described and explained, was then ratified and confirmed by "Owaneca, sachem of Mohegan, son and heire unto Vnchas deceased," and "Josiah, son and heire unto Owaneca," in a new deed, signed by them October 5th, 1685, witnessed by John Arnold and Stephen Gifford, and acknowledged before James Fitch, assistant.

The southern boundary line, it will be observed, is nine miles in length, two east of the river, and seven west, without counting the breadth of the Thames, and the length of Trading Cove to the mouth of the brook, which would make this line nearly ten miles long. This is explained in the deed to be designed as a compensation for "the benefit and liberty of the waters and river for fishing and other occasions," reserved to the Indians.

Of the original so-called "thirty-five proprietors," Miss Caulkins writes as follows:

Who were the original proprietors of Norwich? The current statement that they were just thirty-five in number is based upon the authority of historians writing more than a century after the settlement. Dr. Trumbull in his "History of Connecticut" gives this number, relying, it is supposed, upon a list furnished in 1767 by the Rev. Dr. Lord, pastor of the First Church of Norwich. Dr. Lord's manuscript is extant. He says: "The town of Norwich was settled in the spring of 1660: the Purchase of sd Town was made in ye month of June, 1659, by 35 men."

He then gives a list of the names, which includes several who were minors at that time, and one at least (John Elderkin) whose earliest grant at Norwich was in 1667.

Laying aside, therefore, all subsequent statements and recurring to the oldest records remaining at Norwich from which these abstracts must have been derived, it is found that the original records were very deficient in giving dates to the early grants. Resolutions passed at different periods in the town meetings refer to this defect.

In 1672 a new record of lands was made under direction of the town authorities, by James Fitch, Jr. It was commenced May 1st of that year, and the book contains a registry of the town lands and grants, "so far as copies of said lands were brought in by the inhabitants." The number of land-owners recorded is seventy-eight, three or four of whom were non-residents. In 1681 the inhabitants declaring themselves sensible of a deficiency in their original records, appointed three of the first-comers, Thomas Leffingwell, Thomas Adgate, and John Post, to search for the original dates of former acts and grants, but nothing appears to have been done under this commission.

May 3d, 1684, Christopher Huntington, recorder, at the request of John Olmstead, who, he says, "desireth to have the primitive date set to his record of land, which hath not been done heretofore for the want of an orderly dating by the first recorder, Mr. Birchard," ascertains the true date, and affixes it under his signature—"which date we find out of an antient wrighting which respects our purchase interest, and right, to be in the yeare of our Lord upon the 30th day of June 1659." Again, December 18th, 1694, the town, after adverting to their former negligence in the record of proprietary lands, nominated a committee of six men "to search out and do the best they can to find the names of first purchasers, and what estate each of them put in, and report to the town."

The striking fact is here disclosed that in little more than thirty years after the settlement, the number of the first proprietors, the amount of each one's subscription, and the names of all the purchasers, were not generally known and could not be determined without some difficulty.

No report of the last commission is recorded. Not long afterwards, Capt. James Fitch was employed in the same business. He began a new registry of lands, copying original records where he could find them, stating bounds as they then existed, and affixing dates as nearly accurate as could be ascertained. It is from this registry that the various lists of the thirty-five proprietors have been gathered. Home lots, that seem to have constituted original grants, not having been alienated or purchased, were in general dated November, 1659. But the whole number that appears to be included under this date, either expressly or by implication, is thirty-eight, and it is difficult to decide which of these should be rejected, so as to leave the number just thirty-five.

The following list comprises those against whom not only nothing is found to militate against their being ranked as first proprietors, but, on the contrary, the records either prove conclusively, or favor the idea, that they belonged to that class: Rev. James Fitch, Major John Mason, Thomas Adgate, Robert Allyn, William Backus, William Backus, Jr., John Baldwin, John Birchard, Thomas Bliss, Morgan Bowers, Hugh Calkins, John Calkins, Richard Edgerton, Francis Griswold, Christopher Huntington, Simon Huntington, William Hyde, Samuel Hyde, Thomas Leffingwell, John Olmstead, John Pease, John Post, Thomas Post, John Reynolds, Jonathan Royce, Nehemiah Smith, Thomas Tracy, Robert Wade.

HEAD OF THE GREEN, NORWICH, IN 1836. BUILDING ON LEFT
WAS THE OLD COURT HOUSE, AFTERWARD THE ACADEMY;
THAT ON THE CORNER A TAVERN. THE CHURCH EDIFICE IS
THE "MEETING HOUSE OF THE ROCK," THE FIRST CHURCH
IN THE SETTLEMENT.

Others having original home-lots and all the privileges of first proprietors were· Thomas Bingham, John Bradford, John Gager, Stephen Gifford, Richard Hendy. Thomas Howard, Thomas Waterman, John Tracy, Josiah Reed, Richard Wallis.

Of this second class, Bingham, Gifford, Howard, Reed, Tracy and Waterman, were probably minors when the plantation commenced. They were all married between 1666.and 1670, inclusive, and were all living, except Howard, in 1702, when a roll of the inhabitants was made in reference to a division of land which distinguished the surviving first proprietors from the list of accepted inhabitants. Bingham, Gifford, Reed, Tracy and Waterman were enrolled with the latter, which would seem to settle the point that they were not original proprietors.

Most of these names, however, are necessary in order to make up the charmed number thirty-five. From the position these young men took, and the prominence of their descendants in the history of the town, they seem to have a higher claim to be ranked as proprietors than some of the earlier class. Hendy and Wallis, for instance, of whom we know little more than their names, and, accepting the six minors, we are brought back to the time-honored prescriptive number, thirty-five Stephen Backus, another minor, became a proprietor in the right of his father, William Backus, who died soon after the settlement.

The Town-plot was laid out in a winding vale, which followed the course of the rapid, circuitous Yantic, and was sheltered for the greater part of the way, on either side, by abrupt and rocky but well-wooded hills. A broad street or highway was opened through this valley, on each side of which the home-lots were arranged A pathway was likewise cleared from the center of the settlement to the Indian landing place below the Falls of the Yantic, near the head of the Cove, following the old Indian trail from Ox-hill to Yantic ford. This path, called by the settlers Mill-Lane, was the most eligible route by which the effects of the planters could be conveyed. In some places the forests had been thinned of their undergrowth by fires, to afford scope for the Indians in their passionate love of the chase, and the beaver had done his part towards clearing the lowlands and banks of the rivers. A few wigwams were scattered here and there, the occasional abodes of wandering families of Indians at certain seasons of the year, who came hither for supplies of fish. fruit, or game; and the summits of some of the hills were crowned with disorderly heaps of stones, showing where some rude defense had been constructed in the course of their wars. But in every other respect the land was in its natural wild state. It was a laborious task to cut down trees, to burn the underbrush, to mark out roads and pathways, to throw temporary bridges over the runs of water, and to collect materials for building.

The home-lots comprised each a block of several acres, and were in general river-lands, favorable for mowing, pasture and tillage. Here lay the prime advantage to be gained by a change of residence, the first proprietors being, with scarcely a single exception, agriculturists and farmers.

Of the coming of the settlers from Saybrook, no better description has been given than that of Rev. Dr. Lewellyn Pratt, delivered at the two hundred and fiftieth anniversary of the founding. He says:

I presume that I have been selected to speak this opening word in the public services of this 250th anniversary, as a native and representative of the old town of Saybrook. I am to remind you of "the rock whence ye were hewn and the hole of the pit whence ye were digged."

As we all know, the band of pilgrims who came here in 1659-60 came for the most part from Saybrook. An independent colony had been established there under the leadership of Gov. John Winthrop the younger. It was a colony animated by great expectations. The importance of the location at the mouth of the great river, the prospect and the purpose of building there a large city, and the hope that many prominent men would soon follow, made it an attractive spot to enterprising souls. That settlement was begun in 1635, the same year that Hooker brought his colony through the wilderness to Hartford. Lion Gardiner, an engineer who had seen service under the Prince of Orange in the Netherlands, was induced by Governor Winthrop to come to fortify the place, to lay out the ground for a city, and to "make preparation for the reception of men of quality" who were soon to follow from England. He remained four years and was succeeded by Col. George Fenwick, and he in turn by Maj. John Mason. During the first years, troublesome years of defence against the frequent assaults of the Indians, the settlement had for its center and principal feature the fort which Gardiner had built at the first. About this were clustered the houses, and in this, in the Great Hall, was the gathering place for defense, for transaction of business, and for worship. No church was formed at first, for it was principally a military post, and the chaplain of the post, Rev. John Higginson, was the spiritual guide of the colony. Col. George Fenwick, after the failure of "the men of quality" who were expected to join him in the enterprise, transferred his colony, in 1644, to Connecticut, and soon after, saddened by the death of his wife, Lady Alice, returned with his children to England, and Maj. John Mason was persuaded to receive the investment and to make Saybrook his home. There he remained as leader for twelve years.

Under his administration the colony thrived, and a more extended settlement was made north, east and west. In 1646 a church was formed, and the Rev. James Fitch, who had studied with the Rev. Thomas Hooker and who was recommended by him, became pastor, and Thomas Adgate deacon Mr. Fitch's ministry, whom Trumbull speaks of as a "famous young gentleman" (he was in his twenty-fourth year when he was settled), proved to be a very happy and successful one. Notwithstanding the hostility of the Dutch and the Indians, the plantation grew by the moving in of choice families, some of them from Windsor and Hartford, attracted in part by the popularity of the young preacher. We have meager records of that period, but it seems to have been one that promised well for the settlement, which was now assuming the consequence of a real plantation and becoming something more than a military post.

After a lapse of fourteen or fifteen years, however, we find that a check is to be given to this progress, the intimation of which is clearly marked by this order of the General Court of Connecticut, dated May 20, 1659: "This court having considered the petition presented by the inhabitants of Seabrook, doe declare yt they approve and consent to what is desired by ye petitioners respecting Mohegin, provided yt within ye space of three years they doe effect a Plantation in ye place prpounded."

We would like to know more of his petition and of the list of names signed to it, but no copy has been preserved. The order speaks of the "inhabitants of Seabrook," which seems to imply that a majority proposed to remove; and the fact that Mr. Fitch, their pastor, decided to come with them, also lends color to that view. It is doubtful, however, if the majority actually came. Mr. Fitch may have recognized the greater need of those who were to go into new conditions and who would require his experience and counsel in the organizations they must effect. Apparently, it was not regarded as the removal of the church, although its pastor and deacon came—Saybrook has always dated the organization of its church in 1646, and Norwich 1660—but in all probability the younger and more enterprising of the colony came, and the loss to Saybrook was most seriously felt. For several years, till 1665, the colony and church that were left behind were in a disheartened state.

Many reasons have been surmised for the removal, some of them too frivolous to be accepted, as that which has been so often repeated—that these Norwich pioneers, with Major Mason and James Fitch at their head, were "driven out by the crows and blackbirds that destroyed their corn." We may imagine many reasons: among them, perhaps, was the disappointment that the men who had planned to settle at Saybrook and who would have given peculiar character and standing to that colony had failed to come; and even their representative, Colonel Fenwick, had lost heart in the enterprise and abandoned it. Then, there were the inducements which the friendly Indians here held out and the offer of a large tract of land for settlement.

The peculiar beauty of this section, with its wooded hills, its fertile plains and running brooks, attracted them. The pioneer spirit appealed to them, was in their blood, as in all the colonies at that time. They must go somewhere. So Hooker had come to Hartford, Pynchon to Springfield, Roger Williams to Rhode Island, Jonathan Brewster to Windsor and Brewster's Neck. Probably this Norwich colony had as reasons for the removal some like those given by Hooker's company in their petition for permission for removal to Hartford, which were: 1. "Want of room where we are." 2. "The fruitfulness and commodiousness of Connecticut and the danger of having it possessed by others" 3. "The strong bent of our spirit to remove thither." Probably the "bent of their spirit" was the motive more potent than either of the others of them or both of them together

The act of the General Court of May, 1659, which I have quoted, made as its condition that the settlement must be made within the three years thereafter. Apparently no time was lost; and the advance guard came in the summer of 1659, followed by the remainder of the company the next year.

It was a valiant and goodly band of well-to-do folk of good ancestry, that had been trained by strong leaders, such as Winthrop, Fenwick, Gardiner, Mason, Higginson and Fitch, had been inured to service in a new country, had already attained to a well ordered life under a constitutional government, and were united under the restraining and refining power of the Christian faith. This colony did not begin in a random way, like so many of the early settlements or like so many of the later frontier ventures, by receiving accessions of restless adventurers from this quarter and that till it gradually grew into stable form and condition: it came upon the ground a town and a church. The people were not a miscellaneous company thrown together by chance, needing to be trained and assimilated, but an association carrying their laws as well as their liberties with them; not strangers, each seeking his own advantage, staking out his own claim and defending it by arms; but a band of God-fearing men and women united into a brotherhood each bound to act for the common good. They were not mere fortune hunters or buccaneers coming to wrest their speedy gain and then retire, but founders of a civilized

N.L—1-9

and Christian state in which they could establish homes, and which they could bequeath to their children as a priceless inheritance. They were looking forward to permanence and a future, and they knew that steady habits, manly toil and fine fraternity of feeling must enter into that to make it stable. All the enactments and procedings of those early days reveal a community in which good order, decorum of manners, self-respect and high ideals prevailed. The Christian church was the unifying bond and the guide of their lives. They were cheered and strengthened by the constant charm of its promises, and the rigor of the wilderness and the privations of frontier life were softened by its hopes. I do not know how much they thought of the names they were to transmit. I think some of them would have smiled at the coat-of-arms and the kind of heraldic glory with which they have been crowned, and would have been incredulous of the "genuine" heirlooms that have been handed down; but they did aim to lead honest and honorable lives and to make a community in which it would be safe and wholesome for their children to grow.

It was sifted seed that was brought by Winthrop to his first settlement; and it was sifted again when Fitch and Mason brought it here. Who they were, how they fared, what hostages they have given to history in the lines of noble descent, we are to hear in the days that are to follow. It is a goodly story—the orderly life of those early days; then, the patriotic spirit of the time when the nation was born; then, the enterprise of this later time. Norwich, proud of her ancestry, of the achievements of her sons and daughters, of her well-earned name, and of her lines running out to the ends of the earth, comes to her quarter millennium with devout gratitude to Him who brought us here and who has sustained us. And it surely is not amiss, while, standing by their graves, we honor the memories of those heroic men and women and congratulate ourselves on our heritage, to remind ourselves that

> "They that on glorious ancestors enlarge
> Produce their debt instead of their discharge,"

and, that though these have witnesses borne to them through their faith, "God has provided some better thing for us, that apart from us they should not be made perfect."

Of the life of Captain John Mason, Miss Caulkins gives a full outline so far as it is known:

Every memoir of Mason is obliged to take him up at the prime of life, for of his birth, parentage, and early years, no certain information has been obtained. When he first appears in history, he is in the English army under Sir Thomas Fairfax, fighting in the Netherlands in behalf of the Dutch patriots, against the bigotry and tyranny of Spain.

He is supposed to have emigrated to this country in 1630, with Mr. Warham's company that sailed from Plymouth, England, March 20th, and arrived at Nantasket May 30th of that year. But this cannot be stated with absolute certainty, as he has not been actually traced on this side of the ocean before December, 1632, when he was engaged in a cruise with John Gallop, under a commission from the Governor and Magistrates of Massachusetts to search for a pirate called Dixy Bull, who had for some time annoyed the coast with petty depredation. He was then called Lieutenant Mason, but soon afterward attained the rank of captain. In 1634 he was one of a committee appointed to plan the fortifications of Boston Harbor, and was specially employed in raising a battery upon Castle Island.

In March, 1635, he was the representative of Dorchester to the General Court, but in the latter part of the same year or early in the next, removed with the major part of Mr. Warham's people to the Connecticut Valley. Here the emigrants planted themselves on the western bank of Connecticut river, above Hartford, and founded the pleasant and honorable town of Windsor.

With the residence of Captain Mason at Windsor, all the stirring scenes of the Pequot war are connected. This was the great event of the early history of Connecticut, and the overshadowing exploit of Mason's life. He was instrumental in originating the expedition, formed the plan, followed out its details, fought its battles, clinched, as it were with iron screws, its results, and wrote its history. This war was begun and ended when Connecticut had only 250 inhabitants, comprised principally in the three towns of Hartford, Wethersfield and Windsor. Out of these Mason gathered a band of seventy men, and, passing down Connecticut river, landed in the Narragansett country, and being joined by a band of friendly Indians, marched directly into the heart of the hostile territory, assailed the Pequots in their strongest fortress, destroyed it, laid waste their dwellings, and killed nearly half of the whole nation. This expedition occupied three weeks and two days. The skill, prudence, firmness and active courage displayed by Mason in this exploit were such as to gain him a high standing among military commanders. From this period he became renowned as an Indian fighter, and stood forth a buckler of defence to the exposed colonists, but a trembling and a terror to the wild people of the wilderness.

In 1637 he was appointed by the General Court the chief military officer of the colony, his duty being "to train the military men" of the several plantations ten days in every year; salary, forty pounds per annum. At a later period (1654) he was authorized to assemble all the train-bands of the colony once in two years for a general review. The office was equivalent to that of major-general. He retained it through the remainder of his life, thirty-five years, and during that time appears to have been the only person in the colony with the rank and title of major.

When the fort at Saybrook was transferred by Colonel Fenwick to the jurisdiction of the colony, Mason was appointed to receive the investment, and at the special request of the inhabitants he removed to that place and was made commander of the station. Here he had his home for the next twelve years.

The people of New Haven were not entirely satisfied with their location, and formed a design of removing to a tract of land which they had purchased on the Delaware river. In 1651 they proposed this matter to Captain Mason, urgently requesting him to remove with them, and take the management of the company. This invitation is a proof of the high opinion his contemporaries had formed both of his civil and military talents. The offers they made him were liberal, and he was on the point of accepting, when the Legislature of Connecticut interfered, entreating him not to leave the colony, and declaring that they could by no means consent to his removal. Finding that his presence was considered essential to the safety of Connecticut, he declined the offers of New Haven. If he went, there was no one left who could make his place good; neither had New Haven any person in reserve, who could fill the station designed for him, and therefore the projected settlement never took place. The active disposition of Mason, however, never lacked employment. There was scarcely a year in which he was not obliged to go on some expedition among the Indian tribes, to negotiate, or to fight, or to pacify their mutual quarrels. At one time, his faithful friend Uncas was in danger from a powerful league of the other tribes, but the seasonable preparations of Mason for his relief frightened the foe into peace and submission. At another time he was sent with arms and men to the assistance of the Long Island Indians, against Ninigrate, the powerful sachem of the Nahanticks, who threatened them with extirpation. This service he gallantly performed; but only two years afterwards was compelled to appear again on that Island with a band of soldiers in order to chastise the very Indians, mischievous and ungrateful, whom he had before relieved.

We find him, at the same time and for several years in succession, holding various public offices, all arduous and important. He was Indian agent, Indian umpire, and the counselor of the government in all Indian concerns; captain of the fort, justice of the peace, and empowered to hold courts as a judge; a member likewise of two deliberative bodies, the Connecticut Legislature and the Board of Commissioners of the United Colonies; major-general of the militia at home, and the acting commander in all expeditions abroad. In 1660 he was chosen deputy governor, to which office he was annually re-elected for eight years, five under the old form and three under the king's charter, which united Connecticut with New Haven. The same year he was actively employed, in conjunction with Mr. Fitch and others, in effecting the settlement of Norwich, and also in purchasing of the Mohegans a large tract of land, in behalf of the colony. At this time, also, for nearly two years, he performed all the duties of the chief magistrate of the colony—Winthrop, the governor, being absent in England, engaged in negotiations respecting the charter.

Thus the life of Mason on this continent may be distributed into four portions The first was given to Dorchester, and the remainder in nearly equal parts to the three towns in Connecticut that he assisted in planting—lieutenant and captain at Dorchester, five and a half years; conqueror of the Pequots, magistrate and major at Windsor, twelve years; captain of the fort, and commissioner of the United Colonies at Saybrook, twelve; Deputy Governor and Assistant at Norwich, twelve. He was not chosen Deputy Governor after 1668, but continued in duty as an Assistant, and was present for the last time at the election in May, 1671.

Of the original band of Norwich purchasers, Mason was one of the earliest laid in the grave. He died January 30, 1671-72. According to Trumbull, he was in the seventy-third year of his age. His last hours were cheered by the prayers and counsels of his beloved pastor and son-in-law, Mr. Fitch. Two years before, he had requested his fellow-citizens to excuse him from all further public services on account of his age and infirmity; so that the close of his life though overshadowed by suffering from an acute disease, was unharrassed by care and responsibility. There is no coeval record that points out his burial-place, but uniform tradition and current belief in the neighborhood from generation to generation leave no reason to doubt that he was interred where other inhabitants of that generation were laid, that is, in the Post and Gager burial ground, or first cemetery of Norwich.

From early times, Norwich commerce prospered, since it was the natural outlet for a considerable farming region and, at the same time, had an excellent position at the head of the Thames. Live stock, provisions, lumber, were exchanged at the West Indies for sugar, molasses and rum.

Shortly after the Revolution, Norwich citizens owned over forty vessels engaged in commerce. From the "Norwich Packet" (editor Jonathan Trumbull), we get some idea of the business in the town. The merchants combined shrewdness with industry. The adventurous spirit of the early settlers was not lacking. New industries were starting up The original settlers had laid out their plots "up town," two miles from the "landing." But with the development of commerce and industry came an increase in the activity of the people of "Chelsea" (the landing). Business interests came to be stronger than the farming interests. The city of Norwich, with its center near the landing, had been incorporated in 1784 as a first step in this growth, and by the middle of the nineteenth century "Norwichtown" had become one of its suburbs.

During the Revolutionary War, Norwich, while not subject to immediate danger, as was New London, was nevertheless very active in assisting the Revolutionary troops and in furnishing its own quota. As an interesting extract we quote from Miss Caulkins:

Detachments from the Continental army frequently passed through Norwich. In 1778 a body of French troops, on the route from Providence to the South, halted there for ten or fifteen days, on account of sickness among them. They had their tents spread upon the plain, while the sick were quartered in the court-house. About twenty died and were buried each side of the lane that led into the old burying-yard. No stones were set up, and the ground was soon smoothed over so as to leave no trace of the narrow tenements below.

General Washington passed through Norwich in June, 1775, on his way to Cambridge. It is probable that he came up the river in a packet-boat with his horses and attendants. He spent the night at the Landing, and the next day pursued his journey eastward. In April, 1776, after the evacuation of Boston by the enemy, the American troops being ordered to New York, came on in detachments by land, and crossing the Shetucket at the old fording-place below Greenville. embarked at Norwich and New London to finish the route by water. General Washington accompanied one of the parties to Norwich and met Governor Trumbull by appointment at Col. Jedediah Huntington's, where they dined together, and the general that evening resumed his route to New York, going down to New London by land.

The inhabitants also had an opportunity of seeing Lafayette, Steuben. Pulaski, and other distinguished foreigners in our service. There was some who long remembered the appearance of the noble Lafayette, as he passed through the place on his way to Newport. He had been there before, and needed no guide; his aides and a small body-guard were with him, and he rode up to the door of his friend, Col. Jedediah Huntington, in a quick gallop. He wore a blue military coat. but no vest and no stockings; his boots being short, his leg was consequently left bare for a considerable space below the knee. The speed with which he was traveling and the great heat of the weather were sufficient excuses for this negligence. He took some refreshment and hastened forward

At another period he passed through with a detachment of two thousand men under his command, and encamped them for one night upon the plain. In the morning, before their departure, he invited Mr Strong, the pastor of the place, to pray with them, which he did, the troops being arranged in three sides of a hollow square.

Nearly fifty years afterwards, August 21, 1824, the venerable Lafayette again passed through Norwich Some old people, who remembered him, embraced him and wept: the general wept also.

At one time during the war the Duke de Lauzun's regiment of hussars was quartered in Lebanon, ten miles from Norwich. Col. Jedediah Huntington invited the officers to visit him, and prepared a handsome entertainment for them. They made a superb appearance as they drove into town, being young, tall, vivacious men, with handsome faces and a noble air, mounted upon horses bravely caparisoned. The two Dillons, brothers, one a major and the other a captain in the regiment, were particularly distinguished for their fine forms and expressive features. One or both of these Dillons suffered death from the guillotine during the French Revolution.

Lauzun was one of the most accomplished but unprincipled noblemen of his time. He was celebrated for his handsome person, his liberality, wit, bravery, but more than all for his profligacy. He was born in 1747, inherited great wealth and high titles, and spent all his early years in alternate scenes of dissipation and traveling. He engaged in no public enterprise till he came to America and took part in the Revolutionary contest. The motives which actuated this voluptuous nobleman to this undertaking are not understood, very probably the thirst for adventure and personal friendship for Lafayette. He had run the career of pleasure to such an extent that he was perhaps willing to pause awhile and restore the energy of his satiated taste. Certain it is that he embarked in the cause of the Americans with ardor, bore privations with good temper, and made himself very popular by his hilarity and generous expenditure.

After Lauzun returned to Europe he became intimate with Talleyrand, and accompanied him on a mission to England in 1792, where one of his familiar associates was the Prince of Wales, afterwards George IV. On the death of his uncle, the Duke de Biron, he succeeded to the title, quarreled with the court, and became a partisan of the Duke of Orleans. Afterwards he served against the Vendeans, but being accused of secretly favoring them, was condemned, and executed the last day of the year 1793. Such was the future stormy career of this celebrated nobleman, who as already mentioned, in the midst of friends and subordinates, enjoyed the banquet made for him by Colonel Huntington. After dinner the whole party went out into the yard in front of the house and made the air ring with huzzas for liberty. Numerous loungers had gathered around the fence to get a sight of these interesting foreigners, with whom they conversed in very good English, and exhorted to live free or die for liberty.

As to the effects of the Revolution on Norwich, Miss Caulkins says:

After recovering from the first stunning blow of the Revolution, the inhabitants of Norwich were not only alert in turning their attention to various industrial pursuits, but engaged also in the brilliant chance game of privateering. The war, therefore, while it exhausted the strength and resources of neighboring towns that lay exposed upon the seacoast, acted like a spur to the enterprise of Norwich. New London, at the mouth of the river, was depressed in all her interests, kept in continual alarm, and finally, by the blazing torch of the enemy, almost swept from the face of the earth; but Norwich, securely seated at the head of the river, defended by her hills and nourished by her valleys, planting and reaping without fear of invasion or loss, not only built new shops and dwelling-houses, and engaged with spirit and success in a variety of new manufactures, but entered into ship-building, and boldly sent out her vessels to bring in spoils from the ocean.

In 1781 and 1782 the town was overflowing with merchandise, both tropical and European. New mercantile firms were established—Daniel Rodman, Samuel Woodbridge, Lynde McCurdy, and others—and lavish varieties of fancy texture, as well as the substantial products of almost every climate, were offered for sale. The shelves and counters of the fashionable class of shops displayed such articles as superfine broadcloths, men's silk hose, India silks, blonde lace, Damascus silks, taffetas, satins, Persians, and velvets, gauzes, and chintzes These goods were mostly obtained by successful privateering.

Another class of merchandise, generally of a cheaper kind, and not dealt in by honorable traders, but covertly offered for sale in various places or distributed by pedlers, was obtained by secret and unlawful intercourse with the enemy.

The coast of Connecticut being entirely girdled by Long Island and New York, and the British and Tories having these wholly under their control, it was very difficult to prevent the secret intercourse and traffic of the two parties through the Sound In the latter years of the war especially, a corrupt, underhand, smuggling trade prevailed to a great extent, which was emboldened by the indifference or connivance of the local authorities, and stimulated by the readiness of people to purchase cheap goods without asking from whence they came. Remittances for these goods must be made in coin, therefore they were sold only for cash, which, finding its way back to the enemy's lines, impoverished the country. Thus the traffic operated against agriculture and manufactures, against honest labor and lawful trade. Moreover, it nullified the laws and brought them into contempt.

Against this illicit traffic a strong association was formed at Norwich in July, 1782. The company bound themselves by solemn pledges of life, fortune and honor to support the civil authority; to hold no intercourse, social or mercantile, with persons detected in evading the laws; to furnish men and boats for keeping watch in suspected places, and to search out and break up all deposits of smuggled goods; such goods to be seized, sold, and the avails devoted to charitable purposes

The vigorous manner in which this company began to carry out their principles caused great commotion in the ranks of the guilty parties. Suspected persons suddenly disappeared: sales were postponed; goods which before had been openly exposed withdrew into cellars and meal-chests, or were concealed in barns under the hay, and in hollow trees, thickets, and ravines. Several seizures were made during the season, but the treaty of peace soon put an end to this clandestine traffic, and the association had but a brief existence. Its object, however, was creditable to the patriotism and efficiency of the inhabitants, and a list of the signers gives us the names of sixty-eight prominent men who were on the stage of life at the close of the war, and all within the bounds of the present town.

The following is a list of the members of the Association against Illicit Trade: Samuel Abbott, Elijah Backus, Ephriam Bill, Jonathan Boardman, John M. Breed, Shubael Breed, Samuel Capron, Eliphalet Carew, Joseph Carew, Simeon Carew, Thomas Coit, William Coit, John Crary, Jacob De Witt, Michael Dumont, Thomas Fanning, Jabez Fitch, Joseph Gale, Joseph Peck, Andrew Perkins, Jabez Perkins, Jabez Perkins, Jr , Joseph Perkins, Joseph Perkins, Jr., Erastus Perkins, Hezekiah Perkins, Levi Perkins, Daniel Rodman, Theophilus Rogers, Zabdiel Rogers, Ransford Rose, Joseph Howland, Andrew Huntington, Eliphalet Huntington, Jonathan Huntington, Joshua Huntington, Levi Huntington, Simeon Huntington, William Hubbard, Russell Hubbard & Son, Ebenezer Jones, Joshua Lathrop, Rufus Lathrop, Christopher Leffingwell, Benajah Leffingwell, Jonathan Lester, Elihu Marven, John McCall, Lynde McCurdy, Seth Miner, Thomas Mumford, Nathaniel Niles, Robert Niles, Timothy Parker, Asa Peabody, Nathaniel P Peabody, Andre Tracy, Jr., Mundator Tracy, Samuel Tracy, Asa Waterman, Samuel Wheat, Joseph Whitmarsh, Benajah Williams, Joseph Williams, Jacob Witter,

Dudley Woodbridge, Samuel Woodbridge, Alexander Youngs.

In January, 1781, the inhabitants were divided into forty classes to raise forty soldiers, which was their quota for the Continental army; and again into twenty classes for a State quota to serve at Horseneck and elsewhere. A list of persons in each class was made out, and each taxed in due proportion for the pay and fitting out of one recruit, whom they were to procure; two shirts, two pairs of woolen stockings, shoes, and mittens were requisite for every soldier; arms and uniforms were furnished by the State or country. Each soldier's family was in charge of a committee to see that they were supplied with the necessaries of life, for which the soldier's wages to a certain amount were pledged. The whole number of classes this year to produce clothing was sixty-six. In 1782 only thirty-three classes were required.

In 1783, instructions were given to the representatives to use their influence with the Assembly to obtain a remonstrance against the five years' pay granted by Congress to the officers of the Continental army. The manifesto of the town on this subject was fiery, dictatorial, and extravagant. A few paragraphs will show in strong relief the characteristics of the people—jealous of their rights, quick to take alarm and sensitively watchful over their cherished liberties:

Where is the free son of America that ever had it in idea when adopting the Articles of Confederation to have pensions bestowed on those characters (if any such there be) whose virtue could not hold them in service without such rewards over and above the contract which first engaged them?
For a free people, just rising out of a threatening slavery into free shining prospects of a most glorious peace and independence, now to be taxed without their consent to support and maintain a large number of gentlemen as pensioners in a time of universal peace is, in our view, unconstitutional and directly in opposition to the sentiment of the States at large, and was one great spoke in the wheel which moved at first our late struggle with our imperious and tyrannical foes.

Further instructions were given at the same time to the representatives to urge upon the Assembly the necessity of keeping a watchful eye upon the proceedings of Congress, to see that they did not exceed the powers vested in them, and to appoint a committee at every session to take into consideration the journals of Congress, and approve or disapprove, applaud or censure the conduct of the delegates.

Norwich has the questionable distinction of being the birthplace of Benedict Arnold. We quote from Dr. Hurd's History:

The painful task now devolves upon the writer to chronicle some of the leading events in the career of one whose baseness has been unequaled since the day that his prototype betrayed his master for thirty pieces of silver. The faithful historian will be just to all; hence no attempt will be made to remove the stain which has long tarnished the history of this fair section of country. Benedict Arnold descended from an honorable Rhode Island family, where one of his ancestors, bearing the same name, held the office of Governor for fifteen years. Two brothers of this family, Benedict and Oliver,

removed from Newport to Norwich in 1730   The elder Benedict, the father
of the traitor, soon became engaged in business, and not long after his arrival
in Norwich, married Mrs Hannah King, whose maiden name was Lathrop.
Benedict, the subject of this sketch, was born in Norwich, January 3, 1741.
Early in life he was apprenticed to Dr. Lathrop, a druggist in Norwich, with
whom he remained during his minority   He subsequently embarked in the
same business in New Haven, and while there became the captain of a company of militia   After the battle at Lexington he made a hasty march to
Cambridge at the head of his company, and volunteered his services to the
Massachusetts Committee of Safety   With the rank of colonel in the Continental army, he joined Ethan Allen and assisted in the taking of Ticonderoga in May, 1775   In the expedition against Quebec, in the autumn and
winter of 1775, he took a leading part.   Having been wounded at Quebec
and at Saratoga, his disability was of a character to render him unfit for
active field service, and he was consequently, by Washington, placed in
command at Philadelphia after the place had been evacuated by Clinton
in 1778   He was at this date a major-general in the Continental army.   While
in Philadelphia he lived in a style far above his means, and his haughty
and overbearing manner involved him in a quarrel with the authorities of
Pennsylvania, who accused him before Congress of abusing his official position and misusing the public funds.   After a long delay he was tried by a
court-martial and was sentenced to be reprimanded by the commander-in-
chief.   Washington performed this disagreeable task as delicately as possible,
but did not lose his confidence in Arnold   While in Philadelphia, Arnold
married the daughter of Judge Shippen, a Tory, which connection enabled
him to communicate without discovery with the British officers.   He opened
a correspondence with Sir Henry Clinton, signing himself "Gustavus."

   In the meantime, at his earnest solicitation, he was appointed by Washington, in August, 1780, to the command of West Point, the strongest and
most important fortress in America.   He sought this command with the
deliberate intention of betraying the post into the hands of the enemy   In
compliance with a previous understanding, Arnold and Major André met at
Haverstraw, on the west bank of the Hudson, September 22, 1780, and arrangements were fully completed for an easy conquest of the fortress by the
English.

   On his return to the city of New York, André was arrested as a spy at
Tarrytown, was tried by court-martial, and sentenced to be executed by hanging.   He suffered the penalty of his crime October 2, 1780.   When it became
known to Arnold that André had been arrested, he fled from West Point in
the utmost haste, and in his flight took passage to New York City in the
"Vulture," a British sloop-of-war   He was immediately made a brigadier-
general in the British service, which rank he preserved throughout the war
as a stipulated reward for his treachery.

   Norwich had one signer of the Declaration of Independence, and many
men famous in Revolutionary times.   General Jedediah Huntington was a
leader in the country.

   He was born, August 4, 1743, in Norwich, where he was prepared for a
collegiate course, and graduated at Harvard College with distinguished honor
in the class of 1763   The high social rank of his family is indicated by the
order of his name on the college catalogue, it being the second in the list of
his class, above that of John Quincy.   The master's degree was also conferred on him by Yale College in 1770.   After leaving college he became asso-

ciated with his father in commercial pursuits, and was engaged in this business when the Revolutionary cloud began to lower, and he soon became noted as a Son of Liberty, and an active captain of the militia. The bursting of the storm found him ready, and just one week from the firing of the first shot at Lexington he reported at Cambridge with a regiment under his command, and was detailed to occupy Dorchester Heights. After the evacuation of Boston by the British he marched with his army to New York, and entertained the commander-in-chief on the way at Norwich.

During the year 1776 he was at New York, Kingsbridge, Northcastle. Sidmun's Bridge, and other posts. In April of that year he assisted in repulsing the British at Danbury, Connecticut, assailing the enemy's rear, and effecting a junction with his fellow-townsman, Benedict Arnold.

In July he joined General Putnam at Peekskill with all the Continental troops which he could collect, and in the following September was ordered to join the main army near Philadelphia, where he remained at headquarters, at Worcester, Whippin, Whitemarsh, Gulph Hills, etc. In November, on receiving information of the enemy's movement upon Red Bank, he was detached with his brigade, among other troops, to its relief, but Cornwallis had anticipated them. Having shared the hardships of his companions in arms at Valley Forge through the winter of 1777-78, he, together with Colonel Wigglesworth, was in March appointed by the commander-in-chief "to aid General McDougal in inquiring into the loss of Forts Montgomery and Clinton, in the State of New York, and into the conduct of the principal officers commanding these posts." In May he was ordered with his brigade to the North river, and was stationed successively at Camp Reading, Highlands, Neilson's Point, etc. In July he was a member of the court-martial which tried Gen. Charles Lee for misconduct at the battle of Monmouth, and in September he sat upon the court of inquiry to whom was referred the case of Major André. In December, 1780, his was the only Connecticut brigade that remained in the service. On the 10th of May, 1783, at a meeting of officers, he was appointed one of a committee of four to draft a plan of organization, which resulted in their reporting on the 13th the constitution of the famous Society of the Cincinnati. On the 24th of June, Washington writes that the army was "reduced to a competent garrison for West Point; Patterson, Huntington and Greaton being the only brigadiers now left with it, besides the adjutant-general." General Huntington was also one of the founders of West Point Academy.

On returning from the army he resumed business in his native town, and was successively chosen sheriff of the county, State treasurer, and delegate to the State Convention which adopted the Constitution of the United States. In 1789 he was appointed by President Washington collector of customs at New London, then the port of entry for Eastern Connecticut and Connecticut River, which office he retained under four administrations, and resigned shortly before his death.

Following the Revolutionary War, Norwich developed the West India

Trade, but after the War of 1812 came more and more to develop its water power and went into manufacturing. For the Civil War it furnished over 1,400 men.

The following letters, sent for the 200th anniversary of the settlement of Norwich, give a vivid picture of life in Norwich in the early part of the nineteenth century.

(From Rev. Erastus Wentworth, Missionary to China.)

Foo-Chow, China, June 15th, 1859.

Gentlemen:—After looking forward with pleasurable anticipations for many years to personal participation in the celebration of the bi-centennial birthday of Norwich, the place associated with my earliest and dearest recollections, I find myself, on the eve of that event, sixteen thousand miles away, and effectually debarred from the intellectual treats and social festivities promised by that occasion. It will be some compensation for the disappointment, and no slight gratification, if I may be allowed to contribute by letter a trifle to the interest of the family gathering. It will not, at such a time, be deemed egotistical in me to state that I spent the first eighteen years of my life in Norwich; that my father was born there seventy years, and my grandfather a hundred and seven years ago; and that my family name, by no means an obscure one, in either English or American history, has stood on the town records for one hundred and eighty, out of the two hundred years you are now assembled to commemorate.

Old Norwich!—Who that has been a denizen of the place, especially in early youth, can ever forget its winding valleys and rugged hills; its stony pastures and green meadows, enameled with violets, and buttercups, and daisies, and goldened with cowslips and dandelions; its spreading elms and sycamores; its clear streams, alternating with babbling shallows and cool depths, overhung with willows and alders, and the favorite haunts of roach, trout and pickerel; its gray precipices and romantic falls; its striking contrasts of village quiet and country seat retirement, with commercial activity and city bustle. All these can never be forgotten. With me, neither the pellucid St. Lawrence or noble Mississippi, nor those floating seas of alluvion, mightiest of the brotherhood of rivers in the northern hemisphere, the Missouri and Yang-tse-keang, have ever served to obliterate, or even to dim the images of the Yantic, Shetucket and Thames. The mammoth tree growths of the prairie bottoms of the west, or the giant banians that greet my vision as I write, have never overshadowed the memory of Norwich sycamores and elms. The billowy seas of granitic elevations which stand, a wall of azure, about the valley of the Min, and roll away in endless undulations over the entire surface of the Fo-ke-en province, are not so charming to me as the hills of New England. Society changes, but these natural features remain, and impress themselves upon the minds of successive generations. My earliest recollections of Norwich antedate steamboats and railroads, canals and telegraphs, temperance and anti-slavery. The Yantic, was Backus's iron works; the Falls, Hubbard's paper mills; Greenville, pastures on the banks of the Shetucket, in which curious antiquarians sought for the pile of stones that marked the grave of Miantinomoh. The first and second Congregational were the only edifices really worth the name of churches; and I remember a Christmas pilgrimage on foot from Bean Hill to the Landing to hear the little organ, the only one in town, in the little wooden Episcopal church, that preceded the present elegant structure. Elder Sterry, Baptist, had a little wooden chapel at the Landing, where, as one of his sons said to me in our schoolboy days, "He preached for nothing and furnished his own meeting house." Elder Bentley had a little church on the wharf bridge, which took a fancy to go to sea in the great freshet of 1815. Court house and jail were up town, and the stocks and whipping post still maintained their position at the corner of the old court house I have seen a woman in jail for debt and heard my grandmother tell of the last woman who was taken to the whipping post, and how the people laughed at the sheriff for merely going through the forms of the law, actually flogging the fair culprit "with a tow string."

In my youth, Strong and Goddard were at the head of the bar, and gentle parson Paddock, earnest parson Mitchell, and the solemn parson Strong, occupied the sacred desk. Through life, I have counted it no small privilege to have received the first rudiments of education in Norwich. I mean those initial lessons which preceded colleges and schools, and the rudimental training of pedagogues Smith, Bliss, and Lester, of cruel memory. A child is educated by all those with whom he comes in contact, and the personal excellences, defects and peculiarities of his earliest acquaintances become his models and measuring rods for all the rest of mankind. Bonaparte said, "The world is governed by nicknames"; and the nicknames of a community are a surer index of the character of the wearers than cognomens of illustrious descent or appellations bestowed by godfathers and godmothers. While a few of the nicknames which still cling to the memory of men long since passed from the stage of action, recall eccentricities, peculiarities, and in some instances the meannesses with which our humanity is afflicted, the great majority of them revive the memory of nobleness and excellences worthy of remembrance and worthy of imitation. It is more blessed to be surrounded by good men than great men, by examples of worth than displays of wealth. My memory retains a whole gallery of daguerreotypes of those whom I loved or hated, reverenced or despized, in the days of my youth. I would like to pay a passing tribute of respect to those who for eminent virtues commanded my most unqualified regard. I can only mention Parsons Strong and Austin, Judges Spalding, Shipman and Hude, Erastus Huntington, James Stedman, and Deacon Charles Lathrop, all of whom have gone to the land from which there is no return. It would be easy to extend the list, but my limits will not allow. I cannot refrain from a passing tribute to the memory of two of my schoolmates, recently deceased—Reverend Z. H. Mansfield and Honorable Thomas L. Harris. I would like also to extend the compliments of the occasion to my old Norwich schoolmates, John T. Wait, J. G. Lamb, Rev. William Havens, Hon. H. P. Haven, Huntingtons, Tracys, and others whom I may not here enumerate. I was in Shanghai last year, and on a rude wooden slab at the head of a recent grave I read, "Charles Bailey, Norwich, Connecticut," son of the old uptown jail keeper, and seaman on one of our ships of war. In what part of the world do not the bones of the sons and daughters of Norwich repose! Black-eyed "Tom Leffingwell" lies with his father at the bottom of the ocean, and curly-headed "Bob Lee," slain by Comanches on the plains of Texas, while Ceylon embalms, with the fragrance of Paradise, the remains and memories of Harriet Joanna and Charlotte H. Lathrop. How brief the space over which the life of any one individual extends in the history of our beloved town. Perhaps not a single soul survives that saw its last centennial. Will any single soul live to connect this centennial with that of 1959? This occasion should not pass away without providing enduring monuments of itself for the use of coming generations. If the idea has not already occurred, as I presume it has, I would suggest the erection of a centennial hall of Norwich granite, fire proof, if possible, to contain a museum of town and State relics, and mementos of the past, of our fathers, of the

Indian tribes, and the present generation. In this way, 1859 may shake hands
with 1959, especially if sealed boxes and coffers containing the sayings and
doings, speeches and sentiments of this day, are secured there to be opened
only on the occasion of the next centennial Books, records, portraits, &c.,
would find their appropriate place there, and it would become the favorite
resort of all those who reverence the past and desire to deduce from it useful
lessons for the future.

With a sigh for the Norwich that was, a greeting to the Norwich that is,
and a hail of welcome for the Norwich that is to be, I remain, gentlemen,

ERASTUS WENTWORTH.

(From Hon. Charles Miner, of Wilkes-Barre, Pennsylvania.)

Wilkes-Barre, July 17, 1859.

Gentlemen of the Committee:—Your invitation to be present at the com-
memoration of the two hundredth anniversary of the settlement of Norwich
was received by last evening's mail. You are pleased to add: "Should you,
however, be unable to attend, will you favor us with a letter containing any
facts of interest in your possession in relation to the town or its inhabitants?"

I beg to return my most respectful acknowledgements I can scarcely
conceive anything left in life that would afford me so much pleasure. But
the feebleness of near eighty years admonishes me that, not only is the
visit hopeless, but that if I have anything to say, it should not be a moment
delayed.

Affection for Norwich is entwined with every fiber of my heart. Having
emigrated to Pennsylvania while yet a boy, my time of observation is limited;
and my scene of observation, to little more than the old town or round the
square, fitted, rather, to amuse the grandchildren, than impart instruction or
pleasure to the present generation.

Born February 1, 1780; peace proclaimed 1784; consciousness of memory
is first awakened to the shouts of triumph and the thundering of cannon, at
the old Peck house (then, I think, doubtingly), kept by Mr. Trott (a fiery old
patriot). I mention this as connecting me with the Revolutionary period,
and to say, the drum, the fife, military display, was the pervading fashion
Almost all the older men had served in the French war. Ticonderoga was
yet a familiar theme Nearly the whole of the (then) present generation,
moved by a common impulse, had been down to Boston. The talk was of
Lexington and Bunker Hill General Putnam is recorded as having stopped
his plow in mid-furrow and started. So had it been in Norwich. An anecdote
often told me shows the universal enthusiasm. My father, a house carpenter,
and his journeyman, dropped their tools on the alarm. As the broad-axe
rang, the journeyman said, "That is my death knell!" Breathing the common
spirit, he hied away cheerfully, but returned no more.

My father was on Dorchester heights, as orderly sergeant waiting on
Mr Huntington, afterwards general Jed He used to relate that going the
rounds, or reconnoitering, the British opened fire upon them from Boston
While ever and anon the balls would scatter the earth over them, General
Huntington moved as unconcernedly as if at home in his own meadow.

At the close of the war half the men on the square wore the title of captain. Starting on the south side of the green going down the road east,
taking them in order, there were Captain Bela Peck, Captain Carew, Captain
Nevins, Captain Simeon Huntington, all in sight and nearly adjoining. The
British in possession of New York; the Sound and a hundred miles of the
coast of Connecticut being subject to their invasion, Norwich may be said

to have slept on their arms, liable every minute to be called out. Horse Neck, Rye, Seabrook, New London, were familiar to every man of them. To be sure, as I listened to their war stories, always with interest, sometimes with awe, occasionally with a smile, for they remembered the jokes of the camp, I do not recollect an imputation upon a single man present or absent as wanting in courage or patriotism. It is a pleasure to record anew the assurance that Norwich did its whole duty.

The plays of the boys were battles with the regulars. The charge—the ambuscade—the retreat—"The regulars are coming!"—"The regulars are coming!" Then the rally and renewed charge. Their songs:

> "Don't you hear your gen'ral say,
> Strike your tents and march away."

But to the schools. The old brick school house at the bottom of the lane, below the spacious new jail, knew no recess. Among the earliest teachers within my recollection was Charles White, a young gentleman from Philadelphia, handsome and accomplished. Of his erudition I was too young to judge, but popular he certainly was among the ladies. Newcomb Kinney awakened a high degree of emulation, especially in writing. A sampler was pasted up before six or seven scholars, near the ceiling, on fine paper, on a double arch sustained by Corinthian columns, the upper corners of each sheet bearing a neatly painted quill, with the motto, "Vive la Plume." Within each half arch, near the upper part, in fine hand, a poetical quotation, as suggested by fancy, probably from Hannah Moore's "Search After Happiness," then highly popular. Beneath, in larger hand, successive lines in beautiful penmanship, filling the whole. The Piece painted in water colors—the pride of mothers—master and scholars.

Mr. Hunt, a graduate of Yale, followed. Mr. Macdonald succeeded, and then Mr. Baldwin became the preceptor. The obedience fair—teachers capable and attentive. Discipline preserved without undue severity. Plasant were our school hours. But school is let out. Boyish sports abound,

> "Some chase the rolling circle's speed,
> Or urge the flying ball."

In winter the plain offered a capital opportunity for a trial of skill and courage. Sides were chosen. Each party built a semi-circular fort of vast snow balls, eight or ten rods apart. When the snow was soft and would adhere, all hands were summoned to the work. A line of balls as big as could be rolled was laid in a crescent; outside that another as large. Then with skids a row on the top—then a third row large as could be raised on the submit to crown the work, making a formidable breastwork. Lockers were cut out in the inside to hold great quantities of balls made ready for action. When both sides were prepared, a proclamation was made, and then came the "tug of war." The sport was manly and exciting.

Other plays were popular—most I have seen elsewhere—"Thornuary," nowhere else. Here the uptown and downtown boys were sometimes pitted against each other. There was among us an active fellow named Choate, "Jabe Choate" we called him. Not of Norwich, he was a down-easter. From Boston, I understood. In our little circle he was a Coriolanus, for "When he moved he moved like an engine"—and like our modern crinoline-clad ladies, swept all before him, yet a favorite, for he was brave and clever. I have wondered, if not the father, was he not, probably, the uncle of Rufus, the present idol of Boston?

Mrs. Gildon kept a school a few rods below the plain for small children—

she had a son Charles growing up to early manhood. I do not know their fate. The name is rare. The good school mistress has often been brought to mind when reading Poe:

"If hungry Gildon drew his venal quill,
I wish the man a dinner and sit still."

But Pope's shaft was no dishonor. So eminent an archer stooped to no ignoble game.

Hark! The whole town is in commotion. A company of strolling players have taken possession of the lower part of the court house, and it is converted into a commodious theater. Where slept our puritan thunder! The tragedy of George Barnwell drew many a tear, soon wiped away in smiles by the shrewd follies of Tony Lumpkin, in "The mistakes of a night." The grown-up beaux of Norwich, especially those who had visited New York and got their cue, were in high glee. I have a good mind to name seven or eight. The comic singer of the company displayed some tact—had a good voice, and sang, "Ye Bucks! have att—ye all." (Never having seen the song nor heard it since, I pretend to give only the sound.)

Instead of the pit, the critic's place, the roaring boys had taken possession of seats far back and high up in the amphitheater, and when he came with all the proper accompaniments of tone and gesture to

"D——n ye! I know ye—
Ye are of att ye all,"

It was a signal for a general cheer! And brought down the house with an "Encore."

Several new songs were introduced by the company, and among them the many year popular "A rose tree in full bearing," which Miss Mary Nevins, the fairest rose that ever bloomed, used so sweetly to sing. Passingly—the songs of the period were mainly the hunting songs borrowed from England—

"Bright Phoebus has mounted his chariot of day,
With hounds and horns each jovial morn when Bucks a hunting go."

But these were giving place to the more modern sailor songs of Dibdin. My intimate and ever dear friend, Gerard Carpenter, used to sing admirably—

"To England when with fav'ring gale,
Our gallant ship up channel steered."

What noise is that, which makes the whole green ring again? Mr. Jones, the cooper, residing next to Captain Peck's on the south side of the plain, with his adz and double-driver, holding it in the middle and playing it rapidly on the empty barrel, as he drives the hoop, sounds a reveille to the whole neighborhood, regular as the strains of Memnon.

A truce to these trifles. The Sabbath has come. Everybody went to meeting. It was the pleasantest day of the week. Manning is ringing the bell. Let us note the carriages as they come up. The chaise drawn by that bay, so sleek, he looks as if he had been varnished for the occasion, brings Captain Thomas Fanning and (pardon me, I was then a young man) his two charming daughters. I think he was the attendant of our uptown meeting who came from the nearest landing. That stout black in a wider chaise brings Lady Lathrop, attended by Mr. Huntley and his daughter, a pretty little girl of eight or nine, whoes poetic genius and sweet moral strains have shed a ray of glory, not only on her native town (as Lydia Huntley and Mrs. Sigourney), but over her whole country, and rendered her name a praise throughout the republic of letters Here drives up a double carriage, plain, yet neat. Those spanking bays are full of spirit, they move admirably. They bring the family of Mr. Thomas Lathrop, who occupies the very handsome white mansion on the southern hill bounding the square.

(Note.—Manning has ceased ringing, and is tolling the bell. Mr. Strong will be here presently He comes with his lady, drawn in a plain chaise by a stalwart brown horse, the favorite of many years.)

Observe, as Mr. Strong ascends the steps numbers press round and hand him scraps of paper. They are received as matters of course—six—seven— or eight, as it may happen. We shall see directly what they are. While the psalm is being sung, which precedes the morning prayer, the minister's head is inclined forward as if reading. He rises and reads the slips of paper—one after another, running in this wise: "Z. D being about to take a voyage to sea, asks the prayers of this congregation that he may be preserved and restored in safety to his family."

Several desiring to return thanks for mercies received. I dare not allow myself to state the variety of petitions, relating to ordinary circumstances in life It would seem to have required long habit and a retentive memory to recall them, yet Mr. Strong would touch each, briefly, but appropriately, and with such earnestness and pathos, especially when praying for the sick, as by sympathy swelling in every breast, and made the petition, the prayer indeed of the whole congregation

Of the church music. Roberts, the famed singing master, had been among the voices, and infused his own impassioned soul into the school. The front seats of the gallery—treble—counter—tenor—bass—were all full. "O, that I could describe them to you!" In the pews below were numbers who had caught the inspiration Nay, more, Colonel Zack was among them, himself an organ full of melody and power. Did "The Pilgrims' Song" close the worship of the day, an hundred voices attuned to perfect harmony, joining to swell the strain.

> "Rise, my soul, and stretch thy wings,
> To seats prepared above,"

The whole congregation rose to their feet—entranced.

The life of Mr Strong, the revered, the beloved, his precepts and example, however imperfectly regarded, have been with me through life. His influence for good is yet felt among hundreds of the descendants of emigrants from Norwich.

Monday has come and brings its usual busy throng and varying scenes

Two printing presses were in full operation, that of Mr. Trumbull had been long established, and his paper was always read with pleasure. Busy memory, clinging to everything with child-like delight that relates to Norwich, calls up the anecdote. The fashion of the day was for advertisers to close—"Inquire of the printer." The wit of the town was dying. Mr Trumbull bent over him with his wonted kindness and asked softly, "Do you know me, Mr. Barney?" "If I don't I'll inquire of the printer" Samuel Trumbull, the oldest son, was a young man of a good deal of reading, and of ready wit. He wrote several essays under the head of "From the desk of Ben Hesden." The hint and the name of the essays—"From the desk of poor Robert the Scribe," I am sure I owed him. William Pitt Turner was the Aesop of the press, the poet and satirist, and lashed the foibles of the Bucks of "Att ye all," with no stinted measures Young Trumbull, following in his wake, satirized the younger brood, and I came in, fairly enough, for my share, more proud of the notice than angry at the rod.

The recent member of the Assembly, Gurdon Trumbull, esq., it was my good fortune to form an intimate acuqaintance with, in 1839, at Hartford. (I hope he is with you.) I cannot deny myself the pleasure of adding, that I was subsequently indebted to his partial kindness for several favors done so considerately, and performed in a manner so delicate, as to demand a renewed and more open acknowledgement; mentioned to show how naturally and kindly the heart of the Norwich boys "warm to the tartan."

The other printing office was nearly opposite that of Mr. Trumbull's, close to Collier's brass foundry The paper published by Bushnell & Hubbard. Mr. Bushnell was afterwards appointed a purser in the navy, and died of yellow fever at sea I mention the fact to add, that when in the West Indies, several gentlemen were inscribing the names of wives and sweethearts in a mountain grove—Bushnell declined to do so, lest the thoughtless should desecrate the place by obscene additions, but he wrote a poem addressed to his wife, it is said, of remarkable delicacy and beauty. A man of genius and learning, few were more capable. Has Norwich preserved it?

The rival houses are at war. Small pox has broken out. There is not a moment to delay Two establishments for inoculation start into existence on the Thames, in Mohegan Dr Tracy and Dr ——— preside over that at famed Massapeage Dr. Marvin and Dr. Jewett over the other, at Adgate's. These were prominent points of interest in their day.

> "Friendship to every willing mind,
> Opens a heavenly treasure,"

From lady voices I still recollect as soothing to my feverish and restless spirits. In the main the remembrances were agreeable, redolent rather of frolic and fun than of pain.

Do you see those strange looking men hawking pictures, in broken English? They are French emigrants, thus seeking to win their bread, exiled from home by the revolution, now raging. Listen: "Louis de 16—madame Elizabet" They have pictures of the guillotine, with their executioner, and the head of the king, all ghastly, streaming with blood, which he is holding up Look again—what have they? Beautiful pictures, but so nearly immodest as to make me hesitate to bring to recollection, what was then familiar to everyone in open market. The revolutionists, to cast odium on the royal family, represented an intimacy between the infamous Duke of Orleans and the queen, Maria Antoinette. The polished verse runs thus:

> "Avaunt, rash boy, while I my homage pay,
> Where joys are bred and nestling cupids play."

Another—a sans-cullote sailor, with a red cap and shirt— emblems of liberty and courage. A French man-of-war has captured an English frigate. The sailor sings:

> "When e'er on French decks shouts of victory roar,
> Your crown's a red cap, and tyrants are no more."

The winter assemblys demand special notice. Managed with such scrupulous care, every lady who might desire it was not only invited, but provided with a carriage and agreeable escort. Mr. Lathrop had built an assembly room, with a spring floor, on purpose. There was no formal supper, but tea, coffee, tongue, ham, cakes, and every suitable refreshment in abundance. Collier, with his inimitable violin—Manning with his drum Order, the most perfect, never for a moment, that I saw or heard of, infringed. Contra dances occupied the evening. The stately minuet had gone out of fashion, and the cotillion not yet introduced The lines of a modern song express what was universally felt:

> "The reign of pleasure is restored,
>   Of ease and gay delight."

In their apology, if one be needed, let me add, Washington would have approved, and entered the pleasant occurrence in his journal. The musicians knew their hour, and at 1 the assembly closed. They did not escape the keen edge of satire. The poem of W. P. Turner could be repeated by many emigrants to the Susquehanna, forty years afterward.

The hum of industry is everywhere. Norwich uptown is a bee hive. Every mechanic, and there are few idlers, with every workman, was employed manufacturing hats, tin ware, pewter ware, boots, shoes, harness, coaches, chaises, small carriages, for slaves to draw the children—everything. The West Indies demanded many cargoes. Such was the prosperity of the country around, nearly every farmer would have his chaise. The fact that there were two coach and chaise manufactories in the town fully employed, showing the activity of one branch, will indicate that of others.

Take your stand on the school house steps, and suppose a circulating panorama. Note that drove of horses dashing by. The driver is Lazelle, from the north. Twenty of the sixty are Canadian They are for Howland's brig. Jesse Brown will see they are cared for a week, and send them to New London, when the brig is nearly ready to sail A dozen vessels are preparing at the landing for cargoes, and droves are daily arriving.

Such a demand for horses must create a demand for sires. Luckily, here they pass, each with his groom. That superlatively beautiful bright bay, fourteen hands high, is "Figure," belonging to Haynes, of New London. That monster dark bay following, seventeen hands high, is "Nimrod." The dark chestnut is a favorite Rhode Island pacer. "Count Pulaski" is the last.

What mean those two covered carts with tinkling bells? They are our market. The single one, a daily, from Bean Hill. The double is from Windham, a weekly, but loaded with mutton that would tempt an epicure

Note that dashing gentleman and lady on the fine pair of blacks. They have a foreign air. It is Jackson Brown, supposed to be an agent of the British commissary department They do not stop to have the gate opened, but bound over it as if in pursuit of a fox.

Note that splendid chariot, with servants in livery as out riders. There are two or three pairs of elegant English hunters. They are bounding away in pursuit of pleasure, to the Bozrah great pond, a fishing. It is the establishment of the noted English Lord Bellisais.

Hark! There is music in the court house. An Irish gentleman of titled family, whom the war has embarrassed, with a noble spirit of independence, rather than sit down in indigence and despair, has opened a dancing school, not only here, but in Bozrah, Franklin, and two or three neighboring towns. Ordering his time that he may attend here twice a week, and visit the others once a week, not a minute was wasted.

John C. De Vereaux; that is the gentleman in the open carriage with the hump-backed musician, Howell, by his side. The general prosperity rendered it easy for parents, all round to country, to gratify their children. Would anyone ask—"How did he succeed?" Enquire who, forty years afterwards, was the wealthiest merchant in Utica, and president of the United States branch bank? The answer would be John C. De Vereaux.

Evening approaches—where are the stages? O! here they come up in style to Brown's hotel That from the east, the horses all in a foam, has come all the way from Providence, since morning!

The one from the west is from Hartford What is that under the Hartford stage? It looks like the fore-top-sail of a brig. Lo! it is a sail cloth, so nailed under the bottom as to hang loose and bring down salmon from Hartford, without being bruised, for Brown, like Lathrop, had a pride in setting a capital table, and it is lucky today, as President Adams has just arrived.

Party, the twin sister of freedom, then prevailed, as it ever will, and the morning salute, confidently expected, was marred, as we black cockade federal boys charged, by the intentional failure of our opponents to—"keep their powder dry."

Training day, especially regimental, or brigade, was a great event. The Matross company, commanded then by Roger Griswold, afterwards by Captain Bailey paraded in front of the meeting house; the light infantry, in uniform, near the old Perit house; the common militia company, facing west, on the lower point of the green; companies from the neighboring towns arriving, where the adjutant assigned them their position From an early hour the plain was thronged; the line formed—mark that fine soldier-like bearing man on that stately war steed—that is General Marvin. Accompanied by his aides, in splendid uniform and nodding plumes, music filling the air, the line is passed, the salute given, the column formed; the march is down east and round the square. The band and the brigade of drums and fifes under Collier and Manning, alternating. Passing Governor Huntington's, the salute is repeated, and could not be paid to a worthier, unless Washington were himself present. The windows all round are sparkling with beauty, and we little boys were thrice happy to trudge round on foot, hear the music, and see the pageant.

A marked incident in the exhibition was the assemblage of all Mohegans and Betty Uncas, their queen, with brooms, baskets, blankets, papooses without number. They lined the fence from Eli Lord's to Lathrop's The military dismissed, still the plain is thronged. Here is Captain Griswold, with a dozen of the most active fellows, playing a game of cricket. Yonder is Captain Slocum and a party intent on a wrestling match. Each right hand hold of his opponent's right shoulder. It was a game of skill, rather than of strength—the trip and twitch—the steel trap quickness. The Zouaves could hardly beat them. An adroitness that would seem unrivaled Let the unpracticed, however strong and courageous, beware how he enters the lists, or he will find himself sprawling in mid-air, seeking a resting place on the green turf, flat on his back, amid the cheers of hundreds.

Look! There is a daring fellow climbing up to the ball on the steeple. It makes one's head dizzy to gaze on him. That is John Post—fearless and spry as a wild cat.

Hark! The sounds of revelry proceed from Lathrop's chamber windows. The officers have dined, and prefer punch, such as Lathrop only could make, to indifferent wine The choicest Antigua, loaf sugar by the pail full, lemons, oranges, limes. Merrier fellows, within tempered mirth, never wore cockade or feather.

So with "sports that wrinkled care derides," closed the day The half is not said, yet I feel that I am abusing your patience. When did a native ever begin to talk of Norwich and know when to stop?

From the time the Jewish maidens hung their harps on the willows, and sang of Jerusalem, to the lay of the sweetest modern minstrel, "My native land" has been a cherished theme. Thus with singular pleasure have I run over the scenes of my childhood, and endeavored to sketch, with rapid pencil,

"Norwich uptown, the plain, and round the square," as memory recalls it, seventy years ago, which, with cordial good wishes, is respectfully submitted

From Miss Caulkins we quote the following account of the industrial growth of Norwich:

The enterprise of the inhabitants in the line of manufactures has been frequently mentioned in the course of this history. But the subject will here be retraced, and various undertakings chronicled in their order, as far as data for this purpose have been obtained.

Iron works were established in the parish of New Concord in 1750 by Captain Joshua Abell and Nehemiah Huntington. They contracted with Robert Martin, of Preston, to become the overseer or operator of their works, engaging him to make and refine iron into anconie, to be done workmanlike, and binding themselves to remunerate him with 100 lbs. of bar iron for every 200 anconies he shall make.

Elijah Backus commenced a similar work at Yantic nearly at the same time. These are supposed to have been the first forges erected in New London county. They manufactured blooming and bar iron for anchors, mills, and other uses.

In the year 1766, cutlery as a business made its appearance, and various implements of husbandry, that had before been imported, were manufactured in the town. The Backus iron works obtained great repute, and during the Revolutionary war all kinds of iron work necessary for domestic use, and various instruments of warfare, were made and repaired at the Yantic forges. The same year a pottery for the manufacture of stone ware was established at Bean Hill, which continued in operation far into the present century, seldom, however, employing more than four or five hands.

The making of linseed oil was commenced at Bean Hill in 1748 by Hezekiah Huntington. In October, 1778, Elijah and Simon Lathrop gave notice in the "New London Gazette" that they had erected an oil-mill at Norwich Falls, and were ready to exchange a gallon of oil for a bushel of well-cleaned flaxseed. In 1786, Silas Goodell set up another oil-mill near the falls. This was probably the same that in 1791 was owned by Joshua Huntington. Lathrop's mill was destroyed by fire November 9, 1788. The loss was estimated at $1,500, a considerable quantity of oil and flaxseed being consumed. It was rebuilt the next year. In these mills flaxseed was used to produce the best kind of oil, but inferior kinds of seed were often substituted. The three mills together produced about 9,000 gallons annually, which sold at three or four shillings per gallon.

During the Revolutionary war, iron wire and cards were made at the falls, under the supervision of Nathaniel Niles. Edmund Darrow established at the same period a nailery, which continued in operation nearly to the close of the century.

The business of weaving stockings was begun in 1766, under the patronage of Christopher Leffingwell. William Russell, an Englishman, was the first operator. For many years it was a small concern, limited to two or three looms. But in 1791, Leffingwell had nine looms in operation, producing annually from 1,200 to 5,000 pair of hose, and employing in the manufacture worsted, cotton, linen, and silk. The silk hose ranged in value from 12s. to 20s per pair. Gloves and purses were also woven at these mills, the whole business employing only five operatives. At a later period the business was continued successively by Louis Baral, Leonard Beattie, and William

Coxe. all foreigners, and still later by Jeremiah Griffing, a native of New London.

Stocking-looms were not only employed here, but constructed Before 1790, looms that had been made in Norwich were set up at Hartford and Poughkeepsie—two at each place. Looms were in operation at that period in New Haven, Litchfield, and Wallingford, and it is not improbable that these also were made in Norwich. To accommodate his stocking-looms and other utilitarian projects, Colonel Leffingwell built, after 1780, the range of shops called Leffingwell's row. In 1785, wool-cards were made by James Lincoln in Leffingwell's row.

Paper.—In the early manufacture of this article in Norwich, Christopher Leffingwell stands pre-eminent. His mill upon the Yantic, near No-man's Acre, was erected in 1766. This was the first paper-mill in Connecticut. Leffingwell's mill in a short period produced various kinds of paper for wrapping, writing, printing, cartridges, and sheathing. The quantity annually turned out was estimated at 1,300 reams, the prices varying from 4s. 6d. to 45s per ream Ten or twelve hands were employed. At the outset of this undertaking, a small bounty was granted by the government, to continue for three years. It was not renewed After the year 1790, Andrew Huntington engaged in the manufacture of paper, and erected a new mill upon the Yantic, either on the site of Leffingwell's oil mill, or very near it. Ebenezer Bushnell was for a few years his partner.

Chocolate Mills.—Christopher Leffingwell was first in this department also. His chocolate-mill was in operation in 1770. Another was erected in 1779 by Simon Lathrop. They were both moved by water-wheels, and could be tended each by a single workman The chocolate made was of the best quality and the quantity produced was estimated at 4,000 and 5,000 pounds annually. It sold in considerable quantities at 14d. per lb.; retailers asked 18d.

Clocks and Watches.—This business was commenced in 1773 by Thomas Harland, a mechanician of great skill and efficiency. His watches were pronounced equal to the best English importations. In 1790 he had ten or twelve hands in constant employ, and it was stated that he made annually two hundred watches and forty clocks. His price for silver watches varied from £4 10s. to £7 10s. As at that period watches were far from being common, and it was even a mark of distinction to wear one. Mr. Harland's establishment was a center of the business for a considerable extent of country. Barzillai Davidson, 1775, N. Shipman, Sen , 1789, Eliphaz Hart on the Green by the court house, and Judah Hart at the Landing, in 1812, though not probably to any great extent manufacturers, were yet "workers in gold and silver," and offered for sale handsome assortments of jewelry and time-keepers.

Between the years 1773 and 1780, four fulling-mills with clothiers' shops and dye-houses went into operation—one in the parish of New Concord, one in Franklin, a third at the falls, "near Starr and Leffingwell's works adjoining the Paper Mill," and a fourth on Bean Hill.

In a statement made of the industrial pursuits of the town in 1791, in addition to several establishments already noticed, are the following items: Two nailleries, or machines for making nails, employing eight or ten hands. Fifteen blacksmiths, who make annually about 50 dozen scythes, 150 dozen hoes. 50 dozen axes, and other implements for domestic and agricultural use. Three distilleries. Two tobacconists. Two braziers, and a bell-foundry.

Cotton.—In 1790, Dr. Joshua Lathrop established a cotton factory in the town-plot. He began with five jennys, one carding-machine, and six looms.

This machinery was afterward increased, and a great variety of goods manufactured, probably to the amount of 2,000 yards per year while the project was
continued In 1793, the firm was Lathrop & Eells. The following is one of
their advertisements, March 19, 1793:

> Lathrop & Eells have just finished a variety of Cotton Goods, consisting of Royal Ribs,
> Ribdelures, Ribdurants, Ribdenims, Ribbets, Zebrays, Satinetts, Satin-Stripes, Satin Cords,
> Thicksetts, Corduroys, Stockinetts, Dimotys, Feathered Stripes, Birds-Eye, Denims, Jeans,
> Jeanetts, Fustians, Bed Tickings that will hold feathers.
> The above Goods are well finished, and for durability undoubtedly superior to European
> manufactured Gentlemen, merchants, and others, who feel disposed to encourage home
> manufactures, are invited to call and see for themselves, and may be assured they shall be
> supplied as low as they can furnish themselves from any quarter.

This business could not be made remunerative, and after a trial of eight
or ten years was discontinued.

The manufacturing spirit had been called into exercise to meet the ex-
igencies of the Revolution. Before that time the country had been dependent
upon England for all articles that required combination, capital and machinery for their production. When the intercourse with Europe was renewed,
and commerce again brought the lavish results of foreign labor to our shores,
the crude manufactures of the country declined, most of the imported articles
being cheaper than those made at home. The spinningwheel and loom still
kept their place in families, fulling-mills and carding-machines were patron-
ized, ropes and nails were made; but as a general fact, the workshops and
factories of the country were in Europe. The spirit and enterprise of Norwich
had been wholly diverted into the channels of commerce, and future prosperity seemed to be expected only from the ocean.

At the commencement of the present century, the paper-mill at the falls
was the only establishment of any kind in Norwich worthy the name of a
factory.

The Norwich Falls district, now so busy, bustling, and crowded with
inhabitants, was then a wild, secluded hamlet, consisting of two or three
old mills and the dwelling house of Elijah Lathrop. Beautiful was the place
fur all the purposes of romance and lonely meditation—renowned for echoes
and evergreens, the chosen resort of moonlight parties, curious travelers, and
wandering lovers—but the Genius of Manufacture had only marked it for
his own; he had not yet erected his standard and marshaled his legions in
the valley In relation to manufactures, and in some respects it would apply
to the whole business of the town, this was a period when old things passed
away, and all things became new.

Hemp.—In the year 1803, Nathaniel Howland & Co erected a building
at the falls for hemp-spinning Mr Timothy Lester was engaged as machinist; the best of hatcheled hemp was used, and the warps were spun by a
recently improved machine Looms were soon introduced, duck and canvas
offered for sale in 1804.

The Howlands appear to have been stimulated to this undertaking by a
visit from Mr. Baxter, a noted hemp-spinner from Great Britain, who was
engaged in introducing the manufacture of cordage and duck, by machinery,
into this country He came to Norwich to survey the situation, and was
satisfied with its facilities, but was not himself sufficiently encouraged to
remain and conduct the experiment.

Colonel Howland's mill kept on its way for a few years, employing from
twelve to twenty hands, and throwing a considerable quantity of hempen
cloth into the market. He was encouraged in his operations by the government Proffers were made to him to supply the navy upon cash advances,

and a small bounty was granted by Congress for every bolt of duck produced. But the business could not withstand the pressure of the times, and
was overwhelmed in the general wreck of mercantile affairs, connected with
the embargo and other commercial restrictions of that period.

Manufactures at the Falls.—The rise of manufactures after this period
is intimately connected with several prominent individuals who removed
to the place from other parts of New England—Calvin Goddard in 1807, William Williams in 1809, William C. Gilman in 1816, William P. Greene in
1824. These all in their first coming to Norwich were connected with the
manufacturing interest at the Falls. Though not natives, they are wholly
identified with the place, and by their enterprise and their liberal and enlightened course as citizens, have contributed largely to its prosperity.

Mr. Goddard was a lawyer and statesman, connected with the manufacturing interest only as a proprietor and patron. Having projected an establishment at the Falls, he purchased in 1800 the old Lathrop house and mill-
seats of that district, the saw, grist and oil mills, with the ancient distillery
and tannery lots and privileges, and formed a partnership with William
Williams, Sen., of Stonington, and his sons (Wm., Jr., and Thos. W.),
under the firm of William Williams, Jr., & Co., one of the younger partners
taking the principal agency in the business. In common parlance, however,
the firm was Goddard & Williams.

This company set up the machinery necessary for grinding and bolting
"Virginia wheat and Southern corn"; imported their grain, and obtained
William Weller, an experienced miller from Pennsylvania, for their foreman.
They kept two or three sloops in their employ, sailing to Norfolk, Petersburg, Fredericksburg, and Richmond. In 1812, they fitted out the schooner
"Ann and Mary," and sent her to Cadiz with flour. This was their only
foreign adventure. The war with Great Britain throwing obstacles in the
way of trade with the South, the flour business was broken up, and the company turned their attention to the manufacture of cotton cloth.

The Howland duck factory was changed by this company into a cotton
mill, which began to run in December, 1813, preceding by a few months the
cotton factories at Jewett City and Bozrahville. They began with carding
and spinning, giving out the yarn from the factory to be woven in hand-looms,
but after three or four years the power-loom was introduced, and they turned
out mattresses, nankeens and shirtings in a completed state.

This mill, though of small account in comparison with the gigantic operations of modern times, and by no means a money-making experiment to the
proprietors, merits notice as one of the first cotton mills successfully established in the country, and as leading the way to undertakings in the same
line far more extensive and important. The title of this company was changed
in 1819 to Williams Manufacturing Co. It continued only a few years in
active operation, but its affairs were not settled and the partnership dissolved
till 1833, when they sold out to Amos Cobb and others, agents of the Norwich
and New York Manufacturing Co.

In May, 1813, William C. Gilman, "late of Boston," purchased a privilege
at the Falls of Goddard & Williams, and in connection with the Iron and
Nail Co. established a nailery, which went immediately into successful operation. In this factory the nails were cut by a newly-invented machine with
great rapidity, and while the novelty lasted, visitors were attracted to the
falls to hear the clink of the machine and view the continual dropping of the
nails.

The next company that was formed commenced business with promising
aspects upon a large capital. This was the Thames Manufacturing Com-

pany, incorporated in June, 1823   It consisted of six members, viz , Wm.
C. Gilman, Samuel, Henry and John Hubbard, Wm. P. and Benjamin Greene.
Five of these partners were Boston men, to whose favorable notice the water
privileges that lay unemployed at the falls had been forcibly presented by
Mr. Gilman.

This company purchased the naillery and several other water privileges
at the falls, and erected a large cotton factory, preparing for a business of
considerable extent and value   The corner-stone of the building was laid
with interesting ceremonies, and Judge Goddard delivered an address, welcoming the new company to that secluded seat   William P. Greene, one of
the Boston partners, became a resident in Norwich, and for a few years Mr.
Greene and William C Gilman transacted together the business of the company. Mr Greene then resigned, and Mr. Gilman was afterward the sole
agent of the concern.

The Quinebaug Company, for the manufacture of cotton and woolen
goods, was chartered in 1826   The mill erected by this company on the
Shetucket river was purchased by the Thames Company before it went into
operation, and was considered by its new owners as the most valuable of
their possessions. This mill was the beginning of Greenville.

The Thames Company purchased likewise the mill at Bozrahville, built
by Messrs. Dodge and Hyde in 1815, and in their best days had the three
mills—in Bozrah, at the Falls, and on the Shetucket—in successful operation.

Another company with similar objects and expectations, called the Norwich & New York Manufacturing Co , was incorporated in 1829   Some of
the partners belonged also to the Thames Company, but they were distinct
concerns. To this new incorporation the Thames Company sold the Falls
mill   This company purchased also the mills and machinery of Huntington
and Backus on Bean Hill.

In 1833, a large cotton mill, two paper mills, an iron foundry, nail factory and rolling mill were reported in successful operation at the Falls.

But this prosperity was of short duration. Both the Thames Company
and the Norwich and New York Company became involved in the mercantile
disasters that so widely affected the business of the country, and went down
in the financial crash of 1837. The two mills belonging to the Thames Company were purchased nominally by Mr. Gilman—the mortgages nearly equal-
ing the value—and conveyed by him to other parties: the Quinebaug mill to
Mr Caliph, and the mill at Bozrah to Mr. James Boorman of New York. A
period of great depression and stagnation of business ensued.

Fresh undertakings of a more enduring nature arose out of these reverses.
Two new companies were formed under the auspices of Wm. P. Greene—the
Shetucket Company and the Norwich Falls Company. Both went into pros-
perous operation between 1838 and 1842.

The Shetucket Company purchased the misnamed Quinebaug mill on
the Shetucket. The building was burnt down in May, 1842, and the present
mill, of far greater capacity, standing on the same spot, is called the Shetucket mill. It is the great cotton mill of Greeneville.

The Falls Company purchased the mill at the Falls, which had formerly
belonged to the Thames Company. This has since been enlarged to almost
three times its former size and power, and has kept on from that time to
the present, without any suspension of its acitvity or check to its prosperity.

These companies were established by Mr. Greene, chiefly upon his own
credit, and were kept while he lived under his management and direction.
The business has been gradually extending, and for several years each mill
has had 15,000 spindles in operation.

The manufacture of paper at the Falls has of late years been connected exclusively with the name of Hubbard   Amos H. Hubbard entered into the business in 1818.   Paper was at that time made in the old way; not by machinery, but by hand, sheet by sheet.   Mr. Hubbard very soon furnished his establishment with the modern improvements that diminish the amount of manual labor required   In 1830 he successfully introduced Fourdrinier's machine into his factory   This was the first paper-making machine used in Norwich

The brothers Russell and A H. Hubbard were in partnership in this business for twenty years, but dissolved in 1857   They had two mills—the old wooden building erected by Messrs. Huntington and Bushnell in 1790, and a modern one, built of brick and stone, both of which, with various lots, tenements and water-privileges, were sold by A. H. Hubbard in 1860 to the Falls Company.   Mr. Hubbard then removed his establishment to Greene-ville on the Shetucket.

According to the census of 1860, the great cotton mill at the Falls employed 125 males and 375 females; producing annually six and a half million yards, valued at $450,000

The Falls Company has from time to time purchased the various privileges in its neighborhood, and now controls nearly the whole water power at Yantic Falls, and at the old paper-mill above the falls   The nailleries, foundries, pistol factories, the paper, flour and oil mills, have all disappeared, their seats and privileges passed over to this company, and their various crafts transferred to other localities   In this valley of the roaring waters, in 1860, Cotton reigned the sole and undisputed king.

This sovereignty has been recently invaded by the occupation of a hitherto unemployed mill-seat near the railroad bridge.   Here a large brick building, erected by C A Converse in 1864, furnishes accommodation to a grist mill and the thriving cork factory of Messrs. J. H. Adams and James E. Learned

The cork-cutting business is one of the specialties of Norwich, this being the place where an ingenious machine for transforming sheets of bark into well-shaped corks was invented and set in operation, and where the business is prosecuted with a success that promises to make it one of the permanent industrial pursuits of the town.

The corks used in this country had been mostly imported from Europe, where they were all made by hand.   Vast quantities were required to supply the market, and a machine that would abridge the labor and cheapen the article was a desideratum.   This furnished by the machines invented and patented by the brothers Crocker, of Norwich.

William R. Crocker, the first inventor, after many experiments, brought his machine into successful operation, and procured a patent for it, bearing the date of October 30, 1855   This machine produced from twenty to thirty finished corks per minute, turning them out in better condition than those made by hand   In 1859 the inventor went to Europe, accompanied by a younger brother, to dispose of rights in his patent   On their return in the steamer Hungarian, they both perished in the wreck of that vessel on the coast of Newfoundland, February 15, 1860.

But the business of cork-cutting commenced by them in Norwich, has been continued by Messrs. Barnes & Spalding, the proprietors of their patented machine

Another machine of different structure, but for the same purpose, was invented by a third brother, John D. Crocker, and patented in 1862.   This patent is the one employed in the factory at Yantic Falls.

Uncas Mill.—In the early part of the century, at Bean Hill, in a turn of the Yantic and on both sides of it, we find a grist mill of ancient date, the fulling mill and carding machine of Erastus Huntington and Eber Backus, the stone ware factory of Armstrong & Wentworth, and the machine shop of James Burnham. Mr. Burnham constructed carding machines, looms, and other kinds of machinery, but died on the island of Madeira in 1813.

The establishment of Huntington & Backus was purchased in 1828 for $9,000, by a company organized that year and called the Norwich Manufacturing Company. This company established a woolen mill on the premises, since known as the Uncas Woolen Mill. The ownership has since been several times changed. In 1859, F. B. Loomis, proprietor, the census reported the annual produce 150,000 yards of doeskins, valued at $175,000. Mr. Loomis sold out in 1860 to Wm. Elting & Company. The Elting Woolen Company has since been organized, with a capital of $150,000.

Another woolen mill, at a lower point on the river in Norwich-Town, was run for several years by Peter Lanman. The site is now occupied by a mill of larger size and a group of neat tenements built by A T. Sturtevant.

Timothy Green, of New London, who was then printer to the colony, opened a printing office in this town early in 1773, and in company with Judah Paddock Spooner, his brother-in-law, prosecuted the business until 1778. At that time the people of Vermont had just completed an independent State government, although they were in the asserted limits of the State of New York. Upon invitation of the government of the new State, Green and Spooner removed their office from Norwich to Westminster, Vermont, where they established the first newspaper printed in that State, under the title of "The Vermont Gazette, or Green Mountain Post Boy." The motto of this paper was indicative of the spirit of the times:

"Pliant as reeds where streams of Freedom glide;
Firm as the hills to stem oppression's tide."

The other printing office established in this town in 1773 was by a company consisting of Alexander and James Robertson, who had emigrated from Scotland to Albany, and from Albany came here, and John Trumbull, a native of Charlestown, Mass. In the month of October, in that year, they issued the first number of "The Norwich Packet, and the Connecticut, Massachusetts, New Hampshire and Rhode Island Weekly Advertiser." "The Packet" was continued by this company until 1776, when the Robertsons, being Tories, were obliged to leave Norwich. They went to New York, and on the conclusion of the war took up their residence in the British province of Nova Scotia. Trumbull conducted the paper alone till his death in 1802. The title was then changed to the "Connecticut Centinel," and printed but a short time for the benefit of his widow, Lucy Trumbull.

On the 29th of November, 1791, Ebenezer Bushnell issued the first number of "The Weekly Register." In the issue of that paper of the 7th of June following, Bushnell announces that he has associated with himself Thomas Hubbard "In the Printing and Stocking Weaving business." This firm continued until October 1, 1793, when Bushnell retired, leaving the business in the hands of Hubbard. In 1796, the office was removed from the

Town to the Landing, then called Chelsea Landing, and the title of the paper changed to "The Chelsea Courier" On the 20th of November, 1805, Thomas Hubbard retired from the paper, leaving as his successor his son, Russell Hubbard, who soon changed the title to "The Norwich Courier," by which title it has ever since been known. In February, 1817, Mr Hubbard formed a co-partnership with Theophilus R. Marvin, and under the firm of Hubbard & Marvin, the "Courier" was continued until 1819, when Marvin removed to Boston In April, 1822, the paper was purchased by Thomas Robinson and John Dunham, and continued by them until March, 1825, when it passed into the hands of Dunham, who retained it until 1842. In September, 1842, Dorson E. Sykes assumed the control of the "Courier," and retained it until March, 1859, when he retired, and the paper was purchased by George B. Smith. In the August following, Smith's affairs were involved in bankruptcy, and the "Courier" was managed by his trustee.

In 1803, John Sterry and Epaphras Porter issued the "True Republican," of which Consider Sterry was editor, and continued the same for about four years

In January, 1829, the "Norwich Republican," by Boardman & Faulkner, made its appearance It soon passed into the possession of Adams & Faulkner; they retiring, it was published till April, 1835, by Melza Gardner. At that time it was purchased by Marcus B. Young, its political character was changed, and L. F. S. Foster assumed the editorial charge. The "Republican" was discontinued in 1838.

In May, 1835, James Holbrook issued the first number of "The Norwich Aurora." He continued its publication till June, 1838, when Gad S. Gilbert purchased it and conducted it till March 24, 1841. From that time until August 8, 1844, it was successively conducted by William Trench and Trench & Conklin.

From 1843 till 1848, "The Norwich News" was published by William Faulkner.

Of the other newspapers which have had an ephemeral existence in Norwich, the following may be mentioned:

"The Canal of Intelligence," by Levi Huntington Young, commenced in 1826 "The Norwich Spectator," by Park Benjamin and M. B. Young, commenced in November, 1829; revived in 1842 by John G. Cooley, and continued for a short time "The Norwich Free Press," by M. B. Young, February, 1830. "The Norwich Gleaner," by B. F. Taylor, in 1845. "The American Patriot," by the friends of General Taylor, 1848 "The Norwich Tribune," by Charles B. Platt and Edmund C. Stedman, in 1852 "The Norwich Examiner," by Andrew Stark, in 1853. "The State Guard," by the same publisher, in 1855.

In August, 1859, the press of Norwich was as follows: "The Norwich Courier." published by the trustee of the estate of George B. Smith. "The Norwich Aurora," by John W. Stedman. "The Morning Bulletin," by Manning. Perry & Co., established in December, 1858. "The Weekly Reveille," by Walter S. Robinson (suspended). "The Free Academy Journal," published by the students of the Free Academy.

For the Norwich Jubilee in 1859 the following article was prepared by Ashbel Woodward, M.D., president of the Connecticut Medical Society:

Of the physicians generally of the American colonial period, little is now known. As a class they were unambitious to participate in the deliberations of public councils, or take the lead in advocacy of popular measures, so that only few names became prominently identified with local or general history. Many devoted to the duties of their calling the undivided energies of long and laborious lives, reaping only a scanty pecuniary recompense for the present, and no place at all in the grateful recollection of posterity. Respected and loved by cotemporaries with that respect and love which strikes such deep root and blossoms so beautifully in the chamber of suffering, they were too frequently forgotten when their own generation had passed away.

No systematic account of the early physicians of Norwich has hitherto been given. The materials for such a work are fragmentary, and collectible only with great difficulty and labor. Public records afford little assistance, while the scanty aid they might otherwise render is still further impaired by the general absence of the titular appendage from the names. Another peculiar circumstance of the present case cuts us off from one source of information, which, in many localities, is highly fruitful. During the early colonial period (as has almost always been true in the infancy of nations) the professions of theology and medicine frequently met in the hands of the same incumbent, the cure of fleshly ills being esteemed an incidental concomitant to the cure of the more dangerous maladies of the soul. These clerical physicians, exercising their double vocation amid a people justly celebrated for affectionate attachment to the expounders of the divine oracles, were often minutely remembered and described for after time, in virtue of the popularity of the priestly office. But in Norwich, the two professions were kept entirely distinct from the beginning, so that ecclesiastical writings in all the multifarious forms they then assumed, are wholly unavailing to the biographer of her early doctors.

Of some of these, almost the only memorials are the precarious inscriptions of moss-grown and neglected tomb stones. Others whose days of toil and nights of watching in alleviation of human pain were otherwise forgotten, still live in the hearts of their descendants, and in traditions floating downward in the same current with their blood. The names of several enter largely into cotemporary records, whereby we may infer the prominency of their influence, though the various proceedings they shared in, and the trusts imposed upon them must here be passed in silence as too commonplace for exhumation in our brief tribute to their memory. Yet it should not be forgotten that, as a citizen, one may be pre-eminently useful, and still perform few actions whose recital either interests the attention or quickens the pulses of postrity.

The medical profession in ancient Norwich was more than respectable, was distinguished. As practitioners and teachers, several of its members had few superiors on the continent. As reformers of abuses and fearless advocates of salutary though unpopular changes, they held pace in the foremost rank. In the year 1763, prior to any attempts at medical organization elsewhere on the continent, Theophilus Rogers, with ten others, petitioned the colonial legislature for the charter of a medical society. This movement, made in advance of the age, was negatived in the lower house. Still it indicates one of the most important crises in the history of the profession. The presentation of that unpretending Norwich memorial was the initiative step in a series of efforts which have since resulted in the permanent establish-ment of many flourishing State associations, and within a few years of the national society, which has contributed in a high degree to purify the ranks, elevate the aims and make a real unit and fraternity of the profession in America. In the attempt alluded to, it was not the object of the petitioners to secure any immunities or exclusive privileges for themselves, but to pro-tect the health of the community by additional securities. At that time there was no authority in the state legally qualified to confer degrees in a way to discriminate the man of solid acquirements from the ignorant pretender. Many, without either study or natural aptitude for the exercise of the calling, by shameless vauntings imposed upon a credulous populace, and by assuming their title brought discredit upon honorable men. Our Norwich memorialists wished to strike at the root of this disgusting and rampant empiricism. To shut down the flood gates through which their ranks were inundated by incessant streams of ignorance and charlatanry, to establish a standard of education by making a respectable amount of attainments an indispensable requisite to the acquirement of the title, they asked for the appointment of a committee legally authorized to examine and approve candidates, if found qualified. Thus Norwich, though unsuccessful in her first attempt, was the pioneer in the cause of American medical organization.

As early as 1785, when there were but two medical schools in the whole country, Drs. Philip Turner and Philemon Tracy issued proposals for the delivery of a series of lectures to students on "Anatomy, Physic, Surgery, &c." As additional incentives to induce the "rising sons of Æsculapius" to improve the facilities proffered to them, they tendered the free use of a "complete library of ancient and modern authors," together with "the advantage of being present at capital operations, dissections, &c." The prospectus goes on to state, "Every attention will be paid by the subscribers to render their lectures both useful and pleasing, their constant endeavors will be to facilitate the instruction, direct with propriety the judgment, correct the errors, and increase the knowledge of the pupils in their study."

Another interesting point in the history of Norwich was the long and bitter controversy between the advocates and opponents of inoculation for small pox. At that period this disease was the most formidable scourge of humanity. There was no place of refuge from its ravages, nor means of mitigating the fury of its poison. Inoculation having been practiced with suc-cess in Turkey, had recently, through Cotton Mather's influence, been intro-duced into the colonies Commencing in 1760, for many years several of the more prominent physicians of Norwich struggled assiduously to establish the practice against the inveterate prejudices of the community. A popular vote authorized pest houses, passed after the lapse of a third of a century, shows how obstinately the public contended before yielding to the superior argu-ments of the profession.

The following account of Lincoln's visit to Norwich, prepared by Mr. Francis J. Leavens, has never been published:

One morning in March, 1860, I was standing with three or four of my classmates of the junior class in the Norwich Free Academy when one of the older boys of the senior class came up to us and said, "Boys, if you want to hear a regular western stump speaker, go down to the Town Hall tomorrow night." "Who is he?" we asked, and the answer came, "A man from Illinois named Lincoln, and they say he is great."

A man from Illinois named Lincoln meant nothing to us. We had never heard of him, but we had heard of stump speakers, though we had not seen or heard one. Buffalo Bill's Wild West Show had not begun to make its annual visits to New England, and none of us had been west. "Stump speaker" sounded good to us and we decided to go.

Boys are not apt to be late at anything likely to interest them, and four of us were among the earliest arrivals at the Town Hall. We seated ourselves on the front bench, and when Mr. Lincoln took his place behind the bar that ran along the front of the platform he was not six feet away from us. In fact, when he leaned forward and swung his long arms in gestures it seemed as if we were in danger of being struck.

I will not attempt to describe his appearance; that has been done by many who were intimately associated with him, while artists and sculptors have faithfully portrayed his form and features. I remember that he was dressed in a black suit and that he wore a wide turnover collar and a black silk sailor's tie, both of which were striking and unusual in this region.

At this distance of time I cannot undertake to report what he said, but we four boys sat on that front bench till ten o'clock, our eyes never leaving him, notwithstanding we had to keep our heads raised at an uncomfortable angle as he towered above us. I have heard many famous orators since, but never have I listened to one with such rapt attention, and no one ever made such a deep and lasting impression upon me.

His speech was richly illustrated with stories and was frequently interrupted by vigorous applause. One story I remember was about a young farmer who in some way opened up a nest of large and active black snakes, and as Mr. Lincoln described the terrible combat that followed his body swayed, his long black arms and his fingers were writhing and twisting till even the Laocoon itself was not more realistic. That picture is as plain in my mind's eye today as it was fifty-seven years ago.

The next morning two of us on our way to school reached a cross street and looking down saw two other boys approaching who had also been there. In an instant, without a word, four pairs of arms were writhing in the air and any stranger who had seen us would have surely thought us crazy. All that day, and for many days, those writhing arms were the countersign, and "snakes" the password for the boys who had heard Abraham Lincoln.

After the meeting was over a large number of citizens adjourned to the Wauregan House where Mr. Lincoln was entertained, and had a most enjoyable after meeting with refreshments and more stories from Lincoln. About midnight, as it was known that Mr. Lincoln had to leave for New Haven at six the next morning, the company reluctantly broke up and bid him good night.

There was left, however, one gentleman, Mr. John F. Trumbull, of Stonington, who had come some distance to attend the meeting and was spending the night at the Wauregan. Mr. Trumbull had a very considerable reputation as a political speaker and story teller, and after the others were gone he and Mr. Lincoln sat and talked for an hour in the parlor and then went up stairs together. When they reached the door of Mr Lincoln's room something interesting was unfinished, so Trumbull went in and they talked on till the town clock in the Baptist church nearby struck two, when Mr. Trumbull apologized and went out. Mr Lincoln had removed his coat, vest, collar and shoes and was rapidly preparing for bed when there was a knock on the door and there stood Trumbull. "Oh!" he said, "I have just thought of one more story I must tell you." And they sat down beside each other on the bed and swapped stories for three-quarters of an hour more. It was nearly three when the final adjournment took place, and Lincoln was called at five to make ready for New Haven.

This latter part of the story was told me years after by my friend, Col. H. H. Osgood, who was a member of Governor Buckingham's military staff. The Connecticut State elections at that time were held in April, and Lincoln's speeches in our State were part of the campaign for Governor Buckingham's re-election.

It was through the efforts of Colonel Osgood that Mr. Lincoln came to Norwich. He had heard of the wonderful impression made by the Cooper Union speech, and, as Hartford was one of his first assignments in New England, Colonel Osgood went there and heard him, then, procuring an introduction, invited him to come to Norwich. Mr. Lincoln was pleased with the invitation, but said that it was absolutely impossible, as his route had been carefully laid out and there was no possibility of taking on another engagement. At that time railroad trains were very few and very slow, but Colonel Osgood was familiar with time tables, and he looked over the speaker's schedules and at last said, "You can do it. You can come between Providence and New Haven." "Young man," said Mr. Lincoln, "demonstrate it." So thoroughly did Colonel Osgood demonstrate it that Mr. Lincoln promised to come, and he did come. I shall never cease to be thankful that I was permitted to see and hear him.

Once again I saw him It was in the spring of 1864, during my vacation from college. I was making a visit with relatives in Baltimore and they took me for a day in Washington. We went, of course, to the White House, and while looking about in the East Room, which is always open to the public, the usher stationed in the hall came to me and said, "The President is just coming in from the War Department. If you would like to see him, just come and stand in the doorway of this room" It was at a dark period of the war, heavy fighting had been going on for several days, but without any satisfactory results. The porch door was opened and the President came in, but oh! how changed. His step was slow, his shoulders were bent, and his face told most plainly the story of the great burden that he was carrying. He started slowly up the broad staircase, when a small man who had been standing in the hall ran quickly up behind him and spoke to him as he reached the broad stair, introducing himself as a professor in some fresh water college in Ohio I could not hear much that he said, and I think that the President heard none of it, for he stood there very quiet, but with such a faraway weary look in his burdened face that I felt his thoughts were with the boys in blue and the boys in gray fighting the battle of the Wilderness, while the little man's tongue babbled on. Why is it that there are some ———— who will rush in where angels dare not tread?

A year later, during my spring vacation, the dreadful news of the assassination came one Saturday morning. It was like a national stroke of paralysis, men stopped whatever they were doing and little business was resumed that day. That Saturday night, three other members of the Broadway Church, with myself, having secured several pieces of black cloth, by working till midnight, managed to drape the interior of the church, and Sunday morning Rev. John P Gulliver, who always rose to a great occasion, preached a masterful discourse on the text, "It must needs be that offences come, but woe unto him by whom the offence cometh."*

The following data covering the founders of Norwich were compiled from various sources for the quarter-millenial celebration in 1909:

1. Deacon Thomas Adgate, 1649. Born about 1620; died 1707. One of

those appointed to "dignify the pues." His house was on north end of Lowthrope Meadows.

2. Robert Allyn, 1659. "First constable in the Town." Died 1683, at Allyn's Point

3. Wm. Backus, 1659. Died soon after the settlement. His home-lot was next north of Thomas Bliss, from Washington street to the river. Father of Stephen Backus

4. Lieut. Wm. Backus, Jr., 1659. He styled himself "yeoman," but was known successively as sergeant, ensign and lieutenant.

5. John Baldwin, 1659. Constable in 1696. Ancestor of Judge Simeon E. Baldwin of New Haven. Home-lot on West Town street, near the river.

6. Deacon Thomas Bingham, 1659. Born 1642; died 1730. Home-lot on West Town street above Thomas Waterman and extending to the river.

7. John Birchard, 1659. Born 1628; died 1702. First schoolmaster. Home-lot on West Town street, opposite Samuel and William Hyde.

8 Thomas Bliss, 1659. Died 1688. Home-lot on Washington street adjoining John Reynolds. His house is still standing.

9. Morgan Bowers, 1659. Home-lot on West Town street adjoining John Post.

10. John Bradford, 1659. Son of Governor Bradford, of Plymouth. Townsman in 1671. Home-lot on East Town street west of Huntington lane

11. Deacon Hugh Caulkins, 1659. Born 1600; died 1690. One of the most useful men of his time. Home-lot on West Town street.

1. John Caulkins, 1659. Born 1634; died 1703. Active in town affairs. Home-lot on West Town street

13 Richard Edgerton, 1659. Died in 1692. Townsman and constable.

14 Rev James Fitch, 1659 Born 1622; died 1702. First pastor of First Church in Norwich; held the office fifty-six years Called by Cotton Mather, "the holy, acute and learned Mr. Fitch." Home-lot from Simon Huntington to the river.

15. John Gager, 1659. Died 1703. Constable in 1674 and 1688 He was son of William Gager, "a right godly man and skillful chyrurgeon."

16 Lieut Francis Griswold, 1659 Born 1622; died 1671 Represented the town in the General Court in eleven sessions. Home-lot on West Town street.

17. Christopher Huntington, 1659. First townsman Died 1691. One of the most useful of the pioneers Home-lot on Washington street corner of East Town street.

18 Deacon Simon Huntington, 1659 Born 1629; died 1706 Townsman in 1690 and 1696. Home-lot on south side of East Town street west of Lieut. Thomas Tracy.

19. Samuel Hyde, 1659. Died 1677. Home-lot on north side of West Town street above the rocks.

20. Wm. Hyde. 1659. Died 1682. Townsman in 1673 and 1679. Home-'ot on West Town street.

21. Thomas Howard, 1659. Slain at the Narragansett fort fight in 1675 Home-lot on north side of West Town street below Bean Hill church.

22. Lieut Thomas Leffingwell Born about 1622, died after 1714 Home-lot located on the corner of the present Washington street and Harland road. House occupied by D. H. Torosian in 1909. Leffingwell was famous for bringing relief to Uncas when he was besieged by the Narragansetts. Rep-

---

* There is to be found in Holland's "Life of Lincoln" a brief account of the New England trip, including the visit to Norwich, and also an interview between Mr. Lincoln and Dr Gulliver that took place on the train to New Haven the morning after his speech in Norwich

resented the town in fifty-six sessions of the General Court.

23. Major John Mason, 1659. Born in England; died in Norwich, 1672. Deputy Governor of Colony of Connecticut. Distinguished among the Founders of Norwich. In his hand the sword of the Lord was mighty against the savage Pequots. Firm friend of Uncas and the Mohegans. Valiant soldier; wise counsellor. Home-lot corner of Town street and New London turnpike

24. Dr. John Olmstead, 1659 Born about 1626; died 1686. The first doctor in the town. Home-lot where the Gilman family live, at 380 Washington street.

25. John Pease, 1659. "A sea faring man." Home-lot the last on West Town street at the river crossing.

26. John Post, 1659. "A sea faring man." Home-lot the last on West street next above Thomas Bingham.

27. Thomas Post, 1659. Died 1701. Constable. Home-lot on West Town street, adjoining John Gager.

28. Josiah Read, 1659. Died 1717. Constable. Home-lot on Washington street east of the Coit Elms.

29. John Reynolds, 1659. Died 1702. His dwelling, on Washington street, is one of the oldest in Norwich. Home-lot included Backus Hospital grounds.

30. Jonathan Royce, 1659. Died 1689. Home-lot on West Town street between Allyn and J. Tracy.

31. Rev. Nehemiah Smith, 1659. Born about 1605; died 1686. Home-lot on West Town street north side opposite T. Post.

32. Sergeant John Tracy, 1659. Died 1702. Home-lot on south side of West Town street between John Baldwin and John Pease.

33. Lieut. Thomas Tracy, 1659 Born about 1610; died 1685. Home-lot on East Town street adjoining Christopher Huntington One of the most distinguished of the Founders of Norwich. He and John Mason were witnesses of the deed of Unkos, Owaneco, and Attawanhood, granting nine miles square to the inhabitants of Norwich, for the sum of seventy pounds. First representative to the General Court.

34. Robert Wade, 1659. Date of birth and death unknown. Home-lot south side of West Town street between John Birchard and John Gager.

35. Sergeant Thomas Waterman, 1659. Born 1644; died 1708. Home-lot on West Town street adjoining John Mason Youngest of the Founders, sixteen years of age. He represented the town in the General Court in 1679

OTHER EARLY SETTLERS

36. Caleb Abell, died August 7, 1731. Three of this name are found at an early period among the inhabitants of Norwich—Caleb, Benjamin and Joshua. Caleb married in July, 1669, Margaret, daughter of John Post. Robert Wade transferred to Caleb Abell his house lot, Town street. It was located between John Birchard and Morgan Bowers. He was chosen constable 1684; townsman 1689; appointed to keep tavern in 1694. Gen. Elijah Abell, a gallant officer in the Revolutionary War, born in Norwich, was a descendant of Caleb Abell.

37. Richard Bushnell was born September, 1652; died 1727. Came to Norwich with his step-father, Thomas Adgate. In the earlier part of the eighteenth century, Richard Bushnell was one of the most noted and active men in Norwich. He performed the duties of townsman, constable, schoolmaster, poet, deacon, sergeant, lieutenant and captain, town agent, town

N.L —1-11

deputy, court clerk, and justice of the peace. His dwelling was on the Montville road a mile south of the city. Married, in 1672, Elizabeth Adgate.

38. Samuel Lathrop, died February 29, 1700. Was son of Rev John
Lathrop, of London; came with his father to America in 1634 when about
fourteen years of age. He married at Barnstable, Mass., November 28, 1644,
Elizabeth Scudder. He was a house carpenter, and came to Norwich in 1668.
He had nine children by his first wife. His second wife, Abigail Doane, sur-
vived him and lived to the age of 103 years.

39. John Elderkin, died June 23, 1687. Elderkin's earliest grant at Norwich was in 1667, and was conveyed in 1668 to Samuel Lathrop The next
was at the old landing place below the Falls, where he built a grist mill for
the convenience of the town. Here for a long course of years stood the
mill and the miller's house. Elderkin built the second meeting-house for the
town. Of his first wife nothing is known. His second wife was Elizabeth,
relict of William Gaylord, of Windsor.

40. Stephen Gifford, born about 1641; died 1724. He was an early settler
and is classed as a proprietor by Miss Caulkins. Constable in 1686. His
home-lot extended from Mediterranean lane to the chapel of First Congregational church.

41. Christopher Huntington, Junior, born 1660; died 1735. "The first
born of males in Norwich." Son of Christopher Huntington the Founder.
A man of the highest character, and a prominent contributor to the prosperity of the most vital interests of the town. For near forty years he "used
the office of a deacon well." Town Clerk 1678 to 1691.

42. Elizabeth Hyde, born August, 1660, died at Lyme, 1736. Daughter
of Samuel and Jane (Lee) Hyde, the first child of English parentage born
in Norwich. Married, in 1682, Richard Lord, of Lyme.

43. Col Christopher Leffingwell, born in 1734; died 1810. Pioneer paper
manufacturer. Soldier and patriot in the Revolution Prominent citizen.

44. Major James Fitch, Jr., born in Saybrook, 1647; died 1727; married
(1) 1676, Elizabeth Mason; married (2) 1687, Mrs. Alice (Bradford) Adams.
During his residence in Norwich "he took a leading part in all town affairs,
and served as land-surveyor, registrar, captain of the train-band, and commissioner of boundaries." In 1698-99 he sold his house and home-lot to
Samuel and Simon Huntington, and later made his home in Canterbury. His
home-lot was on the east side of the town Green, and his house probably stood
south and near to the present residence of Wallace S. Allis

45. Governor Samuel Huntington, LL D., born 1731; died 1796. Repre-
sentative in Legislature 1764, and Senator 1773; Associate Judge Supreme
Court of Connecticut 1774; member of Congress 1775-1780 and member of
the Marine Court; signer of the Declaration of Independence; President of
Congress 1779-1781 and 1783; Chief Justice of Connecticut 1784; Lieutenant-
Governor 1785; Doctor of Laws, Yale College, 1779, Governor 1786-96.

46. Benjamin Huntington, LL D., born 1736; died October 16, 1800.
Graduated at Yale 1761, married daughter of Jabez Huntington, of Windham; State Counsellor during Revolutionary War, director of battery built
on Waterman's Point 1775; agent of colony to purchase the "Spy," bought
to watch British; superintended building of the "Defence" 14-gun brig, 1776;
representative from Norwich 1775; member Continental Congress 1784 and of
Constitutional Congress 1789; Judge Superior Court 1793; LL.B. from Dartmouth College 1782; moved to Rome. N. Y., 1796. His body was brought to
Norwich for burial First Mayor of Norwich, 1784 to 1796.

47. Benedict Arnold, born Norwich, 1741; died in London, 1801. General in the Revolutionary army. Distinguished for his heroism at Quebec,

Lake Champlain, Ridgefield, and Saratoga. Detested for his treason and for the burning of New London The house where he was born, on east side of Washington street, below LaFayette street, was destroyed sixty years ago.

48 Aaron Cleveland. The Aaron Cleveland house is now standing on West Town street at Bean Hill next below the meeting-house. Here Aaron "carried on" the hat business, and at the same time wrote poems, essays, lectures, and sermons upon all subjects of the day, social, political and religious. Aaron was great-grandfather of Grover Cleveland (see No 78).

49 William Cleveland, died in 1837. Rev Benjamin Lord purchased a house on the site, next to the Johnson home. This was his residence. This property was held by the Lord heirs until 1830, when it was sold to William Cleveland, grandfather of the President. William built a shop east of the house where he carried on the business of gold or silversmith. This dwelling house was burned in 1852 (See No. 79)

50. Dr. Philip Turner, born in Norwich, 1740; died in New York in 1815 and was buried in St. Paul's churchyard. He was highly distinguished for his professional skill.

51. Joseph Trumbull, the eldest son of Governor Trumbull, and the first Commissary General Continental Army; in 1778 bought the property between the present residence of A. W. Dickey and the house of Mrs. Kelley.

52. Diah Manning, 1760-1815, drum-major of Washington's Body Guard He carried to Major André his breakfast on the day of his execution, bringing it from the table of General Washington. House on Town street, corner Old Cemetery lane.

53. Rev. Benjamin Lord. D.D , was born at Saybrook, Conn , in 1694, and died at Norwich in 1784. For sixty-seven years pastor of the First Church in Norwich. He was graduated at Yale in 1714 and received the degree of D D. in 1774

54. Dr. Solomon Tracy, born in 1650; died in 1732. He was a youth at the settlement of the town. In addition to the duties of his profession he served the town as representative in the General Assembly and as lieutenant in the train-band.

55. Madam Knight (Mrs. Sarah Kemble Knight), born in Boston in 1666, and died in New London in 1727. The greater part of her life was spent in New London and Norwich, where she stood high in social rank and was respected both in church and civil affairs. In 1717 the town of Norwich granted her liberty "to sitt in the pue where she use to sitt in ye meeting-house." A silver tankard which she presented to the church is still preserved. She was remarkable for her versatile gifts and is remembered by her journal of a journey alone on horseback from Boston to New York in 1704.

56. General Andrew Huntington, born 1745; died 1824. John Elderkin sold land on East Town street to Samuel Lothrop, who built a house upon it soon after 1668 Portions of his house were probably incorporated in the present building now owned by Mr. Fitch, which was constructed about 1740, by Joshua Huntington (1698-1745). (See No. 61.) Commissary General, judge and merchant. Lived in this house from 1766 until his death

57. Simon Huntington, Jr., born 1659; died 1736. In 1688-89 Simon Huntington, the proprietor, granted land on East Town street to his son, Simon, who held many civil offices, was deacon of the church from 1696 to 1736. and in 1706 opened "a house of public entertainment." Captain Joseph Carew probably used parts of the house built by Simon Huntington, Jr., when he constructed in 1782-83 the house now occupied by Mr. Kelly. Joseph

and Eunice Carew Huntington and their children occupied this house until 1854.

58. Hon. Jabez W. Huntington, born 1788; died 1847. United States Senator from 1840 to 1847, lived in the Simon Huntington house (see No. 57) after his marriage in 1833 to a daughter of Joseph Huntington. "A statesman of unbending integrity and unswerving fidelity to the interests of the Union."

59. General Jedidiah Huntington, born 1743; died 1818. Fought at Bunker Hill and in many of the most important battles of the Revolution. He entertained both Washington and Lafayette in the house on the corner of East Town street and Huntington lane. He married, in 1766, Faith Trumbull, the daughter of the famous war governor. After the war he held many important positions and in 1789 was appointed Collector of Customs at New London and held that office until his death.

60. General Ebenezer Huntington, born 1754; died 1834. Was the half-brother of Jedidiah. After Jedidiah removed to New London his house was occupied by Ebenezer. He left Yale College when the war commenced and served until the troops were disbanded in 1783. In 1810 and in 1817 he was elected a member of Congress. Major General, Connecticut militia, over thirty years. His four unmarried daughters were "the Ladies Huntington."

61. Colonel Joshua Huntington, born 1751; died 1821. Married, in 1771, Hannah, daughter of Col. Hezekiah Huntington. He was in business at the Landing, but at the call to arms he followed his brothers in giving himself to the service of his country. He was high sheriff of New London county and had charge of the first United States census (1709) in this region. He lived in the house on Huntington lane now owned by Mrs. Theodore F. McCurdy.

62. General Jabez Huntington, born 1719; died 1786. Graduated at Yale College, 1741. "The house in the lane" is today practically unaltered from its condition when it was occupied by Gen. Jabez Huntington, who as the head of the Connecticut troops did much for American freedom. It surely includes a portion of the whole of the house of his father, the first Joshua Huntington, and may include the house built by the founder, John Bradford. General Jabez Huntington was the father of Jedidiah, Andrew, Joshua, Ebenezer and Zachariah. "If the annals of the Revolution record the name of any family that contributed more to that great struggle, I have yet to learn it."

63. Colonel John Durkee, born in Windham, 1728; died May 29, 1782. Leader of 500 men who compelled Ingersoll to resign the office of stamp master for Connecticut. Colonel at Long Island, Harlem, White Plains, Trenton and Monmouth. He was in Sullivan's Indian expedition. Durkee's tavern at Bean Hill was "opposite the home-lot of Mr. Samuel Abell." He was known as "the Bold Bean Hiller."

MEETING HOUSES AND BURYING GROUNDS

64. The first meeting-house stood near the southeast corner of the Green, "with the open Common around it." Of its erection there is no record. It was probably built by a "general turn-out of the inhabitants." In 1668 a small rate was collected to pay Samuel Lathrop "for repairing the Meeting-house." It was in use only twelve or fourteen years. Opposite present Norwich Town post office.

65. In 1673 the town contracted with John Elderkin to build "forthwith a new meeting-house." The building committee were Deacon Hugh Calkins,

Ensign Thomas Leffingwell, Ensign Thoman Tracy, Simon Huntington and William Backus. It was completed in two years Elderkin contracted to build it for £428 This building was repaired and a "leanto" added, in which several new pews were made. These improvements being completed in March, 1698. five of the oldest and most respected inhabitants were directed "to seat the people with due regard to rank." The site of this second meeting-house was on the summit of the hill. It was to serve as a watch-tower, and a garrison post, as well as a house of worship.

66. December 6, 1709, a vote was passed to build a third meeting-house, the dimensions not to exceed 55 feet by 45, to be modeled by a committee of the church, and completed by March 1, 1712. This building was on the rocks near the site of the second meeting-house John Elderkin, 2d, son of the old church builder, was the architect It was completed in December, 1713 A vote was passed to sell the old edifice, which had lasted forty years.

67 The site of the fourth meeting-house was at the corner of the Green, under the rocks, where the present church stands. It is said to have been a "square building, with a front porch or platform," with doors on three sides. It was voted for in 1748, but was not begun until 1753; it remained unfinished for several years. It was completed in 1770. On the 7th of February, 1801, it was destroyed by fire, with several other buildings. The present building, the fifth meeting-house, was built partly by subscription and partly by a lottery.

68. Post-Gager Burial Ground, 1661. In 1661 the town bought this land for a common burial-place. Many of the proprietors and early settlers were interred in this "regular oblong plot," 11 rods long and 7 wide. The last interment was in 1740. In 1872 the present monument was erected to the memory of Major John Mason and the other proprietors. It is on West Town street, half a mile above the Uptown Green. No traces of graves remain.

69. Entrance to Old Burying Ground, 1699. At Norwich Town through Old Cemetery lane near the corner of Town street (the River road), and the Uptown Green; a portion of the home-lot of Rev. James Fitch.

70 Entrance to the Old Burying Ground, 1796 On East Town street, adjacent to the Governor Huntington house, through the Hubbard gates, inscribed by Faith Trumbull Chapter, D A, R, with names of soldiers of the Revolution buried within. A portion of the home-lot of Simon Huntington.

PUBLIC BUILDINGS

71. Court House, 1762. In 1735 the first court house was erected on the south side of the parsonage lot In 1762 a new one was built on the Green near the present watering trough. This was moved across the street in 1798 near the present school, used until 1833, when courts were moved to the Landing, and then used as a school building until 1891.

72. Town and Court House, 1829. Built on north side of Church street. Burned April 11, 1865.

74. Jail, 1815. A third location was chosen in 1815, when the Perit house on the opposite side of the Green was purchased for the county house, and a jail was built on the adjoining lot a short distance back of where the store now stands This lasted until the courts were moved to the Landing, in 1833.

73 Jail, 1759. First jail was at southeast corner of Green. About 1759 a new one was built back of old brick schoolhouse. This was burned in 1786 and rebuilt and used until 1815.

75. Office of Town Clerks. The first town clerk was John Birchard. We have no record of his appointment He was in office eighteen years. Christopher Huntington, appointed 1678, was in office until his death, 1691. Richard Bushnell, 1691, for seven years. Christopher Huntington, Jr., 1698, for four years Richard Bushnell again in 1702, in office for twenty-four years. Isaac Huntington, 1726 till his death, 1764. Benj. Huntington, 1764, in office nearly two years. Benj. Huntington, son of Isaac, 1765, in office thirteen years. Samuel Tracy, 1778, in office one year. Benj. Huntington, 1779, in office until his death, 1801. Philip Huntington, 1801, until his death in 1825, and his son, Benjamin, born 1798, was in office nearly continuously until 1830.

76. Dudley Woodbridge's Store. Dudley Woodbridge, in 1774, purchased of Ebenezer Lord his house and shop on the Green, north and next to where the present chapel stands. He sold goods of every description, groceries, shoes, dress goods, hardware, etc. In 1782, the first post office was established in Norwich; Dudley Woodbridge was the first postmaster, and held the office until 1789. The mails had previously been delivered by post riders. Mr. Woodbridge removed to Ohio in 1789 or 1790.

In 1790 Gurdon Lathrop occupied this store, as a general trader In 1791 it was sold to Joseph Huntington and he formed a partnership with Joseph Carew After October, 1800, the business was carried on by the firm of Joseph and Charles P Huntington On February 7th, 1801, this store and the meeting-house with several other buildings were burned. The Huntington Brothers moved their goods to the store "a few rods N. E. from the Court House." In August they moved to the large, new brick store, which they had had built on the site of the old Woodbridge shop. This building is now the chapel of First Congregational Church.

77 Tracy & Coit's Store. About 1780, Uriah Tracy and Joseph Coit leased from Thomas Leffingwell land upon which they built a shop 50 x 32, in which they carried on for many years an extensive business It was a long, gambrel-roofed, one-story-and-half structure. Uriah Tracy bought in 1790 the Benedict Arnold house, where he lived until his death. Tracy & Coit's Store was one of the representative stores of Norwich.

78. Aaron Cleveland Shop This building formerly stood the next but one below the meeting-house, Bean Hill. It was the shop of Aaron Cleveland, in which he carried on the business of hat making. It was moved across the road and is now known as "Adam's Tavern." President Cleveland was his great-grandson (see No. 48).

79. William Cleveland Shop This building was the one used by William Cleveland as a goldsmith shop, 1830-37. It stood between the schoolhouse and the Johnson home facing the Green (see No. 49).

80 Brick School House. On Norwich Town Green Founded by Doctor Daniel Lathrop in 1783. Now occupied by the Noah Webster Literary Association.

81. Brick School House. On Washington street. Built in 1789. The first school attended by Lydia Huntley (Mrs Sigourney) Now used by the School-house Club

82 Leffingwell Row. Sometimes called "the Long Shop," built by Christopher Leffingwell about 1780, was burned in 1882 with the red store adjoining. Its position near the fork of the roads opposite the residence of General Edward Harland made it a conspicuous landmark It was occupied at different times by Leffingwell's stocking factory, various small shops, by the judge of probate and by the post office.

83. The Teel House, "Sign of General Washington." Built for a hotel

in 1789 on Chelsea Parade, afterwards occupied for a school by William Woodbridge, now the parsonage of Park Church, for many years the residence of General William Williams, who was distinguished for his benevolence and for his interest in the Mohegan Indians. He and his wife, Harriet Peck Williams, gave five acres now the grounds of the Norwich Free Academy, and she founded the Peck Library, now in the Slater Memorial Building. He was born in 1788 and died in 1870.

EARLY INDUSTRIES

84. Stocking Weaving. The business of weaving stockings was begun in 1766 by Christopher Leffingwell with two or three looms. In 1791 nine looms were in operation producing 1,200 to 1,500 pairs of hose annually.

85. Grist Mill. A grist mill built by John Elderkin at No Man's Acre about 1661; was removed about 1667 under agreement with the town, to the Yantic river below the Falls, and a large tract of land was granted to him as compensation in the vicinity of the Indian burying place on Sachem street.

86. Iron Works. The first iron works were established at Yantic in 1750 by Elijah Backus. He manufactured bloom and bar iron for anchors, mills and other uses. The Backus Iron Works obtained great repute and during the Revolutionary War all kinds of iron work for domestic uses and warfare were made and repaired here.

87. Pottery. A pottery was established in 1766 at Bean Hill and continued in operation far into the 19th century. Specimens of this pottery are among the treasured possessions of some of the old residents of Norwich.

88. Linseed Oil Mills. The first linseed oil mill was established at Bean Hill, in 1748, by Hezekiah Huntington, and at a later period the manufacture was carried on extensively at the Falls.

89. Cotton Mill. A cotton mill was established by Joshua Lathrop in 1790 on Lowthorpe Meadows with one carding machine, five jennies and six looms This machinery was gradually increased and a great variety of goods manufactured. In 1703 the firm was Lathrop & Eells

90. Chocolate Mill. The first chocolate mill was established in 1770 by Christopher Leffingwell on the Yantic flats below the Falls. In 1772 Simon Lathrop erected another. This industry was of considerable importance.

91. Paper Mill. In 1766 Christopher Leffingwell began to manufacture paper at his mill on the west side of the Yantic above the Falls, near what are now called Paper Mill rocks. This was the first paper mill in Connecticut. The annual output was about 1,300 reams.

92. Clocks and Watches. Clocks and watches were manufactured by Thomas Harland in 1773. He employed ten or twelve hands and made annually two hundred watches and forty clocks, which were pronounced equal to any imported from England.

93. Fulling Mill. A fulling mill with clothier's shop and dye house went into operation near the present site of the Falls mill in 1773.

TAVERNS

94 Caleb Abel, the third innkeeper of Norwich, probably came from Dedham: he bought the Wade lot in 1677; was constable in 1684, townsman in 1689, and often thereafter; enrolled among the dignitaries with title of Sergeant in 1702, married Margaret, daughter of John Post, 1669, and after her death married Mary Loomer; died August 7, 1731. He was appointed

innkeeper under the date of December 18, 1694, as follows: "The towne makes choise of caleb abell to keep ordinari or a house of entertainment for this yeare or till another be choosen"

95. Deacon Simon Huntington, the first of four successive generations of deacons was the second innkeeper of Norwich. He was married to Sarah, daughter of Joseph Clarke, of Saybrook, in October, 1653; appointed innkeeper 1690, died 1706, leaving an estate valued at £275, including a library of fourteen or fifteen volumes, of the value of about 30 shillings, which we are told was probably a fair library for a layman at that time.

96. Joseph Reynolds, son of John Reynolds, the Founder, kept the ordinary in 1709. He was born in Norwich, March, 1660; married Sarah Edgerton, 1688.

97. Thomas Waterman, born 1644, came to Norwich in 1659 with John Bradford, whose wife's nephew he was; only townsman in 1675, '81, '84; made a freeman in 1681, died June 1, 1708; buried in Society Burial Ground. He was appointed innkeeper in 1679. "Agreed and voted by ye town yt Thomas Waterman is desired to keep the ordinary. And for his encouragement he is granted four akers of paster land where he can conveniently find it ny about the valley going from his house to the woods."

98. Eleazer Lord's tavern on the corner of Town street and the New London turnpike was built about 1770 and for many years was frequented by the lawyers who came to Norwich to attend court.

99 Joseph Peck's tavern on the east side of the Green, overshadowed by a large elm tree, among whose central boughs an arbor was formed and seats arranged, to which on public days friendly groups resorted and had refreshments served—a plank gallery being extended from a window of the house to the bower as a means of access.

100. Thomas Leffingwell, the fourth innkeeper of Norwich, was given liberty to keep a "publique house of entertainment of strangers" in 1700. This tavern was continued for more than one hundred years, and was at the east end of the town plot, and was a noted place of resort in war times. Married Mary Bushnell, September, 1672; died March 5, 1723-24, leaving an estate of nearly £10,000. The interesting features of this quaint old house, within and without, are remarkably well preserved.

101. On the site of the present "Johnson home" was located Lathrop's tavern. Built in 1737 by Nathaniel Lathrop, its prosperity was maintained by his son, Azariah. From here was started the first stage coach to Providence in 1768. In 1829 the property was sold to the Union Hotel Company, who erected the present building, which was later used for a boarding school.

102. Jesse Brown's tavern was erected in 1790 and its proprietor established a stage route from Boston to New York via Norwich. On August 1, 1797, President John Adams and wife stopped over night here. In 1855 the property was purchased by Moses Pierce, who later gave it to the United Workers for the Rocknook Children's Home.

103. It is said that Capt. Samuel Bailey was jailor about 1800, and the accommodations for the jail were on the second floor, and that on the first floor the captain kept what was called "Cross Keys Tavern."

PRESIDENTS OF THE UNITED STATES

104. Millard Fillmore. Capt. John Fillmore, son of John Fillmore, "Mariner," of Ipswich, Mass., born March 18, 1702. He married, November 24, 1724, Mary Spiller, and removed to Norwich West Farms; died there February 22, 1777. Captain John's grandson was Nathaniel, whose eldest son was Millard, born January 7, 1800, in Summer Hill, N. Y.

105. Ulysses S. Grant. On the site of the house of Herbert L. Yerrington stood the original Christopher Huntington homestead. After the death of the first Christopher this was inherited by his son, John (born 1666), who married, in 1686, Abigail, daughter of Samuel Lathrop John had three daughters and two sons. One daughter, Martha, was married to Noah Grant, of Tolland, and became the ancestress of Ulysses S. Grant.

Martha Huntington married, June 12, 1717, Noah Grant, born December 16, 1693 Their son, Noah, Jr., born July 12, 1718, married Susannah Delano, November 5, 1746 Their son, Noah, 3rd, born June 20, 1748, married Rachel Kelly, March 4, 1792. Their son, Jesse, born January 23, 1794, married Hannah Simpson, June 24, 1821 Ulysses S. Grant was born April 27, 1822

106. Rutherford B Hayes George Hayes left Scotland in 1690 and settled at Windsor, Connecticut, 1682 His great-great-great-grandson, Rutherford Hayes, settled at Brattleboro, Vt., and married, in September, 1813, Sophia Birchard. Her ancestry on the male line is traced to John Birchard, one of the thirty-five founders of Norwich Both of her grandfathers were soldiers in the Revolutionary War. Rutherford Hayes removed in 1817 to Delaware, Ohio, where he died five years later, leaving two children On October 4, 1822, Rutherford Birchard Hayes was born three months after his father's death.

107. James A. Garfield. Was the descendant of Major John Mason and Reverend James Fitch, who are recorded among the founders of Norwich (see Nos 14 and 23).

108. Grover Cleveland William Hyde. Samuel Hyde married Jane Lee. John Hyde married Experience Abel. James Hyde married Sarah Marshall. Abiah Hyde married Rev. Aaron Cleveland. William Cleveland married Margaret Falley. Richard Falley Cleveland, born at Norwich, 19 June, 1805. He married Anne Neale, 10 September, 1820, of Baltimore. They removed to Holland Patent, New York, where he died 1 October, 1853. Grover Cleveland was born at Holland Patent, 31 July, 1853 (see Nos 48, 49, 78 and 79).

109 Mrs. Theodore Roosevelt. Edith Kermit Carow, born New York, August 6, 1862, daughter of Charles and Gertrude Elizabeth (Tyler) Carow. She was married at St. George's Church, Hanover square, London, England, 1886, to Theodore Roosevelt. Her grandfather was General Daniel Tyler of Norwich.

OTHER MEN OF DISTINCTION

110. Rev. Hiram P. Arms, D.D., pastor and pastor emeritus First Congregational Church, 1836-82. Born in Sunderland, Mass , 1799. Died at Norwich, 1882

111. Major-General Henry Warner Birge, born in Hartford, August 25, 1825 Died in New York, July 1, 1888. In the War for the Union he passed through the successive ranks from major to brevet major-general. He rendered distinguished services at Irish Bend, in the Red River campaign, and led the forlorn hope at Port Hudson, and was actively engaged in battles of Winchester, Fisher's Hill and Cedar Creek.

112 Isaac Hill Bromley, born in Norwich, March 6, 1833. Captain 18th Regiment Connecticut Volunteers; provost marshal. First editor "Norwich Bulletin"; journalist; humorist; chief editor New York "Tribune," 1891-98. Died at Norwich, August 11, 1898.

113. Hon. William Alfred Buckingham, born in Lebanon, Connecticut, May 28, 1804; died in 1875 Mayor of Norwich 1849-50, 1856-57. Presidential elector, 1856 Governor of Connecticut, 1858-66. U S Senator, 1869-75.

Merchant, manufacturer, philanthropist, generous benefactor of Yale University, the Broadway Church and Norwich Free Academy.

114. Thomas Fanning, born at Norwich, Conn., July 18, 1750; died May 24, 1812. Soldier in the Revolution. Merchant. One of the donors of Chelsea Parade, 1791.

115. Lafayette Sabin Foster, LL.D., born in Franklin, Conn., November 22, 1806; died in 1880. Graduated Brown University 1828. Mayor of Norwich, 1851-53. Speaker Connecticut House Representatives, 1847. United States Senator, 1854-66. After death of President Lincoln, acting Vice-President of the United States. Professor of Law at Yale 1868; judge Supreme Court of Connecticut 1870-76. Benefactor of Yale University, Free Academy and Otis Library. "Great citizen, incorruptible senator, wise counsellor, eloquent advocate, righteous judge."

116. Daniel Coit Gilman, LL D., born in Norwich, July 6, 1831; died in Norwich, October 13, 1908. Graduated Yale 1852. Professor Yale College 1856-72; president University of California 1872-75; president Johns Hopkins University 1875-1901; president Carnegie Institution 1901-04. Delivered historical address at Norwich bi-centennial celebration in 1859.

117. William Charles Gilman, born in Exeter, N. H., 1795; died in New York 1863. Came to Norwich 1816. Established nail factory at the Falls. Extended cotton manufacture from the Falls to Greeneville and Bozrah. Identified for thirty years with the most important manufacturing, financial, educational and religious enterprises in the town. First president Norwich & Worcester railroad. Mayor in 1839.

118. Hon. Calvin Goddard, born at Shrewsbury, Mass., 1768. Mayor of Norwich 1814-31. Judge Supreme Court, 1816. Member of Congress 1801-05. Died in 1842. He lived on the corner of Washington and Sachem streets and owned several acres of land, including the Indian burying place, and mill property at the Falls.

119. William Parkinson Greene, born in Boston, 1795; died in Norwich, 1864. He was graduated at Harvard in 1814; removed to Norwich in 1824; became largely interested in manufactures at the Falls and Greeneville and in the Norwich Water Power Co He was mayor in 1842; first president of Thames Bank, original corporator Norwich & Worcester railroad; second president and liberal benefactor of Norwich Free Academy.

120 Rev. John Putnam Gulliver, D.D., born in Boston in 1819; died at Andover, Mass., 1894 Yale University 1840; D D. Iowa University. President Knox College; Professor Andover Theological Seminary. Twenty years pastor Broadway Congregational Church. Held in honored remembrance as chief promoter of the Norwich Free Academy.

121. Russell Hubbard, born in Norwich, 1785; died 1857. Proprietor of Norwich "Courier." Paper manufacturer at Norwich Falls and Greeneville. A founder and vice-president of Norwich Savings Society First president and generous benefactor of Norwich Free Academy.

122. Thomas Sterry Hunt, LL.D., born at Norwich in 1826; died February 12, 1892. Professor of chemistry at McGill University, 1862-68; professor of geology at Massachusetts Institute of Technology 1872-78. Presented with Cross of the Legion of Honor at Paris, 1855 Honorary member Royal Society of London, 1859. He invented a permanent green ink, first used for "greenbacks."

123. Deacon Jabez Huntington, born in Lebanon, Connecticut, 1767; died in Norwich, 1848. He was president of the Norwich Bank and of the Norwich Savings Society. He and Hezekiah Perkins bought the land, now known

as the "Little Plain," on Broadway in 1811, and gave it to the city for a park. His house is now Mrs. II. H. Osgood's.

124. Charles James Lanman, born in Norwich, June 14, 1795. Yale graduate, 1814. Receiver of public money for Michigan, 1823-1831. Founder of Tecumseh, Michigan. Mayor of Norwich, 1838. Died in New London, July 25, 1870.

125. James Lanman, born in Norwich, June 14, 1769; died August 7, 1841. Yale graduate, 1788. United States Senator, 1819-25. Judge Supreme Court of Connecticut.

126. Doctor Daniel Lathrop, born in Norwich, 1712; died in Norwich, 1782. Yale College, 1733; St. Thomas' Hospital, London, 1737. As an importer of drugs he and his brother Joshua built up a wide reputation and large estates for their day. He left £500 to Yale College, £500 to the First Church of Norwich, and £500 to establish a school on the Norwich Town Green. "Many were the amiables that composed his character."

127 Daniel Lathrop, born in Norwich, 1769; died 1825. Yale College, 1787. Was engaged in the drug business in Norwich. Son of Dr. Joshua Lathrop.

128. Doctor Joshua Lathrop, born in Norwich, 1723; died Norwich, 1807. Yale College, 1743. Merchant; cotton manufacturer; public-spirited citizen; one of the donors of the Chelsea Parade to the inhabitants of Norwich, and contributed generously for improvement of highways. "He devised liberal things and did them."

129. Donald Grant Mitchell (Ik Marvel), born in Norwich, in 1822, near present residence of the principal of the Norwich Free Academy. Died in New Haven, in 1908. Yale graduate and valedictorian, 1841. Distinguished author and landscape gardener. He delivered an oration at the bi-centennial celebration in 1859.

130. Col. George L. Perkins, born in Norwich, August 5, 1788; died September 5, 1888. Paymaster United States army, War of 1812. For fifty years treasurer of Norwich & Worcester railroad. A well-known and prominent citizen of Norwich. In his great age, one hundred years and one month, "his eye was not dim, nor his natural force abated."

131. Capt. Hezekiah Perkins, born in Norwich, 1751; died 1822. He and Jabez Huntington gave to the city in 1811 the land now known as the "Little Plain" for a park. He lived in the house now owned by Mrs. Charles Coit.

132. Major Joseph Perkins. A soldier of the Revolution; member of the Committee of Safety in 1814 Prominent merchant; public-spirited citizen. He with Thomas Fanning and Joshua Lathrop gave Chelsea Parade to the inhabitants of Norwich for a park. He built the stone-house on Rockwell street in 1825.

133. Dr. Dwight Ripley, born in Windham. Connecticut, in 1767; died in Norwich, 1835. A descendant of Gov. William Bradford of Plymouth. He was actively engaged in business in Norwich for over forty years, and built up a large wholesale drug trade on present site of Lee & Osgood's store. He did much for the advancement of Norwich, and left a large family of sons and daughters who are held in honored remembrance.

134. General Alfred Perkins Rockwell, born in Norwich, 1834; died in Boston, 1903. Yale College, 1855. Professor mining in Massachusetts Institute of Technology. Rendered distinguished services in the War for the Union, rising from the rank of captain to brevet brigadier-general, and serving at James Island, Fort Darling, Bermuda Hundreds and Fort Fisher.

135. Charles W. Rockwell, born in Norwich, 1799; died in 1866. During

his residence in Norwich he was distinguished for his liberality and public spirit. In 1833 he built the mansion on Broadway afterwards owned by John F. Slater   He was interested in manufactures at Norwich Town; was four years mayor of the city; was three times elected to the State Legislature, and was for several years United States Commissioner of Customs at Washington.

The following description of Norwich by Henry Ward Beecher, published in "Star Papers" in 1851, and reprinted for the 250th anniversary of the settlement, is given entire:

There are hundreds of villages in Connecticut that are beautiful in various degrees and by different methods; some by the width of prospect, some by their mountain scenery, some by their position on the water, and some, nestled away from all the world, find their chief attractions in their deep tranquility. But in every place the chief beauty must be in what nature has done, or in what man has done naturally. The rocks, hills, mountains; the innumerable forms of water in springs, rills, rivulets, streams, estuaries, lakes or ocean; but above all the trees—these create beauty if it exist at all. It is rare that any place combines to a great degree the several specialties mentioned. A place that is inland, and yet on the seaboard—that has bold, precipitous rocks close at hand, and at the same time is spread out upon a champaign—that unites the refinements belonging to society in large towns with the freshness and quiet of a secluded village, imbosomed in trees, full of shaded yards and gardens, broad, park-like streets, soon opening out into romantic rural roads among pine woods along the rocky edges of dark streams—such a place, especially if its society is good, if its ministers, teachers, civilians, and principal citizens are intelligent and refined, and its historical associations abundant and rich—must be regarded as of all others the most desirable for residence. And such a place is Norwich, Connecticut.

The river Thames is formed by the junction of the Yantic and the Shetucket   Upon the angle of these three streams stands the town. The Shetucket is a black water in all its course, and near to Norwich it has a bed hewed out of rocks, and cliffs for banks. The Yantic is a smaller stream, rolling also over a rocky channel, with a beautiful plunge, just above the town, of seventy-five feet   The Thames is not so much of a river as a narrow arm of the sea, thrust far up inland as if to search for tributary streams. These ribbon-like bays mark the whole northern coast of Long Island Sound   The Thames is navigable for large steamers to its point of formation. The conformation of the ground on which Norwich stands is entirely peculiar. Along the water it is comparatively low, affording a business plane and a space for railroad necessities. The whole ground then rises with sudden slope, lifting the residences far up out of the dust and noise of business into an altitude of quiet. But what is the most remarkable is, that a huge broad-backed granite cliff of rocks bulges up in the very midst of the city, cutting it in two, extending backward half a mile, and leaving the streets to sweep around on either side of it. This masterly old monarch looks down a hundred feet perpendicular, on the eastern side, upon the streets below, its bare rocks and massive ledges here and there half hid by evergreens, and in spots matted with grass and fringed with shrubs. On the western side the slope is gradual, and it is cut half way down to the Yantic by a broad street, nobly shaded with stalwart elms and filled with fine family residences. As one winds his way from the landing up the curving street, about the base of the rock on the eastern side, at evening especially, in twilight, or with a tender moonlight, this wild, uplifted cliff—in the very heart of a city, with forest trees rooted almost plumb above his head—has a strange and changeable uncertainty, at one moment shining out distinctly, and at the next dim and shadowy; now easily compassed by the eye, and then glancing away, if we have imagination enough, into vast mountain spaces. This singular rocky ridge trends toward the north, and gradually loses itself in the plain on which stands Norwich Old Town. There is thus brought together, within the space of a mile, the city, the country, and the wilderness. The residences are so separated from the business part of the town that one who comes first into the upper part of the city, and wanders about under its avenues of mighty elms, and among its simple old houses or its modern mansions, would take it to be a place of elegant repose, without life or business. But if he first lands below, amid stores and manufacturing shops, as for several years we did, he might go away thinking Norwich to be a mere hammering, rumbling place of business. Indeed, there are three towns in one.

The streets skirting the water form a city of business; the streets upon the hill, a city of residences, a mile or two back is the old town, a veritable life-like picture of a secluded country village of the old New England days. What could one want better for a place of retirement? An hour's ride brings you to the seaside; to boats, fishing, lounging, and looking, whether in storm or calm. You may go by cars to old New London, or by boat to Stonington, and then by yacht or other craft to Block Island, or anywhere else you please. There are places for fish—black fish, blue fish, speckled bass, porgies, weak-fish, etc.; there are places for surf-bathing, with waves tempered to all degrees of violence and to every tone from whispering to thunder. If your mood does not take you seaward, half an hour will suffice to bear you inland, among bold and rocky hills, cleft with streams, full of precipitous ravines, and shaded with oaks and evergreens. Or, if you do not wish to roam, you may ascend the intra-urban mountain—the Tarpeian Rock of Norwich, or Mount Zion, whichever your associations prefer to call it—and from its pinnacle overlook the wide, circumjacent country. If you happily own a house upon the western side of Washington street, or, better yet, if you own a friend who owns the house and feels lonesome without you, then you can have the joys of the breezy wilderness at home. For, if you will go back through the garden, and then through a little pet orchard, you shall find the forest-covered bank plunging one hundred feet down toward the Yantic; and there, hidden among shrubs and wild flowers, oaks and elms, you hear no din of wheels or clink of shops, but only the waving of leaves and the sport of birds.

But if there were none of these rare conjunctions of hill, rock, and plain, river and sea, Norwich would still be a beautiful place by virtue of its trees, and especially of those incomparably most magnificent of all earthly trees, elms! A village shaded by thoroughly grown elms cannot but be handsome. Its houses may be huts; its streets may be ribbed with rocks or channelled with ruts; it may be as dirty as New York and as frigid as Philadelphia; and yet these vast, majestic tabernacles of the air would redeem it to beauty. These are temples indeed, living temples, neither waxing old nor shattered by Time, that cracks and shatters stone, but rooting wider with every generation and casting a vaster round of grateful shadow with every summer. We had rather walk beneath an avenue of elms than inspect the noblest cathedral that art ever accomplished. What is it that brings one into such immediate personal and exhilarating sympathy with venerable trees! One instinctively uncovers as he comes beneath them; he looks up with proud veneration into the receding and twilight recesses; he breathes a thanksgiving to God every time his cool foot falls along their shadows. They waken the imagination and mingle the olden time with the present. Did any man of contemplative mood ever stand under an old oak or elm without thinking of other days—imagining the scenes that had transpired in their presence? These leaf-mountains seem to connect the past and the present to us as mountain ridges attract clouds from both sides of themselves. Norwich is remarkably enriched by these columnar glories, these mysterious domes of leaf and interlacing bough No considerable street is destitute of them, and several streets are prolonged avenues of elms which might give a twinge of jealousy to old New Haven herself—elm-famous!

Norwich Old Town, however, clearly has the pre-eminence. Its green is surrounded by old Revolutionary elms of the vastest stature and of every shape and delineation of grandeur. How a man can live there and ever get his eyes to the ground, I cannot imagine. One must needs walk with up-turned face, exploring these most substantial of all air castles. And when pausing underneath some monumental tree he looks afar up and sees the bird-population, that appears scarcely larger than humming-birds, dimly flitting about their secure heritage and sending down a chirp that loses itself half way down to a thin whistle, it seems as though there were two worlds—he in one and they in another Nearly before the fine old-fashioned mansion where Lydia Huntley (Mrs. Sigourney) was brought up are two gigantic elms—very patriarchs, measuring at the base more than eighteen feet in circumference. An old man of a hundred years, a member of Dr. Bond's society, relates that his father selected these trees from the forest, and backed them into town and planted them here. His name should be written on a tablet and hung upon their breasts!

The two elms next south from these, though not as aged as they, may, we think, be regarded as models of exquisite symmetry and beauty. One might sit by the hour and look upon them as upon a picture

No other tree is at all comparable to the elm The ash is, when well grown, a fine tree, but clumpy; the maple has the same character. The horse-chestnut, the linden, the mulberry, and poplars (save that tree-spire, the Lombardy poplar) are all of them plump, round, fat trees, not to be despised, surely, but representing single dendrological ideas. The oak is venerable by association, and occasionally a specimen is found possessing a kind of grim and ragged glory. But the elm alone, monarch of trees, combines in itself the elements of variety, size, strength, and grace, such as no other tree known to us can at all approach or remotely rival. It is the ideal of trees; the true Absolute Tree! Its main trunk shoots up, not round and smooth, like an over-fatted, lymphatic tree, but channelled and corrugated, as if its athletic muscles showed their proportions through the bark, like Hercules' limbs through his tunic. Then suddenly the whole idea of growth is changed, and multitudes of long, lithe branches radiate from the crotch of the tree, having the effect of straightness and strength, yet really diverging and curving, until the outermost portions droop over and give to the whole top the most fault-less grace. If one should at first say that the elm suggested ideas of strength and uprightness, on looking again he would correct himself, and say that it was majestic, uplifting beauty that it chiefly represented. But if he first had said that it was graceful and magnificent beauty, on a second look he would correct himself, and say that it was vast and rugged strength that it set forth But at length he would say neither; he would say both; he would say that it expressed a beauty of majestic strength and a grandeur of grace-ful beauty.

Such domestic forest treasures are a legacy which but few places can boast Wealth can build houses and smooth the soil; it can fill up marshes and create lakes or artificial rivers; it can gather statues and paintings; but no wealth can buy or build elm trees—the floral glory of New England. Time is the only architect of such structures, and blessed are they for whom Time was pleased to fore-think! No care or expense should be counted too much to maintain the venerable elms of New England in all their regal glory!

No other tree more enjoys a rich loam and moist food In summer droughts, if copious waterings were given to the finer elms, especially with diluted guano water, their pomp would be noticeably enhanced. But, except in moist places, or in fields where the plow has kept the surface stirred, we noticed that elms were turning yellow and thinning out their leaves.

CHAPTER VII

OTHER TOWNS OF NEW LONDON COUNTY

Colchester—East Lyme—Franklin—Griswold—Groton—Lebanon—Ledyard—Lisbon—
Lyme and Old Lyme—Salem—Sprague—Stonington—Voluntown—Waterford.

Colchester.—There can be but little doubt but that Nathaniel Foote could
have justly claimed to be the father of Colchester. He was the grandson of
Nathaniel Foote, who early in the seventeenth century emigrated from Colchester, England, to the Colony of Connecticut. His grandson, Nathaniel
Foote (3rd), in the latter part of the seventeenth century was a resident of
Wethersfield, and while there obtained a grant from one Owaneco, a sachem
of the Mohegan Indians, of a large tract of land including a large part if not
the whole of the present town of Colchester. By the terms of this grant,
Foote undertook to distribute the land, except fifty acres retained for himself,
among the settlers thereon. He undoubtedly intended to settle himself upon
this fifty-acre tract, but, his health having failed him, he never personally
took possession.

On October 13th, 1698, authority was granted by the General Court of
the Colony to Captain Daniel Wetheral, Captain John Hamlin, Mr. William
Pitkin, Captain John Chester, Mr. Robert Christophus and Captain Samuel
Fosdick, to lay out a new town at the place called "Jeremiah's Farm," upon
the road to New London, "beginning at the North bound of the Twenty Mile
River and so to extend southward to a river called Deep River and to extend
eastward from the bounds of Haddam seven miles." While these boundaries
are very indefinite, they help to locate today what undoubtedly included the
present town of Colchester and the Indian grant to Nathaniel Foote. On May
11th, 1699, the General Court of the Colony specified by a statute the bounds
of the town more closely, providing that "the north boundary of the town
shall be as formerly at Twenty Mile River, and the south bounds to join
the north bounds of Lyme and the west bounds to join the east bounds of
Middletown and the east bounds of Haddam and the east and northeast
bounds to run to the bounds of Lebanon and Norwich." The town as originally
laid out was included in the county of Hartford, but on October 13th, 1699,
upon the application of Michael Taintor, Samuel Northam and Nathaniel
Foote, it was transferred to the county of New London and received its
name, Colchester. These men apparently were the representative men of
the town at that time and, as Foote's ancestors came from Colchester, England, the strong presumption is that he is the one responsible for its name.

About this time the Indians had begun to cause trouble to the settlers,
and Captain Samuel Mason was appointed by the General Court to make a
settlement with them, which he effected. During this year the first settlement
appears to have been made in the town, unless the designation of "Jeremiah's
Farm" means that there has been a prior settlement upon this territory. But
of this there is no certainty. Foote had laid out his fifty acres, and in 1702
built a home for himself and family, but his health broke down and he died

in 1702, before he was able to occupy it The building, however, was occupied almost immediately, in the same year, by his widow and a large family of children, from whom the Footes of today are direct descendants. The fifty acres thus laid out was located along the westerly side of what is now Broadway, and the frame of the house built in 1702 still stands upon the premises now owned by Mr Frederick G. Bock In 1700 the first white child was born, a daughter (name not given) to John Skinner, and the next year, on November 9th, 1701, was born Mary, a daughter of James Taylor.

Up to about the year 1703, the land in the town, except the fifty acres of Foote's tract and possibly the "Jeremiah's Farm." was held in common by the settlers; but about that time steps were taken for its division among them, and shortly a town measurer was appointed to measure and set off allotments of land to the persons entitled to it. The first grants upon the record appeared to have been made at a town meeting, January 11th, 1703, when a large number of grants were made by the town. The first to be recorded was the one allotted to Samuel Loomis and John Skinner, the latter the father of the first white child, but the description is so indefinite that it is impossible to locate it Then followed the records of a large number of grants, but as the descriptions of none of them are more definite than this first one, it is impossible to locate them. It may be said, in passing, that one of the fields on the north side of Packwood lane was formerly known as the "Loomis lot." This may be the location of that first grant to Samuel Loomis. While these grants cannot be definitely located, it is certain that the first settlement in the town was made upon the property now owned by Mr. Hamilton Wallis.

The first church was erected at or near the corner of Broadway and Packwood lane and, in clearing along the east side of Broadway, a number of old foundations, wells, and graves, have been discovered. There was also discovered what apparently was an old roadway running diagonally from Broadway, which at that time was the ordinary narrow country road, in the direction of the present Packwoodville. Michael Taintor was the first town clerk, and held that office for some thirty years The first selectmen were chosen in 1706, and were Deacon Loomis, Joseph Chamberlain and Michael Taintor.

During the early years of its history, the town and church were one, and therefore the history of the town during these years includes the history of the Congregational church. In 1702 a town meeting had authorized the employment of a minister for the church, and had fixed his salary at forty pounds per annum. In October, 1703, the General Court of the Colony had authorized the organization of a church in the town, and this organization had been effected December 20th of the same year. In 1725 the General Court established a new parish which included the southern part of Colchester and the northern part of the town of Lyme, which they called Salem. This continued as a separate parish, but was not organized as a separate town until 1819 Again, in October, 1728, the General Court created another parish in the western part of the town, which was called Westchester, which still exists under that name and continues to be a part of the town of Colchester. Obviously, upon the creation of these new parishes, it was impossible to call upon the inhabitants of the entire town to support these several parishes or to exercise control over them, and so there was created what were known as "Ecclesiastical Societies" having jurisdiction over ecclesiastical affairs, within the limits of the parishes How these were supported is unknown; whether by some system of taxation, as had been the case before, or by voluntary contributions, cannot be definitely ascertained at this time.

As has been stated, the first church was erected in 1706, at the corner of Broadway and Packwood lane, and was forty feet square. The building was sold in 1709, but the congregation continued to occupy it until 1714, when they removed into a new building erected by authority of the town meeting. This building was thirty-six by forty feet. In the meantime the population of the town had moved from its original location to the site of the present village, possibly because the settlers had found the water supply of the first location inadequate. This second church was erected a little to the east of the present church building, in the middle of what is now the highway. The third church was erected near the last in 1771, and continued for seventy years, when it gave place to the present edifice.

During its early history social lines were sharply drawn in the church. For at a town meeting held January 14th, 1715, it was provided as follows: "The pew next to the pulpit to be the first, second is designated for the second pew and the pews equal to the second, the third is designated for the third pew, fourth for the fourth pew, next the fifth, sixth, seventh, and eighth," the remaining seats were distributed among the remaining members according to their rating on the Assessment list.

Methodism was introduced by circuit preachers in 1706, but the present building was not erected until 1843. The Baptist church was organized and the present building was erected in 1836 Calvary Church was organized in 1865, and the first church erected in 1867. The first Roman Catholic mass was said in 1851 at the residence of John Murphy, and services were held for some time by a visiting priest once a month. In 1854 St. Andrew's Church building was erected, and since then it has had several additions. Within the last ten years a Jewish Synagogue has been constructed on Lebanon avenue.

One of the first matters which engaged the attention of the settlers was the education of their children. Very early they required the selectmen to see to it that their children were "fitted for some lawful employment and not become crude and stubborn; and that children and servants should be catechised once a week in the details and principles of their religion." They were required to submit to examinations on these points by any selectman. It is hard to imagine any of these gentlemen, who have for years composed our board of selectmen, holding up a youngster on the street and examining him in the shorter catechism Just when the schools were founded it is impossible to say, but more than one hundred years ago there was a school for colored children north of the old church, which resulted in the influx of a large colored population. The other schools were generally represented by the rural district school of today, but their surroundings and furnishings were very much rougher.

The celebrated educational institution of Colchester is the well known

Bacon Academy. It was founded through the generosity of Pierpont Bacon, a farmer from New London, who settled in the latter part of the eighteenth century upon a farm about three miles south of the church. By his will he bequeathed his estate to the First Ecclesiastical Society of Colchester for the establishment of a school for instruction in "reading, writing, English, in arithmetic, mathematics, and all such branches of learning for said inhabitants and such instruction to be free to children of the town." The present building was erected and school opened in 1802. It soon had a large student body, which after many years slowly decreased but has now begun to rise again. During its one hundred and thirteen years it has faithfully and successfully educated many men and women who have been successful in all the walks of life. Among those of national reputation are Senator Lyman Trumbull, of Illinois, William H. Buckingham, Governor of Connecticut, and Morrison R. Waite, Chief Justice of the United States Supreme Court. Beginning with an endowment of thirty-five thousand dollars, it has now more than sixty thousand besides its building and equipment.

Another of the institutions of the town is the Cragin Memorial Library, which was erected by Dr. Edwin B. Cragin, a Colchester boy who has achieved a notable success as a physician in the great city of New York, the most difficult of all places in which a young man can command a general recognition of his ability. It has on its shelves more than five thousand volumes.

Colchester has borne its full share in the defense of the nation. When the news of Lexington was heard over the land, seventy of its sons rushed to the relief of Boston. Their names have been preserved, and among them are those of Foote, Jones, Ransom, Bigelow, Holmes, Chapman, Storrs, Rathbone, Taylor, Day, Brown, Higgins, Fuller, Allen. This is the only roster of soldiers of the Revolution giving the residences of the privates. The official roster maintained at the capitol gives the residences of the officers only, so that it has been impossible to determine who of the residents of Colchester rendered services to the country in any of its wars unless they happened to hold an official position, and the roster is so enormous and the names so numerous that it is impractical to go over it and pick out the names of the officers who were from Colchester. This town itself has maintained no list of the men who went from here to the defense of the country.

Many years ago the town boasted of a bank, a savings bank, and was lighted by gas, but all these things have passed away. In early times the only means of transportation available to the inhabitants was the back of a horse. The inhabitants went to church on horseback, the farmer riding, and the wife on a pillion. The farmer carried his pork over the back of the horse and brought back from the market the groceries which the pork had purchased by the same conveyance. The first teaming was by oxen, of goods hauled from East Haddam landing on the Connecticut river, and the first public conveyance was a stage coach over this route. As railroads were constructed, a stage line was opened to Andover and a coach used there can still be seen back of Jonathan Clark's barn. At one time this route had become so important that it boasted of a three-seated coach drawn by six horses, and the coach itself hung on leather straps instead of springs. A coach line was run to

Norwich, which had boat connection with New York. This coach was run by John Talcott, whose descendant ran the last coach out of Colchester. When the Air Line railroad was constructed, this route was discontinued, and the coach made its regular trips between the village and Turnerville. The Air Line railroad was completed in 1873, and the Colchester branch in 1877, when the Turnerville stage was withdrawn. The principal source of freight during the history of the town has been the Hayward Rubber Company. Its freight business was for many years transacted by mule teams hauling large covered wagons over the Norwich road, to and from Norwich. The construction of the railroad, of course, put the mule teams out of commission.

While the principal industry of Colchester has always been farming, its inhabitants, very early in its history, began to avail themeslves of the many water powers found within the town. In 1704 Nathaniel Kellogg and Samuel Gillett obtained the rights to erect and operate a sawmill on "Governors Brook," probably the present location of Elgart's mill. In 1706 J. Deming obtained the rights to establish a fulling mill. In 1708 J. Wright, Ebenezer Skinner and J. Deming were granted the right to operate "Iron Works" on "Jeremy's River," the present location of Norton's paper mill, and afterwards two tanneries were located upon the same stream. In 1720 rights were given to Nathan Kellogg and others for the establishment of a grist and saw mill on Kellogg's land. In 1725 Andrew Carrier and U. Skinner obtained the right to establish a grist mill at Comstock's bridge, and afterwards A. Comstock located a grist and saw mill near the same place. On "Stoney Brook" was also a factory for the manufacturing of nails, in those days hand made.

The most important of all the manufacturing enterprises in Colchester was the Hayward Rubber Company, which was established in Colchester in 1847 by Nathaniel Hayward, a joint inventor with Goodyear of vulcanized rubber. This enterprise, beginning in a small way, rapidly expanded until from a capital of $100,000 it grew, through capitalization of profits, to $500,000, and an output of $2,000.000 per annum. It was finally absorbed by the Rubber Trust and closed. The town had of late years supported a shoe factory and a creamery, both of which have been discontinued. Today the existing manufactories are the feed, cider and vinegar mill of D. Elgart, and two paper mills, operated by H C. Brown and C. H. Norton.

The population has been a fluctuating one both in numbers and composition. In 1756 it had 2,312 inhabitants. It had increased by 1782 to 3,865, which has been the largest population in its history. From this point the population gradually decreased until 1830, when it numbered 2,073. Then the tide rose again, and in 1870 it had 3,383 people. Another decline followed, and in 1900 the population reached the lowest point in its history, 1,991. The tide began to rise again, and the census of 1910 showed a population of something over 2,100. Originally it was peopled by the old New England stock. A list is still extant of the voters of the town in 1725. This list contains many names of residents whose descendants are still with us or have been recently. Among them we find Bigelow (spelled in old times Bigeloo), Gillette (Gillett), Kellogg, Williams, Brown, Clark, Fuller, Swan, Chapman, Taintor, Baker, Foote, Taylor, Strong, Chamberlain, Pomeroy, Hall, Otis,

Palmer, Morgan, Worthington, Ransom, Huntley, Day, Carrier, Adams, Brainerd, and Staples. But the introduction of manufacturing brought in a large
foreign element, from whom are descended some of our most respected inhabitants

In 1821 John R. Watrous, Ralph Isham and David Deming conveyed to
the trustees and proprietors of Bacon Academy one and one-half acres of
land, said land being now the southerly end of the park. The borough of
Colchester was incorporated in 1846. The town is bounded on the north by
Hartford and Tolland counties and by Lebanon; on the east by Lebanon;
on the south by Salem and Middlesex county; and on the west by Middlesex
county.

East Lyme.—East Lyme is bounded on the north by Salem, on the east
by Montville and Waterford, on the south by Long Island Sound, and on the
west by Lyme and Old Lyme. It was originally part of Waterford and of
Old Lyme. It was incorporated as a town in 1839.

The well known story of the "Bride Brook Marriage" refers to a stream
that empties into the Sound somewhat west of Niantic Bay. Miss Caulkins'
poem is an interesting evidence of her ability in verse:

When this fair town was Nameaug,—
A bleak, rough waste of hill and bog,—
In huts of sea-weed, thatch, and log,
     Our fathers few, but strong and cheery,
     Sat down amid these deserts dreary.

'Twas all a wild, unchristian wood,
A fearful, boisterous solitude,
A harbor for the wild-fowl's brood,
     Where countless flocks of every pinion
     Held o'er the shores a bold dominion

The sea-hawk hung his cumbrous nest,
Oak-propp'd on every highland crest:
Cranes through the seedy marshes prest;
     The curlew, by the river lying,
     Looked on God's image, him defying.

The eagle-king soared high and free,
His shadow on the glassy sea
A sudden ripple seemed to be;
     The sunlight in his pinions burning,
     Shrouded him from eyes upturning.

They came, the weary-footed band;
The paths they cleared, the streams they spanned,
The woodland genius grew more bland;
     In haste his tangled vines unweaving,
     Them and their hopes with joy receiving.

Then beasts of every frightful name,
And wild men with their hearts of flame,
By night around them howling came;
     No arms had they but care and caution,
     And trust in God was all their portion

Firm as the rocky coast they stood,
And earnest as the rushing flood,
Disdaining fear, yet fearing God;
    Each man was both a lamb and lion,
    With heart of flesh, but nerves of iron.

They yoked the eagle to the dove,
They tamed the wilderness with love,
Clear light within, clear light above;
    By faith upheld, by foes undaunted,
    Home, freedom, country here they planted.

Great hearts were those that hither came,—
A Winthrop of undying fame,
A Brewster of an honored name;
    Great hearts, the growth of three great nations,
    Laid deep for us these firm foundations.

The angels as they glided by
Some gleams of brightness lent the sky;
And earth's own angels, too, were nigh,—
    The choicest of fair England's daughters
    Came with them o'er the billowy waters.

Now thanks to thee, O God of lands!
Who settlest lonely men in bands,
That brought these angels to our strands;
    The Rose of Eden, heavenly woman!
    To gardens changed these wilds inhuman.

See! like the rose-tree's sudden bloom,
Bright visions break the wintry gloom,
The evergreens breathe forth perfume,
    Love's purple light the scene is flushing,
    A romance into life is rushing.

A streamlet—Nameaug's western bound—
A path by craggy hillsides found,
Meandering to the distant Sound;
    A slender stream, but clear and glowing,
    Down through umbrageous valleys flowing

Forth from a lovely lake it came,
Sweet stream with an ungentle name:
But now, ice-bound, snow-wreathed, and tame,
    No longer sparkling, prattling, leaping,
    The Naiad of the brook was sleeping.

To this fair stream two sledgy trains,
Grotesque and quaint as Lapland wains,
Rushed swiftly o'er the dazzling plains:
    Vast earth before, behind all hoary,
    Embosomed in a shroud of glory.

How still is all surrounding snow!
How dead but for this diamond glow!
The sun's exuberant overflow,
    Filling the air with quivering gladness,
    Relieves earth's spectre of its sadness.

No sounding bells waked nature's ear,
Yet music, flowing sweet and clear,
Rippled the sea of silence drear.
    Cheery they come,—men, maidens, singing,
       *   *   *   *

They meet, here noble Winthrop stands.
Come forth, ye gladsome bridal bands,
Ye snow-capt hills, clap all your hands!
    Ye spicy cedars, green and towering,
    Draw round them all your screens embowering.

The woven nets are lightly spread,
The spruce boughs yield their fragrant aid,
The white smoke o'er them curls a shade,
    And fruits and viands, choice and dainty,
    Flow from the ample horn of plenty.

Her furry wrappings cast aside,
As rosy skies when clouds divide,
Forth steps the conscious, blushing bride,
    A trembling, serious, fadeless beauty,
    Commingling sweetness, love, and duty.

She stood like Summer on the snow,—
No morning dawn around could throw
Such rosy light, so warm a glow,—
    And hovering clouds, with seraphs laden,
    Showered heavenly blessings on the maiden.

She was a dame of fair degree;
Her lover, fearless, bold and free,
Had suffered scaith by land and sea;
    Their hearts long pledged by word and token,
    Now let their sacred rite be spoken

Then hands were clasped, and Winthrop prayed:
The life-long covenant was made;
High heaven a mute attention paid;
    Winds, groves, and hills, with reverence lowly,
    Trembled around a scene so holy.

"Now Sunk-i-paug is Bridal Lake:
Flow, ever flow!"—thus Winthrop spake,—
'Round hearts and homes thy journey take;
    Love's streamlet out of Bride Lake welling.
    God lead a branch to every dwelling.

Franklin.—The town of Franklin, set off in 1786 from Norwich, as were Bozrah and Lisbon the same year, was settled as early as 1710 by nearly fifty families The people of this section of Norwich, known as "West Farms," were allowed to form their own ecclesiastical society in 1716 As settlers increased in number, other societies were formed. The original society lost in power as the others branched off, but recovered under the long and able leadership of Rev. Samuel Nott, whose remarkable service has been referred to in the general history of the county.

The population increased to 2,358 in 1860, but lost by the setting off of

Baltic as a part of the town of Sprague, incorporated in 1861. Its most famous son is perhaps the Hon. Lafayette S. Foster, United States Senator for many years.

The following names are on the World War honor roll of the town of Franklin: Ralph A Armstrong, Frederic K. Armstrong, Ernest C. Ayer, Ray B. Beckwith, Harold B. Capshaw, Walter N. Chappell, John Alton Cox, Charles E. Davis, Clarence Howard Davis, Harold A. Duerr, Charles W. Frink, William C. Hanson, Herbert R. Hoffman, Alfred G. Mason, Edward W. Mason, James J. McCarthy, John N. Muckensturm, Thomas F. Murphy, Louis E. Nolan, Michael O'Hearn, Frederick H. Race, John C. Rother, Anthony Wisneske, Michael Yuschalk.

Griswold.—The town of Griswold is bounded on the north by Windham county, on the east by Voluntown, on the south by North Stonington and Preston, and on the west by Preston and Lisbon The first settler was Eleazer Jewett, from whom the borough of Jewett City (incorporated 1895) takes its name. His tombstone bears the following inscription: "In memory of Mr. Eleazer Jewett, who died Dec. 7, 1817, in the 87th year of his age. In April, 1771, he began the settlement of this village, and from his persevering industry and active benevolence it has derived its present importance. Its name will perpetuate his memory."

The town of Griswold was incorporated in 1815, being taken from the town of Preston Starting in with a small farm, Mr. Jewett developed a grist mill and a saw mill Other settlers came and set up mills on the Pachaug river. An oil mill, a woolen mill, a cotton mill, soon followed, and added largely to the prosperity of the town. While the town of Griswold itself is largely agricultural, its water power has developed large manufacturing establishments, which include the Slater Mill, the Aspinook Company, and the Ashland Cotton Company. Its population in 1910 was 4,233.

Groton.—Groton is bounded on the north by Ledyard, on the east by the Mystic river, which separates it from Stonington, on the south by Long Island Sound, and on the west by the Thames river. It comprised, originally, the part of New London lying between the Thames and Mystic rivers, but was lessened by the incorporaion of Ledyard in 1836. Groton was separated from New London in 1704, but the settlement was well started fully fifty years earlier. Mystic, Noank, and Groton are the main villages of the town. Its name was that of Governor Winthrop's English home in Suffolk county. Of one of its early settlers Miss Caulkins writes:

In 1694, Davie (John Davie, who afterwards became Sir John Davie), was one of the landholders to whom the assembly granted letters patent enlarging the territory of the New London settlement, or colony. The same year he took a prominent part in building the second meeting house in New London, being one of the building committee, which shows the activity of the man in public affairs. He had been previously appointed rate-collector and selectman for the East Side. He took a prominent part in the measures which resulted in the agreement to let the East Side become a separate township, by a vote passed in town meeting, February 20, 1705; and at the assembly, the same year, an act of incorporation was passed. After Mr. Davie had been town clerk about two years, and was one day hoeing corn in Poquonnoc plains in company with John Packer, in the midst of a strife as to which of them should prove the faster, suddenly a messenger appeared at the end of the row and inquired of the barefooted men, with their trousers rolled up, which was named Davie, and, upon being told, he congratulated Davie in these words "I salute you, Sir John Davie," . . . and tradition has it that the town clerk came out ahead of Packer, winning in the hoeing match, and that he did not deign to speak to the newcomer until he had won the wager. This same John Packer afterwards visited his old friend the baronet in England, and they had a good time together. . . Sir John Davie soon went to England and to his estates in Creedy, county of Devon, where he succeeded his uncle of the same name, but he never forgot his American relatives and friends, for he not only showed his beneficent feeling toward the school, the college and the church, but through Governor Saltonstall he made gifts, while living, to his relatives in various colonies.

An interesting item in the early town records of Groton runs as follows:

Whereas, ye money ye law allows for killing wolves is found by common experience to be too little, for commonly there are employed twenty or thirty men, who often spend two or three days about it, and then sometimes swamp them and do not kill them. Such things ye inhabitants of other places have considered, and added considerable money to what the law allows

Therefore, the inhabitants of this town are desired to add ten shillings for killing a wolf, and three shillings for swamping a wolf or wolves; but six shillings if he be killed; and three shillings for killing a grown fox or wild cat, or eighteen pence for a young one, and two pence a head for crows, and a half penny for black birds, which was voted.

In another place we have described fully the Battle of Groton Heights, from which may be seen the patriotism of its citizens. We quote from the town records an interesting proof of the town's attitude:

At a town meeting held June 20, 1774, the following action was taken: This town taking into serious consideration the dangerous situation of the British colonies in North America respecting sundry late acts of the Britsh Parliament, particularly those of shutting up the Port of Boston, the metropolis of the Province of Massachusetts Bay, and abridging their chartered rights, &c., which if carried into execution not only deprives us all of our privileges, but renders life and property very precarious, and as we esteem the inhabitants of Boston, now suffering the tyranny of said acts of Parliament, and in the common cause of America; voted, that we will join with the other towns of this Colony in such reasonable measures as shall be judged best for the general good and most likely to obtain redress of our grievances. Voted, that we esteem a General Congress of all the colonies the only probable method to adopt a uniform plan for the preservation of the whole.

Voted, that if it shall be judged best by said Congress to stop all exports to Great Britain and the West Indies, and all imports from them, we will most cheerfully acquiesce in their determinations, esteeming the benefits arising therefrom mere trifles compared with the rights and privileges of America.

In the War of 1812, Groton men did noble service in several sea fights. It is an interesting fact that during Decatur's enforced idleness in the Thames his midshipmen received instruction in mathematics from a Groton school teacher who became widely known as the originator of the famous "Daboll's Almanac." The father was aided by his son, Nathan Daboll, Jr. This almanac has been published in New London for considerably over a century.

Groton monument, erected in 1831, marks the spot of the famous Revolutionary fight, and many patriotic celebrations have been held at its fort. In the Civil War, Groton took a noble part, furnishing many volunteers and making liberal provision for the support of dependent families.

In Groton is found the oldest Baptist church in Connecticut, dating from 1705. Bishop Seabury, the first bishop of the Episcopal church in the United States, was born in Groton in 1729. He was buried in New London. Over his grave was placed a tablet with this inscription:

> Here lieth the body of
> Samuel Seabury, D D,
> Bishop of Connecticut and Rhode Island,
> Who departed from this transitory scene, ·
> February 25, 1796,
> In the sixty-eighth year of his age.
> Ingenious without pride, learned without pedantry, good without severity,
> He was duly qualified to discharge the duties of the Christian and the Bishop.
> In the pulpit, he enforced religion; in his conduct he exemplified it
> The poor he assisted with his charity; the ignorant he blessed with his instruction.
> The friend of man, he ever desired their good
> The enemy of vice, he ever opposed it.
> Christian! dost thou aspire to happiness?
> Seabury has shown the way that leads to it.

His remains were later removed to St. James' Church, New London.

In the town of Groton, on the east side of the Thames, and about three miles from its entrance, the United States Government established, in 1875, a navy yard, which grew to large proportions during the World War.

Lebanon.—The town of Lebanon is bounded on the north by Columbia, a town of Tolland county, and by Windham, of Windham county; on the east by Franklin and Bozrah; on the south by Bozrah and Colchester; on the west by Columbia, Hebron and Colchester. The town was originally somewhat larger, including a part of Columbia and other territory. The background of its history is laid in the settlement of the General Assembly, first with Uncas, then with his son, Owaneco, who sold to various proprietors a tract called the "Five-mile purchase," which, with several other tracts purchased from Indian chiefs, constituted the original territory of the town. The standard history of the earlier years is a historical address delivered by Rev. Orlo D. Hine, July 4, 1876. We quote freely from this address:

The four proprietors—Mason, Stanton, Brewster and Birchard—evidently designed that the "Five-mile purchase" and "Mason & Fitche's mile" should form the main part of a plantation, and that this street, since called Town street, should be the center, and under their direction the street was laid out, and the land adjoining it allotted. Having in view the earliest establishment and most efficient maintenance of the worship of God and the means of education, the land along the street was divided into home-lots of forty-two acres each, and there were second and third lots lying back of these, and in other parts of the town. Every one taking a home-lot was entitled to a lot of the other divisions. In this they seem to have had in view this ridge, and the possession of meadow-land in the valleys. The second and third divisions, taken from unoccupied land in other parts of the town, were assigned by lot, and hence were literally lots.

This broad street and open common, which became so marked a feature of the place, seems to have been formed in this way: Originally it was a dense alder-swamp When the settlers came to build their houses they would, of course, set them on the dryer ground of the edge of the slopes, extending back on each side. Thus between the lines of dwellings there was left some thirty rods of this swampy space. Of course it was owned by the original fifty-one proprietors of the "Five-mile purchase."

They were organized, had their officers, meetings, and records. They performed acts of ownership of the land in this street, as of other common undivided land in the purchase; and in 1808 (by William Williams and the second Governor Trumbull, as their representatives) gave to Deacon Samuel Buckingham a deed of a portion of the common in front of his premises, and received of him forty dollars as the price. They had meetings at a still later date.

The actual settlement of the plantation began in 1695, and its increase appears to have been rapid, the number of grants and allotments bearing date November that year being more than fifty. The "Five-mile purchase" evidently came then to be fully open for occupancy, and settlers rushed in. They came from different quarters, some from Norwich, others from Northampton, still others from other places in this colony and in that of Massachusetts.

Lebanon has been spoken of as originally a dependence of Norwich. No part of its territory was ever embraced in the Nine-mile square, which constituted the territory of Norwich, or was ever under the jurisdiction of Norwich; and there is no evidence that a majority of the early settlers came from that town—the Clarks, the Deweys, the Trumbulls, the Strongs, came from other places.

The inhabitants held a meeting in 1698, and the earliest record of the town or settlement, as it was properly called, was then made The year 1707. Lebanon stands £5,179, and 135 taxable persons. For a few years the settlement of the town appears not to have been rapid Privations and hardships must have been endured by those who came here, their dwellings must have been log houses among the trees and bushes, with here and there a clearing, and all uncertainty as to the bounds and titles of lands had not ceased to perplex and embarrass.

That there was a great amount of danger or annoyance from the Indians does not appear, the Indians of this section being friendly to the English, in league with them, and very much dependent on them. There is a tradition that some Indians of a tribe at war with the Mohegans—perhaps from a remnant of the Pequots, possibly from the Narragansetts, still farther east in Rhode Island—took a Mohegan child from the house of Mr Brewster, who lived on the Brewster place, near where Hon. Edwin M. Dolbeare now resides, and killed it, dashing its head against the garden fence. This tradition comes reliably from one who lived near the time of the alleged event, and who spoke of it as a fact well known There is also a tradition that the Abel house, which stood where Mr. Robert Peckham's house now stands, was a sort of fort (stockaded, I conclude), to which the inhabitants fled in times of danger.

If the Indians did not seriously trouble the settlers the wild animals did So late as 1730 the town offered a bounty of ten pounds for every full-grown wolf that should be killed. Col. James Clark, of Bunker Hill celebrity, who died December 29, 1826, ninety-six years of age, used to relate to his grandchildren, who are now living, that in his boyhood, as, coming from Norwich in the evening, he reached the low ground near where Mr Jeremiah Mason now lives, he drew his feet up upon the saddle to protect them from the wolves, which he often heard barking and howling in the thickets on each side of the road. Deer and wild turkeys were abundant The first settlers had common corn-lots, which they joined in clearing, fencing, and guarding. I have queried whether they had the fever and ague, and I am sure they had, and must have shaken soundly with it, but probably it did not frighten people away, for it must have prevailed in all the new settlements.

After about 1707 the number of taxable persons ceased to be given in the public records, and only the property list is noted. The list continued steadily to increase, and to gain on the lists of other towns in the colony. In 1730 it was £19,972; 1733,£23,803 and was in amount the eighth in the colony. In 1740 it was £31,709, and was the fifth among the forty-eight towns in the list, and more than that of Hartford or New London; in 1748, £35,570 From 1730 to 1760 Lebanon must have gained rapidly in population and wealth. The colony of Connecticut had greatly prospered. In 1730 the number of inhabitants, according to a census then taken, was 38,000, and about 700 Indian and negro slaves and 1,600 Indians. In 1756, twenty-six years later, the population of the colony, consisting of seventy-nine towns and settlements, was 130,612, an increase of 90,312, and Lebanon then had a population of whites, 3,171, and blacks, 103; total, 3,274. Only five towns in the colony had a larger population, viz.: Middletown, the largest, 5,664; Norwich, 5,540; New Haven, 5,085; Fairfield, 4,455; and Farmington, 3,707; Hartford had only 3,027. In 1774, the year before the battle of Lexington, there were but seventy-six towns and settlements in the colony, some of the smaller settlements having been given up; the population of the colony had increased to 198,010. The population of this town was then, whites, 3,841, blacks, 119; total, 3,960, the largest population the town has ever had. Only six towns in the colony then had a larger In 1784 the population of the State had grown to 208,800, and Lebanon had, whites, 3,827, 4 less than ten years before; blacks, 94, 25 less than sixty years before; total loss, 29 Only eight towns then had a larger population, New Haven having the largest, 7,960 In 1775 only eight towns had a larger grand list than this town, it being then £41,600, equal to $130,300, the pound then being $3 33 1/3. The grand list in 1876 was $1,185,047. Though the population has diminished, the grand list has largely increased. The population of the town in 1870 was 2,211, an increase on that of the two preceding decades; in 1804, Columbia, with a population of about 600, was set off from this town; it now has a population of 891; add this to the present population of the town, and the total is 3,162, showing a total diminution of 798 since 1774 within the territory then constituting Lebanon.

As we have said, the thirty-five or forty years previous to 1774 were a period of great prosperity to the town. Men of character and enterprise came in and grew up here. Capt. Joseph Trumbull came here from Suffield about 1,704, evidently without any considerable means, for when he bought the place which had been occupied by Rev. Joesph Parsons he mortgaged it for the sum of three hundred and forty pounds. He had vigorous traits, became a planter and trader, and at length had a ship which carried cargoes of his own, or belonging to his family.

A fact which comes to us on good authority illustrates the temper of the man. His business often called him to Boston, and sometimes he went as a drover, and he would meet Rev Mr. Wells, who had been pastor here, whose parishioner he had been, and who now lived in Boston Mr. Wells was a little shy of him, and evidently avoided him now and then, in his plain and perhaps dusty attire, as not quite in trim to be familiarly recognized by a Boston gentleman When Mr. Wells came here, where he still owned property, and (meeting Mr Trumbull) accosted him as an old acquaintance, the latter refused to shake hands with him, and turned away, saying, "If you don't know me in Boston, I don't know you in Lebanon."

Trumbull's son, the future governor, after being graduated at Harvard College in 1727, went into business with his father and became a merchant, and engaged extensively in commerce, the War Office, now standing, being his store He and the firms to which he belonged owned ships which traded with London and Bristol. England. Hamburg, Germany, and the West Indies, and took in their caroges at New London and Stonington, and at Haddam, on the Connecticut river. All the trades were carried on here, and it became an important business center Cloth, leather, boots and shoes, saddles and harness, axes scythes, and barrels were made here. Among the town officers appointed every year was an inspector of leather.

The town appointed Jonathan Trumbull to obtain from the General Assembly leave to hold and regulate fairs and market-days, and they were held twice a year. These streets, now so quiet, were a place of concourse and bustle, of exhibition and traffic. which the people of surrounding towns frequented. and to which traders came from a distance, Trumbull being engaged in wide commerce and large business.

After 1743 there was a renowned school here, which Trumbull was an active man in establishing, and it was controlled by twelve proprietors, and which was kept for thirty-seven years by Master Nathan Tisdale. It became so widely known that it had scholars from the West Indies, from North Carolina and South Carolina and Georgia, as well as from the more northern colonies At one time it had students from nine of the thirteen colonies Tisdale was a genius in his profession, and carried the school to the highest stage of prosperity which it ever reached. This helped the intelligence and high character, the activity and pecuniary thrift of the place. As a result of this and other agencies, this town had for many years some of its sons in courses of liberal education, and one hundred and twenty-two are known to have received college degrees. The strong interest in education which long prevailed here accounts for the fact that so many of its sons and daughters have risen to eminence

And from the first, Lebanon has been active in military enterprises. While this town was never directly menaced by the Indians, the frontier towns of this colony and of the Colony of Massachusetts were, and this town was required to aid in the common defense. As early as 1709, Mr. Jedediah Strong, one of the original settlers, and an ancestor of the Strong family, which remained and still has representatives here. was killed in an expedition against the Indians near Albany. This colony sent troops to the defense of the county of Hampshire. Massachusetts. in which in 1704 the Deerfield massacre occurred, and which was exposed to the incursions of the French and Indians In 1709, in an expedition against Canada, in Queen Ann's War, the proportion of troops from this colony was one hundred and forty-seven, and the quota of Lebanon eleven.

In the wars in which the Mother Country was engaged at this period, the colonies were involved—in the Spanish War of 1739; in King George's War: a war with France in 1744 in which Louisburg. in Cape Breton. a very strong place, termed the Gibraltar of America, was taken; in the French and Indian War. which began in 1755 and ended in 1763 with the conquest of the whole of Canada During these wars the seas were infested with hostile ships, and the colonists were exposed on every side. The colonies learned how to raise troops. to equip and supply them. and to tax themselves in order to pay them, and thus were in most important training for the crisis now just before them. The drums used at Bunker Hill were the same which had been used at the capture of Louisburg.

Lebanon. as a town, was among the foremost in this colony in the part it bore in these enterprises and testings. In 1739, Jonathan Trumbull, then young, was commissioned lieutenant-colonel of a regiment raised for an expedition against Canada, he was afterwards colonel, and early had experience in recruiting, furnishing, and moving troops The people of the town were patriotic and spirited. On the surrender of Quebec, in 1759, they observed the general thanksgiving, and Dr. Solomon Williams' jubilant sermon on the occasion of this was published. He says, "For more than seventy years our enemies have been designing our ruin, and formed and projected a settled design to encompass us, unobserved, with a string of forts from Canada to the Bay of Mexico." He regards "the conquest of Quebec, the capital of Canada, as of more importance than has ever been made by the English since England was a nation." He states his reasons, and calls upon the people triumphantly to praise Him who has given such success.

Of course a people thus trained, in such a temper, and having such leaders as there were here in Jonathan Trumbull, William Williams, and others, were all ready, when the Mother Country began to encroach on the liberties of the colonies, to resist them and to maintain their rights. When, in October, 1765, Governor Fitch proposed to take the required oath to enforce the Stamp Act, and called upon his "assistants" to administer it to him, Trumbull was among those who resisted and remonstrated. The governor urged that their allegiance to the king, the oath of their office, the safety of the charter of the colony, and their personal safety, demanded that they administer the oath and aid in the execution of the act Trumbull was ready with the reply that the act was in derogation of the rights of the colony, in violation of the common privileges of English subjects, and that they had also sworn "to promote the public good and peace of Connecticut, and to maintain all its lawful privileges," and these they would treacherously sacrifice by submitting to the demand now made upon them.

When five (the requisite legal number out of the twelve) were found ready to administer the oath, Trumbull refused to be present to witness its administration, and taking his hat hastened from the chamber, leading the six other assistants who, with him, had stood firm. This, with other clear and courageous conduct, showed him to the colonists as fitted to be their first magistrate, and to have their interest in his hands, and he was chosen governor in 1769. He already had large experience in public affairs He had fourteen times represented his town as deputy to the General Assembly and had three times filled the office of speaker; had been chosen assistant for twenty-two years, had been for one year side judge, and for seventeen years chief judge of the County Court of Windham county; had been for nineteen years judge of probate for the Windham district; had been once elected an assistant judge, and four times chief justice of the Superior Court of the colony; and for four years had been deputy governor. He held the office of governor fourteen years, and till within two years of his death.

William Williams was more impulsive and ardent, and fitted to inspire others with enthusiasm. With tongue and pen and estate he gave himself to the cause of the colonies. During the gloomy winter of 1777 he sent beef, cattle, and gold to Valley Forge, saying "If independence should be established he should get his pay; if not, the loss would be of no account to him." With such men active here, we are prepared to find on the town records resolutions like the following: At a town-meeting held 7th December, 1767, a letter received from the selectmen of Boston, as to the oppressive and ruinous duties laid on various articles, and calling for union in some common measures of relief· "Jonathan Trumbull, the selectmen, and others were appointed a committee by themselves, or in concert with committees from neighboring towns, to consider and devise such measures and means as may more effectually tend to promote and encourage industry, economy, and manufactures." Under these oppressions, bearing heavily on it as a port,

Boston appealed to Lebanon, and this town came into full sympathy and concert with it.

The number of men whom this town sent into the War of the Revolution it is now impossible to determine, so many of the rolls of companies are wanting. Some who have given most attention to the papers existing and to all the evidence, estimate that there were periods when as many as five hundred were serving in the army at the same time. Some served for short terms—three months, six months; some were minute-men, called out when the towns along the coast, New London and New Haven, were menaced or attacked This would be one to about every eight of the inhabitants at that time. The quota of this town for the Civil War, from 1861 to 1865, was 206; and the population in 1860 being 2,174, this would be one to about every ten of the inhabitants About one hundred actually went from this town, one to every twenty-one of the inhabitants.

The town records furnish abundant evidence of the resolute effort made to meet the demands for men—which came year after year as the war went on, and tasked the resources and endurance of the colonies—and to provide for the families of those absent in the army. In the later stages of the war, when a given number of men was called for, the number capable of bearing arms had been reduced, and the enthusiasm, which in the beginning had prompted men to enlist, had subsided, the able-bodied men of the town between the ages of fifteen and fifty-five were divided into classes of the same number, ten, and each class was required to furnish a man.

After the religious services on the Sabbaths, and on Thanksgiving and fast-days, especially in 1777, contributions for the suffering soldiers were received in the meeting-houses, when jewelry and every article of clothing and provisions were presented, and the ladies, as individuals and in concert, with the discreet and earnest Madame Trumbull encouraging them and setting them an example, bore their part in these contributions.

How impossible it is for us in quiet Lebanon, as it now is, to picture what Lebanon was and what transpired here during the years of the war, the governor of the State residing here, the counselor and friend and efficient helper of Washington; the Council of Safety, which aided the governor and wielded extensive powers in the conduct of the war in this State and in this part of the country, holding here nearly all of its more than twelve hundred sessions held during the war; messengers from the army and from Washington arriving at and leaving the War Office, bringing and carrying away dispatches; the governor, with the agencies he employed, engaged in procuring and forwarding provisions, clothing, and military supplies, and these streets often crowded with activity of this sort; for seven months at one period the Duke of Lauzun's legion of French cavalry here, some of them in barracks in a lot on the right of the Colchester road, called "Barracks lot," others of them on the Common, a little north of where we are assembled, where still can be seen remains of their ovens and camp utensils; the soldiers now and then stealing wood, and a sheep, a pig, and convicted and punished; a deserter shot; the duke and higher officers having quarters in the house (on the corner), in its original form, now occupied by Asher P. Smith, and some of the officers at Alden's tavern, these gentlemanly officers in their leisure flirting with the fair maidens of the place; gay festivities, at which distinguished guests from abroad were present, frequently occurring; reviews of troops; Washington repeatedly here to consult with the Governor; Lafayette here, according to Stuart in his "Life of Trumbull"; General Knox, Dr. Franklin, Samuel Adams, John Adams, John Jay, Thomas Jefferson, and others Lebanon was certainly then a center of dignity and influence, and was the military headquarters of this part of the country.

With its other important contributions to the War of Independence, this town contributed in Jonathan Trumbull a laborious and efficient War Governor, at the beginning the only loyal governor to whom Washington gave distinguished confidence, on whom he relied in the most trying emergencies, a man discreet, far-seeing, inflexible in following his convictions, eminently God-fearing, and a true patriot; in William Williams, a member of the Continental Congress in 1776-77 and again in 1783-84, a signer of the Declaration of Independence, ardent, self-sacrificing, passionate in his devotion to his country, who one hundred years ago today represented this State, represented this town in that great proceeding in Independence Hall, Philadelphia, in Joseph Trumbull, a commissary-general and the first commissary-general of the national army, whose brilliant career was cut short by an early death, hastened by his strenuous devotion to his difficult duties in organizing this department of the army; in John Trumbull, an aide-de-camp to Washington, an adjutant-general to General Gage, and a painter who acquired a distinguished reputation from his delineation of national scenes and from his portraits of distinguished men of the Revolutionary period; in Jonathan Trumbull, Jr., a paymaster to the northern department of the army, a first aide-de-camp and private secretary to Washington, a member of his family, and enjoying his high esteem. Capt James Clark commanded a company in the battle of Bunker Hill, and was in the battles of Harlem Heights and White Plains. Lieut. Andrew Fitch was in the battle of Bunker Hill, and in the service to the close of the war. John Wheelock, son of President Wheelock, of Dartmouth College, afterwards himself president, served as lieutenant-colonel in the Continental army, and was a member of the staff of General Gage.

Lebanon has done well in the men whom in different periods it has furnished—six governors of States, five of them of this State, who held the office thirty-seven years, and one of them (William A. Buckingham) a second War Governor, and a worthy successor of the first; resolute, indefatigable, large-hearted, vigorous, and upright in administration, and of a character to command universal esteem and affection; Trumbull and Buckingham! names that honor the town, honor the State, honor the nation In all the list of honored men from the beginnings have there been abler, better governors than the Trumbulls, Bissel, and Buckinghams? Four senators in Congress; seven representatives in Congress, and one of them, Jonathan Trumbull, Jr., speaker of the Second Congress; five judges of higher courts, and two chief justices: a colored man in Prince Saunders, connected for a time with Dartmouth College, who was minister from Hayti to Great Britain, and attorney-general of that government; and a large number of ministers of the gospel and other professional men

At the dedication of the War Office in 1891, several noteworthy addresses were made that bear on the history of the town The account of the celebration, edited by Mr. Jonathan Trumbull of Norwich, contains several interesting manuscripts discovered shortly before that date. We quote from the speech of Hon. N. B. Williams, made in presenting the War Office:

Although Lebanon appears to have been exceeded in population by thirteen of the seventy-six towns enumerated in the census of 1774, the excess was in most cases slight, and the population, 3,060, is by no means an adequate measure of the importance of the town in the days of the Revolution. In the grand list of 1776, but ten towns showed a higher valuation of taxable property But most significant of all is the fact that in the awards for services in the Lexington Alarm, but two towns in the State, Windham and Woodstock, were granted larger sums of money as their compensation.

The reasons for a service so largely in excess of any quota which Lebanon might have been called upon to furnish at this time seem evident. Here were the residence and home office of the only colonial governor who asserted the rights of his country as opposed to the oppressive measures of his king, which very fact must have given to that all-potent assemblage of the day, the town meeting, an inspiration and force which it might otherwise have lacked. Owing to the location of the town and the fact that the governor resided there, Lebanon must have been the place where the news from Boston was usually received in the exciting times which led up to the Revolution.

Another point necessary in maintaining our independence was concert of action, and the War Office was the great center of attraction from which such an influence arose, and its associations in this respect are calculated to touch the heart of every patriot. It was in that building that George Washington often met his bosom friend, our first War Governor, and the only one in thirteen colonies in whom he could place implicit confidence. In that office they matured plans for future action. It was there that important war measures originated, dispatches were sent to the army, reports returned, and the war council held over one thousand sessions. During some of the dark days of the Revolution, so dark as to be depressing to ordinary minds, it was the inspiring words that went forth from this council—who believed their cause was the cause of God—that gave hope and cheer to the army and renewed courage to trust in Him who overrules all events, to "keep their powder dry" and "fight on, to victory or to death."

It was military headquarters for this part of the country, and its floors have been trodden by Washington, Trumbull, Adams (Samuel and John), Jefferson, Putnam, Franklin, Knox, and many others of note, both of this country and France. The War Office was the center of influence to keep the fires of the Revolution burning, and this vast assembly shows that it will take more than another century to kill out the fire that burned in the bosoms of the patriots of '76.

I rejoice that there is a society called the "Sons of the American Revolution," formed for the purpose of perpetuating the memory of their fathers and preserving as memorials those relics that are connecting links with the Revolution, and it affords me great pleasure, in behalf of Mrs. Wattles, the donor of the War Office, to present to the Society, through their president, Mr. Trumbull, the key of said office. I do not ask you to keep it in a state of preservation, for what you have already done, and the fact that the blood of the Revolutionary fathers flows in your veins, is sufficient guarantee for the future.

Also a poem composed for the occasion by Mr. Thomas S. Collier:

What is the soul of a nation?
  Lo, is it not deeds well done?
Red blood poured out as libation?
  Hard toil till the end is won?
Swift blows, when the smoke goes drifting
  From the cannon, hot with flame?
And work, when the war clouds, lifting,
  Show the blazoning of fame?
These hold that affluence golden,
  Bright fire of sword and pen,
Which from the ages olden
  Has thrilled the hearts of men.

Not where the trumpets bluster,
  And answering bugles sound,
As martial legions muster,

Are all the heroes found;
But where the orchards blooming
  Foams white the hills along,
And bees, with lazy booming,
  Wake the brown sparrow's song,
By quiet hearths are beating
  The hearts that watch and wait,
With thought each act completing,
  That conquers Time and Fate;
Rounding with patient labor
  The work of those who died,
Where sabre clashed with sabre
  Above war's sanguine tide.

Here was no field of battle,
  These hills no echoes gave

Of that fierce rush and rattle
  Whose harvest is the grave,
Yet where the drums were calling,
  And where the fight was hot,
And men were swiftly falling
  Before the whistling shot,
No soul with hope was stronger
  Than that which blossomed here—
No voice, as days grew longer,
  Was louder with its cheer.

Ah, souls were bent and shaken
  As days grew into years,
And saw no bright hope waken
  To gleam amid the tears—
Heard no call, triumph sounding,
  From mountain side and gorge,
Only the low graves rounding—
  The gloom of Valley Forge;
Yet here a strength unbroken
  Met all the storm-filled days,
Rising sublime, a token
  Of faith, in weary ways.

What built the power, unfolding
  Such glorious purpose, when
War's carnival was holding
  High feast with homes and men?
When grew the thought, whose glory
  Burned like a sun supreme,
Above the fields, all gory
  With battle's crimson stream?
Where bloomed the manhood, keeping
  Such steadfast step and strong,
When the red sword was reaping
  The harvesting of wrong?

Here in the peace, and tender
  Warm light of heart and hearth,
Was born that virile splendor
  Which filled the waiting earth,—
That flame of Freedom, rising
  In broadening waves of light,
The souls of men surprising,
  And lifting them from night:
Here, and in kindred places,
  The fire that all could see
Shone from determined faces,
  And taught men to be free

Why are we gathered together?
  The land is full of peace,
And high in the halcyon weather
  The songs of labor increase
What makes the drums beat, ringing
  Their challenge to the hills?
Why are the bugles flinging
  Swift calls to marts and mills?
Because these walls have cherished
  A memory bright and high;
No name they knew has perished,
  For deeds can never die;

And here, when hearts were beating,
  Half hoping, half in fear,
Strong souls, in council meeting,
  Spoke firm, and loud, and clear.

There was no weak denying,
  There was no backward glance,
But where the flags were flying,
  And red shone sword and lance,
Their words rang swift and cheerful,
  And skies grew bright again,
For those whose hearts were fearful,
  For these were master men;
And one led, who unknowing
  Linked to the land his name,
By earnest manhood showing
  How near we live to fame.

Ours is the sunlit morning—
  Ours is the noontide's gold—
And the radiant light adorning
  The paths once dark and cold;
But the savor of our treasure
  Was the salt of toil, and tears,
And want, that filled the measure
  Of long and bitter years;
We drink the wine of gladness,
  We reap the harvest sheaves,
Whose seed was sown in sadness,
  And the drift of yellow leaves;
With faith, and not with grieving,
  Was built the mighty past;
What good gift are we leaving
  To those who follow fast?
What thought, what deed, what glory
  Shall mark this epoch ours,
And leave our names and story
  High set where grandeur towers?

What thing shall make men cherish
  The memory of today?
Ah, actions will not perish
  Though monuments decay
We see, spread out before us,
  The fairest land of earth,
Loud with the ringing chorus
  That only here has birth:
Ours is the holy duty
  To build, with firmer hand,
This heritage of beauty,
  That it may ever stand;

Our deeds should make more lasting
  The freedom that has grown
From toil, and tears, and fasting,
  And strength of blood and bone.
Then like the blossoms vernal
  That with the spring combine,
Our age will shine eternal,
  To all mankind a sign;
A star serene, yet showing
  Near kindred to the sun,
Whereon these names are glowing—
  Trumbull and Washington.

We quote also from an address by Rev. Leonard W. Bacon:

But a contrast as startling and intense as the canvas of history has ever exhibited was that which was exhibited here on Lebanon green when the French regiments lay cantoned here in winter quarters. Where, in American history at least, could such subjects be found for romance, or for the pencil of historical painter? These representatives of the gayest, most brilliant, most corrupt and vicious court in Europe, what kind of figure did they make in the midst of the severe simplicity of old Lebanon? We are not without some record of their impressions in the journal of the Count de Rochambeau and the travels of the Marquis de Chastellux But the contrast between the foremost personage among the Frenchmen here, the gay Duke de Lauzun, who made his headquarters at the house of David Trumbull, and the serious, precise figure of the governor is drawn already to our hand by the graceful pencil of Donald Mitchell.

And what a contrast it is—this gay nobleman, carved out, as it were, from the dissolute age of Louis XV., who had sauntered under the colonnades of the Trianon, and had kissed the hand of the Pompadour, now strutting among the staid dames of Norwich and Lebanon! How they must have looked at him and his fine troopers from under their knitted hoods! You know, I suppose, his after history—how he went back to Paris, and among the wits there was wont to mimic the way in which the stiff old Connecticut governor had said grace at his table. Ah! he did not know that in Governor Trumbull, and all such men, is the material to found an enduring state; and in himself, and all such men, only the inflammable material to burn one down. There is a life written of Governor Trumbull, and there is a life written of the Marquis (Duke) of Lauzun. The first is full of deeds of quiet heroism, ending with a tranquil and triumphant death; the other is full of the rankest gallantries, and ends with a little spurt of blood under the knife of the guillotine upon the gay Place de la Concorde.

There is another line of pedigree, too, down which the influence of the great names and examples of the Lebanon heroes has descended It is a line not always as easy to be traced as that of natural genealogy, but it is sometimes clear enough. There is the story, for instance, of the country boy who grew up in this old town some fourscore years ago, where, in the vast amplitude of the town street, he marked the traces of the old French camp, and where every house was inhabited with heroic memories and traditions. I love to imagine the handsome little fellow wandering thoughtfully among the gravestones in the old burying-ground, that tell of holy ministers, and brave soldiers, and upright citizens, and pausing to read the four inscriptions on the Trumbull monument, recording the career of one who, by the force and dignity of his character, rose from private station to be the foremost man in all the commonwealth, and, next to Washington himself, the chief promoter of his country's liberty. I love to imagine how that shining example of a Christian patriot dwelt in the young man's mind when he had removed from ancestral Lebanon to Norwich for the beginning of his fair career; and how, in the midst of daily duties in counting-room and church and municipal business, the lineaments of that heroic Puritan character unconsciously reproduced themselves in his mind; and as great events went on, and lifted him as by a rising tide into the highest station in the State, history for once consented to repeat itself, and to complete that impressive parallel on which later historians of Connecticut will delight to dwell, between the great War Governor of the War for Independence. and the great War Governor of the War for the Union and the Constitution.

The following is an extract from a speech of Rev. Dr. Samuel Buckingham, a brother of the War Governor of Civil War time:

Such were some of the people who had the early guidance of affairs and the shaping of public sentiment in this New England town. And such were some of the moulding influences which made the State what it was, and shaped our general government; and wherever they have been carried by emigration, must have been a blessing, as they have been here.

When I was a boy, emigration from this town was going on to " 'hio" —Ohio—"Genesee county," in and about Rochester, New York, and "up country," which meant Vermont. Dartmouth College, under President Wheelock, then "Moore's Charity School" for the education of Indian youth, had been taken up almost bodily and transported from Columbia, then a part of this town, to Hanover, New Hampshire. just across the river And so many of the settlers went with it from this vicinity that twenty or more of the neighboring towns in Vermont bear the names of Connecticut towns from which the settlers came. Indeed, the State had so much of this sentiment in it that it was named "New Connecticut," and the name was only changed because there were other settlements of similar origin taking the same name—like the "New Connecticut" in the Susquehanna Valley, and the "New Connecticut" of Northern Ohio, both of which distinctly show the characteristics of their origin. The springs where mountain streams take their rise, and flow down through fertile plains, and alongside of wealthy cities, to enrich the commerce of the world, and bless its countless inhabitants, are interesting spots to visit, and suggestive of what smaller towns may have done for the world and are likely to do in the future.

The list of Governors which this town has furnished to the State is certainly remarkable, both in number and character, especially considering its population and business. Entirely an agricultural town, with never more than three thousand inhabitants. it has filled the chair of State with such men as these, and for such terms of office: Jonathan Trumbull, Sr , 1769 to 1784; Jonathan Trumbull. Jr , 1798 to 1809; Clark Bissell, 1847 to 1849; Joseph Trumbull, 1849 to 1850; William A. Buckingham, 1858 to 1866. Here are five governors from the same town, holding the office by annual election for one-third of a century, and filling the office with becoming dignity and distinguished usefulness. We do not wonder at the pleasant boast of the people of the town:—"We supply Norwich with butter and cheese, and the State with governors, especially when they want good ones."

The proclamation of Governor Jonathan Trumbull, dated June 18, 1776, is worthy of permanent record:

The Race of Mankind was made in a State of Innocence and Freedom, subjected only to the Laws of God the Creator, and through his rich Goodness designed for virtuous liberty and Happiness, here and forever; and when moral Evil was introduced into the World, and Man had corrupted his Ways before God, Vice and Iniquity came in like a Flood and Mankind became exposed, and a prey to the Violence. Injustice and Oppression of one another. God in great Mercy inclined his People to form themselves into Society, and to set up and establish civil Government for the protection and security of their Lives and Properties from the Invasion of wicked men. But through Pride and ambition, the Kings and Princes of the World appointed by the People the Guardians of their lives and liberties, early and almost universally degenerated into Tyrants, and by Fraud or Force betrayed and wrested out of their hands the very Rights asd Properties they were appointed to protect and defend. But a small part of the Human Race maintained and enjoyed any tolerable Degree of Freedom. Among those happy few, the nation of Great Britain was distinguished by a Constitution of Government wisely framed and modelled to support the Dignity and Power of the Prince, for the protection of the Rights of the People, and under which that Country in long succession enjoyed great Tranquility and Peace, though not unattended with repeated and powerful efforts, by many of its haughty Kings, to destroy the Constitutional Rights of the People, and establish arbitrary Power and Dominion. In one of those convulsive struggles our Forefathers, having suffered in that their native Country great and variety of Injustice and Oppression, left their dear Connections and Enjoyments, and fled to this then inhospitable land to secure a lasting retreat from civil and religious Tyranny.

The God of Heaven favored and prospered this Undertaking—made room for their settlement—increased and multiplied them to a very numerous People and inclined succeeding Kings to indulge them and their children for many years the unmolested Enjoyment of the Freedom and Liberty they fled to inherit. But an unnatural King has risen up—violated his sacred Obligations and by the Advice of Evil Counsellors attempted to wrest from us, their children, the Sacred Rights we justly claim and which have been ratified and established by solemn Compact with, and recognized by his Predecessors and Fathers, Kings of Great Britain—laid upon us Burdens too heavy and grievous to be borne and issued many cruel and oppressive Edicts, depriving us of our natural, lawful and most important Rights, and subjecting us to the absolute Power and Control of himself and the British Legislature; against which we have sought Relief, by humble, earnest and dutiful Complaints and Petitions: But, instead of obtaining Redress our Petitions have been treated with Scorn and Contempt, and fresh Injuries heaped upon us while hostile armies and ships are sent to lay waste our Country. In this distressing Dilemma, having no Alternative but absolute Slavery or successful Resistance, this and the United American Colonies have been constrained by the overruling laws of Self Preservation to take up Arms for the Defence of all that is sacred and dear to Freemen, and make this solemn Appeal to Heaven for the Justice of their Cause, and resist Force by Force.

God Almighty has been pleased of his infinite Mercy to succeed our Attempts, and to give us many Instances of signal Success and Deliverance. But the wrath of the King is still increasing, and not content with before employing all the Force which can be sent from his own Kingdom to execute his cruel Purposes, has procured, and is sending all the Mercenaries he can obtain from foreign countries to assist in extirpating the Rights of America, and with theirs almost all the liberty remaining among Mankind.

In this most critical and alarming situation, this and all the Colonies are called upon and earnestly pressed by the Honorable Congress of the American Colonies united for mutual defence, to raise a large additional number of their militia and able men to be furnished and equipped with all possible Expedition for defence against the soon expected attack and invasion of those who are our Enemies without a Cause In cheerful compliance with which request, and urged by Motives, the most cogent and important that can affect the human Mind, the General Assembly of this Colony has freely and unanimously agreed and resolved, that upwards of Seven Thousand able and effective Men be immediately raised, furnished and equipped for the great and interesting Purposes aforesaid. And not desirous that any should go to a warfare at their own charges (though equally interested with others) for defence of the great and all-important Cause in which we are engaged, have granted large and liberal Pay and Encouragements to all who shall voluntarily undertake for the Defence of themselves and their country as by their acts may appear, I do therefore by and with the advice of the Counsel, and at the desire of the Representatives in General Court assembled, issue this Proclamation, and make the solemn Appeal to the Virtue and public Spirit of the good People of this Colony. Affairs are hastening fast to a Crisis, and the approaching Campaign will in all Probability determine forever the fate of America. If this should be successful on our side, there is little to fear on account of any other.

Be exhorted to rise therefore to superior exertions on this great Occasion, and let all the people that are able and necessary show themselves ready in Behalf of their injured and oppressed Country, and come forth to the help of the Lord against the Mighty, and convince the unrelenting Tyrant of Britain that they are resolved to be Free. Let them step forth to defend their Wives, their little Ones, their Liberty, and everything they hold sacred and dear, to defend the Cause of their Country, their Religion, and their God. Let every one to the utmost of their Power lend a helping Hand, to promote and forward a design on which the salvation of America now evidently depends. Nor need any be dismayed. the Cause is certainly a just and a glorious one: God is able to save us in such way and manner as he pleases and to humble our proud Oppressors. The Cause is that of Truth and Justice; he has already shown his Power in our Behalf, and for the Destruction of many of our Enemies. Our Fathers trusted in Him and were delivered. Let us all repent and thoroughly amend our Ways and turn to Him, put all our Trust and Confidence in Him—in his Name go forth, and in his Name set up our Banners, and he will save us with temporal and eternal salvation. And while our Armies are abroad jeoparding their lives in the high Places of the Field, let all who remain at Home, cry mightily to God for the Protection of his Providence to shield and defend their lives from Death, and to crown them with victory and success.

And in the Name of the said General Assembly I do hereby earnestly recommend it to all, both Ministers and People frequently to meet together for social prayer to Almighty God for the outpouring of his blessed Spirit upon this guilty land—That he would awaken his People to Righteousness and Repentance, bless our Councils, prosper our Arms and succeed the Measures using for our necessary self defence—disappoint the evil and cruel Devices of our Enemies—preserve our precious Rights and Liberties, lengthen out our Tranquility, and make us a People of his Praise, and the blessed of the Lord, as long as the Sun and Moon shall endure

And all the ministers of the Gospel in this Colony are directed and desired to publish this Proclamation in their several churches and congregations, and to enforce the Exhortations thereof, by their own pious Example and public instructions.

Given under my Hand at the Council Chamber in Hartford, the 18th day of June Anno Domini 1776.

JONATHAN TRUMBULL.

There is a marked difference between Jefferson's Declaration of Independence of July 4, 1776, and that solemn proclamation of Governor Trumbull of twenty days earlier, lately discovered by the keen eye of Mr. Hoadly, and characterized, perhaps with a strained use of the word, as "the Connecticut Declaration of Independence." The one starts with an enumeration of self-evident truths, and with a doctrine of human rights, and is grounded on the principles of the Contrat Social of Jean Jacques Rousseau. The other begins with the creation and the fall of man, is grounded on the Holy Scriptures, and is the utterance throughout of a lofty and noble religious faith.

Jefferson's Declaration, accepted as the voice of the American people, is famous thoroughout the world. The proclamation of Trumbull has only just now been rescued from its century of oblivion by the hand of the patient antiquary But we may safely challenge the twentieth century to pronounce between the two as to which is the nobler, more solemnly eloquent, document, and the worthier of the great theme which is common to them both.

Ledyard.—Ledyard is bounded on the north by Preston, on the east by Stonington and North Stonington, on the south by Groton, and on the west by the Thames. From the article written by Captain William T. Cook, over forty years ago, we quote briefly:

The Pequot Indians were the aboriginal inhabitants of this section of the country They were a warlike race, more savage than the surrounding tribes, and more unfriendly towards the whites, although there is no record of any Indian battle taking place within the limits of what is now known as the town of Ledyard.

A favorite place of burial seems to have been on the farm now owned by Mr. William Fanning. An old gentleman who was present at the opening of one of these graves many years ago gives this description of it: A circular opening was dug in the earth, and the body placed in a sitting posture. A stake had been forced into the ground perpendicularly in front of it; a nail was driven into the stake, on which was hung a looking-glass opposite the face of the dead, who was supposed to be a female. Two earthen bowls were also deposited in the grave; these were supposed to contain the succotash to be used as food on the journey to the spirit-land The finding of these articles in this grave shows that the body was placed there after the country was settled by the whites. The glass and bowls dropped in pieces on being exposed to the air. In the grave where another body was laid years after were buried a gun with seven pounds of powder and seven pounds of shot for the use of the hunter when he should arrive at the "happy hunting-grounds" A white man is said to have coveted these then precious articles and hired a man to rob the grave, but his courage failed before the time came for the attempt to be made, and the Indian is supposed to still retain his gun and ammunition.

The last "Retreat" (so-called) of the Pequots is a portion of it situated in the northeast part of this town. This reservation, consisting originally of nine hundred acres, was called in the Indian dialect, Mashantucket. It is now known as "Indian Town" The tribe has been gradually dwindling away, and probably at this day there is not a pure blood left.

Miss Caulkins gives the names of early settlers as follows: Christopher Avery, Robert Allyn, Philip Bell, Jonathan Brewster, William Chapman, Edward Culver, Silas Dean, Edmund Fanning, George Geer, John Hurlbutt, William Maynard, Benadam Gallup, James Morgan, Isaac Lamb, Robert Park, Peter Spicer, Ralph Stoddard, Ezekiel Turner, and William Williams. Other names were added afterwards.

Jonathan Brewster, one of the early settlers, came to America in 1621; his wife Lucretia was one of the original "Mayflower" Pilgrims, and was the daughter-in-law of Elder William Brewster of Plymouth fame. Silas Dean, Jr., born in Ledyard, was graduated at Yale in 1758, and was one of the three commissioners appointed by Congress to urge France to acknowledge the independence of the United Colonies Allyn's Point and Stoddard's Wharf still bear the name of the original settlers in these places Gale's Ferry, as the name suggests, indicates the ocupation of a former proprietor.

The original settlement, then a portion of Groton, soon obtained permis-

sion from the legislature to organize an ecclesiastical society. The parish
was incorporated in 1724 as North Groton. The town of Ledyard was incorporated January 1, 1836, taking its name from Col. William Ledyard, of Fort
Griswold fame. The town contained about 2,000 inhabitants. The population has since that day grown less. Farming constitutes the main occupation of the people. Among the men who have gained national fame is Asa
Whitney, the projector of the first Pacific railroad.

Lisbon.—Lisbon is bounded on the north by Windham county, on the
east by Griswold, on the south by Preston, on the west by Norwich and
Sprague. Originally claimed by the town of Norwich, it was granted on
certain conditions to the Mohegan chief Owaneco and his followers. An
extract from Miss Caulkins' "History of Norwich" shows how difficult it
was for the settlers to deal satisfactorily even with friendly Indians:

On this grant the sachem gathered his special clan, probably some twenty
or thirty families. An annual tribute of ten deerskins was at first demanded
of them, but the scarcity of deer in the vicinity rendered that regulation a
dead letter. Moreover, the village was soon broken up by the war with
Philip, which called the sachem and his warriors to the field and scattered
the women and children among their neighbors. When the conflict was over
a part of this tract was assigned to the Indian fugitives, called Surrenderers,
and in May, 1678, Mr. Fitch reported to the government that twenty-nine
families of this class had settled upon it under the supervision of the English.

By a deed of trust, December 22, 1680, Owaneco assigned to James Fitch,
Jr., the care and disposition of all his lands on Quinnebaug river. A few
years later, absolute deeds of sale of these and other tracts of land were
executed by the sachem in favor of the same Captain Fitch. In 1695, Owaneco
and Samuel Mason, who by his own choice and the authority of the government had been appointed his trustee, requested that a committee of the town
should be empowered to survey the three-hundred-acre grant and fix its
bounds. The next year Captain Fitch, being then proprietary clerk, recorded
the whole grant to himself, as included in the large purchases he had made
of Owaneco in 1684 and 1687. The town entered a formal protest against the
claims of Captain Fitch, particularly to the three hundred acres at Quinnebaug Falls, which had been guaranteed to the Indians with a proviso that it
should not be alienated. The course of Captain Fitch in regard to these Indian
purchases was distasteful to the town, and no clear account can be given of
the basis upon which the difficulty was settled. Apparently the town, after
some murmuring, acquiesced in the claim of Captain Fitch to what was called
the eighteen-hundred-acre grant.

Also:

The settlement of Newent was for many years obstructed by the diversity
of claims arising from a confusion of grants and conveyances. In 1723 a
committee was appointed "to enquire into and gain as good an understanding
as they can come at respecting the Indians land in the Crotch of Quinebaug
and Showtucket rivers."

In 1725 the proprietors of the common and undivided land put an end
to all controversy by giving a quit-claim deed to Captain Jabez Perkins, Lieut.
Samuel Bishop, Mr. Joseph Perkins, and Mr. John Safford of all the Indian
land in the crotch of the rivers, and of all contained in Major Fitch's eighteen-
hundred-acre grant, for the sum of seventy-five pounds money in hand paid
to said proprietors, provided that the Indians shall be allowed to remain and

occupy the tract that had been secured to them. To these purchasers and to those who should claim under them the town confirmed the title of reversion. The Indians dwindled away, and in 1745 the descendants of Owaneco and other principal Mohegans, for the sum of one hundred and thirty-seven pounds, executed a quit-claim deed of the Indian reservation in favor of the English claimants. This instrument, which extinguished the last aboriginal claim to land in the Nine-mile square, was in substance as follows:

Ann alias Cutoih. Betty Ancum widow, Wedemow daughter of Mahomet deceased, Ann otherwise young Ben's wife, all of whom are descendants of Owaneco, late sachem of Mohegan, and the said young Ben of Ben Uncas Jr. and Daniel Panganeck, all of Mohegan, for the consideration of 137 pounds in bills of credit—to Captain Samuel Bishop, Joseph Perkins, Jacob Perkins, John Safford, Joseph Safford, and Solomon Safford, to all of them in proportion as they now possess—do now relinquish all right and title to the tract of 300 acres more or less in Newent, in the crotch of the rivers of Quinebaug and Showtucket, called the Indian Land, abutting southeasterly on the Quinebaug, April 9, 1743.

Witnesses, ISAAC HUNTINGTON,
ASA WORTHINGTON.

Lyme and Old Lyme.—On the north the town of Lyme is bounded by East Haddam and Salem, on the east by East Lyme, on the south by Old Lyme, and on the west by the Connecticut river. This portion of the original town of Lyme is not the oldest portion, though it retains the original name. In 1665 the town of Lyme was set off from Saybrook In 1816 a part of the town was set off with part of Waterford to form the town of East Lyme. In 1855 another portion, as a matter of fact the oldest settled part, was set off to form Old Lyme. The original articles of agreement between Saybrook and Lyme were as follows·

Whereas there hath been several propositions betwixt the inhabitants of east side of the River and the inhabitants on the West side of the River of the towne of Saybrok towards a Loving parting, the inhabitants on the east side of the River desiring to be a plantation by themselves; doe declare that they have a competency of Lands to entertaine thirty families.

They declare that they will pay all arears of rates past and all rates due by the 2 of May next ensuing that belongs unto the towne and ministry, to be brought into the townsmen in the town plots, to wit; Richard Rayment and Abraham Post now in Place. At the request of thos on the east side of the River to abate them ther proportion belongin to the ministry from the furst of May to the latter end of January next ensuing, the towns doe consent ther unto, and in case they have not a minister selected amongst the, then they are to pay rates to the minister on the west side, as formerly, unless a minister be settled amongst them.

In reference to the Lands of hamanasuk, they on the east side of the River doe fully and freely Resign all their Rights, titles, and claims to all and every parcels of the Lands to the inhabitants of the West Side, engaging themselves to afford what help they have amongst them for the Recovery of those Lands, they being Resonably considered for their pains That the Indians at Nehantick have the Land agreed upon by the covenant maid betwixt the inhabitants of Saybrook and them.

The above laid articles being agreed upon by the comites chosen on both sides of the River, the inhabitants east side have Liberty to be a plantation of themselves In witness whereof the comites on both sides have sett to their hands. Signed by John Waldo, William Pratt, Robert Luze, William Parker, Zachariah Sanford, for the west side; Nathan Griswold, William Waller, Renald Marvin, John Luze, Sr., Richard Smith, John Comstock, for the east side.

It would perhaps be fairer to speak of Lyme as North Lyme, for the historic interest of Old Lyme is much greater than that of Lyme itself. In spite of the legal separation of these towns, their history is one from the original settlement until 1855. Miss Martha Lamb, writing for "Harper's Magazine" in 1876, said of it:

It was settled over two centuries ago (in 1666) by an active, sensible, resolute, and blue-blooded people, who gave it a moral and intellectual character which it has never outgrown. Its climate is one of perfect health, and its people live to a great age. The salty, bracing atmosphere tends towards the increase of mental vigor as well as length of years, hence the results which we are about to chronicle. It is a town which has kept pace with the times. It has been near enough the metropolis to partake of its literary culture and many-sided opportunities, and sufficiently remote to escape its dissipating wastes, and it has always maintained a self-respecting inner life. It is exceptionally rich in family reminiscences, occupies in a certain sense historic ground, and possesses elements of national interest. Lyme-Regis is said to have been famous for its physicians. Lyme is, or ought to be, famous for its lawyers, as it has produced more than any other town of its size on this continent, or any other continent, and not only lawyers, "whose trade it is to question everything, yield nothing, and talk by the hour," but eminent judges, senators, and governors, its latest and grandest achievement being a chief justice of the United States.

Lyme was formerly a part of Saybrook, the settlement of which commenced in 1635. The region was selected for the commencement of empire by Cromwell, Hampden, and several English noblemen who had become dissatisfied with the management of civil and religious affairs under Charles I., and fully determined to remove permanently to the wilds of America. They organized a company, and secured a patent for a large portion of Connecticut, and sent John Winthrop the younger to take posession and build a fort at the mouth of the Connecticut, and it was called Saybrook, in honor of Lord Say and Seal and Lord Brook who were foremost in pushing the enterprise It was located on a peninsula, circular in form, and connected to the mainland by a narrow neck, over which the tide sometimes flowed, and was considered safe from any sudden incursion of the Indians. Two great handsome squares were laid out on the rolling land near the fort, designed as a building site for palatial residences.

Colonel George Fenwick was the only one of the original patentees who came to abide in Saybrook. Cromwell and some others actually embarked in the Thames, but were stopped by an order from the king. Colonel Fenwick was accompanied by his young, lovely, golden-haired, sunny-tempered wife, Lady Alice Boteler. She had been reared in the bosom of English luxury and refinement, but could, however, adapt herself to pioneer life, and made her rude home in the quaint fort bright with wild-flowers and merry with laughter. She brought with her a "shooting-gun," with which she used to practice, to the great diversion of her neighbors, and she had "pet rabbits," and a little garden which grew table delicacies. She was fond of out-of-door exercises, and was often seen cantering over the country on horseback. She had few associates: Mrs. John Winthrop, whose home during that period was on Fisher's Island; Mrs. Lake, a sister of Mrs. Winthrop; Mrs. Anna

Wolcott Griswold; and Colonel Fenwick's two sisters (one of whom married Richard Ely), comprised about the whole list. She died after nine years of Saybrook life, and was buried within the embankment walls of the fort. Colonel Fenwick soon after returned to England, where he was one of the judges who tried the unhappy Charles I. He left his private affairs in this country in charge of Matthew Griswold, who erected the monument over Lady Fenwick's grave, which for two and a quarter centuries was an object of sorrowful interest on the treeless, flowerless, desolate bluff which overlooks the flats and shallows of the mouth of the Connecticut river. It is, howeve·, no longer there, but occupies a shady nook in the old Saybrook Cemetery Four years since an enterprising railroad corporation found the world so narrow that it must needs plow directly through this sacred spot, and not only rob us of the last shovelful of earth which our heroic ancestors heaped together, but heartlessly overturn the "quiet couch of clay" upon which Lady Fenwick had so long rested. Her remains were reinterred with imposing ceremonies. Her golden hair was found in a perfect condition, or nearly so, and a lock of it is preserved in an air-tight box in the Acton Library at Saybrook.

Lyme, notwithstanding its uneven surface, has very little waste land. Agriculture and the raising of horses, mules, and horned cattle have been a great source of wealth to the inhabitants, particularly in former years. The shad-fisheries in the Connecticut have also yielded large profits, and shell and other fish have been taken plentifully from the Sound. The town has a thrifty, well-cared-for appearance, even to its remotest borders, and a quiet, unconscious aspect, as if the stormy world had rained only peace and contentment upon its legendary soil and historic homes. It is one of the loveliest nooks on the New England coast, and if its distinguished sons and daughters could all be gathered home, the world might well pause to exclaim, in figurative language, "However small a tree in the great orchard, Lyme is a matchless producer of fruit."

Certainly no town of its size in America can boast a more wonderful list of sons and daughters than Lyme, not only as a "mother of lawyers," but as the progenitor of many famous men in other walks of life. Lyme has produced at least one author of note, Rev. E. F. Burr, for many years pastor of the Congregational church in Lyme, who wrote "Pater Mundi," "Ecce Coelum," and many other well-known volumes.

The beauty of the scenery of Lyme and the convenience of its location have made it a Mecca for artists. Here in recent years Henry Ranger, Louis Dessar, Childe Hassam, and a host of other well-known artists have lived in the summer colony. Lyme, more than any other town in New London county, is unspoiled by the bustle and uproar of our modern age. It still retains the calm and restful aspects of its earlier charms.

The deed for the lands in the town of Preston was signed by the Mohegan chief Owaneco in 1687, and was given in payment for damages to the farms of white settlers by swine belonging to the Mohegans. The early settlers came from Norwich, the first being Greenfield Larrabee, according to Miss Caulkins. A complete list of these settlers may be found in her history of Norwich.

Salem.—Salem, incorporated in 1819, was set off from Colchester, Lyme and Montville It lies south of Colchester, west of Montville, and is bounded on the south by East Lyme and Lyme Its western boundary is East Haddam, in Middlesex county. The whole region was claimed by the Mohegan Indians, who asserted that the purchase from Owaneco was illegal, inasmuch as that sachem had been intoxicated when he signed away the land. The case was long in the courts, being carried to England in the time of Queen Anne. Finally the Indians were made wards of John Mason of Stonington. The matter was really never settled so far as the courts went, but was decided by the event. As a local historian says:

Up to this period in the history of the country the sound of the woodman's axe was not heard, and the wild animals of the forest roamed undisturbed by the white man. The feathered flocks filled the air, and the aquatic bird swam on the bosom of her many lakes in undisturbed quietude; but gradually her hills and her valleys were occupied by the hardy pioneer from the Old World, where they one and all could enjoy the freedom of religious liberty, and be the humble possessors in fee simple of an heritage not immediately under the mandate of kings and potentates, but breath the air of liberty and freedom, and feel that they were lords of their own manors. Society began to shape itself by the stern reason of necessity. Laws were enacted and scrupulously kept, both religious and secular, and the preacher was regarded as a man of such superior mind and intelligence that his word was regarded as the highest authority. The presumption is strong in support of the theory that there were few or no settlers in this town prior to the year 1700, yet tradition says there was in that portion of Lyme now Salem, originally embraced on the two-mile-wide section formerly known as the Lyme Indian hunting-ground.

By various grants of the Connecticut legislature, by land, sales, and immigration, a considerable part of the region was occupied. Music Vale Seminary, founded in 1833, came to have a wide reputation, gaining pupils from widely remote points. It was the first Normal School of Music in the country

Four towns—Bozrah, Franklin, Lisbon, Montville—were set off in 1786, largely from the original town of Norwich (Montville came from New London). Their early history was linked with that of their parent towns. The Fitch family, the Bailey family, and the Hunt family, of Bozrah; the Kingsleys, the Huntingtons and other families of Franklin; the Hydes of Lisbon; the Palmers, the Robertsons, the Jeromes, of Montville, were but a few of the many settlers who moved out from Norwich and New London, made a settlement, established a place of worship, and became independent of parental control. Wherever there was water power, they established mills, and where there was no manufacturing, they created prosperous farming communities

The detailed study of any one of these little settlements will reward the investigator who appreciates the Puritan virtues.

The backbone of American liberty is found in such men and women as these In all the greater enterprises of State and Nation they did their part. The Civil War found them ready to send their boys to save the Union, and the World War again revealed that same loyalty to the ideals of liberty which the founders of our republic had shown, as appears in the military chapter of this work.

North Stonington was originally the North Society of Stonington. The situation of the meeting house was settled only after prolonged disagreement. The General Assembly of Connecticut as early as 1724 passed a vote "that the North Society of Stonington for the future be called by the name of North Stonington." Religious discussions led to a separate party even in this parish, and harmony was not restored till about 1824, when Rev. Joseph Ayer succeeded in reuniting the churches. The actual creation of a separate town took place in 1806, the Legislature insisting on the name North Stonington rather than "Jefferson," the name for which the town meeting had voted.

Sprague.—The town of Sprague was incorporated in 1861, from Lisbon and Franklin, taking its name from Governor Sprague of Rhode Islnad, who started a large cotton mill in what is now the village of Baltic. We quote a local historian:

This town in the rapidity of its growth resembles the changes that often take place in western clearings. Lord's bridge, where the Shetucket was spanned to unite Lisbon and Franklin, and near which the Lord family dwelt in quiet agricultural pursuits for more than a century—father, son and grandson living and dying on the spot—was a secluded nook, without any foreshadowing of progress or visible germ of enterprise. A grist mill, a saw mill, coeval of the first planters, a respectable farm house, with its sign-post promising entertainment, and two or three smaller tenements, constituted the hamlet. Only the casual floods and the romantic wildness of the river banks interfered with the changeless repose of the scene

Suddenly the blasting of rock and the roar of machinery commenced; hills were upset, channels were dug, the river tortured out of its willfulness, and amid mountainous heaps of cotton bags the rural scene disappeared, and Baltic village leaped into existence. In the course of five years more than a hundred buildings, comprising neat and comfortable houses, several shops, a church and a school house, grouped around the largest mill on the Western Continent, had taken possession of the scene, the whole spreading like wings each side of the river and linking together two distinct towns.

The town is bounded on the north by Windham county, on the east by Lisbon, on the south by Norwich, and on the west by Franklin.

Stonington.—The town of Stonington was first settled under the leadership of William Chesebrough, who had come to visit John Winthrop's settlement at Pequot, but preferred the region further east. He built in 1649 a house and settled with his family, supposing he was within the borders of Massachusetts. The General Court of Connecticut, however, claimed jurisdiction of the region. In 1652, after considerable effort, he obtained a grant for himself and his sons. Other settlers came gradually, amongst whom were Thomas Stanton, Thomas Miner, Governor Haynes, Walter Palmer, Capt. George Denison, Capt. John Gallup, Robert Park, and their families. Being repeatedly refused incorporation as a separate town by the General Court of Connecticut, they made a similar request of the Massachusetts General Court. The disagreement between the courts of the two colonies was referred to the commissioner of the United Colonies. A full account of the documents sent and received may be found in the "History of Stonington," written by Mr. Richard A. Wheeler.

The commissioners in 1658 decided that the region east of the Mystic river belonged to Massachusetts, the portion between the Mystic river and Pawcatuck river to be called Southerntown. Rev. William Thompson, who had come to the settlement in 1657, was for two years preacher to the settlers and to the nearby Indians, a remnant of the Pequot tribe which had been defeated by John Mason. The difficulties of the settlers were increased by the claims of certain men from Rhode Island who had secured a title from one of the Pequot chiefs.

The Connecticut charter of 1662, however, fixed the eastern boundary of the colony at Pawcatuck river, which remains the boundary of Connecticut and Rhode Island today. Massachusetts yielded her claims, and the General Assembly of Connecticut issued a charter in 1662. In 1665 the name Southerntown was changed to Mystic, and in 1666 the name Mystic was changed to Stonington. In 1668, according to Mr. Wheeler, there were 43 inhabitants, viz.: Thomas Stanton, George Denison, Thomas Miner, John Gallup, Amos Richardson, Samuel Chesebrough, James Noyes, Elisha Chesebrough, Thomas Stanton, Jr., Ephriam Miner, Moses Palmer, James York, John Stanton, Thomas Wheeler, Samuel Mason, Joseph Miner, John Bennett, Isaac Wheeler, John Denison, Josiah Witter, Benjamin Palmer, Gershom Palmer, Thomas Bell, Joseph Stanton, John Fish, Thomas Shaw, John Gallup, Jr., John Frink, Edmund Fanning, James York, Jr., Nathaniel Beebe, John Reynolds, Robert Sterry, John Shaw, John Searls, Robert Fleming, Robert Holmes, Nathaniel Chesebrough for Mrs. Anna Chesebrough, his mother, Gershom Palmer for Mrs. Rebecca Palmer, his mother, Henry Stevens and Ezekiel Main.

A home-lot was laid out for each inhabitant, and the title was obtained by lottery on the following conditions, namely: "If built upon within six months and inhabited the title would be complete, except that each proprietor must reside on his lot two years before he could sell it, and then he must first offer it to the town and be refused before he could sell the same to any person and give good title. How many of these home-lots were built upon by the then inhabitants cannot now be ascertained."

The young settlement was in special danger at the time of King Philip's War, but kept the Pequots friendly to the English. Captain George Denison was provost-marshal of New London county during the war, and almost every able-bodied man of Stonington took part in it. After King Philip's War the town grew, but in 1720 a portion was set off as North Stonington. The general conditions of a settlement at Long Point, a part of the town of Stonington, are interestingly portrayed in a document from the Connecticut Archives, quoted by Mr. Wheeler:

To the Honorable General Assembly of the Colony of Connecticut to be held at Hartford on the second Thursday of May instant. The memorial of William Morgan, Benjamin Park, John Denison, 4th, Joseph Denison, 2d, Oliver Hilbard, Edward Hancox, Oliver Smith, and the rest of the subscribers hereto in behalf of themselves and the professors of the established Religion of the Colony, living at a place called Long Point in Stonington in the County of New London humbly sheweth, that they are scituate near four miles from any meeting house and that the inhabitants living at said Long

Point are generally poor they living principally by the whale and cod-fishery, there carried on, to the public advantage, by which means within a few years said place has increased to upwards of eighty families among which are twenty widows, seventeen of which have children as families there that the whole number of inhabitants are nigh to five hundred, that there is not among them more than one horse to ten families, so that but very few are able to attend meeting at the meeting-house except those that are robust hardy and used to travel on foot, which are very few, the greater number of said inhabitants consisting of women and children, that thereupon the society have for several years consented to have one sermon preached a said point every Sabbath by their Rev. Pastor, which he has performed and is still willing to continue, but their number has so increased that it is very inconvenient for those that do attempt public worship (as they have no where to convene but in a small school house or private houses) and many more than at present do attend would if there was room to accommodate them; that for the want of a proper place to meet in for the celebrating divine service, many who means the Sabbaths are misspent and may be more and more misspent and pro-phaned, that those who would be glad to build a house and maintain preach-ing and good order among them have been and continue unable of themselves to bear the expense, by which the cause of religion much suffers there, and the good people among them greatly fear the increase of vice and irreligion. That the town of which your memorialists are a part, have lately paid and are liable to pay upwards of one thousand pounds for the deficiency of sev-eral collectors that have lately failed that your memorialists from great neces-sity, by their being very remote from any constant grist mill, have lately con-tributed about £70 as an incouragement to an undertaker to build a wind mill at said point, which with about the same sum lately subscribed by said in-habitants for a schoolhouse, with the great labour and expense they have been at to make roads and causeways to said point, all which with the poor success that attended the last years fishery, and the lowness of markets and the various and different sentiments in the religious denomination of chris-tians among them, viz · First day Baptists, Seven day Baptists and the Quak-ers or those called Friends, are such real grief and great discouragements to your memorialists, who are of the established Religion of this Colony, that they can no longer think of obtaining a meeting-house by subscription or any other ways among themselves

Wherefore they humbly pray that liberty may be granted to build a meeting house for public worship at said Long Point, and that your Hon-ours would in your great goodness grant them a Lottery for raising a sum sufficient for the purpose aforesaid or so much as your Honours shall think proper under such restrictions and regulations as your Honours shall think fit, and your memorialist as in duty bound shall ever pray.

It was not at all uncommon for the General Assembly to grant permis-sion for churches to raise money by lottery in those days. Permission was twice granted to the Long Point settlers to raise £400 by lottery.

At a general Assembly of the State of Connecticut holden at Hartford in said State on the second Thursday of May, being the 12th day of said month, and continued by adjournments until the ninth day of June next fol-lowing Anno Dom. 1785 Upon the memorial of Nathaniel Minor, John Denison 3d and Joesph Denison 2nd, all of Long Point in Stonington, set-ting forth that they with others of the first Society in said Stonington were on the second Thursday of October 1774 appointed Managers of a Lottery granted by the Honorable General Assembly to your Memorialists William Morgan and others of the established Religion of the then Colony of Connecticut for the purpose of raising the sum of £400, to build a Meeting House at said Point. That said Managers proceeded by way of Lottery to raise said sum in Continental Bills toward the close of the summer of 1777, when your Memorialists for whom the Grant was made, not being apprehensive of the depreciation that would attend said Bills and considering the great scarcity and dearness of materials for building said House and the dangers they were then exposed to from the enemy who were then at New York, Newport and Long Island, thought best for the Grantess not then to proceed in building said House, since which the Bills in the Hands of your Memorialists have depreciated to almost nothing except a part which has been turned into Public Securities, Praying that a Judicious Committee may be appointed to examine into the matters of said Memorial and the true State and Circumstances of the money which they hold in trust, put a just value thereon, and that said Committee be enabled to direct said Managers, to raise on said Grant such Sums with what they already have as to make up the £400. Granted by your Honors as per memorial.

Resolved, by this Assembly that said Nathaniel Minor, John Denison, and Joseph Denison 2d be continued as Managers of said Lottery with the addition of James Rhodes and Elijah Palmer of said Stonington, and that the Honorable William Hillhouse and Benjamin Huntington Esqrs, and Elisha Lathrop Esq be and they are hereby appointed a committee to enquire into the state and circumstances of said lottery and liquidate and settle the Accounts thereof, and ascertain the value of the avails thereof in the Hands of said Managers, and in case said Committee shall judge it to be reasonable, they may and they are hereby Authorized and impowered to direct that said Managers proceed to Issue and draw such further numbers of tickets in said Lottery as to raise such sum of money for the purpose of building a meeting House at said Point as shall be thought by said Committee to be proper, not exceeding £400, including what is already on hand as aforesaid and exclusive of the cost of said Lottery, said managers to be accountable to the General Assembly when requested for their Doings in the premises.

James Abbott McNeil Whistler, the great artist, passed his boyhood in Stonington

Voluntown.—Situated in the northeastern part of the county, Voluntown is bounded on the north by Windham county, on the east by Rhode Island, on the south by North Stonington and on the west by Griswold. Its forty square miles of territory supports a population of less than one thousand people who are for the most part farmers. The name "Volunteers' Town" comes from the fact that the land was given in 1700 to volunteers of the Narragansett War. The settlers came mostly from Norwich, New London and Stonington. In 1719 a strip of land to the north was granted in lieu of a portion to the east claimed by Rhode Island.

The village of Pachaug grew up from cotton manufacture on the Pachaug river. The incorporation of the town took place in 1721, but lost the territory of the present town of Sterling in 1794. Voluntown, which till 1881 was in Windham county, was annexed to New London county at that date.

Waterford.—Bounded on the north by Montville, on the east by the Thames and by New London, on the south by Long Island Sound, and on the west by East Lyme, Waterford was incorporated as a town in 1801, being taken from New London. Its forty square miles are devoted chiefly to agriculture and quarrying, though there is some manufacture in the village of Flanders.

CHAPTER VIII

NEW LONDON COUNTY TODAY

A General Review — 250th Anniversary Celebration — The Principal Manufacturing Establishments — National and State Officials — Recapitulation.

It is the purpose of this chapter to make a general review of the recent developments of the county, showing how the present has grown from the past, and summarizing in statistical form many matters that have been discussed in special topics in foregoing chapters.

Topographically, the area of seven hundred square miles is of as great interest to the modern business man as it is to the geologist. The glacial action that left the rocks in the fields, the wearing down of river beds that produced the water power of the county, the deep estuary of the Thames, which offers one of the best harbors on the Atlantic coast, have resulted not only in a wonderful variety of landscape, but also in a remarkable diversity of industries. A climate at once bracing and wholesome, yet not too severe for open air labor throughout the year, has conduced to the success of agriculture and manufacturing. Yankee ingenuity and thrift, combined with a spirit of enterprise and progress, have taken advantage of natural advantages to develop remarkable prosperity. Education, in school and out, has helped to cultivate the best ideals of American citizenship. And while sixty per cent. of the population is either of foreign birth or foreign parentage, the loyalty to American ideals is as strong today in our county as it was fifty years ago. It will be interesting to note some of the public enterprises that have been carried out in recent years.

If some fifty-year Rip Van Winkle were to visit us, the first thing he would note is, doubtless, the improvements in our roads. With State subsidies have been combined local grants to make a splendid network of roadways that make the county at once smaller and stronger than ever before. The most encouraging thing about the situation is that the public is still unsatisfied, and is planning greater things for the future.

Our Rip might not at first comprehend the horseless vehicles that have made good roads a necessity, any more than he could understand the thousand and one other marks of scientific advancement of the age; but he would undoubtedly note a great change for the better, and in a few hours could traverse a region that formerly required days of travel. Were he to come by train, he would be surprised that his train rushed over the Connecticut river and the Thames unimpeded by the need of delay for the ferry. New bridges, indeed, have replaced the former ones, one of which is now used as a highway between Groton and New London, while over the Connecticut is a splendid toll bridge built by the State. He could hardly avoid seeing the million dollar pier built by the State at New London, and, two miles upstream, the large naval base with its fleet of submarines and its wealth of equipment. If he were to ask, he would find that the channel of the Thames has been well dredged, so that ships of good size can sail to its head at Norwich.

A drive up the military highway on the east side of the Thames would reveal Connecticut College on the heights of the western shore, would show him the State Hospitals, one on the east side and one on the west, near Norwich. The tall chimneys lining the river would remind him that in the last fifty years the county has entered more deeply than ever into manufacturing.

If he were to visit Norwich, New London, and Stonington, he would note with approval the many fine public buildings, the memorial tablets and monuments, the public parks, the reservoirs, the improved streets, and the splendid school buildings under construction or in use already. Other buildings for public use such as libraries, Y. M. C. A. buildings, hospitals and church edifices, would show great improvement over those of his day.

All of the advances in modern science, such as the use of electricity for light and power, for the telephone and the street railway, would remind him that New London county with the rest of the world had entered upon a new era in the past fifty years. The points of historic interest to the tourist are well covered in several handbooks. A brief outline of these will serve to show why the tourist and summer visitor have made this county a rendezvous, combining as it does natural charm, healthful climate, and personal ties that reach out all over our land. The real history of New London county would follow its children in their westward migrations and would reveal the pioneer spirit of early days, expanding throughout the upbuilding of many other sections of the United States.

Starting with the western end of the county at the Connecticut river toll bridge, eighteen hundred feet long, one enters Old Lyme, opposite Saybrook, famous for its beauty, unspoiled by modern industry. The meeting house was rebuilt from the same plans as the former one of 1817 which was burned about ten years ago. The plan, said to be copied from the plans of Sir Christopher Wren, is well suited to the simple charm of the town, with its wide streets and overarching elms. In Old Lyme a notable gathering of eminent artists is found throughout the warmer months. Their annual exhibition is a noteworthy event. For permanent exhibits an Art Gallery has been erected on Old Lyme street. The Griswold House (not to be confused with the Griswold Hotel at Groton) is famous for the artists it has entertained, and who have left specimens of their art in the decorations of the house. It is best known as the subject of W. L. Metcalf's "May Day," now in the Pittsburgh Art Gallery. To catalogue the artists who spend their summers in Old Lyme would be a long task. Many who came for a brief stay have built substantial homes on attractive sites. The home of the first minister of Lyme, Rev. Moses Noyes, is now occupied by his descendant, the eminent Judge Walter C. Noyes.

North of Old Lyme is Lyme, with its growing artist colony at Hamburg Cove. Lords Cove, on the east of the main channel of the Connecticut, is a famous hunting resort when rail and ducks are in flight.

The high hills with the picturesque ponds and "Eight Mile River" make Lyme a most attractive summer resort for many cottagers. In industry, the shad fisheries and agriculture furnish the main occupations of residents, though there are a witch hazel factory and small mill.

If we go east from Old Lyme along the Sound, we pass through "Black Hall," settled by Matthew Griswold in 1645 and retained in the family for six generations. The many names of local significance such as Hawk's Nest, Giant's Neck and many others, indicate that the whole shore line has become one great summer resort. Just before reaching Bride Brook, whose story has been told at length in another part of our history, we pass the birthplace of Morrison Waite, former Chief Justice of the United States Supreme Court.

The town of East Lyme, with its Black Point colony (this section was once the reservation of the Niantic Indians), its large settlement at Crescent Beach, and its inns and cottages in Niantic proper, gets much of its living from summer visitors, but has also a considerable business in fisheries, and there is considerable woolen manufacture in the northern part of the town near Flanders village. Here is to be found a camping ground much used by the State militia. The former toll bridge, which succeeded the old Rope Ferry, has been replaced by a handsome bridge constructed recently by the county.

Crossing this bridge, we come into Waterford with its famous Millstone granite quarries. In Waterford was a settlement of the Rogerene Quakers whose adherents gave much trouble in New London in early times. New London, next to the east, will be described later.

After crossing the Thames on the old railroad bridge, given to the adjacent towns by the New York, New Haven & Hartford railroad and converted into a highway bridge, we come to Groton. The industrial growth of Groton will be later described; its ancient history has already been touched upon. To the traveler the Groton of today has many points of interest.

The Monument, not very tall in itself, but situated at the crest of Groton Heights, commemorates the place where Colonel Ledyard and his comrades fell in September, 1781. Near the Monument one may see the remains of the old fort, and close by the Bill Memorial Library, one of many beautiful buildings given for public use in our county. The Hotel Griswold at Eastern Point, Groton, is one of the finest hotels on the coast, and is one of the many improvements made by the late Morton F. Plant, whose estates in East Lyme and Groton are model establishments for the county at large. The shipbuilding village of Noank lies within the town limits. The fine military road from Groton to Norwich takes one up the east bank of the Thames by the Naval Station (Submarine Base), equipped to accommodate several thousand men, with splendid facilities for harborage and wharfage.

The Mystic river, formerly the boundary between Connecticut and Massachusetts, separates Groton from Stonington. In the bay adjacent to Stonington is a stone marking the coming together of three States—Connecticut, Rhode Island, and New York. In Mystic village much building has been done in times past. Here also are made Lathrop's engines, Packer's Tar Soap, and various parts of machinery. Here also, as at the mouth of the Connecticut river, the artists have formed a colony. Stonington is in many respects the Stonington of early days, but the whaler is seen no more. Time was when its seafarers led the fleet in Antarctic voyages. Relics and memorials tell of those days. The steamship line that ran to New York has been abandoned. Its chief industries today are the manufacture of machinery, printing presses, woolens, velvets, and threads. Its population has grown in the last decade from 9,154 (1910) to 10,236 (1920). Pawcatuck village, a part of Stonington, is, economically, a part of Westerly, Rhode Island, Pawcatuck river being the eastern boundary of New London county and of the State.

The most remarkable topographical feature of North Stonington is Lantern Hill, famous for the view from its summit and for the silex that is mined from its sides. A new State road now passes through North Stonington village, connecting Norwich and Westerly. The Wheeler School and Library is a fine structure, one of the many memorials erected in the county by private generosity. The main industry is agriculture. It has the largest area of any town in the county, with a population of 1,144 (1920). Its prosperous farms add much to the variety of scenery in the county.

To the north from North Stonington lies Voluntown, the least easily accessible town of the county. Its 656 inhabitants have, on an average, about four hundred acres apiece. Farming is the main industry, but the manufacture of cotton goods is carried on successfully. Its hills and ponds make it a favorite resort for summer campers.

To the north of Groton lies Ledyard, then Preston, then Griswold, in succession. Ledyard, rich in history and in hills, is crossed by the State highway in its north-eastern corner, and has easy access to the outside world by the railroad running up the eastern shore of the Thames river. This agricultural community is cut up into many hamlets by its rugged contour. On the river front we find Gales Ferry, for a month each year the home of Yale and Harvard oarsmen. Decatur Hill is the most conspicuous landmark for miles around; Allen's Point, Stoddard's Wharf, Fort Point, and Poquetonuck, bring to mind the Indian aborigines, the colonial settlers, and the days of Stephen Decatur.

The town of Preston, today a suburb of Norwich, has within itself Preston City, a village that was once the metropolis of its farming population. Its name, like that of Jewett City in Griswold, reminds us that the West is not alone in place-names based on hopes rather than accomplishments. The Norwich Hospital for the Insane, at Brewster's Neck, marks the modern progress of State and county in social amelioration of the helpless.

Griswold, once a farming village, has become the home of manufactures, which will be described when we consider the industries of the county. West of Griswold lie four children of Norwich—Lisbon, Sprague, Franklin and Bozrah. Their rich scenery and fertile fields have attracted many former residents who have returned to build up and occupy the ancestral farms. Their water power has built up thriving communities at Versailles and Occum (named for Samson Occum of Dartmouth College fame), at Baltic, and at Fitchville.

Of Lebanon, much has already been written. On the Central Vermont railroad, but somewhat isolated from modern industrial growth, she retains her earlier simplicity and charm   One who desires to revive his memories of earlier days can do no better than to visit the village, see the long common, characteristic of early New England settlements, inspect the old War Office, preserved as a historic memorial, survey the broad fields heavy with crops. As the people of the town say, "We supply Norwich with butter and cheese, and the State with Governors, especially when they want good ones." With never more than three thousand inhabitants, it has furnished five governors of the State, who served collectively for thirty-eight years.

The central towns of the county, Norwich and New London, too, abound in monuments of supreme interest to the antiquarian   New London, with its splendid harbor, its State pier (costing over a million dollars), its railroad facilities, its natural beauty, and its successful industries, must become in time a metropolis for Eastern Connecticut. Its face is set toward the future, but its present beauty is enhanced by many an historic memorial

The Shaw Mansion of Acadian memories contains many relics of great interest; the old mill has already been referred to; the Nathan Hale school-house, kept as a museum of Revolutionary relics; the Soldiers' and Sailors' Monument near the railroad station at the foot of State street—these and many more reminders are to be found.   But even more impressive are the buildings of recent times, both public and private.

The Y. M. C. A. building, the Public Library, the Club buildings, the Plant building, the Munsey building, the splendid school buildings, the hospitals, the stores, the parks, the remarkable villas of the summer colonists, combine to make New London a wide-awake, modern city, proud of its past, even prouder of its future. Of its industrial growth we shall soon speak.

As one follows the road up the west side of the Thames, he sees the buildings of Connecticut College so beautifully situated on the hill; he passes through Waterford and Montville, and comes to Norwich, the "Rose of New England." This is the route followed by the old "Mohegan Trail," with slight modifications. Uncasville (in Montville) is well named for the chief, Kitemaug, Mohegan Hill, and Trading Cove, remind us that in this region the Mohegans lingered longest; do, in fact, linger to this day. Montville gets its living today chiefly from manufactures, though there is some farming.

Norwich, on its hills, is at the head of the Thames, where the Shetucket and Yantic join. Rich in interesting memorials, it has many modern buildings and public works of which to boast. In Norwich are a number of parks (the largest, Mohegan Park) aggregating four hundred acres   Norwich is the burial place of Uncas, of Miantonomoh, and of Captain John Mason. The Uncas monument was dedicated in 1833, the Miantonomoh monument in 1841, the John Mason monument in 1871

The most remarkable of the buildings of the last fifty years is the Slater Memorial building given in 1888 by Mr. William A Slater, in honor of his father, John F. Slater, who gave one million dollars for the education of freedmen in the South. This building, with its museum and art collections, belongs to the Norwich Free Academy.

The development of Norwich within the past fifty years has proceeded largely on industrial and commercial lines The Bank buildings, the Shannon buildings, the Otis Library, the Town Hall, the Thayer building, the Backus Hospital, one of the best plants of its size to be found anywhere, the Buckingham Memorial building (formerly the residence of Governor Buckingham, and now devoted to patriotic purpose, under the control of the Grand Army of the Republic and the members of the American Legion), are only a few of its notable structures. New buildings are planned for the immediate future—a new Y. M. C. A. building and a modern school building of splendid equipment on the West Side. The beautiful residences, the noble trees, the sightly streets and parks make Norwich well worthy of its title of the "Rose of New England."

New London county history could be fairly estimated from its names, chiefly Indian, English, and Biblical. Certainly in Norwich these names are significant. Yantic, Shetucket, Quinnebaug, Wauregan, Mohegan, Occum, Wequonnoc, Ponemah, are a few names that will keep the Indian aborigines in mind for centuries to come.

Judge Samuel O. Prentice, in his historical address delivered at the 250th anniversary celebration in 1909, thus refers to the history of Norwich for the past fifty years:

The limits of the city have been extended four times, and those of the town once. In 1874 the Greeneville section was added to the city, as were Laurel Hill and Boswellville in 1875. In 1901 the western portion of the town of Preston was taken into both the town and city, and in 1907 that portion of Mohegan park which lay without the city limits was included in them. In 1870 the completion of the city's fine water supply system, work upon which had been begun in 1867, was fittingly celebrated, and on July 4th President Grant honored the city with a visit, and received the enthusiastic welcome of its people The same year the first street railway line was built. It extended from Greeneville to Bean Hill. It was electrified in 1892, and since that time radiating lines have been constructed furnishing direct and convenient communication with a large portion of Eastern Connecticut. In 1904 the city became the owner of its lighting plant. The year 1873 saw the occupation of the combined court, town and city building, which during the last year or two has been undergoing the process of enlargement to meet the increasing demands upon it The spring of this same year also witnessed the erection at the head of the Great Plain of the monument to the memory of the soldiers and sailors of the Civil War. This theater was opened in 1890 The following year the Otis Library was made free, and in 1892 enlarged, and thus the way prepared for the invaluable work it is now doing. The year 1893 was made memorable by the completion of the William W. Backus Hospital, for whose beautiful location, admirable plant and ample endowment, Norwich owes an inestimable debt of gratitude to Mr. Backus, and to that most generous of her sons, William A. Slater. In 1894 the Masonic Temple was dedicated, and in 1905 the new Post Office was opened.

Fifty years have passed. They have been eventful ones, and have witnessed great changes in the business, industrial and social life of this country. Material prosperity has abounded; the spheres of business activity have wonderfully broadened; industrial growth and expansion have been marvelous, and populations have multiplied and centralized as never before in our history. Many centers of population have increased in numbers and been transformed in character so as to be scarcely recognizable. Riches have been amazingly multiplied, and have fallen to the lot of very many who had not been trained to their use. Extravagance and display have set their alluring examples in many quarters, making simple and unostentatious living harder and less common than it used to be. New standards of various sorts have come to supplant the old, and former ideals have given place to others. The changes which have taken place, however, have been by no means uniform. Cities have prospered and increased, where the country has not to the same extent, or not at all. Some cities have thriven and grown almost in spite of themselves, where others have had to plod their way to larger things. Some communities have found wealth dropping into their laps with the minimum of effort, while others have been obliged to win their achievements by persistent endeavor. Nature's bounty has not been the same to all sections, the advantages of location have not been uniform; and the facilities of transportation, which have played a large part in industrial and business history, have not been shared in equal measure. Norwich has not found itself the beneficiary of some great natural deposit of coal, iron ore, gas, copper or gold to contribute to the expansion of its industries, the increase of its population and its accumulation of wealth. It has not found itself the center of some great industrial development. It has not been favored by exceptional transportation facilities. The great lines of railway passed it by on either hand. It has thus been left without those aids to growth which certain other places have in greater or less degree enjoyed, and it has been compelled to rely for the most part upon the resources and energy of its people for what it has attained. The situation, however, has not been without its compensations. Success won by effort is blessed in the winning. It is blessed in the character it develops, and in the type of manhood it creates. And there has been success. Of this there are evidences on every hand, and the fact that the population has practically doubled within the last fifty years amply attests it. But the conditions have not been such as to invite heterogeneous population of all sorts and kinds to the extent and of the character found in some other localities. Sudden wealth has not come to many, and to many unfit to use it. The new rich do not infest its streets and knock at the door of its society. What has come has been earned, and in the earning, the stability, the solidity and the strength of the old days has not been dissipated. The dignity of the simple life in its best sense has not been lost sight of, nor the standards and ideals of the former days forgotten. There has been retained a closer touch with the country than is common with cities. The ranks of its trade and its professions have been recruited very largely from the surrounding farms and villages, and that influence has been a constantly powerful and wholesome one. The best blood of the country round about, and the most of it the blood of a New England ancestry, has flowed to this center to invigorate its life. As a result of all these influences and conditions, Norwich, it seems to me, is today more truly representative of the old New England spirit, and better typifies the life and thought and sterling character of the fathers, than any other large and growing center of population of my acquaintance.

We may sum up the charms of our county by saying that the only excuse one of our citizens finds for going away in summer is to avoid summer visitors; the only excuse one can have for moving away is the anticipated pleasure of returning to dwell here after his fortune is made.

It will be extremely difficult for the skeptic to find another region of like population that has received so many proofs of the generosity of its citizens in public bequests, as shown in charitable organizations, schools, libraries, and monuments.

And, while all that makes for patriotism and culture has been retained, New London county has progressed in its business development in an impressive way. A brief survey of the main lines of industrial development is here presented. The banking system of the county is presented in a special article.

Taking a large view of the county, we note its abundance of water power. The tributaries of the Yantic and the Shetucket, with numerous smaller streams flowing into the Thames, the Connecticut, and the Sound, are marked with mill settlements. The estuary of the Thames furnishes adequate transportation facilities for Norwich and New London. Stonington has a fine harbor of its own, and the railroad makes the county easy of access for more rapid transportation. One characteristic of the industries of the county is their diversity, so that no one industry determines the prosperity of our communities.

Farming is carried on to a considerable degree in every town but New London, where town and city limits coincide. Dairy farms and market gardens have good markets within easy reach. The farming classes are as a rule prosperous, progressive, and happy. With the good roads and motor vehicles they combine the advantages of country life and urban resources. In Colchester and Montville, considerable colonies of Jewish farmers have settled. Scattered through the county are numerous estates managed more for pleasure than for financial return. But the mass of the farming population is composed of the original independent stock that has been the real backbone of our country

The enlightened policy of the State makes it possible for every child of a rural community to get a high school education at no greater expense than the city child has to meet Free public libraries abound, many of which were given by enlightened citizens. Traveling libraries are sent out by the State Library Committee. The telephone, the motor car, the morning newspaper, the church life, the grange meetings, the trolleys, universal education, and commerce, bind together the county with a solidarity unknown fifty years ago.

Far more important, financially, than the farming, is the cotton industry of the county, which, in diverse forms, is undoubtedly the support of more people than any other form of manufacture. Numerous villages have sprung up around the factories in many places. These villages are many of them model settlements, in which the laborer is encouraged to live in comfort, amidst clean and sanitary surroundings, with play grounds, community centers, social diversions, all of which tend to increase his individual progress and good citizenship. The chief centers of the cotton industry are Norwich, Jewett City (Griswold), Baltic (Sprague) The woolen mills at Hallville (Preston), Yantic (Norwich), and Thamesville (Norwich), do an extensive business The making of bed quilts of many kinds is carried on in the mills of Palmer Brothers at New London, Uncasville (Montville), and Fitchville (Norwich). These mills have a capacity of many thousand quilts a day. The silk industry of the Brainerd & Armstrong Company (New London), and the

J. B. Martin Company (Norwich), has reached large proportions. The ship-building industry follows the shore from Stonington to New London, and many forms of machinery, marine and of other sorts, are manufactured throughout the county.

The paper industry has reached large proportions, one plant at Thames-ville turning out one hundred and twenty-five tons of strawboard daily. The manufacture of firearms, too, is a long-standing and prosperous business. The American Thermos Company has its chief factory in Norwich. To give some sense of the variety of products of our manufacturing districts we submit an outline by districts.

New London manufactures ships and ship machinery, silk fabrics, motors, brass tubing, carpet lining, boilers, printing presses, quilts, paper boxes, electric specialties, underwear, machine tools, vises, poultry feeders, heating apparatus, mattresses, hats and caps, clothing and many lesser products.

Norwich manufactures pistols and other firearms, cutlery, plating, cotton and woolen goods, velvet, silk, paper, steam boilers, boxboard, carriages, pulleys, electric supplies, leather and belting, machinery of many sorts It is the seat of the largest plant of the United States Finishing Company.

Stonington manufactures machinery, printing presses, woolen and velvet goods, threads, Packer's Tar Soap, cotton goods, and goods of less importance.

Griswold's Mills are mostly cotton mills, but at Jewett City we find the Aspinook Company, one of the great bleaching and printing plants of the country.

Groton builds ships, and engines for submarines. Its main industry is looking after summer visitors.

Sprague makes cotton goods, woolens, paper, electricity, hospital supplies and novelties.

Lyme makes undertakers' hardware, birch oil and witch hazel extracts. Waterford makes paper, bleaching and dyeing products, and has large interests invested in quarrying and monumental work. Montville makes quilts, cotton goods, paper boxes, paper, and electricity (Eastern Connecticut Power Company.) Preston with its cotton and woolen goods, Bozrah with bed quilts and shoddy, Voluntown with cotton manufacture, Colchester with paper and leather goods, East Lyme with its granite quarries, menhaden fisheries, woolen goods, dyeing and bleaching, are mainly agricultural, as are the other towns of the county

The varied industries of the county have brought in many allied interests, banking and commercial, too numerous to mention. A list of the main business firms of the county is here attached. Many of them are of such proportions as to merit special articles, and some are referred to in other parts of the history.

The grand list of the county, which does not include non-taxable property of religious, educational and charitable institutions, and public properties of great value, is over ninety-two millions, approximately six hundred dollars per head for each one of its 155,311 inhabitants. Its tremendous banking capital will be touched upon in another article Among the main manufacturing concerns of the county are the following:

American Pants Co., Norwich
American Strawboard Co., Norwich
American Thermos Bottle Co., Norwich
Atlantic Container Products Co., Norwich
Atlantic Carton Corp., Norwich
Atlantic Products Co., Norwich
Atlas Radiator Pedestal Co , Norwich
Bard Union Co., Inc., Norwich
Blue Star Overall Co., Norwich
Brainerd & Armstrong Co., Norwich
Carpenter Mfg. Co., Norwich.
Cave Welding & Mfg. Co , Norwich
Chelsea File Works, Norwich
City of Norwich Gas & Electric Dept., Norwich
Climax Specialty Co., Norwich
Connecticut Cord Iron Corporation, Norwich
Connecticut Pants and Knee Pants Co., Norwich
Connecticut Popcorn Co., Norwich
Coronet Knitting Co., Norwich
Crescent Fire Arms Co., Norwich
Crystal Spring Bottling Works, Norwich
Davis Warner Arms Corp., Norwich
Eastern Pants Co., Norwich
Empire Skirt Co., Norwich
Geisthardt's Steam Saw Mill, Norwich
Glen Woolen Mills, Norwich
Hammond Process Co., Norwich
Hartford Mosaic Marble Co , Norwich
Ideal Pants Co , Norwich
Lang Dye Works, Norwich
Lester & Wasley Co. (Machinery), Norwich
J. B. Martin Co. (Velvets and Silks), Norwich
New London-Norwich Sign Co., Norwich
New York Mineral Water Co., Norwich
Norwich Belt Mfg. Co., Norwich
Norwich Marble & Granite Works, Norwich
Norwich Overall & Skirt Co., Norwich
Norwich Paper Box Co., Norwich
Norwich Wood Working Co., Norwich
Norwich Woolen Co., Norwich
Norwich Woolen Mills, Norwich
Oakdale Cordage Co., Norwich
Parker, Preston & Co (Paints), Norwich
Pequot Brass Foundry, Norwich
Pequot Rug Factory, Norwich
Phoenix Fire Extinguisher Co., Norwich
H. B. Porter & Son Co. (Woodworking), Norwich
Reliance Yarn Company, Norwich
Richmond Radiator Company, Norwich
Saxton Woolen Corp., Norwich
Shetucket Harness Co., Norwich
Thames Valley Mills (Woolen), Norwich
Turner & Stanton Company (Cordage and Small Wares), Norwich
Ulmer Leather Co., Norwich
United Metal Mfg. Co., Norwich
United States Finishing Co., Norwich
Vaughan Foundry Co., Norwich
Winchester Woolen Co., Norwich
John T. Young Boiler Co., Norwich
Admore Woolen Mills Co., Norwich
Glen Woolen Mills, Norwich
Massasoit Mfg. Co., Oakdale
Totokett Mfg. Co., Versailles (Lisbon)
American Chemical Co., (Old Mystic) Groton
Mystic Woolen Co., Groton
Old Mystic Grist Mill, Groton
Hallville Mills (Woolen), Preston
American Thread Co., Stonington
H. F. & A. J. Dawley (Lumber), Preston
Airlee Mills, (Hanover) Sprague
American Velvet Co., Stonington
Laper Fire Alarm Co., Stonington
Morrison Granite Co., Stonington
Ship Construction & Trading Co , Stonington
Venture Rock Bottlery Works, Stonington
William Clark Mills, Stonington
Ponemah Mills, (Taftville) Norwich

Norwich Woolen Mills, Norwich
Federal Paper Board Co., (Versailles) Lisbon
Hygienic Paper Co., Lisbon
Brigg's Mfg. Co. (Cotton), Voluntown
Voluntown Grist Mill, Voluntown
Booth Bros. & Hunicane Isle Granite Co., Waterford
Jordan Mill, Waterford
Millstone Granite Quarries, Waterford
Norwich & Westerly Traction Co., Westerly
Holmes Motor Co., (New Mystic) Groton
Yantic Mills (Cotton), Norwich
Baltic Mills (Cotton), Sprague
Shetucket Worsted Mills, (Baltic) Sprague
Federal Felling Co., (Clarke Falls) North Stonington
Columbia Kid Hair Curler Mfg. Co., Colchester
Hills Turning & Saw Mill, East Lyme
Menhaden Oil & Guano Co., East Lyme
Monumental Works, East Lyme
American Thread Co, (Glasgo) Griswold
Mutual Hair Goods Co, Groton
Electric Boat Co., Groton
General Ordnance Co., Groton
Groton Iron Works, Groton
Groton Marine Railways, Groton
Lake Torpedo Boat Company, Groton
New London Ship Engine Co., Groton
Shay Fertilizer Co., Groton
Vanadium Metal Co., Groton
Glengarry Mills, (Hanover) Sprague
Smith's Mills, Sprague
Ashland Cotton Co., (Jewett City) Griswold
Aspinook Co., (Jewett City) Griswold
Blissville Mills, Griswold
Jewett City Textile Novelty Co., (Jewett City) Griswold
Slater Mills, (Jewett City) Griswold
Ingalls Co. (Lumber), Norwich
Royal Silver Co., Lyme
Chagnon Huggard Co., Montville
Johnson & Co., Montville

Palmer Bros (Quilts), Montville
Pequot Mills, Montville
Eastern Conn. Power Co., Montville
Robertson Co., Montville
Standard Package Co, Montville
Thames River Specialties Co., Montville
Uncasville Mfg. Co., Montville
Allen Spool & Wood Turning Co., Stonington
Climax Tube Co, Stonington
Mystic Gas & Electric Co., Stonington
Mystic Lace Mills Co, Stonington
Mystic Marine Railway Co., Stonington
Mystic Woolen Co, Groton
Packer Mfg. Co. (Tar Soap), Stonington
Robinson Silk Co., Stonington
Rossie Velvet Co, Stonington
Standard Machine Co, Stonington
Sutton's Spar Yard, Stonington
Anchor Knitting Mills, New London
Babcock Printing Press Mfg Co., New London
Auto Radiator & Lamp Co, New London
Bingham Paper Box Co., New London
Brainerd & Armstrong (Silks), New London
Casey Granite Works, New London
Cedar Grove Monumental Works, New London
Conn. Iron & Metal Co., New London
Conn. Power Co., New London
Conn. Turbine Mfg Co, New London
Hawthorne Sash & Door Co., New London
Holland Skirts Mfg. Co., New London
Lenox Shirt Factory, New London
Long Island & Fisher's Island Brick Co, New London
Mohegan Cotton Mills, New London
New England Carpet Lining Co., New London
New England Collapsible Tube Co., New London
N. E. Dress Mfg. Co., New London
N E. Pants Co, New London

New London Boiler Works, New London

New London Granite & Marble Works, New London

New London Marine Iron Works Co., New London

New London Vise Works, New London

Automatic Feeder Co., New London

Putnam Furniture Mfg. Co., New London

Reliable Skirt Mfg. Co., New London

Sheffield Dentifrice Co., New London

Standard Brass & Copper Tube Co., New London

Standard Ice Cream Cone Co., New London

Submarine Boat Co., New London

Thames River Lumber Co, New London

Thames Sheet Metal Works, New London

Thames Tow Boat Co., New London

DeWhiton Machine Co., New London

Wilson Planing & Molding Mill, New London

General Machine & Electric Co., (Noank) Groton

Groton Iron Works (Noank Branch)

The reader may learn from the preceding list, incomplete as it is, that a citizen of New London county has little need to go elsewhere for food, clothing. or weapons From cutlery to tombstones, the county is well-nigh self-sufficient. And the manufacturing establishments, as a rule, are placed so as to interfere very little with the beauty of residential sections. Even in mill villages, the prospect pleases. Many a worker is renting for two or three dollars a week a home that could cost four times as much in the city. Home gardens are allotted to all who seek them. Free hospital service, a complete system of health inspection by competent nurses, good schools, ample play grounds, all tend to protect young and old. Most of these improvements have come in the last three decades.

In public affairs the county has continued to do its part for State and country. Out of twelve United States Senators who have served since 1860, New London county has furnished three. Its list of Representatives has been an honorable one It has furnished but one Governor since 1880, Hon. Thomas B. Waller, of New London. One Lieutenant-Governor, two Secretaries of State, two State Treasurers, three Speakers of the House, have come in the last fifty years from this county. In the General Assembly New London county has three Senators and thirty Representatives.

In this county are four boroughs—Stonington, 1801; Colchester, 1846; Jewett City, 1895; and Groton, 1903. Its population has increased over twenty per cent. in the last twenty years Of the total population, approximately sixty per cent is either foreign born or of foreign parentage. The process of Americanization is going on apace, largely through the influence of the public schools In many cases these new-comers have a lively sense of the blessings of liberty. They are thrifty and industrious They are acquiring property and therefore feel that they have a stake in the welfare of the community. Bolshevism does not thrive in New London county. In every Liberty Loan drive the county went far over its quota. For the Red Cross, as for distinctly local improvements, its people are generous contributors

The two hundred and fiftieth anniversary of New London was celebrated on May 6th, 1896, when the Soldiers' and Sailors' Monument was dedicated. Miss Charlotte Molyneux Holloway prepared the Historical Sketch of New London, which, with many splendid illustrations, was published by Messrs. G. C. Morgan, R I. Waller and H. H. Morgan. In it may be found a detailed account of many of the gifts of generous citizens to the community. The programme of the celebration reads as follows:

May 5th, 1896, evening meeting at the Armory, of 3rd Regiment, Connecticut National Guard.

Concert, 7.30 to 8 p. m., 3rd Regiment Band.

Meeting called to order by His Honor James P. Johnston, Mayor of New London.

Prayer, by Rev. John R. Stubbert, pastor of Huntington Street Baptist Church.

Music, "Star Spangled Banner," by a choir of four hundred school girls.

Address, "The Founding of the Town," by Walter Learned.

Hymn, "Speed Our Republic," chorus.

Poem, "New London," George Parsons Lathrop, LL.D.

Speeches by Hon. Charles A. Russell, Member of Congress; Hon. Orville H. Platt, Senator; Hon Thomas Weller, ex-Governor.

Music, "America."

May 6th, 10 a. m.—Laying of corner stone of a monument to John Winthrop the Younger, in Bulkeley Square.

Introduction by Mr. Alfred H. Chappell, president Board of Trade.

Prayer, Rev. James Bexler, Second Congregational Church.

Address, "The Founder of the Town," Rev. S. Leroy Blake, D.D., First Church of Christ.

Music, "Our Flag is There."

Laying of corner store, Grand Master James H. Welsh, Grand Lodge of Connecticut Free and Accepted Masons.

Music, "America."

Benediction, Rev. Alfred P. Grint, St. James Episcopal Church.

11 a. m.—Dedication of Soldiers' and Sailors' Monument, on the Parade, presented by Sebastian D. Lawrence, Esq.

Introduction, Mr. Alfred H Chappell.

Presentation of Monument by the Donor.

Acceptance by the Mayor, Hon. James P. Johnston.

Music, "Battle Hymn of the Republic "

Address for the Army, Hon Joseph R Hawley, Senator.

Address for the Navy, Rev. George W. Smith, president of Trinity College, Hartford.

Music

2 p m., Grand Military and Civic Procession.

8 p. m., Grand display of fireworks

At this time was also published "A Brief History of New London," by Carl J. Viets, publisher.

In 1909 was celebrated the 250th anniversary of the founding of Norwich. A complete account of this celebration, edited by Mr. William C. Gilman, was published in 1912. Its illuminating introduction of over fifty pages gives a full and inspiring statement of the growth of the town from 1859 (date of the two hundredth anniversary) to 1909 Wit, charm of style, and wisdom, are combined in this account of the "Rose of New England." The celebration lasted three days; the official programme covers four full pages. The table of contents of the volume gives a skeleton only of a remarkable three-day "feast of reason and flow of soul."

Statistics and outlines, buildings and streets, are the superficial evidences of the prosperity of the county. The real county beneath all these outward forms may be seen only in the lives of its people. The moral tone of the citizens, their customs, their activities in a thousand ways, have to be seen to be appreciated.

New London county needs a "Joe" Lincoln to set forth the real nature of its citizens. Only those who rise to fame are recorded in the pages of history, but the observant citizen of any of our towns sees going on every day before him a process of growth and struggle worthy to be described by a master hand.

Difficulties are being surmounted, characters are being formed, generous deeds are being performed today, as in times past Undoubtedly our communities have their peculiar traits, as do individuals. The heritage of the past and the present environments combine to give a special tone to the life of each community. New England reticence, Connecticut individualism, and local needs, have given to our county a character of its own. It is this intangible part of our assets that constitute our best possession. Mr. William

C. Gilman, editor of the "Norwich Quarter Millennium," quotes Judge Nathaniel Shipman's words about Norwich, "It is inexpedient for us to do anything more than simply to say we loved the town when we were boys, we love it now when we are men, and we want to say so."

The same words and sentiments about every town in the county would show the charm that is felt by former residents. Our cities and towns have not been over-standardized. The same sort of individuality that makes people interesting, still imparts to many of our communities a local color easily perceived by the visitor. One hears in our towns but rarely the loud protestations of the western "booster," but finds a surprising number of men who, after great success in the competition of the large cities, are content to settle in the home of their boyhood days. They feel much like the Cape Cod captain who came back from voyaging the world over to settle near the tip of the Cape. Said he, "I've been 'round the world eight times. I've seen 'most every country. But, I'm satisfied right here, and I don't care if I never go west of Barnstable again in my life."

CHAPTER IX

MISCELLANEOUS INFORMATION

The Various Cities and Towns — Financial Condition of County — Officiary of New London and Norwich—Important Events.

At various times local business organizations have issued pamphlets descriptive of the commercial opportunities afforded by the county. We quote freely from one such prospectus printed seven years ago:

On each side of the beautiful Thames river are twelve miles of available territory, suitable for factory sites. On the west side lie the tracks of the Central Vermont railway, on the east those of the N. Y., N. H. & H. railroad, and sufficient depth of water for wharfage purposes on any of its factory sites. There is not a sheet of inland water in the United States that gets the free advertising that comes to the Thames river every year when the great college regatta focuses the eyes of the whole civilized world and draws thousands of the youngest, fairest and best of humanity to this same fourteen miles of the Rose of New England. This of itself is an advertising asset of no small proportion.

We quote right here the reason the president of one of our newest and largest industries gave for moving his plant from New York to Norwich-on-the-Thames: "We consider the property on both sides of the Thames river between Norwich and New London superior to any other property within the zone desired, and, for that matter, within the United States, for the following reasons: First—You have more than thirty-eight million people within twelve hours' ride. Second—You have 144 cities of 10,000 people and over within the twelve hours' radius. Third—You have parts of sixteen states within twelve hours by rail and all of Eastern Canada and direct trunk line connections therewith. You have the cheapest hydro-electric power in all New England, which with your gas works and water plant (two large reservoirs) are owned and operated by your municipality. You have low cost of living, abundant labor, little, if any, labor troubles, favorable freight rates, both rail and water, splendid climate, and are surrounded by lands which, if properly cultivated, are rich in production. These are the advantages for manufacturing in Norwich that have convinced our board of directors that our removal from New York to your city is a move in the right direction and may be of interest to those who read these facts, as they are the reasons for inducing other manufacturing industries to locate here. Our company by its removal from Manhattan Island to your city has estimated that it will effect annual economies aggregating $44,000."

Norwich, agriculturally, is not unlike the towns that bound it on the north, east, south and west, hence a general description will satisfy the reader who may take a deep interest in rural life. Opportunity awaits the man who engages in agricultural pursuits in any of the towns surrounding Norwich. Close proximity to a ready market, easy access to trolley lines, best of State and macadam highways, rural telephone service, rural free delivery and parcel post, all go to make farm life hereabouts that of a country gentleman. Dairying and market gardening constitute today the real business being developed and nurtured on most of the farms in Eastern Connecticut. Stock raising and the fattening of beef for market, we believe, is one of the natural outcomes of the high cost of living, and he who early gets the habit will reap the greatest benefit. Salem, Bozrah, Lebanon and Franklin, towns to the west and north of Norwich, are devoted wholly to agricultural pursuits, the town of Lebanon perhaps being the more noted of the four for its fertile farms and their prosperous owners and well-kept buildings Lebanon Green, a street three miles long, is one of the historic points of interest of the town, and was the home of Jonathan Trumbull.

Preston, east and south of Norwich, has a small factory village known as Hallville A good sized woolen mill is engaged in manufacturing high grade woolen cloth for men's suitings. etc. The property is known as the Hall Brothers' Woolen Mill. The land is fertile and many good farms are to be found in Preston.

Sprague, eight miles north of Norwich, because of its being intersected by the Shetucket and Little rivers, has three thriving mill villages within its borders. Baltic, the largest, is a busy village of some 3,500 inhabitants and is the seat of town government. Located here is the model plant of the Baltic Mills Company, employing about 1,500 hands, engaged in the manufacture of a fine grade of cotton goods. There are also mills manufacturing woolen goods Abundant power is furnished by the damming of the Shetucket river. Hanover, in the town of Sprague, has as its chief industry the Airlie Mills, employing 100 hands engaged in making ladies' woolen dress goods The factory is located on the Little river, a tributary of the Shetucket, joining the latter at Versailles, where the third village has a factory engaged in making hospital supplies, employing 100 hands. Located on the eastern border of the town is the paper mill known as the Eastern Straw Board Company, making a coarse roofing and building paper. Power is taken from the Little river.

Lisbon is a small town adjacent to Sprague. and lies northeast of Norwich. It has the distinction of not having a store, post office or factory within its limits Agriculture is the principal occupation, and like many other towns in Eastern Connecticut, a large revenue is derived from summer boarders, who come here every year in goodly numbers.

Bozrah possesses many good farms, a charming recreation resort and some industries. Gardner's Lake, a pure body of crystal water three and one-half miles in length, one and one-quarter miles in width and sixty feet in depth, affords excellent fishing and boating, while its thickly wooded and grassy slopes offer many opportunities for summer homes. The largest industry in the town is the quilt mill of Palmer Bros at Fitchville, a quaint and picturesque village, five miles from Norwich, on the Yantic river.

Griswold lies east of Lisbon and eight miles from Norwich. Jewett City, the only village of any size in the town, has a borough form of government. Located here are the original Slater Cotton Mills, in operation continuously since late in the eighteenth century. The Aspinook Bleachery, employing many hundred people : the Jewett City Textile Novelty Company, engaged in finishing cotton goods. furnish employment to a large number of operatives. The Ashland Cotton Company, manufacturers of plain cotton cloths. The American Thread Company. making all kinds of thread, have a modern factory located at Glasgo, on the western border of the town. It is the only factory in the village and employs 150 hands.

Voluntown is one of the most easterly towns of Connecticut, on the Rhode Island line. The only village in the town bears the same name. Located here are the cotton mills of the Briggs Manufacturing Company, some three in number, furnishing the principal means of support of residents. Voluntown is twelve miles from Norwich and seven miles from the nearest railroad, all freight being delivered at Jewett City, on the Norwich & Worcester division of the N. Y., N. H. & H. railroad. Agriculturally, the town is not very progressive; large farms can be purchased for a few hundred dollars.

The great dairy prospects of this section of New England are most notable. Milk is being shipped to the ready markets of Boston and Providence in large quantities from nearly every farm, as all are within easy access to the railroad. The advent of the suburban trolley system has already doubled the amount of shipments. Milk cars are attached to all early trains and it is a most interesting sight to see from twenty-five to one hundred farmers, representing as many farms, with their teams in the early morning delivering their cans of milk to the many receiving stations along the lines, leaving full cans and taking back empty ones for the next day. And don't think for a moment that the farmer is not posted on the news of the day. That theory has long since been exploded. With the four bright newspapers published in Norwich, two daily and two weekly, the farmer knows every day all that has happened throughout the world during the past twenty-four hours.

Every town has its Grange, giving ample opportunity for social intercourse for the whole family, and a rare chance to gather knowledge. Norwich Grange is one of the most progressive of the State, having a membership of 125 active men and women, and during the winter lectures are given by professors from the State Agricultural College that prove not only entertaining but highly instructive as well. We cannot paint the picture of the future farm life and its prospects, both in the town of Norwich and its environment, in too vivid colors. There is no better market garden outlet in any rural section of the United States than right here in any of the towns briefly referred to, while orchards consisting of apple, peach and pear trees are beginning to interest the thrifty husbandman of the soil.

The greater the industrial development of a State, correspondingly greater and more valuable must become its agricultural output and land values, inseparable and useless each without the other.

Come to Norwich, Connecticut, the Rose of New England, an Eastern city with Western progressiveness, "The Coming City of the East."

New London's greatest asset is her harbor. Here is the natural entrance to the great coming of the North and West, but not only this: The increasing congestion of shipping trade at New York and the correspondingly increasing difficulty and expense of securing dockage at that port for new lines of steamers are as constantly attracting attention to the opportunities afforded at New London; when the docks are completed (they have since been completed), a vessel destined for New York can discharge her passengers and freight at New London and deliver them in New York at greater economy of time and money than by proceeding along the slower channel to New York. The development of this million-dollar enterprise will inevitably greatly stimulate local business and opportunity, not alone for a day but for years to come. History and observation abundantly illustrate the natural industrial and commercial development of great cities, with their development as great ports.

Second to her harbor as an asset is New London's seashore. By this is meant not only her Ocean Beach and the Pequot estates and properties bordering the harbor, including the unsurpassed hotel site formerly occupied by the old Pequot House which was burned some years ago, but the entire territory between the Connecticut river and the Rhode Island State line and extending up the Thames river toward Norwich.

Thousands are added to the summer population of this section during "the season," which, unfortunately, for visitors often must end when the schools for their children reopen at home. The proximity of river, harbor and sound makes it a favorite resort for yachtsmen and the owners of motor craft without lessening in any degree the usual attractions of the open country. Detailed notices of Crescent Beach, Niantic, Groton, Mystic and Stonington are included later in this sketch.

First—To the large manufacturer: In these days of keen competition, every avoidable expense possible must be eliminated by the manufacturer; among these expenses are avoidable charges for transporting both raw material and finished product. Hence, accessibility to supplies and to markets are of vital importance in selecting a location. Being a junction point of the New Haven railway system, and also that of the Grand Trunk of Canada, it is evident that New London's railway facilities cannot be surpassed, and in addition it has opportunities for securing the waterway competition of the whole world; not only this, but in some cases raw material may be unloaded directly from the vessel to the factory on one side and the finished product reshipped by water, or it may be loaded onto cars on the other side of the factory.

Second—To the employee and the smaller manufacturer: It should be remembered that the natural attractions of this region appeal with as much force to the intelligent, desirable employee as to the more exclusive, so-called, residential classes; as freely as their children, may his little ones enjoy the delights of the sea and the sands at Ocean Beach.

Another thing to remember is that self-respecting, contented, coöperating employees are essential to the manufacturer and the city's welfare. Satisfying suroundings secure satisfied citizens. New London's policy is to provide adequately for them; not how great alone, but how well shall New London grow, is the principle of many citizens; to make it a good city for all of us to live in. At the present time it is doubtful if any city in New England has a greater percentage of good streets and sidewalks or of thrifty public shade trees.

Until recently the above considerations had little weight in determining the policy or location of manufacturing plants; today, however, in many progressive communities they have much weight in influencing city planning for the future. It is believed that with the smaller manufacturer, particularly one who desired to assimilate with the best life of his new city, they should receive very favorable consideration. Such men with healthy enterprises will be most heartily welcomed to New London. Moderate rates for power and as favorable conditions as possible will be provided. Bear in mind the fact that goods shipped in the afternoon or evening, even heavy freight by boat, from New London, can be delivered in New York the following morning; equally prompt shipments are received from New York.

An opportunity to personally discuss local conditions and possibilities is solicited. A number of small water power privileges, one of considerable size and well equipped, are available in this vicinity.

Groton, just opposite the city of New London, is one of the very few localities where valuable water transportation rights remain unabsorbed by railroad or other powerful corporations. Definite information regarding specific properties on Groton Bank or properties bordering the railroad will be supplied to interested parties on application to the Groton Board of Trade. The New Haven Railroad Company controls valuable properties both below and above the bridge. Manufacturers or others desiring to avail themselves of these privileges will receive very favorable consideration from the company.

Mystic, a village in both the townships of Groton and Stonington, naturally blends the one with the other, thus completing the most splendid bit of shore line east of Thames river. Whether one seeks location for a factory, a recreation spot for summer, or a home site, Mystic offers peculiar advantages. Industries of world-wide reputation are already here; there is room for more. Artists of repute find in Mystic and environment permanent charm and inspiration for their talent; their recommendation brings others who become enthusiasts. City-jaded folk find in Mystic's beauty, quiet and simplicity, a panacea for tired bodies, weary minds. The sea, the country, the hills, the lowlands—all nature at her best is Mystic's glorious asset to offer the vacationist. Would you build yourself a home "far from the madding crowd," but within easy access, overlooking the sun-kissed waters of the Sound, or up the Mystic Valley? Would you buy some dear old farmhouse dating back to Colonial days, with the possibilities it would be a joy to develop acres surrounding it for the farm you have always planned to own; the farm where you and the wife, the children and their children may get in tune with life? Has that time come yet? Then buy a ticket for Mystic on the Shore Line, about half-way between Boston and New York. Look up the secretary or president of the Men's Club; tell him your errand, and he will try to show you that Mystic, Connecticut, has all the characteristics of the ordinary New England village extraordinarily developed.

Stonington offers unusual inducements as a place of summer residence. It is situated directly on the Atlantic Ocean, indeed, it is the only town on the main line of the New Haven railroad between New York and Boston with an ocean frontage. It also lies between Stonington Harbor, a safe anchorage for yachts, protected by three Government breakwaters, and Little Narragansett Bay, a picturesque sheet of water on the farther side of which, three miles distant, is situated Watch Hill, one of the most famous summer resorts of New England. Between Stonington and Watch Hill a passenger steamer makes frequent trips during the summer season.

This situation, on ocean, harbor and bay, gives Stonington remarkable advantages for sailing and other aquatic sports. The town is the headquarters for an extensive fishing industry, bluefish, cod and mackerel being among the varieties of edible fish that abound in the nearby waters. The ocean breezes reduce the temperature in the heated months, so that the mercury customarily registers from five to ten degrees below the temperature in neighboring communities, while in winter the nearness of the salt water tends to prevent the extreme cold experienced farther inland.

In the last few years Stonington has taken on new life as a summer resort. Many city residents have purchased or built homes in the borough and vicinity, and a first-class summer hotel, to which the name of the Stonington Manor Inn has been given, has been established on the outskirts of the borough, in the midst of a beautiful estate of field and forest, ninety acres in extent. There are also a number of inns and boarding houses within the settled portion of the town.

The township of Stonington contains 10,000 inhabitants. Stonington borough has a population of 2,500, and is situated half-way between the eastern and western boundaries of the township. The town was settled in 1649: the first house in what is now the borough was erected in 1752. In 1814 the place was the scene of a three days' bombardment by a British squadron, which was marvelously repulsed by a handful of defenders with three small cannon. This event was elaborately celebrated, with the aid of State and town appropriations, on August 8-10, 1914.

Stonington has the quality of quaintness to an unusual degree. No nearby community possesses quite the same element of old-world charm. It has a free library with nearly 7,000 volumes and liberally endowed, an excellent union high school with over 200 students, five churches, express service to New York, Providence and Boston, trolley service to New London, Mystic and Westerly, improved automobile roads, and a delightful variety of back-country scenery within easy reach. Its Board of Trade would appreciate the opportunity of acquainting any interested persons still further with its advantages as a place of residence, either for the summer season or all the year round.

The town of Montville is situated on the west side of the Thames river, midway between Norwich and New London. It is especially fortunate in its location, having a deep water front, best of steam and trolley service, as well as being intersected by the broad macadam boulevard that connects Norwich on the north and New London on the south. The Oxoboxo river furnishes power to many industries.

Salem, a naturally very productive farming township, northwest of New London, has been comparatively isolated, and its prosperity retarded because of inferior roads, but now with the reconstruction of the Hartford Turnpike, largely by State aid, through Waterford, Montville, Salem, Colchester, Marl-borough, Glastonbury and Hartford, a new era for the town of Salem is assured.

Beautiful Niantic by the Sea! This village is situated on the Connecticut shore of Long Island Sound, seven miles west of New London, on the main line of the N. Y., N. H. & H. railroad midway between Boston and New York, and on the Lincoln highway running from California to Maine. It also connects with New London by trolley.

The village derives its name from the Niantic Indians, who once occupied this stretch of the north shore, fishing upon the waters of sound, lake and rivers, and hunting in its woodlands. The village has a population of about 800, with 1,900 inhabitants in the entire town of East Lyme, of which the village is a part. This village offers exceptional opportunities to manufacturers and home-makers. For the most part the land is comparatively level, and many acres finely located could be secured at reasonable prices.

Lake Niantic, a beautiful sheet of crystal water, is encircled by the village. This lake is principally fed by springs, covers about twenty-five acres, and is a never-failing reservoir This body of water is available for manufacturing purposes. The one-quarter mile spur track of the railroad reaches to the lake, passing directly by Luce's factory, a three-story building formerly occupied by the Knickerbocker Typewriter Company, now for rent. The Technical Equipment Company, engaged in the manufacture of brass valves and gauges, occupy the factory on the east side of the village. The streets are well kept and lighted by electricity. There are four churches—the Baptist, Methodist Episcopal, Congregational, and Episcopal. The Roman Catholic, at Crescent Beach, one-half mile away, is open during the summer season

Splendid farms adjoin the village The soil for the most part is loam, with gravel subsoil, and especially adapted for the cultivation of fruit, vegetables and grain As means of enjoyment, the fishing, bathing, boating and hunting cannot be surpassed anywhere on the Atlantic seaboard.

Crescent Beach, a summer resort, one-half mile away and connected with the village by steam and trolley, has a summer population of 1,500 people, while Pine Grove, the same distance from the center of the village, has one hundred cottages and is the summer home of about five hundred people. There are two good hotels, and an efficient livery stable. The train and trolley service meet every need both for travel and transportation. Everyone visiting the village for the first time is charmed with its location and general appearance, and expresses the wish to visit it again During the summer season many visitors from all parts of the world visit the village and nearby beaches Niantic is also the summer headquarters for the National Guard of the State, who, by their presence, each year attract many friends and visitors.

Recently a Village Improvement Society has been formed for the purpose of rendering the town more attractive, and to promote its business interests. Any further information or description of the village, its conditions and the advantages which it offers, will be cheerfully given.

The town of Ledyard, a quiet farming community, is situated on the east shore of the Thames river, directly across from Montville. Peach growing and strawberries furnish the big output from the farms The only

village in the town is Gales Ferry, on the N. Y., N. H. & H. railroad, noted
for being the headquarters of the Yale and Harvard crews while training for
the college regatta.

The village is composed, in a large measure, of summer cottages. Boating and fishing attract thousands to shores of the Thames, and shore property is steadily rising in value in all the towns that border on this beautiful
stream.

From an article in the "New England Magazine," written by Mr. Henry
R. Palmer, we quote the following description of Stonington:

When Longfellow wrote of "the beautiful town that is seated by the
sea," he was thinking of Portland; but his tender song applies to Stonington.
If the town is not strictly beautiful, since it has no fine buildings and stately
streets, still it is set in the midst of a pleasant country and the charm of the
sea wraps it about. A mile from the shore its roads wind their way through
overhanging woods, and the traveler loses his sense of the ocean, except as
its scent is borne to him on the breeze. But from every hilltop the sea is
disclosed. It stretches in soft expanse as far as the eye can reach. On clear
days the white cliffs of Montauk and Block Island come into view. A dozen
tall lighthouses cast their glow over the evening waters. There is salt in the
air and in the speech of the fishermen. It is the sea that gives the town its
distinctive note.

Also a description of the whaling industry in its prime:

Shortly after 1830, the whaling industry took the place of sealing as
the chief maritime resource of Stonington. Captain Charles P. Williams fitted
out, first and last, no less than twenty-eight whaling ships; Charles Mallory
of Mystic, on the western borders of the town, nineteen; John F. Trumbull,
eleven; and other individual owners or firms, half a dozen. The industry
reached its climax in the forties, when fortunes were made in single voyages,
and the Arctic and Antarctic seas were stripped of the profitable monsters.
The whalemen sought the Southern Ocean first, and in their zeal sailed it
from east to west, sometimes circling the world. When the whales became
scarce in that portion of the globe, the intrepid venturers made their way
north and found even greater prey in the waters of Alaska and Kamschatka
Their voyages lasted sometimes but a few months, at other times they extended over four or five years. During this prosperous period. Stonington
was a live commercial town. The fitting out of a whaleship required much
time and industry, and the sorting of cargoes made the harbor front a busy
and interesting place. Oil casks, anchors and rigging, lumber and spars, were
strewn about. Sailors lounged at the corners or leaned over the bar at the
taverns. They wore blue trousers and roundabout jackets and black ties
knotted in sailor fashion. They were a jovial, happy-go-lucky lot and bent
on rough-and-ready pastime when they got ashore. The taverns rang with
the scrape of their fiddles and the clatter of their hornpipes; and once when
two ships sailed into port the same day, the rival crews, boasting of the
prowess of their favorites, formed a ring on Water Street and held high fistic
carnival. As fast as one contestant measured his length in the dust, another
took his place, while a crowd of villagers packed the street and cheered the
valiant. There was little brutality; when a man went down he was "out of
the game." One young fellow of fine physique maintained his place in the
ring against a large number of fresh comers. One blow of his fist was enough
for each of them. A distinctive American artist like Mr. Pyle could make a
lively picture of the scene.

The annals of whaling are tinged with tragedy. A Stonington captain died at sea, and his wife, who had accompanied him on the voyage, brooded over his death till one morning her room was found empty, with the window at the stern of the vessel open. Accidents on shipboard were followed by rough but effective treatment in the absence of a doctor, as when an unfortunate colored seaman injured his leg so severely that amputation became imperative. The captain—a stern disciplinarian accustomed to strict measures—consulted with his ship-keeper, and together, after the suffering man had been lashed to a ring in the deck, they sawed off the offending limb and seared the arteries with fire.

The township of Stonington contains eight thousand people, only two thousand of whom live at Stonington borough. The remainder are divided between Pawcatuck, which is practically a part of Westerly and has about four thousand inhabitants; Mystic, at the western extremity of the town, with fifteen hundred more; Old Mystic, three miles to the north of Mystic, with a population of five hundred; and an extensive farming district. Pawcatuck is a busy community with manufactories of textile goods and printing presses. Mystic is a picturesque village set in a charming valley, with cotton and velvet mills. At the southwest corner of the town is Mason's Island, a part of the grant to Captain John Mason, the Indian fighter, and still in the possession of the Mason family; and just beyond it is Mystic Island, the extreme southwestern limit of Stonington authority. The town for the most part is rocky, and the superabundance of "stones" may account for the name of "Stonington" received from the General Court in 1666. Regarding this name, ex-Judge Richard A. Wheeler, the "historian of the Pequot country," writes in a recent letter: "I have searched as with lighted candles all of our New England records to learn the origin of the name of Stonington, but thus far have failed. I have two books entitled gazetteers of all the known civilized nations of the world, one published in London in 1782 and the other published in Philadelphia in 1806, in neither of which does the name of Stonington appear except as a place in Connecticut. So the name or word Stonington may have been coined, I think, by one or both of our representatives, viz., Thomas Stanton, Senior, or Samuel Cheesbrough." Be this as it may, it has taken firm root in American nomenclature, and been grafted on new communities in several States of the Union. To all of these old Stonington sends greeting and best wishes on her two hundred and fifteenth birthday.

From an article in the "Architectural Record," by Mr. M. W Pentz, we quote regarding Stonington:

There remains, as far as I know, only a single place which has preserved to any marked degree its Colonial atmosphere, and that is Stonington. Here progress has been asleep, its population has barely doubled in a hundred years; its old sea trade is dead beyond hope of recall Grass grows in its streets; its wharves are tenanted only by a few motor boats and unused steamers of the Sound lines; its glory has departed. It is kept alive by a few textile factories and a great machine works, but its principal industry is summer boarders, fortunately not so numerous as to change its ancient tone. The resident population, aside from the descendants of its original settlers, is composed largely of Portuguese from the Azores Islands, descendants and relatives of the daring sailors who once formed the crews of its fishing vessels. Here they furnish the factories with labor and form an element both picturesque and useful.

I suppose the trees have grown up, some houses have been reshingled, a few new shops have been built, but in the old portion of the town so little has been changed that the effect is precisely what it must have been a

hundred years ago. The railroad station is on the neck of land which separates the old town from the mainland, no trolley passes through the streets
and only a couple of side tracks to the unused pier of the steamship company
exist to change its appearance   Even these wabble around so unobtrusively
through the back yards that they are almost invisible, and I have never seen
a train upon them. I suppose to preserve the franchise they must occasionally
run some cars, but it is probably done in the middle of the night, when everybody is asleep and there is nothing else to do

Immediately beyond the green is the south end of the point, a grassy,
quiet place with a lovely view of the water on three sides, and the delightful
old stone lighthouse in the center. This is a splendid place to sit and dream
and if you try hard enough you can easily fancy Admiral Hardy's ships fighting away without doing any harm except for what a modern lawyer would
term the damages for mental anguish of the inhabitants; who, after all, do
not seem to have been much alarmed   In the harbor not far from the point
is a monument which marks the corner betw᭙ n the States of Connecticut,
Rhode Island and New York, and as a small boy I went out there and sat
with my legs curled around it "in three states at once."

Turning back from the green toward the square, on Main street, one
passes more exquisite examples of the old work, of which the most charming
is the house known to the youngsters as "Miss Katty's," and the Wayland
residence, which in some ways is the show place of the town. Almost opposite the Wayland house is the old library, a typical house of the early times,
when two-story houses were taxed by the King and when one-story houses
went free. Still on Main street is the Second Congregational Church, an
interesting example of church architecture of the early nineteenth century,
although not in detail as good as the earlier work   Several cross streets
connect Main and Water Streets and where there is width enough little side
streets project like spurs from them, each lined with residences, quaint or
dignified as the fancy of the owner dictated. The customs house still flies
the flag of the Revenue Service, and I suppose the collector has occasionally
something to do, yet looking through the window one sees only a couple of
old gentlemen half asleep over the newspapers and a collection of dusty and
mildewed leather-bound books.

Peace and a certain sleepy dignity are the characteristics of the old town.
It is unable to get much excited about anything; changes and advances in
civilization are infrequent; the authorities there appreciate the loveliness of
the place and are anxious to keep it as untouched as possible.

The following figures give some idea of the financial situation of the
county at present. The list shows the number of people in each town and
city in New London county who paid the Federal tax on their incomes, and
whether the tax was based on incomes over or under $5,000 a year:

	Over $5,000	Under $5,000		Over $5,000	Under $5,000
Bozrah	0	29	New London	256	2,732
Colchester	1	49	North Stonington	1	1
East Lyme	9	78	Norwich	215	2,805
Franklin	1	7	Old Lyme	7	41
Griswold	14	520	Preston	0	4
Groton	28	546	Salem	0	1
Lebanon	0	8	Sprague	8	318
Ledyard	0	30	Stonington	55	980
Lisbon	0	0	Voluntown	3	21
Lyme	4	45	Waterford	7	132
Montville	6	101			

The State Senators from the three Senatorial Districts, called Ninth, Tenth, and Eleventh, till 1906, and thereafter Eighteenth, Nineteenth, and Twentieth, have been as follows:

Ninth District	Tenth District	Eleventh District
1890-92		
Stephen A. Gardner	Charles F. Thayer	Alex. C. Robertson
1892-94		
Stephen A. Gardner	S Ashbell Crandall	Alex C. Robertson
1894-96		
Benj H Lee	William H. Palmer, Jr.	Wm. F. Gates
1896-98		
Benj. H. Lee	Lucius Brown	John N. Lewis
1898-1900		
James Pendleton	John H. Barnes	Henry C. Burnham
1900-02		
James Pendleton	Wallace S Allis	Frederick J Brown
1902-04		
Thomas Hamilton	Nelson J. Ayling	Arthur M. Brown

Eighteenth District	Nineteenth District	Twentieth District
1904-06		
William J. Brennan	Reuben S. Bartlett	Austin I Bush
1906-08		
Charles B. Waller	Alonzo R. Oborn	Harley P. Buell
1908-10		
Fredk. P. Latimer	William I. Allyn	George H Bradford
1910-12		
Bryan F. Mahan	Charles S. Avery	Angus Park
1912-14		
Alton T. Miner	Charles S. Avery	Frederick A. Johnson
1914-16		
Lucius E. Whiton	John H. Barnes	Benjamin H. Hewitt
1916-18		
James R. May	John H Barnes	Frank H. Hinckley
1918-20		
William C. Fox	William B. Wilcox	Elisha Waterman
1920		
C. C. Costello	Allyn L. Brown	James Graham

The Mayors of Norwich have been as follows:

Benjamin Huntington, 1784-96; John McLaren Breed, 1796-98; Elisha Hyde, 1798-1813, Calvin Goddard, 1814-31 (resigned).

Since 1831, elected annually—James Lanman, 1831-34; Francis Asher Perkins, 1834. Charles W. Rockwell, 1835, 1838, 1846; Charles J. Lanman, 1838; William C. Gilman, 1839: John Breed, 1840-42; William P Greeve, 1842-43; Gurdon Chapman, 1843-45; John Breed, 1845; Charles W. Rockwell, 1846, John Dunham, 1847-49; William A Buckingham, 1849-51, LaFayette S. Foster, 1851-53; Erastus Williams, 1853-55: Wm. L Brewer, 1855; Wm. A. Buckingham, 1856-58; Amos A. Prentice, 1858-60; James S. Carew, 1860-62; James Lloyd Greene, 1862-66: Lorenzo Blackstone, 1866-70; James A. Hovey, 1870-71: James Lloyd Greene, 1871-75, Hugh H. Osgood, 1875-76; Charles Osgood, 1876-77; Hugh H. Osgood, 1877-86; Increase W Carpenter, 1886-88; A. Ashbel Crandall, 1888-92; Calvin L. Harwood, 1892-96; Frederic L Osgood, 1896-1900; Charles F. Thayer, 1900-08; Costello Lippett. 1908-10;

Charles F. Thayer, 1910-12; Timothy C. Murphy, 1912-16; Allyn L. Brown, 1916-18; Jeremiah J. Desmond, 1918-20, Herbert M. Lerou, 1920-22.

Mayors of New London:

Richard Law, 1784-1806, 22 years; Jeremiah G. Brainerd, 1806-29, 23 years; Elias Perkins, 1829-32; Coddington Billings, 1832-35; Noyes Billings, 1835-37; Jirah Isham, 1837; Francis Allyn, 1838-41; George C. Wilson, 1841, died July 20, 1841; Caleb J. Allen, August 12, 1841, resigned June, 1843; Andrew M. Frink, 1843-45, resigned; J. P. C. Mather, 1845-50, resigned August; Andrew C. Lippett, 1850-53; Henry P. Haven, 1853-56; Jonathan N. Harris, 1856-62; Hiram Wiley, 1862-65; Frederick L. Allen, 1865-71; Augustus Brandegee, 1871-73; Thomas W. Waller, 1873-79; Robert Coit, 1879-82; George E. Starr, 1882-85; C. A. Williams, 1885-88; George F. Tinker, 1888-91; George Williams, 1891, resigned in two weeks; Ralph Wheeler, 1891-93, resigned after two years; A. J. Bentley, 1893-94; James P. Johnston, 1894-97; Cyrus G. Beckwith, 1897-1900; M. Wilson Dart, 1900-03; Bryan F. Mahan, 1903-06; Alton T. Miner, acting Mayor five months in 1905; Benjamin L. Armstrong, 1906-09; Bryan F. Mahan, 1909-15; Ernest E. Rogers, 1915-18; E. Frank Morgan, 1918-21.

The "New London Day" recently published an edition celebrating its fortieth anniversary, which contains much valuable information. Among other information, it printed the following chronological review:

1880—Population of New London, 10,537.
1881—Charter granted Smith Memorial Home, Masonic street.
1882—Petition recorded from telephone company, asking permission to set poles through the street.
1882—State Armory land sold by Coit heirs to State of Connecticut, November 9.
1885—Permission granted by common council to O. L. Livesey "for J. A. Jenny to erect poles for trying out the experiment of lighting the city by electricity without cost to the city."
1885—City meeting voted to install sewer system.
1888—Nameaug schoolhouse built. First of present modern structures.
1889—Thames river railroad bridge opened for the use of the New Haven and Boston and Providence railroads.
1890—Pequot Casino Association organized July 12.
1890—Lyceum Theater opened. First play, "The Wife," by the Frohman Company, April 7.
1890—Nathan Hale Grammar School erected.
1891—Williams Memorial Institute erected.
1891—Montauk avenue opened. First called the Boulevard.
1892—New London Street Railway began running cars.
1893—Ocean Beach and Lewis' woods sold by T. M. Waller to the city.
1893—Winthrop School erected.
1894—Saltonstall School erected
1894—Shiloh Baptist Church, colored, organized.
1896—Post Office building erected.
1896—Mohican building erected.
1896—Brainard Lodge, F. & A. M., altered Universalist Church, Green street, into lodge room.
1896—Robert Bartlett School opened.
1898—First Church, Christian Scientist, organized, June 26.
1898—Police Station, Bradley street, erected.
1899—Norwich and Montville trolley road began operation.

1899—St. Mary's Parochial School started.
1905—Thames Club destroyed by fire, rebuilt.
1906—John Winthrop Club organized.
1906—New London Vocational School erected.
1907—East Lyme and New London trolley line started.
1907—Harbor School erected.
1908—Pequot House destroyed by fire.
1908—Elks' Home built, corner-stone laid August 13.
1908—Swedish Congregational Church dedicated.
1909—All Souls' Church, Huntington street, building permit issued.
1909—St. Joseph's Roman Catholic Church, Montauk avenue, corner stone laid May 30.
1909—Southwest Ledge light first turned on, November 10.
1910—Lawrence Free Hospital opened.
1910—Ship and Engine Company leased factory site in Groton from New Haven railroad. Purchased same in 1911.
1911—Fund of $134,196 14 raised to secure location here of Connecticut College by popular subscription up to March 1.
1912—Harbour Club building permit issued.
1913—Manwaring building erected
1914—Union Lodge, A. F. and A. M., erected new building, Union street
1915—Montauk Avenue Baptist Church rebuilt.
1915—Plant building erected.
1916—Y. M. C. A. building erected, Meridian street.

The lists of Representatives from the various towns of the State have been as follows for thirty years:

Bozrah—1890-92, William F. Bogue; 1892-94, John J. Gager; 1894-96, William J. Way; 1896-98, E. Judson Miner; 1898-1900, William Kilroy; 1900-02, William Kilroy; 1902-04, Wareham W. Bentley; 1904-06, Wareham W. Bentley; 1906-08, John S. Sullivan; 1908-10, John F. Fields; 1910-12, John F. Fields; 1912-14, John S. Sullivan; 1914-16, Nelson L. Stark; 1916-18, John J. Sweeney; 1918-20, John J. Sweeney; 1920, Elijah S. Abel.

Colchester—1890-92, James R. Dutton, Milton L. Loomis; 1892-94, Frank B. Taylor, Clarence H. Norton; 1894-96, Wm. E. Harvey, Howard C. Brown; 1896-98, Edward M. Day, William Daudley; 1898-1900, Addison C. Taintor, Edward E. Brown; 1900-02, Joseph E. Hall, Charles H. Daudley; 1902-04, John R. Backus, Amatus R. Bigelow; 1904-06, David S. Day, Edward C. Snow; 1906-08, Samuel N. Morgan, Guy B Clark; 1908-10, Edward T. Bunyan, Samuel McDonald; 1910-12, Asa Brainard, Harry Elgart; 1912-14, Harry Elgart, Daniel T Williams; 1914-16, Daniel W. Willи̯ams, Curtis P. Brown; 1916-18, Edwin R. Gillette, Jacob J. Elgart; 1918-20, Samuel Gellert, William K. Raymond; 1920, Albert H. Foote, George Cutler.

Griswold—1890-92, James H. Finn; 1892-94, Frederick H. Partridge; 1894-96, John Potter; 1896-98, Ira T. Lewis; 1898-1900, Samuel S Edmond; 1900-02, Arthur M. Brown; 1902-04, Albert G. Brewster; 1904-06, Arba Browning; 1906-08, Jonas L. Herbert; 1908-10, John W. Payne; 1910-12, J. Byron Sweet; 1912-14, Alfred J. L'Heureux; 1914-16, John Potter; 1916-18, John F. Hermon; 1918-20, Wm. H. McNicol; 1920, John T. Barry.

Groton—1890-92, Charles H. Smith, Amos R. Chapman; 1892-94, William R. McGavhey, Everett L Crane; 1894-96, Charles H. Smith, Judson F. Bailey; 1896-98, Robert P. Wilbur, Donald Gunn; 1898-1900, Wm. H. Allen, Ralph H. Denison; 1900-02, Wm. H. Allen, George A. Perkins; 1902-04, Benjamin F. Burrows, Albert E. Wheeler; 1904-06, Simeon G. Fish, Edward F. Spicer; 1906-08, Frederick P. Latimer, Benj F. Burrows; 1908-10, Charles H. Smith,

Everett L. Crane, 1910-12, Percy H Morgan, Edward E. Spicer, 1912-14, Christopher L. Avery, Allen W. Rathbun; 1914-16, Charles T. Crandall, Charles H. Kenyon; 1916-18, George R. Hempstead, Frank E Williams, 1918-20, Charles H. Smith, Irvin E. Crouch; 1920, Charles H. Smith, Howard A Edgecomb.

Lebanon—1890-92, Isaac G. Avery, Frederic Gates; 1892-94, William C. Blanchard, Fred J. Brown; 1894-96, Hobart McCall, Robert E. Turner; 1896-98. George A. Mills, George A. Fuller; 1898-1900, Llewellyn P. Smith, Edw. H McCall; 1900-02, Charles B. Strong, Charles H. Loomis; 1902-04, Charles S. Briggs, Charles B. Noyes; 1904-06, William H. Geer, George H. Hewitt; 1906-08, Charles A. Perkins, Fred'k O. Brown; 1908-10, Isaac G. Larkin, Elisha Waterman; 1910-12, George H. Hoxie, Myron R. Abell; 1912-14, Frank K. Noyes, Wm. A. Watson; 1914-16, Frederick N. Taylor, James A Thomas; 1916-18, Edward A Hoxie, Wm. T. Curry; 1918-20, Karl F. Bishop, Edward W. Jones; 1920, Stanton L. Briggs, Arthur E. Hewitt.

East Lyme—1890-92, E. K. Beckwith; 1892-94, Arthur B. Calkins; 1894-96, George P. Hill; 1896-98, Arthur B. Calkins; 1898-1900, John F. Luce; 1900-02, Arthur B. Calkins; 1902-04, James R. White; 1904-06, John T. Beckwith; 1906-08, Frederick A. Beckwith; 1908-10, Washington I. Gadbois; 1910-12, Clifford E. Chapman; 1912-14, Jay V. Beckwith; 1914-16, Marion R. Davis; 1916-18, Asahel R. DeWolf; 1918-20, Charles R. Tubbs; 1920, Julius T. Rogers.

Franklin—1890-92, John M. N. Lathrop; 1892-94, Clifton Peck; 1894-96, Clayton H. Lathrop; 1896-98, James H. Hyde; 1898-1900, Frank B. Greenslit; 1900-02, Azel R. Race; 1902-04, Frederick S. Armstrong; 1904-06, Walter S. Vail; 1906-08, Abial T Browning; 1908-10, Frank A. Rockwood; 1910-12, James H. Hyde; 1912-14, Frederick W. Hoxie; 1914-16, C. Huntington Lathrop; 1916-18, Frank I. Date; 1918-20, Herman A. Gager; 1920, Charles B Davis.

Ledyard—1890-92, George W Spicer; 1892-94, George W. Spicer; 1894-96, Charles A. Gray; 1896-98, Nathan S. Gallup; 1898-1900, Jacob Gallup; 1900-02, Daniel W. Lamb; 1902-04, Daniel W. Lamb; 1904-06, William I. Allyn; 1906-08, William I Allyn; 1908-10, Frank W. Brewster; 1910-12, William I Allyn, 1912-14, Isaac G. Geer; 1914-16, Joseph D. Austin; 1916-18, William I. Allyn; 1918-20, William I. Allyn; 1920, Henry W Hurlbutt.

Lisbon—1890-92, John G. Bromley; 1892-94, John G. Bromley; 1894-96, James E. Roberts; 1896-98, Charles B Bromley; 1898-1900, James B Palmer; 1900-1902, Frank E. Olds; 1902-04, Calvin D. Bromley; 1904-06. Harry L Hull; 1906-08. John M. Lee; 1908-10, Ira C. Wheeler; 1910-12, Herman E. Learned; 1912-14, James T. Shea; 1914-16, Francis H. Johnson, 1916-18. James Graham; 1918-20, James Graham; 1920, Henry J. Kendall.

Lyme—1890-92, Stephen P. Sterling, Robert M Thompson; 1892-94, J. Elv Beebe, Ephriam O. Reynolds; 1894-96, Roswell P. LaPlace, J. Greffin Ely; 1896-98, James L. Lord, E. Hart Geer; 1898-1900, Samuel W. Jewett, J Raymond Warren; 1900-02, James Daniels, James E. Beebe; 1902-04, Lee L. Brockway. J. Raymond Warren; 1904-06, Frederick S. Fosdick, William Marvin; 1906-08, J. Raymond Warren, William Marvin; 1908-10, Nehemiah Daniels, John S Hall; 1910-12, J. Warren Stark, Harold H. Reynolds; 1912-14, Charles W. Pierson, John S. Hall, 1914-16, John S Hall, Charles W. Pierson; 1916-18, Ray L. Harding, J. Lawrence Raymond; 1918-20, J. Lawrence Raymond, Hayden L. Reynolds; 1920, J. Warren Stark. Arthur G. Sweet.

Montville—1890-92, Charles A. Chapman; 1892-94, John F Freeland; 1894-96. George N. Wood, 1896-98, George N. Wood; 1898-1900, Moses Chapman, 1900-02. Joseph F. Killeen, 1902-04, George H. Bradford; 1904-06, Robert C. Burchard; 1906-08, Robert C. Burchard; 1908-10, Dan D Home; 1910-12, Frederick A Johnson; 1912-14, C. Everett Chapman; 1914-16, Matt A. Tinker;

1916-18, George H. Bradford; 1918-20. Edwin F. Comstock; 1920, Frank W. Browning.

New London—1890-92, George C. Strong, Walter Fitzmaurice; 1892-94, George C. Strong, Walter Fitzmaurice; 1894-96. Frederick H. Parmalee, Charles R. Boss; 1896-98, Robert·Coit. Cyrus G. Beckwith; 1898-1900, Frank B. Brandegee. Charles B Whittlesey, 1900-02. Charles B. Whittlesey, William B. Coit; 1902-04, Henry Lambert, William B Coit; 1904-06, Daniel M. Cronin, Charles B. Waller; 1906-08, Lucius E. Whiton. Carl J. Viets, 1908-10, Lucius E Whiton, Daniel M. Cronin; 1910-12, Nathan Belcher, Lucius E. Whiton; 1912-14. Abel P. Tanner, James R May; 1914-16, Frank Q. Cronin, Cyrus W. Brown; 1916-18, William A. Holt, William C. Fox; 1918-20, William A. Holt; George Goss; 1920, Ernest E Rogers, Morris B. Payne

North Stonington—1890-92, Cyrus H. Stewart, George W. Edwards; 1892-94, S. Curtis Eggleston, Latham Hull, 1894-96, Amasa W Main, George F. Coats; 1896-98, Amasa W. Main, George F. Coats; 1900-02, George D. Thompson, E Frank White; 1902-04, George D Thompson, E. Frank White, 1904-06, Calvin A Snyder, Latham Hull; 1906-08, Calvin A. Snyder, Herbert Richardson; 1908-10. Frank H. Brown, Chester S. Maine; 1910-12. Richard B Wheeler, Charles Lyman Stewart; 1912-14, Frank H. Brown, Thurman P Maine; 1914-16, Clarence E. Palmer, Lyle C. Gray; 1916-18, George H. Stone, Horace G. Lewis, 1918-20, George H. Stone, Malcolm E. Thompson; 1920, Irving R. Maine, N Frank Maine.

Norwich—1890-92, Gardiner Greene. Jr. George C Raymond; 1892-94. William C. Mowry, William H Palmer, Jr., 1894-96, Gardiner Greene. Jr, Joseph Brewer; 1896-98, John H. Barnes, Currie Gilmour; 1898-1900, Currie Gilmour, Edwin W. Higgins; 1900-02. George Greenman, James H. Lathrop; 1902-04, George Greenman, James H Lathrop. 1904-06. Frank T Maples. Herbert W. Hale; 1906-08, Tyler Cruttenden, Henry W. Tibbits; 1908-10. Henry W Tibbits. Charles B. Bushnell; 1910-12, Frederick Dearing, John F Craney, 1912-14, John F. Craney. William T. Delaney; 1914-16. Albert J Bailey, Joseph H Henderson; 1916-18. Albert J Bailey. Joseph H. Henderson, 1918-20. Patrick T. Connell, Joseph F. Williams; 1920, George Thompson, C. W. Pendleton.

Old Lyme—1890-92, Lyman Chapman; 1892-94. Henry Austin; 1894-96. James T. Bugbee 1896-98. John H Noble; 1898-1900. Frank I Saunders; 1000-02. Joseph S. Huntington; 1902-04, John H. Bradbury; 1904-06, John H. Bradbury; 1006-08, Eugene D. Caulkins; 1908-10, John H. Noble; 1910-12, John H. Noble; 1912-14. Thomas L. Haynes; 1914-16, Joseph S. Huntington; 1916-18, Harry G Pierson; 1918-20, Robert H Noble; 1920, Harry T. Griswold

Preston—1890-02, Frank W Fitch. Charles W Kingsley; 1892-94. Henry E Davis. William H Burnett: 1894-06, Austin A. Chapman, Appleton Main; 1896-98, Charles F. Boswell, Charles B. Chapman; 1898-1900, Daniel L. Jones, Gilbert S. Raymond; 1900-02, Adolphus D. Zabriskie, George M. Hyde, 1902-04, George A. Frink, John H. Davis; 1904-06, Edward P Hollowell, John H. Davis. 1906-08. Luther C. Zabriskie, Alexander C Harkness, 1908-10. Arthur E. Shedd. James F. Thurston; 1910-12, Walter MacClisien, Hollis H Palmer; 1912 14, Henry M Betlerig, Allen B Burdick; 1914 16, Eekford G Pendleton, William B Mitchell; 1016-18, James B. Bates. John P. Holowell; 1918-20, John P Holowell, Beriah E Burdick; 1920, E. G. Pendleton, Joseph E Carpenter.

Salem—1890-02. Alvah Morgan, 1892-94. Edwin H. Harris; 1894-96, Alvah Morgan; 1896-98. Albert Morgan;1898-1900. Frank S DeWolf; 1900-02, Alvah Morgan; 1902-04. John H. Purcell; 1904-06. Howard A Rix, 1906-08. Sydney A Dolbeare; 1908-10, Elmer M. Chadwick; 1910-12. Ernest L. Lati-

N L.—1-16

mer; 1912-14, Lewis Latimer; 1914-16, J. Frank Rogers; 1916-18, Carl H. Rogers; 1918-20, James Lane; 1920. William B. Kingsley.

Sprague—1890-92, William Ladd; 1892-94, Thomas H. Allen; 1894-96, Thomas H Allen; 1896-98. Ebenezer Allen; 1898-1900, Henry Buteau; 1900-02, Joseph Quinn; 1902-04, Harold Lawton; 1904-06, Augus Parker; 1906-08, Raymond J. Jodoin: 1908-10, Raymond J Jodoin; 1910-12, John H. Brown; 1912-14, Irenee L. Buteau; 1914-16. Irenee L. Buteau; 1916-18, Irenee L. Buteau; 1918-20, Raymond J. Jodoin; 1920. William G. Park.

Stonington—1890-92, Silas B. Wheeler, Warren W. Chase; 1892-94, George R. McKenna. Arthur G. Wheeler; 1894-96, James Pendleton, Henry B. Noyes, Jr.; 1896-98. James Pendleton, Elias Williams; 1898-1900, Frank H. Hinckley. George H. Maxson; 1900-02, Frank H. Hinckley, George H. Maxson; 1902-04. William H. Smith, Charles F. Champlain; 1904-06, Charles F. Champlain, Peter Bruggenam: 1906-08, Eli Gledhill, William J. Lord; 1908-10, William F. Broughton. Albert G. Martin; 1910-12, Joseph W. Chesebro, John R. Babcock; 1912-14, Joseph W. Chesebro, Herman L. Holdridge; 1914-16. Elias F Wilcox, Bourdow A. Babcock; 1916-18, Elias F. Wilcox, Bourdow A. Babcock: 1918-20. Nathaniel P. Noyes, Frederick Boulder; 1920, Frederick Boulder, Nathaniel P. Noyes.

Voluntown—1890-92, John N. Lewis: 1892-94, Henry C. Gardner; 1894-96, George W. Rouse; 1896-98. Charles E. Maine; 1898-1900. Ezra Briggs: 1900-02, Oregin S. Gallup; 1902-04, Edward A. Pratt; 1904-06, James W. Whitman; 1906-08. Elam A. Kinne; 1908-10, E. Byron Gallup; 1910-12. Azarias Grenier; 1912-14, William H Dawley, Jr.; 1914-16, Stephen B. Sweet; 1916-18. Constant W. Chatfield; 1918-20, Constant W. Chatfield; 1920, Thomas A. Brown.

Waterford—1890-92, John L. Payne; 1892-94, James E. Beckwith; 1894-96, William C Saunders; 1896-98. Frederick A. Jacobs; 1898-1900. Albert H. Lauphere, 1900-02. Albert H. Lauphere; 1902-04. Albert H. Lauphere; 1904-06, Edward C. Hammond; 1906-08. Selden B. Manwaring; 1908-10, Frederic E. Comstock; 1910-12. Albert H. Lauphere; 1912-14, Albert H. Lauphere; 1914-16. Stanley D. Morgan; 1916-18, John C. Geary; 1918-20, John C. Geary; 1920. William Ellery Allyn.

LIBRARY CONNECTICUT COLLEGE FOR WOMEN

CHAPTER X

EDUCATIONAL INSTITUTIONS

Connecticut College—Norwich Free Academy—Bacon Academy—Bulkeley School—
Williams Memorial Institute — New London Vocational School — Mystic Oral
School for the Deaf.

The greater number of the following narratives of notable educational
institutions are contributed by authorities of recognized knowledge and ability. The first, relating to Connecticut College, is by President Benjamin T.
Marshall, head of that institution.

CONNECTICUT COLLEGE, NEW LONDON

The foundations of Connecticut College were laid, not only in the fine
purposes and industry of the incorporators, but also in the faith they held in
women, and in their conviction that within the State of Connecticut there
should be a modern, progressive college for women, that should provide these
forms of higher education for women to which in recent years they have
aspired in increasing numbers, and for the privileges of which they have now
for many years demonstrated their indisputable qualification.

But there is also the glow and ardor of romance in the story of the
college. for how else shall we describe the experience of the young institution
whose hand was sought by a score or more towns and cities, who also
promised lavish gifts. Was it not romance, and was it not high gallantry,
that moved New London to sue so ardently for the hand of the college and
to present so promptly the gifts it promised, in the form of lands and funds?

The college will never forget the splendid enthusiasm of New London,
its corporate body, and its citizens, nor their significant and munificent gifts.
The coming of the college afforded New London a chance to demonstrate a
spirit of unity and of devotion to education which became in a real way the
revival of a civic pride and spirit which has characterized the city unmistakably in these recent years.

To serve and honor the city, which has served and honored it, will be
always a dominant factor in the purpose and life of the college; for it recognizes that by virtue of its character and purpose it should be the purveyor
to the city of opportunities for culture through lectures, exhibitions. musical
programs and conferences of various kinds, and seek to encourage the people
of the city to avail themselves of its ever-widening and increasing privileges.

The relations of city and college each to the other were begun under
happiest auspices. May they never cease to be reciprocally joyous and profitable. While the city goes about its daily business, the "College on the Hill"
moves faithfully and eagerly forward in the prosecution of its program, in
devotion to its distinctive ideal.

What the college is and what it aims for, how it does its work, and in
what spirit and with what results, the following paragraphs aim clearly to
state. They are presented as the official statement of the college through its
president.

1. The need for more women's colleges. For many years there had been

among educators and all persons interested in the higher education of women a recognition that more women's colleges of high grade were greatly needed, since the women's colleges already existing were either filled to capacity or over-crowded.

Connecticut College came into existence to meet, so far as it was able, that well-defined need of more high-grade, centrally located colleges for women. It became, in fact, a necessity in this new era for women, which has given them the full rights of suffrage. Within the State the need was accentuated by the fact that Wesleyan had determined to be solely a man's college; and in the mind of Wesleyan Alumna, and in the minds of friends whom she had gathered about her, the idea and purpose to have a woman's college within the State of Connecticut took root, assumed form, and became an established fact.

2. The Specific Need. There was further recognized the need of colleges specifically for women, which should definitely contemplate the tastes, talents, aptitudes, ambitions, potential service and possibilities of women in social, literary, educational, secretarial, business, professional and administrative positions; and should, coupled with the cultural and literary and scientific studies which serve as backgrounds and resources, those subjects and that training in them which give a vocational emphasis, and stimulate and equip the student to become in a sane, balanced and concrete fashion, both socially minded and socially efficient.

Courses coming under this description may be cited as those of home economics, fine arts, music, economics and sociology, secretarial studies and office practice, library science, physical education.

3. The Purpose and Ideal of the College. The effort to meet these needs generally and specifically is expressed in the purpose of Connecticut College, namely:

To offer college work of grade and value second to none; to offer technical work worthy of college credit; to prepare for professional work in all branches where women are needed.

In short, to maintain, with high standards, and to conduct with highest efficiency, a curriculum prepared to develop each woman's peculiar talents toward her most effective life work.

4. The Practical Fulfillment of Purpose. The practical operation and demonstration of this purpose and ideal is seen in the inclusion in the curriculum of the familiar college subjects—the ancient and modern languages and literatures, mathematics, chemistry, physics, botany, zoology, history, political science, economics, sociology, philosophy, psychology, education, biblical history, and literature; and, with their specific technical, vocational, artistic, domestic and social values, the following: Music, fine arts (including drawing, painting, design, interior decoration, mechanical drawing and ceramics) home economics (including foods, nutrition, household management, institutional management), library, science, secretarial studies and office practice, physical education (required of all students throughout their course).

It should be noted that there are courses, in their respective departments, for the training of teachers in Latin, English, French, music, physical educa-

BRANFORD HOUSE

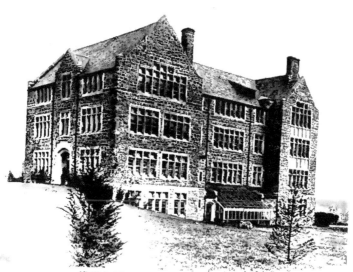

NEW LONDON HALL

BLACKSTONE HOUSE.

tion, besides the courses in education; courses in chemistry are, some of them, conducted with reference to their applications of that science, and a course in psychological chemistry, in its relation to home economics, is a particularly progressive and timely piece of work; that courses in mathematics, such as the theory of investment and statistics, have a direct practical value; that courses in economics and sociology are presented and prosecuted with sympathy toward, and understanding of, the instincts, interest and aptitudes and specific adaptability of women to social problems and social work.

The work in fine arts and in music is not merely theoretical, which method would tend to superficiality, but is also technical, coördinated, expressional, creative. Thus action and accomplishment are elevated to their rightful place in granting full credit to studio work; and action (creative work) is seen to be as essential to any worthy sort of appreciation in the realm of art as laboratory work is essential for the correct evaluation and esteem of any science. In this policy certain results are already unmistakably evident. There has come to be: (a) a respect for the use of the hand; (b) a higher grade of work in the studio; (c) greater enjoyment and satisfaction in the work; (d) a realization that education does not mean cessation from all work of the hand.

5. Broad and Balanced Curriculum—Values and Results. Because of the breadth of opportunity in major subjects offered in the preceding list (the regularly accepted academic majors, complemented by a number of majors in technical courses we can demonstrate that:

(a) There is a much larger percentage of students who find courses that lead to direct activity and expression, than in other colleges.

(b) There is an appreciable increase in the educational value of the institution from the very distinct and varied types of mind and of personality that are attracted by a diversity of courses.

(c) There is a more liberal and appreciative academic student, who has learned that arts are not superficial, but fundamental; and a more cultured and better technical student, by reason of required courses in foreign language, English literature, science, history and social science.

The trustees and faculty are united and enthusiastic in the loyal undertaking of this program. They are convinced of its soundness, practicability, and high value. Their confidence and enthusiasm are justified by the superior quality and large number of students who have sought admission, a number which every year has exceeded the capacity of the college.

6. The college has attracted superior students in large numbers from several States. Students now enrolled in the college number approximately 380; the largest number, we believe, ever known in an American College in its seventh year. Students come from twenty-one different States. Several students have transferred from other colleges, to find in Connecticut College more nearly what they wanted and needed, than they could find elsewhere, and several girls have entered Connecticut College attracted by its offerings, who, from their early years, had fully purposed to enter other and older women's colleges. The college has graduated three classes, the class of 1919 with sixty-eight who received degrees, and the class of 1920 with sixty-

nine who received degrees, and the class of 1921. We believe that no other college in America can cite such large figures for its first three classes.

7. Complete Student Self-government. No argument attempting to justify the existence and service of the college would be complete that did not stress the value and significance of the system of full student self-government, granted by the faculty to the student body from the first   The system provides for a complete control of all the life and activity of the students, except in strictly academic matters.   It is organized as a representative democracy, and functions with reality. efficiency, good judgment, and we believe, with increasing success.

The counsel, suggestion, and experience of faculty and administration is always available, and is frequently sought, and in all more vital matters is always requested.

In managing their own affairs as a real democracy, students are trained in responsibility, coöperation, initiative, in forming judgments, in making choices, in creating policies, in establishing tradition, and maintaining college morale, and in official duties and committee work learn valuable lessons in tact, appreciation, discrimination and in administration and execution.

8. The Spirit of the College—Loyalty, Enthusiasm. Coöperation, Confidence.   The undoubted effect of this organization of the students has been to develop a spirit of true democracy, without religious or social or class prejudices; to stimulate respect for work in all its forms, particularly with reference to students working their way through: there is tolerance and good will and sympathy; the bases of the organization are work, responsibility, liberty, solidarity, and a type of girl is being developed who is entirely free from pedantry and cant; she is open, sincere, unselfish and of sound judgment and initiative, able to deal with people and with situations, yet without conceit or assumption.

Through all the activities of the college, both in its academic and social side, there breathes an intense spirit of loyalty and of enthusiasm.   From the beginning the students were made, by the administration and the faculty, to realize how much the morale and spirit of the college were in their keeping, and they have grown in intensity of appreciation and responsibility for the highest character in college life.

The spirit of coöperation is cultivated in the fact that the college does things together.   It meets every day for Chapel, every Sunday for Vespers, every Tuesday for Convocation, as a college body, faculty and students merging; and it undertakes an interest and a support of outside activities in college-wide fashion.   When called upon to give, as for instance during the war, to the Students' Friendship War Fund, to the United War Campaign, and more recently in aid of the students and professors of the colleges in central Europe, it organizes its efforts as an all-college affair, pours its energy, its enthusiasm, its zeal, its gifts, into one common effort, and the result is issued with the seal and endorsement of the entire college upon it.

There is in all the life of the college great confidence in the institution, a splendid satisfaction in its work, great happiness in its fellowship, and a fine sense of challenge in the richness, variety and wholesomeness of its entire

ABOVE, WINTHROP HOUSE. IN CENTER, THAMES HALL, REFECTORY. BELOW, GYMNASIUM.

The spirit of coöperation, understanding, unanimity, which prevails, may be expressed when we say that in the four years of the present administration there has not been in the board of trustees a single divided vote; and in the faculty, on no vital point, anything but practical unanimity.

9. Favorable and appreciative attitude of educators and institutions toward Connecticut College. The attitude and favor and good-will, confidence and commendation on the part of educators and of presidents of other women's colleges has been very cheering. Without exception, the older colleges have welcomed Connecticut College into the sisterhood, have declared that it was greatly needed; that the kind of work it is doing is essential and is well done, and that its future is bright and challenging. The comment of President MacCracken of Vassar is perhaps as significant as any, when, after speaking of several forward steps in the education of women in America in recent years, he says:

Among these steps the most important is undoubtedly the founding of Connecticut College at New London, and all friends of higher education for women have welcomed its entrance into the field, because it is clear from the general trend of registration that women will in increasing numbers seek the college degree.

Visitors to the campus, representing other colleges, presidents, deans, registrars, official committees of visitation with specific errands, have spoken uniformly of their pleasure in the visit, of the distinct impression of industry, vigor and worth in which the college work is done, and congratulated the college on its site, on its work, and on its prospects. Organizations, whose representatives have come to give counsel to the students with reference to future occupation, representatives of social organizations seeking superior material, for graduate study in schools of social service, have expressed themselves in such language as this:

"In conference, the students ask most intelligent questions."
"Know what they want."
"Have a knowledge of the factors in social and industrial situations more than students of other colleges visited."

The college has freely been granted the counsel of the Russell Sage Foundation, whose aid in planning various lines of community work under the auspices of the sociology department has been offered.

Graduates of the college have gone forth to social work or to advanced study on the basis of the work done here, and have been given practically a year's credit in advance over the graduates of other institutions, whether in graduate study or in active positions on the staff of charity or social organizations.

10. Record of Graduates: Variety in activity and service, and gratifying success. All that precedes, which is an effort to justify the existence of the college, finds its concrete, and we believe unanswerable justification in the quality of the product of the college in its graduates and in the nature and quality of the service they are rendering in their present fields.

There are 180 alumnae of the college, graduates in the first three classes,

1919, 1920 and 1921. The director of the college appointment bureau reports that these graduates are largely engaged in the work toward which their major work in college particularly fitted them.

The success and gratifying service of such graduates, from whom we have received definite returns, is due, not alone to the careful and able training by a competent faculty, but also to that spirit of enthusiasm, of loyalty and coöperation which has characterized the college since its inception, a passion to do whatever they do worthily, and to count constructively by rendering a specific service to society.

There is a profound confidence in the college on the part of the trustees, faculty, students and friends of the college alike. They take pride in its genuine, though modest accomplishment, and they feel confident of its future and hopeful and zealous of its maintenance and expansion along the lines projected from the beginning and faithfully followed to this moment, so far as years of war and relatively unincreased endowment have permitted.

The preceding paragraphs, we trust, constitute a sufficient and genuine justification of the existence of the college. Our conviction is that the college was opened to meet both a general and a specific need, that it established for itself a splendid purpose and a high ideal, and it set itself vigorously and conscientiously to the practical fulfillment of that purpose. It has offered a broad and balanced curriculum of soundness, practicability, undoubted values and of high promise It has summoned to itself superior students in large numbers from a wide area. It has cultivated in them a passion to do whatever they do worthily, and to count constructively, whether by helping to brighten a home and elevate the life of a family, or by rendering some more specific service to society at large.

It has already developed a peculiar, significant and exalted spirit, which is recognized as distinctive, strong and exceptional. It has won from the beginning and in increasing measure, the welcome, the appreciation, the regard and commendation of its sister colleges, their leaders and all educators who have come to know it; and chiefly, and above all, it has contributed in its graduates a group of women who are undertaking specific tasks toward which the college unmistakably directed them, following their natural bent, ambition and equipment, and they are doing, each in her own place, the world's work in a way that is worthy, noble and commendable, to the credit of the college they love, to the honor of their own lives, and as a rare and distinctive contribution to the life of America.

NORWICH FREE ACADEMY

This historical sketch of the Norwich Free Academy is by Rev. Lewellyn Pratt, D.D., formerly president of the corporation.

The next oldest of the private schools of the county is the Norwich Free Academy. The following account of its early days was delivered by Dr. Lewellyn Pratt, its president, in 1906, on the fiftieth anniversary of its opening:

OLD BRICK ACADEMY. DEDICATED IN 1846; DEMOLISHED

The story of the fifty years of the Norwich Free Academy is very simple compared with that of Winchester, Eton, Rugby, Harrow and other great schools of Europe, with their five and six centuries of achievement, and yet the history of these fifty years, given in any fair completeness, would require more time than I can take today I must content myeslf with a mere introduction to what is to follow in the addresses of these two days.

For many years before 1856 the need of improvement in the schools of Norwich had been keenly felt, and various attempts had been made to bring them together into some system and to establish schools of a higher grade. The discussions that immediately preceded the organization of the Academy aroused much opposition, but they directed attention to the need and strengthened the determination to find some way by which an advance could be made. The opposition was so decided that it did not seem feasible to wait for a vote of the town to make that advance, nor altogether safe to trust to that to maintain it, if by chance it could be made Under the leadership of the Rev. John P. Gulliver—to whom as the organizer more credit is due than to any other one—the plan of an endowed academy, which should be so correlated with the grammar schools that it should take the place of the high schools, then being formed and developed in Massachusetts and Connecticut, and at the same time so independent of political control and free to accept all approved methods of education as to bring and keep it in close connection with the higher institutions of learning, was adopted. A group of men was found in Norwich far-sighted and public-spirited enough to grasp and welcome the idea, and with singular generosity to furnish the means by which it could be realized. All honor to those men of faith and self-sacrifice who, without expectation of pecuniary return for themselves, gave freely of their wealth for that which the public would soon have been almost compelled to do by increased taxation, devised the plan which has stood the test of time and bestowed a benefaction which is to bless many generations!

Some of you may recall the verses with which Mrs. Sigourney celebrated the spirit of this benefaction, which were read at the opening of the school:

> There's many kinds of stocks, they say,
>   That tempt the speculators;
> But what is safest held, and best,
>   Might tax the shrewdest natures.
> Sage Franklin said in earlier days,—
>   And now the wisest bless him,—
> "Who pours his purse into his brains,
>   No man can dispossess him."
>
> And so, the people of my love
>   His theory have tested,
> And for their children and themselves
>   A glorious sum invested —
> And by this dome, for knowledge rear'd,
>   Which no dark mortgage fetters,
> Have nobly made a race unborn
>   Their everlasting debtors.

And as in old historic times,
    Though exiled and unnoted,
The Roman citizen with pride
    His honored birth-place quoted:
So I, with quickened heart this day,
    Warm orisons addressing
Ask, for these native rocks and dales
    Our Father's richest blessing.

The aims of the founders, as set forth by them when they applied for their charter in 1854, were: 1. To excite in the minds of parents, guardians and children a deeper interest in education. 2. To stimulate scholars in primary, intermediate and grammar schools to higher attainments in the elementary branches. 3. To elevate the standard of education in the town and vicinity. 4. To furnish the facilities for a higher education for our sons and daughters so cheaply that the poorest can enjoy them, and so amply that the richest shall be grateful for the privilege of receiving their benefits

The great aim of the plan was the betterment of all the schools, and its immediate result was the consolidation of two of the districts and the building and equipment of larger and more commodious schoolhouses, and since that time there has been steady advance of the standard in the schools of the town and vicinity. Starting in 1856, a small school, we mark some tokens of steady growth. At its opening there were eighty scholars with five teachers. The present enrollment, including those in the Art and Domestic Science departments, is about four hundred and fifty, with twenty-three teachers. The original endowment was $50,000, with $36,000 more invested in building and equipment. In spite of the fears expressed that an endowed school would suffer by the decline of interest after the original donors should pass away, the endowment, through the same self-sacrifice and public spirit that characterized them animating their descendants, has increased to ten times the original amount, and the investment in lands and buildings and apparatus to more than eight times what it was at first. In the first years there were only the Classical and English departments. To these have been added the Art, the Manual Training and the Domestic Science departments, while the two original divisions have been enlarged and enriched, keeping pace on the one hand with the advanced requirements of our leading colleges and on the other with the need of more thorough scientific and practical courses for those who finish their school life in the Academy and enter upon the duties of domestic and business life. A notable part of the equipment, to which attention was called by speakers at the opening of the school, was the establishment of the Peck Library. This has been steadily increased by the income of its separate endowment till it now numbers thirteen thousand nine hundred and eighteen volumes of carefully selected books, which are in constant use by the school. A promising and most important department of Normal Training was projected and carried on for seven years, giving to the public schools a number of well trained teachers who have by their successful work and the high positions they have attained vindicated the plan that was proposed. This, because of difficulties of adjustment that were encountered, was abandoned in 1896 During these fifty years there have been graduated

FREE ACADEMY—ABOVE, AT LEFT, SLATER HALL, LIBRARY AND MUSEUM, WITH
ART DEPARTMENT IN REAR; IN CENTER, MAIN ACADEMY BUILDING. BELOW,
REAR VIEW; AT LEFT, MANUAL TRAINING BUILDING; CENTER, MAIN ACAD-
EMY BUILDING; AT RIGHT, SLATER HALL, SHOWING ART BUILDING

from the academy 1,310, and from the normal department 81. As many more have taken a partial course in the school. These twenty-six or twenty-seven hundred are now scattered in almost every State of the Union, and many are in foreign countries.

From the first the school has not been restricted to narrow town limits. The original donors, while primarily aiming to benefit the schools of the town, took a large view of the position of Norwich in its relation to the surrounding community, and, regarding it as a commercial center for the towns around, they planned that it might become an educational center for the vicinity, and on condition of a moderate payment opened its doors to those from other places who could successfully pass its examinations. One of the first scholarships established was specially designated by its giver as for the benefit of scholars from his native town, many miles distant. Later, when an addition of $50,000 was added to the endowment, one of the conditions made by the donors was that "the academy should be open to scholars from any quarter." And several of the scholarships given since were to be offered to out-of-town pupils on equal terms with those of the town. "Greater Norwich"—and Norwich once included greater territory—has been considered as sharing the benefit: and well has that expectation been justified not only by the numbers that have been attracted hither—some to become permanent residents—but by the character of those who came and the credit they have reflected upon the school. The amount received for tuition the last year from these out-of-town pupils was nearly equal to the whole income of the first year. As a high school for Norwich, the academy has been a great gift to the town, relieving it of a vast amount of taxation during these fifty years; and as something more than a high school, an academy, it has been a great gift to Eastern Connecticut. In its present enrollment, seventy-five are from beyond the narrow limits of present Norwich.

The school was fortunate in the large and liberal views of the founders and in their wise purpose to keep it free for all time from the contingencies of politics and to give it a stable character by placing its control in the hands of a self-perpetuating board of corporators who might be free to study its interests and make far-reaching plans without fear of sudden displacement or reversal.

It was fortunate in its location in this beautiful spot in historic Norwich. Here, in the midst of homes of wealth and culture, it has found a wholesome atmosphere and congenial soil. The questioning of early days has given place to pride in its possession, and the generosity of its early friends has been well sustained by their successors.

It has been specially fortunate in the character and ability and work of its chosen leaders to whom the great task of development has been committed

It has had four principals:

1. Professor Elbridge Smith, a man trained in the best schools of Massachusetts at that time, from 1856 to 1865. The work of the beginning from almost chaos was in his hands. He proved himself a good organizer and disciplinarian, and amid the discouragement of the day of small things and of the period of formation, and then of almost disbanding because of the

drafts made by the spirit of patriotism in the time of the Civil War (from the small numbers then connected with the school, fifty-six enlisted in the army), he carried the work through its early stages wisely and well.

2. Professor William Hutchison, who succeeded him from 1865 to 1885, who brought to the school a large and inspiring spirit, and by his sympathetic relation with his pupils, his broad common sense and wide interest in all that concerned the town, gave to the school an acknowledged place in the affections of the people. What tributes were paid to his memory at our Fortieth Anniversary! Any school is fortunate in such a memory.

3. Professor Robert Porter Keep, who came in 1886 and whose term in office was next to the longest in its history, ending in 1903. Professor Keep was a scholar of great attainment, worthy of a place in university work, who with singular and untiring devotion gave himself to the cause of secondary education, and saw here opportunities for development and growth that had scarcely been dreamed of before. To him we owe in large measure the Art department, the Normal, the Manual Training and Domestic Science departments, and a position among educational institutions recognized by scholars throughout the country. His rank among scholars, his acquaintance with the best schools of this country and Europe, and his belief in this school and its possibilities, were guarantees of its worth and constantly reflected credit upon its name. A large debt of gratitude is ever due to him from the Norwich Free Academy

4 It is not proper that I should speak here today as I would like of him who now holds the office of principal, Mr. Henry A. Tirrell.

With these principals have been associated a long list of faithful teachers, who, for a longer or shorter time, have given their best work to the school and wrought themselves into the lives of the pupils. So well chosen have many of these been, that the academy has proved a favorite recruiting station for instructors and professors for many of our colleges and universities.

The school has been fortunate, too, in its scholars. While, unlike some academies which draw their pupils from a wide field and who have largely those of wealth and position, we draw our pupils alsomst exclusively from the immediate neighborhood and offer its privileges alike to rich and poor, yet we claim for the academy that in good order, in the development of character, in training for life's work, in actual attainment, the graduates here will compare favorably with any school in the land, and in loyalty no high school can equal it, and few if any academies surpass it. The cabalistic "N. F. A." inspires many a heart and wins everywhere a loud acclaim.

It was with sublime faith that the founders of this academy entered upon their great undertaking, and the work that was done by them, the extent of the grounds, the scale of the building, the endowment of the library, indicated that they were planning for a large future. Nobly has their confidence been justified and sustained. The academy has always held a high place in the thought and affection of the people of this city. Ministering to the growth and reputation of the town, it has been the constant recipient of gifts for its enlargement and expansion. Notable among these was the gift of this building with its Museum of Art, unsurpassed in the country except in the great cities, and the creation of the unique and excellent Art Department, through the filial love, the loyalty to his *Alma Mater* and the pride in native place of William A. Slater. Besides this, the bequests of Hon. Jeremiah Halsey, of Hon. Lafayette S. Foster, W. W. Backus and of Col. Charles A. Converse, with the special additions of $31,000 in 1867, of $50,000 in 1876, made by many of the most influential citizens of Norwich, and of $50,000 by an unnamed donor, with many other contributions of money, scholarships, prizes and collections, show the appreciation in which it has always been held. We believe that this interest does not flag, and that the committal of the academy in the opening address of 1856 to the future generations for their support will be honored by the residents of the city and the alumni of the school, and that the plans for enlargement now imperatively demanded by the success of the past and the increasing needs of the present will meet with hearty response

I close with the words of Dr. Gulliver in 1886 at the dedication of the Slater Memorial Building. He said, "I close, citizens of Norwich, by commending this noble school to your love, to your constant care, to your benefactions, to the possession of your estates when you and yours have ceased to need them, and to your prayers for that Divine blessing in which the institution began and with which it shall continue and increase until in the holy words oft uttered on this very spot, 'she sends out her boughs unto the sea and her branches unto the river, so that the hills are covered with the shadow of it and the branches thereof are like goodly cedars.' "

The foregoing summary by Dr. Pratt takes the school to the year 1906 Since that date more than a thousand pupils have been graduated, making a total of about twenty-five hundred. More than twice that number have attended the school for a part of the regular four-year course Although the academy is a local school, its graduates are found scattered over the world, only about a third of them now remaining in Norwich. The list of alumnae is slightly larger than the alumni list. Among the names are many honored for success in the professions, and many more who have become useful and influential citizens in other lines of work. During the Civil War 58 boys served the Union when the school numbered not more than 85 boys. In the World War over three hundred graduates entered the service, of whom eleven made the Supreme Sacrifice.

The school at present numbers over six hundred, and offers various academic courses, in addition to special courses in practical arts and in craft work. In its Slater Museum and Peck Library it has an equipment hardly equalled in any other secondary school In addition to its valuable plant, the school has an endowment of about three-quarters of a million dollars, the income of which is available for the various needs of the academy.

BACON ACADEMY

The following narrative of this famous old school is by Mr. Samuel A. Willard, of Colchester:

The beginnings of Bacon Academy were in the will of Pierpoint Bacon, his estate, inventoried at $35,000, was left to the "Inhabitants of the First Society of Colchester for the purpose of supporting and maintaining a school in said First Society at such place as the Inhabitants of said First Society shall agree upon near the meeting house in said Society."

The largest town in the State by the census of 1800 was Stonington, with a population of 5,347   Colchester had 3,163, of which perhaps rather more than one-half lived in the "First Society."   Mr. Bacon's gift opened great opportunities to this small community, and at the same time placed upon it grave responsibilities.   The first problem was how to manage the bequest, which was largely in lands, and to arrange for the development of the school.   It was soon evident that the Society meeting was not the place to handle this business, and a committee was appointed to secure a charter from the General Assembly.   For the purposes of caring for and administering the fund and carrying on the school in accordance with the terms of the will, the inhabitants of the First Society were incorporated under the name of the Trustees and Proprietors of Bacon Academy.

There were two unusual features in this charter which make the management of the school unique.   They are well worth attention.   The first was the composition of the board of trustees.   There were to be twelve trustees, five of whom were to be non-resident in said Society, and by the charter and subsequent amendments the seven resident trustees were to hold office for a term of four years, and at each election at least four of the seven must be persons who had served during the previous term   The second provision to be noted is the manner in which the trustees were to be chosen.   The voters of the First Society in public meeting duly warned were to nominate the trustees; these nominations were to be sent to the State Senate; the Senate is to appoint and the Governor to approve.   Some machinery, perhaps, but the procedure gave dignity and permanence to the governing body, and separated the school from petty local influence.   The school is and always has been a free public school, supported by endowment.   The non-resident trustees on the first board as mentioned in the charter were "His Excellency Jonathan Trumbull, the Honorable Zepheniah Swift, the Honorable Roger Griswold, General Epaphroditus Champion, the Reverend Henry Channing."   The resident trustees named were "The Reverend Salmon Cone, Colonel Daniel Watrous, Major Roger Bulkeley, Joseph Isham, John R. Watrous, Asa Bigelow and Ichabod Lord Skinner," all men of affairs and representative citizens of Colchester.   This all shows "that men eminent for their services to the church and the state thought it not beneath them to manage the concerns and direct the interests of the school founded by Mr. Bacon's bequest."   It has been of great assistance to the school that a part of the board was able to view matters detached from local interests.   Some of the other non-resident trustees during these intervening years have been Eliphalet A. Bulkeley, first president of the Aetna Life Insurance Company of Hartford; Reverend Abel McEwen, of New London, William A. Buckingham, Connecticut's War Governor; Charles J. McCurdy, lawyer, of Lyme; Morgan G. Bulkeley, another Connecticut governor; Charles N. Taintor, president of the United States Savings Bank of New York City; Edwin B. Cragin, M.D., of New

York; Edward M. Day, lawyer, of Hartford, and Michael D. O'Connell, lawyer, and judge of probate in Stafford Springs

With the organization complete, the next important factor in determining the success of the school was the principal, who must by his scholarship and personality interest, enthuse, develop and direct the youth committed to his charge. The first principal was John Adams, Yale 1795, and a teacher of successful experience The choice was a most fortunate one, and the school at once took foremost rank. Two months after the school was opened, 206 students were enrolled, of whom 63 were from out of town. Mr. Adams left in 1810 to accept the principalship of Phillips Academy, Andover, Massachusetts. Able successors followed him, and the school continued to grow in numbers until in 1835-36 the enrollment was over 400, including 125 "scholars from abroad." The following year the attendance probably reached high water mark The catalogue contains the names of 425 scholars, 137 of whom were from out of town, and 32 of these were from out of the State. It must have been a problem to accommodate all these pupils in a village which at that time had a population of only about 1,200 . "To accommodate these students or their families, almost every family of the village rented a part of the house or took boarders." Gradually high schools were started in other towns, and the out-of-town attendance fell off, but the school maintains its high standard, fitting for college, and also making special effort to adapt itself to the community needs.

There have been some thirty-five different principals since the school opened All but two or three were college graduates, and twenty-two were graduated from Yale. Several of the earlier masters had served as tutors there. They were a fine body of men, and their influence and example were an inspiration to many a Colchester youth and led him to continue his studies beyond the high school. There are no statistics extant of the number who went from the academy to college during the first seventy years. One who had given some time to looking this up has a list of seventy-five Bacon Academy students who had graduated from colleges before 1870. Since Mr. Burnette became principal in 1869 up to the present, about sixty-five of the graduates have completed a course in some college or university, and some twenty others have entered but were compelled to withdraw before finishing the course on account of ill health or lack of funds. Last year there were eighteen graduates from the school continuing their studies in higher institutions of learning The enrollment of the school for the last few years has been about eighty-five.

The original endowment has been increased by gifts from Asa Otis, S. Lewis Gillette, Judah Lord Taintor. Lewis E. Stanton, Charles E. Jones, James F. Cutler, Hamilton Wallis, Charles N Taintor, and a fund of $10,000 given at the Centennial by the alumni. The present fund is about $100,000.

The list of men and women who have received a part of their preparation for life work in the academy is a long one. A few may be mentioned without reference to the chronological order of their attendance at the school:

Morrison R Waite, chief justice U. S. Supreme Court; Lyman Trumbull, U. S. senator from Illinois; John T. Wait, lawyer and member of Congress,

Norwich; George Champion, missionary to Zululand, Africa, David Trumbull and James Trumbull, who lived for years in Chili, South America; William Larrabee, governor of Iowa, Joseph Selden, editor, East Haddam; William A. Buckingham, governor of Connecticut; Elisha Palmer, James D Mowry. Lewis A. Hyde. Welcome A Smith, Norwich; Charles Wetmore, M.D., missionary physician in Sandwich Islands; Rev. James T. Hyde, D.D., professor in Chicago Theological Seminary, Lewis E Stanton, lawyer, Hartford: Silas A. Robinson, judge of Connecticut Supreme Court, Middletown; Rev Ezra H. Gillett, D.D., professor in New York University; John E. Gillette. Catskill Station, New York; Ralph Smith Taintor, Saybrook; Charles N. Taintor, president United States Savings Bank, New York City; James U. Taintor, secretary Orient Fire Ins. Co., Hartford; Judah Lord Taintor, publisher. New York City; John E. Leffingwell, president Farragut Ins. Co., New York City; Edward Sheffield Bartholomew, sculptor, Hartford, Harriet Trumbull (Mrs. George J Brush). New Haven; Catherine Olmstead (Mrs Erastus S. Day), Colchester; Sebastian Lawrence, banker, New London; S. Lewis Gillette, business, Boston, Massachusetts; James S Foote. M.D., professor Creighton Medical College. Omaha, Nebraska, Charles W. Haines, lawyer. Colorado Springs; Rev. Curtis M. Geer, Hartford Theological Seminary, Frank D. Haines, Portland, judge Superior Court. Connecticut; Park Benjamin, journalist, New York City; Henry C. Demming. Hartford; Henry W. Bigelow. manufacturer, Boston; Henry Marsh. California; Rev. Charles N Ransom, missionary, South Africa; John T. Swift, professor University. Tokyo, Japan; Rev. Florence O'Shea, Pittsburgh, Pennsylvania; Rev. Michael Sullivan, LL.D., Hartford; Rev. Eugene Sullivan, Portchester, New York; Rev. Timothy Sullivan, East Hartford; Edward M Day, lawyer, Hartford; Eliphalet A. Bulkeley, first president Aetna Life Ins. Co., Hartford; Morgan G. Bulkeley, governor of Connecticut, Hartford; Theron Clark, registrar Brown University, Providence; Edwin B. Cragin, eminent surgeon and professor, College of Physicians and Surgeons, New York City, Michael D O'Connell, judge of probate, Stafford Springs; Rev. James T. Champlin, president Colby College. Maine, Charles Brand, lieutenant-commander U. S. Navy, John W Brand, treasurer Institution for Savings. Springfield, Massachusetts; Martin Shugrue, assistant professor, Massachusetts Institute Technology, Boston; Almira Lathrop (Mrs. Solomon T. Swift). Colchester; David S Day, lawyer, Bridgeport; Mary R. Willard (Mrs Edwin B. Cragin), New York City; Margaret Weeks (Mrs. J. L. Shipley). Springfield; Leonore Bartlett (Mrs. B F. Parsons). Georgia. Caroline Swift (Mrs. D W. Willard), California; Lewis E. Sparrowe, investment broker, New York City; Thomas S O'Connell, M D., East Hartford; Richard T. O'Connell, judge of probate, East Hartford; Rev William B. Sprague. LL.D., noted divine, Albany, New York; Rev. Nathaniel Hewitt, D.D., Bridgeport; Frederick W. Lord, M.D., member of Congress. Greenport, L. I.; W Henry Foote, Romney, Va.; Rev. E Goodrich Smith, Washington, D C.; Samuel A. Bridges, member of Congress. Allentown, Pennsylvania, Charles J McCurdy. lawyer, Lyme, David H. Raymond, judge in Indiana when it was a territory; James Raymond, Westminster, Maryland; Henry M. Waite, chief justice Supreme Court Connecticut; Samuel A Talbot, attorney-general, New York State; Ebenezer Jackson, member of Congress. Middletown, Charles J. McCurdy, lawyer, Lyme; Charles J. Watrous, U. S. District Judge, Texas.

These are a few of the hundreds who have had a share in the benefits of Mr. Bacon's gift to Colchester How much such a legacy means to a place so small that otherwise it would not have had a high school! The following taken from a letter written by the Honorable Samuel A. Bridges in August,

1853, acknowledging an invitation to attend the Semi-Centennial of the Academy, indicates the way a non-resident pupil regarded the matter:

By it they (the citizens of Colchester) have been elevated in the enjoyment of privileges far above many of their neighbors. To them the name of "Bacon" has given a distinction of which others would like to boast. Through his bountiful munificence the elder portion of them have lived to see their children first taught in his academic halls elevated to the pulpit, the bar, and the bench. How many important influences at the expiration of the half century radiate from that grand center! This is no less true now that 117 years have passed. The original gift supplemented during the last twenty years by the generosity of other friends does not in any way relieve the town in its support of schools, but provides opportunities for the education beyond the graded schools, for community work and for Americanization work beyond the usual lot of small communities.

THE BULKELEY SCHOOL, NEW LONDON

The following account of the Bulkeley School has been prepared by its principal, Mr. Walter A. Towne.

The founder of this school was Leonard Hallam Bulkeley. Mr. Bulkeley was a descendant of Rev. Gershom Bulkeley, the second minister of the Colonial church, and a son of Captain Charles Bulkeley, who was associated with John Paul Jones, who in command of the "Bonhomme Richard" harried English commerce so effectively during the war for American Independence. One is rather safe in saying, consequently, that the foundation fund of the school had its beginning in the prize moneys of these gallant but precarious adventures.

Mr. Bulkeley was a merchant of modest pretensions, whose place of business was very near the school which now bears his name. He was born December 22, 1799, and died December 19, 1849. He left an estate valued at something less than $25,000 to found a secondary school which should be free to boys of New London. In his will he provided that the funds should be kept intact until the trustees, who were named in the will, should decide that they were justified in the erection of the schoolhouse.

There were five trustees named by Mr. Bulkeley, viz.: John P. C. Mather, Nathan Belcher, Henry P. Haven, William C. Crump, and N. Shaw Perkins, who served continuously until his death in 1905. This official board decided in 1870 that the estate had increased so considerably in its careful management that they were justified in beginning operations. Accordingly, plans were secured from the famous architect, Mr. Eidlitz, and upon a lot presented to them by the city they erected a very substantial and attractive building. How little they anticipated the growth of the city may be seen from the fact that the school provided seating capacity for only forty-two boys in the main study hall.

The school was opened in September, 1873, for the admission of boys, under the direction of Eugene B. Collester as principal, who had graduated from Amherst College the preceding June. Mr. Collester resigned in 1880, and afterwards lived in Minnesota. The next principal of the school was

N.L.—1-17

Ely R Hall, Yale '72, and previously a teacher in Hopkins Grammar School. Mr Hall remained in charge of the school until 1888, when he moved to Woodstock, Connecticut, and was principal of the academy of that town until his death in 1920. The conduct of the school was then placed in the hands of the writer, who has remained in charge until the present (1921).

The ordinary custom of secondary schools in having a curriculum of four years leading to graduation was followed until 1884, when the course was changed to one of three years, with the privilege of an additional year for boys desiring to enter college. This plan was followed until 1910, when the school restored its original plan of a course extending through four years.

Bulkeley School is the successor of the New London Grammar School, established in 1713, and maintained jointly by the town and the income of a gift of two hundred and fifty acres of land given by Robert Bartlett, who died in 1676 Nathan Hale was one of the masters of this school, which was discontinued in 1873 and the Robert Bartlett foundation was given to the trustees of Bulkeley School. The funds of the school have been enhanced by various legacies and gifts, notably from Asa Otis, Henry P. Haven, and George F. Tinker.

The building was very much enlarged since 1873, and now accommodates about two hundred boys. The graduates number about 850, of whom 275 have entered college or other institutions of higher learning. Many of the graduates have attained eminence in public life. At the present time the school has a graduate in both houses of the National Congress as well as in the Connecticut Legislature. They are found in the faculties of the United States Military and Naval Academies and various colleges. About two hundred were engaged in the activities of the recent European war.

The foregoing facts constitute the visible history of Bulkeley School, but its real history and the apology for its foundation are to be found, like those of every school, in the lives of those who have come within its influence, and will never be known until the day when all things shall be revealed and we shall see each other face to face.

WILLIAMS MEMORIAL INSTITUTE

Mr Colin S Buell, principal, gives the following account of this school.

The Williams Memorial Institute is a secondary school for girls, founded by Mrs. Harriet Peck Williams, of Norwich, Conn., as a memorial to her son, Thomas W. Williams, 2d, a whaling merchant of New London. Mr. Williams died suddenly in 1855, leaving the bulk of this property to his mother. One parcel of this property was a lot on which he had planned to build a house. The mother decided to give this lot and the funds left her by her son to found a school.

The school was opened in September, 1891, with about 100 pupils, taken over from the "Young Ladies' High School," a public school of the city of New London. In order to make the school free to the girls of New London, the city agreed to pay the nominal fee charged to all girls.

As the years went by the school increased in numbers beyond all expectation, in spite of the fact that a Vocational School was founded and flourished greatly. The number of girls at present enrolled is about 325.

The graduates of the school number about 1,100, and are scattered over the world. Over 50 per cent of them are, or have been at some time, teachers. Many of them have attended the leading colleges, and have won the highest honors. Some are now professors in colleges of America and of foreign lands. The majority of the alumnae are, at the present time, occupying the places which are the natural heritage of women—wives and mothers

In 1917 a member of the board of trustees bought the property adjoining that of the institute and presented it to the school The property now consists of about six acres of land in the city, with two large buildings, greenhouses, etc.. tennis courts, out-door basketball court and room for sports of various kinds. From the very beginning the school has insisted on physical training. A teacher has been in charge of the gymnasium, and all girls go to work there twice a week.

NEW LONDON VOCATIONAL HIGH SCHOOL

The following is from the pen of Mr. F S Hitchcock, principal.

The origin of this school dates back to the early boyhood of its founder, Mr. William H. Chapman, and represents a plan on his part, not necessarily to lessen labor, for he believed in work, but to enable young men and women to attack the problems of life with intelligence, with a love of industry and skill, and with a greater certainty of achievement worthy of their best efforts.

William Henry Chapman was born April 8th, 1819, in East Haddam, Middlesex county, Connecticut, and traces his ancestry from Robert Chapman, a native of Hull, England, who came to America in 1633 and settled in Saybrook, Connecticut Another ancestor, Sir John Chapman, was at one time Lord Mayor of London. Mr. Chapman spent his youth in the country. As a boy he was normally healthy but not vigorous. He was fond of reading and inclined to seek seclusion to gratify this taste From biographies of business men he gained help for his personal plans and problems. He was educated in the public and private schools of his native town and in Bacon Academy, Colchester, Connecticut. He keenly enjoyed historical literature.

In 1837 Mr. Chapman began as a clerk in a drygoods store in New London, which proved to be the beginning of a long and successful business career. He was president of the Union Bank (chartered 1792) for forty-six years, and was president of the Savings Bank of New London from 1866 until the time of his death in February, 1912. From 1875 until February, 1912, he was a deacon in the Second Congregational Church of New London, and active in religious work. During the Civil War he was town treasurer of New London, and throughout his life his ecclesiastical, educational and financial interests led to active participation in constructive service to the city.

About 1885 Mr. Chapman began to take interest in public education, and from reading and observation came to believe the culture and training which characterized the instruction of his youth should be supplemented by courses in the productive activities of life. About 1891 the annual reports of Charles

B. Jennings. acting superintendent of New London schools, began to contain
a plea for the introduction of industrial arts into the public schools. Manual
training, mechanical arts and trades schools were being advocated and established throughout the country, and in 1901 Mr Chapman decided to give
$100,000 for a building and equipment to furnish instruction to girls in dress-
making, millinery, domestic science and home economics; to boys, the tools,
appliances and machinery for training in handicrafts by which all might be
helped in obtaining a livelihood The intention was to present to the city
the facilities for teaching the domestic and industrial arts, but the cost of
maintenance was a problem, and he later contributed securities of a par value
amounting to another $100,000 to make it possible to start the institution.
To safeguard the investment and to insure the carrying out of his idea, he
secured from the Legislature articles of incorporation which were approved
May 11th, 1903. Section 1 reads: "Resolved by this Assembly, that Walter
Learned, Alfred Coit, Charles B. Jennings, James Hislop, George Whittlesey,
Frederick S. Newcomb, Lucius E. Whiton and George H. Holmes, all of the
city of New London, together with such other persons as may hereafter
become associated with them and their successors, be and they are hereby
constituted a body politic and corporate by the name of The Manual Training
and Industrial School of New London. The mayor of the city of New London
and the president and secretary of the board of School Visitors of the city
shall be ex-officio members of the corporation." At that date Hon. B. F.
Mahan was mayor, Dr. John G. Stanton was chairman, and Mr. Carlos
Barry secretary, of the Board of School Visitors of New London

The establishment of an institution of this type proved to be a task for
the board of trustees involving thought, correspondence, visitation and discussion which required time The original building was far enough completed
to be used in the fall of 1906, and the school opened October 1st of that year.

The responsibility of equipment and organization of the school was vested
in Frederick St. John Hitchcock under the title of principal. He was born
in Westfield, Massachusetts, August 1st, 1865. of English ancestry, educated
in New England public schools and the Massachusetts Institute of Technology. He had eighteen years of experience in teaching in high schools and
technical branches before coming to New London. From this preparation and
experience, and by conference with the founder of the school and its board of
trustees, the present institution was developed

The experience of other institutions was constantly kept in mind, and by
inspection or correspondence the activities of technical and vocational schools
elsewhere, were helpful in these early days The Massachusetts Institute of
Technology, Mechanic Arts High School in Boston, the Rindge College,
Manhattan Trade School, Hebrew Technical Institute of New York, Pratt
Institute of Brooklyn, the Williamson Free School and Drexel Institute in
Philadelphia, Hampton Institute, Virginia, and Georgia Technical Institute,
were visited and studied for ideas. A committee of manufacturers, mechanics
and individual educators and teachers from New England and New York was
formed for advice and suggestions. The conclusion reached was that a course
should be planned for no special class or group, but for normal youth, age

about fourteen, with the first eight grades of the public schools completed or equivalent preparation, as an entrance requirement. Students with less schooling on account of poor opportunity, but with maturity of mind and body fitting them for "catching up" and pursuing the course without being a drawback to their associates, to be admitted on six weeks' probation.

In mechanical arts and trades the fundamental principles were sought by analysis, only as much taught in a day as could be received with keen interest; the amount of information and skill in each subject to be comprehensive enough to be of practical use. "Manual training" does not reside in the hand, but principally in the brain and in the mind," and "First think out your work, then work out your thought," two quotations from Dr C. M. Woodward, represented the angle by which technical skill was approached.

The age of eighteen was decided upon as a desirable average for graduation, to give time for development of body, mind and character through a four years course. That the substantial development of skill in mechanical arts might lead to further interest and opportunity, the related mathematics, science and social and political history were included in the course of study. One year of civics and four of English gave a base, from which English literature and social and political duties and problems could be taught or discussed. After the third year, a group of students observing that at graduation a career in the industries would have greater opportunity for them if their education was continued in a technical college, a request came for language enough to pass entrance examinations. This was given out of school hours for a period of five years, and finally was added to the regular schedule of the school.

After the first year all machinery and equipment of the school was installed by students, and after the third year all repairs to machinery were part of the regular instruction. Practically all small tools within the scope of the equipment have been made by students from the beginning.

The four years course in general woodwork, pattern making, draughting, tool forging and machine shop experience, combined with English, civics, history, mathematics, sciences and modern languages, has placed the young men who have graduated as follows: 77 per cent in the trades or vocations taught in the school, 12 per cent went to college, and 11 per cent. are at work in other occupations.

Of the girls who have completed the four-year domestic art and science courses, together with English, civics, history, literature, mathematics, sciences and modern languages, 64 per cent are employed at vocations or teaching the branches studied in the school, 24 per cent. continued their education in summer schools or by going to college, and 12 per cent. who attended especially with reference to the efficiency, independence and contentment afforded, have taken a measure of those attributes into their homes.

The skill and earning capacity of graduates leads a large percentage of them to take up work immediately in the productive vocations, but the scope and thoroughness of the academic courses maintained enables students of good scholarship to enter colleges, either by examination or by certificate. A fair percentage of the young men have been accepted in colleges and technical schools and more are planning to continue their education in that way

Considerable difficulty in obtaining teachers has been experienced from the first Competent instructors in the trades could make more money in the industries than as teachers. Those at the heads of departments teach because they enjoy the life and service. The dressmaking, ladies' tailoring and millinery are carried to a degree of skill and excellence seldom found outside the trades. The analysis of the work may be copied by anyone, but the morale and efficiency of the department of domestic art has attracted some notice outside New England. A superintendent from the Middle West visited the school some years ago, and spent the day in copying details of the course in domestic art. Upon leaving he expressed his thanks for information obtained and stated: "That is just what we want in our city, one matter troubles me, however; that is teachers. Where do you get yours?" Answer: "We generally make our own." "Well, but you had to start somewhere. What do you have to pay a woman like the head of that department?" Answer: "That is a somewhat embarrassing question " "There is no secret about it is there?" Answer: "No!" "But you would not stand in the way of her advancement, would you? We could offer much more than that." Answer: "Well, if you are going to ask her to leave here, perhaps you ought to be told more about her " "Is there any 'out'* about her?" Answer: "Not that we know of, except that she married the principal about eighteen years ago, and they are educating their own children here." The practical tailoring, millinery and art needlework have closely approached professional excellence from the beginning, due in part to the technical accuracy sought, but due more to the personality and example of motherly refinement, dignity and efficiency of the teacher matron of the domestic art department, Mrs. E. L. Cheney Hitchcock.

In the shops and laboratories as well as in the tailoring rooms, competent heads of departments have extended their work by employing graduates of the school as assistants. Mutual helpfulness carried through the four years of study and practice has developed a constant supply of those who want to teach as a vocation The most skillful have been glad to get experience for moderate wages under their old instructors, and the school profits by their eagerness to earn a recommendation to superintendents seeking teachers skilled and experienced in mechanical arts.

The very practical work of the students has brought appeals for extending the work to smaller groups in grade schools and social service centers. Senior boys have taught mechanical drawing and general woodwork in the Y. M. C. A., Mystic Oral School and Montville. Senior girls have conducted classes in cooking or dressmaking in Mystic Oral School, Montville, and in the social service centers of New London The work in Montville was started under the auspices of Mrs. Frederick A. Johnson, and has been instrumental in directing many toward a full four years high school course which later on they completed. Most of the extension work carried on by students was done evenings, on Saturdays, or during vacations The immediate benefits have usually been followed by increased attendance at the Vocational High School.

Throughout the early years of the school the problem of maintenance

---

* "Out," a colloquialism meaning any weakness.

was serious. The intention of the donor was to furnish buildings and equipment for practical instruction to youth of high school age, but the costs of materials, teachers, etc., were expected to be borne by the city or by the payment of tuition. New London started by paying $500 per year, and when the amount some years later had advanced to $700 an effort was made to get aid from the State. The basis of approval by the State included forty-eight weeks of school of eight hours per day, per year, consisting of 50 per cent academic and 50 per cent. shop work, each student confined to one trade which must be followed to completion.

Ordinarily, 85 per cent. of the vocational students have to earn a part or all of the cost of their education out of school hours. The longer day and longer school year would have made attendance impossible for a large number. Four hours academic work as taught in other high schools would have been acceptable, but in practice the subjects required failed to include those which form a basis for culture and make the way open to further training after graduation. No parents would consent to that plan. Neither would they consent to deciding upon one trade for children at the age of fourteen. Another factor leading to the abandonment of State aid was the cost of equipment and teachers for the long hours of shop work required. No reduction of expense would result for the city, but a large reduction in attendance would follow. The four years technical high school course was continued free to resident students and paid for by the city. Non-resident students met the increased costs by an advance in tuition. The struggle for support doubtless had a tendency to increase the attendance and advance the standards of the school. The threatened loss of all cultural training developed an appreciation of it, and English history, civics and general science received an impetus which sent an unusual number of graduates on to technical schools and colleges. One effect of the stimulated interest in English was the success of students in competition with other schools for literary prizes. A second prize of ten dollars offered by the Colonial Dames of America was awarded to Samuel Bittner, a junior in 1918. The Connecticut gold medal together with fifty dollars in gold from the Sons of the American Revolution was awarded to Louise Ernst, a sophomore in 1915.

In connection with the English and history classes, the school has given several plays each year which at first were staged in the history room of the school. The seating capacity soon proved to be inadequate, and the Lyceum Theater was used for "Higby of Harvard" in 1912. In 1914, through the bequest of $28,000 under the will of Mrs. Ellen Tyler Chapman, wife of the founder of the school, a fine auditorium was added to the building. A series of debates, prize speaking and plays became part of the student activity each year. "Mice and Men," "The Cricket on the Hearth," "Little Lord Fauntleroy" and the "Birds' Christmas Carol" were enthusiastically supported by students and the public. The profit from the plays so far exceeded the expense that valuable pictures and many articles of furnishing and equipment were added to the institution. The school glee club and orchestra formed a beginning from which a general public interest in good music has grown. Musicians of national reputation and accepted merit have found the acoustic properties of the school auditorium to be excellent. The audiences have been large and appreciative. Much of the achievement in dramatics and musical work is due to the talent and energy of Miss Eva M. Sherburne, teacher of English in the school.

In 1911, when the Hartford Graduate Club, represented by Mrs E. V. Mitchell, Miss Mary Partridge, and Miss Elizabeth Wright, came to New London looking for a site for the Connecticut College for Women, and the city of New London proposed to raise $100,000, the short term campaign plan was proposed and carried out under the auspices of the New London Vocational School. Professor Ralph L. Cheyney of the Y. M. C. A. College, Springfield, Massachusetts, outlined the plan of the campaign. Frederick S. Hitchcock, principal of the Vocational School, in consultation with Mr. C. S. Ward, member of the international committee of the Y. M. C. A., organized the details of the drive. A committee consisting of Mr. Hitchcock, Mr. Alex. Campbell, superintendent of the New London Gas and Electric Company, and Rev. James W. Bixler, pastor of the Second Congregational Church, went to Philadelphia, where Mr. Ward was conducting a million dollar campaign. The organization and methods of work in that drive were practically duplicated in New London under the direction of these three men, with the addition of Mr. F. Valentine Chappell of New London. The Vocational School having suggested the plan of the business organization, was by its equipment and personnel able to carry on a large share of the practical work

From President Burton, of Smith College, a statement of what Smith College has done for Northampton, obtained by Mr. Hitchcock, was used as a business argument in favor of the college. The office management organized at the school was soon transferred to the larger office equipment of the Gas and Electric Company. The special directory and card indexing of the city began at the school with students' help, and was finished in the larger offices under the same management by paid stenographers and clerks. The filing cases and small articles were made entirely by students. In the rush to complete larger projects, carpenters and sign painters from outside the school were employed. The Daily Bulletin used at headquarters, the twenty-foot clock on the "Evening Day" building and the thirty-foot thermometer on the First Congregational Church lawn were made in this way. The clock, with materials furnished by Mr. Theodore Bodenwein, was begun on the school shop floor, but the sections would not go through the largest door, and it was transferred to the floor of the Konomoc Hose House. The lettering was done under great difficulty by A. Francis Watson, and the clock erected on the Day building by B. B Gardner, in a morning of drizzle of sleet and rain. The thermometer in three sections was erected by the New England Telephone Company. Noonday lunches were a feature of the campaign, and with a hastily improvised kitchen they were managed and served by Miriam Marstow and relays of girls from the domestic science department of the Vocational School.

In the College campaign, practically every individual, group, club and corporation united as with one mind to carry out a single plan, with every personal and business interest merged into an organized whole. The city awakened to a collective conscious effort and did what it set out to do The Vocational School was only one factor among many contributing to the object sought. New London has done several bigger things as a city since 1911, but the school was ready in mind and skill and equipment to furnish its quota of service and coöperation when the opportunity came.

Upon the declaration of war with Germany, a large number of graduates and seniors volunteered in the army and navy, and several were promoted on account of their mechanical skill and general academic training. The remaining students were organized to put over the many drives to support hospitals, the Knights of Columbus, Young Men's Christian Association, Red Cross, Hebrew Welfare Association, and the Salvation Army, as well as for the sale of bonds. During the summer seasons many worked independently, and with the Boys' Working Reserve to increase the production of food. Under the auspices of the domestic science department, instructive courses were given in the school auditorium teaching better methods of conserving food in the home, and a series of demonstrations and lectures was carried over a period of two years for the benefit of housekeepers and women desiring to prepare for service by nursing. One by one the male teachers enlisted until every eligible man had gone. Women served well in their places where possible, but most of the academic branches of the school being correlated with technical work in shops and laboratories, made it difficult for women to do the work of men. Toward the end, senior boys carried some of the classes in mathematics and sciences It was in a way a strain upon the student teachers and the classes, but the spirit under which they strove together brought no apparent loss to either. The student teachers have since done well in technical colleges, and some of the students have done the same. An added interest and application to study seem to have offset such weakness as there was in formal preparation.

During the fifteen years of its life to the present time the New London Vocational School has carried the approval of the State Board of Education for acceptable work as a high school. Making school work a business as much as storekeeping, manufacturing or office work, with that absorbing interest that leads to success, has helped somewhat Keeping such standards in academic work, parallel with shop and laboratory practice, as would give a combination of thought and skill, have developed self-respect and a strong school spirit. Contact with and practical service to the interests of the city and the homes, has brought increasing attendance and financial support. In regard to the dignity of labor, Ruskin said, "We are always in these days endeavoring to separate intellect and manual labor; we want one man to be always thinking and another to be always working, and we call one a gentleman and the other a laborer, whereas the workman ought to be thinking some of the time, and the thinker to be working some of the time, and both

MYSTIC ORAL SCHOOL FOR THE DEAF

Miss Clara M. H. McGuigan has the written the following account of this school

Home School, was founded in 1869 by Zerah Colburn Whipple. Zerah Whipple was descended on the Whipple line from Samuel Whipple and Elizabeth Eddy of Providence, Rhode Island, who removed to Connecticut prior to 1712 Samuel Whipple was an iron manufacturer and a successful business man. His mills were built on Saw Mill river, near Pocquetannock. No doubt from this line Zerah inherited his ingenuity and mechanical skill. When only a boy he made himself a very good violin, and later, as an aid to his work in teaching the deaf, he invented the Whipple's natural alphabet, an ingenious pictorial alphabet representing the positions of the lips, tongue, etc., in producing the elementary English sounds. He was also descended from the Wolcotts and Griswolds of Connecticut, families empowered with great intellectual and executive ability. His Bolles, Hempstead, Waterhouse and Rogers blood gave literary ability, musical and oratorical talent, and religious zeal. Two Scotch families, Grouch and Douglass, added strength to his fine English blood. Having the remarkable family inheritance that he did, it is no wonder that Zerah Colburn Whipple was endowed with the vision and ability of a genius. The inspiration for his work came from his grandfather, Jonathan Whipple, who had taught his own little son Enoch, deaf from birth, to talk and read the lips.

Jonathan Whipple was also endowed with all of the talents of his remarkable ancestors, but perhaps religious zeal was paramount. He was the first president of the Connecticut Peace Society, and the extent of his charities was boundless. He was a natural scholar himself, and gave his children a good common school education in the little red school house of his district, but he did so much for the poor and friendless that he hadn't the means left for the higher education of his children, so although all, including Enoch, had college minds, none had college advantages.

Enoch Whipple owned a farm and blacksmith shop adjoining his father's farm. He spoke and read the lips so well that he did business for years with an iron manufacturer in Norwich without anyone suspecting he was deaf. He married a cousin, a hearing woman of great literary ability. Their evenings were spent in reading the best books of literature, travel, etc., and their home with its extensive library was the gathering place for all the ambitious children in the neighborhood. They had the bound volumes of the "Century Magazine" from its first issue to the one at the time of their death, and their book-cases were filled with hundreds of fine books on every conceivable subject.

Zerah Whipple grew up in his grandfather's home. He imbibed his religious zeal and inherited his remarkable talents. He loved and admired his uncle Enoch and his cultured wife. He spent many evenings with them in their delightful home. As he grew to manhood, he began to wonder why other deaf people could not be taught to talk like his uncle Enoch, and his grandfather convinced him they could. He determined to make teaching the deaf and dumb to speak and read the lips his life work

He advertised for pupils, and November 15, 1869, a young lad of twelve years from a wealthy Quaker family of Wilmington, Delaware, was brought to the Whipple home in Ledyard Connecticut, for instruction. The old

grandfather showed Zerah how to begin his work in bringing speech to the
dumb lips of the boy, and Zerah quickly acquired skill in teaching and
obtained gratifying results. Although this boy was twelve years old when
his education began, he acquired good, intelligible speech, was a fine lip
reader, and had a liberal education when he left school at the time of Zerah's
death in 1879. His taste for good literature was formed. He regularly subscribed for the leading magazines, was familiar with Dickens and other good
writers, and was able to take his place in the class of society in which he was
born and look after his own and his mother's business interests.

Other pupils came from all over the United States, and the old gambrel-
roofed farm house had to be enlarged to accommodate them. All of the
family were pressed into service as teachers except the dear mother, who
was "Mother Whipple" to them all. The results were remarkable, for
Enoch, who lived next door, was their model. He it was the parents saw and
talked with when they brought their children to the school, and speech like
his or approaching it was what they paid for and expected. Most of the
pupils came from distant States, but the fame of the school soon began to be
talked about in Connecticut. Parents of deaf children who hadn't money visited the school and wrote letters begging Mr. Whipple to find a way to give
speech to their children. There was no school in Connecticut but the sign
school at Hartford where deaf children could be educated free. Then it was
that Zerah Whipple applied to the legislature of Connecticut for State aid
This was granted July 24, 1872. From that time children from families in
poor and moderate circumstances have had the privilege, if they so desired,
of having their children educated by what is known as the Pure Oral Method.

By the Pure Oral Method is meant giving a deaf child speech and lip
reading in an oral environment, so that he will unconsciously, by force of
habit, use speech altogether in communicating with his fellow-men—in other
words, restoring him to society. Now this can be done more or less perfectly according to the ability of the child, the ability of the teacher and the
child's environment. If we want our child to acquire French and talk French
naturally and fluently, we place it in a French school in France, where it has
a French environment. Such a method of procedure is absolutely necessary
in acquiring fluency in any language. It is the same with speech for the
deaf. A deaf child in order to acquire speech and use it spontaneously must
have a speech environment. No school that teaches signs and finger spelling
can give its pupils a speech environment. The child easily masters signs
and finger spelling, and as they are easier at first, it will use them instead
of speech. So it is in the schools called Combined Schools, where they have
what is called an Oral department, speech is relegated to the class rooms
and seldom if ever used elsewhere. In such schools the children think in
signs and translate into speech when they use it. In Zerah Whipple's school
this was not true. The pupils thought in speech and used speech as their
mother tongue. Speech soon became spontaneous and natural. Because of
this difference between Oral and Sign and Combined Schools, the Mystic
Oral School has continued its work and because of this difference it is still
needed

In a short time the Whipple School outgrew the farm house and its additions. The beautiful summer residence of a retired sea captain was purchased from his heirs, and in 1874 the pupils were transferred to their new home. There is where the school is still situated. It is in the town of Groton, about a mile from the village of Mystic. It is said the old sea captain selected this site for his home because it commanded the most wonderful view of land and sea to be found on the southern coast of Connecticut. It is on a high hill overlooking river, village, valley and sound. It has country, seashore, and almost mountain air combined. The Mansion, as it was called, seemed particularly well adapted to fill the requirements of the Whipple Home School, and it grew slowly in numbers and flourished until 1879, just ten years after its establishment, when its enthusiastic and gifted principal died.

His loss was in a way irreparable, but as the members of his family had always assisted in teaching, they were able to go on with the work. His brother-in-law, Frank Whipple, who had been his partner for a time, became its principal and did excellent work. He finally sold out his interests to an uncle and aunt, and though retained for a while as a teacher, eventually he left Connecticut and went to California to teach speech to the deaf in the State School at Berkeley.

For ten years longer the school was conducted with varied degrees of success according to the efficiency of the teachers employed. Advertising ceased with Zerah Whipple's death. The private pupils were gradually withdrawn and placed in other schools or taught by a private teacher at home until none but State pupils remained. As the school was not endowed and had to depend almost entirely upon the State appropriation for its maintenance, and as this was only $175 per capita per annum, it was impossible to secure experienced teachers and provide up-to-date equipment in the home.

In 1895, Hon. O. Vincent Coffin, then governor of Connecticut, visited the school and completely reorganized it. Its name was changed to the Mystic Oral School for the Deaf, and the per capita appropriation was raised to $200 per year. Dr. Clara M. Hammond McGuigan, daughter of the former principal and first cousin to Zerah Whipple, was asked to assume the responsibility of the school as its superintendent.

Dr. McGuigan was a graduate of the Connecticut Normal School at New Britain, of the Mystic Valley Institute at Mystic, and of the Woman's Medical College of Pennsylvania at Philadelphia. She had taught in the public schools of Ledyard and Groton, and had been principal of the Ivoryton School in Essex. She had been resident physician for fifteen months in the City Hospital of Philadelphia, and had received special training in work with the deaf from both Zerah and Frank Whipple. She was the wife of a physician, and was not dependent upon the school for her support, consequently she could and did use the State money for the betterment of the school instead of taking an adequate salary.

Dr. McGuigan at once engaged Miss Ella Scott as principal, a teacher who had had eleven years experience teaching in the Clarke School at Northampton, Massachusetts, probably the best school for the deaf in the world

1902

MYSTIC VALLEY INSTITUTE, MYSTIC

Miss Scott came to Mystic full of courage and enthusiasm, with the determination to make the Mystic School as much like her model at Northampton
as possible She taught trained teachers to assist her, and did brave work.
The school was soon incorporated, and in five years had doubled in numbers.
More room was needed, so a large addition, subscribed to by friends of the
school, was built and occupied. The work of reorganizing and building up
the school had worn upon Miss Scott so that when she was offered a fine
position as a private teacher of a little girl in Canada she resigned to accept it.

Other efficient principals followed Miss Scott, but owing to lack of funds
the work was arduous and discouraging, so no one held the position longer
than five years. The principals under Dr. McGuigan's superintendency were
as follows: Miss Ella Scott, 1895-1900, Miss Alice H. Damon, B A., 1900-04;
Miss Frances E. Gillespie, 1904-07; Misses Jane and Eleanor, associate principals, 1907-12; Mr. Tobias Brill, 1912-17, Dr. C. M. H. McGuigan, superintendent and principal, 1917-18, Mrs. Sara Small Temple, 1918-19; Miss Addie
L. Landers, acting principal, 1919-20; Mr. Walter J. Tucker, 1920-21.

In 1895 the school numbered 18 pupils; in 1900 there were 36; in 1910
it numbered 54, and at the present time there are 82 pupils in school, and
about 50 on the waiting list.

The per capita apportioned by the State of Connecticut for the support
of the school has been as follows: 1872-95, $175; 1895-1901, $200; 1901-03,
$225; 1903-07, $250; 1907-15, $275; 1915, $300; in each of the last four periods
there was an allowance of $20 for clothing when necessary.

By 1909, the building with its addition was inadequate. It was unsafe
to house so many deaf children in a frame building, so the State Legislature
was appealed to and eventually $17,000 was appropriated for a fireproof
dormitory. This was built and occupied in September, 1911. This was built
for fifty or sixty children, and not for eighty, so another new building is now
needed to relieve congestion and to form the first unit of a model school on
the cottage plan.

Four States have sent their deaf wards to the Mystic School: Connecticut,
1872 to the present time; New Jersey, 1876-1882; New Hampshire, 1897-1902;
Vermont, 1898-1912.

A member of the Board of Charities of Massachusetts visited the Mystic
School and recommended sending its pupils to Mystic when it hadn't accommodations for them within its own borders, but as the room at Mystic was
limited, no effort was made to secure Massachusetts pupils.

The course of study prescribed includes lip reading, speech, language,
technical grammar, arithmetic, geography, United States, General and English
history, physiology, American and English literature, and some algebra. In
1904 one pupil, having completed the course, graduated. In 1907 two pupils
graduated. In 1910 there were two graduates; in 1913, two graduates; in
1918, three graduates; and in 1919, one graduate. Three of these pupils
afterwards entered high school for the hearing.

In addition to the speech, lip reading and academic studies taught, each
child is trained along one or more industrial lines. The various industries
that have been taught in the school are as follows· For boys—Printing, farm-

ing, cabinet work, carpentry, chair caning, hammock netting, cobbling, tree pruning and spraying, waiting on table, assisting cook, cooking, etc. For girls—Gardening, basketry, pottery, embroidery, crocheting, knitting, sewing, dressmaking, housework, cooking, millinery and weaving.

Almost without exception, the pupils of this school have gone out into the world well equipped to earn their own living and to be a credit to their school, their families and their State.

Practically from the time of its organization the school has maintained a small normal class. Over fifty teachers have finished the course and rendered valuable service in bringing speech to deaf children in this and other States.

During all the years Dr McGuigan superintended the school, she looked forward to the time when either some wealthy person would endow it or the State would purchase it so its work could go on unimpeded by private management and lack of funds. The endowment did not materialize, so in 1919 a bill for the purchase if the school by the State of Connecticut was passed by the legislative body, and the school would at once have become a State school had its board been assured it would be continued. This assurance was not given, so the deeds were not signed Dr. McGuigan continued the work and waited for a more auspicious time.

Before the legislature of 1921 came into being, the new governor, Hon. Everett J. Lake, expressed himself as favorable to the continuance of the Mystic School, so relying upon the hope that he and the new legislative body would make proper provision for the future of the Mystic Oral School, the deeds were signed and the school passed over to the State It is now a State School. It is the only Pure Oral School in the State. It represents the most advanced method known in the education of the deaf Its situation for such a school is ideal, and with proper provisions for its future, new buildings and equipment. it can be made the equal of the best school for the deaf in the world

Dr McGuigan resigned as superintendent, and Mr. Walter J. Tucker was appointed to the place. He was an oral teacher of long standing. He had held the position as principal of the Wright Oral School of New York, and his wife was also an experienced oral teacher of the deaf. They seemed particularly fitted to go on with the work.

Though not the first oral school in America, it was one of the first Hampered always by lack of funds. it has grown and has done good work. Its influence has been far-reaching and its pupils are its best advertisement.

CHAPTER XI

RELIGION IN NEW LONDON COUNTY

The following History of Religion in New London County, beginning on this page and ending on page 314, is by the Rev. W. Hulbert, pastor of the First Church of Christ, in Croton The remainder of the chapter is by contributors and staff writers:

In this southeastern corner of Connecticut, religion of an advanced type has for these two hundred and seventy-five years and more proved its fundamental place in human society The Indian tribes preceding foreign settlements had their peculiar religious cults which doubtless were also basic to their political and social life; but as far as we can know these show no trace of development in form of worship or substance of creed, and especially interest us only in their contacts with the more advanced faiths of their successors. For more than a quarter of a millenium, now, New London county has witnessed almost every development of religion characteristic of the New World, and especially of New England.[1]

It is true, the temporary decline in ethical ideals did not afflict the infant seventeenth century settlements here with anything like the fanatical craze which would burn a "witch" or smother a "Quaker," or even exile a Roger Williams, as was the case in the Massachusetts colony. Indeed, at intervals we note, on the contrary, an unexpected breadth of handling of issues that might easily have taken a harsher turn, as when in 1702 the Rev. John Keith and the Rev. John Talbot, working under the auspices of the Society for the Propagation of the Gospel in Foreign Parts, coming from Providence, crossed the Ferry (Groton Banks) to New London and were graciously received, particularly by the authorities, even though they came to champion the Church of England. The first mentioned of them says in his journal:

"September 13th, Sunday, Mr. Talbot preached there (New London) in the forenoon and I preached there in the afternoon, we being desired to do so by the minister, Mr. Gurdon Saltonstall, who civilly entertained us at his house, and expressed his good affections to the Church of England. My text was Romans viii:9. The auditory was large and well affected Colonel Winthrop, Governor of the Colony, invited us to dinner at his house and kindly entertained us, both then and the next day."

Again we have the story of Jesse Lee, the pioneer of Methodism, in 1789 preaching with popular acceptance in the identical county court house our eyes rest upon today in New London. A few years later, Bishop Asbury,

---

[1] New London county as constituted in 1666, when the Connecticut Colony was divided into four counties under the new charter obtained in England by Governor John Winthrop, Jr., in 1662, embraced a much larger area than it does today. It stretched from the much disputed Rhode Island boundary westward across the Connecticut river to the Hammonasset river, being the western border of the modern Clinton, taking in all the Saybrooks (Killingworth and Chester). To the north it embraced gradually (until 1726) the larger part of the modern Windham county (with the exception of Woodstock, claimed by Suffolk county, Massachusetts) and a small part of the modern Tolland county We must be content with a hazy notion of this whole northern border. When Windham county was established in 1726, the Northern townships of New London county were added to several from Hartford county to constitute the new area. When Middlesex county was formed in 1785, New London county lost historic Saybrook, with Killingworth and Chester, retaining all east of the Connecticut up to East Haddam.

of the same Communion, had a similarly favorable reception. In 1793 the Rev. John Thayer, a Roman Catholic missionary, was allowed the use of the old First Church at Norwich Town by Rev Joseph Strong, its pastor, in speaking to a miscellaneous audience, when he undertook to prove that the Roman Catholic was the only true church of Christ. The discourse was accounted by the local press to be "learned and vigorous," and the speaker was given a further hearing in the same place on the following Sunday evening

These incidents are typical of the freer conditions that generally prevailed in the Connecticut Colony, following the Plymouth precedent and doubtless influenced to a degree by the still freer attitude of the Rhode Island Plantation. Voting, in New London county, was never confined to church members, as was the case in Massachusetts and New Haven, but the suffrage was open to all reputable male citizens. While the historian of New London county has to call attention to many instances of narrowness and petty religious persecutions in the earlier colonial life, he can yet report better conditions in these respects than were customarily found in other parts of New England or in the British Isles and the continent of Europe.

The first religious organization in the county (the First Church of Christ) came to New London as an already organized body from Gloucester, Massachusetts, bringing a modified connection between Church and State. To these virile, simple-hearted founders the Bible was a law-book for the infant colony, as well as a book of religion, and many decisions in the early courts took their precedents direct from Scripture. All freeholders originally were taxed for the support of the churches, and many of the disturbances and quarrels which arose were essentially economic; for a parish was loath to lose any of its paying constituency through the secession of outlying communities who claimed the right to carve out their own parishes. Indeed, the location of churches seems to have caused more trouble than any other question that arose in those early days.

Church attendance at the first was compulsory, and a large number of cases of discipline came about thereby. "Separatism" caused the nearest approach to martyrdom to be found in all these annals, bringing to the front men and women who claimed the right to worship as their consciences dictated. The record gives us case after case of that form of persecution. Extreme personalities were ready to go the limit in self-assertion. Possibly the still freer conditions that prevailed in Rhode Island may have helped to this end. The famous Rogerenes boldly denounced what they called "the idolatry of the Sabbath," and took delight in disturbing meetings, and in the punishments which inevitably followed. New London county took its full share in the long contest which at last brought complete separation of Church and State (about 1750) and placed on a voluntary basis both church attendance and church support. But in the meanwhile, Baptists, Adventists, Roman Catholics, Episcopalians and Friends, as well as all free thinkers, had, for the most part, a hard time of it during the first century of the local history.

We get a happier outlook on things when we note that New London county shared in all the theological movements that helped fashion the religious, educational, social and political life of Southeastern Connecticut. Whatever our modern outlook may be, all this past now seems to have been essential and fundamental in the developing life. The looser bonds of the Cambridge Platform (1648) which fostered the spirit of independency gave place gradually to the closer associational and constitutional ties of the Saybrook Platform (1708). The more formal life of the churches, that succeeded the pioneer fervor, and under which the "half-way covenant" allowed a kind of church membership which did not necessitate deep religious convictions, was powerfully invaded by the preaching of the Great Awakening in the third, fourth and fifth decades of the eighteenth century, when Jonathan Edwards, George Whitfield and Eleazar Wheelock championed reasonable evidence of true "conversion" as essential to church membership.

The inevitable demoralization of the war of the American Revolution struck the religious life in New London county hard, in spite of the patriotic fervor that centered about the celebrated Land Office in Lebanon and the heroic defence of New London in 1781 The massacre at Fort Griswold took every male member of the Groton church except an aged invalid who could not get out to share the glory of that September day Loss of life generally in the homes in the county, abject poverty, the emigration of many enterprising families to newer settlements in Vermont, New Hampshire, New York and Ohio, laxness of morals and the inroad of a deistical philosophy from France and England, as well as lack of well-equipped men for the ministry, the taking of many efficient pastors for much-needed chaplains in the army, the temporary clouding of the loyalty of those churches in the county planted and fostered by the Church of England, and the loss of substantial citizens who could not go back on the old flag of England, and who, often as the result of bitter handling by their neighbors, migrated to Canada—all these and many more obstacles like them contributed to give an alarming setback to organized religion in New London county We may well be astonished that the combined results were not worse than they were, and that the recovery, checked by the alarms of the War of 1812, was as good as it was. It all shows a virile stock of men and women who could think through the changing, freer conditions into the larger life of our day.

To the aid of the traditional Congregational churches came that of other types of religious life and feeling, which, in turn, laid solid foundations of religious faith and greatly stimulated, directly and indirectly, the older forms Particular attention here is called to the conscientious contentions of the various types of the Baptist invasion from Rhode Island, which rapidly permeated the whole county as soon as the initial friction quieted down, and affected especially the sections east of the Thames river Social ostracism, oft imprisonment as "Separatists," fines, nor any other obstacles, could keep these sturdy contenders for freedom of worship and a literal obedience to the commands of their Master from swinging forward, often with a marked evangelistic force, in all these communities. With these came the Adventists of various hues, who seemed still more extreme in their ideals and methods

At the opposite poles came the liturgical groups, on ancient and approved foundations, which sought to build solidly the Kingdom of God. The Episco-

N L—1-18

pal churches established their orderly worship in all the centers and with chapels in selected rural places. They had the honor of presenting to their American communion its first Bishop, who, as an infant, had been baptized in a Congregational church (North Groton or Ledyard) by his own father, then a temporary supply there. (See page 305.)

As immigration brought in ever-increasing numbers of followers of Rome from Ireland and the Continent of Europe, Catholic churches thoroughly organized their constituencies throughout the county and rendered an inestimable aid to law and order, as well as to religious fervor.

The Methodist Episcopal churches sprang up in the tracks of Jesse Lee and Bishop Asbury, the pioneers of Methodism. They did vital service in all the centers and reached out to the farthest limits of the rural districts Their freer expression of religious life and feeling brought a general benefit to all the communities where they were established

In the deistical atmosphere of a century and a half ago, when the conception of an absentee God had so generally displaced that of the immanent, Divine Personality of the Bible for both orthodox and free thinker, the stage was set for a battle royal in New England, as well as old England, between the somewhat decadent orthodoxy and the many who styled themselves "Unitarian" as against the semi-theistic tendency of the traditional theology, under the soubriquet of "Trinitarian." New London county was not markedly influenced by this movement, which in many other sections swung the leading Congregational churches under the lead of Harvard College over onto the Unitarian side of the controversy Doubtless the Saybrook Platform (1708) (see page 287) and its Consociation organization kept the churches of Connecticut more in line.

In this connection, however, it should be noted that for nineteen years the First Church of Christ in New London had a pastor, Rev. Henry Channing, just out of Yale College, who during his pastorate from 1787 to 1806 held views that later were counted "Unitarian," but yet which, with only slight modifications of phraseology, do not seem far from modern orthodoxy.[a]

But at the close of the ministry of Mr. Channing in 1806, the religious leaders of the orthodox Congregational churches of New London county set

---

[a] "Profession and Covenant" used by Rev. Henry Channing at the First Church of Christ" in New London from 1790 to 1806:

"In the presence of Almighty God, the Searcher of hearts, and before this assembly, you profess your unfeigned belief in the Holy Scriptures as given by divine inspiration, your acceptance of all the doctrines contained in them and your submission to the whole will of God revealed in His Word.

"You do now acknowledge the Lord Jehovah, the one loving and true God, to be your God; and, relying upon divine assistance, do promise to walk humbly with God

"Professing repentance of all your sins and faith in our Lord Jesus, you sincerely receive Him as He is offered in the Gospel as the Teacher from God—the High Priest of our profession—and the King and Head of the church, believing that there is none other name under heaven given among men whereby you must be saved.

"Depending on the Holy Spirit for sanctification, consolation and spiritual strength; and, receiving the Word of God as the only rule of your faith and practice, you submit to the brotherly care of this church of Christ, and to the discipline He hath established in His church

"You do now solemnly give up yourself and all that you have unto God, promising that you will endeavor to walk as becometh the Gospel of Christ, that you may give no cause for others to speak evil of it on your own account, but that the name of God may be glorified in you. Thus you profess and covenant."—Blake, Vol. II, p. 22

themselves against this plan of church life which seemed to accept membership on the basis of a good moral character and not by conversion or deep
conviction, and which had little or no interest in missionary endeavor and
became more and more self-contained and intellectual   The sterner Calvin-
ism of Puritanism had a revival and the Westminster Confession and Catechism came again into vogue, as a deeper call of God was recognized in powerful revival movements that set in. The winning of an expanding continent
and of a world lying in sin and misery appealed to the orthodox churches of
the county of all denominations. The desperately shattered condition of the
post-Revolutionary churches, with the aftermath of the war of 1812, had its
healthful reaction. Slowly the churches gathered themselves together for an
emphasis upon a Biblical faith, pressing the claims of the Scriptures through
the Bible Societies upon every home in the county, and by the establishing
of Sunday schools for the organized study of the Bible. The Connecticut
Home Missionary Society helped the churches reach all neglected places in
the State and county and to reach out to all regions whither Connecticut
people had migrated—in Vermont, New Hampshire, New York, and especially
in the Western Reserve of Ohio. The best and the worst of humanity followed the western trail, and the call for the establishment of religion in the
new sections appealed successfully to the churches of this county, which sent
its finest men and women as pioneers, and, along with them, churches, schools
and ministers.

Soon the call came from further afield and the whole world of needy
humanity came home to the hearts of these earnest Christians, and the
orthodox churches of New London county began that steady and copious
stream of benevolence and self-surrender for foreign work which has grown
with the years. As the New London and Norwich sea captains took America's commerce to the ends of the world, so the educator and missionary took
America's deepest religious character and discipline to nations still in the
shadow of idolatry.

Closely linked to this broad development, with its wholesome local reaction, came the zeal for reform. The Groton Monument was built by a lottery
scheme, as were many churches and colleges of those early decades of the
nineteenth century. But the conscience of the churches steadily developed
until all gambling, like duelling, was outlawed. The same deepening of
conscience was stirred by human slavery and did its full share in the awakened nation, first with abolition societies and later with the stern tramp of
soldiers marching southward. The equally grave curse of intemperance became more and more evident. In 1811 we note the occurrence of an ecclesiastical ordination at the Groton Congregational Church. On the expense
account was a large bill for "liquor" That was quite in order in those days.
But soon thereafter we see ministers and churches reacting from this growing
evil in society, and temperance organizations sprang up throughout the
county and made no compromise with the use of alcoholic drink until at
length the Eighteenth Amendment made an outlaw of it also. The Groton
Banks Temperance Society was one of the earlier active agencies to bring
this about Orphanages, asylums, hospitals, followed with the marked im-

provements in education. In every one of these vital reforms the churches of the county have taken a leading part, originating most of them.

The distinctive work for young men and later for young women among all denominations seemed to grow out of the needs made manifest by the Civil War. The Christian Endeavor movement came speedily to Southeastern Connecticut, followed by the Baptist Young People's Union and the Epworth League, the Knights of King Arthur, the Camp Fire Girls and the Boy and Girl Scouts. Later the Knights of Columbus and the Holy Name Society took their strong places in the life of the Catholic churches.

The Brotherhood of St. Andrews and men's clubs of various names have been established in many of the churches, and have added marked strength to the work of the churches. Perhaps the most active of all these men's organizations is "The Layman's League." This is an interdenominational organization. It has been especially efficient in New London and throughout the southern townships of the county. Mention should be made of the Baraea classes that have gathered large groups of men for continuous study of the Bible in various parts of the county, and especially in Norwich and New London.

Never has the modern force of free, voluntary, coöperative, religious organization shown itself more powerful and fundamental in New London county than in the services rendered by the churches of the county in the Great War (1917-18). The note of patriotism rang true and convincingly from every pulpit. Honor rolls and flags arose in every place of worship. No organization within these churches failed to do its part. Proclamations from Governor and President were read so frequently at the services that it became evident that, whatever the pressing need, the churches were a chief avenue to the intelligence, the hearts, the conscience and the pockets of the several communities of the county.

The close relation of the churches to education in New London county has been marked from the first. The common school at once followed the church in every community. Academies and, later, high schools, sprang up in all the centers, fostered at first in pastors' studies until separate buildings were inevitable. Norwich Free Academy in the northern section still retains the old name. It also does the high school work for Norwich and its environs. Indeed, the remains of most of the old academies are seen in the form of endowed high schools, like those in New London, North Stonington and Mystic. The Norwich Free Academy furnishes us with a typical New England scene. The camera brings into view the monument to Uncas, the Mohegan Indian chieftain who sold the nine-mile tract to the original settlers of Norwich Town, then the ancient colonial mansion, once a tavern that harbored George Washington and is now the parsonage of the Park Congregational Church, and in the background to the right the fine lines of the Gothic Park Church, and the Free Academy to the left.

The famous Plainfield and Lebanon (Moor's Indian Charity School) schools were in territory once a part of the county. Eleazer Wheelock, founder of Dartmouth College, was a strong leader in the churches of the county.

The Collegiate School of Connecticut (later Yale College) began its work in the parsonage of Rev. Abraham Pierson, at Killingworth (now Clinton), then an important part of New London county. In 1707 we find its three lower classes established at Saybrook Point, and practically in charge of Rev. Thomas Buckingham, the pastor. The minister of the First Church of Christ in New London, the Rev. Gurdon Saltonstall, was prominent in all those early days in the institution, and later as Governor of the Colony had the influence that finally located the College at New Haven.

The Connecticut College for Women, located in New London, was not so directly the outcome of the churches as was Yale University, but in all the initial steps leading to the starting of the College and the choice of its location and in the raising of nine-tenths of its funds for its first half dozen crucial years, the pastors and the churches of Greater New London were most active and influential. It is recognized that no other single agency ever established in the county has promised so large and pervasive and unlimited a spiritual power for this section of the State. Already it has become the center of activities in close coöperation with the churches of all denominations, as well as with the schools.

Before closing this brief general introductory review of the religious development in New London county through the churches, just a word must be said as to the marked reaction of the various denominations on one another within these two hundred and seventy-five and more years. The original churches in the Colony of the Congregational type have had a steady development from the first. While keeping to the autonomous principle, they have coöperated more and more closely in associational forms and have been largely influenced by the free and warm-hearted spirit of Methodism and the worshipful and orderly ideals of Episcopacy. In turn, the principle of autonomy, fostered by the Congregational as well as the Baptist communions, has had a marked influence on Methodism and Episcopacy, bringing in each of these denominations a strong laic representation to the front and making it so that each individual self-supporting church has practical control of its ministry and its local work. At the same time the centralizing tendency in the Episcopal and Methodist churches has powerfully affected the plans for efficiency in the more loosely ordered communions. Of late this decided harmonization of interdenominational methods and spirit has brought to the front the Federation ideal which resulted in the Federation of the Churches in New London and Vicinity. The coöperative spirit has promise in it of large things in the future work of the churches of the county.

It has been the fashion to speak of "the good old days" in the church and family life of New England. While the latter seems to be passing through a critical phase and, as yet, has not reached the turning of the road, it is not a too optimistic judgment to say that church life as a whole was never in better condition in New London county than it is today. In all outward ways the outlook is reassuring. The growth in membership, in benevolences, in brotherhood, in coöperative efforts and in missionary zeal, since the Great War, has been unprecedented.

II.

THE COLONIAL STATE CHURCH IN NEW LONDON COUNTY

It is now established that organized religion came first to New London county in 1651, when the Rev. Richard Blinman arrived at the five-year-old settlement near the mouth of the Pequot (Thames) river, bringing with him a substantial majority of his church, which he had previously organized on Congregational principles (1642) at Gloucester (Cape Ann) Massachusetts. The total absence of all records of any other formal organization of a church in the new colonial venture, and the definite statements later as to the fact of a church already being in existence and in full career there, with Mr. Blinman as its pastor, have led inevitably to the above conclusion. The Norwich Town church came there full-fledged from Saybrook (organized there 1646) under the lead of its pastor, Rev. James Fitch; just as Rev. Thomas Hooker brought his Newtown (Massachusetts) church to Hartford, and the Plymouth (Massachusetts) church had come from Leyden, Holland.

The Rev. Thomas Peters had been associated from the first (1646) with Governor John Winthrop, Jr., in the beginnings of New London, and doubtless had conducted occasional services in the rude log huts in the clearing on the west bank of the river before the arrival of Mr. Blinman and his followers. The accomplished Governor was not unmindful of religion, and all labor ceased in the little settlement as the sun went down of a Saturday evening, except as emergencies of war arose. The smoke curled up from the chimneys of a score or more of crude log huts, as a Sabbath of rest had come. The guard kept watch without the stockade, and the goodman of each home had his weapons close at hand. As the shades of night fell and the owl hooted from the primeval forest trees that hemmed them round, and mothers quieted the restless children to sleep, the voice of Psalm and prayer might be heard from the hearts that appreciated the Divine protection amid the haunts of wild beasts and the skulking Pequot. We can see the little company, in 1647 increased by a number of families, among them the Governor's own, gathered reverently of a Sunday morning in the most convenient audience room available to listen to Scripture exposition and Puritan sermon; and for them, too,

> "The sounding aisles of the dim woods rang
> To the anthem of the free."

The advent in 1651 of the church-colony from Gloucester, Massachusetts, under the lead of Mr. Blinman, at once brought together all the forces of religion. The Governor and his family and all the older settlers took their places with the new-comers in the regular parish life now fully established, it being the thirty-fifth church to be planted in New England under colonial

---

* The story is told of a couple (Jonathan Rudd being the man) that desired to be married by the Governor. This prerogative belonged for nearly a generation to the civil magistrate About 1685 clergymen were legalized to perform the ceremony as well as the magistrates. John Winthrop could not legally overstep the boundary into the Connecticut colony to render such a service, even though he had been formerly at the head of the Saybrook colonial enterprise. So he made his way through the snow that winter's day to the stream separating the two colonies. Beside its frozen waters on his own territory he pronounced the eager couple to be man and wife. Hence Bride Brook and Bride Pond or Lake, near the modern Connecticut Farm for Women in Niantic.

jurisdiction. Their first minister was of Welsh extraction and brought with him from Gloucester the ancestors of the Calkins, Coits, Averys, Lesters and others, in all over twenty families, with a total of one hundred souls.

The earliest place for worship was a transformed barn owned by Robert Park, situated on "Meeting House Hill," near which in 1653 a place for burial was set apart. A drum called the assembly for worship in the crude structure Plans were at once laid for the erection of a regular church building on the south side of the old burial ground This first church was completed and first used in 1655. It seems to have been a modest place of worship, but with a tower commanding wide views down the river and harbor, being a point of civic and military importance as well as the religious center. It had galleries and a high pulpit, being probably quite the best building in the settlement.

The parish extended from the Pawcatuck river to Bride brook, which was considered the western edge of the Massachusetts jurisdiction under which, at the first, John Winthrop, Jr., was operating It also extended northward somewhat indefinitely through Montville to the Norwich line and included the modern Ledyard and North Stonington One of the earliest records speaks of Thomas Miner, who had moved to Pawcatuck in 1652, and Captain Denison as having serious differences of opinion with their minister, Mr Blinman, over the proposed erection of a town of Mystic and Pawcatuck, which conflict was healed two years later Minister's rates were levied by the voters over this wide-extended parish. Mr. Blinman undertook to hold occasional services in the more remote sections, especially to the east across the Thames river. He was deeply interested in preaching to the Indians.

The short pastorate of Mr Blinman came to an unexpected end in 1658 for no special reason that can be ascertained.[*] He was accounted a man of learning and high ability, and a natural leader. On occasion he was sent to the General Court of Massachusetts to represent Pequot on business of importance He was a non-conformist and Puritan of the straightest sect, a sturdy, frugal pioneer, who well set the pace for the religious development of the settlement and the county.

For three years the parish of Pequot (changed to New London in 1658 by order of the General Court of Massachusetts) sought a successor for Mr. Blinman. In the meanwhile they were supplied by preachers when available. Sometimes a Mr John Tinker, rate-maker, collector and commissioner, as

---

[*] It is surmised that he was not in harmony with the more and more prevalent plan of the "Half-way Covenant," a modification of church membership not anticipated by the founders of New England, who expected that those who should become members of the church would give reasonable proof of "regeneration," and that children of only such should be baptized But a large number of the children of the first colonists did not seek admission to the church and so the grandchildren were left without baptism, with terrible consequences in case these died before they themselves were baptized at their own instance The pressure became so great that during the last half of the 17th century the churches gave temporarily a new plan to such, whereby parents of good standing in the community, whose parents in turn had been members of the church, could bring their children for baptism, even though they themselves were not full members They had to make certain acknowledgements of a purpose to give themselves to God in Christ, to endeavor to walk according to the rules of that holy religion all their days and bring up their children to fear God Under these conditions of a "Half-way Covenant" their children could be baptized

well as an assistant in the affairs in the Colony and licensed to distill and retail liquors, often "exercised in public at religious meetings until the arrival of the new minister." The open town meeting at this time and for several generations following passed upon all business affairs of the church, including the calling of the minister. The Colonial legislature also had spiritual oversight of creed and discipline.

It was during this interval that matters most important for the church life of the county (to be) were occurring elsewhere. The crushing of the Pequots by Captain John Mason in 1637 in the famous Mystic battle, had left Uncas, friend of the English, the leading Indian chieftain of the Mohegan-Pequot remnants, with his residence at the head of the Pequot estuary (Norwich). The southern section of what was to be the county was taken as spoil of war by the English, leaving all the northern watershed of the Thames more or less under the political control of Uncas and his tribe. In August, 1659, he signed the famous deed of transfer of the "nine-mile" tract to Captain John Mason and his compatriots, following permission from the General Court of the Colony to plant a settlement on the Yantic; and so "Norredge" became a legal township in 1662.

In 1646 the Rev. James Fitch had organized a church at Saybrook as we have seen. In 1660 he, with a majority of his churchmen, moved to the fertile banks of the Yantic and founded the Norwich Town Congregational Church. The first crude structure for religious purposes in this new settlement was erected on the southwest corner of the "Green" or "Plain," with a sun dial and a horse block at the door, and served its purpose for twelve years.

Mr. Fitch, in this old First Church, gathered about him a remarkable group of men and women, who, with their descendants, were destined to render the world as fine a human result as any company of the same number has ever done on this continent. The parish extended throughout the nine-mile tract, which was made a legal township in 1662, as has been noted. It faced somewhat different problems as a church and community than those found in the adjacent seaport settlement of New London. The center of Indian life was near at hand. Mr. Fitch learned the Mohegan language and sought to christianize the accessible tribes. On a Sunday morning the settlers near and far rode in for the church services, their wives on pillions behind them. Every available hitching post on the Green was preëmpted, as the serious-minded men and women, and children, too, filled the crude meeting house under the lead of the much beloved pastor. While it was the social event of the week, it also had to do with eternity, as they listened attentively to the elaborate exposition of Scripture, and the prayers, and sang out of the Old Bay Psalm Book the hymns lined out by the leader.

When the structure became inadequate, they built a new church on the top of the steep hill to the northwest of the Green. Rumors of war with the Indians kept the Norwich settlers restive, and so they made their church a fortress and a watch tower. In 1673 they began to hold services on this almost inaccessible height, helping the young and the old and the feeble up the winding path. The guards kept watch beside the stacked rifles of the men during the service.

Mr. Fitch was incapacitated by a stroke of palsy in 1674, and Jabez Fitch, his son, just out of Harvard, was asked to succeed. He helped them out a year or so and then went off to complete his studies. In the meanwhile King Philip's War (1675-78) threw the whole settlement into confusion Uncas with his Mohegans stood faithfully by his English friends. Fugitives from every point of the compass poured in upon them, and a special settlement was arranged for these on the Shetucket river near Norwich.

At last (1699) Rev. John Woodward was inducted into the pastorate, his parish covering, besides the nine-mile tract, Canterbury and Windham. In 1708 Captain Rene Grignon, a Huguenot from France, presented the town with a bell, which was hung in a separate tower on the summit of Meeting House Hill, ringing every night at nine o'clock and for Sunday services.

But to return to the settlement at the mouth of the Thames. The year 1661 saw Rev. Gershom Bulkeley (Harvard 1655) preaching in the old First Church of Christ in New London. He came of fine family connections in both New England and old England, and brought to the settlement his young wife, Sarah Chauncey, only daughter of President Chauncey of Harvard. With them came also his cultured, widowed mother, a daughter of Sir Richard Chitwood of England. This second spiritual leader of New London was a man of marked strength of character and of decidedly anti-democratic leanings. His ideals of a more centralized form of church government led to differences of opinion with his parishioners; so, rather than foment strife, he wisely relinquished the pastorate in 1665. He took this measure under the kindly protest of his people, who had voted to give him "liberty of conscience and utterance." He was a learned man, skilled in languages and medicine. After a decade as pastor at Wethersfield, Connecticut, he retired to the practice of medicine. His gracious mother remained in New London to the end of her life. His descendant, Leonard Bulkeley, was the founder of the Bulkeley school in the same place. Another descendant was the Hon. Morgan G. Bulkeley. Governor of the State.

We now come to a more settled condition of church affairs in New London. The new Colonial charter, which John Winthrop, Jr., secured from the government of Charles II in 1662, allayed some of the disputes in Southeastern Connecticut by defining Pawcatuck river as the eastern boundary of the newly constituted Colony. Massachusetts had claimed a large section of territory hereabouts, but gracefully yielded the township of Southertown, which now became a part of Connecticut. The New London parish by that arrangement extended to the Mystic river.

Rev. William Thompson had come as a missionary to the Indians in 1667, when the Massachusetts General Court had granted 8,500 acres to a tribe of Pequot Indians under the chieftainship of Harmon Garrett. Beside preaching to the natives, Mr. Thompson held services in the homes of the planters (Cheesebrough, Miner, Wheeler, Palmer, Stanton, Denison, Gallup, etc.), who were restive at having to go so far to church as New London. Considerable controversy thus arose in the attempt to erect a separate church in Mystic and Pawcatuck. The Commissioners of the United Colonies had rendered a decision in 1658 that all land east of the Mystic river should belong to Massachusetts, and a township of Southertown had been constituted, embracing also territory afterwards ceded to Rhode Island. A humble meeting house seems to have been erected in 1661, where occasional preaching was had. Southertown was renamed Mystic (1665) and later (1666) Stonington.

In the meanwhile the planters of this section had called Rev. James Noyes to take charge of the religious life and development in the region east of the Mystic river. Thus began a long and very important ministry of over fifty years (1719). For ten of these years the young minister was content to preach as a licentiate and delayed his ordination until 1674, when a new church building was erected near the present "Road Church," and the ecclesiastical organization was fully established (June 3, 1674). The ministry of Mr. Noyes was of far-reaching importance. He and his brother, Rev. Moses Noyes, of Old Lyme, were important factors in the founding of Yale College. The Stonington pastor entered into all the life of his extensive parish and shared with his people to the full the hardships of the Indian wars. He seems to have been skilled as a physician as well as a minister, and received public recognition for his services in the Narragansett war.

This venerable church furnished the Colony and the State with a long line of able ministers who entered into all the developments of spiritual, educational and social life in Southeastern Connecticut. During the long pastorate of Rev. Ebenezer Rosseter (1722-62) there was controversy as to the location of a new church edifice. This resulted in the erection of two buildings, the "West," near the old site on Agreement Hill (1729); the other the "East," or the "Centre" church, at Putnam Corner. This latter society called as pastor Rev. Nathaniel Eells in 1733. In 1762, at the death of Mr. Rosseter, the two churches were brought together under the ministry of Mr. Eells.

In the meanwhile the North Society in Stonington (now North Stonington) was incorporated by an act of the General Assembly in 1720 and was organized in 1721. After the customary controversy as to the location of the church building and the pressing problem of the "Half-Way Covenant," occasional preachers were succeeded by Rev. Ebenezer Russell, who was ordained (1727) at the time the church itself was fully organized. After the death of the first pastor (1731) came the remarkable pastorate of Rev. Joseph Fish (1732-81). In spite of a large "Separatist" defection in 1742, the ministry of Mr. Fish was notable, especially all through the Revolutionary War.

For thirty-six years after his death the church had no settled pastor, showing the sad case of spiritual decline everywhere manifested in the country at large and in New London county in particular. In 1817 the "Separatist" and "Regular" churches at last came together and reunited under the ministry of Rev. Joseph Ayer.[5]

At the conclusion of the Narragansett War the territory north of North

---

[5] The following installed pastors have since served this church: Rev. Peter H Shaw, 1837-39; Rev. Myron N. Morris, 1846-52; Rev. Stephen Hubble, 1853-69; Rev James R Bourne, 1873-79; Rev. John W. Savage, 1881-84; Rev. Wm B. Cary, 1884-1900; Rev. Edwin Judson Klock, 1900-1908; Rev. F. M. Hollister, 1909-1914; Rev. O D. Fisher, 1915—.

Stonington was set aside for a new township, which was named in honor of the volunteers of that war, Voluntown. All well accredited soldiers of that fierce struggle were granted land in the new township. But it was a long time before its rather remote fastnesses were made accessible. Pioneers finally flocked in in numbers enough to warrant the "gathering" of a church, and in 1720 the Onconk or "Line" church was built, one-half the structure in Voluntown and the other half in Sterling.

But we must not forget that the western part of what was New London county, as constituted in 1666 and for something over a century and a quarter (1785), embraced the huge township of Old Saybrook, stretching east and west of the Connecticut river from Bride brook (Niantic) to the Hammonasset river (Clinton). In this territory there was an earlier development of organized Christianity than in that now within the county limits. Governor John Winthrop, Jr., had first essayed to establish a colony at Saybrook Point (1635) in opposition to the Dutch claims. High ambitions seemed to have centered about this strategic spot. During the contemporaneous civil disturbances in England it was dreamed that here, at the mouth of the Connecticut river, a mighty commonwealth might be planted and fostered with the great Cromwell at its head and John Milton to be its chief literary ornament. Two Puritan noblemen, Lord Say and Lord Brook, were the leaders. The lingering glory of this dream may have had something to do with the location later at Saybrook of the Collegiate Institute of Connecticut in 1701. But the early dream faded, and John Winthrop, Jr, gave over the enterprise to George Fenwick, who in turn sold out his rights to the Connecticut Colony in 1644. Two years later (1646), on the very year of the founding of the New London settlement, the Old Saybrook (Congregational) church was organized under the pastorate of Rev James Fitch, as we have seen. He left in 1660 with a large portion of his flock to found Norwich and to establish a church there.

From the first the Saybrook settlement and its parish included all the territory east of the Connecticut river and south of East Haddam as far as Bride brook in Niantic. But the broad estuary of the Connecticut made it very difficult for the settlers east of it to attend their church at Saybrook. Occasional preaching services were held in that eastern section of the parish, and in 1666, the very year New London county was legally constituted by the General Assembly, Rev. Moses Noyes began to preach regularly east of the river. In 1668 a log meeting house was erected, which served the purpose until 1689. Then a more fitting structure replaced the original crude edifice. Its site was determined by lot, after the usual sharp differences of opinion. After Mr. Noyes had been preaching for twenty-seven years at Black Hall or Old Lyme, on March 27, 1693, he was installed and the church regularly organized. His very distinguished pastorate lasted until 1722. He played a most important part in the founding of Yale College (at Saybrook from 1701 to 1716) and was a leader of eminence throughout the county and the colony.

Rev. Jonathan Parsons, the third pastor, was an ardent participant in the movement of the Great Awakening, which spread throughout New

England. He was eminent as a theologian and a revivalist, receiving into the membership of his church 288 members within fifteen years. A successor, Rev. Stephen Johnson, was also eminently successful in his pastorate of forty years. The outcome of these labors and the increased opening up of the county to settlers were the organizations of the Niantic church (1724), that at Lyme (1725), at Hamburg (1727), at Salem (1728), and Grassy Hill (1746).

Indeed, the religious activities in the southwestern part of what is embraced in New London county of our day were more notable during its colonial history than those found in any other section of Southeastern Connecticut, as the result of revival interests prevalent there. It was to have been expected that this region would be a stronghold of Congregationalism. But the early pre-Revolutionary promise was not fulfilled. A large colony of religious recalcitrants migrated as a body to the Western Reserve in Ohio and founded the town of New Old Lyme in Ashtabula county.*

But we are far afield from the story of the "Old First" at New London,

---

* The writer is familiar with the modern New Old Lyme, where only in recent years has there been established an "Orthodox" church. "Free Love" and "Spiritualism" and other "isms" originally prevalent there seem to indicate that the inhabitants went westward partly at least to escape the moral restraints of religion. The writer knew the clergyman who founded the Presbyterian church in New Old Lyme about 1895. He was generously assisted by a thoughtful local merchant nominally a Spiritualist, who endowed the Academy there and eventually left his homestead for a parsonage.

---

7 *Rogerenes, Rogerene Quakers, Rogerene Baptists.*—This peculiar sect or social group under one or other of these names took its name from John Rogers, son of James Rogers who came from Milford, Connecticut, at the instance of Governor John Winthrop, Jr., about 1655. John Rogers, the son, grew up in the membership of the First Church of Christ in New London. He seems to have been a man of a strong, eccentric nature, while in 1674, while at Newport, Rhode Island, came under the influence of a small Sabbatarian church and there experienced a marked religious upheaval, which set him off in his new career. Later he formally united with that body by immersion Still later he was much influenced by preaching of the Friends (Quakers). Finally he broke with the Sabbatarians and established his own order, which was neither Sabbatarian or Quaker.
Among the tenets of the new sect were the following items of creed and practice:
1. Theologically it held to the orthodox views concerning God and the Trinity.
2. It sought to follow literally the teaching of Jesus Christ and the Apostles.
3. It put aside the Puritan "Sabbath" (Lord's Day) as a day of the week more sacred than the other six and it inveighed against what it called the "idolatry" of Sunday, although holding its stated services on that day.
4 It emphasized the sacredness and lawfulness of work on all seven days of the week, and boldly practiced it on Sunday as against colonial law.
5. It abjured priestcraft and the salaried profession of the ministry, and refused to pay the legal church tax.
6. It proclaimed public prayers to be pharisaic, especially the "long prayer."
7. It undertook to oppose the whole scheme of the regularly established church and welcomed punishments, fines, imprisonments. A craze for persecution led to most extravagant practices.
8. It used strictly New Testament methods in dealing with the sick, and would not call in the aid of the regular physician. The reader has noticed that many clergymen practiced medicine on occasion
9 The matrimonial experiences of John Rogers, leading him to practice what he considered to be plurality of wives with an Old Testament sanction, and the ignoring of the legal colonial ceremony of wedlock, offered an example fruitful of unfortunate family conditions outside the law among his followers.
It will be seen at once how inevitable was the conflict between the ordered evolution of ecclesiastical life in New London, Connecticut, and this erratic movement. Refusal to attend church services or to pay the ministerial tax, working in the fields on the Lord's Day as well as traveling on Sunday, all were indictable offenses calling for fine or imprisonment. Often the acts committed were so contemptible that justice had hard work getting seasoned with mercy. No orderly assembly of Christians in the county could reckon on an undisturbed meeting. Violent noises outside the buildings were indulged in. The mischief-makers boldly came into the services, arose in their places and undertook to dispute with the preacher.

which we left just as it was calling Rev. Simon Bradstreet to its pastorate in 1666 This was the very year that New London county was fully constituted under the new colonial charter, embracing the four townships of Saybrook, New London, Stonington and Norwich. Mr. Bradstreet served the church as preacher four years before his regular ordination in 1670 Here begin the first obtainable records of the church. The threatening "Half-Way Covenant," though spreading among the Connecticut churches, was not yet preached or practiced in the New London church. It was under this pastorate that the Rogerene disturbances began to be troublesome, gradually spreading throughout the county and among all denominations.[1]

The ordination of Mr. Bradstreet in October, 1670, was the first of many succeeding such services to be held in New London county. During his pastorate (about 1685) ministers were given legal right to officiate at weddings, although this privilege did not take from the civil authorities their prior right. During his ministry a new church edifice was erected, not without serious differences of opinion as to the location, high up on the southwest corner of Meeting House Green, now Bulkeley Square. The tower still retained the aspect of a watch tower, looking far down the estuary of the Thames and about among the hills and valleys surrounding the little settle-

---

brought in all sorts of handwork and flaunted their illegal industry before the worshipers; and in every other conceivable way attempted to spoil the service. On one occasion a Rogerene trundled a wheelbarrow filled with saleable goods into the morning worship of the old First Church, and, before anyone could hinder, reached the communion table and the obtruder turned and in stentorian voice offered his wares for sale. On the whole the entire community and the churches and the ministers were more persecuted than the Rogerenes, who were in a fair way to make all law contemptible.

New London county today is filled with stories true and apochryphal as to the strange and often ridiculous doings of these social conspirators It cannot be seen that their outrages hastened the abatement of the Puritanical scheme of compulsion They continued until the death of John Rogers in 1721, which was soon followed by the death of Governor Saltonstall

For forty years thereafter the Rogerenes kept out of the court records. The leadership was then in the hands of wiser men, such as John Bolles, John Waterhouse and John Culver The conciliatory attitude of Rev. Eliphalet Adams of the First Church had much to do with this interregnum of hostility between the Rogerenes and their neighbors Printed pamphlets and books and itinerant speakers carried their doctrines widely in New England. Settlements were made as far afield as in portions of the Western Reserve in Ohio. One of these may have been New Old Lyme, of which mention has been made In the meanwhile gradual intermarriages led to a less acute contention. The Rogerenes seemed to have prospered in business ways in spite of all financial requisitions upon their property for fines and taxes

The coming to New London as pastor in the First Church of Rev Mather Byles, Jr., in 1757 soon brought on a "counter-move" on the part of the Rogerenes which was at its zenith in 1764-66 Mr Byles began to preach against the Rogerenes and to incite renewed discipline against Sunday labor and travel, the holding of unauthorized meetings, abstention from regular church services and the administration of the sacraments by unauthorized persons. Court records once more abound with cases of trial, fine and imprisonment But the close of Mr Byles' ministry (1768) largely brought to an end the offensive tactics of the Rogerenes. A general plan prevailed among the churches to ignore utterly the disturbances of the malcontents The Revolutionary War now impended. Many Rogerenes proved patriots to the American cause The sect seems to have subsided, as the freedom of church attendance and voluntary payment for church expenses and a simplification of ecclesiastical pulpit garments and ministerial manners prevailed

Today a small remnant of the sect may be found in the southeastern corner of the township of Ledyard, popularly known as Quakertown Education in public schools, the modern newspaper, less stringent sumptuary laws and the new age, have combined to make the Rogerenes practically indistinguishable from their neighbors "Quaker Hill," "Bolles' Woods" and many another local designation, recall to mind the places and personalities connected with this strange and often amusing religious episode in the long story of New London county.

ment. The building was not completed until 1682, at the very close of Mr. Bradstreet's ministry.

As we have seen, the eldest daughter of First Church of Christ in New London had been fully established in Stonington in 1674, not without friction with the mother church or among its own membership. The dividing line between the two parishes was placed at the Mystic river. But even this did not stop the restiveness of the increasing numbers dwelling on the east side of the Thames. These more distant families were under the leadership of Captain James Avery. In 1684, as soon as the old "Blinman Church" building in New London was superceded by the "Bradstreet Church," this strong man of the eastern part of the parish bought the old church building for six pounds sterling, separated it into parts and floated them one by one around to his farm in Poquonnock, and set it up as a part of the homestead he was erecting. At one time or another this famous landmark was used for informal religious services.

In 1687 there came to the New London church by far the most outstanding ecclesiastical figure ever connected with the county, the Rev. Gurdon Saltonstall, then a man of twenty-one years of age and only three and a half out of Harvard College. He was not ordained in the pastorate of the First Church until November 25, 1691, and remained in that position until elected Governor of the Colony in 1708. An aristocrat by birth and temperament, large, tall and commanding in person and voice, a natural leader among men, he began at once to exercise qualities of personal initiative which spread his reputation throughout the colony. Early in his ministry the first bell in the county was hung in the church tower and used both for church services and for civil functions.

The "Half-Way Covenant" had, by this time, spread widely in Connecticut and Massachusetts, and there was a serious declension in spiritual power clearly discernible everywhere it went. The low morale led in 1692 in Massachusetts to the Salem witchcraft delusion. New London county was fortunately free from that most unchristian religious and civil declension. Mr. Saltonstall was the first clergyman in New London actually to take advantage of the new law permitting a clergyman to perform the marriage ceremony. He was a powerful preacher, somewhat stern in church discipline and provocative of trouble with the Rogerenes. His severe attitude toward restive parishioners east of the Thames, especially toward Captain James Avery, widened the previous estrangements. These culminated in 1702 in a request to the General Assembly for a separate church organization in that portion of the parish and township. This was consummated in 1704. On the 8th of November of that year, Rev. Ephraim Woodbridge was ordained as the first minister and the First Church of Christ in Groton fully organized. In 1705 Groton township was set off from New London, and the Ecclesiastical Society of the church received its permanent name. On the year following (1705) the First Baptist Church of Groton was organized at Old Mystic.

But in spite of elements that awakened opposition within and without the church, Mr. Saltonstall was a man of singular power as a preacher and as a man. His influence spread throughout the colony to such an extent that at the death of Governor Fitz-John Winthrop (1698-1707), his parishioner, all eyes turned to this pastor as the most fitting successor in the gubernatorial chair. This political advancement occurred on January 1, 1708, after a pastorate of nearly twenty years, or sixteen years after his ordination.[*]

In the meanwhile, matters of very considerable moment had been occurring in the northern portion of the county. The First Church of Christ at Norwich Town, after the disturbances of the Indian wars, had experienced a notable expansion. To the east across the Shetucket river on land purchased from the Mohegan Indians, the inhabitants were granted a township charter under the name of Preston, in 1687. They set at work at once to have an organized church of their own. They were a sturdy band, with household names such as Brewster, Standish (of "Mayflower" descent), Park, Tracy, Richards, Tyler, Fobes, Morgan, Witter, Welch, so ran the names, who cleared the forests and tilled the rich lands of Preston. In faith they built a church and, after long search, secured Rev. Salmon Treat to be their minister. He was ordained at the organization of the church on November 16, 1698. This was the beginning of a fruitful pastorate extending through forty-six years. One of the important results of his ministry was the peaceful establishment of the North Church of Preston (now Griswold) in 1720.

At this last-mentioned church the Rev. Hezekiah Lord, immediately on its organization, took up the pastorate, which lasted until 1761. These were

---

[*] Gurdon Saltonstall was re-elected colonial Governor from year to year until his death in 1724. The unprecedented elevation of a clergyman to this high office was fully justified by the wise statesmanship exhibited by the incumbent. Thomas Hooker, Gurdon Saltonstall, Lyman Beecher and Horace Bushnell are four out of a score of Connecticut clergymen who proved powerful factors in the building up of the State and the nation. As Governor, Mr. Saltonstall at once exercised his leadership by summoning at Saybrook, with the assent of the General Assembly, a Synod to examine ' the defects of the discipline of the churches of this government arising from the want of a more explicit asserting of the rules given to that end in the Scriptures." Hence that memorable though small ecclesiastical gathering at the next Commencement season of the Collegiate Institute (later Yale College) then established at the mouth of the Connecticut river. On September 7, 1708, this Synod brought forth the famous "Saybrook Platform," which was successfully to contest place with the "Cambridge Platform" (1648) in the approval of the great majority of the churches of Connecticut. An important exception to this approval occurred in the Governor's old church, New London First, of which he still remained a member and a regular worshipper. Nor did it stand alone. The "Saybrook Platform" was accepted by the General Assembly, which "ordained that all the churches within this government that are or shall be united in doctrine, worship and discipline, be and for the future shall be owned and acknowledged by law; provided always that nothing herein shall be intended or construed to hinder or prevent any church or society that is or shall be allowed by the laws of the government, who soberly differ or dissent from the united churches hereby established, from exercising worship and discipline in their own way according to their consciences."

By law, the churches of each county were to form one or more "consociations" or Standing Councils before which all cases of discipline, difficult of settlement by the local church, should come, as well as certain matters having to do with ordinations, installations and dismissions. In similar fashion the ministers of each county were to be formed into "Associations" which should in turn send delegates annually to a "General Association" of colony-wide representations. The latter is still in existence, though now not a delegated body, except as any regularly settled Congregational minister in the State is invited to attend. The Saybrook Platform remained legally in effect until 1784, and as a recognized standard for more than a half century after that.

Governor Saltonstall also was influential in the final settlement of Yale College at New Haven. At its first Commencement at that place he pronounced an oration in Latin (Sept. 12, 1718) and its Latinity was accounted of high grade. He ever stood high in the councils of the College. What with Indian and French wars, Colony disputes, high prices, territorial adjustments with Massachusetts and Rhode Island, the times called for leadership of a high order, and the Governor was easily the foremost man in the colony in his time.

the difficult pioneering days at that end of the county. Mr. Lord was succeeded by Rev. Levi Hart in a still more distinguished ministry lasting from 1762 to 1808. Mr. Hart had studied theology with the famous Dr. Bellamy, of Bethlehem, Connecticut, and married his daughter. He had one of those remarkable life-ministries in Griswold, exerting a lasting influence in his own parish and widely over the State. His wisdom and charity handled the "Separatist" movement in his section so effectively that no opposition congregations were "gathered" there. He took great interest in Home Missions in Connecticut and northern New England, resulting in the organization of the Missionary Society of Connecticut, the oldest one in the country.

Between Norwich and Preston, on a narrow strip of territory about twelve miles long, later joined to Preston, in what was before that called East Norwich, we find the "Long Society" (Fifth Congregational Church of Norwich), established in 1726. Rev. Jabez Wight was pastor there for fifty-six years.

But over a quarter of a century before this, came the settlement of Lebanon and the founding of its First Church of Christ in 1700 in what was to become a famous historic center during the War of the Revolution. In 1702 it was included in New London county. The "five-mile" purchase from the Indians had come in 1697. The pioneers began the opening out of the land in the following year and the town was formally organized in 1700, the church being there practically from the first (organized November 7, 1700). The meeting house was built at the west end of the "Green," near what became later the "Land Office" of Governor Trumbull.

Within twenty years the growth of the wide-extended community called for the establishment of a North Parish or Second church, in what was styled Lebanon Crank (now Columbia) (1720). There fifteen years later (1735) Rev. Eleazar Wheelock, son of Deacon Ralph Wheelock and Ruth Huntington (Norwich), was settled. From these two foci of religious life the uplifting influence of the Lebanon churches spread widely. In the First Church there were two remarkable pastorates, together covering over a century—that of Rev. Solomon Williams, D.D. (1722 to 1771), and Rev. Zebulon Ely (1782 to 1824). From these two churches there grew up the Goshen Church (November 26, 1729), Exeter (1773), and Liberty Hill. Largely owing to the schools established in Lebanon proper (Tisdale's Academy) at North Lebanon (Moor's Charity School) and at Plainfield (Academy) the homes of those pioneers sent forth within a century over forty ministers.

In close connection with this development, the churches of Plainfield and Canterbury were organized. There seems some dispute as to just which county the credit for those earlier years shall go. But it is certain that the impetus came from the south. The Plainfield church was organized in what was then called the Quinebaug Plantations, on January 3, 1705. They called their first pastor from Norwich, Rev. Joseph Coit, who originated in New London. He ministered to the church for forty-nine years. The Canterbury church was organized in 1711, while its parish was in New London county. Together with Plainfield, it brought forth men and women of wide influence in the nation at large. Moses Cleveland, the founder of the metropolis of Ohio, went forth from Canterbury.

The First Church of Colchester, on the Connecticut river watershed, was organized in 1703, soon followed by the Westchester church in the same township in 1729. Rev. John Bulkeley, son of Rev Gershom Bulkeley, M.D., whom we met in New London as pastor of the First Church, was the first pastor of the Colchester church, beginning a long line of distinguished ministers. The temporary house of worship was exchanged for a better after 1709, and in 1771 a new structure came, which was counted "the finest in the colony." The Westchester parish in the northern part of the township had an equally strong development with a faithful series of influential pastors, beginning with Rev. Judah Lewis.

There was a long controversy with the alleged Indian owners as to the southern portion of the town of Colchester, which delayed settlement for many years, but at last a township of Salem was set off by the General Assembly, made up of portions of south Colchester and northern Lyme, and settlers came in. A church was organized in 1728, as previously noted.

The Norwich Town church went strongly forward under the pastorate of Rev. John Woodward for a decade, giving forth helpfulness in every direction, as we have seen. Mr. Woodward was one of the delegates to the Saybrook Synod, of which he was the secretary, and thus largely responsible for the Platform adopted in 1708. On his return he found he could not carry his church with him. The friction thus arising paved the way to a rupture of the pastoral relation in September, 1716. In the meanwhile a new church building was erected, after the usual quarrel over the location, near the site of the old one on the Meeting House Hill. This new house of worship was opened for use in December, 1713. Mr. Woodward retired from the ministerial profession and spent his last days on his farm in West Haven, Connecticut.

That section of Norwich called "West Farms," a few miles to the northwest of the Green, constituted the most fertile section of the "nine-mile" tract, and was portioned out in sections to the occupants of the Town Plot. This new region was gradually cleared and settled by some of the leading citizens of Norwich. A notable lot of families established themselves there. Efforts had been making for some years to secure a separate ecclesiastical society in that flourishing section. When two score families there set about getting this done, their requests were granted and on October 8, 1718, Rev Henry Willis was ordained pastor and a church organized, what is now known as the Franklyn church. The new building was barely housed in, and use was made of the old furniture of the former Norwich church at the start.

Mr. Willis, though a graduate in 1715 of the Connecticut Collegiate Institute at Saybrook (later Yale College), was a strong adherent of the Cambridge Platform (1648) as distinguished from the Saybrook Platform (1708), which quite pleased his people for twenty-six years. But by that time friction arose in the parish; Saybrook adherents made trouble. "Separatist" movements were under way and, in spite of the powerful revivals of the Great Awakening, the pastorate came to an end in 1750.

N L —1-19

But about the time of the founding of this strong daughter of the Norwich church, a new pastor came to that church, Rev. Benjamin Lord, who was ordained November 20, 1717, also, at the first, a strong opponent of the Saybrook Platform. On April 30th of that same year the church had voted to sustain itself by contributions rather than by the old State-Church rate, anticipating the Old First at New London by ten years. We note a revival in 1721 and great activity during the times of the Great Awakening, which was judiciously favored by Mr Lord, who, however, revolted at many of the eccentricities that arose

The Lisbon church (Newent) was organized in 1723 with Rev. Daniel Kirkland, whose pastorate lasted until 1752.

We now turn back again to the southern part of the county and to the First Church at New London. The remarkable ministry of Rev. Gurdon Saltonstall terminated by his election to the governorship. It was followed by the still more fruitful ministry of Rev. Eliphalet Adams, extending from 1709 to 1753. He was the last pastor ordained by the township, showing the changing order, as church and State began to be separated Three hundred and eighty-seven persons were added to the church membership during this long ministry. The powerful revival interest incident upon the Great Awakening impressed itself upon the old church, especially in 1740-41 The Half-Way Covenant, introduced into the church during the previous pastorate, still continued, although there was a manifest difference between those admitted on deep conviction during the revival period. The children of all those living exemplary lives and whose ancestors had made a "serious profession of religion" were baptized

In October, 1772, the North Parish (Montville) was constituted a distinct parish, the church organized, and Rev. James Hillhouse installed as pastor He continued in this position for fifteen years. His successor, Rev. David Jewett, was ordained October 3, 1739. A dance (strange to say) and a supper gave this occasion the title of the "Ordination Ball."

The East Lyme (Niantic) church was organized in 1724, its parish being known as "The Second Ecclesiastical Society of Lyme," with Rev. George Griswold as pastor. This minister, of high social rank and a graduate of Yale College, was a strong preacher and widely useful as a spiritual leader.

On January 23, 1727, the Old First Church of Christ in New London formally broke away from the old order of township direction and organized the "First Ecclesiastical Society of New London," an incorporated body which took over the financial responsibility for the conduct of the church, as distinguished from the old plan of universal taxation for the support of the ministry. The other churches of the county did the same. This placed the churches of other denominations on an equal footing financially and the new day was ushered in.

In 1727 a "Relief" law was passed by the General Assembly of the Colony, exempting the members of the Church of England from compulsory attendance on the Puritan State-Church and payment of minister's rates, provided there was a regularly ordained Church of England minister established and performing the duties of his office

The revolution or evolution involved in this change went down to the roots of the matter. It did not come suddenly, but spread steadily all over the county, the Colony (later State) and New England. It was in harmony with the growing democracy, and came as a matter of justice and common sense. We have noted all along the tendencies to break away from the old established order of things, as "Separatist" congregations sprang up in almost every section of the county. Good Yankee common sense prevailed. A glimpse of it is seen in the provisions of the "Saybrook Platform," where other possible types of religious organization were clearly in mind. The close proximity of Rhode Island, with its broader handling of this same problem from the first, doubtless had a strong influence. The lack of a Biblical New Testament precedent for the old New England order was a weakness. Doubtless, too, the mighty upheaval of the Great Awakening had much to do with the structural change of organized church life. A new individualism pervaded the community, and the church life felt the transformation. A State-Church more and more seemed an inconsistency. Other denominations were pressing in, even though their adherents were asked to pay the church tax for the regular ministry. Two Baptist churches and one Episcopalian church were already firmly established within the county and others came thick and fast. The story, whose brief outline we are following, now breaks up into strictly denominational divisions, which we must trace out one by one.

III.

THE CONGREGATIONAL DENOMINATION IN NEW LONDON COUNTY

The Congregational churches in the territory of what is now known as New London county, at the time of the gradual transition from the position of a State-Church to the independent status of its sister denominations, numbered about a score, the most of which were under the leadership of strong pastors. These took over by natural inheritance all that had been developing in the religious activities in more strictly pioneer days. The advantages in this situation clearly outbid the disadvantages and gave the denomination a powerful leadership with all its responsiblities.

It is hard to date the beginnings of the transition, for this was largely left to local conditions. The movement seems to have been accelerated by the "Great Awakening" and the sense of fair-dealing with the groups of worshippers outside the State-Church. Out of it all came, among other things, our Congregational autonomy. Its story begins clearly in the Colonial period (1737-1783). From then to 1852 came the period of theological conflict, the establishment of theological seminaries, reconstruction after the Revolution, evangelical revivals, revived study of the Bible through Sunday schools, and the upbuilding of missionary societies for home and foreign work and the beginnings of systematic efforts for the well-being of the negro (1846). With the Albany Convention (1852), Congregational polity began to realize its continent-wide responsibilities. The Connecticut churches had anticipated much that later became constituent elements in this denominational self-consciousness, and for that very reason in New London county and in the

State found it a little harder to adjust themselves to the more radical central-ization adopted by the whole denomination in recent days.

Rev. ·Eliphalet Adams at the time of the transition was in the heyday of his ministry at the First Church of Christ in New London. He was a man of peace and good will and of much learning. He spoke the Indian languages and preached on all possible occasions for the Mohegans, Pequots and Niantics. He received into his church several of the Mohegan sachems Benjamin Uncas, third of the name and sixth Sachem, he received into his own family. He coöperated with Samuel Occum in the establishment of Indian schools. August 31, 1735, the First Church meeting house (the Saltonstall building) was struck by lightning during the service, with one fatality and others seriously injured. After some controversy the building was repaired in 1746 and served the organization for another half century (1785). Under Mr. Adams' kindly handling, the Rogerene troubles quieted down. His preaching was sought for all over the colony. He was methodical, tactful and constructive. Under such a ministry the church survived easily the withdrawal of "Separatists" and the sharing with the Episcopal church of St James founded in 1725, in the religious life of the community.

Indeed, in 1724 Mr. Adams had been invited to the presidency of Yale College, of which he had been a trustee since 1720 Two years after that (1722) President Timothy Cutler, D.D , and one of his principal coadjutors, had embraced Episcopacy. After debates "that shook Congregationalism throughout New England" (said President Quincy of Harvard), it was de-cided that the teachers at Yale in the future must assent to the Saybrook Platform. A strong man was needed to head the College, and Mr. Adams was elected president. However, he declined the honor and went on with the pastorate.

His name does not appear as one of the lights of the Great Awakening He was not unsympathetic, and was glad to see great good come to his parish and the county from the movement. But his wisdom and serenity were much exercised to curb the eccentricities that abounded in the meetings held under the leaders of that type. In 1741 Mr. Adams found himself in the midst of a powerful revival interest, and eighty-two persons were received into the church. The Separatist movement in New London grew out of the eccentric preaching of John Davenport, and some one hundred withdrew from the First Church. Only the personal force and wisdom of Mr. Adams prevented a fatal schism Along with this conserving work he yet had a rare breadth of spiritual and practical earnestness. He was active in helping build a rector's house at Yale, and also encouraging a Congregational move-ment at Providence, Rhode Island, lending a hand wherever he could promote a good work or word. His long and faithful ministry came to a close with his death in 1753 He had been for many years acknowledged "in every respect the most superior person" in the Colony of Connecticut

The story of the Old First in New London from the death of this beloved pastor and citizen (1753) to 1835, takes the church through the greatest political and theological controversies of America, including the French and Indian war, the American Revolution, the founding of the United States of

America, the War of 1812, the unexpectedly firmer grasp of slavery on the expanding Republic, the consummation of the freedom of the Church from the State, and the great schism among the churches of New England resulting in the "Unitarian" defection, as well as the beginning of the splendid record of the "orthodox" churches in the establishment of the Home and Foreign Missionary enterprises, the founding of schools and colleges and theological seminaries, and the upspringing of notable spiritual awakenings that far more than made up for all the losses.

The pastorate of Rev. Mather Byles, Jr., in the First Church in New London (1757-68), was chiefly marked by the fact that he was the first pastor in the county to be inducted into his office in the modern Congregational way. A brilliant man, he lacked the judicial temper of his predecessor and soon had awakened the animosity of the Rogerenes, who broke out in vigorous rebellion against his drastic methods of law enforcements. But the real cause of the brevity of his ministry in New London was a strong leaning to Episcopacy, which at last led him to resign and seek Episcopal ordination.

The still shorter pastorate of Rev Ephraim Woodbridge (1769-76), a grandson of the first pastor of the Groton church, was marked by his strenuous opposition to the Half-Way Covenant and his exaltation of the principle of church membership based on genuine conversion. A revolutionary spirit was in the air, and a spiritual decline manifest throughout the country. All denominations lost ground in New London as well as everywhere. Young Woodbridge heroically set himself against all the obstacles But the death of his wife and his own physical frailty were too much for him, and he died September 6, 1776.

A long interval occurred before a successor was found (1776-87), during which the building of a new meeting house was gotten under way (1785) to be finished and dedicated under the ministry of Rev. Henry Channing (1787-1806). New London by the first United States census (1791) had 2,465 inhabitants, of whom 138 were blacks and of these 95 were slaves. This pastorate was notable for its relapse to the extreme into the Half-Way Covenant heresy on the part of minister and people. Church membership involved simply a record of good moral character. The number of members at the beginning was down to twelve males and forty-seven females. Mr. Channing received in all two hundred and forty-five persons and baptized five hundred and seventy-five, going thus the limit of comprehensiveness. On another page may be found the form of admission to membership used, which was accounted to be "Unitarian" in principle by his orthodox brethren all over the county. At the same time considerable care was taken as to cases calling for discipline of conduct not befitting a Christian. In 1798 the church entered heartily into the formation of the Missionary Society of Connecticut. The Unitarian tendencies of Mr. Channing led to considerable feeling in the church, leading to hesitancy of financial support and finally to his resignation in 1806. It is interesting to note that the dismissing council voted "they unanimously and affectionately concur in recommending him as a minister in regular standing in the church of Christ."

Turning to the north of the county, we find the long pastorate of Rev. Benjamin Lord at Norwich Town coming to its close in 1784. For six years he had been assisted by Rev. Joseph Strong, who now entered upon another half-century of service. This was a most critical era of reconstruction, in which the Norwich church rendered signal assistance to all the pastorless churches in that whole region Mr. Strong was a man of a most genial temperament and held firmly to the new orthodoxy in the reaction from the Unitarian movement. The church entered into all the strong forward movements of this new evangelical Congregationalism, especially into its missionary zeal. From 1829 until his death in 1834, Mr. Strong had Rev. Mr. Everest as colleague. Mr Everest resigned in 1836, and the church called Rev. Hiram P. Arms, who was installed in 1839

The Franklin church kept its strong leadership under the pastorates of Rev. John Ellis and Rev Samuel Nott, which stretched over a century, beginning in 1753. During that time the Franklin church sent forth men and women of national and international reputation. Indeed, few regions in New England during that period were so fruitful in character and human achievement as the northern townships of New London county. During the storm and stress of the Revolutionary days—as someone has expressed it— "the Land Office in Lebanon was for the nonce the capital of the United Colonies." The Bozrah church was established in 1739, the Hanover church in 1766, Jewett City (Griswold 2nd) in 1825, and Mohegan church in 1832

The pastorate of Rev. Abel McEwen, D.D., at the First Church in New London (1806-1854), brought that venerable organization into the use of its present imposing edifice and into the modern life of the denomination Beginning with a reaction from the latitudinarianism of his predecessor, the ministry of Dr. McEwen struck a strong, virile note at a time when religion in New London county was perhaps at its lowest ebb and a majority of the churches pastorless, he being at the beginning the only settled pastor, as he used to say, "in a territory fifty miles long and twelve miles broad." He instituted the weekly prayer-meeting. A "Sessions House" was built on the site of the present Parish House on Union street (1819) to accommodate all the social activities of the church, especially the newly established Sunday school. The church, under the leadership of Dr. McEwen, threw itself into the Home Mission work in the county. In 1815 the Consociation of New London County was organized, this being the last county in the State to do so, "two uncompromising conservators of independency" having died. The year following (1816), the Domestic Missionary Society of Connecticut was formed under the lead of Dr McEwen and Rev. Mr. Hart, of the Griswold church. Pastors rapidly began to be called to the churches. The world-call for missions was not unheeded, and in 1819 a member of this church, Harriet Lathrop, married Rev. Mr. Winslow, and they sailed for Ceylon as foreign missionaries In 1821 the ladies of the church formed the Foreign Missionary Society. Mr. Asa Otis became a member of the church in 1834, and eventually left to the American Board of Commissioners for Foreign Missions over a million dollars

The spiritual quickenings that came with these varied enterprises showed themselves in large and stable accessions to the church. Several notable revivals stirred the waters. At length it became manifest that the "Old First" could not handle the growing responsibilities. The story of the founding of the Second Congregational Church in New London is most refreshing. The members of the First Church practically built the new edifice, and started off this fourth daughter in a strong way. During necessary repairs on the old church, the daughter welcomed the mother church to its services for several months. Whereupon, leaving the new organization to carry on its work unfettered, Dr. McEwen started again to put his own church in working order under the new conditions. The empty seats were soon filled and both churches went on rejoicing. The pastorate closed with the building of the modern church edifice, which remains as peculiarly the monument to this remarkable spiritual leader. It expresses the solidity of his character, possibly suggesting, too, a certain reserve and stiffness in a rather puritanical aspect of his earnest career. His resignation from the pastorate came in 1854, with graciousness after nearly fifty years of most active and fruitful ministry. He remained for six years an honored worker in the church and county, when (1860) he was gathered to his fathers, honored and lamented by the whole community.

The water privileges of the upper end of the Thames estuary gradually brought Norwich into trading connection with the whole world. About the Landing Place there grew up a community called Chelsea, which finally required church privileges of its own. In 1751 such an organization was effected. The growth was slow, and it was not until 1761 that a regular minister was settled over the new parish, Rev. Nathaniel Whittaker. His pastorate was interrupted by a long absence in England as an agent seeking funds for Moor's Indian Charity School of Lebanon, Connecticut, and later Hanover, New Hampshire. Rev. Ephraim Judson succeeded to the pastorate in 1771. He too had an interrupted ministry, being called off as chaplain during the Revolutionary War and being much of the time in poor health. This intermittent service came to an end in 1778, and for eight years there was no successor.

In 1786 came the division of the huge township of Norwich, taking away all the upper and eastern portions of the "nine-mile" tract. The year following, Rev. Walter King was installed over the Second Church, as the Chelsea organization began to be known. The meeting house was burned in 1793, and Mr. King's congregation enjoyed for some months the hospitality of the neighboring Episcopal church during the rebuilding. Mr. King was a man of deep earnestness. In 1811 a controversy over the academic question of marrying a dead wife's sister led to the dissolution of the pastorate.

A brief ministry of Rev. Asahel Hooker was followed by that of Rev. Alfred Mitchell in 1814, who started the series of powerful spiritual leaders, making the Second Church of Norwich a worthy competitor in good works with the First Church in New London. It grew rapidly in numbers, wealth and standing in the county. Its readiness to be the leader in a new era of Congregationalism was indicated in every turn. Mr. Mitchell took an active part in all constructive missionary politics. The Second Church was notable especially in standing back of the Sunday school work begun in Norwich in 1815. The death of the pastor in 1831 was a severe blow to the church

The short pastorate of Rev. James T Dickinson prepared him for the Foreign Mission field in 1834. The Rev. Alvan Pond succeeded in a ministry of twenty-nine years (1835-65), a period of steady growth for the church and community. Soon it appeared that one church could not care for the religious life crowding in, and in 1842 what was called the Fifth Society was formed by a colony of ninety-eight persons going out, who organized what was known for over eighty years as the Broadway Congregational Church, now again, with the mother church, making the United Church. That the new venture did not seriously deplete the strength of the mother church is seen in the fact that the fire of 1844 destroying its edifice did not keep its strong constituency from building of granite on its present site what was at the time the finest church structure in the county. With its membership ever growing in influence, culture and spiritual and evangelical progressiveness, the Second Church of Norwich became a power in Eastern Connecticut. Then followed the pastorate of Rev. Malcolm McG. Dana, D.D. (1864-74), which carried on the strong work of the church. The feeling that its helpfulness to the community would be increased by removal to the suburban district near the Academy led to marked differences of opinion with the majority of his parishioners, and in 1874 Dr. Dana resigned and, with one hundred and five of his old members, formed the Park Congregational Church Rev. William S. Palmer, D D., came to the Second Church in the autumn of that year (1874) and began a fruitful ministry of fifteen years The difficulties at the opening of the pastorate were gradually overcome. Dr. Palmer began with two hundred and forty members and closed with three hundred and fifty-one. During his ministry the Christian Endeavor Society was organized, and special work was done for the Chinese. Dr. and Mrs. Palmer did a strong and wide work, and their influence was felt in the State and the denomination at large. The pulpit was supplied for three years by Rev Leonard Woolsey Bacon, D D., when Rev Cornelius W Morrow was installed.

As we have seen, the year 1842 was notable in Norwich for the establishment of what became the Broadway Congregational Church. No new church enterprise in the county ever started off with better opportunities. The short pastorate of Rev. Willard Child (1842-45) was succeeded by the epoch-making ministry of Rev. John P Gulliver. D. D (1846-65). With a genius peculiar to himself, he took hold of his problem in harmony with his brethren in the ministry and worked it out from the community standpoint. The story of his local work for education is told at length elsewhere and may not be repeated here. A disastrous fire in 1854 led to the building of "Broadway" Church, now the home of the United Church. Under his lead the church stepped out into the larger life of the denomination and has ever since played a strong part in its life at home and abroad.

Dr. Gulliver's successor was Rev Daniel Merriman (1868-75), who carried on the tradition of strength and breadth, as also did his successors, Rev. L T. Chamberlain (1877-83) and Rev. Nelson Millard, D.D (1884-87). In 1888 began the powerful pastorate of Rev. Lwellyn Pratt, D D , who had already in a variety of spheres accomplished a life work. He gathered up the lines of service developed by his predecessors and added yet more of his own, increasing in power for nearly a score of years. In 1906 he laid down the burden of labors which were too much for his weakening physique, but remained a loved adviser until his death in 1913.

Side by side with the development of these two urban churches, the old First at Norwichtown had gone on its way under the pastorate of Rev. H. P. Arms, who lived to preach an emeritus sermon on the fortieth anniversary of his ministry in 1876. Since that date the Old First at Norwichtown has gone on her steady way, holding a strong position in the Association.

The Park Church started off on her vigorous life, as we have seen, under the pastorate of Dr. Dana in 1874. Her beautiful house of worship, in a superb location, adjoining the group of the Academy buildings, with a powerful ministry under Dr. Dana (1874-78), Rev. Leonard Woolsey Bacon, D.D., and Rev. Samuel H. Howe, D.D., have made the Park Church a bright light in the Association and State and throughout the denomination.

The Greenville Church in Norwich (Third Congregational) had been established (1833) in a suburb where the water privileges began to attract manufacturing interests. Its pastorates were short for over a half century of its life, but it is closing the century with the long and faithful ministry of Rev. Charles H. Ricketts. In 1867, as the manufacturing interests moved further up the stream, the Taftville Church was added to the Norwich group, doing its helpful service to a fine constituency of people mostly connected with the mills established there. The Second Congregational Church of Stonington was organized in 1833 and the Mystic church in 1852, and with the Groton church have given the shore section of the county a steady and vigorous Congregational ministry.

At the Old First at New London the pastorate of Dr. McEwen was succeeded by that of Rev. Thomas P. Field, D.D., after an associate pastorate from 1856 to 1860, closing in 1876. Dr. Field brought to New London from his professorship of literature at Amherst College, culture and learning, and a spiritual leadership, as well as a wide reputation throughout religious and educational circles. A revival in 1858 led on to a steady growth throughout his strong ministry. Rev. Edward Woolsey Bacon (1877-87) and Rev. S. Leroy Blake, D. D. (1887-1902), succeeded, each with a fruitful service. Dr. Blake wrote in two volumes the story of the church he served.

Rev. J. Romeyn Danforth, the present pastor (1922), came in 1903 and has carried on with distinction the high-grade service of the church. He has represented the denomination in her national councils for many years, and proved a wise councillor in the American Missionary Association. The war opened the heart of this church, and it rendered valuable service, social and religious, to the soldiers and sailors, who accepted to an unusual degree its hospitalities. Its Young People's Society was especially active in this work and has since been carrying on strongly. The Old First Church was incorporated in 1919 in harmony with the modern plans of best church organization, and the venerable ecclesiastical society voluntarily closed its long and honorable career. It added deaconesses to its efficient organization. At the

time of epidemics its parish house has been used as an emergency hospital.
Mr Danforth entered widely into the religious and philanthropic life of the
community. The Smith Memorial Home. the Mohegan fund, the Tinker
Bread fund, the Rotary Club, the Masonic and Odd Fellows orders, claim him.

As we have seen, the Second Congregational Church started off in 1835
with the warmest favor of the Old First, and has grown into the stature of
a powerful leader among the churches of the denomination in the State and
country. It worshipped in its original building until its destruction by fire
in 1868, just after a thorough repair. At that time the present main building
was erected, one of the finest in the State, especially after the addition in
recent years of the Church House, fully equipped for all lines of church
activity. The early pastorates were comparatively short, with intervening
supplies, and the names of Hurlbut, Huntington, MacDonald, Boies and
Edwards (1845-57) make up the rapid succession. During the pastorate of
Rev. G. B. Wilcox (1859-69) two hundred and seven persons were received
into the membership, and the Bradley Street Mission (since the Learned
Mission) was founded (1859). Many still living will recall the edifying
ministry of Rev. Oliver Ellsworth Daggett (1871-77), during which he
received 156 new members Rev. John Phelps Taylor, D.D. (1878-83),
brought a learned and distinguished equipment to the pulpit of the Second
Church. He was followed by Rev. James Gibson Johnson. D.D. (1885-91),
who will be remembered by a still larger group for his genial and effective
ministry. But it was not until the eighth pastor of the Second Church that
it was able to hold a strong man for a full quarter of a century, the Rev.
James Wilson Bixler, D D., who rounded up his uplifting ministry from 1891
to 1016 with a power rarely surpassed in the annals of Connecticut. The
membership of the church grew from 413 to 622. Under the ministry of Dr.
Bixler the church was incorporated and the ecclesiastical society eliminated,
a men's club established, the Whiton chimes mounted in the belfry, the
Harris manse erected and endowed, as well as the Harris organ installed and
the Church House built, completing the superb working plant of church.
There were several revivals during this pastorate, notably the one under the
leadership of Rev J. Wilbur Chapman. D.D , in 1894. The influence of Dr
Bixler pervaded the community, and no important organization in the city
failed to receive the strong impress of his congenial personality He was
especially a leader in the establishment of the Connecticut College for Women
on its noble site in New London. He retired from his long pastorate to take
an honorable position in Atlanta Theological Seminary. The ministry of
Rev. J Beveredge Lee, D D., began in 1917 with every promise of a full
utilization of all the successes of the eight preceding pastorates.

The Congregational churches of New London county came up to the
end of 1920 with a total membership of 5,332 in the thirty-two churches of
that order within the area of the county, twenty-eight of which are connected
with the New London Association of Congregational Churches and Ministers.
This Association is the direct descendant of the Colonial Association, a clear
record of which we have as early as 1750. It took its present form during
the readjustments in the denomination early in this century. The constitution

under which it is working was adopted May 10, 1921, and harmonizes with the general modern pattern throughout the denomination. It is now a strong, efficient body, continuously existent through its executive committee and carrying on its united work through this and the standing committees, with an annual meeting in May and a semi-annual meeting in the autumn. The traditional autonomy of the individual church has been sacredly preserved. Never was this scion of its New England ancestry so strong in numbers, organization, material equipment, and social and religious powers. The year 1921 brought into its membership more new members than any year in a generation.

At this writing (1922) the pulpits are filled with strong, united men, all of whom have at heart the whole work in the Kingdom of God in the county, in most cordial relations with all the sister denominations.

IV.

THE BAPTIST CHURCHES IN NEW LONDON COUNTY

Second in arrival on the field to begin their heroic struggle for the upbuilding of religion in New London county, came the Baptists from Rhode Island. The border line between the two colonies was greatly confused at the first, but got straightened out when Governor John Winthrop, Jr., brought back from England his new charter for the Connecticut Colony (1662), and Massachusetts graciously gave over her claims in these regions the Pawcatuck river becoming the boundary. The contest for entire religious liberty soon crossed this Rubicon and asserted itself in the State-Church territory of Connecticut. At first in individual homes and then in groups the work began. The lowering of the original Puritan standards and the incoming of the "Half-way Covenant" into the State-Church parishes led to a real need for the strong assertion of individual conversion, and with this came the necessity for individual initiative along the whole line of religious as well as civil development. These groups of colonial Christians contended for a simple form of faith and practice which they attempted to draw directly from the New Testament records. Each organization formed a complete and autonomous democracy, and was linked by a common belief to all similar bodies, soon forming into free associations of such. A baptism (immersion) of faith was required for church-membership and, with more or less insistence, the communion was administered only to such believers. The result in church life brought out a remarkable staying quality. Today (1922) the Baptists have the largest number of churches and of communicants of any denomination in the county, and a very conscientious and vital hold upon the whole religious and ethical life hereabouts.

The beginnings were naturally east of the Thames river. On the very year that the General Assembly of the Colony set off Groton township from New London (1705), the First Baptist Church of Groton was organized at Old Mystic, the venerable "Mother" of all that followed. The story of the Wightmans—father, son and grandson—in establishing the principles for which the denomination has ever stood in this county, is a truly remarkable and heroic one. At the first, individuals and families west of the Thames, sympathizing with this movement, connected themselves with this first church. But in 1710 the First Baptist Church, in what was later called Waterford (1801), was organized as the second Baptist church in the Colony. Stephen Gorton was ordained its pastor in 1726, and for a generation went widely over the western part of the county preaching his faith and practicing its rites. Some trouble interrupted his labors, arising out of personal matters and doubtless partly out of disturbances connected with "Separatist" movements connected with the revival enthusiasm of the "Great Awakening". A majority of his church stood by him and seem to have been disfellowshipped with him by the other Baptist churches in the vicinity. At any rate, the minority went off and continued the First Church under the leadership of Elder Peckham.

We have record of special contentions throughout the whole of that period before the Revolutionary War against the State-Church system, and the proclamation of religious liberty by these earnest folk, who suffered hardship for their faith at the hands of the Puritan church leaders. They had to share the obliquy of all the Non-conformists (Rogerenes, Separatists, Adventists, etc.), in disregarding many rules and laws and customs of the Colony. This came to a climax about 1748, when a lodgment of the venerable Elder Peckham and his intrepid colleague, Green, and many of their followers in New London jail in the winter time, with no fire or bedding and with insufficient food, gave wide publicity to the matter. This local persecution called forth deepest sympathy and a signal protest from the ranks of even their opponents. The president of Yale College issued at once, on hearing of the affair, a pamphlet on "The Essential Rights of Protestants," in which he gave a scorching rebuke to the intolerance of the existing laws and set forth the rights of conscience and the principles of civil and religious liberty. This had much to do with the overthrow of the old and impossible system, and of bringing in the new order more in harmony with the American ideal. The larger freedom that ensued gave great encouragement to the increasing numbers of conscientious Baptists in the county.

In the meanwhile, in the north-eastern part of the township (Waterford, later) the second Baptist church had been established (1730), which in later years seems to have been reorganized by the Board of the Connecticut Baptist State Convention and is sometimes called the "Quaker Hill" church. In 1741 came the North Stonington First, in 1765 the North Stonington Second, in 1767 the Salem Baptist church, in 1769 the East Lyme church, in 1775 the Stonington First, and in 1780 the Scott Hill church in Colchester. The Stonington church has had a long and most honorable career, and is a leading religious force in the eastern section of the county

The name of Nathan Howard appears as the second pastor of the Old First at Waterford. His rare personality greatly endeared him to the people. His long illness and sudden death in 1777 brought a grievous blow to the cause he represented. Baptist pastors for the most part in those days earned their own livelihood in various occupations, especially in farming. Elder Howard was an expert fisherman as well as a fisher of souls. He discovered in the Sound a prolific fishing ground, ever since a favorite resort. It appears on the mariners' charts as "Howard's Ledge".

In 1775 there began in the First Church at Waterford that remarkable succession of the Darrows. Elder Zadok Darrow had grown up in the church, and in so high a regard was he held that the mantle of the beloved Howard fell on him. In the midst of a general decline of religion in the county, we find this ardent apostle of a vital faith covering in his activities wide sections, being wellnigh omnipresent, like a second Athanasius. The seed thus scattered was to bear abundant fruitage. In his day (1789) was formed the "Groton Conference" of Baptist churches as well as the "Stonington Conference". In 1817 came the New London Baptist Association, embracing the churches of that order west of the Thames. In that same year the Groton and Stonington Conferences were merged into the "Stonington Union Association".

Elder Zadok Darrow passed away in 1827, in the 99th year of his age He was succeeded by his grandson, Francis Darrow, who had been converted in the great revival of 1794, and who had been for a long time an assistant to the older man. The strong ministry of the younger Darrow of more than forty years averaged seventeen immersions a year, totaling about seven hundred converts. A large number of these became ministers of the Gospel

The widespread fruitage of the labors of the Wightmans and Darrows is seen in the rapid organization of Baptist churches all over New London County, beginning with the First Church at Norwich in 1800. Within the half century following, twenty-five churches were founded in territory now included in the county, not to speak of many more outside This makes up more than half the number and much more than half the strength of the entire Baptists in the county.

In 1804 the Baptists moved into New London proper and established the First Baptist Church, thus making straight the way for its long and growingly powerful service at the heart of things. Mention must be made here of the particular helpfulness of this church in the Great War. At considerable personal sacrifice its building was enlarged and fully equipped and placed at the disposal of the soldiers and sailors at this important centre of war activity Its pastor, Rev Charles R. McNally, donned the uniform and served as Army and Navy Pastor in New London under the auspices of the Northern Baptist Convention and the Connecticut Baptist Convention. The church has since then been active through its pastor, Rev. Chester H Howe, and its members in the Federation of Churches in New London and vicinity, of which federation Mr Howe was the first president.

Lebanon (1805), North Lyme (1810), Moodus (1810), Preston City (1815), Chesterfield (1824), North Stonington Third (1828), Packerville (1828), Colchester Borough (1830), Bozrah (1831), Voluntown (1832), and Jewett City (1840), followed in rapid succession. Special mention may properly be made here of the long and successful pastorate at Colchester of Rev. B. D. Remington

That year of 1840 was signalized by the organization of the Norwich Central Baptist Church, which has grown steadily and become a power not only for its own denomination, but for our common Christianity in the county Of recent years the names of Herr, Wright, Slocum and Purkiss have made the pastorate of that church notable in the State.

In that same year (1840) the Montauk Baptist Church of New London was founded, and which now worships in its attractive new church in the southern section of the city The zeal and success of the denomination in New London is evidenced in the founding of the Huntington Street Baptist Church in 1849, which is rejoicing at this writing in the long and fruitful ministry of Rev. Joseph A Elder (1899—). In close connection with the origin of this enterprise is found the name and fame of Elder Jabez Swan, whose remarkable personality became a constituent part of New London tradition. His influence was widely felt throughout the county, as he exercised his evangelistic gifts, sooner or later, in almost every Baptist community. His piquant remarks have come down like proverbs in the whole region round about, linking his personality up to the Wightmans and Darrows as outstanding religious influences in the county.

In 1842 came the establishment of the Montville Union Baptist and Lake's Pond, while Niantic (1843), Ledyard (1843), Groton Heights (1843). and Noank (1843), came on in rapid succession, the most of them being the results of special revival interests. The Noank and Groton Heights churches stand strongly up in the list of vigorous workers The long pastorate of Rev. George R. Atha at the Groton Heights church calls for special comment.

The Old Lyme Church was established in 1846, Stonington Third in 1846, Poquonnock Bridge in 1856, and Mystic Union in 1864. The latter is a strong church and with promising signs of enlarged work The Grace Memorial (1871) at Norwich, Fitchville (1887). Laurel Glen (1894), and Mt Calvary (1903), in Norwich, also are the more recent organizations, as well as the Shiloh (Colored) Baptist Church (1894) in New London.

A word should be said at this point as to the Stonington Union Sabbath School Convention, which was founded in 1858 and is still a vigorous exponent of the religious life of the Baptist churches east of the Thames river in New London county. The last few years have seen strong and united work within the Stonington Union Association under the lead of a special missionary who works with the pastorless churches in that section.

A roster of the Baptist pastors at this writing (1922) in New London county shows the names of thirty pastors and missionaries at work in these forty-three churches It is probable that never in the history of the county has there been a more effective body of Baptist ministers serving these organizations. The membership of the Baptist churches of New London county totals 6,173. of whom 4,856 are put down in the last report as "resident members." There seems to be a tendency to co-operate with other denominations in the county wherever practicable. Special efforts are made to this end in the rural districts. Strong men are at the helm, and the future looks bright for the co-operative labors for the religious well-being of the county as far as this earnest fellowship and bring it about

V.

THE EPISCOPAL CHURCH IN NEW LONDON

Rt. Reverend Chauncey Bunce Brewster, D D , Bishop of Connecticut.
Rt. Reverend E Champion Acheson, D.D., Suffragan Bishop of Connecticut.

Rev. J. Eldred Brown, Archdeacon of the New London Archdeanry.

Place	Church or Mission	Communicants
Black Hall (Old Lyme).....St. Ann's Mission........................		52
Rev. Johnson, Missionary in Charge		
Colchester. .... Calvary Church		19
Rev. Theodore D. Martin, Rector		
Groton................Bishop Seabury Memorial..		82
Rev. Frederick W .Haist, Rector		
Jewett City............... Episcopal Mission		
Archdeacon Brown in Charge		
Mystic....................St. Mark's Church		173
Rev. John Beauchamp, Rector		
New London...............St. James's Church....		707
Rev. Philip Markham Kerredge, Rector		
New London............... Pequot Chapel		
Niantic....................St. John's Chapel......................		75
Rev. Johnson, Missionary in Charge		
Noank..................... Grace Chapel		22
Rev John Beauchamp, Priest in Charge		
Norwich.................... Christ Church		396
Rev. Richard D. Graham, Rector		
Norwich................... Trinity Church		277
Rev. J. Eldred Brown, Rector		
Norwich..................St. Andrew's Church................. ...		200
Rev. William H. Smith, Rector		
Poquetanuk................St. James's Church...		115
Rev. Thomas H. M. Ockford, Rector		
South Lyme..............St. Michael's Church....................		13
Rev. Johnson, Missionary in Charge		
Stonington................ Calvary Church		131
Rev. Frederick R. Sanford, Rector		
Yantic..................... Grace Church		121

2,382

The reader has noted on previous pages glimpses of the beginnings of
Episcopacy within the borders of New London county. It seems clear that
it did not spring out of the original Puritan settlers, but grew up gradually and predominantly from newcomers, especially those interested in shipping and commerce. These at an early date showed a tendency, both in
New London and Norwich, to form social groups of a less austere type
than prevailed, whose members craved for themselves and their families
the liturgical forms of worship to which they had been accustomed elsewhere, and particularly in the old country. But still there are notable
instances where they did not fail to do their part in honoring religion in

their new domiciles even in its puritanic form. We find record of the payment by such of the minister's rate and of the rental of pews, as well as other indications of a general goodwill toward their more or less uncongenial spiritual surroundings. When the time came that they could honorably and legally proceed to do so, they began to organize themselves into churches after their own desires. Descendants also of some of the leading founders of the colony (Winthrops, Saltonstalls, Bulkeleys, etc.) are found co-operating in this later development.

It is evident that New England presented quite a serious problem to the Church of England Boston and Plymouth gave no encouragement except among the British officials and their families. Early efforts to set up Episcopacy in Boston were stigmatized by the unfortunate tyranny of Andros. But King's Chapel was opened in 1689, though under bitter opposition from the Puritan leaders Newport, Rhode Island, was more congenial, and in 1698 Trinity Church was founded there, soon followed in 1707 by the famous Narragansett Church. But if New England was to be won back to the Church of England, the Colony of Connecticut must be the key to unlock the door.

The report of Rev. Dr. Bray to the authorities in England as to his investigations in New England and elsewhere led in the very year of the founding of what grew into Yale College (1701) to the establishment of the Venerable Society for the Propagation of the Gospel in Foreign Parts. Mention has been made of the visit of the early New England missioners (Messrs. Keith and Talbot) from this Society to New London in 1702, and of their cordial reception at the hands of Governor Fitz-John Winthrop, and Rev. Gurdon Saltonstall, pastor of the First Church of Christ there. Near to the south-western edge of the Colony, at Stratford, the first Episcopal church was started, with grave opposition, almost leading to a riot in 1706, and fully established in the years following.

In the early struggles to get onto its feet, the Collegiate Institute of Connecticut (Yale), originally situated within the boundaries of New London county at Saybrook and later moved to New Haven (1716), sought to build up a library. A consignment of two hundred books was sent over from England for this purpose by Sir John Davie, a recent resident of Groton (Ct.) and was followed soon by seven hundred more from an agent of the Institute in London. A few years later, Bishop Berkeley, who was seeking to establish in the Bermudas a college for the education and civilization of the American Indians and who was residing during the time of futile waiting in Rhode Island, before his return to England, was induced to add his valuable library to the Yale collection (1731). The eagerness with which the instructors and students of the college absorbed the contents of the books, embracing as they did the finest assortment of contemporary literature in England, together with a number of controversial, philosophical and theological books vindicating the Church of England as against the Puritans, proved to be more effective in winning favor for Episcopacy in Connecticut than all the efforts of the Venerable Society for the Propagation of the Gospel in Foreign Parts. By 1722 the president of the college and other principal instructors and a group of most influential Congregational clergymen in the vicinity boldly proclaimed their adherence to Episcopal views, to the consternation of the trustees and the Congregational constituency throughout the Colony. Needless to say, resignations were called for, and the college trustees put up bars against a repetition of a like invasion. There is no telling what would have happened had the young men been more patient, and thus more deeply inoculated the Congregational ministry of Connecticut with churchly ideals before letting the break come.

One of the students, profoundly affected by this episode at New Haven, was Samuel Seabury, born July 8, 1706, to John Seabury, a deacon in the First Church of Christ in Groton, Connecticut. Young Seabury left Yale at the rupture, followed President Cutler to Boston, and finished his course at Harvard (1724). But he still kept the Congregational connection, and prepared himself for its ministry. We find him soon married to Abigail Mumford, of Groton, Connecticut, and preaching as a licentiate at the North Groton (Ledyard) Church, where his second son, Samuel, was baptized. His wife was daughter to one of the most devout and influential members of the Episcopal church in New London, though living in Groton. The combination of the death of this young wife, the strong influences from that side of the family, the formative episode at Yale, the intimacies fostered with Cutler in Boston and Johnson in Stratford, Connecticut, (soon to become president of King's College in New York City), and other powerful adherents of the Church of England, at length induced the elder Rev. Samuel Seabury in 1731 to demit his Congregational ministry. As a widower he went to England, was ordained by the Bishop of London, and returned to America in 1732 as a missioner of the Venerable Society for the Propagation of the Gospel in Foreign Parts. He was stationed at New London, and soon married Elizabeth Powell, an ardent Episcopalian lady of the Narragansett, Rhode Island, church.

Ever since the mission of Messrs. Keith and Talbot in 1702, the Episcopal contingent in New London had been growing, gathering to itself many elements of strength. As a port of entry, with its official collector of customs, a group of English families somewhat different from the staid Puritan strain began to be formed, of people who had been reared in the older English traditions and who craved the forms of worship that followed the church year, with Christmas and Easter emphasized, and the venerable Episcopal liturgy. On June 6, 1725 a subscription had been begun for the erection of a "church for the service of Almighty God according to the Liturgie of the Church of England as by law established." The names of Mumford, Merritt, Buor and Goddard appear at the first, followed later by the Winthrops and Saltonstalls. The first church building (undedicated because of the absence of a Bishop) was erected on the Parade. It was built of oak, and had a bell, being first used in 1732. Rev. Samuel Seabury, Sr., was its first rector. Wide interest was taken in the establishment of this church, subscriptions coming from as far afield as Newport and New York. The belfry was surmounted by a staff at the end of which was a gilded ball at the summit. Once upon a time as a group of Indians was

N L—1-20

parading by, one of the Red Men shot an arrow at the ball and the arrow's head became embedded so deeply in the ball that it became a fixture

In the meanwhile, another of the Yale group reached through the library. Rev. Ebenezer Punderson, had been ordained in his twenty-first year as pastor of the North Groton Congregational Church, succeeding Rev. Samuel Seabury, Sr. After only two and a half years of service, Mr. Punderson suddenly announced to his congregation that he planned to seek Episcopal ordination. Strong effort was made to keep him, but in vain. A number of his parishioners in the northern part of the township and over in the town of Preston, came together and established the St. James's parish of Poquetanock, just over the border in Preston. After being inducted into the Episcopal ministry by a new ordination, Mr. Punderson made the Poquetanock church the basis of a most extensive work for the cause he had espoused. The reactions from the extravagances of the Great Awakening proved helpful for the growth of his more orderly and dignified conduct of religious services.

The faithful ministry of Rev. Samuel Seabury, Sr, in New London terminated in the acceptance of a call from the church at Hempstead, Long Island, in 1743. That year was marked by the strange extravagancies of the followers of Davenport who got the people to burn books and costly clothing, the leader himself bringing the flames a pair of expensive velvet breeches as his sacrifice of luxury St. James's Church, as it was now called, was without a rector until the coming of Rev Matthew Graves, a native of the Isle of Man, who served the church until the days of the American Revolution. He was a bachelor, peculiar in manner, retiring in disposition, and who gave offense to his Episcopal brethren by attending the ordination of a Congregational minister. The growth of St. James was quiet and steady. When the revolt of the Colonies took place, Mr Graves could not violate his oath or go back on the old flag, even though George III. was not a wise ruler His church people, however, were filled with patriotic colonial fervor Things came to a crisis, when on November 14, 1778, the church voted that the clergyman must pray for Congress and the United Colonies. Mr. Graves brought on a riot by attempting to pray for the royal family. He was sent under a flag of truce to New York, where he died soon after. During the Benedict Arnold raid (September 6, 1781), the church, probably because of the notorious American sentiments of its members, was burned to the ground. This catastrophe laid low the activities of St. James throughout the remainder of the war. But on the signing of the treaty of peace in 1783 and on Easter Monday morning, we find the usual annual meeting held (April 25, 1783) and the project of rebuilding was undertaken.

The origin of Episcopacy in Norwich is somewhat obscure Services seem to have been held in private houses in Chelsea (Norwich) by Rev. Samuel Seabury, Sr., and later by Rev. Ebenezer Punderson until his removal from Poquetanok to New Haven in 1751. An edifice for worship was constructed on the site of the present Christ Church about 1750 Eighty subscribers assisted. Between 1751 and 1763 the new organization got on with lay readers and occasional clerical supplies. In that year, Rev. John

Beardsley came from England, serving Christ Church for five years. He was succeeded by Rev John Tyler in 1769, whose long ministry of fifty-four years (to 1823) seems to be one of the record ministries in the county.

In the meanwhile, Samuel Seabury, Jr., had grown to manhood, and was graduated from Yale College in 1748. He went to Scotland to study medicine, but was led to change to the study of theology. He was ordained a deacon by the Bishop of Lincoln and as priest by the Bishop of Carlisle. Returning to America, he served several churches or missions in New Jersey before marrying and settling down as rector at Westchester, New York. During the Revolution he was a royalist, and served as chaplain in the British army.

Upon the proclamation of peace, the Connecticut clergymen asked Mr Seabury to go to England and seek consecration as their Bishop. This he undertook to do. But such was the bitterness in England over the issue of the war that they refused to consecrate one who would not swear fealty to the British ruler. Whereupon Rev. Samuel Seabury, Jr, went to Aberdeen, Scotland, and was consecrated November 14, 1784, as a Bishop by a Bishop in the disestablished Episcopal Church of Scotland. He returned to America in 1785 via Newport, Rhode Island, and took up his residence in New London. His wife having died, his daughter took charge of his home. He at once took up the local work as rector in addition to the burden of his extensive diocese, to which Rhode Island was soon added. He began preaching in the new court house, until in September he could consecrate the new St. James's Church, then located on Main street.

The erection of this new edifice was a heavy task to the little company of faithful ones left after the war. A cupola was added in 1794, in which a French bell, brought by Captain Hurlbut from the West Indies, was hung. To New London from all over the United States came candidates for holy office for consecration. Innumerable problems came to Bishop Seabury for solution. He had much to do with the adaptation of the Book of Common Prayer to American uses. Here his connection with the Scotch branch of Episcopacy was especially marked. On February 25, 1796, at the age of sixty-seven, he was suddenly stricken down by apoplexy and left his many burdens to others.

His son, Charles Seabury, was elected rector on March 28, 1796, and continued the local work until 1814. As noted elsewhere, these were years of greatest spiritual decline everywhere in New England, and it was especially so in New London county. Salaries of clergymen and cost of living were on a starving basis. When this pastorate came to an end, St. James was content to get on for a while with a lay reader. Rev. Solomon Blakeslee found three years (1815-1818) as long as he could carry on the work. His leadership was, however, signalized by the installation of the first church organ in New London. Rev. Bethel Judd was the succeeding rector (1818-1832). While of the "evangelical school", he strenuously asserted the divine right of Episcopacy. During his ministry a Sunday school was established at St James. Mr Judd had an admiring parishioner in a Colonel Walbach, a Roman Catholic, who had a pew in St James. When Bishop Cheverus of

Boston came to administer the rites of the Catholic church in New London, the rector had him preach in his pulpit. Not to be outdone in courtesy, the Congregational minister opened also his pulpit to the genial Catholic Bishop, who preached on "Martha and Mary".

The short ministry of Rev. Isaac W. Hallam (1833-34) was followed by the long and fruitful labors of Rev. Robert A Hallam (1835-1877). During the enlargement of the church building, services were held by invitation in the Second Congregational Church. The growth of St. James steadily advanced under this wise ministry, calling for still larger facilities. On November 3, 1847, the cornerstone of the present beautiful gothic structure in which St. James worships was laid. Three long years of heroic struggle brought the consecration day (June 11, 1850). Mr. Hallam was formally constituted rector on August 1st of that same year. In 1855 the will of Jonathan Coit, Esq., of the Second Congregational Church, gave the community a thrill when it announced that each Protestant church in New London (seven in all) had received a substantial bequest. The sum of $3,000 came to St. James.

The present parish house was erected in 1859 as a rectory. In 1867 the church was enlarged by the addition of a vestry. In 1872 an associate clergyman was appointed (Rev Robert M. Duff), who was active in the beginnings of the Bishop Seabury Memorial Church in Groton (1875). Dr. Hallam's long and blessed ministry terminated with his death in 1877 Rev. William Buckingham, the associate minister from 1876, succeeded as rector until 1885 The year following, Rev Alanson Douglass Miller began a short ministry (1886-1889), when Rev. Alfred Pool Grint, Ph.D , came for a service of nineteen years. In 1896 the centenary of the death of Bishop Seabury was commemorated. In 1900, on St. Barnabas Day, the fiftieth annniversary of the consecration of the present place of worship was observed. In 1910, Rev Philip Markham Kerredge began his work at St. James, during which the growth has gone on steadily. The installation of an organ in memory of Mrs Morton M Plant equipped the stately church to voice the deepest things of the spirit. Under its ministry a strong, broad, Christian fellowship is drawing all Christians together.

All this while, the Norwich phase of the Archdeaconry developed apace. The name "Christ's Church of Chelsea" was first used in 1785 as the ministry of Rev. John Tyler began to gather up the broken fragments after the Revolution days. In 1789, Christ's Church was moved to a more central part of Norwich, and dedicated by Bishop Seabury in 1791. The revered rector was also an adept in medicine, and went far and wide among all types of people in Norwich, healing the body as well as the soul. In 1823 he was succeeded by Rev. Seth Paddock, under whose administration the parish greatly expanded from sixty to nearly four hundred families in a score of years. It was during the succeeding ministry of Rev. William F. Morgan that the new parish of Trinity Church was set off in the growing city, with Rev. Edward O. Flagg for its first rector. Both churches have had a distinguished ministry. The succession at Christ Church has such names as Walden, Banks, Binney, Geisy, Nelson (now Bishop of Albany), Emery, Davies (now Bishop of Western Massachusetts) The present rector, the Rev Richard R. Graham, is (1922) rounding out ten years of strong service. The rector of Trinity Church is also Archdeacon, the Rev. J. Eldred Brown.

In the meanwhile, Calvary Church was established in Stonington in 1847, with Rev. Junius Marshall Willey as rector. Its beautiful church was designed by the distinguished architect, Upjohn. St. Mark's of Mystic was organized into a full parish in 1865. In Norwich came a third parish in due course of time, St. Andrew's, and later another at Yantic. The missionary zeal of the Archdeaconry has added a number of smaller churches, chapels and mission stations, as set down in the roster at the beginning of this statement. It is as true of these Episcopal churches as it is of the churches of the other denominations, that today the ministry and the churches average as well if not better than at any time in the past and look forward to a strong future in closer relations with the common heart of Christianity throughout the county. The Archdeaconry embraces sixteen churches, chapels and other places of worship within New London county, several of them ranking with the most beautiful specimens of architecture in the State. It has a company of a dozen devoted clergy, who have leadership over 2,382 communicants and many more than ten thousand parishioners.

VI.

METHODISM IN NEW LONDON COUNTY

No phase in the development of religion in New London county is more picturesque than that of the work done under the auspices of the Methodist Episcopal Church. Though it was the latest of the larger Protestant bodies to enter and cultivate this field, and thus escaped all but the very minor and quite negligible persecutions incident to any religious propaganda, Methodism came to do a most needed work. The imagination follows the circuit rider as he made his way about the county from sympathetic house to house and from class-meeting to class-meeting, then from school-house to school-house and finally from church to church, pressing home in free utterance of prayer and sermon the vital things of a plain gospel.

We are particularly attracted by the heroic figure of Jesse Lee, who passed through the southern part of the county in 1789. Tradition tells of his preaching at Lyme and Niantic, but the date of September 2, 1789, comes clearly to view, as on that Wednesday he preached in New London at the newly-built court-house the first sermon under Methodist auspices. His reception seems to have been most kindly, according to a New London precedent, and the fervid apostle of a faith that was stirring the English-speaking race on both sides of the Atlantic was impressed with the hunger for warm-hearted and vital religion in New London. We will recall that the pastor of the First Church of Christ in New London at the time was Rev. Henry Channing, who was accounted a Unitarian in faith, and was receiving into membership into his church on the basis of reputable moral character, going to the limit in applying the spirit of the "Halfway Covenant." The Episcopal Church there was at a low ebb in its somewhat formal religious life. Baptists had not yet entered this seaport town. Indeed, Connecticut as a whole

seemed to need something that Methodism could give, and was the open
door to all New England On September 25th of that same year (1789),
Jesse Lee organized at Stratford, Connecticut, the very first Methodist church
in New England, where some eighty years before Episcopacy, not without
opposition, had also found its open door to Connecticut.

In 1791, Bishop Asbury came through New London on his way to Lynn,
Massachusetts, and preached by way of paying for the hospitality received.
In 1793 a Methodist conference held at Tolland, Connecticut, appointed
George Roberts the elder in charge of all work in Connecticut The State
was organized into five circuits, of which one was the New London circuit,
embracing all Eastern Connecticut from the Massachusetts line to the Sound.
In October of that year (1793) a "class" was formed in New London, and
Elder George Roberts began preaching in the court-house. One early convert was Epaphras Kibby, who in 1798 began his work as a travelling preacher,
known throughout New England, carrying on a ministry sixty-seven years in
length We have seen elsewhere the mighty stirring of waters in New London county during a general revival in 1794, and Methodism must be given
credit for its pervasive power. Throughout the circuit 219 persons were now
gathered into "classes," and thirty-nine of these joined the Methodist membership in New London. One of these was Daniel Burrows, who became a
local preacher, a member of Congress, and one in the convention that adopted
the present State Constitution On July 15, 1795, Bishop Asbury held a
conference in the home of this Daniel Burrows, when nineteen preachers
were present. In 1798 the first church was built. On a Friday it was "raised,"
and on the Sunday following it was dedicated, Jesse Lee and Bishop Asbury
being present and preaching. This first Methodist church building (completed in 1800) stood on Golden Hill, at the corner of Union and Methodist
streets On April 17, 1808, a second conference was held in New London,
with fifty preachers in attendance. The little church not being large enough,
the authorities of the First Church of Christ (Congregational) courteously
tendered their church for the ordination services, Bishop Asbury officiating
and preaching. In 1816 a revival of exceptional proportions swept the whole
region round about, affecting all classes in the community and all denominations Its principal human agency is manifested by the fact that three hundred persons were received at that time into the Methodist church.

This made it necessary to build a new church. The original structure
was sold and removed (to be again used, however), and the new building
was erected on the old site in 1818. In that year the New London church
at its own request was made a station, and Rev. Asa Kent was placed in
charge Of necessity, a careful reorganization of the church ensued which,
with many other causes, brought many years of discord to New London
Methodism By 1820 one hundred and fifty persons were admitted into the
church, sixty-eight names were removed from the roll, twenty dropped,
three persons withdrew, and twenty-four were expelled.

In 1820, Rev. Elijah Hedding (afterwards Bishop) came to the charge.
He found in the church a "boisterous element" that overtaxed his strength,
and he had to leave with broken health In 1827 things came to a crisis in

the church, with disagreements among trustees, church people and minister, which led to an open rupture. In 1829 the church building was shut by the trustees against the members, who thereupon secured the use of the original church building. The trouble brewed for ten years. Then (1830) a new board of trustees with Rev. James Potter (1831-2), managed by good administration and firm discipline to settle the difficulties. Some were expelled, others withdrew. A revival ensued But bitter contention over the slavery question led forty members to form a Wesleyan Methodist Episcopal church, which discarded the bishopric, and were given the use of the church building by the trustees.

The original Methodist church was now reduced to one hundred and fifty-five members. The meetings were held as best they could be, finally in the court house. Here the work prospered, a gracious revival added largely to the membership, a project for a new building went forward, and the new sructure on Washington street was dedicated in 1842.

In the meanwhile, the larger work of the New London circuit went on apace. Jesse Lee had preached the first Methodist sermon in Norwich Town, in the home of Mrs. Thankful Pierce, on June 25, 1790. Bishop Asbury had secured an enterprising audience at 8 a. m. on July 20, 1795, and a "class" had been formed in 1796 with Solomon Williams as class-leader. The "Norwich North" Methodist church building was dedicated in 1831, Erastus Wentworth, Esq., a local Congregationalist, materially assisting. The conversion of his son Erastus in the ensuing revival amply repaid him. This was the Rev. Erastus Wentworth This church had a steady career, broken by a marked revival in 1857, when sixty were received into the church.

Early in that century, at the Landing, a Methodist church had been organized and a meeting-house erected But the great flood of February, 1824, had swept away the building. Baptists, Universalists, Congregationalists and Episcopalians hastened each to offer the bereft Methodists a place for worship The General Assembly at Hartford voted to have the Governor issue a proclamation to all churches in the State to set aside a certain Sunday for raising funds to help replace the Methodist church at Norwich Landing. This netted $463.32, and the new house was dedicated in 1825 and was called the Sachem Street Church The East Main Street Methodist Church, in another part of the city, had been organized and its meeting-house dedicated in 1816. In 1854, the Norwich Central Church was organized and endorsed by the Conference. It dedicated its meeting-house in 1859. At last, in 1895, through the wisdom and indefatigable energy of Presiding Elder E. Tirrell, aided by the pastors of the three churches, a consolidation was accomplished, which secured the approval of the Quarterly Conference. The new church was called the Trinity Methodist Episcopal Church of Norwich It has fully justified the wisdom of those who brought it into existence. It has had a succession of strong pastors. On its quarter of a century milestone it reported (1920) a membership of four hundred and seventy-two, which has since had a marked increase. Its present (1922) pastor, Rev. R. L. Roberts, has the work strongly in hand and the prospects are most cheering.

But the genius of Methodism is quite as much seen in its rural activities.

Colchester was reached as early as 1806, though a church was not built until 1842. Methodism did a distinctly valuable work at that point as long as the mills were active. Since the closing of these, the church has dwindled, and is now little more than a supplied preaching station.

The Gales Ferry Church is a successful rural exemplar of Methodism in New London county. George Roberts preached here at an open air service in 1793, and for ten years there were occasional services in homes or out under the sky. A class was formed in 1803 under the leadership of Ralph Hurlbutt. In 1806 he was licensed to exhort, and in 1810 to preach, becoming practically the pastor. He is set down in the histories as their first preacher, 1806-1840. An abandoned building formerly used by an old Separatist Congregational Church, three miles to the east of Gales Ferry, was purchased and moved (1803) to the site of the present church. In 1859 the present church edifice was dedicated, and later there came a parsonage. The laymen and women of this church have been especially active. Its memberbership in 1920 was 54.

The Old Mystic Methodist Church dates from 1826, ten years after school-house services had been held. The first pastor lived and preached in the home of John Bennet for a year. In 1827 the mill proprietors (Hydes) became deeply interested in the organization, and the school-house was re-opened. In 1831, Rev. Daniel Dorchester was appointed to the Mystic Circuit (including Griswold, Preston and North Stonington). The church building came in 1849, only to be destroyed by fire in 1851. The Jubilee was celebrated in 1876.

The prosperous Uncasville church dates from 1829, when a small society was formed not without opposition. But in 1835 the first meeting-house was erected and the work put on a strong basis. Revival after revival blessed the church. In 1872 the present fine structure was erected, and later a chapel added. Rev. Charles Smith is in the midst (1922) of a strong pastorate. The church is an active member of the Federation of Churches of New London and vicinity.

The Griswold or Voluntown organization (Bethel) dates back to 1841. In that year the meeting-house was erected on land deeded for 999 years. In that same year (1841) the Mystic (Bridge) Church was started, connected at first with the old Mystic organization. It was the outcome of a great revival in which the famous Elder Swan (Baptist) of New London co-operated with the Methodist pastor, Rev. Benjamin C. Phelps, at Old Mystic. At the close of the meetings, both Baptist and Methodist converts went down into the river together and were baptized by immersion. In 1842 the first settled minister was appointed at Mystic. The present church was erected in 1867. Rev. Jerome Greer is (1922) in the midst of a very successful pastorate in Mystic and Noank.

Jesse Lee, en route through Lyme, preached, as tradition would have it, on September 1, 1789. The growth of Methodism, however, was very slow. In 1843 a church was dedicated, largely through the assistance of Stephen Peck, who, tradition says, had been a leader of a rough opposition gang. At a meeting in a private house he had arisen as a sign for a riot to begin, when a cat leaped upon his back from a bureau and so frightened him that before the meeting was over he had yielded to the earnest appeal of the preacher. The Methodist work does not seem to have thrived in this region, and in 1920 a membership of only twelve was reported.

The same year (1842) the traditions of the preaching of Jesse Lee in Niantic bore fruit and a church was organized. This had been preceded by class-meetings and itinerant preaching. A church was built at that time. In 1873 the present edifice was erected, and later a parsonage. In 1882-83 a large number of Swedish Methodists joined the church. In 1890 an Epworth League was established. Rev. G H. Wright is the present pastor (1922), and the membership stood at ninety-three in 1920.

The Jewett City church was started in 1874 with a class and a Sunday school. A revival service in that year was followed by a church organization in 1875. Baltic, Gardner Lake and Versailles were other points where small groups of Methodists formed churches, and where, at one time or another, organizations have been active.

In 1863 a band of Abolitionists came out from the Baptist church in Noank, and seem to have kept together for a number of years In 1878, after a revival service, a Methodist church was built. This organization is linked by a common pastorate with the Mystic (Bridge) Church

We left the Methodist Church at New London just moving into the Washington street meeting-house in 1842. Here, after all its ancient troubles, the church greatly thrived. On June 4, 1843, it celebrated the semi-centennial of Methodism in New London. Revivals and steady growth by 1854 had made the building inadequate to the needs of the organization. The difficult project was carried to a successful issue, and the imposing Methodist church building on Federal street (now the Jewish Synagogue) was dedicated in 1856. The legacy from Jonathan Coit, Esq (Congregationalist), was a substantial aid in this effort

In this much enlarged equipment, Methodism in New London forged ahead under a series of able pastors. A parsonage was secured in 1882 through the activities of the Ladies' Aid Society. Bishop Ames presided over a conference here in 1864, and other conferences were entertained in 1877 and 1891. In 1893 the centennial of the advent of Methodism in New London County was duly commemorated.

The lengthened pastorate of the late Rev. C Harley Smith (1911-1918) in the Federal Street Church will be long remembered by the present generation.

In 1918 began the pastorate of Rev Myron T. Genter. It soon became evident that Methodism in New London needed a much ampler equipment for its strong development Fortunately, it had kept a solid unity in the city, and had a host of friends on the outside. With marked heroism, the pastor and his official board took hold of the project. Land was secured for a new structure directly north of the old court house in which Jesse Lee preached in 1793. With rare business sagacity, the project was carried through, and the beautiful church, with ample equipment for social purpose, was dedicated by Bishop Edwin H. Hughes, November 13, 1921. The dedication came at the close of a series of evangelistic services in the church and community conducted by Rev. Dr. Milton S. Reese. One most interesting and inspiring event following the dedication services was the welcoming of one hundred and twenty-seven new members as the first official act in the newly consecrated building. This brought the entire membership up to seven hundred and nine. The church and its pastor have been active in the Federation of the Churches of New London County and Vicinity since its origin in 1920.

Thus it is seen that while Methodism in New London county stands fourth in numbers among the Protestant bodies, it has been a powerful element in the spiritual development of the Kingdom of God in south-eastern Connecticut. The New London county contingent of the Norwich District under the administration of Rev. William H. Bath as superintendent, includes eighteen churches and preaching stations, with about twelve hundred members. They form a strong harmonizing element in the religious life of the county.

VII.

OTHER RELIGIOUS BODIES IN NEW LONDON COUNTY

Scattered throughout New London are a large number of Protestant denominations with one or more small organizations doing faithful work for the Kingdom of God. In New London there are the Evangelical Lutheran Church, the A. M. E. Zion Church, All Souls' Church (Federated Universalist-Unitarian)* and the First Church of Christ, Scientist, together with a number of auxiliary organizations like the Learned Mission and the Salvation Army. The Y. M. C. A. and the Y. W. C. A. form the specialized institutional work for young men and women by the churches. In Norwich there are also similar groups of organizations, the Universalist Church being of long standing in that community. The data for all this scattered effort is not easy to gather.

THE YOUNG MEN'S CHRISTIAN ASSOCIATION

Among the many organizations which have come into existence in this county during the past sixty years, none has proved more effective or valuable than the Young Men's Christian Association. On June 1, 1867, in the town of New London, forty-seven young men met and organized a "Y. M. C. A.," which has existed continuously up to the present day with increasing value to the churches and the community, and from which thousands of young men and boys have carried influence and inspiration into other States and perhaps into foreign lands. As the years passed, Associations were formed in other towns in the county, but their history is brief, the work having been abandoned for various reasons, principally lack of trained leadership.

In those early days the activities of this Association were largely of a religious nature, and therefore did not appeal to young men of all classes. At the same time the social feature was recognized by the directors as somewhat necessary; they also encouraged the formation of a Literary Society, which became a means of benefit to those who were interested in it.

*See page 321

Three years later, in 1870, the records showed a decided increase in the membership and in the amount of work which had been accomplished. More religious meetings were being held in different sections of the town, a building fund of $1,000 had been accumulated, and other features which had been added were attracting the favorable attention of the public.

For the next decade the work moved on in the usual way, with the emphasis still on the religious phase, but during the period 1880-1900, the last twenty years of the nineteenth century, the scope of the work was broadened, and in 1885 the first general secretary, Mr. R. F. True, was chosen to guide the Association's affairs and to devote his whole time to carrying out its important program for young men and boys. Mr. True assumed his duties in December, and the movement advanced steadily. After two years he resigned, but he had demonstrated to the directors that a general secretary was essential to the success of the Association, and the vacant position was soon filled by Mr. A. L. Willis, who had been an active worker in the New Haven Association for a number of years. Efficiency in all departments characterized his administration. Particularly noticeable were the increased membership and the greater prominence given to the physical department.

After the departure of Mr. Willis at the end of two years, a temporary secretary served for a few months. Then, on June 1, 1891, a permanent secretary was secured in the person of Mr. F. H. Law, a graduate of the International Training School of Springfield, Massachusetts, who filled the position four years. When he gave it up and left the city, he had the assurance that his labors were much appreciated and that the directors and members greatly regretted his decision.

Mr. Law was followed by Mr. Richard W. Mansfield, who had coöperated with him as assistant secretary. Mr. Mansfield remained in charge of the Association for seventeen years, doing a constructive work. A building was secured in the form of a residential home, to which a gymnasium was added as a valuable asset to the property. The whole plant was valued at about $20,000. Mr. Mansfield made numberless friends. When he resigned as the executive head of the Y. M. C. A., he was given the position of city missionary, which he still occupies to the great satisfaction of all the people of the city.

The next in chronological order was Mr. Charles A. Green, formerly of New Jersey. In the four years which he served as general secretary, dating from 1913, he did a noble work. The old property was disposed of and a new and commodious structure, erected at a cost of about $150,000, was dedicated on February 16, 1916. A few months later, Mr. Green was called to a larger field, and Mr. John C. Church succeeded him at New London, continuing in office until 1920. The present general secretary is Mr. Clyde L. Williamson. The work of the organization is in a prosperous condition and the outlook for the future is most encouraging.

The foregoing facts pertain to the town and city of New London, but the Y. M. C. A. movement in the county, even in those remote days, was not confined to that one place, for in 1870 the young men of Norwich organized an Association which flourished for a while, then was discontinued for the time being, because the necessary support from the community was with-held   After several years had elapsed, interest was re-created in the welfare of young men and boys, and a new Association was organized in 1885, which has been doing a most excellent work throughout the past thirty-seven years, with the loyal approval and liberal financial support of the public-spirited citizens.   One building was provided and dedicated in 1897.   At this writing a new and more modern structure is being erected and the old one is soon to be sold.

The activities of this Association have been broad.   The members have obtained rich benefits for themselves, but they have also endeavored to carry out the purpose of the Y. M. C A. Brotherhood—"A work for young men, by young men."   Nearly four decades ago the "Rose of New England" found its place among the Young Men's Christian Associations of America. Through the intervening years it has strengthened a host of young men and boys physically, socially, educationally and religiously, or has provided them with employment or homes, or has given them helpful counsel and advice.

The board of directors are to be congratulated upon their success in securing such efficient men as leaders for the work.   As they have come to the field in turn and assumed their duties and discharged their responsibilities as general secretaries, they have seemed to be, each one, performing his part in the same infinite plan.   Beginning with Mr. C. K. Flanders and continuing in succession, the list contains the names of Messrs. R. S. Ross, I. V. Cob-leigh, O E. Ryther, F. H. Merrill, F. R. Starkey, W. A Morse, and Edwin Hill, who is in the field today, having the confidence of all the people.

It would not be possible to express in financial terms or in statistics what has been done by these two organizations.   Suffice it to say that the time and money invested in both have produced results far beyond what the most sanguine could have anticipated.   Because of it all, Connecticut has better sons, better fathers, better citizens, better laymen as well as ministers, to direct Christian activities.

The most recent development of the Y. M. C. A. movement in New Lon-don county is what is known as the "County Work," which was begun on March 10, 1919, under the direction of State County Work Secretary, Mr. Harry Hedley Smith.   On that date a county organization was effected on the Y. M. C. A. basis, and a committee was elected.   The same plan is in operation today and the committee consists of the following: Benjamin T. Marshall, chairman, New London; W G Park, vice-chairman, Hanover; Allyn L. Brown, vice-chairman, Norwich; Ralph H. Melcer, treasurer, Montville; George H. Bathgate, East Lyme; Frank Palmer, Bozrah; E. T. Bunyan, Col-chester; Frank E. Robinson, Griswold; C. W. Allyn, Groton; Otto Pultz, Lebanon; Reginald L. Lord, Lyme; Hadlai A. Hull, New London; E. E. Rogers, New London; H. M. Swinney, Niantic; C. E. Carpenter, Norwich; Harry M. Clark, Norwich; Dr. A. L. Stebbins, Colchester; Fred H. Topliff, Versailles; James Cooper, Mystic.

A county secretary, Mr. C. A. Pipher, is in charge of the work, with an office at 102 Thayer building, Norwich.   There are twelve groups organized in thirty-two committees in the county, in which effective work is being carried on

This is only a brief statement, but to the thoughtful reader it cannot fail to indicate to a high degree the power of the Young Men's Christian Association in the building of manhood in the local community and the county, and also in the larger spheres of the State and the country.

VIII.

ROMAN CATHOLIC CHURCHES

The Roman Catholic churches of New London county are in the Diocese of Hartford, which also embraces the entire State of Connecticut, and with officiary as follows: Rt Rev. John J. Nilan, D D., Bishop; Rt. Rev. John G. Murray, Auxiliary to the Bishop, Rt. Rev. Monsignor Thomas S. Duggan, Vicar General; Rev. William H. Flynn, Chancellor and Secretary.

The manager of the Diocesan Board for the Protection of Dependent Children for New London county is Rev. John N Broderick, of Norwich. The Diocesan director of the Holy Name Society and district director of New London county is Rev. William A. Keefe, of Norwich.

There are seventeen parishes in New London county, of which there are in the city of New London three parishes; in the town of Norwich, five. These and the other churches are as follows:

St Mary's Star of the Sea, New London—Pastor, Rev Timothy M Crowley, LL.D. Assistants—Rev. Alexander Wollschlager and Rev. John J. McGrath.

St. Joseph's, New London—Pastor, Rev. William C. Fitzsimons

Our Lady of Perpetual Help, New London—Pastor, Rev Paul Kosczyk

St. Patrick's in Norwich City, 205 Broadway—Pastor, Rev. M. H. May. St. Patrick's Parochial School is in charge of teachers from the Convent of the Sisters of Mercy, Sister Loyola, Superior, with nine other sisters resident there.

St. Mary's, 192 North Main street, Norwich—Pastor, Rev. W. A. Keefe. The Parochial School maintained by the parish is in charge of Sisters of Mercy from the Convent of Mary Immaculate, Sister Anacletus, Superior, eight sisters being under her care

Sacred Heart Parish at Norwich Town—Pastor, Rev C. W. Brennan

Sacred Heart Parish of Taftville—Pastor, Rev. U. O Bellerose. The parish has a Parochial School requiring in its various grades and departments sixteen teachers, Sisters of Mercy, Mother Geraldine, Superior

St Joseph's (Polish), 120 Cliff street, Norwich City—Pastor, Rev. Ignatius Maciejewski

St. Patrick's Parish of Mystic—Pastor, Rev. W J Fitzgerald.

Sacred Heart Parish of Groton—Pastor, Rev. William Fox.

Our Lady of the Rosary Parish of Jewett City—Pastor, Rev. John Mc-Cabe.

St. Andrew's Parish of Colchester—Pastor, Rev Philip J. Mooney; assistant. Rev. Daniel Sullivan.

St. Joseph's Parish of Occum—Pastor, Rev. Frederick Oessureault.

St. Mary's Parish, Stonington—Pastor, Rev James E O'Brien.

Immaculate Conception Parish of Baltic—Pastor, Rev. William T. O'Brien.

St. Thomas's Parish, Voluntown—Pastor, Rev. Ludovic Paradis.
St. John's Parish, Uncasville—Pastor, Rev. John F. Quinn.

Legally, St. Mary's Star of the Sea Roman Catholic Church of New London is St. Patrick's Corporation. The name St. Mary's Star of the Sea has been the recognized name of the parish for half a century. The church had its inception in the first mass ever sung in the city, about 1840, by Father Filton, who was then pastor of a church in Worcester, Massachusetts. The first service was held in a building on Washington street, a second mass being celebrated by the reverend father in a building at the corner of Bank and Bleinman streets. These services created an interest among the Catholics of New London, and soon afterwards St. John's parish was formed, and a chapel was erected on Jay street. Father Filton was followed by Father Brady, who in 1848 was succeeded by Rev. James Gibson, the first resident pastor He remained with the parish two years, Rev. Peter Blenkinsop becoming pastor in 1850; Rev. P. Duffy in 1851; then Rev. F. Stokes, who in October, 1852, gave way to Rev. Thomas Ryan, under whose pastorate a new church, St. Patrick's, was erected on Truman street, below Blackhall street. That church was consecrated May 4, 1855, the Jay street chapel being retained by the parish and used for church purposes. Father Ryan remained with St. Patrick's parish until 1858, and then was succeeded by Rev. P A. Gaynor, who remained until 1866. During that period he organized St. John's Literary Society, and started it on its long and useful career. In 1866 Rev. B. Tully became pastor, and while his pastorate was a short one, he left an indelible impress upon the history of the parish through his purchase of the large lot at the corner of Washington and Huntington streets. In August, 1867, Rev. P. Grace, D.D., became pastor, and he, too, made church history by beginning the erection of the present large and well planned structure in which the congregation worships in everincreasing numbers. Father Grace remained but a short time, being followed by Rev. E. A. Connor as pastor, he having as assistant Father Furlong. Father Connor continued building operations, and also organized St. Mary's Benevolent Society. He died in 1871, Father Furlong having temporary charge of the parish. Rev. M. Tierney became pastor in May, 1872, and during his short pastorate organized Star of the Sea Total Abstinence Society. In January, 1874, Rev. P. P. Lalor was made pastor, and under him the parish became St. Mary's Star of the Sea, and the large granite structure, one of the finest in the State, was completed and dedicated in May, 1876, with imposing ceremonies. Father Lalor was succeeded in 1879 by Rev. Thomas Broderick, whose pastorate extended over a period of four years, Rev. Thomas Joynt coming to the parish on May 28, 1883. The present pastor, Rev. T. D. Crowley, LL.D., succeeded Father Joynt as pastor, July 22, 1910. The congregation is a large one, about thirty-five hundred worshippers attending service every Sunday morning, five masses being celebrated, the children having a special mass in the basement. The Sunday school numbers eight hundred scholars. St. Mary's has a Convent of Sisters of Mercy, who are in charge of the parochial school, of which Rev. John J. McGrath is principal. The school course covers eight grades;

the graduating class of 1922 numbering seventy-two. There are twelve teachers, including special instructors in music, art, and domestic science.

Under Dr. Crowley's pastorate the church tower with its flaming cross was completed, the marble altars placed in the church and the interior redecorated and renewed

A Norwich newspaper item of November 14, 1793, recites· "On Friday evening John Thayer, a Catholic missionary, delivered to a large audience at the Rev Joseph Strong's meeting house (First Congregational) a learned and ingenious discourse in which he undertook to prove that the Catholic church was the only true church of Christ." This missionary priest delivered another doctrinal sermon the Sunday evening following, and with this excepton there is no mention of a Roman Catholic service until 1831, when a priest from Worcester, Massachusetts, then the nearest Catholic mission, began occasional visits. The first mass was celebrated in the town about 1840 by Rev James Filton, who about the same time visited New London. The first sacrament recorded as administered in Norwich was the baptism of Catherine, daughter of John and Eleanor Connolly, by Father Filton, May 15, 1836. The first Catholic marriage in Norwich was also performed by Father Filton, June 30, 1840, when he united John Savage and Mary Melvin.

St Mary's Mission was organized and a chapel begun in 1843. The church, small, but sufficiently large to accommodate the congregation, was first occupied for religious services March 17, 1845 In May of that year, Rev. John Brady was placed in charge of the Norwich Mission, he being followed by Rev William Logan, who was succeeded by Rev Peter Blenkinsop, who remained in charge of Norwich and neighboring missions until September, 1851. There were then three thousand Catholics residing in Norwich and vicinity, over whom Rev Daniel Kelly was settled as pastor in 1851; he remained until August, 1866, when he was succeeded by Rev Peter Kelly. St Mary's Chapel had been enlarged several times to meet the demands of the congregation, and under Father Kelly a beginning was made toward building the much needed new church, he buying two adjoining lots on Church street. On March 17, 1867, ground was broken for the building, but the church authorities disapproved the location, and it was abandoned for church purposes Father Kelly was succeeded soon afterward by Rev. Bernard Tully, who a few months later was followed by Rev. Daniel Mullen, who became pastor January 20, 1868. Father Mullen, after careful consideration, selected a plot on Broadway, about in the center of the scattered parish, which extended from Yantic on the north to Thamesville on the south and west, and to Greeneville and part of Preston on the east Ground was broken March 17, 1870, and a new church was erected in the most substantial manner The cornerstone was laid July 13, 1873, and work continued until the fall of 1877 under the direction of Father Mullen who died during the last months of the year, leaving the church uncompleted. It was estimated that up to that time, $200,000 had been spent in the construction of walls, roof, and tower up to the peak of the roof then in course of completion

Rev. P. P. Strahan became pastor in April, 1878, and at once assumed responsibility for the completion of the church, and so energetically did he prosecute the work that it was possible to use the building by March 17, 1879, when the first mass was celebrated. On September 28, 1879, the church was dedicated, Archbishop Gibbons, of Baltimore, later Cardinal, and now gone to his reward, preaching the sermon. A fitting honor was paid Father Filton, who offered up the first mass in Norwich thirty-six years before, and who built the first Catholic church there, in making his presence a feature of the occasion. This great church, a fine specimen of ecclesiastical architecture, now known as St. Patrick's, seats nearly two thousand people, while the basement, reserved for the children, seats one thousand. St. Mary's Church seats twelve hundred, and the Church of the Sacred Heart in Norwich Town seats four hundred.

St. Mary's congregation has continued to worship in the old church on Central avenue, but a handsome church edifice built of Weymouth granite is nearing completion, Rev. William A. Keefe is the present pastor.

St. Patrick's parish is under the pastorate of Rev. M. May. Both parishes in all their departments are in a prosperous condition.

Until 1872, Taftville Catholics were under the pastoral care of the church at Norwich, but in October of that year they were placed under the care of the church at Jewett City, mass being celebrated in the town hall. In 1874, Rev. John Russell succeeded to the pastorate, and to his zeal and energy the Catholic church that crowns the Taftville hills, is due. That church was dedicated April 18, 1878. The present pastor of Sacred Heart parish is Rev. U. O. Bellerose.

The early Catholics of Jewett City received spiritual consolation from Father McCabe, of Danielson, a missionary priest whose district then included several Connecticut counties. In 1861, Rev. James Quin, stationed at Moosup, was given jurisdiction over the town of Griswold. In April, 1866, he purchased the church of the Second Congregational Society. Father Quin was succeeded by Rev. Ferdinand Bolenger, who in turn gave way to Rev. James B. Reynolds, who became the first resident pastor at Jewett City. Father Reynolds, of delicate constitution, succumbed to the hardships of his large mission field, and after a short pastorate died, in December, 1874. In January following, Rev. John Russell became pastor, continuing until June, 1878. During his pastorate the church was greatly enlarged and embellished. In June, 1878, Rev. Thomas P. Joynt became pastor, and under him the congregation erected a new and appropriate parsonage. The present pastor is Rev. John McCabe.

Prior to 1850, Rev. James Felton, of Boston, Massachusetts, preached in Pawcatuck for the benefit of the Catholics there residing. There was no Catholic church there, and his services were held in the open air. He was, however, tendered the use of the Union meeting house, the trustees offering it to the preacher whenever he needed it. For five years Father Felton continued his pastoral ministrations, Father Daley succeeding him, and followed after a year's service by Father Duffy, who remained two years, then being succeeded by Rev. Thomas Dray, who remained six years.

St. Mary's Roman Catholic Church at Stonington was founded in 1851, and the same year Rev. P. Duffy built a church there by subscriptions from Catholics in Stonington and vicinity. The church was dedicated in 1851 by Bishop O'Reilly, who later was lost at sea with the ship "Pacific." The present pastor of St Mary's Church is Rev James E O'Brien.

The church property at Mystic Bridge was purchased from the Methodist Episcopal congregation there and was dedicated as St. Patrick's Church in 1870, Rev. P. Lalor, the first pastor. The present pastor is Rev. W. J. Fitzgerald.

IX.

ADDITIONAL CHURCH HISTORY

A Universalist Society was formed in New London in the year 1835, and occasional services held, but no church was erected or regular minister established until 1843, when a brick church edifice was erected on Huntington street, which was dedicated March 20, 1844, Rev. T. J. Greenwood the first pastor. He continued over the church four years and then resigned, the church being sold by the trustees the following year, the Third Baptist Church purchasing the property. In August, 1849, the Universalist Society bought a former Episcopal church on Main street, that was later sold, the society then worshipping in Allyn Hall until the erection of a new church, corner of Greene and Starr streets, which in 1896 was sold to Brainard Lodge Masonic Corporation and is used as a Masonic Temple The present beautiful church on Huntington tsreet is known as All Souls' Universalist Unitarian Church A union of the two congregations, Universalist and Unitarian, was subsequently effected. The pastor of All Souls' Church is W C. Greene, 26 Prospect avenue.

In the fall of 1772, John Murray, a Universalist preacher, visited Norwich, and in Dr. Lord's church (First Congregational) preached the first sermon ever delivered in Norwich in open advocacy of Universalism. For several years thereafter, John Murray paid Norwich annual visits, and about 1791 a society was formed and Elhanan Winchester, an eloquent preacher of the Universalist faith, visited Norwich in 1794, Rev. John Tyler, of the Episcopal church, allowing him, as he had Mr. Murray, to preach in his church. Near the close of 1820 the present Universalist Society was founded under the name, "Society of United Christian Friends in the Towns of Norwich, Preston and Groton " The first meeting of the society was at the home of Paul Harvey, in Preston, with David Tracy as moderator, and Gurdon Bill as clerk A committee was chosen to draft a constitution, and later at Poquetanoc the society organized by the election of the proper officers In 1821, under the preaching of Rev. Charles Hudson, later a congressman from Massachusetts, a deep interest was aroused and the first meeting house of the society erected. That church was dedicated July 21, 1821, Rev. Edward Mitchell preaching the dedicatory sermon. In 1836 the name was changed to the Universalist Society in Norwich, and the present organization of the church began February 6 of that year with eighteen members. A new church was dedicated in 1841, and on November 15, 1848, was rededicated, having been enlarged. The present Universalist Society, the Church of the Good Shepherd, is located at 148 Broadway, Rev. George H. Welch, pastor. The present church edifice was erected by the society in 1910.

Other denominations and sects maintain congregations in the county, and all sections are furnished with churches and Sunday schools in which the people may worship according to their own belief. There are two churches dedicated to the faith as taught by Mary Baker Eddy, the First Church of Christ (Scientist) at New London, and the First Church of Christ (Scientist) at Mystic. A society of the same faith has been founded in Norwich with reading room in the Thayer building, but a church organization has not yet been effected. The church at New London is located at the corner of Hempstead and Granite streets, the reading room at 315 Plant building. The Mystic church maintains a reading room at No. 5 Grand street.

The churches of all denominations in New London county are admirable for their beauty, size and furnishings, while the small country churches show by their neat and well kept condition that a love of the church as handed down from their forefathers in this and other lands, exists in the hearts of the people.

CHAPTER XII

COURTS AND LAWYERS

"The establishment of courts and judicial tribunals where society is protected in all its civil rights under the sanction of law, and wrong finds a ready redress in an enlightened and prompt administration of justice, is the first necessity of every civilized community. Without such protection the forces of society in their changeable development, even under the teachings of the pulpit, the direction of the press, and the culture of the schools, are exposed to peril and disaster from the turbulence of passion and conflicts of interest, and hence the best and surest security that even the press, the school and the pulpit can find for the peaceful performance of their highest function, is when protected by and entrenched behind the bulwarks of the law, administered by a pure, independent and uncorrupted judiciary.'

The New London County Bar has from its beginning numbered among its members able jurists, talented advocates and safe counsellors. Here many have lived, flourished and died, while others still are upon the stage of action, who have been prominent in the advancement of the interests of the county and figured conspicuously in the councils of State and Nation.

The first county court was held in New London county June 6, 1666, Major Mason presiding, John Allyn, assistant, Thomas Stanton and Obadiah Bruen, commissioners. A court was also held September 20, 1666, Major Mason, Thomas Stanton and Lieutenant Pratt, of Saybrook, occupying the bench, with Obadiah Bruen, clerk. In June, 1667, Daniel Wetherell was appointed clerk and treasurer. Major Mason was the only magistrate in the county, and when his health broke and he was seldom able to attend on court, the General Court after 1670 nominated assistants to hold the court annually in New London. In May, 1674, Major Palmes was invested with the authority of a magistrate for New London county, but was never chosen an assistant, though often nominated as one.

In 1676, Captain John Mason, eldest son of Major Mason, was chosen assistant, but the same year in December he received his death wound in the Indian fight. The next assistant from New London county was Captain James Fitch, about 1680; Samuel Mason, of Stonington, being appointed soon afterwards. As long as Major Mason lived there was no other magistrate in the county and he generally held his courts at his home in Norwich, a fact which irritated New London, and in October, 1669, County Court Clerk Wetherell, who lived in New London, petitioned the General Court on behalf of the commissioners and obtained an order for an assistant or magistrate to hold a court at New London at stated times. After Major Mason's death there was no chief magistrate resident within the county bounds until May, 1674, when the records show the appointment already noted. "Maior Edward Palmes is invested with magisterial power throughout New London county and the Narragansett country."

The first Prerogative Court in the county was held at Lyme, April 13,

1699, the next at New London, August 28 following, Daniel Wetherell, judge. This court henceforward relieved the county court from the onerous burden of the probate of wills and the settlement of estates. The justices of the peace in New London in 1700 were Richard Christophers and Nehemiah Smith, the former judge of the probate court in 1716

The Supreme Court was held in New London for the first time in September, 1711, the court being held in the meeting house, no court house having then been erected Prior to 1711 the Superior Court had sat at New Haven and Hartford, but in 1711 it was made a Circuit Court, each county of the State to have two annual sessions. Richard Christophers was one of the assistant judges and Captain John Prentiss, county sheriff. After an unsuccessful effort in 1720 Norwich successfully petitioned the General Court that the Supreme Court in March and the Superior Court in November might hold their sessions for New London county in that city, and thus Norwich became a half county seat after a long and determined fight for her share of the courts.

The Connecticut Superior Court is deemed to be open for business for civil business only at New London on the third Tuesday in September and the first Tuesday in February, and for criminal business only on the first Tuesday in May. At Norwich the court opens for criminal business only on the first Tuesdays in January and September. Sessions for civil business only open at Norwich on the third Tuesday in January, the fourth Tuesday in May and the first Tuesday in November

The Court of Common Pleas for New London county opens at Norwich on the first Tuesdays of October and February; at New London on the first Tuesdays of August and April. For criminal business the court opens at Norwich on the second Tuesdays in February, March, August and September; at New London on the second Tuesdays in April, May, June, October, November, December and January.

The City Court of New London has civil jurisdiction only, such jurisdiction being limited as to amount of claim to $500; return days, the first Tuesday of each month. The police courts of New London and Norwich have criminal jurisdiction only, fines to the amount of $200 or a jail sentence of six months, or both, being the limit of penalty that may be imposed. The town courts of Griswold and Groton have civil jurisdiction in cases not exceeding $300, and in criminal cases may impose a fine not exceeding $200, a jail sentence of six months, or both. Return days are the first and third Mondays of each month.

Judges of probate are elected on the Tuesday after the first Monday in November in the years having an even number The term of office is two years, beginning the first Monday in January following their election. The following embraces the names of the districts into which New London county is divided, and the towns in each district the year the court was constituted, and the judges elected November 2, 1920:

New London District—New London and Waterford Constituted at the May session of the General Court held in 1666, as a county court Judge. Arthur B Calkins.

Norwich District—Norwich, Franklin, Griswold, Lisbon, Preston, Sprague, Voluntown. Constituted in October, 1748, from New London Constituted in October, 1748, from New London. Contains the records of Voluntown. Judge, Nelson J Ayling.

Bozrah District—Yantic Constituted from Norwich, June 3, 1843 Judge, Wareham W. Bentley.

Colchester District—Constituted May 29, 1832, from East Haddam Contain East Haddam records from October session of 1741 to May 29, 1832 Judge, Harley P. Buell.

East Lyme District—Niantic Constituted June 2, 1843, from New London. Judge, Austin I. Bush.

Groton District—Noank. Constituted May 25, 1839, from Stonington. Judge, Arthur P. Anderson.

Lebanon District—Lebanon. Constituted June 2, 1826, from Windham. Judge, George E. Briggs.

Ledyard District—Ledyard. Constituted June 6, 1837, from Stonington. Judge, Samuel E Holdridge.

Lyme District—Hadlyme, Rural Free Delivery. Constituted July 5, 1869, from Old Lyme Judge, William Marvin.

Montville District—Constituted June 27, 1851, from New London Judge, Dan D Home.

North Stonington District—Constituted June 4, 1835, from Stonington. Judge, Charles C. Gray.

Old Lyme District—Old Lyme. Name changed from Lyme to Old Lyme July 5, 1869. Contains the records of Lyme from June 4, 1830, to July 24, 1868. Judge, Robert H. Noble.

Salem District—Constituted July 9, 1841, from Colchester and New London Judge, Henry A. Rogers.

Stonington District—Constituted at the October Session, 1766, from New London. Judge, Elias B Hinckley

The number of the justices of the peace in each town may be equal to one-half the number of jurors to which such town is by law entitled. They are elected biennially in each town at the electors' meeting held for the election of State officers and hold office from and after the first Monday succeeding their election If any person elected fails to take the oath of office before the tenth day of January succeeding his election, he shall be deemed to have declined the office and an election to fill the vacancy may be held Under this law New London county has elected 174 justices of the peace, apportioned among the towns of the county as follows:

Bozrah	3	New London		29
Colchester	5	North Stonington		3
East Lyme	5	Norwich		33
Franklin	4	Old Lyme		7
Griswold	6	Preston		2
Groton	19	Salem		2
Lebanon	3	Sprague		6
Ledyard	3	Stonington		15
Lisbon	5	Voluntown		1
Lyme	3	Waterford		12
Montville	8			174

Before the Revolution, the commissions of notaries public in the colonies emanated from the Archbishop of Canterbury. The commission of Elisha Hall, dated August 30, 1721, is registered in the office of the Secretary of State. The governor was first authorized in 1784 to appoint one or more notaries public in the State of Connecticut "as the commercial interests thereof may render it necessary or convenient." In 1838 notaries were empowered to administer oaths and acknowledgements of deeds. In 1800 there were fifteen notaries in the State; in 1812 there were thirty-two; and in 1827, sixty-four. Now there are literally thousands.

The following New London county lawyers have risen to the high office of Chief Justice of the Supreme Court of Connecticut: Gurdon Saltonstall, 1711-12; Jonathan Trumbull, 1766-69; Matthew Griswold, 1769-84; Samuel Huntington, 1784-85; Henry M. Waite, 1854-57; John D. Park, 1874-89.

Of these, Gurdon Saltonstall, Jonathan Trumbull, Matthew Griswold and Samuel Huntington were also Governors of Connecticut; Jonathan Trumbull and Samuel Huntington were members of the Continental Congress; Jonathan Trumbull was a United States Senator from Connecticut, having previously served as Congressman. These were the giants of the New London bar who rose to the highest eminence, but there were many, many others less prominently in the public eye, but men of the strongest intellectual powers, men of learning and culture, who played well their part in the great drama of life and reflected credit upon their ancient and honorable profession The following names in addition to those already mentioned won recognition and fame through their splendid powers, and will long be remembered:

Asa Spalding, who with his brother, Judge Luther Spalding, settled in Norwich in 1797, at the time of his death in 1811 was counted one of the richest men of his section. He was without patrimony or special patronage, but by force of native ability, sound judgment and integrity built up an extensive practice and filled many offices of trust. Asa Spalding, Judge Luther Spalding and Dr. Rufus Spalding were contemporaries in Norwich, and there they were buried, all in the same burial ground.

Elisha Hyde, a lawyer of good repute and mayor of Norwich fifteen years, was most deeply beloved for his genial spirit and great benevolence. He died December 16, 1813, aged sixty-two years.

Joshua Coit, Harvard 1776, practiced in New London, was a member of the Legislature several times, and congressman 1793-98, his death occurring September 5, 1798.

Elvin Perkins, Yale 1786, was presidential elector, member of congress, judge of the County Court, mayor of New London when he died, September 27, 1845.

General Elisha Sterling, born in Lyme, Yale 1787, and Cyrus Swan, of Stonington, men of a high order of talent, practiced outside New London county. Major Nathan Peters, a Revolutionary hero, after the war became a learned and able lawyer. He died in Norwich in February, 1824.

Jeremiah Gates Brainard, judge of the County Court for twenty-two years, resigned in 1829, his health failing. He was most democratic, affecting little dignity on the bench, but was regarded as an excellent judge, one who dispatched business promptly and won public confidence. His son, William E. Brainard, was for a long time a leading lawyer of New London.

Richard Law, Yale 1751, practiced in New London and attained the highest eminence. He was prosecuting judge of the County Court, justice of the Supreme Court of Connecticut, delegate to the Continental Congress 1777-78, and 1781-84, United States district judge after the adoption of the Constitution, a friend of Washington, long mayor of New London, and with Roger Sherman revised the Connecticut Code. He died while United States circuit judge, January 26, 1806. He was a son of Jonathan Law, a colonial governor of Connecticut, and father of Lyman Law, Yale 1791, speaker of the Connecticut Legislature and member of Congress, 1811-1817. He studied law under his honored father, and practiced in New London, where he died, February 3, 1842.

James Stedman, Yale 1801, settled in Norwich in 1806, and there died May 18, 1856, aged seventy-six. He was for many years clerk of the County Court.

George Burbank Ripley, Yale 1822, did not practice his profession very long, but turned to the soil. He filled a number of municipal offices, was judge of probate a number of years between 1850 and 1858, in which year he died. He was a man of high literary and scientific attainments, warm-hearted and generous, one of the best known and best loved men in his county.

Calvin Goddard, Dartmouth, settled in Plainfield, Connecticut, in 1791 and was a member of Congress, 1801-05. He settled in Norwich in 1807, and in 1815 became a member of the Connecticut Supreme Court. He was elected mayor of Norwich and held that office seventeen years. He died May 2, 1842, aged nearly seventy-four.

James Lanman, born in Norwich, June 14, 1769, son of Peter and Sarah (Coit) Lanman, was graduated from Yale, class of 1788, studied law, and rose to prominence. He was United States Senator 1819-1825, judge of the Supreme Court of Connecticut three years, and mayor of Norwich, 1831-34. He died August 7, 1841, aged seventy-two.

Benjamin Huntington, LL.D., Yale 1761, was one of the most honored and honorable men of his period. He was State Counsellor during the Revolutionary War, member of the Continental Congress in 1784, member of the Constitutional Convention of 1789, and in 1793 was appointed judge of the Supreme Court of Connecticut. He died in Rome, New York, October 16, 1800, and was buried in Norwich by the side of his wife, who was a daughter of Colonel Jabez Huntington, of Windham.

Roger Griswold, LL.D., settled in Norwich when first admitted to the bar in 1783, and soon acquired distinction as an able advocate and vigilant public official. He was a member of Congress, 1795-1805, and in 1801 declined appointment as Secretary of War. Later he was a justice of the Supreme Court of Connecticut, lieutenant-governor, and in May, 1811, was elected governor, receiving the honor of a re-election in 1812. He was also a presidential elector. Judge Griswold received the degree of LL.D. from Harvard University. He died in Norwich, October 25, 1812, aged fifty years.

Joshua Coit, born in New London, October 7, 1758, died there September 5, 1798, of yellow fever. He was a graduate of Harvard, 1776, studied law, and practiced in New London until his death. He served in both the Connecticut Legislature and the National Congress.

Joseph Williams, of Norwich, Yale 1798, was admitted to the New London county bar in 1801 and practiced in Norwich about thirty-three years, retiring from practice in 1833. then becoming a partner in the Merchants' Bank. After seven years of banking he returned to the office practice of law, and was also secretary-treasurer of the Norwich Fire Insurance Company, 1819-55. During the last years of his life he was president of the Norwich Savings Society, the oldest bank in Norwich. For twenty-five successive years Joseph Williams was treasurer of New London county; for thirty-nine successive years he was a justice of the peace; for twenty-two years he was an alderman of Norwich, and a member of the Legislature four terms. He was a director of the Norwich Bank over thirty-five years, and president of the Norwich Savings Society from its organization in 1824 until his own death, November 28, 1865, aged eighty-six, being at the time of his death the oldest native male citizen of the city.

Jeremiah Halsey was born in Stonington, Connecticut, in 1743, died August 25, 1829, and is buried in Preston. Connecticut. He was admitted to the New London county bar in June, 1770, and began practice in Preston, where he married Esther Park. He enlisted shortly after the battle at Lexington, was at Crown Point and Ticonderoga, and on May 1, 1775, was commissioned a lieutenant by Governor Trumbull. He was commissioned a captain of the armed sloop "Enterprise," June 21, 1775, and continued in service on Lake Champlain until December, 1775, when he was commissioned a captain in the Continental army. He was commissioned lieutenant-colonel, February 29, 1780, and was in service until the war closed After the war he returned to the practice of law. He is described as a man of tall, commanding figure, of sanguine temperament, persuasive address, combined with great force and energy of character.

Marvin Waite was born in Lyme, December 16, 1746, died in New London, June 21, 1815. He was admitted to the bar in 1769, and the same year settled in New London. He was an easy and effective speaker, and stood high in his profession. It was said of him that he studied men as carefully as he studied books, and that his thorough knowledge of human nature gave him a great advantage in the trial of jury cases. He won friends easily, his pleasing personality aiding him greatly in the public career which he began very early. He was nineteen times elected to the Legislature, was for several years judge of the old county court for New London county, was a presidential elector in 1793, and voted for General Washington. When Washington retired, Judge Waite became a disciple of Thomas Jefferson and was one of the leaders of that faith in Connecticut. Throughout his entire professional and public career he was held in the highest esteem as a man of highest integrity.

Jirah Isham, born in Colchester, Connecticut, in May, 1778, died in New London, October 6, 1842. He was a graduate of Yale, class of 1797, and was admitted to the bar in 1800, locating in New London. He was for several years State's attorney for New London county, was judge of probate for the New London district, and mayor of the city. He stood high in his profession, was fluent, ardent and graceful as an orator, and popular socially. During the War of 1812 he was commissioned major general of State militia, and for a time was in command of troops stationed at New London.

The acknowledged leader of the Eastern Connecticut bar for many years prior to his death, it may further be said of Henry Strong that he was without a superior in the State. He was the youngest son of Rev. Joseph and Mary (Huntington) Strong, his father an LL.D , who prepared his son for college. Henry Huntington, born in Norwich, August 23, 1788, entered Yale at the age of fourteen and was graduated with honors, class of 1806 For two years after graduation he taught school and studied law, then for two years was a tutor in Yale and a law student. In 1810 he was admitted to the bar in New Haven, but at once returned to Norwich, where he was in practice until his death, November 12, 1852 He is described by contemporaries as "one who by the ability, integrity, fidelity and diligence with which he discharged his various duties, imparted dignity and respectability to the profession, and caused his own name and memory to be held in honored remembrance " He was naturally well adapted for a lawyer, being quick, logical and able to separate the false from the true in evidence. He seized upon the strong salient points of a case and presented them in the most convincing manner. He scorned all trickery or deception, and met his opponents in a case fairly As a public speaker he was earnest and at times impetuous. He was most eloquent, and possessed a wonderful power of language which he well knew how to command at the bar or elsewhere to rebuke, commend, or in vindication of the right. He refused all offers of political preferment and they were many, with the exception of a seat in the State Senate Yale conferred upon him the honorary degree of LL D in 1848, he having declined a law professorship in Yale Law School He was a consistent Christian and a liberal contributor to charity

Henry Matson Waite, ancestor of Marvin Waite, of previous mention in this chapter, was born at Lyme, Connecticut, February 19, 1787, and there died December 14, 1869, full of years and honors He fitted for college at Bacon Academy, Colchester, and in 1806 entered Yale in the sophomore class He was graduated with high standing in 1809, then for three years taught school and studied law, gaining admission to the New London county bar in 1812. He finally located in Lyme, where he continued in active, successful practice until his elevation to the Supreme Court bench in 1834 He was an able lawyer, learned in the law, and a very successful advocate His strength lay not in his oratory, however, but in questions of law, patient research, discriminating power and directness of argument In 1834 he was elected a judge of the Supreme and Superior Courts and in 1854 was made Chief Justice, an office he held until reaching the constitutional age limit (seventy years) in February, 1857. During that period (1834-57) Judge Waite enjoyed the perfect confidence, respect and esteem of his contemporaries of the bench and bar, and won public confidence to a very high degree He was careful in forming his legal opinions, but firm in upholding them. Connecticut reports show that he was not infrequently in a minority and sometimes stood alone in his opinions, but not often were his decisions revised by the ultimate judgment of the bar. Of him it was said: "He contributed his full share to the character of a court whose decisions are quoted and opinions respected in all the courts of the United States and the highest courts of England." Yale conferred upon him the honorary degree of LL D. in 1855. Judge Waite married Maria Selden, daughter of Colonel Richard Selden, of Lyme, and granddaughter of Colonel Samuel Selden, an officer of the Revolution. The eldest son of that marriage, Morrison R. Waite, became Chief Justice of the Supreme Court of the United States. Another son, George P. Waite, was a member of the New York bar at his death, and a younger son, Richard Waite, rose to eminence at the Ohio bar.

The career of Lafayette S. Foster was one of brilliancy and useful lesson. He was of early Puritan ancestry, born in Franklin, near Norwich, November 22, 1806, but began life as a penniless and friendless lad, depending upon his own energy and ability for everything. He secured a good education and after graduation from Brown University studied law, located in Norwich, and rose to eminence in his profession. In 1870 he was elected to the Supreme Bench of Connecticut, serving until 1876, when he was automatically retired through reaching the age limit. After his retirement from the bench he resumed law practice and so continued until his death, September 19, 1880.

His public service was long continued and valuable. He represented Norwich six terms in the General Assembly, being thrice elected speaker. He was mayor two years, and from March 4, 1855, until March 4, 1867, was United States Senator from Connecticut, elected first as a Whig and later as a Republican. After the war, Senator Foster favored a speedy restoration of the Southern States to their constitutional relations with the Federal Government and was antagonistic to the radical leaders of the Republican party, a fact which operated against his election for a third term. When Andrew Johnson succeeded President Lincoln, Senator Foster became Vice-President and president of the Senate, holding until 1867, when his term as Senator expired. In 1872 he supported the Liberal movement, and in 1875 ran for Congress on a Democratic Liberal ticket, polling a large vote, although defeated. He supported Hayes in 1876, and the same year declined a legislative nomination. He was a man of polished manners, and was a delightful conversationalist, well read, apt in quotation, quick at repartee, brimful of genial humor, kindly in spirit; he entertained most bountifully, and with his gracious wife dispensed a generous hospitality. He was a devout member of Park Congregational Church, Norwich.

Charles Johnson McCurdy, son of a lawyer who was a graduate of Yale and grandson of a Scotch-Irish Presbyterian who came from County Antrim in the North of Ireland, was born at Lyme, Connecticut, December 7, 1797. He was graduated from Yale with high honors in 1817, studied law, was admitted to the bar in 1819, began practice in Lyme, and in 1856 was appointed a judge of the Superior Court. In 1863 he was advanced to the Supreme

Bench, holding until his retirement in December, 1867, through the operations of the constitutional age limit. After his retirement, Judge McCurdy
delivered courses of lectures before the students of Yale Law School, the
University conferring upon him the honorary degree of LL.D   Judge Mc-
Curdy was active in public life, serving ten terms in the Connecticut House
of Assembly between 1827 and 1844, and in three of those years was speaker
of the House. In 1832 he was State Senator, and in 1847 and 1848 was
lieutenant-governor. During his legislative career he brought about that
great reform in Connecticut law by which interested parties to a lawsuit may
be witnesses. In 1851 he represented the United States at the Austrian Court,
his course as a diplomat being highly commended by other countries than his
own. Judge McCurdy passed the evening of his life at his farm in Lyme,
hallowed by memories of Washington and Lafayette, both of whom were
there entertained.

Morrison R. Waite, who became Chief Justice of the United States Supreme Court in March, 1874, was born in Lyme, Connecticut, where his
ancestors settled a century before the Revolution. He entered Yale at the
age of sixteen, and was graduated with honors in 1837 at the age of twenty-
one. He began the study of law under his eminent father, Chief Justice
Henry Matson Waite, but went West before finishing his studies, becoming
a member of the Ohio bar. His career as lawyer and jurist was one of brilliancy and success, culminating in the highest honor that the lawyer can attain
His career belongs to the judicial history of Ohio, but New London county
gave him birth and here that career had its beginning.

John Turner Wait, another member of the distinguished Wait family of
New London county, was born in New London, August 27, 1811. He prepared for college at Bacon Academy, Colchester, spent two years at Trinity
College, then studied law, gaining admission to the New London county bar
in 1836. He was State's attorney, 1842-44, and from 1846 until 1854. His
law practice was very extensive, and for many years no important case was
tried in the New London county courts that the name of John Turner Wait
did not appear in as counsel. He was widely known beyond the confines of
his own courts, and his appearances were frequent in State and Federal courts
in other parts of the State. He was unquestionably one of the ablest advocates
in his State.

Prior to the Civil War, Mr. Wait acted with the Democratic organization, and was four times the candidate of his party for lieutenant-governor,
each year running ahead of his ticket. In 1860 he supported Stephen A.
Douglas for the presidency, but, being a strong Union man, he thereafter
acted with the Republican party. In 1864 he was presidential elector at large
on the Lincoln-Johnson ticket, State Senator 1865-66, and in 1867 member of
the House from Norwich, and unanimously chosen speaker of the Forty-fifth,
Forty-sixth and Forty-seventh Congresses In Congress, Mr. Wait was a
powerful advocate for a protective tariff and for the interests of his State.
He took special interest in pension legislation, in the marine and fishing
interests of the State, the improvement of Connecticut harbors, the con-

tinuation and improvement of the New London Navy Yard, and in support of some of these delivered elaborate arguments on the floor of the House. He gave a son to the Union cause, Lieutenant Marvin Wait, of the Eighth Regiment, Connecticut Volunteer Infantry, who was mortally wounded at the battle of Antietam. ·

Jeremiah Halsey, a native son of Preston, New London county, won high distinction at the bar of his county, being contemporary with and a worthy associate of those eminent lawyers—Henry Strong, Lafayette S. Foster, John Turner Waite, and others of that period. He was a paternal grandson of Colonel Jeremiah Halsey of Revolutionary fame, and a maternal grandson of Elder William Brewster, of the "Mayflower." Delicate in health, he was not able to pursue college study, and finally went South seeking health in the milder climate of Georgia. At Hawkinsville, in that State, he began the study of law, and was there admitted to the bar, April 23, 1845. The next four years were spent in further legal study, and travel for the benefit of his health, he finally in 1849, at the age of twenty-seven, opening a law office in Norwich in company with Samuel C. Morgan. In April, 1863, he was admitted to the bar of the United States Circuit Court, and to practice at the bar of the United States Supreme Court on February 24, 1870. He practiced with great success in all State and Federal courts of the district and State, and Connecticut reports show that he made many elaborate and effective arguments before the Supreme Court of the State, arguments that will ever be monuments of his great ability and learning as a lawyer. Professional, not political distinction, was his high ambition. He was a Whig in politics and, later a Republican, holding several positions in public life, but never seeking an office of any kind; yet he so won public confidence and esteem that he was chosen without an effort on his own part to win public place. He was sent to the Legislature from Norwich in 1852, 1853, 1859 and 1860, and was appointed by the governor in 1853 a member of the commission charged with the erection of a new State capitol at Hartford, a work completed in 1870. In 1853 he was elected Norwich city attorney, an office he held eighteen years, then resigning. He was long a warden and vestryman of Christ Protestant Episcopal Church of Norwich, and a man highly respected.

Henry Howard Starkweather, like Jeremiah Halsey, was a native son of Preston, New London county. He studied law under the eminent Lafayette S. Foster, and in 1850, at the age of twenty-four, he was admitted to the New London county bar. For several years he was associated in practice with Edmund Perkins, of Norwich, but after a decade of successful law practice he entered public life, giving little attention to his profession after 1861, when he became postmaster of Norwich A Whig in politics, he was in at the birth of the Republican party, and one of its founders in eastern Connecticut. He was elected a member of the Legislature in 1856, was a delegate to the National Republican Conventions of 1860 and 1868, and in 1867 was elected to Congress, and died in Washington during the session. A man of strong common sense, inflexibly honest, ever governed by principle, a philanthropist and a Christian gentleman, the remembrance of his virtues is fragrant.

John Duane Park, LL.D., the last member of the Supreme Court of Errors of the State of Connecticut to sit from New London county, like the two men whose record precedes this review, was born in the town of Preston, New London county, April 26, 1819, son of Benjamin Franklin Park, son of Elisha Park, son of Rev Paul Park, son of Hezekiah Park, son of Robert Park, son of Thomas Park, son of Sir Robert Park, who with wife and three sons came from England in 1639 and settled in Boston, Massachusetts. After completing a thorough academical education he began the study of law, in 1845 entering the office of the eminent Lafayette S. Foster, and in February, 1847, was admitted to the New London county bar. He began practice in Norwich and there continued a private practitioner until called to the bench, he winning high rank as a learned and able lawyer. In 1854 he was elected judge of the New London County Court, and in 1855 represented Norwich in the State Legislature. At that session of the Legislature there was a radical change made in the courts of the State, the county courts being abolished and all the business of those courts transferred to the Supreme Courts. Four new judges of the Supreme Court were elected under that law, of whom John Duane Park was one. He served under that election as a judge of the Supreme Court until 1863, when he was elected to succeed himself, but a year later was called higher by election to the bench of the Supreme Court of Errors. In 1872 he was re-elected a judge of that court, and in 1873 was elected Chief Justice of the Supreme Court, thus reaching the highest State honor a member of the bar can attain. He served with ability in that high office until 1889. In 1861 Judge Park received the degree of A M. from Yale, and in 1878 the degree of LL D. from the same institution.

James Albert Hovey, of Norwich, a judge of the Superior Court of Connecticut, was of Windham county birth, son of Jonathan and Patience (Stedman) Hovey. He was admitted to the Windham county bar in December, 1838, having acted as clerk of the Probate Court of Hampton district while pursuing his legal studies He had also been prominent in military life, serving as captain of the local company, as major of the Fifth Connecticut Regiment of militia, and for three years as its colonel. In 1841 he settled in Norwich, New London county, and from that year until 1849 Colonel Hovey was associated in practice with General Cleveland, under the firm name Cleveland & Hovey. When the bankrupt act of 1841 went into effect, he was appointed general assignee in bankruptcy for New London county, an office he held until that act was repealed, Colonel Hovey settling during his term about one hundred and sixty bankrupt estates. In 1842 and 1843 he was executive secretary under Governor Cleveland, and from June, 1849, until 1854 he was senior alderman of Norwich, and for the same time an ex-officio judge of the City Court At the organization of the Uncas Bank in 1852, he was elected president of that institution, and when it became the Uncas National Bank he continued president until 1873, when he declined further re-election, having held the office twenty-one years. In 1850-51-52-53-54 he was judge of the New London County Court, and in 1851-52 for about six months also discharged the duties of judge of the County Court of Windham count , owing to the sickness and death of Judge George S. Catlin His record on the county bench was remarkable, but one of his judgments being found erroneous when reviewed by the Superior Court and the Supreme Court of Errors. From 1854 until 1876 he was in the private practice of his profession in Norwich, but in that year he was elevated to the bench of the Superior Court. During his term as judge of that court he was called at times by the Chief Justice to sit upon the Supreme Court of Errors, and in some important cases prepared and delivered the opinion of the court; these opinions may be found in Connecticut Reports, Volumes 45, 46, 47 In addition to the official positions enumerated, Judge Hovey represented the town of Norwich in the Legislature in 1851, and in 1870 was chosen mayor of Norwich. During his term as mayor he prepared a revision of the city charter with some important amendments, which were later approved of by the common council, the County Court, the voters, and General Assembly. Judge Hovey was for more than three decades a trustee of the Savings Society of Norwich, and of the Chelsea Savings Bank of Norwich from its organization in 1858.

S T. Holbrook, a law student under Jeremiah Halsey, was judge of the Norwich probate court, 1856-68, judge of the court of common pleas for New London county in 1873, and in 1878 was again elected judge of the Norwich district probate court. He was a member of the State Legislature from Norwich in 1873 and again in 1876.

George Pratt, a graduate of Yale, studied law under the eminent John Turner Wait of Norwich, and in 1859 was admitted to the New London county bar, and opened an office in Norwich, where he practiced with great success until his early death, June 4, 1875 He was four times elected to the State Legislature, once from Salem and three times from Norwich He ranked high in his profession, adding to a well-disciplined mind legal knowledge, sound judgment, tact and discrimination. As an advocate he was earnest, direct and forcible, commanding from the court close attention when arguing.

George Willard Goddard, son of Major Hezekiah Goddard, son of Daniel Goddard, a lineal descendant of William Goddard who came to New England in 1665, was born in New London, July 3, 1824. He was graduated from Yale, class of 1845, and was admitted to the New London county bar in 1848, having pursued law study under Walker & Bristol, of New London, in Yale Law School, and under the eminent Lafayette S. Foster, of Norwich Mr. Goddard began the practice of law in New London in 1848, and during his long career filled many offices of trust, professional and civic. He was for many years a member of the examining committee of the New London county bar; was chosen town agent in 1848; clerk of the probate court in 1855; member of the Legislature in 1856, and in 1859, his eyesight failing, he practically retired from the practice of his profession. From July 4, 1864, to July 4, 1867, he was judge of the probate court for the New London district, and from 1862 until 1865 had been judge of the New London police and city court. In 1871 he was elected alderman, and several years later retired to the Vauxhall farm in the town of Waterford, near New London.

William H Potter, although never a member of the New London county bar, was for a number of years judge of the probate court for the Groton district, a justice of the peace, and so eminent a citizen that he does not inappropriately appear in this chapter. He was a son of Colonel William H. Potter, grandson of George Potter, a descendant of Vincent Potter, one of the judges who condemned Charles I. of England to death. William H. Potter was born at Potter Hill, Rhode Island, August 26, 1816. His father moved to Waterford, Connecticut, in 1820, and there his education was begun. He was a graduate of Bacon Academy, valedictorian, going thence to Yale in 1836, but health and eyesight failing, he could not finish, but later received from Yale an honorary A.M. After leaving college he began teaching, and in 1840 became principal of Mystic River graded school, and there married a daughter of Deacon Elisha Rathbun. During the years 1851-55 Mr. Potter was principal of Brandon Academy, in Mississippi, and on his return again became principal of the Mystic River graded school, a post he long filled. In 1865 he was appointed assistant assessor of internal revenue, holding until 1869, when he resigned, having been elected a member of the General Assembly. In 1872 he was elected State Senator from the seventh district, and as chairman of the committee on education had a large share in moulding the entire educational code of the State, revising every law pertaining to colleges, academies, common and normal schools. He was said to have been one of the few legislators always at their post when possible, and kept his own time, refusing pay for any time absent, a practice also scrupulously followed by his father, Colonel Henry Potter, while a member of the Lower House. In 1872 Professor Potter was elected a member of the State Board of Education, and a trustee of the State Normal School. After four years of service he was re-elected to the same office by a Legislature opposed to him politically. Dr. Northrop, secretary of the board, bore witness to Professor Potter's faithfulness and usefulness during the eight years he served the State as a member of the Board of Education. In 1876 he was elected judge of the probate court for the Groton district, an office to which he was repeatedly re-elected. He was also a justice of the peace and a notary public. In politics, Judge Potter was a Whig, later a Republican. He became a member of the church in 1831, was for more than three decades a deacon of Union Baptist Church of Mystic River, a teacher in Sunday school, for twenty years clerk of Stonington Union Association, later its corresponding secretary; for many years statistical secretary of the Baptist State Convention, later a member of its board of managers; for several years was a trustee of Connecticut Literary Institute at Suffield; and in 1881 took an active part in the Centennial Celebration at Groton. While acting as probate judge he also conducted an insurance and real estate business. Judge Potter wrote many historical sketches of churches and communities, and was widely known as a peacemaker, many disputes having been brought to a happy settlement through his counsel.

Daniel Chadwick was born at Lyme, January 5, 1825, and was graduated from Yale, class of 1845, and studied law under later Chief Justice Henry M. Wait, Lafayette S. Foster, and later Chief Justice Morrison R. Waite in Ohio.

Mr Chadwick was admitted to the New London county bar in 1847, and practiced law at Lyme until his retirement, with the exception of three years, 1854-55-56, when he was practicing in Baltimore. He was a member of the State Senate in 1858 and 1864; member of the Lower House in 1859; State's attorney for New London county for fourteen years: was appointed United States attorney for New London county in November, 1880; and served as government director of the Union Pacific Railway Company for four years beginning in April, 1877.

George Coit Ripley, youngest of the sons of George Burbank Ripley, was born in Norwich, August 25, 1839. He was graduated from Yale, A.B., 1862, and at once entered the Union army, serving until the close of the Civil War with the Tenth Regiment, Connecticut Volunteer Infantry. He studied law under Jeremiah Halsey, and in October, 1867, was admitted to the New London bar. He began practice in Norwich and there continued with success until his retirement. He served the city as councilman, clerk, recorder and attorney, and as a member of the State Legislature.

Contemporary with many of these men who have won high distinction at the bar and in public life noted in these pages, and yet an actor on the stage from which they have passed, is Thomas M. Waller, nestor of the New London county bar, of which he has been a member more than six decades; a lawyer of high repute, a citizen of public spirit and patriotism; a veteran of the Civil War; ex-speaker of the Connecticut House of Representatives; ex-mayor of New London, and the oldest officer of the State of Connecticut now living, having been Secretary of State 1870-71, and Governor 1883-1885.

Thomas M. Waller was born in New York State in 1839, son of Thomas C and Mary Armstrong. He was doubly orphaned at the age of nine years, and was later adopted by Robert T. Waller, of New London, and thus became Thomas M. Waller. He was educated in New London public schools, finishing with graduation from Bartlett high school. He chose the profession of law, and in 1861 was admitted to practice at the New London county bar. He hardly began professional practice in New London before he enlisted as a private in Company E, Second Regiment, Connecticut Volunteer Infantry, and with that command went to the front. He later developed serious eye trouble which caused his discharge from the army for disability. From the army he came again to New London, which has ever since been his home. He rose rapidly in professional rank, and until his virtual retirement commanded a large and influential clientele. He is yet a member of the New London county bar. From 1875 until 1883 he was State's attorney for New London, and his son, Charles B. Waller, is the present judge of the County Court of Common Pleas

A Democrat in politics, Mr. Waller early took an active part in public affairs, and represented New London in the General Assembly of the State in 1867-1868-1872 and 1876, serving as speaker of the House during the last session. He was Secretary of State in 1870-1871, and in 1883 was elected governor of Connecticut. President Cleveland appointed him consul-general at London, England, a post he ably filled until 1889, then resumed law practice in New London He was a member of the Constitutional Convention of 1902, serving as one of the two vice-presidents of that body. He served New London as mayor, and his public service has been both long continued and valuable.

Walter C. Noyes was born at Lyme, New London county, August 8, 1865, son of Richard and Catherine Chadwick Noyes. After completing his studies at Cornell he studied law, and in 1886 was admitted to the New London county bar. He was very successful as a practitioner, and rose to a high plane of professional success. From 1895 until 1907 he was judge of the Court of Common Pleas for New London county, leaving that position for service as judge of the United States Circuit Court, Connecticut second circuit. He continued as circuit judge for six years, then resigned and returned to private practice, locating in New York City. Judge Noyes is now general counsel for the Delaware & Hudson Company, but conducts a general law practice. He was a delegate from the United States to the International Conference on Maritime Law held in Brussels in 1909-1910, and is an authority in that branch of the law. He is the author of "The Law of Inter-Corporate Relations," 1902, and "American Railroad Rates," 1905. Judge Noyes retains his home in Lyme, his birthplace; his city residence, 405 Park avenue, New York City.

Frank B. Brandegee, son of Augustus and Nancy Christina (Bosworth) Brandegee, was born in New London, July 8, 1864 He is a graduate of Yale, A.B., 1885, and after graduation, following in the footsteps of his father, he studied law and became a member of the New London bar, being admitted in 1888. He located in New London, where he was in practice for many years, being ten years corporation counsel for the city of New London. An ardent Republican, he early entered public life. He was elected a member of the Connecticut House of Representatives in 1888, the year of his admission to the bar, he then being twenty-four years of age. He was again elected in 1899, and at the following session of the House was chosen speaker. He was a delegate to the National Republican Conventions of 1888, 1892, 1900 and 1904, and had then become a State party leader. In 1902 he was elected to fill out an unexpired term in the Fifty-seventh Congress (1902-3) and was re-elected to the Fifty-eighth and Fifty-ninth Congresses, but did not serve his last term, resigning to accept election as United States Senator from Connecticut to fill out an unexpired term, 1905-1909. At the close of his term he was re-elected to serve the full term of 1909-1915; was again chosen to represent his State for the term 1915-1921, and then was paid the honor of a fourth term in the Senate, 1921-1927. He has held many important committee assignments, and is one of the men of the Senate who exert a strong influence in the work of that body. He is a member of many organizations, political and social; his clubs, the University, of New York; the Metropolitan and Chevy Chase, of Washington; the Hartford, of Hartford, the Union League and Graduates, of New Haven; the Thames, of New London; and the Colonial, of Meriden, Connecticut. His home is in New London.

Richard Patrick Freeman, son of Richard Patrick and Mary Belle

(Magenis) Freeman, was born in New London, April 24, 1869. He completed classical study with graduation from Harvard, A.B., 1891, then entered Yale Law School, whence he was graduated LL.B., class of 1904. He was admitted to the New London county bar the same year, opened a law office in New London, and there has since successfully practiced his profession. He was regimental sergeant-major of the Third Regiment, Connecticut Volunteer Infantry, during the war with Spain in 1898, and from 1901-1908 was major and judge advocate of the Connecticut National Guard. He is a Republican, and since 1915 has represented the Second Connecticut district in the Lower House of Congress. Congressman Freeman is a member of the Masonic order, and of the Congregational church. His home is in New London.

Lucius Brown, son of Daniel and Mary (Stanton) Brown, was born in the town of Griswold, New London county, May 5, 1846. He is a graduate of Brown University, Ph.B., class of 1866, and of Albany Law School, LL.B., 1868. He was admitted to the bar of New London county in 1868, and practiced alone in Norwich until 1878, when he became senior of the firm of Brown & Perkins. He was judge of the city court of Norwich, 1894-1913; member of the State Senate, 1871, 1877, 1878, 1879, and chairman of the committee on judiciary in 1877 and 1878. He is president of the Norwich Savings Society; a trustee of Brown University since 1908; is a trustee of Connecticut Literary Institute; is a Republican in politics, and in religious faith a Baptist.

Gardiner Greene, son of Gardiner and Mary Ricketts (Adams) Greene, was born in Norwich, August 31, 1851. He is a graduate of Norwich Free Academy, 1868; Yale University, A.B., 1873; Columbia University Law School, LL.B., 1877. He practiced law in Utica, New York, 1877-78, then returned to Norwich, was admitted to the New London county bar in 1878, and from that year until 1910 practiced very successfully at that bar, and in all State and Federal courts of the district, rising to high and honorable rank as a lawyer of learning and skill. In 1910 he was elected a judge of the Superior Court of Connecticut, an office he now holds. Judge Greene is a Republican in politics, and in 1891 and 1895 represented his city in the Connecticut Legislature. In 1902 he was a member of a commission appointed to revise the statutes of the State, and has always been the devoted public-spirited citizen. He is a devout Christian, a trustee of Berkeley Divinity School, Middletown, Connecticut; senior warden of Christ Church parish, Norwich; and in 1907, 1910, 1913, 1916 and 1919 sat as a lay delegate in the General Convention of the Protestant Episcopal church. He is also a trustee of Norwich Free Academy, a member of the American Bar Association and the Connecticut Bar Association. His college fraternity is Delta Kappa Epsilon; his Yale society, Wolfs Head.

Edwin Werter Higgins, son of Werter Chapin and Grace Agnes (Taintor) Higgins, was born in Clinton, Connecticut, July 2, 1874. After completing his studies at Norwich Free Academy he entered Yale Law School, whence he was graduated LL.B., class of 1895. In that year he was admitted to the New London county bar, the same year settled in Norwich, and has there been in continuous practice until the present (1922), a lawyer of high standing and a citizen whom the people have delighted to honor. He was corporation counsel, 1901-02, for the city of Norwich, and prosecuting attorney in 1905. His business is large, and its course embraced a receivership of the Hopkin & Allen Arms Company. He is a member of the American and Connecticut State Bar Associations, and highly respected as a lawyer of ability and skill In public life Mr. Higgins has made an equally creditable record. He was a member of the General Assembly in 1899, member of the Republican State Central Committee, 1905-1906; health officer for New London county, 1900-1905; delegate to the Republican National Conventions in 1904 and 1916; and when Frank Brandagee resigned his seat in the National House of Representatives to become United States Senator from Connecticut, Mr. Higgins at the special election held October 2, 1905, to choose a successor, was elected to fill out the unexpired term. When that term expired in 1907, Mr. Higgins succeeded himself and sat as representative from the Third Connecticut district for eight years in the Fifty-ninth, Sixtieth, Sixty-first and Sixty-second Congresses, 1905-1913. Mr. Higgins is a member of the Sons of the American Revolution; Phi Sigma Kappa; and in religious faith is a Congregationalist.

Arthur M. Brown, son of George W. and Sarah F. (Young) Brown, was born in Jewett City, New London county, September 24, 1877. After completing public school study at Norwich Free Academy, he cruised around the world for two years as quartermaster on a private yacht, and upon his return began the study of law. In 1901 he was admitted to the New London county bar, and has since practiced his profession continuously in Norwich, his home, however, in Jewett City Since 1902 Mr. Brown has been counsel for the borough of Jewett City; since 1904, counsel for the town of Griswold; since 1905, health officer for the county of New London; and since 1901 has been treasurer of New London county. In 1901 he was elected a member of the Lower House of the State Legislature; in 1902 was a member of the Connecticut Constitutional Convention, and in 1903 was chosen State Senator. He is a member of the Masonic order, a Baptist in religious faith, a Republican politically, and a man of strong ability who has won the perfect confidence of the public.

Bryan Francis Mahan, son of Andrew and Dora (Dougherty) Mahan, was born in New London, May 1, 1856, and there his life has been spent He is a graduate of Bartlett High School and of Albany Law School, LL.B., 1881, and the same year was admitted to the New London county bar. He opened law offices in New London, and there has continually practiced until the present. His public career has been notable. He has served the city of New London as prosecuting attorney, postmaster and mayor, his legislative district as member of the General Assembly in 1882-83; as State Senator in 1911-12; and in 1912 was a member of Congress from the Second Connecticut district, serving in the Sixty-third Congress, 1913-1915. He accomplished a great deal for his native city while in public life, the appropration of $1,000,000 for the development of New London harbor being secured through his efforts. In politics Mr. Mahan is a Democrat.

Abel P. Tanner, son of Abel and Clarissa (Waterous) Tanner, was born in Groton, Connecticut, July 7, 1850, and since 1875 has been a member of the New London county bar and in active practice at that bar. After completing public school study with graduation from high school, he entered Brown University, when he was graduated A.B., 1875. He then pursued a course of law study, and in 1875 was admitted to the bar. He practiced law in Mystic, 1875-1882, then located in New London, his present home and seat of practice. He was corporation counsel in 1912-13, and in 1913 represented his city in the Connecticut General Assembly. In 1906 Mr. Tanner was elected president of the New London Bar Association, and through successive re-elections has held that office for several years. He is a Democrat in politics, and has frequently been the nominee of his party for high office, notably presidential elector in 1896, and for Congress in 1904.

Charles B. Waller, son of Thomas M. and Charlotte (Bishop) Waller, was born in New London, July 27, 1875, and there resides, and like his father, the ex-governor, is an honored member of the New London county bar. He completed his classical education at the University of Minnesota, then prepared for professional life at Yale Law School, receiving his LL.B. with the graduating class of 1896. He was admitted to the New London county bar the same year and began practice in New London. He rose rapidly in his profession and in public esteem, being elected to the Connecticut House of Representatives in 1905, and to the State Senate in 1907. When in 1907, Walter C. Noyes resigned his positon as judge of the Court of Common Pleas for New London county to go upon the bench of the Superior Court, Mr. Waller was appointed by Governor Woodruff to fill out the unexpired term. He assumed the duties of his office September 28, 1907, and has held the office continuously until the present, 1922.

The following is a list of the members of the New London county bar who now (1922) occupy positions of trust in the judicial life of the State or county, or positions of importance in national affairs:

Frank B. Brandegee, of New London, United States Senator from Connecticut, 1905-1927.

Richard P. Freeman, of New London, Member of Congress from Second Congressional district.

Gardiner Greene, of Norwich, Judge of Superior Court of Connecticut (term expired August 31, 1921).

Christopher L. Avery, of Groton, Judge of Superior Court, 1920-1928.

Allyn L. Brown, of Norwich, Judge of Superior Coourt, August 31, 1921-1929.

Hadlai A Hull, of New London, State's Attorney for New London county.

George E. Parsons, of Norwich, Clerk of New London County Courts.

Harry L. Peterson, of Norwich, Assistant Clerk.

Richard W Mansfield, of New London, County Probation Officer.

Robert McBurney, Court Messenger at Norwich.

William N. Tubbs, Court Messenger at New London and Librarian of the Law Library.

John M. Thayer and Gardiner Greene, of Norwich, State Referees.

Charles B. Waller, of New London, Judge of Court of Common Pleas for New London county; term expires February 2, 1925

Lewis Crandall, of Norwich, Clerk of that Court

Charles S. Whittlesey, of New London, Prosecuting Attorney of same Court.

S. Victor Price, Judge of City and Police Court of New London

Lewis Crandall, Assistant Judge.

Daniel M Cronin, Prosecuting Attorney

Clayton B Smith, Assistant Prosecuting Attorney.

Clayton B. Smith, Clerk of same Court.

John H. Barnes, Judge

Henry H. Pettis, Assistant Judge

Lee R. Robbins, Prosecuting Attorney

Tetley E. Babcock, Clerk of the City Court of Norwich

Arthur M Brown, Judge.

Henry H. Burnham, Prosecuting Attorney and Clerk.

John T. Barry, Assistant Prosecuting Attorney and Clerk of Town Court of Griswold (post office, Jewett City).

Warren B. Burrows, Clerk and Prosecuting Attorney of town of Groton

Arthur B. Calkins, Judge of Probate Court of New London District.

Nelson J. Ayling, Judge of Probate Court of Norwich District.

Wareham W. Bentley, Judge of Probate Court of Bozrah District.

Harley P. Buell, Judge of Probate Court of Colchester District.

Austin I Bush, Judge of Probate Court of East Lyme District

Arthur P. Anderson, Judge of Probate Court of Groton District.

George E. Briggs, Judge of Probate Court of Lebanon District

Samuel E Holdridge, Judge of Probate Court of Ledyard District.

William Marvin, Judge of Probate Court of Lyme District

Dana D. Home, Judge of Probate Court of Montville District,

Charles C. Gray, Judge of Probate Court of North Stonington District

Robert H. Noble, Judge of Probate Court of Old Lyme District

Henry A. Rogers, Judge of Probate Court of Salem District.

Elias B Hinckley, Judge of Probate Court of Stonington District.

George Cutler, Member of Connecticut House of Representatives

John T. Barry, Member of House of Representatives from town of Griswold.

Attorneys at law, members of the New London county bar (Manual 1921):

Arthur P. Anderson	Thomas F. Dorsey	S. Victor Prince
Guy T. Arms	Richard P. Freeman	Charles L Smiddy
C L. Avery	Charles A Gallup	William M. Stark
Nathan Belcher	John G. Geary	Clayton B Smith
William Belcher	Philip Z. Hankey	John F. Sullivan
Max Boyer	Benjamin H. Hewitt	Abel P. Tanner
Frank B. Brandegee	Charles E Hickey	Thomas E. Tolland
Warren B. Burrows	Perry J. Hollandersky	John H. Walker
A. B. Calkins	Charles H. Hull	Charles B. Waller
Charles Chadwick	Arthur T. Keefe	Thomas M. Waller
Alfred Coit	Frederick P. Latimer	Tracy Waller
William T. Connor	John J. Lawless	Charles B. Whittlesey—
Lewis Crandall	Harry Learned	All of New London.
George J. Crocicchia	Morris Lubchansky	
Daniel M Cronin	Bryan F. Mahan	Frank H. Allen
Frank Q. Cronin	Frank L. McGuire	Wallace S. Allis
Marion R. Davis	George C Morgan	Herman Alofsin

Nelson J. Ayling
Telley E. Babcock
Albert J. Bailey
John H. Barnes
Leslie L. Brewer
Traver Briscoe
Allyn L. Brown
Arthur M. Brown
Lucius Brown
Henry H. Burnham
Edward T. Burke
Charles W. Cassidy
Andrew B. Davies
Jeremiah J. Desmond
R. M Douglass
Frank N. Gardner
Gardiner Greene
John D. Hall,
Edwin W. Higgins
John P. Huntington
Charles V. James
Edwin C Johnson
Thomas J. Kelly
Arthur F. Libby
Earl E. Mathewson
Hibbard E. Norman
W. Tyle Olcott

George E Parsons
Edmund W. Perkins
Harry L. Peterson
Henry H. Pettis
Virtume P. A. Quinn
Lee Roy Robbins
Thomas M. Shields
William H. Shields
William H. Shields, Jr.
Charles L Stewart
John M. Thayer — All-
of Norwich.

Erastus S. Day, of Col-
chester
Austin I. Bush, of East
Lyme
Marion R. Davis, of
East Lyme
Arthur M. Brown, of
Jewett City
Henry H. Burnham, of
Jewett City
John T. Barry, of Jew-
ett City
Arthur P Anderson, of
Noank

Arthur P. Anderson, of
Mystic
Albert Denison, of Mys-
tic
F. H. Hinckley, of Mys-
tic
Fred P. Latimer, of
Mystic
George R. McKenna, of
Stonington
Charles A. Gallup, of
Waterford (post of-
fice, New London).
Harry B. Agard, Henry
W. Rathbun, both re-
siding in Westerly,
Rhode Island.
William N. Tubbs, of
New London

J. Frank Corey, of Nor-
wich, and Edith M.
Rathbun, of Stoning-
ton, are Commission-
ers of the Superior
Court, but are not
members of the bar.

This list is from the Connecticut Register and Manual published by the State, 1921.

The pages that follow are dedicated to the memory of Solomon Lucas, Seneca S. Thresher, Augustus Brandagee, and Jeremiah Halsey, men whom in their lifetime the members of the New London county bar have delighted to honor. The chapter finishes with an eloquent address historical in character

SOLOMON LUCAS—The memorial meeting of the New London County Bar in honor of the memory of Solomon Lucas, long State's attorney for New London county, was held in Norwich, November 9, 1906 Addresses were delivered by State's Attorney Hadlai A. Hull, Abel P. Tanner, Jeremiah A Desmond, and John H Barnes. Mr. Tanner's address follows.

A conspicuous member of this bar for many years, a leader in his chosen profession, has reached the mystic shore that all the dead have reached and whence it is said no voyager returns Today we come as friends to speak his eulogy, to tell who and what he was, and what he did, and we strive to preserve for future times some measure of his fame. In choosing his niche in memory we come again upon the names of illustrious men who have been lawyers here—Pratt, Foster, Crump, Lippitt, Hovey, Park, Halsey, Wait, Brandagee, these were giants in our profession and it is some consolation to reflect that in distant years our brother will be reckoned among these classic men

Solomon Lucas was born in Norwich, Connecticut, of English parentage, in 1835 At that time Andrew Jackson was President of the United States and a little while before had coined the famous: "The Union, it must and shall be preserved." Curiously indeed, when twenty-six years later our friend came to this bar (April, 1861) that sentiment had become the slogan of the North in the momentous issue of the Civil War. Already its people had been startled by the fall of Sumter, when for the first time in this Republic they saw the American flag lowered in surrender to foes who were their own countrymen. In this exciting period Mr. Lucas was chosen to the legislature of this State. His distinguished townsman, William A. Buckingham, was governor, and though differing from him in politics he helped sustain the loyal purpose of that splendid man. But retiring at the close of the session of 1863, never to hold political office again, he devoted the remainder of his life to the practice of law.

Mr. Lucas was a man of consummate ability and worth A child of plain New England people, starting in life poor and with many limitations, he rose by his own exertions to the highest rank in his profession—he was for seventeen years State's Attorney for this county—and he finished his eminent career with credit and honor. His life is an object lesson to every American boy who climbs the winding ways to wealth and fame. We see the slender country boy working on the farm for his board and clothes, we see the student in the law school at Albany laying the foundation for future success, we see him as a country schoolmaster teaching others the way of knowledge, toiling for the meagre wages of fifty years ago, we see him later in the office of Counsellor Wait, the eager student exploring the sources of the common law; at last we see him at the bar practicing in all the courts of the state, the apt and finished lawyer of his time In all conditions he was a candid, sincere, useful man The friend of social order, he sought in modest ways to raise the standard of civic duty. He was an accomplished advocate, a brilliant cross examiner, in argument fluent, forcible and convincing A careful manager, but aggressive, and with marvelous endurance, he expressed his cause with vigor, and once engaged he never left the field until the last maneuvre had been tried and the last stand had failed. And yet as a counsel he was usually sound, the cautious adviser who never failed.

It would be superfluous to call him a fearless prosecutor, an honest and faithful public servant. In the coming years we will cherish a grateful remembrance of his fidelity in official station and the virtue and simplicity of his private life He did not claim to be a perfect man Doubtless he had the faults and foibles, the infirmities which are common to our race His continuity of purpose and the desire to always accomplish what he undertook, may have sometimes made him seem severe; but to those who knew him at home and in the social circle he was considerate, he was affable, he was kind We shall not recall unmoved his death in the court room when absent from home and family friends After all there is no pathos like that of the unspoken farewell when fate overwhelms us at the bend in the road But in this world we cannot always live. Here where blossoms wither at last, the oak ceases to be clothed with the leaves of spring And so our friend "after life's fitful fever" rests unperturbed in the serenity of death, as when some craft on ocean currents tossed for many days, lies in the calm of the last harbor with sails forever furled.

Mr. Lucas was a consistent, active member of the Congregational church Imbued in life with the faith of the Christian fathers, he carried through all the years the solace of unfailing hope. He was conversant with the metaphor of the ancients, they to whom each day was a symbol of human life—the crimson of morning, the midday of splendor; the waning afternoon; the gold of sunset, the creeping shadows, and at last the darkness of the night—and he believed that somewhere "night wakes up morning for the endless day."

And so we, sustained by the same hope, will look to meet again these classic men, in brighter spheres where strife and conflict never come and friendship never fails.

SENECA S. THRESHER—On July 2, 1920, the New London County Bar assembled at Norwich in a memorial meeting held to honor one of the county's old and able attorneys, Seneca S. Thresher, Abel S. Tanner delivering the address, which follows in part:

A citizen of the far past, Seneca S. Thresher, in life's afternoon, became a solitary figure among men He belonged to a generation that is dead. Coming to Norwich nearly sixty years ago to begin professional life, he was longer in continuous practice than any other lawyer of this county, so far as I know. The nestor of this bar, holding its chairmanship by the privilege of age, he cherished its customs and traditions, waged its legal contests without rancor, and retired at 87, with his mental vigor still complete. I call to mind very distinctly my first acquaintance with him, and with equal distinctness, the last conversation in the shadow of death. These meetings—the first and the last—stand out in memory like the terminals of a long journey, and forty-four years lie between.

I first knew S. S Thresher as a fellow delegate in a political state convention in the city of Hartford, in 1874. He was chairman or secretary of the platform committee and read to that convention the resolutions on which Charles R. Ingersoll was chosen governor for the second time. Up to 1872, Mr Thresher was a Republican, and I a Democrat, but lately come of age. Thereafter, he, too, was a Democrat to the end of his life. He may have had ambition and coveted public office, but he did not communicate that fact to me, and so far as I know, held no important office beyond that of justice of the peace and of prosecuting agent somewhere in the 70's He was, presumably, content to illustrate Pope's famous lines:

'Honor and shame from no condition rise;
Act well your part, there all the honor lies"

And then, again, he may have pondered, sometimes with regret, the proverbial ingratitude of republics.

As the committee have informed us, Mr. Thresher was a child of Massachusetts, born in the quaint town of Swansea, in that corner of the State where dwelt so many of Puritan origin in the early colonial days. It has been facetiously remarked that a man should choose his ancestors with great care. Mr. Thresher's ancestors were chosen for him among the sturdy pioneers One of his kindred was among the patentees of Rehoboth 300 years ago, when most of New England was a wilderness where the Indian chanted his hymn to the Great Spirit, and the white man answered, sometimes, the call of the wild. He came also of good fighting stock. His people on both the paternal and maternal side, served in the Colonial wars and in the War of the Revolution, and one of them received the thanks of Congress for bravery in the field.

In 1832, when Mr. Thresher was born, this country was favored by exceptionally great men Calhoun was vice-president; Webster and Clay were in the senate, and Andrew Jackson was president of the United States. Many of our presidents have been noted phrase-makers, inventing epigrams that have lived, but no saying attained such wide celebrity as that coined by Andrew Jackson, in 1832, when he said: "The Union, it must and shall be preserved." In 1862, when Mr. Thresher was admitted to this bar, that phrase had become national. It had swelled to the chorus of the Union, heard above the roar of battle when a million men from the North resolved that the Republic should endure, that slavery should not live, and that the Union should not die. Mr. Thresher was among the list of the lawyers of this county in the great Civil War period. Of his contemporaries in 1862 only two are left: ex-Consul Day of Colchester, and former Governor Waller; both octogenarians going serenely down the declivity of life. The rest have from this mortal forever disappeared. They were among the greatest lawyers this county has produced. In the presence of these men Mr. Thresher did not, himself, seem so great and, doubtless, by some he was overshadowed. But, all things considered, he was a master in his profession and deserves to be classed with the great lawyers of his time.

He was essentially a self-made man. Lacking some early advantages, he, nevertheless, by close application, attained to a degree of learning hardly surpassed by many academically trained. He was conversant with the fundamental principles of the common law. He knew its sources, its possibilities and its limitations. He was a skillful pleader under the old regime when pleading was a fine art, and knew the value of concise and lucid statement. He knew, likewise, the importance of careful preparation—the utility of assembled facts and forces and abundant material. He knew that the law, like the God of battles, is often on the side of the heaviest battalions. He was a competent examiner who extracted information from varied sources, from the willing, the hesitant and the unwilling. In argument he was ready and fluent, often with a voice, both quaint and droll, that revealed his Puritan lineage and traits and Yankee derivation; but he was forceful, impressive, convincing, sometimes psychologic. He was a man of positive convictions always firmly entertained and frankly avowed and stoutly defended.

In his strong personality there were three main characteristics: The humorous, the stoical, and the optimistic. He was a lover of comedy and the drolleries of the stage. A reader of Mark Twain, whom he slightly resembled, he had the blessed sense of humor that chloroforms trouble and makes us forget. In disaster he was undaunted, calm and evenpoised. Though misfortune came to him as it comes to all, he met it unflinchingly, with no demonstration of weakness, and of suffering he gave no outward sign. Above all he was optimistic. He had the rare faculty of inspiring confidence in desperate situations, often finding loopholes which others had missed. And so, it was not always a false hope he raised. In litigation he was as successful as the average trier. He early cultivated the acquaintance of hope, and, in all his career, hope never deserted him. It abided with him in affliction and trouble. It was with him in sickness and health and in joy and sorrow. It sat by him at the bed of death and, when the end was reached, he and hope stepped into the shadows, hand in hand. He has crossed the boundary line of the great unknown, and will long be missed from this broken circle.

AUGUSTUS BRANDEGEE—Augustus Brandegee, youngest of the three sons of John and Mary Ann (Deshon) Brandegee, was born in New London, Connecticut, July 12, 1828, died at his home in Pleasant street, in the city of his birth, November 10, 1904. John Brandegee was a cotton broker of New Orleans, Louisiana, when war broke out a second time with Great Britain, and fought with Jackson at that famous battle of New Orleans on January 8, 1815. Mary Ann Deshon was of Huguenot ancestry, a daughter of Captain Daniel Deshon, who in 1777 commanded the armed vessel "Old Defense," which was built by the State of Connecticut.

After attendance at Union Academy, New London, Augustus Brandegee finished preparing at Hopkins Grammar School, New Haven, entered Yale in 1845, and was graduated fourth in his class in 1849. He then pursued professional study at Yale Law School for one year, then entered the law office of the eminent Andrew C. Lippitt, and after admission to the New London coutny bar in 1851 became Mr. Lippitt's partner. They dissolved partnership in 1854, when Mr. Brandegee was elected to represent New London in the Connecticut Legislature.

The Whig party was then in the throes of dissolution after the disastrous political campaign under General Scott, and the proposed repeal of the Missouri Compromise had stirred the moral sense of the nation to its foundations. Mr. Brandegee, with the ardor of a young and enthusiastic nature, threw himself into the anti-slavery movement. Although the youngest member of the House, he soon developed talents of a very high order as a parliamentarian and debater and became its leader. He was appointed by Speaker Foster, afterward Senator, a member of the judiciary committee, also chairman of the select committee to carry through the "bill for the defense of liberty," a measure the practical effect of which was to prevent the enforcement of the "fugitive slave" law in Connecticut. He was also chairman of the committee on the Maine Law, and as such carried through the Assembly the first and only prohibitory liquor law ever passed in Connecticut. Mr. Brandegee was largely instrumental in the election at that session of Speaker Foster and Francis Gillett to represent the anti-slavery sentiment of Connecticut in the United States Senate.

Returning to his practice, Mr. Brandegee was elected judge of the city criminal court of New London. In the enthusiastic campaign "for free speech, free soil, freedom and Frémont" which followed the anti-Nebraska excitement, he took an active and conspicuous part. He made speeches in the principal towns and cities of Connecticut, and soon became noted as one of the most popular and well known campaign orators of his party. He was chosen as one of the electors of the State on a ticket headed by ex-Governor Roger S. Baldwin, and with his colleagues cast the electoral vote of Connecticut for the "Pathfinder" and first presidential candidate of the Republican party—John C Frémont.

In 1858 Mr. Brandegee was again elected to represent the town of New London in the Connecticut House of Representatives, and in 1859 he was a third time chosen. Although selected by his party then in a majority as their candidate for speaker, he was obliged to decline the office on account of the death of his father. In 1861 he was for a fourth time elected to the House, and was honored by being chosen its speaker. This was the first "War" session of the Connecticut Legislature. The duties of a presiding officer, always difficult and delicate, were largely enhanced by the excited state of feeling existing between the two great parties, and the novel requirements of legislation to provide Connecticut's quota of men and means for the suppression of the rebellion. The duties of the chair were so acceptably filled by Speaker Brandegee that at the close of the session he was presented with a service of silver by Henry C. Deming, the leader of the opposition, in the name of the members of both political parties, without a dissenting vote.

In the stirring events of the period of 1861-65, Mr. Brandegee took an active part His services were sought all over the State in addressing patriotic meetings, raising troops, delivering flags to departing regiments, and arousing public sentiment. In 1863 he was elected to the Thirty-eighth Congress as representative from the Third Connecticut Congressional District, and in 1865 he was re-elected. Although the youngest member of the body in which he sat, he took a prominent position, and was selected by Speaker Colfax as a member of the committee on Naval Affairs, at that time, next to Military, one of the most important committees. He was also a member of the committee on Naval Accounts, and chairman of a special committee on a post and military route from New York to Washington

Mr Brandegee continued a member of the national House of Representatives during the reconstruction period, acting with the most advanced wing of the party, and was trusted and respected by his contemporaries, among whom were Garfield, Blaine, Schenck, Conkling, Dawes, Winter Davis and Thaddeus Stevens. He was admitted to frequent and friendly intercourse with President Lincoln, who always manifested a peculiar interest in Connecticut, and who was wont to speak of Governor Buckingham, its executive at that time, as the "Brother Jonathan" upon whom he leaned as did Washington upon Jonathan Trumbull.

In 1864 Mr. Brandegee was a member of the Connecticut delegation to the National Republican Convention held at Baltimore which renominated President Lincoln, and to that delegation it was largely due that Andrew Johnson was selected instead of Hannibal Hamlin for the vice-presidency, Connecticut being the first State to withdraw its support from the New England candidate.

In 1871, against his earnest protests, Mr. Brandegee was nominated for the office of mayor of the city of New London. He received very general support and was elected, but resigned after holding office for two years, being led to this by the exacting requirements of a large and growing legal practice. In 1880 he was chairman of the Connecticut delegation to the National Republican Convention held in Chicago, and nominated Senator Washburn for the Presidency. His nominating speech attracted favorable notice in the convention as well as throughout the country, and won him wide reputation as an orator and party leader. In 1884 he was again chairman of the Connecticut delegation to the National Republican Convention, also held in Chicago, and placed in nomination General Hawley as the candidate of his State for the Presidency.

During the last decade of life, Mr. Brandegee gradually retired from public affairs and devoted himself almost exclusively to the legal affairs of Brandegee, Noyes & Brandegee, a leading law firm of New London, of which he had been a member since 1892. He was urged by the leaders of his party to accept the nomination for governor, and was talked of as an available candidate for the United States Senatorship, but he steadfastly declined this and all other public offices and honors, preferring to devote his entire time and energies to professional work.

Mr Brandegee married Christina Bosworth Their daughter, wife of

Major M. G. Zalinski, of the United States army, and their son, Frank B. Brandegee, survived their father. The son, then Congressman from the Third Connecticut District, once represented by his father, now United States Senator from Connecticut, an office to which he was elected a year after the death of his father

As a lawyer, Augustus Brandegee ranked as one of the foremost in his profession; as a politician, one of the highest ability and integrity; and as a citizen, one of the most respected and honored.

The following memorial was the tribute paid by Judge Walter C. Noyes to his friend and contemporary, Augustus Brandegee, December 31, 1904, at a special meeting of the Superior Court, held to pay respect to the memory of Mr. Brandegee, Judge George D. Stanton and Colonel Allen Tenny, of Norwich. Judge Noyes said:

Augustus Brandegee, a leader of the New London county bar for half a century, is dead During all that time he reflected honor upon this bar. He gave to its members an example for emulation. He has left us a memory which is a benediction. We strive through this memorial to show that we appreciate what he was and what he stood for.

He was a learned lawyer. Coming to the bar filled with the learning of the classics, he readily absorbed the law written in the books, and yet was always more than the book lawyer. He never failed to appreciate that the law is not an abstract science, but a rule of action for men. Mercy and charity ever came to him as the hand maidens of legal principle. He approached the trial of a cause with diffidence. He participated in the trial as a master.

He was a brilliant orator. Convention, legislature, congress and court thrilled with his eloquence. In manner unexcelled he clothed his thoughts in language chaste and beautiful. and drove his words deep into the hearts of his hearers. He stood for high ideals through all his public life. At a time when the Abolitionist met scorn and contumely, he labored zealously to free the slave. A member of Congress through the war, he became the trusted friend of Lincoln, and rendered signal service for the cause of the Union. And then and ever after he put aside official station for the simple life.

He was a knightly man—hypocrisy, shame, expedients, pretensions—the whole brood of lies and deceits—were his enemies. He fought them all his days and when the end came, passed over God's threshold with escutcheon unstained and with plume untarnished.

Eulogies were also delivered by Solomon Lucas, Frank T. Brown, Hadlai A. Hull, Edwin W. Higgins, and Judge Ralph Wheeler, of the Superior Court, the last named saying:

It was not my good fortune to become acquainted with Augustus Brandegee prior to the year 1868, at which time his great intellectual and moral forces coupled with the training received in the schools and at his Alma Mater, Yale, had enabled him to attain a position of eminence in political life and in his chosen profession He had already brought many honors home to his native city and state

At the date mentioned there were many able men in the practice of our profession in New London county. Among them were Lippitt, Wait, Hovey, Foster and Halsey—men learned in the law, and some of whom had devoted their lives almost exclusively to its practice.

Though younger than most of them, Mr. Brandegee had already easily taken rank among the first as a lawyer. He was a great lawyer, advocate and orator, a man of great resources, fidelity, diligence, force and efficiency in every situation, and under all circumstances. He loved the practice of his profession, and for that reason resolutely refused to accept nominations to high political offices after his service in Congress. He preserved his youthful enthusiasm late in life, was most hearty and vivacious and entertaining among his associates, but would sometimes assume a brusqueness of manner which might lead to some misunderstanding of his real nature. His personality was most interesting. He had a great heart as well as a great intellect—was helpful, generous and magnanimous. He would give time and effort, and do much for others, and for any cause which interested him.

His was a great soul and through what experiences and by what struggles that soul reached hope, faith and rest, may not be known to us, but we may be sure they were attained.

JEREMIAH HALSEY—At a memorial meeting held to honor the memory of Jeremiah Halsey, one of the giants of the New London county bar, one of the speakers was Augustus Brandegee, another "giant" of that bar. His address follows:

The melancholy privilege of age assigns to me the duty of formally seconding these unanimous resolutions of the bar expressing the sentiments of the professional brethren at the loss of their great leader. The proprieties of the occasion do not permit any labored or extended review of his life, his character and abilities, but it is fitting that while still standing in the shadow of our great loss, we place upon the imperishable records of the court this last feeble tribute of our respect, admiration and love for our departed brother.

Jeremiah Halsey was born at Preston, Connecticut, February 8, 1822. He was admitted to the bar in 1845. He practiced continuously in all the courts of this State for just half a century, and died at Washington, D. C., on the 9th of February, 1896, in the ripeness of his fame, and the full maturity of his powers.

He was a great lawyer; great in every department of that profession that calls for the exercise of the highest and most varied powers of human intellect. Whether he stood before the learned judge or a jury or an arbitrator or a committee of the General Assembly, or other tribunal upon whose decision the lives, the property, and the rights of men depend, he was master of himself, his subject and his audience. In that wonderful system founded upon the principles of everlasting righteousness wrought out by the wisdom of ages and sanctioned by the experience of mankind, at once the handmaid and the sure defense of human society which men call law, he was easily *"primis inter pares."* The principles of this system he had explored to their deepest foundations. His comprehensive and philosophical mind had sought out their reasons, their applications and their limitations. He knew how and when to apply them in their rigor, and when to make them elastic enough to meet the requirements of an ever changing and ever advancing civilization.

He was no mere "case lawyer" such as the weaklings of our profession, whose sole requirements consists of a catalogue of authorities and whose ill digested citations only serve to "make confusion more confounded." He was not one of those who darken counsel with "profane and vain babblings," "striving," as saith an apostle, "about words to no profit but to the subverting of hearers." He rightly divined the word truth, seeming by an intuitive alchemy to know how to separate the dross from the pure gold, how to marshal, to reinforce, explain, apply, and if needs be to reconcile, the authorities. He loved the law—to him it was not a trade for hire, nor even a profession for furnishing one's daily bread, it was rather a sacred ministration. He looked upon it as that portion of the scheme of eternal justice committed to man by the Supreme Law Giver for the advancement of the human race, a rule of righteousness to be administered here, as at once a preparation and a foretaste of the more perfect law of the Grand Assize, when we shall no longer "see as through a glass darkly, but face to face." A judge was to him a representative of Him of whom it was written: "Justice and judgment are the habitation of His throne." A court room was a sacred temple, and while he ministered at the altar he had no part or lot with those who in the outer courts "were changers of money and sellers of doves."

And for this part in the noblest of all professions, Providence had endowed him with great and peculiar gifts of intellect, temperament and character. And these fitted into and worked in harmonious action with one another as in the most nicely adjusted piece of mechanism ever devised by the skill of man. His intellectual equipment was of the highest order. He possessed a mind strong, vigorous and acute, capable of close and continuous application, and of comprehending the most abstruse and complicated problems. Nothing seemed too high, nothing too deep, nothing too hidden or involved as to baffle or obscure that penetrating vision. When once he had grasped the underlying principles of a case, he followed that clue through all the Daedalian windings and turnings of the labyrinth to its logical results as though guided by the fabled thread of Ariadne. He was not unmindful of the rule, "Stare decisis," but he looked beyond the decision to the reasons and the philosophy of it, and if it had not these credentials he boldly challenged it as not having entered by authority through the lawful door of the fold, but as a thief and robber that had climbed up some other way.

To this clearness of vision there was added a lucidity of statement which has never been surpassed in our time by any member of the Connecticut bar. What he saw so clearly, he had the faculty of so expressing that his hearers saw it as clearly as he did himself. This is a rare gift and if it be not eloquence, it is akin to it. It was a delight in some tangled and complicated cause rendered still more tangled and complicated by the efforts of others who had struggled hopelessly in the Serbonian bog, to listen to the pure clean-cut Anglo-Saxon with which he extricated and unfolded the real issue and stripped it from all incumbrances. He rarely made excursions outside his argument by way of illustration into general literature, but at times there would come a flash of humor to irradiate and illumine, as lightning sometimes comes from a clear sky as a warning of the approaching thunder.

It was to these two masterly qualities—perspicacity and perspicuity—clearness of vision and clearness of utterance—more than all others, I think, was due the great reputation which he achieved among his brethren all over the State. It was on account of these that he always received the undivided attention and confidence of the judges, who while not hankering after the dry husks of the law for their daily bread, still, it may be presumed, prefer argument to eloquence and demonstration to rhetoric.

In him was happily united to these qualities a temperament which acted in harmony and gave them full opportunity for exercise and development. He was calm, serene, self-poised and equable, no matter how important the issue, or how desperate the contest. Whether victory or defeat hung trembling in the balance—amid the smoke and confusion of the battle, "amid the thunder of the captains and the shoutings"—like the great Marlborough, he was imperturbable. He never lost his selfpossession. He never failed to employ all his resources. He never retreated till the last man was brought up, and the last gun was fired, nor until all was lost save honor. And his fight was always in the open—a fair fight and no favors. There were no mines or countermines, no breaches of armistice, no firing upon flags of truce—"*Noblesse oblige.*" The law and the testimony, truth and honor, right and justice, these and nothing more and nothing less. were his watchwords

It was these and such qualities as these that placed him in the front rank of our profession and caused his name to become a household word in our State from the river Bronx to the Providence Plantations. But he was more than these—he was a pure, spotless, honest, simple, unaffected, truthful, just, honorable, white-souled, gentleman There was never one so conspicuous who bore honors more unostentatiously. There was never one whose life had been spent in contest and in combat, more free from "envy, hatred, malice, and all uncharitableness" He was "not slothful in business, but fervent in spirit, serving the Lord" "When the ear heard him it blessed him, and when the eye saw him it gave witness to him"

I may not on this public occasion draw aside the veil which covers our personal relations. But it may be permitted me to say that to me he was more than a Brother in Law. For forty years we have been associated in the battles of the bar, always together, except as I remember on only two or three occasions. He was my inspirer, my guide, my counsellor and my friend. "We took sweet counsel together and walked in the courts of law as friends.' We have been together in many a hard fought battle, have sympathized in many a defeat, and have rejoiced together in many a well earned victory. It was assigned to me as "junior" to lead the "light brigade and dash at the enemy with sound of battle and slashing broadsword"—but I knew full well, whether in attack or retreat that behind me was drawn up the heavy artillery and that my great commander stood there as fixed and immovable as "the Rock of Chickamauga"

His personal appearance harmonized with the disposition of his mind and character. He was tall and slim, with straight black hair, a pale intellectual countenance, the eye of an eagle, and that prominent nose which is the unfailing sign of indomitable will and forceful character. His manners though mild and affable, were decorous and dignified, inviting friendship while repelling undue familarity. There was an indescribable something about his fellow-citizens, as a man by all men with whom he came in contact. "His "that Goodness had come that way." One knew at his mere presence—here is a man to be trusted, and he was trusted—as a counsellor by his clients, as a lawyer by his brethren, as a legislator by his constituents, as a neighbor by his fellow-citizens, as a man by all men with whom he came in contact. "His life was gentle and the elements so mixed in him that Nature might stand up to all the world and say, This was a Man."

Alas, Alas! The inexorable law of human existence, which spares not rich or poor, young or old, great or humble! "He hath given his honors to the world again, his blessed part to heaven, and sleeps in peace." He has gone "to join the innumerable caravan which ever moves to that mysterious realm where each shall take his chamber in the silent halls of death." And so for a season we bid our brother "Farewell." He has fought a good fight. He has kept the faith. He has walked circumspectly amid the pitfalls of life. He has rejoiced not in iniquity, but has rejoiced in truth He was first pure and then peaceable. He provided things honest in the sight of all men. He recompensed to no man evil for evil. He overcame evil with good, in all things showing himself a pattern of a perfect Christian gentleman.

As we stood by his open grave banked with flowers and watered by tears, as in the presence of the judges who honored him and whom he loved, as we committed "earth to earth, ashes to ashes and dust to dust." as we caught the solemn refrain of the church he loved so well: "This corruptible hath put on incorruption, and this mortal hath put on immortality," our hearts responded to the triumphant pæan, "Yea—even so—it is well."

"Death is swallowed up in victory."

The effect of Mr. Brandegee's beautiful eulogy upon his large audience is indescribable. He spoke with the fullness of deep feeling, at times solemnly, gently, then again like a trumpet, making every word a live thing, his voice filled with tears as he spoke of his personal love and association, and to a man his listeners turned away their faces lest the gushing of their own tears be seen. When the speaker finished, John T. Wait, after a moment of deep silence, asked Messrs. Lucas and Wait, who were to speak, if they wished to add their testimony to that of Mr. Brandegee, they could only shake their heads in negation. A master had painted the portrait. And thus the memory of Jeremiah Halsey was honored.

Abel P. Tanner, of New London, one of the oldest members of the New London county bar, was chosen to deliver the historical address on the occasion of the rededication of the New London County Court House in the city of New London, September 16, 1910. Mr. Tanner deeply interested his large audience, and his address is so full of value that it is here preserved in full:

The committee to whose unfailing politeness I owe this invitation to speak, informed me not very long ago that I was the oldest attorney in active practice at this end of the county. If correct in their assupmtion, it will account this afternoon for my appearance here in "history." For the courtesy I have received from the commissioners and the bar and the public as well, I am extremely grateful—more than I can tell. But with that acknowledgment, I think my friends are mistaken, both as to my age in the profession and my place in the line. To the cold indictment of silvered age, I am still loath to plead guilty. And yet, young as I am, or imagine I am, for it is said a man is no older than he feels, I have begun to note the waning afternoon; already I perceive that the day is far spent, and though the future may have many allurements, that the years of my activity will be few. Still we are all hurrying on to some place in the distance where the line is mustered out; and from its last bugle note, no marchers "come back." And it is a pretty long line, though we count only those who have practiced law in this town—from John Winthrop, the younger, to the last hopeful accession—and it reaches far back into the past.

Courts of justice have sat in this our city, with few interruptions, consecutively, two hundred and fifty years—more than half the distance back to the discovery of this western world—and during much of that time New London was the only county seat. In 1660, the General Court, which was the Legislature, also established a primitive tribunal here, known as the "Assistants" court, composed of one assistant and three commissioners. A curious feature of it was, that the assistant was really the foreman, and the commissioners did the assisting. As its jurisdiction was limited to exactly two pounds, or about $10 of our money, and it could only punish for trifling misdemeanors, it has always seemed to me that putting four judges into one court session was using a good deal of ammunition on pretty small game.

The first judge of this earliest court in New London was John Tinker, a liquor dealer, but, like our distinguished ex-mayor, the judge was popular not only in New London, but elsewhere as well.

After a time, the Assistants Court by process of evolution became the County Court, with only a single judge, but with much larger judicial powers, and it existed a hundred and eighty-eight years.

The county itself was formed in 1667, with Norwich as an inconsequential member. But Norwich waxed and grew. It grew a little uncomfortable—at times, discordant. Occasionally it made strenuous efforts to get out of the "Wigwam." It even petitioned the General Court in 1674 for liberty to attach itself to Hartford county; and, would you believe it, it's dissatisfaction was mainly with the way justice was being administered here in New London, for the rest of the county; and Norwich, in its complaint, used plain language. I will read you a sample: "If we must continue as we now are, we beseech you to improve some method by which courts of justice shall be so managed that peaceable and innocent people will not be oppressed."

But though Norwich did not succeed in breaking away from the county, it was nevertheless able to steal a march on New London, and the very next year secured the judge of the County Court. After that, it is conceivable that it gave New London, occasionally, a dose of its own medicine.

Many years after—a great many years—Norwich, apparently not satisfied with having the judge and the court, began to reach out for the court house, and even cast covetous eyes at the jail. And there is a tradition, if I may call it such, that men from Norwich came down here once and undertook to carry off both these institutions bodily. I have not been able to verify this charge of grand larceny from any authentic record; but in a copy of the "People's Advocate,' a newspaper published back in the 40's, there appears this unique paragraph:

"A Norwich citizen has the custom house, here, in view. We knew Norwigians had been trying to carry off the court house and the jail, but we thought the custom house was safe. Well, the lighthouse is at their service whenever they conclude that we have light enough without it."

As a further confirmation, I may remark that, chancing to be here in 1865 at a Fourth of July celebration, while viewing the numerous floats in line I discovered a miniature copy of the old court house on which were these words: "Too old to go to Norwich."

But in 1843 a conspiracy was actually formed with Stonington to abolish this county seat and center all the courts and paraphernalia at Norwich. And how that must have grieved New London, to think that Stonington could do this thing—Stonington, that was once a part of New London, in the days when its first settler, William Chesebro, was a member of our town government, and Stonington was a child after our own heart! Naturally, public furor was high. In New London the matter was a party issue between the Whigs and Democrats. (At that time, there was no Republican party, though there were "Insurgents.") The Whigs affected to treat the subject with indifference, but a great meeting subsequently assembled in this building and one of its resolutions was as follows:

"Whereas the people of Norwich—grasping despoilers—seem determined to concentrate all public institutions at that place, to the great injury of our people, therefore, Voted that a committee be appointed consisting of Codington Billings, Charles Douglass, and Andrew C. Lippitt, to take steps to keep the court house where it is, with all our rights and privileges."

And now New London began to make efforts to get out of the basket. A petition was drafted, praying the Legislature to create a new county in this district, with New London as the big township, and Norwich left out. Fortunately the General Assembly turned down both propositions; and thus ended this "Tale of Two Cities." Happily there is no longer a conflict between these two communities—nothing but the friendliest rivalry. So that, when

New London generously congratulates Norwich on her own magnificent court house, the presence of her citizens here this afternoon is evidence that Norwich, with equal courtesy, returns the compliment.

The first Superior Court in this State was created in 1711, and made a Circuit Court, with two sessions annually in each county, with Richard Christophers, of New London, as one of its judges   And here, strange to say, there was as yet no court house owned by the public in eastern Connecticut. When the Superior Court sat in New London, it was given accommodations in the old meeting house of the First Congregational Church   Even that was later struck by lightning and nearly torn in two. The first court house erected for use in this county was located in New London in 1724, while Gurdon Saltonstall was governor. It stood forty-three years on a corner of the town square, not far from what is now the intersection of Hempstead with Granite street. It was a common, unpretentious, frame building, 24x48, without cupola or tower, and cost the munificent sum of forty-eight pounds—equivalent to about $250 of our money. Manifestly, the cry for municipal economy in New London is not wholly of modern origin. The building was paid for, in part, by the sale of some common lands which the county owned up in "Mohegan."

Not far from the court house stood the first jail ever erected in this county; and close to the jail, on another part of the Green, was the First Congregational meeting house, with its regulation steeple, destined to be one of the watch towers of the Revolution, wherein (as some poet has said) "Liberty its lasting vigil keeps." But the other auxiliaries of defence, such as the powder magazine, etc, were stored in the court house, and the whole was put in charge of Mr. Solomon Coit, a man of consequence. But I do not find that he received any other compensation for his janitorship except the privilege of having his Christian name attached to the most impassable road in New London—Stony Hill, which for many years was called Solomon street   To some it suggested a relation with the wisest of men; and when I perceived this trifling with a great name, I thought of the line from Shakespeare: "To what base uses we may return."

In 1776, for some cause which is not quite clear to us now, a change was made, and thence until 1781 the court house stood on the Parade. It sat a little west of the present Neptune building, on the space which gets its name from the presence of a fortress there in former years. Close to the water's edge on this old site, stood the common jail; and off to the southwest, but still within the circumference of vision, was that other emblem of civilization, the Gallows Tree.

What this court house was, whether a newly constructed building or one transported there from the former site, we do not know. My own opinion is that it was moved there—probably in sections. Moving wooden buildings is not an unknown industry in New London, even in our day; and the colonists were inured to habits of economy

I need hardly say that this court house was consumed by fire during Arnold's invasion, with many other public and private buildings, in that Valhalla of war which "spread woe and desolation throughout this region"; and for three years thereafter the courts of this county were without a home   But in 1784, while Richard Law was mayor, a committee was appointed to provide a new building   The County Court naturally selected the old Parade site. But many objected that it would some time be wanted for commercial purposes; and eventually the new court house was located at the head of this street, on the site of the first school house building here, with a little additional land given by Joseph Coit. And for fifty-five years this building stood out here, in what would now be the middle of the street opposite; though at that time there was no street running to the south, and Broad street, as we know it now, did not exist. In 1839, at the suggestion of Major T. W Williams (new streets having been opened all around it), the building was moved on to the present site, on land procured of Mr Williams, and here it has remained seventy-one years.

This court house, of necessity, has a judicial as well as a materialistic and sentimental history; but the noted causes that have been heard here, and the distinguished lawyers concerned in them, in forgotten years, would make a story longer than I can tell, or you would patiently hear. The argument of Patrick Henry against the Tory, Hook, would suffice to give it lasting fame.

The court room, as originally constructed, had a gallery on three sides as an extra accommodation to the public, but as interest in legal proceedings declined, and other halls were built for public use, this gallery was removed. The present alteration has somewhat curtailed the space railed off for the general public, although I have no doubt that what remains will be ample, but if interest in court proceedings continues to diminish, as it has in the past, the next alteration may reduce this public space to an "Amen corner." To some of us this decay of judicial sentiment is not a hopeful sign.

But though interest in judicial proceedings may have waned, the citizens of New London have never lost affection for the building itself. Through all vicissitudes they have clung to it, through good reports and evil, with a tenacity that at times has seemed pathetic. I confess that for many years I did not know the reason why. There was nothing classic or imposing about the old building; and Miss Calkins, the historian, writing as early as 1854, called it "commonplace," and "generally regarded as an unsightly blot, disfiguring the neighborhood where it stands." But continued agitation of the subject matter has developed a more intimate knowledge of its early history; and though my views have not changed as to a more enduring edifice, I have come to understand more clearly the cause of this devotion to an ancient relic.

In the first place, there is between town and building, a community of interests. The erection of the court house was contemporaneous with the incorporation of the city; and thus starting out together, they have kept even pace through all the current years and shared a common destiny. And, then, there are its cherished and hallowed associations This court house is a connecting link with the great historic past It carries us back to colonial days—to the men who were conspicuous in the great Revolutionary drama. Those concerned in its building had shared the privations, the sufferings and the disasters of the seven years' war. Some of them had stood at Concord and Lexington and the slopes of Bunker Hill. They have shared the gloom of Long Island; the exhilaration of Saratoga, the despair of Valley Forge; and they have felt the wild contagion of joy when Yorktown proclaimed "Cornwallis is taken." They have seen the British flag hauled down, and in its place, above the dome of a new nation, the Stars and Stripes appear. They saw the rise of constitutional government: they saw their country grow strong and great; they saw it spread westward towards the Pacific and south to the shores of the Rio Grande, and the stars of added States burst into blossom on the blue of its flag. And these men, in a way, transmitted this structure as a heritage to our time. Around this site cling also legal memories that will always be dear to our profession. For great lawyers have here pressed their suits to final issue, and great judges have voiced their sound opinions, and pronounced their benediction. Indeed, in these crude temples of justice throughout the new republic, was laid the foundation of a jurisprudence that has become distinctively American, and which bids fair in time to supplant the more cumbersome system of Continental Europe. When I was a child it was the habit of lawyers to quote the common law of England, and cite Law Reports. Today, the English Law Reports are hardly cited more often than the Code Napoleon, or the Pandects of Justinian, in that Rome that crumbled long ago.

In this quaint structure, consummate statesmen have discussed the science of government; religious reformers enjoyed the right of speech; and great orators have electrified the people of their time. Here Cowan and Marshall charmed with their eloquence, and Daniel Webster defended the Constitution of the United States.

A center of social festivities, here our citizens greeted for the last time the gallant Decatur in the War of 1812; and later, voiced their enthusiastic welcome to General Lafayette. In the Civil War this was a center of patriotic devotion, consecrated alike to the living and the dead.

We who wished a new court house have never lacked reverence which was due to the old. But we wanted to preserve this site to further generations. And today we share in whatsoever pride there is in this completed work. We congratulate the commissioners on what they have done. We are pleased with the remodeled appearance of this building—with its white front and green blinds, suggesting to some of us the happy homes of childhood that we can never go back to. But especially are we pleased with its beautiful interior, presenting to the visitor a succession of surprises, which culminate in this elegant court room—one of the finest in the State. We thank the architect, Mr. Donnelly, for his splendid ideals; and we are grateful to the builder, Mr. Douglas, for clothing these ideals in material form. And lastly, we congratulate ourselves on the choice of this site—a vindication of our fathers' judgment when they pronounced it the most convenient and best of all locations. And we are confident that whatever happens, whether this structure shall quickly perish, or endure for generations to come, its location will never be abandoned as a court house site, but preserved to future times. And that future is our inspiration. We believe that posterity will look up to this proud eminence and be glad; glad that here the figure of Justice still holds aloft the golden scales; that civic taste abides; that government endures; and that civilization does not fall.

A meeting of the bar of New London county was held in the Court House in Norwich, on Friday, June 30, 1922, in memory of four of its members who within the year had appeared before the Great Judge—Erastus Sheldon Day, William B. Coit, Franklin H. Brown and Joseph T. Fanning. Resolutions with reference to Judge Day, prepared by a committee consisting of Thomas M. Waller, Lucius Brown, John M Thayer, Gardiner Greene and Abel P. Tanner, were read by Judge Brown Judge William H. Shields delivered the following fervent eulogy:

Hon. Erastus Sheldon Day, of Colchester, in New London county, died at his home there on August 2, 1921, at the advanced age of eighty-five years, following an illness of only a few days' duration. Mr. Day was born in Colchester on July 7, 1836, and was the son of Mr. and Mrs. Elihu Marvin Day, who both died many years ago. He received his early education in the public schools of his native town, which was supplemented by his later attendance at Wilbraham Academy. Upon the completion of his academic course he pursued the study of the law for one year with Ralph Gilbert, Esq , a practicing lawyer at Hebron, and later took up his legal studies at Hartford for two years in the law offices of Welles & Strong, and with the firm of Strong & Nicholas, their successors. He was admitted to the bar at the breaking out of the war of the Southern Rebellion, at Hartford, on March 18,

1861, and thereupon took up the active practice of his profession in his native town in the village of Colchester and became a busy and prominent lawyer in that section of the State at the New London County Bar, from 1861 to 1897, thirty-six years. In the same year that he was admitted to the bar in 1861, Mr. Day married Catherine Gardner Olmstead, daughter of Jonathan and Elizabeth Olmstead, of Westchester, Connecticut. Mrs. Day died at Clifton Springs, New York, on August 15, 1910.

In 1897 Mr. Day was appointed by President McKinley, United States Consul at Bradford, England, which office he held for twelve years, from 1897 to 1909. In 1909 he resigned the consulship and returned from England to the United States to his home in the village of Colchester, and retired wholly from the activities of the law and politics. Early in his career, Mr. Day attached himself to politics and became an active and ardent member of the Republican party, staunchly adhering to and advocating the principles of that party. In the years 1862, 1864 and 1874, Mr. Day was chosen and sent from Colchester as a representative of that town in the General Assembly of Connecticut. In the year 1863, Mr Day was chosen Secretary of the Senate, and performed the duties of that office throughout the term of the sessions of that body. Later for five years, 1886 to 1891, Lawyer Day held the place of chairman of the Republican State Central Committee of Connecticut, and as such had charge and direction of the State and national campaigns of the Republican party in Connecticut in those years. Those political offices held by Mr. Day brought him a State-wide acquaintance with the prominent, influential and leading men in political and legislative life and public affairs of the State, and those prominent men of various activities in turn came to know and respect Mr. Day as a leader for his ability, integrity, fairness, sound judgment and unselfishness in his relations to them and to the subject matters in which they were interested or concerned. His fidelity and loyalty to clients, friends, and fellow men were firm and true and he enjoyed the reputation of being reliable and dependable in every case or exigency. His plighted word was never known or heard to be broken.

A generation and more ago and for many years about that time, there was an extensive legislative legal practice before the General Assembly of the State in which the services of the ablest lawyers were engaged at the capitol. Those legislative cases generally involved large interests and expenditures and in some instances vast results. The parties to those causes were variously towns, cities, railroads, insurance companies, and industrial and other corporations and occasionally directly the State itself. Those cases were exhaustively prepared pro and con on the law and the facts and long hearings were held before designated committees of the General Assembly with witnesses and counsel participating, where arguments of counsel at length were had as before a court and jury. For a long time Mr. Day was one of the foremost lawyers in the most important of those contested legislative cases and trials. Through that legislative law practice Mr. Day was further brought into close relation and acquaintance with the most prominent lawyers and citizens of Connecticut, and gained the reputation of a sound, skillful and able lawyer in that important branch of law practice.

Oftentimes his counsel and advice were sought by party leaders and candidates regarding impending party conventions and nominations, and by governors concerning appointments about to be made by them of persons to high State offices. In many instances Mr. Day's opinions and recommendations were effective and led to nominations and appointments of the very best men to public office. In late years in his reminiscences of those stirring political times and events, Mr Day took much gratification in recounting and discussing the good records and achievements in office of those prominent State officials whose selection came about through his quiet and impartial influence and sound judgment.

Mr. Day had no desire to attain for himself any office in the State. It was well known that he had no personal ambition whatever in that line to serve, and those approaching him for his advice and judgment knew his mind was open and free from any office-seeking desire on his part to affect or prejudice his action or judgment And so he was the more readily and confidently and frequently approached by others for his help, advice and judgment in political affairs.

He had friends in every part of the State and in the highest offices of the State, many of whom were under obligations to him for courtesies extended and essential help freely, cheerfully and gratuitously given in important matters to them. Had Mr. Day any aspirations for public office, he could have had nominations and appointments to such places as he might have chosen. It may be truly said of Mr. Day that had he shown and expressed the aspiration and ambition, he could have easily attained the highest judicial office in the State—judge of the Superior Court, or State's Attorney of his county, or even the governorship of his State. He chose the plain and simple life, and was contented to make his home and law office in the small and isolated village of Colchester, where persons having occasion sought him out for his wise counsel, advice and aid.

Mr. Day was tall in stature, erect in carriage, spare in build, had an open and pleasing countenance and altogether he possessed an impressive and commanding figure and in the ordinary gatherings of men about him he appeared to overlook and tower above his associates. He was always familiar, cordial and pleasant to his fellowmen and brethren of the bar. His general manner was one of human interest and sociability He entertained no prejudices or dislikes against persons because of racial, religious, political or other differences from him. The station, high or low of one's life, did not move him from the equipose of a wellbred man There was nothing querulous or critical-minded in his attitude or dealings, he was at all times broadminded and ever equable in the most trying circumstances, and was what we may well call an all 'round good-natured man.

At the bar in the trial of causes to the judge and to the jury, he had an easy and complacent bearing and was sure of himself and his cause, and by his demeanor provoked no hostility, but rather enlisted the full attention, consideration and favor of the trier and his fellow lawyers. In his advocacy and arguments he was sensible, zealous, reasonable, fair and convincing, and was susceptible and respectful to the force of an argument against him. He had absolute self-control and poise, and in the heat of all contentions never allowed anger, recrimination or personalities to enter the discussions on his part, or himself to be provoked thereto by his opponents

Surviving Mr. Day were two daughters, Misses Elizabeth Day and Susan I. Day, both of whom lived in the home with their father; and two sons, Edwin M. Day, of Hartford, and David S. Day, of Bridgeport, well known, able lawyers at the bar of this State.

Judge Shields was followed by Attorney Abel P. Tanner with the following eloquent eulogy on Mr Day·

Colonel Rapier, in the Peninsula Campaign, censuring an archaic military custom, once said of the English soldier that he was never officially commended in that campaign for distinguished service

I fancy the same could have been said sometimes with equal truth of Erastus S Day. He controlled the destiny of his party in this State for years, with phenomenal success, lifting others into prominence, while he, with characteristic self-effacement, toiled in the background and carried on unseen. In the exceptionally fine tribute to him, drafted by Judge Shields, is a summary of his political activities, the positions he filled, the offices he held and the various honors conferred upon him. It is not a lengthy statement, for the positions, after all, were not many, and the honors conferred were not always distinguished. We are constrained to turn from the record and think of the places he could have had for the asking, in any attempt to appraise his political career. Erastus S. Day could have had any office in the gift of this State. He could have been its governor without doubt; he could have sat on its highest bench; he could have been a national figure and been classed with the statesmen of his time, if, forsooth, he had cared. Apparently he didn't care. He was temperamentally indifferent to the lure of public office. In political classification he was of that number who ask for nothing and always get it. He sat at the civic banquet board where politicians gathered, and ate the bread there served, without carping at its quality. He cheerfully passed the delicacies on to the neighboring guests without first helping himself, and if the dish came back empty, as it generally did, he never complained. He helped others to secure some coveted positions of honor and trust which they filled passing well; but they seldom helped him—he never asked them to do so—and—he did not help himself. Hence, his name is not written on the scroll of fame. Yet he was intrinsically great. There is a greatness that we call innate—that inheres in the person—and there is a greatness that is conferred from without. The greatness that exists in the person survives; it will cross the final tide; but the greatness that is conferred will stop at the water's edge. E. S. Day was personally great. He was forceful; he was intellectual; he was faithful; he was honest; he was stalwart and true. Like the City of God, he stood four-square. He was a competent and resourceful lawyer who served his clients well. He was congenial and democratic in his contact with his fellow-men. He never drew a line of distinction on account of color, or race, or the size of a bank account. He believed that in the country "beyond the stars" there will be no caste, and no prestige of manufactured greatness, that no artificial barriers will separate in the clime where earthly glory fades, and wealth no longer dictates its own terms. He did not believe it is a crime to be rich, or a virtue to be poor, but he knew that in this life "money talks," that it is sometimes deaf, but never dumb, but he believed that in the other it will be mute where character has the floor, and the gold of the Indies will not buy as much as the widow's mite.

Today we construct a kind of mental figure of him as we knew him, and others knew him, and place it in the sacred crypt where other figures stand, to meet the gaze of future generations when we have disappeared. The figure may lack detail—it may be incomplete—it may be overdrawn, but it corresponds in some degree to the man we knew as he crossed life's solemn stage.

Mr. Day was born July 7th, 1836, the last year of Andrew Jackson's administration. He died, as the minutes show, on the second of August, after a life of eighty-five years. He came to this world and departed from it in the cheerful summer time when fields and mountain sides are green; he came and left amid the scent of summer flowers, but he left with the snows of winter on his head. He had taken life's seven steps. To use another's phrase, "In him the four seasons were complete, and spring could never come again." But when the sun had set and the shades of evening were merging into night, almost it seemed the end of a "Perfect Day."

Many years ago I conversed with one who had lived in Colchester when Judge Day was young, and who knew him well. Our talk was mainly of him, and one curious remark of my acquaintance has bridged the gap of time. He said, "When clients come, Day always tells them to settle and keep out of the law." Strange advice for a lawyer, yet not without scriptural authority "Settle with thine adversary quickly," was the counsel of the wisest of mankind.

Erastus S. Day was by nature conciliatory and pacific. He delighted in compromise as the culmination of the diplomatic art But he wanted honorable compromise. He was no money-changer in the Temple where principles are bought and sold, and he despised the cheap barter of the market place His motto was. "To your God, your country, and your friend, be true." He was essentially a peacemaker, and the peacemaker ranks high in New Testament literature. Christ said on the Mountain of Olive, "Blessed are the pure in heart for they shall see God"; but he said of the peacemakers, "They shall be called the children of God."

Mr. Day was an exemplification of New England manhood and courage. he had the virtues of the Puritan with few of his faults When you had conversed with him you felt that you had met the traditional New Englander of every generation. You had met the man of Concord and Bunker Hill and Yorktown's Heights. You had met him at Lundy's Lane and Cerro Gordo; you had met him at Cold Harbor and Appomattox; you had met him even in Flander's Field and in the glory of Chateau Thierry, where the Stars and Stripes mingled with the tri-color of France; and the lion and eagle and the lily moved side by side. Call this rhetorical extravagance if you will; but let me cite a single reminiscence.

In 1863, when Mr. Day was a member of the General Assembly at twenty-seven, the Honorable Henry C. Demming, of Hartford, then a member of Congress, invited him to Washington, and when he arrived he took him to the capitol to meet Abraham Lincoln Now Mr. Lincoln in those days was overrun with callers, callers from everywhere. Clergymen called to tell him how God wished him to conduct the war, lawyers called to advise about "the Constitution as it is, and the Union as it was" Editors came to tell him how to make both peace and war. He was bored to death with callers; only his inimitable humor saved him from utter distraction, nevertheless, he greeted his visitors cordially and, after a few minutes' conversation, he took the young lawyer by the hand and said, "Mr Day, come up to my house, I want you to meet Mrs. Lincoln and the children." With that strange insight of his, he penetrated the character of his guest and knew that he stood in the presence of one of the yeomanry of New England.

Mr. Day was almost the last of the lawyers of the great Civil War period, and I cannot take leave of the subject without some mention of them. When I came to Norwich in war time to a great political demonstration, there were, approximately, fifty lawyers in New London county, and one of them, Judge Day, was at the age of twenty-eight, but on the excursion steamer which brought us here, there was a still younger lawyer, the president of the club which had chartered the boat, then called the "Ulysses." He was a trifle below medium height—of slender build, with classic features and black hair, and beardless face. and glasses that glinted in the sunlight; brilliant in the court room, magnetic on the platform, attractive on the street, he had all the graces of the orator, with a voice and gesture that charmed, and an eloquence that stirred the multitude to action—that lawyer was T. M. Waller at twenty-four, then the youngest member of the New London County Bar.

But time has wrought its changes and sixty years have mingled with the silent yesterdays. That cheering throng has vanished, and with it the three hundred, more or less, on that excursion boat They have crossed the strange frontier; and somewhere, in some inlet of the sea. the ribs of the "Ulysses" dissolve in the ebb and flow of the tide. Today, of those fifty lawyers who practiced here in war time, he who was the youngest member is all that is left, and he is old and white-haired now. In a little while you will be constrained to say in melancholy accents. "The last of all the Romans—fare you well."

I commend these resolutions to the memory of Judge Day, with every feeling of respect. He has reached his journey's end, "the wine of life is drawn," his sands are run, and Fate turns the hour-glass no more His career is finished; his life is ended, his work is done; "the rest is silence."

Judge Webb closed the memorial session with a few remarks and upon motion of Judge Shields the resolutions and eulogies were ordered to be incorporated in the court records.

CHAPTER XIII

EARLY MEDICINE AND MEDICAL MEN

By Charles B. Graves, M D., New London

The rude and primitive character of the life of our pioneer ancestors is well illustrated by the state of medicine in early colonial times. What was true of the country at large was no less true of New London county. A few adventurous physicians, or at least persons who practiced "Physic," came with the first immigrants, like Samuel Fuller of the "Mayflower," Giles Fermin of Ipswich, Mr. Pratt of Cambridge, and our own honored John Winthrop. For many years, however, the colonists were greatly lacking in skilled medical service. It is true that as many as one hundred and thirty-four are named by Savage as physicians belonging to the first three generations, that is, up to 1692. Many of these, however, were ministers and others who practiced medicine more or less in addition to their regular vocations. But there is no doubt that the number of trained and educated physicians in the whole country before 1700 was pitifully small. The rigorous conditions of life in the new settlements and the entire absence on this side of the ocean of medical centers of learning and research, the utter lack of hospitals and libraries, and the meager pecuniary returns, were distinctly repellent. This last consideration was voiced by Giles Fermin (Steiner,[1] p. 2, quoting Hutchinson): "I am strongly sett upon to Studye divinity; my studies else must be lost, for physic is but a meane help." Pratt also had similar troubles, as noted by Governor Winthrop "But he had long been discontented because his employment was not so profitable to himself as he desired, and it is like he feared lest he should fall into want in his old age." (Packard,[2] p. 12.) Nevertheless, with growth of the population of the colonies, the number of physicians did gradually increase Some few of these had a college education. A very small proportion had medical degrees, mostly obtained in England or Scotland.*

Not until 1765 was a medical school established in this country. In that year the sixteen year old University of Pennsylvania organized a medical department. This was closely followed in 1768 by the Medical School of Kings College, in the city of New York, of which the College of Physicians and Surgeons of the University of New York was a direct continuation. The year 1783 witnessed the founding of the Harvard Medical School, 1798 that of Dartmouth. So that down to the year 1800 there were only four medical schools in the whole United States. According to Packard[2] (p. 156), "It has been estimated that at the outset of the War for Independence there were upward of three thousand five hundred practitioners of medicine in the colonies of whom not more than four hundred had received medical degrees." Even until well down into the 19th century the general custom was for the young aspirant to the medical profession to repair to some physician of established reputation and put himself under his tutelage. In fact, he was apprenticed to

---

* Superior figures refer to authorities cited at end of this chapter.

him for a certain definite term. It frequently happened that the preceptor was father, uncle or other relative of the student. Oftentimes it was some nearby prominent doctor. In other cases a special reputation drew scholars from a greater distance. For a local example, in 1753 a grandson of Joshua Hempstead, the diarist, was apprenticed for a year or more to Dr. Ezekiel Porter of Wethersfield. Certain eminent practitioners such as Dr. Jared Eliot of Killingworth, Drs. Norman Morrison and Lemuel Hopkins of Hartford, and Drs. Philip Turner and Philemon Tracy of Norwich, maintained what were in fact small private medical schools, and had a considerable following of students. The life of the medical apprentice had its hard and unpleasant features. Many of his tasks were decidedly menial. Taking care of the doctor's horses, running errands, preparing and putting up medicines are samples of the duties falling upon him. On the other hand, his opportunities were often great. Such book-knowledge as he acquired was doubtless helpful, but the most important and directly valuable part of his education was obtained by precept and example of an old and experienced practitioner. He accompanied the doctor on his daily rounds, was introduced into the household of his patients, and thus had abundant intimate bedside instruction. Of equal importance to his future success was his chance to learn from an older, successful man the art of meeting people and tactful conduct in the sickroom. As Dr. Russell[1] says: "The fortune of many a brilliant man has been marred by his ignorance of a pleasant entrance and by his want of a graceful departure." Not, to be sure, that a gracious manner was always characteristic of the noted men of those days. Quite the contrary, all too often a brusqueness of manner and a rudeness of speech either natural or gradually acquired were characteristic of men of marked ability and large following. If backed by practical success and especially by a kind heart, such mannerisms were forgotten. On the other hand, then as now, such peculiarities, associated with a self-confident manner and an authoritative tone, often cloaked real mediocrity. Not only was the instruction practical and intimate, but it was also broad. The doctor until recently, and more especially in early days, was *par excellence* a general practitioner. His practice ran the gamut of all diseases and injuries, and he had to do his best with any condition that might arise. As a rule, also, he carried the responsibility alone, but in important cases consultations were not infrequently resorted to. Furthermore, there were no apothecaries or drug stores, and he was obliged to prepare and dispense his own medicine. Besides the old familiar drugs, native herbs were also used to a considerable extent. His was also a family practice, and the close bond of doctor and patient was often unbroken for two or three generations.

Under such conditions the medical novice found his education. Not always was his lot a hard one. To the satisfaction of good work done and the sense of power born of his new knowledge and training, there were oftentimes added other amenities. The intimate relationship established between the doctor's family and the medical student in many instances ended in a romance as a result of which the young man later married one of his preceptor's daughters. Such were the conditions generally obtaining as regards the training of doctors down to the early nineteenth century. A survival of the old custom seen in the retention of preceptor in addition to the course in a regular medical school, did not die out entirely until the fourth quarter. It is worth while occasionally to attempt to visualize the life of an old-time practitioner, if only that we may contrast it with present-day conditions. Dr. Russell[a] (p. 208-210) has given a good description, from which I quote:

"The doctor was usually a familiar in the household, and while he was the subject of criticism and gossip, was yet retained in service longer than at present. The opportunity for change was not convenient, and then, too, there was, I suspect, a stronger bond of union between patient and physician than generally prevails at this day; for the intercourse which was begun with the father was continued with the children, until death broke the bond which had united them so long.

"The physician who was in demand generally traveled long distances, and, consequently, was much away from home. Starting early in the morning, a tedious ride was before him, always on horseback in the early days, and it was quite unknown when he would return. The regular office hours of the modern doctor were altogether beyond his knowledge. and probably beyond his belief. He knew nothing of ease and leisure, but plodded on in his daily calling, his round of duty as tiresome and endless as that of the farmers' wives all over the country. He expected to find his dinners where time had conveniently placed him.

"The saddlebags of leather held precious drugs, which were carried about from day to day. When borne into the house, the opening must have excited the wonder of the children as much as the tin trunk of the peddler at a later period. A store of powders, pills, and tinctures, syrups, and electuaries, compounds under names not now known by us, roots and leaves, enabled him to prescribe freely, and probably effectually; he carried with him a little of everything which was needed for immediate use."

The charges seemed very small, a shilling or even less per visit, with some increase due for mileage being the common fee down nearly or quite to 1800. After that, fifty cents was the usual charge. However, such a sum must be considered in relation to the purchasing power of money at the time, and relatively would not be as small as it looks at first sight Medicines, however, seem to have been quite costly, at least the charges for them represent a considerable part of the expense of medical attendance. Competition was not lacking. Besides the clergymen and school-masters who frequently attended the sick, there were midwives who had a large share of the obstetric practice, and also men who bled or pulled teeth. The universal prevalence of all sorts of superstitions is a characteristic of those early times which is familiar to all, but which may be mentioned as hampering the efforts of the clear-headed medical men and delaying medical progress.

Another outstanding feature of those times was the almost utter lack of sanitary knowledge and practice among all classes of people, and of course among the immigrants. The consequences of such ignorance had a profound influence upon the life of the colonists, which reached down to comparatively recent times. The early narratives and correspondence are full of references to the ravages of illness, especially epidemic diseases, and some of the most striking and interesting aspects of our early history have to do with such occurrences. The conditions under which the early immigrants crossed the ocean, by reason of overcrowding, poor and insufficient food, and the length of the voyage, not only led to great mortality on the passage, but so undermined the health of those that survived as to leave them very ill prepared to contend with the hardships and rigorous conditions of the new country whither they were bound.

A striking instance is related by Packard[1] (p. 65). "Upon a voyage to Virginia in 1618 by Francis Blackwell, there were one hundred and eighty of them crowded into a very small vessel. Disease broke out among them and proved fatal to Blackwell and the captain of the ship. By the time Virginia was reached, one hundred and thirty deaths had occurred on the vessel." As is well known, of the one hundred "Mayflower" pilgrims, just half died during the first winter, probably from scurvy. Such devastations were due largely to the debilitated condition brought about by the voyage, which made them an easy prey to infectious diseases, and moreover found them unable to resist the severe climatic conditions of the new land when associated with overcrowding combined with unsuitable and inadequate food.

The rudimentary knowledge of sanitary science was reflected in the very meager sanitary legislation of early times. Down to near the close of the 18th century such laws as were passed were occasioned usually by particular emergencies, and almost invariably were concerned with preventing the spread of small pox (vid. Lindsley[2]).

Epidemic Diseases.—It goes without saying that the conditions just described were especially favorable to the invasion and spread of infectious diseases. From the beginning, it was such visitations that were especially dreaded. A few years before the Pilgrims landed, the Indians of the Massachusetts Bay region had been all but exterminated by an epidemic which has been diagnosed by some as small pox and by others as some form of infectious fever. Without doubt there were infectious diseases in New London county from the beginning, but the first reference known to me occurs in Thomas Minor's[3] diary, where, February 8th, 1657-58, he mentions a case of measles in his own family.

Rev. Simon Bradstreet,[4] who was the second minister of the First Church of New London, records in his diary that July and August, 1670, were sickly in various places, mentioning "Lime and Stonington." The same diarist, after mentioning two deaths occurring in New London in 1683, says: "They both dyed of a malignant feaver wch was very severe thro: this Colony."

Of all the diseases to which the colonists were subject, the most dreaded, as is well known, was the small pox. The oft-quoted passage in Macaulay will bear repetition Calling it "The most terrible of the ministers of death," he says: "The small pox was always present, filling the church yards with corpses, leaving in those whose lives it spared the hideous traces of its power, turning the babe into a changeling, at which the mother shuddered, and making the eyes and cheeks of the betrothed maiden objects of terror to the lover "

The first mention of the disease in New London county known to me, occurs in the diary of Manasseh Minor[5] of Stonington, where in 1689-90 he

records several deaths from the small pox   It is probable that the same outbreak affected New London at that time, as appears from Miss Caulkins'[1]
quotation from the court records: "June 1690. The Court adjourned to first
Tuesday in August on account of the contagious distemper in town." The
year 1700 marked the reappearance of small pox in Stonington, and Manasseh
Minor mentions cases occurring in that town from time to time during that
and the two following years, with at least five deaths caused by that disease.
It was part of a very severe and widespread epidemic which reached its
height in Boston in 1702.

The diary of Joshua Hempstead,[1] which begins in 1711 and continues to
1758, has a number of references to small pox. Under date of April 18, 1719,
he notes cases brought in by vessel, and May 9th "Ephraim Avery was buried
on Powder Island. he died with the Small Pox on bord of Capt King."

Powder Island, a small islet a little below Fort Trumbull on the west
side of the Harbor, was one of the earliest quarantine stations. Miss Caulkins'
(p. 474) says: "The beautiful beach along the mouth of the river, north of the
lighthouse, was for many years used as a kind of quarantine ground. At
various periods, the small-pox has been a scourge to the town. Between
1750 and 1760, vessels were continually arriving with this disease on board.
The selectmen were the only health officers, and it fell to them to dispose of
the sick, and to the town to defray most of the charges. At the White Beach
and Powder Island, such vessels were usually stayed, and there many a victim
to the perilous infection was cast into the earth as a thing utterly abhorred."

Hempstead records its presence again in 1721 and 1730. In the first year
the Governor and Council sat at New London and made regulations with
regard to small pox. In the latter and following years Hempstead made
entries which give an idea of his official duties in connection with such cases.
June 22nd and 27th, 1730, he was at court with Justice Plumb "about moving
G. Buttolphs Brig down to Powder Island." In 1732, November 8th: "Sent
a post to the Govr at Hartford Concerning the Small pox." In 1733 the disease was introduced from the Barbadoes. He writes: "I ordered them to
Ly at Powder Island until further orders." Other minor invasions took place
in 1746-48. Late in 1752 there were five deaths out of eight cases. November
4th he says: "I was with the Selectmen att the Harbours mouth taking Care
of Capt Thomas Eames & Crew in a Brigg from New york. Divers of his
men & himself Sick with the Small pox." On the 12th he records deaths
"att the white-beach in Peter Lattimers House." —"buryed yesterday by one
of the Sand Banks." On December 8th: "I was most of the day with Mrss
Chapman Adam and Hurlbut Selectmen Removing Hannah Preston in Jas
Harris's House She is taken with the Small pox. Widow Hobbs is prest
to Nurse her & we Carted Harris's Household Stuff to Doctor Coits house."
Two days later: "Sund 10 fair. Mr. William adams pr all day. in the toren
I Stayed at home to assist in the small pox affair. they have fenced the
Highway up from Trumans Corner to Holts & across the hill from Holts
Corner to Hills Lot." In 1756 and '57 it appeared again, and in the latter
year some of Hempstead's own relatives were affected and moved "to the
lighthouse so called below the harbours mouth."

As is well known, the practice of inoculation of small pox was introduced in Boston in 1721 by Dr. Zadiel Boylston. The fact that there is no mention of the practice in Hempstead's diary would go to show that it was very late in getting a foot-hold in this part of New England. It was at first everywhere bitterly fought, recognition of its value both in and out of the profession being very slow. The first law bearing upon the subject passed by the Connecticut General Assembly was in 1760, prohibiting the practice in any town except by written consent of the major part of the civil authority and selectmen. The next year it was forbidden altogether. This prohibition was renewed and confirmed no less than twelve times in the ten years to 1769, when it was declared in force for the future. In 1777, however, inoculation was legalized, subject to such restriction as boards of health might impose. (Lindsley.⁴)

In the latter part of the century, inoculation hospitals came into vogue. These also met with strenuous opposition at first. The conflict was particularly bitter in Norwich (Caulkins,¹⁰ pp. 427-8), beginning in 1760, when the town voted down the following proposition: "Will the town approve of Dr. Elisha Lord's proceeding to inoculate for the Small pox, under any regulations whatever?" The question was brought up again from time to time by those believing in the practice, but always with the same result. "The popular feeling was excited almost to violence whenever the faculty brought up the question" In 1773 a hospital for inoculation was opened by Drs. Philip Turner and Jonathan Loomis on an island off the Stonington shore. They were soon obliged to give it up, however, on account of the violent opposition of the dwellers on the mainland. Miss Caulkins¹⁰ states that: "In April, 1774, Dr. Loomis was arrested and committed to prison on the charge of having communicated the infection of small pox by inoculation to two persons in Stonington. He escaped from his cell after a few days' confinement, and the Norwich jailkeeper, Sims Edgerton, advertised him and offered a reward for his apprehension, as would have been done in the case of a notorious criminal." Dr. Elisha Tracy, also, although recognized as a distinguished and skillful physician, was, according to Dr Woodward¹¹ (p. 176), presented by two grand jurors of the county "for communicating the Small-pox by inoculation to Elijah Lathrop and Benjamin Ward, both of Norwich aforesaid, and sundry other persons against the peace, and contrary to the laws of this State." He plead guilty, and "was held in a recognizance of sixty pounds, to appear and answer before the county court." Further efforts were made by Drs. Elihu Marvin and Philemon Tracy in 1787 to get permission to open a hospital for inoculation, subject to the control of the selectmen, but in vain. As the next best thing, however, they found two suitable sites near the river in the town of Montville, and there, together with Drs. Jeremiah Rogers and David H Jewett of Montville, as their associates, they at last were able to carry on the practice unhindered. Not until 1795 did the town of Norwich vote authority to Drs. Tracy and James W. Whiting to open in the following spring an inoculation hospital within the town limits under the regulation of the civil authority.

So far as New London is concerned, there appears no evidence of any strenuous controversy. Miss Caulkins⁶ gives the town record of June 23.

1777, as follows: "voted almost unanimously to admit of inoculation of small pox agreeably to a resolve of the General Assembly in May last." In the '90s there were two such hospitals in the town, one kept by Dr. Thomas Coit, Jr., the other by Dr. Samuel H. P. Lee.

A few years later, following Jenner's immortal discovery in 1799 of the efficacy of vaccination as a preventive of small pox, inoculation became a thing of the past. Vaccination was taken up in this country with remarkable promptness. One of the first physicians in Connecticut to adopt and push the practice was Dr. Elisha North, then living in Goshen, but later a resident of New London. Other physicians of the county who were early advocates and users of the method were Drs. John R. Watrous of Colchester, and Dr. Vine Utley of East Lyme. It appears from Dr. Watrous' ledger that he frequently employed Dr. Utley to come up to Colchester and do his vaccinating. The ordinary charge was six shillings. Thus in 1805-06 items like the following are not infrequent: "To 2 inoculations for Kine Pock by Doct Utley -0-12-0." (Dr. John R. Watrous, mss. Ledger C.) With the general adoption of the practice epidemics of small pox became more and more rare.

Passing to other infectious diseases, the first mention of the occurrence of measles in this county, so far as I know, occurs in the diary of Thomas Minor[8] of Stonington. He writes under date of February 8th, 1657-58, "Joseph had the measles." In the winter of 1713-14 New London was severely visited with the disease, according to Hempstead,[9] and there were seven deaths in two months. This outbreak, which continued until 1716, was probably the latter part of the general epidemic of measles in America which Webster[10] says prevailed in 1713. Hempstead notes also several deaths from the disease in 1740, coincident with a state-wide epidemic of severe character. Undoubtedly other outbreaks have taken place at more or less irregular intervals, but, as applying to our county, precise information is lacking.

Of other infectious diseases special mention should be made of diphtheria. In 1689 there was in New London a severe epidemic of what was probably this disease. Miss Caulkins[9] quotes the town clerk's record as follows. "An Accompt of severall persons Deceased by the present Distemper of sore throats and ffeaver which Distemper hath passed through most familys & proved very mortall with many Especially to those that now have it in this more than ordinary Extremity of hot weather, the Like haveing not been knowne in ye Memory of man." There were twenty-five deaths in the town that summer, most of them from the epidemic disease.

The first record in Hempstead of diphtheria occurs July 23rd, 1726, when a child of four "died with a distemper of the throat" He notes it again in 1731 and '36. In the latter year there were fourteen deaths in New London from the disease during seven months. He calls it variously, "throat distemper," "sore throat distemper," and what he speaks of as "canker" was doubtless the same disease. Cases were frequent also in 1743-44 and 1751-56.

Dysentery, "bloody flux," is another disease which terribly ravaged the settlements in early times. The first notice of it in our region known to me occurs in Hempstead's diary, where cases are cited in September and October, 1722. It is not, of course, to be supposed that this was its first appearance.

Frequently after that, it afflicted the inhabitants, as in September and October, 1729, when he records five or six deaths from "bloody flux which distemper prevails much in this town." It appeared again in 1734 and 1753.

During the last fort.· years of the 18th century many parts of Connecticut were sorely ravaged by this and other infections. It is not unlikely that New London county may have suffered in like manner, but thus far no records of such have come to my notice.

Another disease that took a heavy toll was what was called then pleurisy, "malignant" or "putrid," but which was probably in most cases what is now called pneumonia. The first record of it that I have seen, though it had doubtless occurred earlier, is in Hempstead's diary in 1731, where the entry is: "Died of a Pleurisy Taken Tuesday & buried on Saturd." From then on that disease is mentioned as a frequent cause of death. Later in the century, in 1761, 1781, 1789-90 and 1793, there were epidemics of this disease, probably often with influenza, in other parts of the State. Whether New London county shared in those outbreaks I have no present means of knowing. We have, however, Dr Vine Utley's[12] account of an epidemic of influenza with pneumonia in Waterford and Lyme in 1813 Of the other infectious diseases, except for Hempstead's mention of whooping cough, there seems to be little or nothing on record.

Of malaria, however, there is somewhat more to be said. It was probably present from the early years of the settlement, as it was known in the New Haven colony practically from the beginning. Thomas Minor[*] under date of August 20, 1670, writes: "hanah had her ffirst fit," and the next year, May 25th, he notes: "My wife had a fit of ague." In 1668 Mr. Bradstreet[*] mentions "Feaver and ague" as "very prevalent toward the westward, especially at Guilford." Throughout almost the whole of Hempstead's diary, at least until 1751, there are frequent allusions to cases of this disease, occurring both in New London and Stonington. The same is true with what was probably typhoid fever, called by Hempstead "nervous" or "long" fever. Both diseases were probably more or less endemic in our area at that time. I have no knowledge of the prevalence of malaria in New London after Hempstead's time until well toward the middle of the next century. There seems to have been an intermission of greater or less duration, for, as stated by C. W. Chamberlain[13]: "It reappeared in New London county in 1837 lasting till 1843. There were a few cases each year."

There were epidemics also of doubtful nature. Quoting from another article by the author[14] (p. 73): "In 1724-25 New London was visited by a very malignant epidemic in the course of which there were thirty-five deaths in February and March Hempstead in his diary says 'fryd 5th (March) fair warm & pleasant wether overhead. but the Most sorrowfull time yt Ever was seen in N. London for Mortality their Lyes now this morning. 6 persons dead & I negro woman of Groton.' Unfortunately, not the slightest clue as to the nature of this disease is given us."

In the same paper[15] (p 75) another epidemic of uncertain character is thus described: "In 1746 a peculiar disease appeared among the Mohegan

Indians. By Webster it is conjectured to have been of the same nature as an epidemic which occurred in Albany, New York, at the same time, and which Dr. Cadwallader Colden called a nervous fever, and Dr. Douglass yellow fever. It began in August and ended with frost. The sick Indians were attended by Dr Elisha Tracy of Norwich, whose son, Dr. Philemon Tracy, gave Webster his information. The disease, quoting Webster, 'began with severe pain in the head and back followed by fever, and in three or four days the skin turned 'as yellow as gold,' a vomiting of black matter took place and generally a bleeding at the nose and mouth till the patient died. These are the words of the old Indian as penned by my informant.' Dr. Tracy was affected with the disease but recovered. About one hundred died. This outbreak seems to have been confined to the Indians. Its nature must remain in doubt, but the possibility of its having been yellow fever cannot be excluded. That disease had raged in the South in 1741-42, and, as stated, in 1743 a 'bilious plague' which was probably the same disease prevailed in New York "

Some special interest attaches to the epidemic of yellow fever of 1798. It had been imported before, but it had never got a foothold, due without doubt to the fact that the patients had not been accompanied by the mosquito carrier. As regards this outbreak in New London, I will quote again (Graves,[11] pp. 82-85): "We have what is probably a fairly accurate contemporary account of this outbreak issued in pamphlet form by Charles Holt, publisher of 'The Bee,' a New London paper of that period. Furthermore, the 'Medical Repository' of New York for the year 1799 contains three letters to Dr. Mitchell, the editor, on the subject, two from the Rev. Henry Channing, and one from Dr. Thomas Coit, both residents of New London. The first victim was Capt. Elisha Bingham, who kept the Union Coffee House on Bank street, in the most populous part of the city. He was suddenly taken August 22 and died after four days. A few days afterward his wife, son and daughter were taken down, and all died. Others in the neighborhood were soon stricken and the disease spread rapidly. Following the first few cases 'the next week witnessed no less than 25 deaths.' It is stated by Holt that within a small space there were fifteen houses inhabited by ninety-two persons of which number ninety were infected by the disease. Thirty-three of this number died and two only escaped the fever. The disease remained practically confined to an area extending about thirty rods north and the same distance south of Capt. Bingham's house, and twenty rods in width. According to Holt, the 'mortality within the aforesaid limits was equal to that among the same number of inhabitants in any part of Philadelphia in the same length of time' 'It is not surprising that this visitation created a genuine panic in the town. A large proportion of the inhabitants, who at that time in the compact part of the town numbered about 2,800, removed to a greater or less distance.' According to Holt, even the physicians, except for two who were ill, left the city, 'excepting Dr. Samuel H. P Lee, to whose lot it fell alone and unassisted to combat the fury of the dreadful pestilence. And his conduct on the occasion was such as will call the warmest sentiment of gratitude and esteem from the citizens of New London, as long as the memory of the Yellow Fever shall exist in their minds He cheerfully sustained the arduous task of visiting and supplying with medicine thirty to fifty patients daily, notwithstanding the great fatigue and danger of infection to which he peculiarly exposed himself." Holt's account is followed by Miss Caulkins': "For a large part of the eight or nine weeks that the epidemic lasted he carried the whole load. He received much assistance, however, from a Mr. Gurdon J. Miller, who, though not a physician, was skilled in caring for the sick, which he did without compensation Moreover, during the latter part of the time, a relative, Dr. James Lee from East Lyme, and Dr. Amos Collins of Westerly, Rhode Island, came to his aid. Dr. Lee himself had an attack of the disease near the end of the epidemic" Holt writes: "In the discharge of the important duty to which he so nobly devoted himself, he was seized with the prevailing disorder, but after a struggle of a few days was happily preserved from falling a sacrifice to his humanity." He received the public thanks of the Committee of Health of the Town, which had been especially appointed for this emergency and which was untiring and most efficient.

"There were," according to Holt, "more than 350 cases and ninety deaths." Rev. Mr Channing, however, gives the figures as follows. "We ascertained with a precision to be relied on that the whole number of persons whose complaints clearly indicated the pestilential, or, as it is called, the yellow fever, did not exceed 246, and I give it you as a very important fact, on which you may rely, that, of the above number, 231 cases were clearly traced to the spot where the sickness commenced; that is, the patients were conversant, or had been in that part of the city a few days before they were seized."

Holt says: "Two or three solitary instances, indeed, occurred, where the disease was taken from an infected person, without any previous communication with the contagious spot. General Marvin, an eminent physician of Norwich, was attacked while attending Mr. Stewart, at Mr Haughton's, seven miles from the city, and went home and died But no other person, it is believed, was taken off by the disorder without having been nursing or otherwise in the infected spot; and in general those who lived at only a few rods distance, and avoided any nearer approach, were as secure from the effects of the fever as though they had removed an hundred miles in the country." In 1803 Yellow fever reached New London again, but according to Miss Caulkins' "The disease came from abroad and did not spread among the citizens. There were only very few cases."

Of the dreaded spotted fever, or cerebro-spinal meningitis, which was such a scourge in other parts of Connecticut in 1807 and 1823-25, New London county seems to have had no distinct outbreak of any importance. There were apparently a few cases in Waterford in the early '30s, which were seen or attended by the veteran Dr. North.

In 1832, at the time of the great epidemic of cholera in New York, when there were, according to Wendt, 2,030 cases, with 852 deaths, a few cases appeared in New London, as in New Haven and Hartford. The "New London Gazette," August, 1832, contains the following note about it:

"Cholera.---The notice published in the papers of Boston & N.Y of the

Cholera in this city, has a tendency to alarm our friends and connections abroad, & to interrupt the business between us & the country. The cases which occurred were—Mrs. Dart, who died on Winthrop's Neck and was found by the attending physician in collapsed state; two boys who had eaten a quantity of green peaches, and died before medical aid could reach them, Mrs. Briggs, their mother, who in the absence of her nurse and in a high state of perspiration, left her bed and went to an open window; and Mrs. Pollus, recently from N. Y., who had taken salts the day before her death without consulting a physician. All the women were afflicted with a diarrhoea several days previous to applying for medical aid. These are all the deaths that have occurred for 14 days past, with the exception of one person who died of old age. No case of the cholera now exists in this city that we know of. The confidence of the public in the practice of our physicians remains undiminished; and we have no doubt that when medical aid is applied for in the early stages of the cholera, it will be successfully combatted."

Medical Organization.—New London county, and especially the town of Norwich, is distinguished by the fact that here was made the first move in this State having for its purpose the organization of the profession and its recognition by the State. In September, 1763, eleven physicians of Norwich petitioned the General Assembly for an act to incorporate the physicians of the State and to provide for examination and licensing of candidates for practice. This memorial was signed by the following: Theophilus Rogers, Joshua Downer, Cyril Carpenter, Php Turner, Obadiah Kingsbury, Joseph Perkins, Physician, Elisha Tracy, Moses Morris, John Barker, Elisha Lord, Ebenezer Robinson.

The petition was negatived, but the attempt was no less significant. Dr. Woodward[1] well says: "The presentation of that unpretending Norwich memorial was the initiative step in a series of efforts which have since resulted in the permanent establishment of many flourishing State Associations, and within a few years of the National Association, which has contributed in a high degree to purify the ranks, elevate the aims, and make a real unit and fraternity of the profession in America. In the attempts alluded to, it was not the object of the petitioners to secure any immunities or exclusive privileges for themselves, but to protect the health of the community by additional securities. At that time there was no authority in the State legally qualified to confer degrees in a way to discriminate the man of solid acquirements from the ignorant pretender." They wished "to establish a standard of education by making a respectable amount of attainments an indispensable requisite, to the acquirement of the title," and they "asked for the appointment of a committee legally authorized to examine and approve candidates if found qualified."

The rebuff which their petition received at the hands of the General Assembly did not entirely discourage the New London county physicians. Even if they could not gain recognition by legislative action, they could at least form themselves into an association which would secure to them at least some of the benefits of organization. In fact, in September, 1775, a voluntary society was formed calling itself the New London County Medical Society. Dr. John Barker was elected as first president, and was annually re-elected up to the time of his death in 1791. "It is said that at the earlier meetings, which were held monthly, Dr Philip Turner gave lectures on military surgery." (Woodward.'*) Further than that, little or nothing is known of the doings of this society. It is beyond doubt, however, that it must have been a powerful factor both in elevating the professional standards of its members and in developing an *esprit de corps* among them.

The direct offspring and close successor of the voluntary organization just mentioned was the still flourishing New London County Medical Association, which came into being with the incorporation of the Connecticut Medical Society in May, 1792, the year following Dr. Barker's death. Naturally, much interest attaches to the first meeting. The original record reads as follows:

"At a meeting of the Physicians and Surgeons of New London County on the 4th Tuesday of Sept. 1792, agreeable to the act of the General Assembly passed in May last incorporating a Medical Society in the State of Connecticut—

"Voted: By a majority present, that the following gentlemen be members of said society for this County, viz "

Then follows a list of names and residences beginning with "Doctr Theophilus Rogers, Norwich," forty-four in all. There is a question whether there may not be a duplication in the names of John Watrous and John R. Watrous. I have been unable to learn whether or not there were two men named John Watrous. Dr. Theophilus Rogers was chosen chairman, and Dr. Simon Wolcott clerk. Unfortunately the members present were not listed, nor was the place of meeting stated, though it was probably Norwich. Some of those thus voted in apparently did not accept their election   Three of the names do not appear again in the records, and in the case of eight others there is only one further mention, always in connection with the abatement of taxes.

Unfortunately, the early records are very meager. Not until 1811 do we find given the names of those present at the meetings and a list of the members. In that year there were ten present, and the total membership was given as twenty-one. The next year, out of twenty-five members sixteen were present at the meeting, a large proportion considering the delays and difficulties of travel at that time. It is probable that the membership and attendance during those early years did not vary greatly from the foregoing figures

The original list of what may be called charter members contained the names of several men of mark in their day, not only eminent in their profession but conspicuous also for qualities which make for good citizenship. Such were Dr. Theophilus Rogers of Norwich, son of a distinguished physician of the same name, leader of the memorialists of 1763, and incorporator of the State Medical Society; Drs. Thomas Coit and Simon Wolcott of New London, the two most eminent and highly regarded physicians in the south part of the county; Dr. John R. Watrous of Colchester, a Revolutionary surgeon of note, six times president of the State Society, and long the most

prominent practitioner of his region; Dr. Philip Turner of Norwich, one of
the ablest surgeons of his time, Surgeon General of the Eastern Division of
the Continental army, later in association with Dr. Philemon Tracy carrying
on a school at Norwich for training young men as physicians and surgeons;
and the two Downers of Preston, father and son, who rushed to the aid of the
wounded at Fort Griswold.

During the first twenty-five years following its organization in 1792,
there were admitted to its membership several men destined later to become
noted in the exercise of their art. Among these, special mention may be
made of Drs. Samuel H. P. Lee of New London, William Hyde of Stonington, Vine Utley of East Lyme, George and Nathan Tisdale of Norwich,
Thomas Miner then of Lyme afterward of Middletown, Richard Noyes of
Lyme, Richard P Tracy of Norwich, Elisha North, Nathaniel S. Perkins,
Archibald Mercer and Dyer T. Brainerd of New London.

These early meetings were held sometimes in Norwich, "at Mr. Jesse
Brown's," sometimes in New London "at Miner's Coffee House," and again
"at Mr. Haughton's Tavern at Montville," which was a sort of half-way house.
Later on, the meetings were held alternately in Norwich and New London,
and the practice has continued until the present day.

With the lapse of time and increase of population the membership gradually increased until about 1830 from thirty-eight to forty-one members were
listed, and the attendance varied from eleven or twelve to eighteen or twenty.
About this time, too, the names begin to appear of men well remembered by
the older members of the present time. Of these may be mentioned Drs. R. A.
Manwaring, I. G. Porter, Ashbel Woodward, Mason Manning and Elisha
Dyer, Jr. During the '30s the list of members ran from thirty-eight to fifty-
nine, with an attendance of eleven to twenty-one; during the '40s, from
fifty-seven to sixty-five were taxed as members, and from twenty to twenty-
five attended the meetings. About that time the New London City Hotel
and the Merchants' Hotel in Norwich were generally the meeting places.

The association has always included in its membership most of the representative medical men of the county. During its long and honorable past
it has exercised a powerful influence for good, fostering good will and mutual
respect among its members, raising and maintaining ever higher professional
standards, and directly and indirectly in various ways working for the general
good of the public.

Early Physicians.—The shortcomings of the following account none can
realize more keenly than the author. With the scanty leisure at his disposal, he has found it impossible at this time to attempt a complete list of
the former medical men of the county, or to give more than sketchy treatment
of lives which deserve the fullest possible biography If the other towns had
been as fortunate as ancient Norwich in having an Ashbel Woodward, there

The author wishes here to acknowledge his indebtedness to Mrs Elisha E Rogers of
Norwich, Miss Celeste Bush of Niantic, and Mr R B Wall of New London, who have
kindly supplied him with facts of interest and importance

would be little left for the late-coming medical annalist. As they were not so favored, it is hoped that even this cursory and inadequate gathering together of scattered records may be not without interest.*

As pointed out by Dr. Steiner in his interesting Historical Address: "Of the three classes of medical practitioners—the priest physician, the regular physician, and the empiric or charlatan—Connecticut appears to have possessed them all." It is well known that the very earliest physicians of many parts of the colony often belong to the first class. This was not true in general of New London county, and as for its first physician, he must certainly be placed among the regular physicians, although not actually holding the medical degree. This county may well be proud of the distinction of its claim to John Winthrop the Younger, first Governor of Connecticut, as its earliest and one of its most famous physicians. The story of his life has been told so often that only an outline may be recalled here. Born in England, February 12th, 1605-06, he first came to America in 1630. Founder of Saybrooke, later of New London, he resided in the latter town until in 1657 he became the first Governor of the Colony. After that time he lived chiefly in Hartford. He died in Boston, April 5th, 1676. Having a marked taste for the natural sciences, a good knowledge of medicine for his time was among his accomplishments, which his generous and sympathetic temperament led him to practice so far as other demands upon his time would allow. A considerable amount of correspondence and other data are extant showing the wide range of his interests, and the high degree of confidence reposed in his knowledge and skill by all classes of his fellow citizens.

There were probably others practicing the healing art in this county contemporaneously with Winthrop, but we know next to nothing about them. Unless made prominent by some other activity, as in church or politics, their very names are apt to be forgotten with the lapse of time. For several generations after the founding of the colony it was too often true, as Dr. Woodward[1] (p. 167) says, that "many devoted to the duties of their calling the undivided energies of long and laborious lives, reaping only a scanty pecuniary recompense for the present, and no place at all in the grateful recollection of posterity."

As regards the early physicians of Norwich, I can add nothing to Dr. Woodward's admirable accounts, and almost all my facts are drawn from that source. We are indeed fortunate in having such accurate and full biographies written by one skilled in historical and genealogical research. Of the profession as a whole in Norwich, Dr. Woodward has this to say: "The medical profession in ancient Norwich was more than respectable; was distinguished. As practitioners, several of its members had few superiors on the continent As reformers of abuses and peerless advocates of salutary though unpopular changes, they held a place in the foremost rank." Of the following, some belonged to Norwich proper, others to that part which was called at first Norwich West Farms, and afterward Franklin.

Dr. John Olmstead (or Holmstead) appears to have been the very first medical man of the place. He was from Saybrooke in 1660 and practiced both in the town proper and at West Farms. "He was something of a surgeon, and is said to have had considerable skill in the treatment of wounds, particularly those caused by the bite of the rattlesnake. He was fond of frontier life, and enjoyed to a high degree the sports of the chase." He died in 1686.

Dr. Solomon Tracy, born about 1651, came to Norwich with his father, Lieut. Thomas Tracy and family, in 1660 He studied with the last-named, and practiced both in Norwich and Franklin. Miss Caulkins[10] says: "He must be remembered among the solid men of the first generation. Very active in all town affairs." He died July 9th, 1732.

Dr. Caleb Bushnell, born May 26, 1679, married January 9th, 1699-1700, Ann Leffingwell, and had one son and five daughters. "Captain Bushnell, as he was more generally called, died February 18, 1724-25, having accumulated by sagacity in business an estate of about £4000." He held various town offices.

Dr. David Hartshorne was the earliest physician to actually settle in Franklin. He was born in Reading, Mass., in 1656, and moved to Franklin about 1700 He was "highly esteemed as a physician, and was a leading man both in civil and ecclesiastical affairs." He died November 3rd, 1738.

Dr John Sabin, born in Pomfret, 1696, early removed to that part of Franklin called Portapaug, where he built up a large practice. He died March 2nd, 1742

Dr. Thomas Worden studied with Dr. Hartshorne, and lived near the present village of Baltic. He died 1759.

Dr. Theophilus Rogers was born in Lynn, Mass., October 4th, 1699. He studied in Boston, and practiced there for a time. Later he moved and settled in Norwich West Farms, where he resided until his death, September 29, 1753. "While he possessed firmness and good judgment as a physician, his natural timidity was excessive. It is said that he built his house very low between joints in order to avoid danger from high winds, and covered the windows with wooden shutters, to keep out the glare of lightning. Whenever called abroad in the night, he preferred to have someone accompany him."

Dr. Joseph Perkins was born in Norwich, in 1704, and graduated from Yale at the age of 23. Dr. Woodward writes of him: "Having enjoyed the best medical instruction obtainable, he opened an office in the present Lisbon. Possessed of brilliant talents, ardent in the pursuit of knowledge and venturesome in experiment, he became distinguished as a daring surgeon. Most of the capital operations of the circumjacent country were performed by his hand. . . . Dr. Perkins was also a man of piety, patriotism and benevolence." He married, July, 1730, Mary, second daughter of Dr. Caleb Bushnell, before mentioned. "His eldest son, Dr. Joseph, became an eminent physician in his native town; was the father of Dr. Joseph Perkins, late of Norwich, and Dr. Elijah Perkins of Philadelphia, who died in 1806." Another son, Dr. Elisha Perkins of Plainfield, was the famous inventor of the "metallic tractors" which for a time were all the rage both here and in Europe The first Dr. Perkins died July 7th, 1794. He was a memorialist of 1763.

Dr. John Barker was an eminent physician of Franklin, born in Lebanon, 1729. He studied with Dr Joseph Perkins and began practice about 1750. "As a physician, Dr. Barker enjoyed an enviable popularity both with the public and the profession. He was extensively employed in consultation throughout eastern Connecticut, and great deference was yielded to his opinions. . . . He was a man of sparkling wit, quick perceptions, sound common sense, and, not least, generous heart. It was to these strong and noble traits of character that he owed his success, for he was not graced with elegance of person or polish of manner, nor did his pointed repartees derive their force from any fastidious selection of words." He was also popular as a medical teacher. He was one of the original memorialists of 1763, and was the president of the voluntary New London County Medical Society from its formation in 1775 until his death, June 13, 1791. He was evidently a man of marked originality and great force of character.

Dr. Obadiah Kingsbury was a student of Dr. Barker. He was born in 1735, and practiced in Franklin. "Though dying in 1776 at an early age, he accumulated by his industry a handsome estate." He also was one of the memorialists of 1763.

Dr. Nathaniel Hyde, another student of Dr. Barker, was born in Franklin in 1746, and located in his native town. "He was a judicious practitioner, though his remedies were chiefly of a domestic character. His field of labor was limited, and he had abundant leisure, which was devoted to reading and meditation. . . . He is said to have done most of his business on foot." He never married, and died in 1832. He was a charter member of the New London County Medical Association.

Dr. Benjamin Ellis was born in Franklin, in 1752; "he studied with Dr Joshua Downer of Preston, and settling in Franklin acquired an extensive practice, particularly in the department of obstetrics." He died in 1825. He also was an original member of the County Medical Association.

Dr. Elijah Hartshorne, another native of Franklin, was born in 1754. "He studied with Dr. Philip Turner, and located in the southern part of his native society. Dr. Hartshorne was a careful and judicious practitioner. His field was a circumscribed one, and he did his business on foot." His name appears in the list of original members of the County Medical Association. He died in 1839.

Dr. Theophilus Rogers, Jr., was born about 1731, married, March 25th, 1754, Penelope Jarvis of Roxbury, Mass., and had one son and three daughters He studied with his father, and established himself at Bean Hill. "He was noted for rigid adherence to etiquette and nicety in matters of dress and appearance. Habitual courtesy, graceful manners and skill in the winsome play of conversation threw a charm around his presence which was felt alike by young and old." He was very active during the Revolution, and a member of the committee of safety. He headed the memorialists of 1763, was an incorporator of the State Medical Society, a charter member and the first chairman of the County Medical Association. In 1798 the honorary degree of M. D. was conferred upon him by the Connecticut Medical Society.

Dr. Elihu Marvin was born in Lyme, about 1753, a graduate of Yale in

1773, and a student with Dr. Theophilus Rogers, Jr., of Norwich, whose daughter he later married. In 1777 he entered the army in Colonel Durkee's regiment as adjutant. He wintered at Valley Forge, and won a high reputation as a brave and efficient officer. After the war he was a leader in reorganizing the militia, and, rapidly rising in rank, was appointed brigadier-general in 1793. In 1798, when the yellow fever broke out in New London, Dr. Marvin went to New York to study the disease in order to qualify himself for its treatment. Upon his return he was called to attend one or more patients with that disease. Holt states that he took the infection "while attending Mr. Stewart at Mr. Haughton's, who lived at Montville," and died a few days afterward. To quote Dr. Woodward again: "Like many noble brethren in a calling around which dangers thicken frightfully when 'pestilence walketh in darkness and destruction wasteth at noonday,' he offered his life in the devoted endeavor to ward off the blow of the destroyer from others. His death sent a pang through the community, falling crushingly upon an amiable wife and six small children." "Dr. Dwight Ripley, an intimate and valued friend, was with him much in his brief illness of four days, and, with his father-in-law, Dr. Rogers, was the only man who had the courage to assist in preparing his body for burial." (Salisbury,[17] VIII, p. 166.) He died September 13, 1798, and was buried in Chelsea Landing burial ground. He was an original member of the County Medical Association.

Dr. Benjamin Wheat was born in Cambridge, Mass., in 1709, the son of Dr. Samuel Wheat. He studied with his father, and when twenty-one years old moved to Norwich, where he lived a little below Bean Hill. He had many students, and a practice which extended over thirty years.

Dr. Elisha Tracy was born in Franklin, 1712, a graduate of Yale, 1738, and studied medicine with Dr. Theophilus Rogers, Sr. "He possessed thorough classical scholarship and was well versed in medical literature." He was a member of the committee which in 1775 was appointed to examine all candidates for positions of surgeon and surgeon's mate in the army. His activity in relation to small pox inoculation has already been noted. He was a memorialist of 1763. He died in 1783, "widely beloved and lamented."

Dr. Philemon Tracy, son of the preceding by his second wife, Elizabeth Dorr of Lyme, was born May 30, 1757. "Having enjoyed the professional teachings of his father and Dr. Philip Turner, he practiced medicine in his native town for more than fifty-five years. His forte lay in the patient and thorough investigation of chronic diseases, especially those which, from their complications, demanded deep research and accurate discrimination. Honorable as a counselor and faithful as a physician, his services were extensively sought both at home and abroad." Mrs. Sigourney[18] has left a word-picture of him which deserves quotation:

"I think I see now that cautious mentor-like person, so grave and courteous, his countenance marked with deep thought and kindness—Dr. Philemon Tracy. I remember him among my benefactors. From his father he inherited medical skill and, monopolizing the principal practice of the city, yet let the pressure of his business be ever so great, he studied a new case as a faithful clergyman does a sermon. He happily avoided the extremes which my Lord Bacon has designated: 'Some physicians are so conformable to the humor of the patient that they press not the true treatment of the disease, and others are so bound by rules as to respect not sufficiently his condition' But the practice of our venerated healer was to possess himself of the idiosyncrasies of constitution as well as of the symptoms of the disease, to administer as little medicine as possible, and to depend much on regimen and rousing the recuperative powers to their wonted action. His minute questions and long deliberation inspired confidence, while the sententious mode of delivering his prescriptions gave them a sort of oracular force."

He was an incorporator of the Connecticut Medical Society, an original member of the County Medical Association, and several times Fellow of the State Society. He received the honorary degree of M. D. from the Connecticut Medical Society in 1816 He was blind for several years before his death, which occurred in 1837, at the age of eighty.

Dr. Philip Turner was one of the most distinguished men in the medical profession that Eastern Connecticut has ever produced. He was born February 25, 1739-40. He studied under Dr. Elisha Tracy, whose daughter Lucy he afterward married. In 1760 he was appointed assistant surgeon in a regiment at Ticonderoga, and this was renewed in 1761. He became widely acquainted and popular with the English surgeons, and was thus "afforded opportunities for improvement rarely enjoyed by men from the Colonies." He continued in service until the peace of 1763, when he returned and took up private practice in Norwich. With the breaking out of the Revolution he immediately entered the army again. Dr. Woodward states that he was with the Connecticut troops on their first campaign before Boston. "He was also with the army in New York in 1776." In 1777 he was "appointed Surgeon General of the Eastern Department of the army, which position he ably filled to the end of the war. He then returned to his private field of labor where he stood unrivalled as an operator" "The late Dr. Shippen of Philadelphia remarked that he had never either in Europe or America seen an operator that excelled him" In association with his brother-in-law, Dr. Philemon Tracy, he instructed many students and lectured upon the essential medical branches. Dr. Turner was a memorialist of 1763, an incorporator of the State Medical Society, and an original member of the County Medical Association. About 1800 he moved to New York, and soon afterward was appointed surgeon to the staff of the United States army, which position he held until his death in the spring of 1815

Dr. Richard Tozer was a student of Dr. Benjamin Wheat. He lost his life in the Louisburg expedition in 1745, being surgeon's mate under Dr. Norman Morrison.

Dr. Jonathan Marsh was born in Wethersfield, but settled in Norwich, and became prominent as a surgeon, especially in bone setting. He served as surgeon in the expedition against Crown Point in 1755-56. He died in 1766. His son Jonathan, born 1754, was also somewhat famous in the treatment of fractures He was an original member of the County Medical Association in 1792, and died April 18th, 1798.

Dr. Elisha Lord was born in Norwich, August 10, 1726. In 1755 he was appointed by the General Assembly surgeon's mate in the Crown Point expedition and he was noted as of Farmington. In 1758 an Elisha Lord went as surgeon in the Canadian invasion, and is then said to be of Canterbury. They were probably one and the same person. In 1759-60 Dr. Elisha Lord was surgeon of the First Regiment, and principal director of hospital stores. He was also surgeon of the First Regiment against Cuba, in 1762. He was one of the memorialists of 1763. He died March 16, 1768.

Dr. Dominique Touzain is mentioned by Miss Caulkins as follows: "On the grave stone of Colonel John Durkee is the following memorial: 'In memory of Doctr. Dominie Touzain who was lost in a hurricane in March 1782 in ye 31st year of his age.'" Additional facts have been kindly supplied to me by Mrs. Elisha E. Rogers of Norwich. He was a French surgeon who came from Latrille, France. He was engaged in the Revolutionary War with the American forces, were captured by the British, and paroled in 1779. He subsequently came to Norwich, where he married Anna, daughter of Colonel John Durkee. He appears to have gone as surgeon on privateering expeditions. The date on the stone seems to be incorrect, as he was known to be living in March, 1783, and was then about to set out on a voyage.

Dr. Richard Proctor Tracy, son of Dr. Philemon, was born 1791, and in 1816 graduated in medicine at Yale. He lived in what was called the Dr. Tracy house, at the foot of Mediterranean Lane, as had his father before him He joined the County Medical Association about 1816, and continued a member until his death, March 17, 1871. Dr. Tracy was noted among his contemporaries not alone for his professional learning and skill, his kindly and genial disposition, but perhaps even more for his wide acquaintance with the best in English literature and for his quaint and original humor. He was affectionately called "Dr. Dick." He never married, and was the last of his family to live in the old homestead. In his obituary notice Dr. Woodward" (1871) remarks: "Thus ends in Norwich the line of medical succession in that family, which commencing with Dr. Solomon, fifth son of Lieut. Thomas, and grand-uncle of Dr. Elisha Tracy, continued for one hundred and eighty years"

Dr. John Turner, oldest son of Dr. Philip, was born in 1764, and died in 1837. He seems to have been a man not only of great professional skill but also of a peculiarly gracious disposition. "Not to mention the heart ever welling forth sympathy for the suffering, the tongue that spoke no words to the sick but words of consolation or cheer, the generous bearing of Dr. Turner toward his medical brethren, his freedom from professional jealousy, and his exertions to promote their welfare, indicated the true nobility of the man." He was an original member of the County Medical Association.

Dr. Gurdon Lathrop was born December 6th, 1767, in Norwich, graduated from Yale in 1787, and married Lucy Ann, daughter of Dr. Philip Turner. He became a member of the County Medical Association in 1793, and died in 1828.

Dr. Lemuel Boswell was a contemporary of Dr. Marvin, and possessed an extensive practice at the Landing.

Dr. Worthington Hooker, born March 2nd, 1806, a graduate of Yale, 1825, M. D. Harvard, 1829, was an active member of the County Medical Association, and in active practice in Norwich from 1830 to 1852. In the latter year he moved to New Haven to accept a professorship in the Yale Medical School. The history of his later life belongs to New Haven Suffice it to say that for the next fifteen years, till his death, November 6th, 1867, he led an extremely busy life, did an enormous amount of writing and other work, and left a highly honorable record.

Dr. Ashbel Bradford Haile was born at Putney, Vermont, May 29, 1806. He was a graduate of Yale in 1835, and in 1842 received his medical degree from same college. Immediately afterwards he settled in Norwich, where, except for three or four years spent in California, he resided until his death, March 8, 1880 He was a member of the County Medical Association from 1842 until his death The author of the obituary of Dr. Haile, Dr. L. B. Almy[19] (1880), says of him: "He always took a firm stand against the numerous forms of quackery, and was steadfast in his endeavors to keep it down, so far as possible. He was . . . a liberal Christian, a genial gentleman, devoted husband and father, and a successful, well-informed, hard working physician."

Dr. Benjamin Fordyce Barker was in practice in Norwich, and a member of the County Medical Association from 1842 to 1849. In the latter year he moved to New York, where he later attained a national reputation.

Dr. Benjamin Butler was born January 30th, 1764 In 1787 he issued a circular announcing that he had been "regularly educated by the learned Dr. Philip Turner in the sciences of Physics and Surgery." He afterward moved and settled in New York State. His name is among the charter members of the County Medical Association. At the time of the yellow fever epidemic in New London, the "Connecticut Gazette," issue of October 24th, 1798, published among the list of donors the name of Dr. Benjamin Butler as contributing "ten fat sheep."

Dr Ashbel Woodward, one if the most distinguished physicians of eastern Connecticut, was born in Willington, June 26th, 1804. Having taken his medical degree at Bowdoin in 1829, he immediately settled in Franklin, and there he lived and worked for the remainder of his long life. He joined the County and State Medical Societies in 1830, was always greatly interested in their welfare, and to near the close of his life took a prominent part in their meetings. He was elected chairman of the County Medical Association frequently, and was Fellow of the State Society no less than fifteen times. He was also president of the Connecticut Medical Society in 1859-60-61, delivering very able presidential addresses, "Historical Account of the Connecticut Medical Society," "Medical Ethics," and "Life" In the Civil War he was examining surgeon of volunteers, and also saw service at the front as surgeon of the 26th Connecticut. The following is taken from the obituary notice by P. C. Woodward, M D.[19] (1886):

"As a physician Dr. Woodward was known for quickness and accuracy of perception. In the sickroom nothing escaped his attention He was especially successful in desperate cases, detecting with the rapidity of intuition the slightest change in the condition of the patient and anticipating every emergency."

Notwithstanding his arduous practice, Dr. Woodward found time to follow up certain extra-professional hobbies which interested him, and considering his limited time did a remarkable amount of writing. Besides his medical papers, he wrote biographies and memoirs, and a treatise on Wampum. He took the keenest interest in local history and genealogy, the results of which appear in his "History of Franklin" and in his sketches of early Norwich physicians. The latter are models of their kind, and we medical men of this generation owe a deep debt of gratitude to Dr. Woodward for rescuing from oblivion so many of these old-time predecessors of ours and making them live for us again. He possessed the joy of the collector, too; rare books and pamphlets, coins, Indian relics, and especially town and county histories and genealogies all came his way.

"During his long term of active service Dr. Woodward ministered in sickness to at least six successive generations, and from the beginning to the end commanded the unqualified confidence of his clientage. Often appealed to for counsel and guidance, he was never known to discuss or even mention a matter that came to his knowledge in the sacredness of profesional intercourse. Scrupulous in performing the work of each day, thorough in all undertakings, intolerate of sham and pretense, direct in aims and methods, he pursued uncompromisingly the paths marked out by his conceptions of duty."

There were not a few other medical men who were for a longer or shorter time before 1860 identified with Norwich, and it is a matter for regret that their names only can be entered here. Some of these were: Drs. Robert Bell, George and Nathan Tisdale, William P. Eaton, Chauncey and Reuben Burgess, Elisha Dyer, Jr., Jonathan W. Brooks, Benjamin F. Roath, John P. Fuller, John D Ford, Jeremiah King, Benjamin D. Dean, Horace Thurston and Daniel F. Gulliver.

Of the other towns surrounding Norwich, Preston is conspicuous as the home of the two Downers. Dr Joshua Downer was born in Norwich, August 6, 1735, married, February 25, 1762, Hulda Crary, and died July 11th, 1795. He was one of the memorialists of 1763, an incorporator of the Connecticut Medical Society and an original member of the County Medical Association. He was surgeon of the 8th Regiment in the Revolutionary War, and assisted in caring for the wounded at Fort Griswold in 1781. He lived in Preston City, in a large old house at the north end of the village.

His son, Dr. Avery Downer, was born in 1763, and succeeded his father. He was present and assisted his father in ministering to the wounded after the battle of Groton Heights. He was assistant surgeon in 1782. An original member of the County Medical Association, he always took a prominent part in all its activities. He was chosen Fellow of the State Society every year from 1800 to 1816, inclusive, and frequently after that. He was also elected chairman of the County Medical Association no less than twenty times. In 1817 the Connecticut Medical Society granted him the honorary degree of

M. D. He was the last survivor of the battle of Fort Griswold. His death occurred in 1854 at the age of 91.

Dr. Bishop Tyler was a member of the County Medical Association from 1811 to 1816 and again in 1842-43. But beyond that I have no knowledge of his career.

Dr. Eleazer Butler Downing was born in Canterbury, December 15, 1786. He studied with Dr. Fuller of Plainfield, and at Philadelphia, and began practice in Preston City in 1811. He joined the County Medical Association in 1814, was elected Fellow a number of times, and continued a member until his death, January 20th, 1870. He was surgeon in the army in the War of 1812. At one time he seems to have kept a tavern, as the Medical Association met in 1838 "at the Inn of Doct. Eleazer Downing, Preston." The little village in the south part of Preston called Poquetannock had its physicians in old times. Of these may be mentioned Drs. Benjamin Harris, Thomas W Gay, Henry C. Randall, and Phineas Hyde.

Griswold had several substantial physicians in early times, among them Dr. Rufus Smith, who was a member of the Medical Association from 1813 to 1830. Dr. Lucius Tyler lived in Jewett City. He joined the Medical Society in 1817 and continued a member until his death in 1847. He was chosen Fellow of the State Society for ten of those thirty years.

Dr John C. Tibbitts was also a resident of Jewett City He joined the Medical Society in 1824, served as clerk in 1828-29, and was several times chosen Fellow of the State Society He appears to have moved away in 1841.

In the town of Lisbon one of the leading physicians was Dr. Jedidiah Burnham. He was born in Lisbon in 1755, "studied with Dr. Joseph Perkins, Sr., and for a time practiced in his native town. Late in life he removed to Ohio, where he died in 1840" He was an original member of the County Medical Association

Dr. Luther Manning was born in Scotland, Connecticut, in 1748. He settled in Lisbon, and continued there in active practice until near the time of his death, May 7th, 1813 According to the "History of New London County,"[59] he was assistant surgeon in the Revolutionary army, and was on duty at New London when the town was burned, September 6th, 1781. He was an original member of the County Medical Society, continuing until 1812. He had two sons who became physicians—Luther in Scotland, Connecticut, and Mason, whose long and active professional life was mostly passed at old Mystic. Dr. Vine Smith was a member of the County Medical Association from Lisbon from 1824 till 1852.

The fine old town of Lebanon was seldom without one or more solid practitioners. Dr. Joseph Comstock was a member of the County Medical Society from 1826 to 1861, and was several times chosen chairman and Fellow of the State Society.

Dr. Erastus Osgood joined the Medical Society in 1826, and continued a member until 1867. The latter part of his life he practiced in Norwich. Drs. Charles H Dutton and Elisha Hutchinson were practitioners in this town from about 1828 until 1835.

Dr Ralph E. Greene was the son of Dr. Daniel Greene of Auburn, Massachusetts, and was born September 15, 1815 He was a graduate of Amherst in 1835 After completing his medical studies he assisted his father several years, and then settled in Lebanon He joined the Medical Society in 1844, continuing a member until his death. July 30, 1845, he married Sarah C. Dutton. He died in Lebanon, May 20, 1874

At Bozrah, the first physician would appear to have been Dr. Christopher Huntington He was born in Norwich West Farms, and was "grandson of Christopher the first male child born in Norwich. Dr. Huntington appears to have been the sole physician of New Concord (Bozrah) during its early history." (Woodward.")

A later and better known physician was Dr. John Scott. He was born in Groton, "studied with Dr. Elisha Tracy and settled in Bozrah. He possessed great professional merit, taught many students, and died at an advanced age." He died February 3rd, 1834, age 88.

Of Dr. Earl Knight, not much is known. He joined the County Medical Society in 1824 and died in 1832. Something seems to have interfered with his success, as in the 1830 record he is noted as "bankrupt," and his dues abated.

Dr. Samuel Johnson was born in Bozrah, July 1st, 1805. He studied with Drs Earl Knight and Joseph Peabody of Montville, attended the College of Physicians and Surgeons in 1828, and graduated from Yale, M. D., in 1829. He immediately settled in Bozrah, where he continued to practice during the rest of his long life He married in 1836 and left three sons. He had students at various times. His obituary notice by Dr S. L. Sprague" (1879) of Norwich ends as follows: "Dr. Johnson was sincere and earnest in his convictions of duty. He possessed a quick perception of the nature of disease, and was keen in diagnosis. He was an agreeable man to meet in consultation. having kindness of manner. honesty of purpose. good judgement and practical common sense."

Colchester has been distinguished for several remarkable physicians. The Rev. John Bulkley, son of the Rev Gershom, was one of the earliest, joining the two professions as his father did before him. His son John, though more conspicuous in the law, is also said to have practiced medicine to some extent.

Dr John Richard Watrous was in his day one of Connecticut's shining lights in the medical profession, as well as one of Colchester's most distinguished citizens. He was born in Colchester, March 16th, 1754. He saw military service during the whole of the Revolutionary War, and was one of the committee of eighteen appointed to examine candidates for the positions of surgeon and surgeon's mate Such experience combined with marked native ability gave him a lasting prestige. He was an incorporator of the State Medical Society, of which he was president from 1807 to 1812 He was also an original member of the County Medical Society, served as clerk twice, was chairman six times, and was repeatedly elected Fellow of the State Society. In 1804 he received the honorary degree of M. D from the Connecticut Medical Society. He maintained a high standing in the community, was most successful as a practitioner, and was widely consulted, especially as a surgeon. Dr.

N I —1-23

Watrous was three times married. He died December 13th, 1842. A full and interesting account of his life is contained in Dr. Russell's article.'

Dr. Thomas Skinner was an original member of the County Medical Society, was chosen Fellow in 1794, and had his tax abated in 1802. A little later Drs. Elijah Butts and John Billings were physicians in Colchester, but of them little is thus far known

Dr. Frederick Morgan was born in Groton, September 6, 1791. He was a graduate of Yale in 1813, after which he taught, and from 1816 to 1818 was a tutor in Yale College. Having in the meantime been reading medicine with Dr. John O. Miner, of his native town, he was able to secure his medical degree from Yale in 1819. He settled in Colchester in 1820, where, except for the years 1824 to 1831, which were passed in Middletown and Ellington, he lived and practiced the remainder of his life. He early married the daughter of Dr. John R. Watrous, and they had six sons and two daughters.

Dr. Morgan took a keen interest in the welfare of his home town, was trustee of Bacon Academy for many years, and deacon of the church for about forty years. He was a member of the County Medical Society from 1822 to 1876 "Dr. Morgan brought to his profession a high order of intellect, a sympathetic heart, and a conscientious fidelity to duty. He preserved throughout life the studious habits formed in his youth, and these, aided by a tenacious memory, gave him a well-stored and highly cultured mind. . . . His patients felt that with professional skill he brought to them a heart tenderly alive to suffering, and his kindly sympathetic face brought sunshine to many a darkened home. The poor had always a friend in him. He gave them freely his professional skill, and often went beyond his means in supplying them with food and raiment." (Woodward," 1878.) He was also greatly interested in antiquarian lore, and was "the standard authority on all matters of local history." He died June 18th, 1877.

Other physicians of Colchester were Drs. Ezekial W. Parsons, Jonathan Dodge, and James R. Dow.

Dr. Melancthon Storrs may be mentioned here, although his life belongs mostly to Hartford county. New London county, however, claims the first decade. He was a graduate of Yale in 1852, and M. D. '53. Soon afterward he settled in Colchester, where he continued to practice until the breaking out of the Civil War. In 1861 he was appointed surgeon to the 8th Connecticut Regiment, and continued in service until July, 1865, being staff surgeon during the last year. At the close of the war he settled in Hartford, which continued his field of work until his death in 1900. He was a member of the New London County Medical Association from 1856 to 1865.

At Montville, two physicians are listed among the original members of the County Medical Association—Dr. David H. Jewett and Dr. George Rogers. The former has already been mentioned in connection with inoculation for small pox. Dr. Joseph Peabody was a prominent physician of the town for many years, and the latter part of his life was spent in Norwich. Other physicians who practiced here in the '30s and '40s were Ephraim Fellows, Henry C. Beardsley, and Jedediah R. Gay.

Dr. John C. Bolles is well remembered by the older medical men now living. He was a graduate of the Vermont Medical College in 1840. He joined the County Medical Association in 1841, was clerk in '46, several times elected Fellow of the State Society, but withdrew in 1861. In 1885 he rejoined the society and continued a member until his death.

New London.—In the early part of its history, following John Winthrop, New London had as a resident one who later acquired much reputation as physician and surgeon. The Rev. Gershom Bulkley became the second minister of the First Church of New London in 1661, and while he was never regularly settled or ordained, he remained and preached until 1667, when he removed to Wethersfield. There is no evidence that he practiced medicine while living in New London. He must, however, have taken it up not long afterward, for by 1675 he had obtained sufficient experience and reputation as a practitioner to be sent out as surgeon of the force against the Narragansett Indians   He was largely employed in that capacity during the Narragansett War. In October, 1686, he was licensed to practice by the General Court (Russell,[2] p 94) He was a man of extensive learning, marked ability and force of character, and exercised great influence in the colony. Two of his sons, while far less distinguished than their father, were well known as practitioners of medicine

According to Miss Caulkins' (p. 231) the first notice of any physician in New London was in 1662. On May 19th that year a man named Robert Chanell "died suddenly, having been well in the morning and at 2 o'clock P. M. he lay dead. The verdict of the jury was rendered in accordance with the opinion of 'John North, professor of Physick,' who being summoned on the occasion, declared that his death was occasioned by unseasonable bathing after inordinate drinking" She states also that "he was probably the Dr. John North that died in Wethersfield in 1682."

The New London County Court Records contain the following: "1687. . . . This court grants liberty unto Mr. Charles Bulkley to practice physic in this county, and grants him license according to what power is in them to do." He was a son of the Rev. Gershom, born in New London, in 1663. He settled in his native town but died young, leaving one child. "His father speaks of him as deceased in an instrument dated Dec 2nd, 1709." (Russell,[2] p 115). His daughter Hannah married, May 18th, 1709, Richard Goodrill of Glastonbury.

Joshua Hempstead in his diary, May 6th, 1715, notes: "Doctr Stephenson Died," and the next day: "I was at home & made ye Docters Coffin & yn at his funeral." Nothing further is known of him. In 1716, Hempstead's wife became very ill following child-birth on July 30th. August 4th he writes "my wife very Ill Mr Winthrop came to visit her in ye Evening used means for her Relief & Mr Miller Let her blood in. Sund 5 fair. My Dear Wife Died about half an hour before Sunrise." A few days later, two of his children were taken very ill, Joshua with "a Sore Throat & fevar," Rashel with "a feaver & flux." Joshua was taken Extream bad about Midnight. I called Mr Jer Miller ye Schoolmaster and physition who readyly gat up Came to See him & tarr ed al night using Such Means as he thought most proper" The next day however he records: "my Dutyful Son Joshua Died about Noon like a Lamb being 17 years & 20 days old a patren of patience."

"Mr. Jer Miller" was Jeremiah Miller, graduate of Yale in 1709 He "studied medicine, and in 1711 settled in New London" (Dexter," Vol. I, pp 83-84) Miss Caulkins' (p 399) states that "he was engaged as principal of the grammar school in New London, in 1714, and continued in that situation for twelve or fifteen years." March 2nd, 1717-18, he married Mary, second daughter of Governor Gurdon Saltonstall. He was one of the leading citizens of the town and held several positions of much responsibility. From 1732 to '47 he was Representative in the General Assembly, and was justice of the peace for many years. According to Dexter," in 1737 he was "appointed naval officer of the port of New London, being the only port for the entry and clearing of large vessels in the colony—and so continued until his death." He died March 15th, 1756. On the previous day Hempstead makes the following entry: "Mr Miller was taken this aftern about 2 Clock with Convulsion fitts. I went to visit him in the Evening, he had 10 or 12 they Say after Sunset & vomited but then Soon Lay Still in a Doze & So I left him as in a Slumber his family & friends around him."

Of Dr. Charles Acourt, Hempstead on February 28th, 1726-27, notes that he had to "assist on an Arbitration between Majr Merriot & Doctr Accourt &c." Again on March 9th: "I was on the Arbitration between Majr Merriot & Doctor Accourts Administrators." The only other item about him that I have found is contained in the proceedings of the Governor and Council in New London, July 28th, 1721, which is quoted by Dr. Russell' (p. 222). The sheriff having a warrant from the Governor "to search for and seize whatsoever he might find imported into the Colony out of the piratical ship . . . he had taken a negro boy, supposed to be about 12 or 13 years old, at Dr. Accourts in Say Brook." I am informed by Mr. R. B. Wall that in the New London land records there is a deed by Samuel Richards to Charles Accourt, 1739-40. which proves that his house stood on the west side of the Mill Brook, "northward from the bridge," making it probable that it was the old Bulkley-Hallam house. This Accourt bought several other pieces of property, and as there is no record that he sold anything, he probably lived in New London until his death. Hempstead's note would imply that Dr. Accourt had died in 1727 Whether the Accourt of the land records was of his family does not appear.

Hempstead records the death of Dr. Giles Goddard, January 31st, 1757, "aged between 50 & 60 He hath been decrepid with the Gout &c Several years & of late Confined to his house & Bed" Dr Goddard was one of the subscribers June 6th, 1725, contributing "for the building and erecting a Church for the service of Almighty God, according to the Liturgie of the Church of England as by law established." (Caulkins,' p. 440) Dr. Goddard was of Groton, but soon after settled in New London. He was one of the first vestrymen of the Episcopal Society, elected in 1732. He seems to have had a high reputation for professional skill and to have enjoyed the respect and confidence of his fellow-townsmen. Hempstead frequently records his professional activities from 1737 on. He resided on Bradley street in 1743.

Dr. Guy Palmes was contemporary with Dr. Goddard. Hempstead makes the following entry, March 27th, 1757 "Dr. Guy Palmes Died before noon aged near 50 I suppose with ye Dropsie." He was apparently the son of Andrew Palmes of New London, who was baptized October 1st, 1682, and died in 1721, and grandson of Major Edward Palmes. Dr. Palmes was also "an early and important member of the Episcopal Society" (Caulkins,[8] p. 444). He is mentioned several times by Hempstead, and it is evident that he stood high in the profession. In 1745 he was living on Bank street.

Dr. Thomas Coit, Sr., came a little later than the two last mentioned. Hempstead's first mention of him is on December 9, 1752. Miss Caulkins[8] (p 476) says of this period: "Dr Thomas Coit was the principal physician He had nearly the whole medical practice of the town for forty years commencing soon after 1750." I gather the following from "The Coit Family," by Rev. F. W. Chapman.[11] He was the only child of Thomas and Mary Prentiss Coit, born August 15th, 1725. He "settled in his native place as a physician and spent there an honorable life . . . dying June 5th, 1811, aged 86." His first wife was Abigail Richards, by whom he had four children. He married for his second wife, Mary Gardiner, by whom he had nine children. He is buried in Cedar Grove Cemetery, New London, his monument bearing the following epitaph: "He was ever ready to pour Wine and Oil, into the wounds of the afflicted, and regulated his actions by the strictest rules of Piety; and died in the full belief of the redeeming love of his Lord and Master."

Dr. Coit lived in the old Coit homestead, which stood where the Armory now is. He was undoubtedly one of the most prominent medical men of his day in eastern Connecticut, and had a long and honorable career. He was one of the incorporators of the State Medical Society, and an original member of the New London Medical County Association. In the Colonial Records of Connecticut he is down for medical services in 1773. (Russell,[8] p. 146.) At the time of the yellow fever epidemic he was active in attending patients during the first fortnight of the outbreak, and until he himself was taken ill with the disease.

In Miss Caulkins[8] (p. 478) we find that about 1764 "Dr. Thomas Moffatt was controller of the customs, and esteemed also as a skillful physician, in which line he had some practice" He was an Englishman, and a friend of Rev. Mather Byles, who in 1768 suddenly severed his connection with the old First Church, of which he had been minister for over ten years. Mr. Byles conveyed his house to Dr. Moffatt as security for repayment to the church of £240 which had been given him upon settlement. Just when Dr. Moffatt left New London is not known, but about 1777 it was represented that he had "withdrawn from America in a hostile spirit and had since been in arms against her" (Caulkins,[8] p 511), so his goods were confiscated He lived for a time in the Byles house, north corner of Main and Douglas streets

A Dr. Samuel Brown lived on the southwest corner of Bank and Golden streets about 1781 He married the daughter of Alexander McNeil, a baker, who owned much real estate which was sold about 1782 by the doctor and his wife. No further information about him has thus far come to light.

Another prominent physician of the latter part of the 18th century was

Dr. Simon Wolcott. He was the son of Dr. Alexander and Mary Richards Wolcott of Windsor, and was born about 1748. He lived first on the west side of Bank street, north of Pearl, later on Coit street, and finally in the Giles Mumford house on Federal street, lately the parish house of the Episcopal Church. He married (first) Lucy Rogers, (second) Charlotte (Woodbridge) Mumford having three children by each wife. He was surgeon of the 6th Regiment in 1775. Just before the attack on New London, September 6th, 1781, he had gone out on a fishing trip off Montauk Point with Mr. Nathaniel Shaw. Having discovered the British fleet, it was too late for them to return to New London Harbor, so they "were obliged to run into Poquonnuck Creek to escape capture" (Caulkins,* p. 548). Dr. Wolcott attended for five months Captain Adam Shapley, who was wounded in the battle of Groton Heights. His bill against the State of Connecticut for his professional services is extant, the charge being at the rate of a shilling a visit. He was clerk of the voluntary New London County Medical Society which preceded the present organization, was an incorporator of the Connecticut Medical Society, and an original member and first clerk of the present New London County Medical Association. He was also frequently elected chairman of the later organization, and Fellow of the State Society. He was one of the foremost medical men of his time and was highly esteemed both in and out of the profession. Dr. Wolcott owned considerable land in the vicinity of Ocean avenue, and was a thrifty and prosperous citizen. He died April 7th, 1809, aged 61.

Dr. Cornelius Coningham was born in Ireland, in 1746. When he settled in New London is not known. There is good reason to believe that he was for a time surgeon at Fort Trumbull. He died in New London, in 1820.

Dr. Samuel H P. Lee has been already mentioned in connection with the yellow fever epidemic. He was born probably in Lyme, August 5th, 1772. He was named for Maj. Gen. Samuel Holden Parsons, a cousin of his father and his commanding officer. Dr. Lee's father, Capt. Ezra Lee, won distinction in the Revolutionary War as the navigator of the first submarine used in warfare, David Bushnell's "Turtle." His great-great-grandfather was Thomas Lee (2d), who lived in the old Lee house in East Lyme. His mother was Deborah Mather of Lyme. He married Elizabeth Sullivan, daughter of the purser of the British frigate "Cygnet," which lay in New London Harbor. They had a son, Dr. Henry Sullivan Lee, who graduated at Yale in 1823. Dr. Lee had an unusual number of medical relatives—Drs. John Lee of Sharon, John Allen Lee of Clinton, New York, Tully Lee of Hartford, Daniel Lee of Lyme, James Lee of New London, and it is not improbable that he may have studied with one or other of these men. Part of his education, however, was obtained in New York, for with the record of his election to membership in the New London County Association in September, 1793, it is stated that he had "produced letters testifying his having acquired sufficient knowledge to practice physic and surgery from Doctor Bailey of New York and sundry other gentlemen." Dr. Lee was an active member of the County Medical Association, having been clerk in 1811-12-13, and Fellow of the State Society from 1806 to '14, inclusive, and again in 1816 and '19. He was the author of two prize essays delivered before the Convention of the State Society, one in 1794 on "Autumnal Bilious Fever," and the other in 1796 on "Cynanche Tonsillaris." In 1795 he was operating a small pox inoculation hospital. In addition to his medical practice, Dr. Lee carried on an extensive drug business. This was located on the southeast corner of Main and State streets, and at one time also on Bank street, near where the Hotel Royal is now. He later lived in a house on Federal street, which had previously been the residence of Dr Wolcott, and it was in this house that he manufactured his famous New London Bilious Pills. Reliable tradition has it that at the time of the yellow fever he was driven about the city night and day by his faithful black, visiting the sick, often falling asleep between the calls and sometimes in the patient's house, so overcome was he from loss of sleep. It is told of him also that in sleighing times he would drive about the city in a fine sleigh drawn by two white horses. He was a successful business man, and bought and sold much real estate. Dr. Lee was also one of the founders of the whaling industry in New London, having fitted out the "Dauphin" in 1804, and the "Leonidas" in 1806. He moved to New York in 1838, where he died January 7th, 1863, at the age of 91. He is buried in Cedar Grove Cemetery.

Dr. James Lee was a cousin of the last named. He practiced first at the "head of the river," East Lyme At the time of the yellow fever epidemic he assisted Dr. S H. P Lee Later he moved to New London, where he built what was called the Brandegee house on State street, standing on the site of the present Crocker House. In 1812 he sold out his New London realty and moved to Trenton, New Jersey He was an original member of the County Medical Association, which he served twice as clerk and which twice elected him Fellow of the State Society He was dismissed at his own request in 1805.

Dr Samuel Seabury, Jr, was the son of Samuel Seabury. Yale 1748, Bishop of Rhode Island and Connecticut. He lived at first in Groton, later in New London on State street, in what was subsequently Dr Brainerd's house. He was an original member of the New London County Medical Association He died at the age of 29, in 1795, and was buried in the Second Burying Ground.

Dr. Thomas Coit, Jr., the son of Dr. Thomas and Mary Gardiner Coit already referred to, was born in New London, April 2nd, 1767, married November 29th, 1789, Mary Wanton Saltonstall, and settled in his native place He probably studied with his father, and for some time practiced "along side of his father, and therefore distinguished from him as young Dr. Coit." (Chapman.") Dr. Coit had eight children, the last born October 28th, 1808. He was an original member of the New London County Medical Association in 1792, and always took an active part in its doings, serving as clerk 1806-10, and chosen Fellow of the State Society for eleven years in succession, 1803 to '13. He was last returned as a member in 1839. About 1795 he operated a small pox inoculation hospital in competition with Dr. Lee. He received the honorary degree of M. D. from the Connecticut Medical Society in 1817. About 1825 Dr. Coit lived in a house on the corner of Main and Douglas streets. Dr Coit was a worthy successor of his father, a credit to his family name, and left a highly honorable record both as a medical man and as a leading citizen.

Of Dr. Thomas H. Rawson, our present knowledge is confined to the mention of him in connection with the yellow fever, the fact of his advertising later "Dr. Rawson's Worm Powders, Prepared by Thomas H. Rawson, member of the Conn. Med. Soc.," and finally the record (Proc. Conn. Med. Soc. 1792-1829, Reprint, 1884, p. 112) of his expulsion from the Connecticut Medical Society, October 17th, 1804, on account of his failure to answer to the charge of "making and vending nostrums, contrary to the bye-laws of the institution, and the expressed principles thereof." He belonged originally to Hartford county.

Dr. Winthrop Saltonstall, born in New London, February 10, 1775, was a graduate of Yale in 1793, and in 1796 had the degree of M. D. from Columbia. There is reason to believe that he never practiced in his native town According to Dexter[6] (Vol. V., p. 83), he settled and engaged in practice at Port of Spain in Trinidad, and "he died there after a short and painful illness from yellow fever June 20 (or 27), 1802, in his 28th year. He was unmarried."

Drs. Luke and Charles Douglas were brothers, sons of Richard Douglas, a Revolutionary War veteran They were born respectively in 1788 and 1792. It does not appear that either of them practiced medicine in New London Charles had formerly been a practitioner in Washington, D. C., but later returned to New London and lived in the family home on Green street. The old gambrel-roofed house is still standing, and now occupied by the office of Mr. William S Chappell. During the latter part of his life Dr. Douglas held many political offices

Of Dr. Joseph Woodbridge Lee I only know that he died young, at the age of 31, October 10th, 1795

Dr. William Graham was listed among the original members of the County Medical Association, was again elected in 1793, but in 1810 he was readmitted, having been "out of the State some years." Nothing further is known of him

During the early years of the 19th century, several men settled in New London who later became eminent in the profession. One of the most noted of these was Dr. Elisha North, who moved here from Goshen, Connecticut, and settled in 1812. He was already at that time a man of wide reputation in the State. Only a summary of his life can be given here; indeed, little or nothing could be added to the admirable biographies already published, viz., the earlier one by H Carrington Bolton,[22] and especially the full and admirable one by Dr. Walter R. Steiner.[23] Dr. North was born at Goshen, January 8th, 1770 He studied at first with Dr. Lemuel Hopkins of Hartford, and later at the University of Pennsylvania in 1793-94, but did not graduate. He practiced in Goshen until 1812. He was already famous for the fact that he was one of the earliest and most enthusiastic advocates of vaccination in this State, and for his study of the spotted fever outbreak in 1807-8. At the time of his advent in New London he was in the prime of life and at once took a high rank in the profession and in the community. Immediately after settling in New London Dr. North joined the County Medical Association, and continued an active and honored member until his death. He served as clerk in 1814-15, and was several times chosen chairman and Fellow of the Connecticut Medical Society. In 1813 the Connecticut Medical Society granted him the honorary degree of M. D. Dr. North is famous also for his eye infirmary, the first in this country, which he opened in 1817. He writes of it as follows. "We had attended to eye patients before that time, but it occurred to us then, that we might multiply our cases of that description and thereby increase our knowledge by advertising the public in regard to an eye institution. This was done and we succeeded: although not to our wishes in a pecuniary view of the case. Our success, or exertions, probably hastened in this country the establishment of larger and better eye infirmaries (i.e., for larger cities)." (Steiner,[22] p. 11.)

Dr. North was the author of a considerable number of works both medical and philosophical. Among them are his books on spotted fever already mentioned, "Outlines of the Science of Life," "Rights of Anatomists Vindicated," "The Pilgrim's Progress in Phrenology," and several technical medical papers. "Besides being known as a writer and man of mark, North is also distinguished for having invented four forgotten surgical instruments—an improved trephine, an eye speculum, a trocar, and a new form of catheter. The first two were exhibited before the State Medical Society in 1821, and the last two had the indorsement of four New London physicians." (Steiner,[22] p. 19.) Bolton[21] states that in his practice he "exhibited a remarkable degree of caution, deliberation, and careful reflection. When concerned with the health and comfort, and we may add the moral welfare of his patients or friends, he exercised a conscientious care and thoughtfulness that preserved him from unsafe enthusiasm or dangerous and extreme views. As a consulting physician he enjoyed the confidence and friendship of his brethren, and was much valued for his philosophical habits of mind in cases of difficulty and uncertainty." About 1824 he lived for a time on a farm in East Lyme, and while there became interested in peat as fuel. The "American Journal of Science" for 1826 contains an article upon the subject from his pen. Dr. North was a man of quaint and original humor, and several anecdotes are extant illustrating this phase of his character. He died in New London, December 29th, 1843. A large granite monument marks his grave in Cedar Grove Cemetery.

Dr. Samuel Huntting was a contemporary of Dr. North, but died August 4th, 1818, at the comparatively early age of 42. Little is known of his life.

Dr. Archibald Mercer appeared in New London the same year as Dr. North. He was born in Millstone, New Jersey, December 1st, 1788, graduated from Princeton, 1807, and studied medicine in Philadelphia. Dr. Mercer joined the Medical Society in 1812 and continued an active member until his death. He received the degree of M. D. from Yale in 1827. Dr. Mercer lived on State street, in a house which was some years ago bought by the Y. M. C. A. He was a man of marked ability, stood well in the profession, and taught many students. One of New London's streets was opened by and named for him. Dr. Mercer died October 3rd, 1850

Dr. Dyer Throop Brainerd was another member of this group. He was born in New London, June 10th, 1790, of a conspicuous and honorable Connecticut family, descended in direct line from Daniel Brainerd of Haddam. Dr Brainerd's father, Hon. Jeremiah Gates Brainerd, Yale 1779, was a distinguished lawyer and for many years judge of the Supreme Court of the State. Dr. Brainerd was named for Gen. Dyer Throop of East Haddam, with whom his father studied law. The poet-lawyer, J. G. C. Brainerd, was a brother of the doctor, as was William F. Brainerd, an eminent lawyer of New London. Dr. Brainerd was a graduate of Yale in 1810, and received the honorary degree of M. D. in 1827 from the Connecticut Medical Society. He settled in New London in 1813 and lived in an old house on the north side of State street, between Union and Main. He became a member of the County Medical Association in 1813, served as clerk in 1816-17, and was chosen Fellow of the State Society seventeen times. In the winter of 1819-20 Dr. Brainerd attended a course of medical lectures in New York. He was military surgeon at New London in 1813-14, and from 1814 onward for many years was surgeon in the Third Brigade (Brainard"). He was also for a long period U. S. Marine Hospital Surgeon at this port. Dr. Brainerd was a man of mark, enjoying in high degree the respect and friendship of his fellow practitionists, and the esteem of his fellow citizens. He was also a prominent Mason, Brainerd Lodge having been named for him. Dr. Brainerd never married, and died February 6, 1863.

The fourth member of this eminent group was a scion of a family long distinguished in the annals of Eastern Connecticut. Dr. Nathaniel Shaw Perkins was born in New London, February 11th, 1792, son of Elias and Lucretia Woodbridge Perkins, and grandson of Dr. Joseph Perkins of Norwich. After attending successively Dr. Dow's School in New London, the Bacon and Plainfield academies, he entered Yale, from which he graduated in 1812. He took up the study of medicine with Dr. Elisha North of this city, but after a short time he went to Philadelphia and completed his medical education at the University of Pennsylvania. Directly thereafter he settled in New London in 1815, where he remained in constant practice for fifty-five years. Dr. Perkins early joined the County Medical Association, served the County Association as clerk for a short time, and was frequently elected a delegate to the State Society. He was licensed to practice by the Connecticut Medical Society, and received the honorary degree of M. D. from Yale in 1829. Dr. Perkins married Ellen Richards of New London, and was the father of fourteen children, of whom only six survived him. He died May 25th, 1870, at the Shaw Mansion on Bank street, now the home of the New London County Historical Society. Dr. Perkins was truly the well-beloved physician, and his death was mourned by all, rich and poor alike. Much might be written of his charming personality, and his benevolent and sympathetic disposition, which endeared him to a very wide circle not only of the wealthy and cultivated but as well of the obscure and needy who called upon him for help. An obituary notice by Dr. Isaac G. Porter was read before the New London County Medical Association and published in the State Proceedings for 1871. By natural tastes and thorough training, Dr. Perkins was well fitted for his calling, and he left behind an enviable record of long, arduous and faithful professional achievement.

Dr. James Rogers was born in Waterford in 1785, and his early practice was carried on in that town. He later moved into New London, so that, as he said, he would not have to take all his pay in vegetables. He died in 1851, and was buried with Masonic honors in Cedar Grove Cemetery, in land which had formerly been a part of the farm belonging to his wife. Miss Caulkins' wrote of him: "He was noted for his benevolent medical parctice. He was peculiarly the physician of the poor."

Dr. James Morgan was born in England, March 20th, 1802, but early came to this country with his parents, who settled in New London. He began the study of medicine with Dr. Mercer. His medical education seems to have been unusually thorough, as he is said to have attended lectures in Boston, London, and Philadelphia, graduating at the last-named place in 1828. He settled in New London in 1829. Directly afterwards he joined the County Medical Association, of which he continued a member until his death. He was several times elected Fellow of the State Society. In 1831 he married Miss Charlotte Mercer, daughter of his preceptor. Dr. Morgan had a high reputation as a practitioner and especially as a surgeon. He was also regarded as unusually skilled in the treatment of diseases of the eye. The obituary notice of him by Dr. L. S. Paddock[19] (1860) has this high praise of Dr. Morgan as a man: "He was always the friend of the poor; his charities were liberal in proportion to his means, and his gratuitous professional practice was large. No man was in so humble circumstances as to be refused the Doctor's services, and the expectation of pecuniary compensation was not a motive in his friendly attentions and intercourse with the sick. As a man he was warm-hearted and sincere, generous and upright in all his dealings." He died July 3rd, 1859.

Dr. Robert Alexander Manwaring is well remembered by scores of people yet living. He was born in New London, August 2nd, 1811, son of Christopher and Mary Wolcott Manwaring, and died in the same house, on Manwaring Hill, September 1st, 1890. He began the study of medicine with Dr. Mercer in 1829, after which he completed his medical training at the Harvard Medical School. His first practice was in Gales Ferry, where he settled about 1832, and where he remained until 1841. After an interval of several years passed in New London, he removed to Greenville, in Norwich, where he practiced until 1850. He then returned to New London, where he lived and worked continuously until his death. May 15th, 1845, he married Ellen, daughter of Hon. Noyes Barber of Groton During his whole professional life Dr. Manwaring was a member of the County Medical Association. An obituary notice[18] (1891) by Dr. A. W. Nelson contains the following: "A busy man, he was seen early and late about town among the rich and the poor with equal readiness and acceptance. . . . No man has ever been more pleasantly known among all classes, for he had a just and proper mixture of wit and humor, so that his words were always fresh and effective and not too many. . . . His understanding of general and professional subjects was wide. He was of the speculative and reflective type, turning over things in his own mind, not especially seeking originality, but a safe conclusion by the way of sound common sense." Dr. Manwaring's only son, Wolcott Barber Manwaring, left at his death in 1905 the homestead and all the other property of his estate to found a children's hospital in memory of his parents, to be called the Manwaring Memorial Hospital. The fund is accumulating in the hands of the trustees until such time as it is deemed adequate to carry out the purpose of the donor.

Another eminent New London practitioner whose professional life extended over several generations and whose memory is cherished by many still living, was Dr. Isaac G Porter. He was born in Waterbury, Connecticut, June 29th, 1806, but spent most of his early life in Farmington, where his father was minister of the church. He graduated from Yale in 1826, after which he taught for several years, partly in New London as principal of the Young Ladies' Academy. His medical studies were pursued at first in New Haven, later at the University of Pennsylvania, where he graduated in 1833. Immediately thereafter he settled in New London, which from that time on was the field of his life work. Dr. Porter joined the County Medical Association that same year, and always took a very active part and a keen interest in its meetings and other activities. He served as clerk in 1835-36, was many times chosen chairman, and Fellow of the State Society. In 1866 he was vice-president of the Connecticut Medical Society, on which occasion he read an address entitled: "Medico-Chirurgical Lessons of the War." His presidential address delivered before the State Convention the following year was upon "Self-restorative power." From 1861 to '67 he was post surgeon at Fort Trumbull, where he was busily occupied not only in the care of hospital patients but also in the examination of recruits, thousands of whom passed through his hands. Dr Porter was a frequent contributor to medical journals, especially the "American Journal of the Medical Sciences." In fact, he has probably to his credit a longer list of published articles than any other New London physician before or since

Dr. Porter married, September 12th, 1833, Williamina Davis of Philadelphia. Their only son, Captain Edward Leighton Porter, a promising lawyer in Norwich, was killed in action at Winchester, Virginia, June 15th, 1863. Dr. Porter himself died of old age, April 30th, 1892. Dr. Porter loved his life-work, and his enthusiasm for the never ending study of medicine held out to the end. The scientific side especially appealed to him. Keen perceptions, close study of his cases, logical deductions, and cautious treatment, combined to build up for him a large and permanent success.

Dr. Seth Smith was a son of Dr. John L Smith of East Lyme, where he was born October 14th, 1823. He graduated in medicine at the New York University in 1845, after which he established himself in this city. He early entered the drug business, which he carried on in addition to the practice of medicine until 1871, but chronic ill health was a more or less constant handicap in the pursuit of his chosen calling. He left a substantial estate for the establishment of an old ladies' home to be called "The Smith Memorial Home." This benevolent institution has now been in operation for many years, and has brought peace and comfort into the closing years of the lives of many old and homeless or dependent gentlewomen. Dr. Smith died April 18, 1878, in the fifty-fifth year of his age   He was a member of the County Medical Association, serving as clerk for several years until 1858, when he was dismissed at his own request. He rejoined the society in 1876, and thereafter was a member until his death.

There were other New London physicians who are deserving of more adequate notice, but whose names only may be mentioned here. Such were: Drs Abel T. Sizer, Charles C Cone, David P. Francis, Archibald T. Douglas, Albert Hobron, Frank D. Brandegee, Robert McCurdy Lord, Henry Potter, and William W. Miner, all practicing in New London before 1860.

Passing now to the towns of Groton and Stonington, one of the earliest physicians of whom we have record was Dr. Dudley Woodbridge. He was a member of an eminent family, remembered especially for its able clergymen. Dr. Woodbridge was born April 21st, 1705, probably in Center Groton, son of the Rev. Ephraim Woodbridge, first minister of the town of Groton. He married, in 1739, Sarah Sheldon of Hartford. He was a graduate of Harvard College in 1724. He began practice in Old Mystic, but a few years later he bought the "Whitehall Farm" in that part of the town of Stonington just east of Mystic river. He erected and occupied until his death the house which still stands there. Joshua Hempstead refers to him in his professional capacity several times from 1729 on, having called him to attend members of his own family living in Stonington. His last note referring to him occurs in 1755. The Colonial Records for 1771 note Dr. Dudley Woodbridge of Groton as one of a committee   He died October 4th, 1790 (Wheeler,[25] p. 693-4).

Dr. Charles Phelps of Stonington, born September 22, 1732, "came from Hebron, Connecticut, and took up his abode in Stonington, now North Stonington, where he built him a residence near the foot of Cosatuc Hill   He afterwards removed to Stonington, where he spent the remainder of his life. He was one of the leading physicians of his day and generation, holding the office of judge of probate of the town and other offices" (Wheeler,[25] p. 538). He married (first) Hannah Denison, and (second) Sally Swan, having in all fifteen children. Dr. Phelps was one of the incorporators of the Connecticut Medical Society, and an original member of the New London Medical Association. His name does not appear again, however, in the records of that organization, probably on account of his advanced age.

Drs. William Hyde, father and son, were for many years leading practitioners in Stonington. The former was born July 21st, 1783. The son was born in Stonington, October 27th, 1808. He graduated from the Harvard Medical School in 1830, and practiced in Stonington until his death, September 25th, 1873   His reputation was high, and he had an extensive consultation practice. Both father and son were members of the County Medical Association during nearly the whole of their professional lives.

Dr. William Robinson joined the County Medical Association in 1827, but the next year he is noted as exempt from taxation by reason of being over sixty years of age. In 1828 he received the honorary degree of M. D. from the Connecticut Medical Society   He died about 1847.

Dr. George E. Palmer was born in Stonington, April 15th, 1803. He began the study of medicine and graduated from the college of Physicians and Surgeons in New York in 1825. He immediately settled in his native town, where he practiced for over forty years. He was twice married and left numerous descendants. As a physician he was held in high regard by the public, and was popular with his fellow practitioners. He was moreover prominent as a citizen, being seventeen times elected to the office of warden of the borough. He joined the County Medical Association in 1828, was chosen chairman in 1856 and '67, and was elected Fellow of the State Society upwards of ten times. He died May 8th, 1868.

Dr. Thomas P. Wattles was a practitioner in North Stonington. He also entered the County Medical Association in 1828, and was clerk in 1832-33-34. He died in 1854, age 54 years.

Dr. John Owen Miner was for many years a much esteemed physician of Groton. He was born January 9th, 1762, and lived to an advanced age. He dwelt near the old village of Center Groton. He was an original member of the New London County Medical Association, and seemed to have been very faithful in attendance and to have taken a prominent part in its activities. He served as clerk in 1804-05, was chairman no less than ten times, and in the twenty-three years from 1800 to 1822 he was chosen Fellow of the State Society twenty times. In 1815 the Connecticut Medical Society granted him the honorary degree of M. D. He died about 1851.

Dr. Phineas Hide was born in Franklin, in 1749. He practiced first in Poquetannock, but the most of his life work was done in Mystic. He served as surgeon in the Revolutionary War, both in the army and navy.

Drs. Amos Prentiss, Sr. and Jr., may be mentioned as charter members of the County Medical Association in 1792.

The following physicians were also residents of Groton or Stonington at one time or another: Daniel and William Lord, Asher Huntington, Jonathan Gray, James Noyes, Asa Spalding, Alfred Bailey, Andrew T. Warner, Thomas J. Wells, Mason Manning, Edward York, David Hart, Henry C. Brown, Alvah Gray, Horatio Robinson, John P. Wells, Edwin Bentley, John Smith, Joseph Durfee, Orrin E. Miner, Benjamin F. Stoddard, Elias F. and A. W. Coates.

The town of Lyme has been favored with a long line of able practitioners. One of the earliest of record was Dr. Eleazer Mather. He was born November 17th, 1716, and graduated from Yale in 1738. "He settled in Lyme (Hamburg Society), where he was a useful physician, selectman, magistrate, etc." (Dexter,[26] I, p. 607.) He married, November 15th, 1741, Hannah Waterhouse (or Watrous) of Lyme, by whom he had six sons and one daughter. He was one of the committee of eighteen appointed at the time of the Revolution to examine candidates for the positions of surgeon and surgeon's mate (Russell,[*] p. 199). Dr Mather died November 2nd, 1798. On his tombstone he is called: "an eminent physician and a man of universal knowledge."

Dr. Samuel Mather, son of the preceding, was one of the original members of the New London County Medical Association, of which he was chosen chairman in 1804, '09 and '10. He was chosen Fellow of the State Society at its first meeting in 1792, and several times later. In 1804 the Connecticut

Medical Society conferred upon him the honorary degree of M. D. He was dismissed by his own request on account of advanced age in 1813.

Dr John Noyes, another charter member of the County Medical Association, was several times chosen Fellow of the State Society, and was chairman in 1803, after which his name does not occur again on the records.

Dr. Thomas Miner was a member of the New London County Medical Association for four years from 1810 to 1813; after that he removed to Middletown, and became later one of the most distinguished Connecticut physicians of his time, and a medical author of considerable prominence.

Other physicians of Lyme who came later were Drs. John C. M. Brockway, who lived at Hamburg, Richard Noyes, who was a member of the County Medical Society for sixty-two years; Sylvester Wooster, Marvin Smith, Richard Warner, John D. Rogers, Oliver Kingsley, Reuben L. Miner, John Noyes, and William W. J. Warren.

In East Lyme, near the village of Flanders, there were three physicians who deserve mention: Dr. John L. Smith, who was a practitioner there for many years, a member of the County Medical Association from 1813 to his death, December 20th, 1860; Dr. Austin F. Perkins; and Dr. Vine Utley. The latter is especially noteworthy for his early work in vaccination, and as a contributor of articles to the "Medical Repository of New York." He was a member of the County Medical Association from 1807 to 1819. His son, Leander Utley, became a prominent physician in Providence, Rhode Island.

Looking back at the lives of these old-time medical men, I think one may truly say that as a class they do not fall far short of Stevenson's estimate—"to have shared as little as any in the defects of the period, and most notably exhibited the virtues of the race." They chose a calling, arduous and toilsome, and with all shades of native ability and educational advantage they did their work for the most part well and faithfully, striving manfully according to their lights to bring comfort and healing to the sick, and to further the welfare of the communities in which they dwelt. Numbered among them were some few gifted, forward-looking puissant men, the equals of any of their time and country.

REFERENCES

1. Steiner, Walter R., M D : Historical Address, "The Evolution of Medicine in Connecticut, with the Foundation of the Yale Medical School as Its Notable Achievement." New Haven, 1915.

2. Packard, Francis Randolph: "The History of Medicine in the United States." Philadelphia, 1901.

3. Russell, Gurdon W, M D.: "An Account of Early Medicine and Early Medical Men in Connecticut" Proc Conn Med Soc, 1892

4 Lindsley, Charles A., M D. "The Beginning and Growth of Sanitary Legislation in Connecticut" Proc. Conn. Med Soc., 1892.

5. "The Diary of Thomas Minor" Stonington, Conn, 1653-1684; Ed by S H Miner and G D. Stanton, Jr, N.Y., 1899.

6. "N. E. Hist.-Genealog. Reg," Vol 9, pp 43-51.

7 "The Diary of Manasseh Minor," Stonington, Conn., 1696-1720, published by Frank Denison Miner and Miss Hannah Miner, 1915

8. Caulkins, Frances Manwaring· "History of New London, Connecticut." New London, 1852

9 "Diary of Joshua Hempstead of New London, Connecticut," Coll N. L Co. Hist Soc. Vol. I, 1901.

10. Caulkins, Frances Manwaring: "History of Norwich, Connecticut," 1866

11 Woodward, Ashbel, M D : "Biographical Sketches of the Early Physicians of Norwich." Proc. Conn. Med. Soc., 1862.

12. Webster, Noah: "A Brief History of Epidemics and Pestilential Diseases." Hartford, 1799.

13 "Medical Repository," N. Y., New Series, Vol. 2, p 213, "History of the Mortal Epidemic that appeared in the Towns of Lyme and Waterford, Connecticut, 1813," by Dr. Vine Utley of Lyme, Connecticut.

14. Chamberlain, C. W.: "Malaria in Connecticut." Rept. Conn. State Board of Health, 1881.

15. Graves, Charles B., M.D   "Epidemic Disease in Early Connecticut Times." Proc. Conn Med. Soc , 1920.

16. Woodward, Ashbel, M.D.: "Centennial Anniversary of the New London County Medical Association." Proc Conn Med. Soc , 1876.

17 Salisbury, Edward Elbridge and Evelyn McCurdy: "Family Histories and Geneologies," 1892

18. Sigourney, Mrs. Lydia Huntley · "Letters of Life," 1866.

19. Proc. Conn. Med. Soc., various years.

20 Hurd, D. H.: "History of New London County " 1882.

21. Chapman, Rev. F. W.: "The Coit Family." Hartford, 1874.

22. Bolton, H. Carrington: "Memoir of Dr. Elisha North." Proc. Conn Med. Soc., Hartford, 1887

23. Steiner, Walter R., M.D · "Dr Elisha North One of Connecticut's Most Eminent Practitioners." 1908.

24 Brainard, Lucy Abigail: "Brainard-Brainerd Genealogy." Hartford, 1908.

25. Wheeler, Richard Anson: "History of the Town of Stonington." New London, 1900.

26. Dexter, Franklin Bowditch: "Biographical Sketches of the Graduates of Yale College, with Annals of the College History." N. Y , 1885

CHAPTER XIV

NEW LONDON COUNTY PRESS

The "New London Day"—"Norwich Bulletin"—"Cooley's Weekly"

In another part of this history has been printed an outline of the early history of the press in New London County. The following accounts bring this record to date. From the "New London Day" we print by permission Mr. Theodore Bodenwein's account of his experience in building up this paper to its present position of influence:

This is the third time I have been called upon to write the history of "The Day." The first time was in 1894, three years after I bought the paper, and the second time was five years ago, after twenty-five years of ownership and service to the community. Would that some better qualified person assumed the task, now that the period of forty years ago—the birth of "The Day"—is the epoch to be commemorated.

I did not enter the employ of "The Day" until six months after the paper was started, or in December, 1881, so what I write about the early days of the paper comes to me partly from observation and partly through report. Elsewhere in this issue John C. Turner, sole survivor of the trio which founded "The Day," contributes a very interesting and witty article on New London journalism forty years ago, but he modestly refrains from giving a close-up view of the early days of the paper.

"The Day" was founded mainly to give Major John A. Tibbits, a well-known lawyer and politician of that period, a vehicle through which he could air his political views. The major, as versatile a man as ever graced an editorial chair, had been at a previous time editor of the "Evening Star," and upon that luminary's purchase by the New London Printing Company in 1873, had become financially interested in its successor, the "Evening Telegram," but C. I. Shepard had a controlling interest in that paper, and I judge, although my information on this point is hazy, Major Tibbits was not able to dictate the policy of the paper, so he concluded to start one of his own.

Those were days when politics cut more of a figure in men's careers than at present, and Maj. John A. Tibbits, lawyer, writer and orator, lived on political expectations all his life. So much for the motives behind "The Day's" inception.

The partnership which undertook to publish "The Day" was composed of John A. Tibbits, John C. Turner and William J. Adams. Of course, Tibbits was to be editor. Turner was to handle the telegraphic and local news and Adams was to be the business manager. The only other member of the staff was John McGinley, city editor and reporter.

John C. Turner in the seventies had been city editor of the "Telegram" and at the same time city clerk. On the "Telegram" the city editor was also the paper's only reporter. Newspapers in those days did not run very much to local news and if they turned out a column and a half an issue that was considered an extraordinary quantity. Turner was exceedingly popular in those days as reporter and city clerk, just as he was later as town clerk. He knew everybody in the city—not so difficult a feat in a city of less than ten thousand inhabitants. He had left the "Telegram" about five years before "The Day" was ushered into the world, to engage in journalistic labors in other cities and was, I suppose, induced to come back to his native heath by Major Tibbits.

N L – 1-26

John A. Tibbits, although a comparatively young man, had an interesting career. He had served in the Civil War with distinction and had been severely wounded in an engagement He was a lawyer by profession, but gave most of his time to the lure of politics. Journalism to him was incidental As a writer he had few equals, especially as a descriptive writer The ease and facility with which he wrote in long hand was remarkable. His penmanship was like copper plate and his copy was seldom marked by changes or interlineations It was no unusual task for him to sit down in an afternoon and turn out enough editorial copy to last a week He could turn his hand to any kind of newspaper writing with equal facility. He had a vivid imagination and a keen sense of humor. During the trial of the Cramer murder case in New Haven, he reported the event for "The Day" and for a week or more he daily produced a highly interesting story of the trial that filled the entire first page of "The Day" But he was erratic and occasionally, when his services were needed the most, he was unaccountably missing. Not that his habits were bad, but because he had found some need for a trip to Washington or Hartford or some other point on a political errand So it was on the last day of the Cramer trial. He left for New Haven the same as usual, but that evening he failed to return on his usual train with a pocket full of copy and next morning "The Day" lacked its usual front page story.

William J. Adams was an active, energetic local man, who had made quite a lot of money, it was said, in fortunate speculations and by various enterprises He was the lessee of Lawrence Hall, the city's only amusement place, and most of the theatrical productions of the period came here under his auspices He was also the city bill poster, a business quite different and of more importance than it is now. Among his other activities he handled the circulation of the "Evening Telegram" for many years, personally distributing the papers each afternoon to the newsboys. The circulation was around one thousand copies, I should judge It was printed in the basement of the wooden building on Green street, south of L Lewis & Co's store, now occupied by sundry small shops, and the boys took turns in running back behind the building through an alley way to the basement to gather up a supply of papers as they came from the fly of the printing press. The press was a slow-running affair, which threw the papers out at the rate of about ten a minute. Charlie Allen, a colored man, caught the papers as fast as the fly delivered them and as quickly as twenty-five or more were collected handed them over to a waiting boy. The papers were then brought up to Adams in a room off the street and here on a counter he folded them with a speed and accuracy that was marvelous, and then counted them out to the carriers

John McGinley, although a New Londoner by birth, had long been living in New York City, and had been a buyer for a linen concern, a very responsible position which frequently took him to England The firm suspended business and somehow he was asked to try his hand at reporting. He had no previous experience, but he did have a large fund of information, a ready command of language a genial personality and a happy faculty of making friends and keeping them. He also had a fine sense of humor and he took to reporting easily and wrote many clever things

Of the original "Day" force, with the exception of John C. Turner, I know of but two who are still living—Samuel T Adams and William H. Rolfe. Adams was a compositor on the "Evening Telegram" and when "The Day" started he was placed in charge of the latter's composing room Two or three years later he was promoted to telegraph editor, replacing John G. Lynch, and he held that position until Major Tibbits in 1889 was appointed United States Consul at Bradford, England, by President Harrison, when he was made managing editor He held that position until 1891 when the paper passed into my control

William H Rolfe was the telegraph operator who took the press report for "The Day" when the paper started. In its early days "The Day" always managed to have a good telegraphic news report, although the cost came very high. Rolfe was an expert telegrapher, and as typewriters had not come into use at that time he had to take the news report sent in code from the wire in long hand. This required very rapid writing and it was generally the custom among telegraphers taking press copy to write without lifting the pen from paper so that nearly all the words were connected, but as they were sufficiently apart there was no difficulty in reading them At the very start of the paper there came the exciting episode of President Garfield's assassination and the press wires were loaded with news, causing an unusual strain upon the operator taking the report Despite the hard work and long hours, Rolfe stuck to his job with the loyalty and grit that has always been characteristic of him while at his work, until his right arm was swollen twice its usual size and he was forced to lay off. Subsequently he left New London and spent ten years or more at his occupation in New York City, but about sixteen years ago he returned to "The Day" as Associated Press operator and has been with the paper ever since in that capacity. During his absence he had perfected himself in the use of a typewriter, an accomplishment made necessary by the great increase in volume of words sent in the press reports Mr Rolfe had the unusual faculty of taking the most rapid and complicated wire report on a typewriter and at the same time keeping up a lively conversation with a chance visitor and not make a break or a skip in his copy.

The paper was launched on the morning of July 3, 1881. It had quarters on the second floor of the stone building on Bank street now owned and occupied by Darrow & Comstock. There were two stores beneath, one on the corner occupied as a saloon and the other by C. C Calvert, father of W. S. and DeWitt C., both doing business here now. Entrance was effected by an outside stairway There could not have been much money invested in the plant, probably a few thousand dollars.

Preparations for starting the paper had been under way for some time In order to create reader interest, great secrecy was observed as to the name the paper was to assume. The title "The Day" was evidently evolved by Major Tibbits himself There had been many newspapers with title of "Star," "Sun," "World," etc., and the idea of the owners of the new paper was to adopt a name that would be original. I never heard whether the major originated it or whether he came upon it in one of the works of Thackeray which mentions a publication that was called "The Day"

To keep the title a dark secret, not even the compositors setting advance copy were let in, and wherever the name should have appeared, three letters were substituted, whatever letters the imagination or fancy of the writer dictated The idea on the night of publication was to take these out and insert "DAY." This was done, but so well were the dummy titles distributed and so numerous that not all of them were eliminated when the paper went to press very late, with the results that as the combined office force seized the first copies off the press and eagerly scanned the freshly printed pages there were exclamations like this "Hey, stop the press, it says here 'The Cat,'" and "Here's another title that hasn't been changed, 'The Bat,'" or again, "Oh, Lord! Here's one more—'The Dog.'" At last, however, all the corrections were made and "The Day" began its career.

It was a four-page, six-column sheet, printed on a flat-bed country press and it presented an attractive appearance The captions over news items were extremely modest in regard to size of type, a fault not then recognized in the journalistic profession. James Hislop, dry goods merchant, had a two-column advertisement on the first page and the rest of the paper had con-

siderable advertising. Mr. Hislop always was a firm believer in "The Day"
as an advertising medium and never failed to use it.

The arrival of "The Day" was eagerly awaited by the townspeople and
it had a good sale. The first issue came out on a Saturday morning. It was
late in getting out—a condition modern newspapers have not entirely overcome—and everyone connected with it, from editor to printer's devil, was
completely tired out. The next day was Sunday and the following Monday
was a holiday. Of course on the Fourth of July everyone connected with the
paper left for parts unknown. Then fate decreed that one of the biggest news
events of the century should occur. President Garfield was shot Sunday afternoon in the Washington railroad station. The dreadful news was flashed
along the wires and reached New London, but not enough of "The Day's"
mechanical force could be found to issue an extra and the paper lost a great
opportunity to score a beat. Not until Tuesday morning could it tell its
readers what had occurred on that eventful Sunday, and a perusal of Tuesday's issue fails to disclose any account of the shooting, the incidents of the
crime being passed over as if everyone knew all about them and "The Day"
began its chronicle of the event by reporting the condition of the patient and
the disposal of the murderer.

"The Day" soon became a good newspaper from the standpoint of the
period, but it was quickly found by the owners that the field was not large
enough to support two daily newspapers. The proprietors after a few months
found their capital exhausted and decided to seek financial help So a stock
company, with a capital of $10,000, was organized. The stockholders included
Frank H. Chappell, Augustus C. Williams, Robert Coit, Mason Young,
Frank L. Palmer, James Greenfield and others. At this time John C. Turner
decided to relinquish his connection with "The Day" and departed for
Paterson, N. J., where he remained for many years on "The Guardian" William J. Adams also disposed of his interest and returned to his amusement
enterprises and bill posting. Later he suffered business reverses and died
poor.

With the help of new capital "The Day" returned to the conflict It was
to be a war to the death between it and its evening contemporary To divide
the advertising patronage in the evening field, in December, 1881, "The Day"
launched a small afternoon daily, called "The Penny Press" It was a little
four-page sheet to which everybody contributed a bit of his brightest, and
it made a hit. A one-cent newspaper was then a novelty. "The Penny Press"
was at once in great demand. After the novelty of issuing it wore off, however, it was left to take care of itself, and it became a dull and tame affair.
It survived over a year, however, until "The Day" establishment was moved
from Bank street into the Brainard Block on Main street, occupying one
store on the street, and two upper floors. To such an extent was "The Penny
Press" regarded by its publishers as an ephemeral affair that no attempt was
made to preserve a file of it and none is known to exist today

But I am getting ahead of my story. I should say something of the
surroundings in which "The Day" found itself when it was ushered into the
world. Its office and composing room was, as already noted, on the second
floor of the stone building in Bank street now occupied by Darrow & Comstock. Entrance had to be effected by climbing a long pair of stairs on the
outside of the building. The floor it occupied was divided in two, the front
room being used as business and editorial room. In the rear was the usual
complement of type cases, stands and press to be found in small newspaper
offices of those days. The stationary engine designed to supply motive power
for the press was located in the northeast corner of the rear room.

"The Day" started off with forty advertisers whose announcements filled
ten columns. Merchants from 1881 to 1891 and even later did a very much

different kind of newspaper advertising than they are doing at the present time. Up to twenty-five years ago, nearly every merchant contracted for a certain amount of space, usually only a few inches, and ran some kind of announcement every day in that space, but seldom did any of them change the copy of their advertisements oftener than once a week, and many of them did not change their copy more than twelve times a year It was easy for the newspaper publisher to calculate how much advertising space he was going to carry every day because none of the advertisers varied the size of their advertisements, except at rare intervals. So that the size of the paper could be permanently maintained whether it was four or eight pages. In 1881 there was no elasticity in the size of newspapers. The maximum size was eight pages ("The Day's" was only four) and when advertising crowded the columns too much, a supplement was issued of two pages or whatever number was required. This supplement had to be folded into the main paper by hand. Presses were not built to print a varying number of pages. Nearly all the daily papers forty years ago were printed on flat-bed presses into which the sheets were fed by hand and printed on one side at a time. After one side was printed the sheets were turned over and printed on the reverse. Sometimes a folder was attached to the press so that the papers would come out folded, but often the circulation was so small that folding by machine was deemed unnecessary.

When "The Day" acquired its big type revolving web press in 1883, that machine was considered the highest development in a printing press. It printed from hand-set type imposed in semi-circular turtles, which were clamped onto a large cylinder.

"The Day" was printed on a web of paper by the impression from the type in these turtles or forms. It was a cumbrous contrivance but considered a great advance upon a flat-bed press, as it would turn out papers at the rapid rate of 1,200 an hour.

It was found after "The Day" ceased experimenting with the one-cent paper scheme that in order to handle a sufficient volume of advertising at the low rates current, four pages would not be sufficient, and so the plan of making two press runs of four pages each was adopted and the two sheets folded together by hand to make an eight-page paper.

The type revolving web press soon became obsolete and was superseded by presses using sterotype plates clamped on cylinders, instead of the cumbersome brass turtles containing hand-set type. When printing from semi-circular plates was found practical, improvements were soon made in printing machinery so that a variable number of pages could be printed at will.

Soon after I obtained control of "The Day" in 1891, indication of an evolution in advertising became manifest. Some advertisers began to contract for variable space so that they could run large advertisements on certain days. David S. Machol, a local clothing merchant, I think was the first to use half-page advertisements, one or two days in the week. This practice was more and more observed until it was no longer possible to print a paper with the same number of pages every day.

When I bought "The Day" I immediately put into the press room a Babcock two-feed Dispatch press which would print 2,500 copies an hour. I thought this capacity would be all "The Day" would need for many years. In 1894, three years later, when the plant was moved from the old stone residence in Bank street, opposite Tilley, to the newly built brick building a short distance above on the same street, erected for its use by F. H. & A. H Chappel, a new press was purchased, called the Cox Duplex, which while it printed from a flat bed, used a roll of paper and was capable of printing according to the guarantees of the manufacturers, 5,000 complete papers, folded, per hour. This press answered the purpose very well for a few years, but as we wanted to get more than eight pages of seven columns each we then bought a Hoe stereotype press, giving us a product of eight pages, eight columns each; printing on this press was from stereotype plates, and we could get a speed of about 10,000 an hour. Making stereotype plates was going into a new branch of the business, and we were doubtful of the result However, after a period of experimentation, the art of stereotyping lost its terrors It soon developed that this third press was not up to the requirements of "The Day's increasing business and so another one was purchased two years later with a capacity of sixteen pages. This press answered the purpose for about ten years, when it was replaced by a press of still larger capacity, the one "The Day" is using at present, a Hoe Right Angle Quadruple, having a maximum output of thirty-two pages and printing up to sixteen pages at a speed of 24,000 an hour, and from sixteen to thirty-two pages at 12,000.

During its second year in its Bank street location "The Day" moved its establishment to the Brainard Building on Main street, where it occupied a store on the ground floor and two floors above. The press room was located in the rear of the store

In 1882, Thomas M. Waller, a New London lawyer and orator and fervid Democrat, was elected governor of the State. Probably that intensified the desire of the Democrats of the city to have a newspaper organ, both of the existing papers being Republican. At any rate, a group of well-known Democrats purchased the "Evening Telegram" in 1883 from C I. Shepard and others who were interested in that paper, and brought one of the writers of the Brooklyn "Daily Eagle," F. Dana Reed, here to manage it for them. Up to this time the "Telegram's" staff consisted of John G. Crump, editor, Julius T Shepard, Jr., news editor, and Walter Fitzmaurice, reporter Fitzmaurice stayed with the paper in his former capacity when the Democrats assumed control Reed was a man of considerable ability, more literary than business-wise, perhaps, and he did his best to put the "Telegram" upon a profitable basis, but he found it increasingly difficult Both papers at this time were having a hard struggle to meet their expenses and the "Telegram" had the least financial backing upon which to call when the ghost failed to walk.

Some time previous to the demise of the "Telegram," some bright genius on "The Day" conceived a plan of selling the paper at one cent a copy and giving it a State-wide circulation. This was soon after the establishment had been moved to Main street. The scheme was entirely practicable by reason of the unequalled railroad facilities New London had at that time. Early morning connections could be made with cities and towns in all directions At this time also a one-cent daily newspaper was a novelty and the field open to "The Day" was unoccupied The metropolitan papers were not then selling at one cent a copy and had not secured so enormous a circulation throughout this State as they have since

A startling tragedy befell the paper in 1885 Fred S Perry, an eccentric individual living on Franklin street, taking offense at a fancied affront in an article that had been printed in the paper, walked into the business office on Main street one morning and demanded of Ezra C. Whittlesey, the business manager, who was counting over some money given him by a newsboy, if he was editor of the paper Mr Whittlesey made some reply without looking up, when Perry, without further parley, pulled out a revolver and shot him in the body. The wound was fatal and the victim only survived the shooting a few days. He was tried, convicted and found guilty of murder in the second degree and sentenced for life, but subsequently confined in the state insane asylum

During the early history of "The Day" a great deal of attention was paid to what is termed newspaper style. Greater thought oftentime was paid to

the matter of capitalization of words and abbreviations of titles than the
gathering of news. The editors and proofreaders were very fussy in requiring
a close adherence to the rules they laid down. Since that time there has been
much elimination of so-called style in newspaper composition. At one time
Italics were used to designate the names of newspapers and foreign words,
and small capitals were also used for titles. When linotype machines were
brought into use they did not carry italics or small capitals, and, consequently,
the use of this special kind of type face was abolished in the interest of speed
and economy. There is yet what is called newspaper style, a good many
papers having a composition style peculiar to themselves, but everywhere
there is more latitude used in newspaper composition than there was formerly.

Newspaper ethics also were peculiar forty years ago, especially in New
London and perhaps some other New England communities. It was customary to leave out the names of non-advertisers in news reports wherever
this was possible. If the display window of a State street store was smashed
by a runaway horse dashing into it and it so happened that the storekeeper
was not an advertiser, the newspaper account would fail to mention his name
or the name of his store, and instead merely allude to "a State street store."
This would appear as very small and petty at this time, and "The Day"
discarded this kind of journalism many years ago. However, the practice is
still in vogue and carried to greater length in certain small newspapers to
include individuals who may not stand in their good graces. Such individuals
may take a prominent part in public affairs, but in accounts of those happenings have their names purposely omitted. This is not true journalism. It is
perverting the power of the press. Fortunately, papers which indulge in such
absurd tactics have so little circulation that they have no influence and their
maliciousness falls flat.

The circulation of "The Day" when it was founded was about 1 000 copies
and, as has already been described, it grew at one time to 16,000 as a one-cent
paper, and fell back again around 2,000 copies, when the price was put back
to two cents. It must have been about this figure in 1885. In 1891, when
I purchased the paper, I had difficulty in finding a paid circulation of as many
as 1,000 copies In 1895 the circulation had increased to 3,145. In 1900 it
had grown to 4,600. In 1905 it was 6,109. In 1910 the average was 6 892 By
1915 it had jumped to 8,536. Then came the World War and with it a substantial increase in "The Day's" circulation. In 1916 it was 9,140, in 1917 it
was 9,780, and in 1918 it had increased to 10,939. In the latter part of 1919
"The Day" was forced by the extraordinary increase in cost of production
to increase its selling price to three cents a copy and its average circulation
that year was 10,579. The year following, 1920, it slightly increased and was
10,701.

Evidently up to the time of the great war the growth in "The Day's"
circulation represented to large extent the growth of population within New
London and vicinity. Since the close of the war all the war-time activities
which brought many thousands of people here have ceased and naturally
there has been a great drop in the number of trans'ent residents, yet "The
Day's" circulation has steadily maintained itself around 10,500. The only
explanation for this extraordinary gain, which appears to be permanent, in
"The Day's" circulation at the advanced price of three cents a copy is, that
it has secured a greater hold upon the confidence and affection of the people
of New London and vicinity and that a larger proportion of the inhabitants
of this territory have become regular newspaper readers with "The Day" as
their favorite Perhaps it should be mentioned in this connection that "The
Day" has never employed any kind of circulation scheme to bolster up its
circulation and that all its readers must have been attracted to it voluntarily
because they liked its character and its superiority as a news purveyor.

"The Day" remained in its Main street quarters until 1891. In 1889 Major Tibbits finally secured something like adequate recognition of his services to his party by appointment as United States consul at Bradford, England. Upon his departure Samuel T. Adams was made managing editor, John McGinley reporter, and Charles W. Whittlesey business manager. Somes, the preceding news editor, had left some time previously and been replaced by John G. Lynch. The spirited rivalry of its morning contemporary, established in 1885, was making itself felt and the business of "The Day" was not profitable. In fact. it never was profitable. One move to reduce its expenses was to transfer its quarters to Bank street into a stone dwelling owned by the Chappell Company. This was about the last place one would pick out for a newspaper office, but it had to do. One side of the lower floor was occupied as a dwelling and "The Day" had its business office on the other side. its composing room on the second floor, its job office in the rear of the business department, and the press room was in an addition in the rear. The big press was moved on a truck from Main street to Bank without taking it apart and that was considerable of a mechanical accomplishment. Here is where I found it in the fall of 1891, when I took possession.

My connection with "The Day" had been spasmodic. I had been employed in various capacities in the job printing department and in the composing rooms, both on the "Penny Press" and "The Day" until 1883. Then for about a year I worked in the composing room of the "Evening Telegram." Upon the demise of that paper, four of us, John G. Lynch, Walter Fitzmaurice, George A. Sturdy and myself, began the publication of the "Morning Telegraph." This paper paid more than expenses at the start and for quite a number of years afterwards. In 1890 I disposed of my interest. John G. Lynch had already dropped out of the concern. Later George A. Sturdy also sold out his interest. I bought it in 1901 from Walter Fitzmaurice, conducted it five years at a loss, then gave it, free of all incumbrances, to my editor, Frank J. Brunner. He couldn't make it pay expenses, and finally disposed of it. The "Telegraph" passed through many vicissitudes later. It suspended in 1920.

In September, 1891, I secured control of "The Day" and the subsequent history of the paper was told by me five years ago, when "The Day" issued a special edition commemorating twenty-five years' progress under my management. It will not be necessary at this time to repeat the history of the paper during that time, as it is familiar to "Day" readers.

There is not much to add to the history of "The Day" since 1916. The period between 1916 and 1921 has been a trying one for newspapers. There was a paper shortage during the war and a great increase in the cost of production generally. The payroll of "The Day" has jumped from $600 per week in 1914 to $1,600 in 1921. Its paper bill rose from $12,000 in 1914 to $36,000 in 1920. These costs seem likely to remain permanently.

In 1918 it had to increase its selling price to three cents a copy, and at various periods it was forced to increase its advertising rates. The loyalty of its readers proved remarkable. The number lost by the increase in price to three cents was negligible. Advertisers also responded cheerfully to the increased rates, realizing that the service rendered them by "The Day" was worth the rate charged.

The volume of business done by "The Day" in its early life I have no means of ascertaining, but in 1891 and 1892, the first year of my ownership, the gross receipts were less than $25,000. By 1900 they had increased to $37.532.12. and in 1910 to $61,042 31. By 1920 the business had expanded so that the gross receipts of that year were $219,771.23

It has been the constant aim of "The Day" to keep fully up to the times in the handling of news. It has sought every means to make its contents and appearance pleasing to the people of Eastern Connecticut. That it has succeeded, is evidenced by its constantly increasing circulation. "The Day" has added many improvements in the past five years; it has strengthened its news and feature service, increased its force of workers, installed the newest machinery and labor-saving devices in place of some less efficient, and only recently added one column to each page, thus giving its readers each day from twelve to twenty columns additional reading matter and illustrations. "The Day" feels that the public looks to it to supply it with a complete, up-to-date newspaper, and that the paper will be remiss in its duty if it fails to do so.

The "Norwich Bulletin" thus told the story of its beginning and career, in its fiftieth anniversary issue:

The Norwich Bulletin, at the age of fifty years, appears this morning before its many friends and readers, extending kindly greetings and sincere good wishes to all. As the rudder guides the ship, so will the lessons learned of experience, that most severe yet kindest teacher, influence its future course, inducing it to be not only abreast of the times, to be at once clean, bright and reliable, and to so well fill its allotted place that its influence will be for good and the best interests of mankind.

This paper, of Norwich birth, has been of, with and for its city, its people and the great public by which it is surrounded since first it saw the light. It has been of, in, and with the community, through war and peace, through trial and triumph, through adversity and prosperity, it has grown with its growth, matured with its development and ripened with its unfolding until it stands today upon the firm foundation established not alone by its own efforts, but by the kindly reciprocal favors of its clients and friends, whom it has endeavored these many years to faithfully serve.

The Norwich Bulletin at this time, taking as it does the full reports of the Associated Press, printing special telegraphic news, reporting fully sports and all items of interest in this and neighboring towns, publishing up-to-date domestic departments, special papers and correspondence, and presenting in miscellaneous articles the best thoughts obtainable from other and original sources, supplying the needs of the financial, commercial, scientific, literary, artistic, musical, political and religious interests, and in short, reflecting in every issue all that can be gathered from the four corners of the earth, is in the fore ranks as a model newspaper. Contrasting this modern development with that of more than a century ago, it may be interesting to return to those times and learn of conditions prevalent in the days when the Bulletin's ancestor, the Weekly Register, began its life in 1791.

When the old-time paper appeared amid "these struggling tides of life," less than nine years had elapsed since the close of the Revolution. George Washington was serving his first term as President of the United States, and John Adams his single one as Vice-President; the thirteen original States, with the addition of Vermont, which had been admitted March 4, 1791, comprised the Union; Connecticut's Senators, then serving in the Second Congress, were Oliver Ellsworth of Windsor, and Roger Sherman of New Haven; Samuel Huntington, Esq., was the Governor of Connecticut; and Benjamin Huntington, LL.D., was then in office as the first Mayor of Norwich, a portion of which place had been incorporated as a city in May, 1784. The population of the country was then 8,929,214, of the State 237,846, and of Norwich (after the division of the town) 3,284, the center of the United States being twenty-three miles east of Baltimore The President's Cabinet was composed of Thomas Jefferson of Virginia, Secretary of State; Alexander Hamilton of New York, Secretary of the Treasury, Henry Knox of Massachusetts, Secretary of War; and Edmund Randolph of Virginia,

Attorney-General. Samuel Osgood of Massachusetts was Postmaster-General, but was not included in President Washington's official family.

At that time the Sabbath began at sun-down on Saturday and ended at the same hour on Sunday; travel was by stage-coach, sailing vessels, and locally by the "one-hoss shay"; wood was the universal fuel and was burned in open fireplaces before which in the wintry time our ancestors could warm but one side of their persons at a time, the other portion being subjected at times to a temperature in the vicinity of the zero point; flint and steel served the purposes of the later lucifer match, and tallow dips furnished the necessary artificial light. Norwich Town and Bean Hill supplied the social, religious, political and commercial life of the town, the former being furnished with the meeting-house, postoffice, flag-staff, half a dozen stores containing all useful commodities, the court-house, whipping-post, pillory, jail, several printing establishments, and Lathrop's, Peck's and Brown's taverns, the latter presenting several stores and the wayside inns known as Hyde's and Witter's, both sections being possessed of various small manufactories. Rev Joseph Strong, pastor of the First Church, officiated in the fourth building of that society, which was completed in 1790, stood on the site of the present edifice, and succeeded that which previously crowned "ye summit of ye Greate Rocke." African slavery was in vogue, but although the practice of holding human beings in bondage gradually abated, the system was not legally abolished in Connecticut until 1848—thirteen years before the outbreak of the Civil War. Middle or Main street at the Landing had been opened at an expense of £100 in 1790, one year before the birth of this paper, that section being in the vicinity of the confluence of the Yantic and "Showtucket," which forms the Thames, and distinct from the portion first called the Landing, which was at the head of the cove below Yantic Falls, near which at an earlier date stood John Elderkin's flour mill, which was accessible from the town through Mill lane (now Lafayette street) and which point was the original landing place for Indian canoes. This paper had been in existence less than a year when the old Indian trail from Norwich to New London was shortened to a distance of fourteen miles and opened in a crude and primitive way to public travel as the first turnpike in the United States. Toll began Tuesday, June 26, 1792, the rates ranging from 1d for man and horse to 9d. for a four-wheeled vehicle. No bank was established in Norwich until June 21, 1796, and the insurance business, which has become a factor, was of but two years' earlier birth.

Mr Bushnell was born in Lebanon, September 13, 1757, a son of Ebenezer and Elizabeth (Tiffany) Bushnell of that place, and a descendant in many lines of the Puritan fathers of New England. He graduated at Yale in 1777, studied law, returned to Lebanon, and there married for his first wife, August 14, 1780, Tryphena, a daughter of Dr John and Jerusha (Huntington) Clark, of that town. He located in Norwich as an attorney, where he married his second wife, November 18 1876, Susanna, a daughter of Capt Russell and Mary (Gray) Hubbard of New London, and subsequently of Norwich. He was a man of ready wit, of varied information, of fluent tongue and facile pen, bright, well-balanced and enterprising. After his retirement from journalism, he entered the United States navy and became paymaster of the ship "Warren." While serving in this capacity he died at Havana, Cuba, in July or August, 1800, at the early age of 43. His widow married for her second husband and as his third wife, January 30, 1803, Deacon Robert Manwaring, formerly of New London, but then of Norwich who died March 29, 1807, and was survived by her until April 9, 1814. Both are interred in the old burying ground at Norwich Town, near the enclosed Huntington lot, where memorial stones indicate their graves.

The Weekly Register's natal day was November 29, 1791, when Ebenezer

Bushnell issued the first number "24 rods West of the meeting-house," in a building at Norwich Town which stood on the home-lot of Sergt Thomas Waterman, one of the thirty-five original proprietors of the town, whose deed bore date November, 1659 The house was built by Elijah Adgate about the year 1779, had successive owners until October 25, 1781, when Ephraim Baker of Norwich in consideration of £100 deeded to Mr. Bushnell "about thirty rods of land, be the same more or less, with a dwelling house thereon standing, on the south side of the meeting-house rocks (so called) on the south side of the town street" This building stood nearly opposite John Trumbull's printing office, whose newspaper, the Norwich Packet, was still in existence The Weekly Register was a twelve-column, four-page journal, 10 x 17 inches in size, which was changed to one of sixteen columns, Tuesday, February 14, 1792, the dimensions remaining unaltered.

Chelsea in Norwich, a district so well established in early days, but now so vaguely understood, and to many of the inhabitants of the present day so utterly unknown, was of indefinite and unestablished bounds, extendtending from about the Norwich Town line southerly to the Landing, easterly to the Shetucket and westerly along the bank of the Thames. East Chelsea, originally a most unattractive portion, was subject to inundation with every freshet, and the receding waters, leaving an accumulation of stones, boulders, ice and rubbish on the swampy slopes of the rivers, became known also as Swallowall West Chelsea developed into the ship-building center, the high ground in the vicinity being called at varying times Oak Spring Hill, Baptist Hill and Mount Pleasant. The commercial center, a part of the West Side, the Falls district and the choicest residential portion were included within the limits of Chelsea.

The first number of the "Chelsea Courier," a four-page, sixteen-column paper, 11 x 18 inches, appeared Wednesday, November 30, 1796, and contained the following "conditions":

1. The Courier will be printed at Chelsea, on Wednesday, and delivered to city subscribers in the forenoon
2 It shall be printed on good paper of Royal size.
3. It shall contain the most important Foreign and Domestic intelligence, together with such original productions, &c, as shall be thought deserving of public attention.
4 The price to subscribers will be one dollar and sixty-seven cents per annum, exclusive of postage
5 One-half of the subscription will be expected on delivery of the first number

Thirteen and a half of the sixteen columns were devoted to reading matter, in which appeared items of foreign intelligence of as late date as September 28 The remaining space was devoted to advertisements, among which was one by the editor, who announced as for sale "at his office in Chelsea" a long list of books, in which were included Ash's Grammar, American Revolutionary, Arabian Nights' Entertainment, Baxter's Saints' Rest, Bunyan's Visions of Heaven and Hell, Complete Letterwriter, Dilworth's Arithmetic, Elliott's Medical Pocket Book, Fordice's Addresses, Goldsmith's Works, Hervey's Meditations, Occum's Hymns, Penitential Cries, Vicar of Wakefield and Zimmermann on Solitude

Messrs Robinson and Dunham continued their close business relations three years, when their copartnership was dissolved March 30, 1825 On that date the following notice appeared "With the present number we complete the third volume of the Courier, and with it the senior editor ends his labors as one of its conductors and proprietors, having disposed of his right and title to this paper to his partner"

Mr. John Dunham then assumed full charge of the Courier, which he

published in the basement of the Dunham block, a wooden building on
Shetucket street, the site of which is now covered by the brick block in
which at present are the ground floor offices of the Adams Express Company
and the New London County Mutual Fire Insurance Company. The paper
was conducted with ability and success for more than sixteen years, at the
end of which period, on September 15, 1841, Mr. Dunham announced his
retirement. His successor, Rev Dorson Ebenezer Sykes, then assumed
charge, and assured subscribers that the principles of the great Whig party,
so ably advocated by his predecessor, would continue to guide the political
course of the paper, that his editorial brethren of all political creeds would
be treated with the courtesy becoming a self-respecting journal and that his
readers would be furnished with the news of the day presented in acceptable
and pleasing form.

The Courier at this time was a twenty-eight column, four-page weekly,
18 x 24 inches in size, well printed and of attractive appearance. Its new
management however, felt that it had outgrown its old quarters in the Dunham block, and therefore announced October 20, 1841, that "The office of
the Norwich Courier is removed to the third story of the building on the
corner of Water and Dock streets, a few rods below the Post Office." This
was the building which still stands on the southeast corner of Little Water
and Market (formerly Dock) streets, and is now owned by Dr. Patrick Cassidy. It was then numbered 51 Water street, where the paper was printed
by J G Cooley. A temporary change of office quarters was made in 1843,
as the Weekly Courier announced March 28 of that year that "The publication office of the Norwich Courier is removed to 117 Main street, next
door east of the Quinebaug Bank, at which place the Editor may be found
at all times, during office hours." This was in the block now occupied by
Gilbert's furniture store, the bank and the office of the paper being on the
second floor.

Monday, March 7, 1842, in addition to the Weekly Courier, appeared
a new venture of the enterprising management. "The Norwick Courier,
edited and published by D E. Sykes, is issued every afternoon immediately
after the arrival of the Eastern Mail, at 51 Water street. Office third story."
This eight-cent a week, one-cent per copy daily, was a sixteen-column, four-
page sheet, 12 x 17 inches, which gave up the ghost August 13 following, and
was succeeded three days later by the Tri-Weekly Courier, a paper of the
same size, which was issued Tuesdays, Thursdays and Saturdays at six
cents a week, or two cents a copy. The Weekly Courier appeared before
its readers January 11, 1846, "materially enlarged," not by increase in size
but by additional length of columns, which while somewhat augmenting the
news, editorial and advertising space, detracted somewhat from the former
handsome appearance of the paper.

In a few years the journal removed to Chapman's block, Main street,
Franklin Square, occupying a room over the present electric street car waiting room, the proprietor having his editorial sanctum at the northwest corner, overlooking Main street, Franklin Square, and what is now Rose alley.
A fire occurred in this building about the year 1852, destroying some files
of the Courier and other property, and compelling a removal to the three-
cornered, or "flat-iron" building which occupied the corner of Main and
Shetucket streets, which, with the adjoining property of the Norwich National Bank, was subsequently demolished to make room for the present
Shannon block. The last change of location under Mr. Sykes' management
was about the year 1858, when the Courier was removed to the Chelsea
building, Franklin Square, on the southwest corner of Main and Ferry streets,
over the store now occupied by Mrs Edwin Fay. Saturday morning, February 26, 1859, on his retirement from the paper, Mr. Sykes published his inter-

esting editorial farewell as follows

"Seventeen years ago last September, the Norwich Courier contained the vale-
dictory of our respected predecessor, John Dunham, and the introductory notice of
our accession to the editorial chair.

"Through summer heat and winter snow, through rain and shine, through good
report and evil report, we have held our way from that day to this, failing not in our
weekly intercourse with our patrons and friends; and for seventeen years this day,
adding to those hebdomadal visits a tri-weekly call upon such of our acquaintances
as signified their desire to see more of us

"The Courier 'still lives' and speaks for itself in the enlarged, improved appearance, and the favor it has met with at the hands of its friends and supporters Of our
faithfulness as a political paper, the columns of our living contemporary, the Aurora,
and of our defunct friends, the Norwich News, Norwich Tribune, Norwich Evening
Advertiser, and we know not how many besides, will show the dire necessity laid
upon them, as political opponents, to pull every wire, turn every stone, and speak
every word which could, by any possibility, ensure our utter and entire demolition
and annihilation

"We cannot leave the editorial chair without expressing to our friends and
subscribers our appreciation of their good will Many of them—nay, almost all, we
regard as personal friends; and those of whom we have failed to please, who have
parted company with us, we consider not as enemies, for the terrible mandate, 'stop
my paper,' that greets an editor's ear in every time of political excitement, is not
irrevocable, and we, in common with our brethren of the quill, have learned to wait
patiently until the tide sets back To our correspondents, we tender our thanks: to
our advertising friends, without whose aid no town or city like Norwich can sustain
a good paper, we present our acknowledgments for favors received, and our best
wishes that, acting on the 'live and let live' principle, their various trades, occupations
or business may so flourish as to fill their coffers and satisfy their desires To our
constant friends who have sustained us in our constant labors, by sympathy, cheerful
words and kindly deeds, we offer our grateful thanks

"Of our successor it is not needed that we multiply words Though a compara-
tive stranger to this community, he is no stranger to Connecticut For the last four
years his connection with the Springfield Republican—one of the best daily papers
in New England, and largely circulating in Connecticut—has rendered it necessary
for him to keep himself thoroughly informed upon the current political events and
interests of our State He enters, therefore, upon his editorial duties under circumstances peculiarly favorable both to himself and to the public Of his plans and
purposes with reference to the future interests and management of the Courier, we
leave him to speak for himself Knowing what we do of those plans and views, we
feel the highest confidence that nothing is wanting but a cordial and liberal support
on the part of the public to ensure to this community a daily journal second to no
other paper in Connecticut With a hearty God-speed to our successor, and a sincere
God's benison upon our readers, young and old, we lay down our worn and weary
pen "

Mr. Sykes' successor as editor, publisher and proprietor of the Courier.
was George B Smith, a young printer from Springfield, whose introductory
appeared March 1, 1859. The establishment retained the old quarters in the
Chelsea building, from which were issued the Daily and the Weekly Courier
The new editor informed the public that "This journal will continue to be
devoted to the highest interests of this community," "and to the inculcation
of those political principles that were intended by the framers of the Constitution to underlie the whole system of government, and that are now represented by the Republican party." "The Weekly Courier will be issued each
Saturday," and "will be the largest, and we are sanguine enough to believe.
the best weekly newspaper in Connecticut."

Mr Smith's high aims and sanguine hopes were doomed to early and
bitter disappointment, and Norwich, that "graveyard of newspapers," appeared about to claim another victim Possessed of excellent taste and fair
business abilities, he was, nevertheless, almost at the outset of his career
beset with financial difficulties against which he struggled manfully, yet
vainly. At the expiration of seven months, unable longer to continue, he
retired, and the paper reverted to Mr. Sykes.

The issue of Saturday, August 20, 1859, contained a notice to this effect, when the former editor was compelled to resume the arduous duties which he thought had been forever relinquished. Under these adverse circumstances, Mr. Sykes decided to publish only a semi-weekly paper, and announced that "The days of publication will be Wednesday and Saturday of each week, and the paper will be issued in time to be sent off in all directions by the earliest mails on the mornings of those days, or by the earliest trains, stages, post-riders, etc. The city, Norwich Town, Bean Hill and Greeneville subscribers will be supplied by carriers as heretofore, and care will be taken that this is done with fidelity and promptitude." In addressing advance subscribers the editor wrote:

"Although the paper has come under its new management seriously encumbered with the subscription contracts of the late publisher, and although their repudiation by us would cause but a trifling loss, individually, to subscribers who have paid in advance, while their fulfilment by us would involve a heavy sacrifice, and, although no legal or moral obligation rests upon us to pay these debts, yet, rather than permit the lowering of the good name of one of the oldest journals in Connecticut or New England, or allow a sin of this sort to stain its escutcheon, the responsibility of satisfying these claims is hereby voluntarily assumed by us, and Daily and Weekly subscribers will be furnished with the Semi-Weekly issue until the dates when their prepaid subscriptions shall expire"

The reasons given for the non-issuance of the Daily Courier were thus given:

"Many readers will naturally be anxious to know the reason why the Daily Courier is not continued Our answer is that our idea of what such a paper ought to be could not be carried out, except at a heavy pecuniary sacrifice on the part of the publisher   Outside of Norwich but little advertising support can be relied on for a daily paper, consequently, the duty of sustaining it must belong to the city   That responsibility it has had a fair opportunity to assume, but has declined, guided in the matter, we believe, by circumstances which would have decreed otherwise had they all been considered. These reasons have been of a pecuniary character—a large number of our citizens being unable or disinclined to incur the expense of a daily, and many of our business men having yet to discover the benefit of liberal advertising in a local paper, established for the advantage of local interests   We think the truth is included in what we have said, and none can regret the facts more than we do   So soon as we see, or believe we see, the time to have arrived when better and brighter prospects for remunerative support justify a renewal of the experiment, we shall not be slow in taking advantage of the change."

December 7, 1859, it was announced that on and after Thursday, January 5, 1860, the publication of the Norwich Weekly Courier would be resumed. It was claimed that the paper would contain more reading matter than would any other weekly journal published in Connecticut, and that its news would be fresh up to the hour of publication. It was gently hinted, also, that the New Year would be "a good time to subscribe."

With the issue of the Semi-Weekly Courier of Wednesday, June 6, Mr. Sykes retired from the paper for the second time, and in this instance was succeeded by H C Kinne. At the top of the first column of the second page appeared the

AMERICAN REPUBLICAN TICKET.
For President,
ABRAHAM LINCOLN, of Illinois.
Vice-President,
HANNIBAL HAMLIN, of Maine

Mr Kinne continued the publication in the Chelsea building, Franklin Square, which has been the paper's home for so long a time

Friday, August 20, 1860, he announced that "We this day commence the publication of the Courier as a Daily Evening paper   Those who have previously received the Semi-Weekly by carrier will be furnished with the Daily till further arrangements can be made The Semi-Weekly will be continued for the benefit of our country readers so that we are now issuing the Courier in three forms, Daily, Semi-Weekly and Weekly As we are circulating a thousand dailies within the limits of the town, transient advertisers will appreciate the value of the Courier as a medium of communication with the people."

Mr. Kinne's proprietorship of the paper was of limited duration, as he died in a few months, when the journal once more reverted to Mr. Sykes The latter gentleman finally disposed of the property to Manning. Perry & Co., the proprietors of the Norwich Morning Bulletin, who issued their first number of the Weekly Courier, December 15, 1858, in the Chelsea building. The paper was 16 x 21½ inches in size, its eight pages containing forty-eight columns In this issue the publishers informed the public that

"We believe the readers of both the Eastern Bulletin (the weekly edition of the Morning Bulletin) and the Norwich Weekly Courier will without exception be gratified to learn that, by the consolidation of the two papers, they are hereafter to be furnished with the largest and best weekly in the State Under the arrangement now perfected, we shall continue to send all paying subscribers of each paper the Norwich Weekly Courier in its present form The advantages resulting from this consolidation to subscribers and advertisers, as well as the publishers, will be readily appreciated Many of our readers will recognize with pleasure an old familiar name and face, many others—readers of the Eastern Bulletin—will give cordial greeting to well-known features that come to them new titled, and many more we hope will find it to their interest to make acquaintance with us during the year ahead

"The Courier has heretofore been issued as a daily evening paper, a semi-weekly and weekly In place of all these we shall issue the Norwich Bulletin daily, and the Norwich Weekly Courier on Saturday morning of each week"

This issue whose whole number was 285, contained twenty-six columns of reading and twenty-two of advertising, all well arranged and presenting a harmonious whole.

January, 1861, the presses, type and accessories were removed from the Chelsea building to Chapman's block.

The Courier, erratic hitherto only in its occasional changes from Weekly to Semi-Weekly and to Daily, appearing at different times in one, the other or all of these forms, now settled permanently as the weekly visitor in thousands of homes where its presence became ever welcome and where its beneficent influence will forever continue.

In the autumn of 1858, Mr. J Homer Bliss, a practical printer and a fluent and forceful writer, feeling that the time was propitious and that Norwich would generously respond to the effort, induced William D Manning and James N Perry to consolidate their printing offices and issue a daily paper which would achieve popularity by its enterprise in fully reflecting the local news and its liberality in presenting the telegraphic intelligence of the world The last-named, whose establishment was on the middle floor of Chapman's block, was the fortunate possessor of a power press, the momentum for which was obtained from the machine shop of Peleg Rose, which fronted on what is now Rose alley, and is at present occupied by Powers Brothers as a fish market At the suggestion of Mr. Henry Hugh Osgood, Isaac H Bromley was selected as editor, and became a member of the firm of Manning, Perry & Co., the other partner in which, whose name did not appear, being J Homer Bliss The title "Bulletin" was suggested by Mr. Bromley as being almost a synonym for "the latest news," and because of its originality, few, if any newspapers having then adopted it Accommodations facing Franklin Square were secured in Franklin hall, Chapman's block, where was born and from which was issued December 15, 1858, the first number of the Norwich Morning Bulletin, a twenty-four column, four-page journal, in size 16 x 21 inches. This number contained eleven columns of reading and thirteen of advertising matter, and as an initial issue indicated the high position the paper was destined to attain in the journalistic world. The editor thanked the brethren of the press throughout the State "for the many kind notices with which they have generally heralded our coming," and paid his respects in true Bromley style to the "Hartford Post and New London Star, for having put into tangible shape and deniable form, a report, which has been somewhat industriously circulated throughout the district—with how much malevolence we are unable to say—that the main object with which this paper was started was to influence the congressional nomination of this Third District."

In their prospectus the publishers announced that the Eastern Bulletin would be published weekly, and would contain, in addition to editorial and other original matter, the current news of the week, a summary of telegraphic items, foreign, State and local news, market reports for the week, carefully prepared, marine intelligence, agricultural matters and literary selections.

Mr. J. Homer Bliss, the projector of the Bulletin, soon retired, yet in his Plainfield home today views with satisfaction the present results of his initial efforts of half a century ago. Two of the other three partners, Messrs. Manning and Perry, are still with us as residents of Norwich.

September 4, 1860, Charles B. Platt of Norwich became a partner in the Bulletin, retiring Mr. Perry, and three days later the firm name of Manning, Platt & Co. appeared as publishers and proprietors This copartnership was dissolved October 31, 1863, and was succeeded by the Bulletin Association, a joint stock company organized for the purpose, the president and directors of which held their first meeting November 30 following The capital stock, all paid in, was $25,000, of which the president, James D. Mowry, held 230 shares, and the directors, Messrs. Isaac H. Bromley, Joseph H. Starkweather and Albert H. Almy, owned 310, 230 and 230, respectively. The company erected the Bulletin building on Main street in 1867, which was then numbered 127, but is now 85, which has since been the home of the paper.

The name of Campbell & Co., as publishers and proprietors, appeared Thursday, July 6, 1871, but disappeared with the issue of Friday, February 28, 1873, being succeeded Monday, March 3, following, by that of the Bulletin Company. The administration of the former was evidently unsatisfactory to the stockholders, as on the last-named date it was explained that

"A newspaper is not a philanthropic enterprise, without regard to pecuniary profits Of all classes of men, an editor should have the least thought of himself, and the most for others. It is their interests, rather than his own, which he is summoned to promote. Consequently, piques of any sort and peculiar ideas of his own have no rightful place in his paper. People want a paper principally for the news, and this they shall have so far as we are able to give it. We do not consider it to be a part of our duty, however, to fill the news out by any imaginings of our own in order to make it more sensational. Truth shall not be lost sight of, nor shall the character or reputation of men be assailed without sufficient reasons; while the pleasure, good and prosperity of all our readers shall be ever kept in view."

The Bulletin Association retained its building but disposed of the paper, presses, type and other accessories to the Bulletin Company, a corporation formed for the object, the present and a majority of the directors of which held their first meeting March 15, 1873. The capital stock of $50,000, all paid in, was held as follows: H. H. Osgood, 300 shares; Albert S. Bolles, 200, Lorenzo Blackstone, 200; H B. Norton, 200; T. P. Norton, 200; A. W. Prentice, 100; John F. Slater, 100; Charles Bard, 100; E. N. Gibbs, 200; W. R. Wood, 80; W. R. Burnham, 40; Sabin N. Sayles, 100; James Lloyd Greene, 50, and Gardiner Greene, 50. The Eastern Bulletin was consolidated with the Courier at the time of the latter's acquisition by Manning, Perry

& Co, and the paper continued under the old and honored name as the weekly edition of the Norwich Morning Bulletin

Many years later, as the citizens of this place, New London, and the neighboring towns had so long been accustomed to the early and regular appearance of their favorite paper, filled to overflowing with local and world-wide intelligence and all that appealed to literary, artistic, musical, scientific, religious and general tastes, it was thought that the word "Morning" in the title became superfluous. It was therefore eliminated, and from August 1, 1895, the ever-welcome visitor has appeared as the Norwich Bulletin

During the earlier days of The Bulletin the old style of hand composition was in vogue, when seven men were able to set only from fourteen to eighteen columns of matter in a night. During the second term of Alonzo H. Harris' management, The Bulletin was equipped with Mergenthaler linotype machines and a web rotary press, which greatly facilitated the work of the plant. The linotype machines were invented by Ottmar Mergenthaler, and reasonably perfected in 1886, to do plain composition, and were first used by the New York Tribune. They have since been greatly improved, and are now adapted to fine newspaper and job work.

Linotype machines are operated by finger keys, as is the typewriter, but there the similarity between them ends. The former works automatically, making and bringing, ready for the press or stereotyping table, bars of type metal, each bearing, properly justified, the type to print an entire line. The machine does not set the type, but evolves a slug, or line of metal, upon which the characters are cast, ready to print from. With this paper's improved facilities, three employees can, in a single night, furnish thirty columns, and, with the aid of operators during the day, the capacity may be increased to forty-five or more. The present daily average of The Bulletin is thirty-five columns. The advance made in machinery is shown from the fact that with the old Washington hand press 100 four-page papers could be printed in an hour—with our modern web power press 200 eight-page papers can be printed and delivered folded per minute.

The officers and editors of The Bulletin have been as follows

Presidents—Col. Hugh Henry Osgood, Norwich, February 28, 1873, to March 11, 1884. Amos W. Prentice, Norwich, March 11, 1884, to March 11, 1889. Col. Hugh Henry Osgood, Norwich, March 11, 1889, to October 21, 1899. Henry H Gallup, Norwich, March 5, 1900, to March, 1908. Chas. D. Noyes, March 4, 1908, present incumbent.

Business Managers—The first manager, who certainly did well his part, was James N Perry, Norwich, December 15, 1858, to April, 1859. Charles Black, from April, 1859, to September 4, 1860 The managers since that day have been: Charles B. Platt, Norwich, September 4, 1860, to October wich, secretary and treasurer, July 14, 1874, to March 7, 1875. William Fitch, New London, secretary, treasurer and business manager, March 8, 1869, to December 3, 1874 Elisha C. Rice, Norwich, 1874 to 1875 Charles E. Dyer, Norwich, secretary, treasurer and business manager, December 14, 1875, to April 30, 1880. Alonzo H. Harris, Norwich, April 30, 1880, to May 7, 1884. Charles Elisha Dyer, Norwich, secretary, treasurer and business manager, May 7, 1884, to January 25, 1888. Alonzo H. Harris, Norwich, January 25, 1888, to October 1, 1898. W. H. Oat, Norwich, October 1, 1898, present incumbent

Secretaries and Treasurers—Albert S Bolles, Norwich, secretary and treasurer, February 28, 1873, to July 14, 1874. Waterman R. Burnham, Norwich, secretary and treasurer, July 14, 1874, to March 7, 1875. William Fitch New London, secretary, treasurer and business manager, March 8, 1875, to December 3, 1875 Charles Elisha Dyer, Norwich, secretary, treasurer and

N L—1-27

business manager, December 14, 1875, to April 30, 1880. Albert S. Bolles, Norwich, secretary and editor, December 14, 1875, to January 1, 1881. Alonzo H Harris, Norwich, secretary, treasurer and business manager, 1880, to May 7, 1884 Charles Elisha Dyer, Norwich, secretary, treasurer and business manager, May 7, 1884, to January 25, 1888 Alonzo H Harris, Norwich, from January 24, 1888, to October 1, 1898 Charles D Noyes, treasurer, October 1, 1898, present incumbent. Isaac H. Bromley, Norwich, December 15, 1858, to 1862, when he entered the Union army as the captain of Company C, 18th Regiment—Management; original control B. M. Fullerton, Springfield, Mass., 1862 to 1865 —Platt and Gates management. Isaac H. Bromley, Norwich, 1865 to July 5, 1871.—Gates management William H. W. Campbell, Salem, Mass., July 6, 1871, to February 28, 1873 His pen name was "Kham."—Spalding's control Albert S Bolles, Norwich, February 28, 1873, to May 18, 1874. Sturtevant's control. E. J. Edwards, Springfield, Mass, May 18, 1874, to December 14, 1875.—Osgood regime. Albert S. Bolles, Norwich, December 14, 1875, to January 1, 1881.—Dyer and Harris: Osgood regime A. P. Hitchcock, New Lebanon, N. Y., January 1, 1881, to August 1, 1885.—Harris and Dyer, Osgood and Prentice regime Edward H Hall, Geneva, N. Y, August 1, 1885, to June 25, 1888.—Dyer and Harris: Prentice regime. A. P. Hitchcock, New Lebanon, N Y., 1888 to 1893 —Harris, Prentice and Osgood regime. A. Walton Pearson, Newburyport, Mass., since March 17, 1893; Dyer, Harris, Dyer, Harris and Oat; Osgood, Gallup and Noyes regime.

Assistant Editors—William H W Campbell, Salem, Mass.; with Bromley. James Hall, Geneva, N. Y., with Campbell, Edwards, Bolles and Hitchcock. Edward H. Hall, Geneva, N. Y.; with Hitchcock. W. H. H. Hale, New Haven; with Hitchcock. Miss Ella A Fanning, Norwich; with Pearson.

Night Editors—Henry Hall, Geneva, N. Y.; with Fitch and Dyer Amos A. Browning, Norwich; with Dyer. Edward H. Hall, Geneva, N. Y.; with Dyer L. R Southworth, Woodstock; with Dyer. Walter A Littlefield, Boston, Mass; with Dyer Edward H Hall, Geneva, N Y, with Harris. W. H. H. Hale, New Haven; with Harris. William C. Thompson, Norwich; with Harris. Albert A. Sparks, Norwich; with Harris and Oat.

City Editors—William Fuller, Hartford; with Bromley Henry P Goddard, Norwich; with Bromley Henry Wing, Norwich; with Bromley. Henry E. Bowers, Norwich; with Bromley. William Fitch, New London; with Campbell. John Rathbone, Norwich; with Fitch Stiles Stanton, Stonington; with Fitch and Dyer Edward Thomas, Norwich, with Fitch. Thomas Hull, Stonington; with Fitch. Amos A. Browning, Norwich; with Dyer Stiles Stanton, Stonington; with Dyer. John Rathbone, Norwich; with Dyer. A Walton Pearson, Newburyport, Mass., with Dyer. Harris; Dyer and Harris William C. Thompson, Norwich; with Harris. Frederic W. Carey, Norwich; with Harris. Julian R. Dillaby, Norwich, with Harris, Oat. Harvey M. Briggs, Norwich; with Oat.

Sporting Editor—William Peet, Clinton with Oat
Assistant City Editor—Charles F. Whitney; with Harvey M. Briggs.
Reporters—Luther K. Zabriskie; with Pearson. Leslie T. Gager; with Pearson.

The Norwich Bulletin has now been four years in its new home, Nos 62-74 Franklin street, not far distant from its first habitation and within sight of the spot where its infantile years were passed. Although changes have occurred in stockholders, officers, editors and employees, The Bulletin, as the child of The Courier and the grand-child of the Weekly Register, remains steadfast in its devotion to principle and to the best and highest interests of its patrons, its State and its country, and will ever thus continue.

Isaac Hill Bromley, one of the founders and the first editor of The Norwich Bulletin, won for himself an enduring national reputation as one of the able and brilliant editorial writers of his time. His first editorial in The Bulletin, to be found in our fac-simile of the first issue presented to our readers today, not only marks out the policy of The Bulletin for its first half century, but shadows forth the quality of the editor who made his mark in the nation by his masterly and brilliant work and who honored every position in life to which he was called. Mr. Bromley was a native of Norwich and a graduate of Yale, and had represented the town in the Legislature and this district in the Senate prior to his entering upon his editorial career. He had conducted the paper but a short three years, when the war broke out and he answered to the call of his country and went to the front as captain of Company C of the Eighteenth Connecticut Volunteers, and a year later he was appointed provost marshal for this district and continued in that office till the close of the war. He then returned to the editorial management of The Bulletin, which he directed until 1868, when he became a stockholder and editor of the Hartford Evening Post. In 1872 he became an editorial writer of the New York Sun, and then went to the New York Tribune, where he continued from 1873 till 1883, after which he went to the New York Commercial Advertiser as editor for a few months. During the Presidential campaign of 1884, he edited the Post-Express of Rochester, N. Y., and in 1891 he returned to the New York Tribune, with which paper he remained until his death on August 11th, 1898, in this city. Mr. Bromley was a government director of the Union Pacific Railroad from 1882 until 1884, and in 1885 was appointed assistant to the president of the Union Pacific Railroad.

Editor Bromley's guaranty for The Bulletin in the first issue was as follows:

"We intend to furnish the community with a good family newspaper, as well as a political journal, and we shall admit nothing into its columns that has the least savor of impropriety. We shall exercise the same care over our advertising columns, as over the editorial and other reading matter, and the wives and children of our subscribers may feel assured that they can read the whole sheet through without being disgusted or shocked by the miserable catch-penny advertisements that stare readers in the face from too many of our otherwise respectable newspapers."

This has continued to be the policy of The Bulletin for a half century, and it is to be hoped that it will ever continue as the honorable record of the paper which today, with the Yale lectures upon Journalism, which he endowed and that bear his name, stand as his best monument.

Mr. James N. Perry, of the firm of Manning, Perry & Co., first owners and printers of The Bulletin, was born in Lebanon, and learned the trade of a printer in New London. He came to Norwich when twenty-one years of age and established himself in the job printing business with Horace R. Woodworth, buying out the printing business of James M. Stewart. In 1858 he and Mr. William D. Manning, under the copartnership title of Manning & Perry, merged their business and associated with them J. Homer Bliss and Isaac Bromley for the publication of The Bulletin in Franklin hall, Mr. Perry acting as business manager a few months, when Mr. Charles Black succeeded him. Mr. Perry then went to the mechanical department, from which he retired in 1860. when he was bought out by Mr. Charles B. Platt. He continued in the employment of The Bulletin job office for some time and then accepted a position as an accountant. Mr. Perry has been the bookkeeper for J. P. Barstow & Co for twenty-six years and is still in active life and esteemed by all who know him.

William D Manning was born in Norwich at the Falls October 19, 1818, and has spent practically all his life here, being identified with the printing business exclusively When a boy he went to Philadelphia to learn the trade of a machinist, but soon returned here and became an apprentice in the office of Hon. John Dunham, who then owned The Norwich Courier. With him in the same office as an apprentice boy was John G Cooley. For twelve years after serving his time as apprentice, Mr. Manning was foreman for Ebenezer Sykes, who bought The Courier of Mr. Dunham, later making it a tri-weekly, and moved it away from Market street. For a period he had full charge of the paper during Mr. Sykes' illness. About 1853 Mr. Manning purchased of Mr. Dunham his job office in Shetucket street, which had been closed, and conducted it with marked success for about five years, although his capital at the start was but $1.25. In 1858 there were three job printing offices closed because of the amount of lottery business being done here at that time There was a question as to what would be done with so much type as there was in these job offices, and it was suggested to Mr. Manning that a daily paper be started here. Favoring the idea, he consulted some of the prominent Republicans of the town and received so much encouragement from Hon. H. H. Osgood, Hon. Henry Starkweather and Edmund Perkins that it was decided to launch a daily, James N. Perry consolidating his office with Mr. Manning's, and with them were J. Homer Bliss and Isaac Bromley as partners, the firm name being Manning, Perry & Co. The suggestion of the daily is said to have been made to Mr. Manning by Homer Bliss.

The name was suggested either by Colonel Osgood or Mr. Starkweather, and the first paper was published on December 15, 1858, on Franklin Square, over the car station, in what is now Foresters' hall. With Isaac Bromley as an editor, the paper was a success from the start and the Tri-Weekly Courier soon abandoned the field and was taken in by The Bulletin in January, 1859 Editor Bromley's leaving was a severe loss to the paper, and, in fact, against the wish of the editor himself, for, as he told the owners then, he had placed his salary so high to the Hartford people that he never believed they could afford to pay it About that time, Charles Platt succeeded Mr. Perry as the business manager and Mr. Manning continued at the head of the job and mechanical end of the business for thirty-three years. When Mr. Platt entered the firm the name was changed to Manning. Platt & Co., and the paper saw one of its most prosperous periods during his managership.

After Mr. Platt's death, a company was formed and Mr. Manning disposed of his interest in the paper, but continued to be the foreman of the job department for a number of years longer Mr Manning taught the principles of the trade to many young men. When he mastered the calling, printing was in a primitive state, and most of the work was done on hand presses. Address cards were printed with a "proof planer" In those days printers boasted that type could never be set by machinery unless inventors could make brains. Mr. Manning has lived to see the perfection of typesetting machines and linotypes, and presses that will print rapidly in five colors from a roll of paper Although out of the business for twenty years, he still feels at home in a printing office.

John Homer Bliss was born in Hebron, Connecticut, August 4, 1832 son of John Flavel Bliss and Mary Ann Porter of that place, being a lineal descendant of Thomas Bliss, one of the founders of Hartford, 1640, and also of John Porter and wife, Anna White, pioneer settlers in Windham, 1639 After receiving a liberal education under the tutelage of the late General Calvin Daggett of Andover, he entered the printing office of the Norwich Courier in 1848, then located in the room directly over the present waiting room of the trolley roads on Franklin Square; and experienced the various vicissitudes incident to the life of a printer's "devil" and newsboy. In 1852 he went to Waterbury, Connecticut, and was for a year and a half a compositor in the office of The American, then located in the original Gothic hall, opposite the corner of the public square at North Main street, Cook & Hurlburt being the publishers In 1854 he returned to Norwich, and in 1858 formed the project of a daily paper, and finally induced the consolidation of two job printing offices—W. D. Manning's on Shetucket street and James N. Perry's on Franklin Square—and the Norwich Morning Bulletin, so well and favorably known in eastern Connecticut, was the child of that union.

In 1876, Mr Bliss commenced the compilation of family statistics, the result being the publication by him of the "Bliss Family Genealogy" in 1881, during a temporary residence in Boston. In connection with this work he made many valued acquaintances and friends, among them being the late George S. Porter of Norwich For several years succeeding 1876 he was a contributor over the signature of "Xylo" to the Printers' Miscellany, a trade paper published in St John, New Brunswick, as many of the older printers in Norwich may remember.

In the spring of 1881 he became connected with the Attleboro Advocate as compositor and contributor under the editorial management of Mr. Mowton, remaining there until January, 1887, when he removed to Plainfield and soon afterward became connected with the Plainfield and Moosup Journal as compositor, and has for some twenty years been the local reporter for that paper, and for several years has furnished news items for The Bulletin. Mr. Bliss is eminently pacific in disposition, is very domestic and regular in habit, seldom indulging in so-called visits and then only at the call of business; and, at the age of seventy-six, is in possession of all his faculties—a wonderfully well-preserved specimen of humanity, whose good nature it is to extend to all his earnest wishes for their continued happiness and prosperity.

Daniel W. Tracy, the present foreman of The Bulletin, was the first compositor engaged when the establishment of the paper was a fact, and he had a hand in its birth and has always had a live interest in its progress. He was born in Preston June 13, 1839, learning the printer's trade in the Aurora office under the tutorship of the late John W Stedman, and has been a sturdy representative of the craft for over half a century.

John Trankla, The Bulletin's first pressman, came to Norwich in 1853, and entered the employ of James M. Stewart, who did a printing business in the Chapman building on Franklin Square, as a hand-pressman doing miscellaneous work, there being no power job-printing presses in Norwich at that time William N Andrew, superintendent of The Bulletin job printing department, was then roller boy. Mr. Stewart sold his plant to Messrs. Woodworth and Perry of New London in 1854. During that year a part of the plant was temporarily moved to a barn back of St. Mary's Catholic Church, where miscellaneous printing was secretly done for several months, for the reason, it is presumed, that like Guttenberg, they were afraid that the powers would discover the primitive art. In 1858 the Stewart plant was consolidated with the printing business of W. D. Manning, for the purpose of having an outfit for the publication of the Norwich Morning Bulletin, under the firm title of Manning, Perry & Co Mr. Trankla was hired by the new company to take charge of one of the first power Adams printing presses, printing The Bulletin for thirty years, the files for that period still giving evidence of his painstaking work. During his employment the firm changed several times, but "John" was always found running the press which printed The Bulletin

The night of the blizzard, March 12, 1888, he had to procure a carriage to take him to work. That night he caught a severe cold, which developed into pneumonia. He never regained his health, and he passed away on November 20, 1888.

The "Norwich Evening Record" was established as a Democratic party organ by John G. Lynch, May 22, 1888, and during the first two years of its existence it changed ownership three times. On May 1, 1890, it was purchased by Cleworth & Pullen, publishers of "Cooley's Weekly," and has since been conducted as an independent local newspaper, free from any political party control, and in the interest of the whole people. On April 1, 1893, the plant was moved from 151 Main street to larger quarters in the Osgood building, 101-103 Broadway, opposite City Hall, where it still remains.

Since January, 1906, shortly before Mr. Cleworth died, the paper has been owned and published by Frank H. Pullen, under the name of Pullen Publishing Company. From time to time the paper and its plant have been materially enlarged and improved, and as a member of the Associated Press, "The Record" has striven to fill its own particular evening field, covering Norwich and the nearby towns to the satisfaction of its steadily increasing clientele. The subscription rate is two cents per copy, or six dollars a year and local advertisers who use its columns regularly and freely have always found "The Record" a most profitable medium for reaching the evergrowing number of people who buy in Norwich, the natural trading centre of Eastern Connecticut.

"Cooley's Weekly," an independent newspaper, was established July 15, 1876, by John G. Cooley, who was widely known in this section, having published newspapers in Norwich many years before, and afterward conducting a successful printers' warehouse and advertising agency in New York City. By somewhat sensational methods and the popular price of "Fifty Cents a Year and No Postage," it soon attained a large circulation throughout Eastern Connecticut. After Mr. Cooley was incapacitated by illness, the paper was continued for several years by his son, John G. Cooley, Jr.

In 1888 the business was purchased by Allan Cleworth and Frank H. Pullen, both long connected with the Lowell, Massachusetts, "Courier." Under the firm name of Cleworth & Pullen, they assumed control on October 4th of that year. Mr. Cleworth died February 27, 1906, and the publication has since been continued by Mr. Pullen under the name of Pullen Publishing Company. Since May 1, 1890, it has been issued as the weekly edition of the "Norwich Evening Record," but under its original name. It is still a favorite in the rural districts and with many former residents of Norwich who have moved away.

www.ingramcontent.com/pod-product-compliance
Lightning Source LLC
LaVergne TN
LVHW012207040326
832903LV00003B/168